Institutions, Incentives and Economic Reforms in India

Institutions, Incentives and Economic Reforms in India

edited by
Satu Kähkönen
Anthony Lanyi

Sage Publications
New Delhi • Thousand Oaks • London

First published in 2000 by

Sage Publications India Pvt Ltd
M-32 Market, Greater Kailash, Part 1
New Delhi 110 048

Sage Publications Inc.
2455 Teller Road
Thousand Oaks, California 91320

Sage Publications Ltd
6 Bonhill Street
London EC2A 4 PU

Published by Tejeshwar Singh for Sage Publications India Pvt Ltd, and typeset by Siva Math Setters, Chennai and printed at Chaman Enterprises, Delhi.

Library of Congress Cataloging-in-Publication Data

Institutions, incentives and economic reforms in India/edited by Satu Kähkönen, Anthony Lanyi.

p. cm.

Includes bibliographical references and index.

1. India—Economic policy—1966– 2. Privatization—India. 3. Tax incentives—India. 4. Finance—India. I. Kähkönen, Satu. II. Lanyi, Anthony.

HC435 .18328 338.954—dc21 2000 00-024741

ISBN: 0-7619-9415-7 (US-hb)
81-7036-894-4 (India-hb)

Sage Production Team: Rishi Iyengar, Arpita Das, Anil Verma and Santosh Rawat

This volume is dedicated to Mancur Olson, Principal Investigator and Chairman of the IRIS Center until his untimely death in February, 1998. His tireless and enthusiastic leadership was responsible for the success of the IRIS/India Projects, of which the present volume is one of the major outputs, and his outstanding contribution to modern social science was one of the principal inputs in the thinking behind the studies published herein.

Contents

PART III
Reforming Public Goods Delivery

PART IV
Agricultural Parastatals and Rural Governance

PART V
Reforming the Industrial and Financial Structure

List of Tables

List of Figures

Acknowledgements

We wish to thank the US Agency for International Development for the financial support and encouragement that made this volume possible. We are deeply grateful to Sarah Bell, Kimberly Brickell, Maria Coppola, Jeremy Highsmith and Brian Steinhardt for help in organising the research programme and conferences out of which this volume grew, and preparing this book for publication.

Introduction

The Institutional Basis of Economic Reforms

Anthony Lanyi

For nearly two decades, a 'silent revolution'[1] has been sweeping through the devloping world,and more recently through the 'second world' of economies in transition from an economic system of central planning to a market-based economy. This is a revolution of economic reforms, involving both macroeconomic stabilisation and structural reforms. The latter involve, inter alia, the replacement of government restrictions and controls by market-based incentives; introduction of clearer economic rationales for fiscal policy and other government interventions in the economy; and privatisation or restructuring of public sector enterprises. Such reform packages have achieved positive results for many countries that introduced them in the 1980s; for those—Chile and some Asian countries—that were already moving in that direction earlier, the outcome has been even more striking. Among the 'transition' economies, those countries in Central and Eastern Europe (including the Baltic republics) that undertook reforms at an early stage already show strong signs of offsetting the initial fall in output that inevitably followed the break-up of the Council for Mutual Economic Assistance (CMEA) trade arrangements.[2]

In this broad setting, India is something of an anomaly: although a third world, not a second world country, its reform process began only in 1991 (after occasional minor reforms in the 1980s), and while the reforms were followed by a spurt of economic growth, the remaining reform agenda is still long and per capita income is still far below that of middle-income developing countries. India still has far to go to attain a number of important intermediate goals, such as achieving a balanced fiscal position, thereby ending the drain on the country's resources created by an inefficient public sector; further developing financial markets capable of mobilising the vast savings needed for the greatly increased infrastructural and other investments required for sustaining a higher rate of output growth; making labour markets sufficiently flexible to facilitate structural changes in the economy; allocating more resources for investment in human capital (especially in the rural areas) in order to create a healthy and literate work force; and completing the process of liberalising foreign trade and investment in order to make India a full partner in a growing world economy.[3]

These policy prescriptions are largely in line with the 'Washington consensus',[4] and are largely accepted by those concerned with Indian economic policies both inside and outside the country, despite occasional evidence in the local press of some hankering after the good old days of central planning. What is less easily agreed upon, or understood, is *why* it has been so difficult even to start the reform process, *why* this started so much later in India than in other countries that have a much less competent corps of civil servants and economists in their upper echelons than India has enjoyed for many years and *why* it appears to be so difficult to continue the reform impetus. What we are just beginning to understand, especially in large and complex countries such as India and Russia, is that being able to define a proper set of policies is only the first step toward transforming the economies of these countries. For economic policies to bring about their desired results, there must be the right institutional and political underpinnings to these policies; otherwise, the reforms will be only partially successful, or entirely fail, or possibly even lead to outcomes that are worse than the initial situation.

Our understanding of the institutional basis of economic development has greatly increased in recent years, thanks to the efforts of a number of economists, political scientists, legal scholars and sociologists. The term 'new institutional economics', which is sometimes used to refer to a wide range of studies in this field, belies a multidisciplinary approach that characterises this work.[5] A premise of this approach is that a proper set of institutions is essential for economic growth and development. A country cannot achieve economic progress and efficiency simply by having the government *not* interfere in the economy. A thriving market economy does not emerge automatically. It requires institutions that most people in the economically developed economies take for granted, but that many developing countries are lacking.[6]

'Institutions' in this sense are understood as the 'rules of the game' that govern the economy and economic policymaking. They include the fundamental legal, political and social rules that establish the basis for production, exchange and distribution. Examples of these are the rules governing elections, government administration, banking practices and the legal structure. The rules can either be formally written down and enforced by government officials or unwritten and enforced by informal sanctions.[7]

This approach represents a change from the earlier thinking that development depends most critically on the availability of natural resources and physical and human capital. In the early post-war period, when economists turned their attention to economic development, they thought that raising the ratio of investment to income was the way to launch a country onto a sustainable path of high growth. In the 1960s, after the remarkably successful Marshall Plan assistance in Europe and the disappointing experience of foreign aid in many of the less-developed countries, the concept of capital was broadened to include human capital, the lack of which was considered another critical obstacle to development in poor countries. The experience of recent decades, however, demonstrates that although physical and human capital accumulation are necessary for economic growth and development, they are not sufficient; this is shown by certain countries where growth rates have been low despite high rates of physical capital accumulation and rapid expansion of education. This experience has led economists to reconsider the determinants of economic growth and in doing so to explore the incentive structures that lead to physical and human capital accumulation and to technological progress. As a result of these studies, economic policies and institutions now appear as key factors in economic growth.

Among such policies and institutions, those that appear to be especially crucial include: well-established property rights and enforceability of contracts; civil law and order, and an honest, independent judiciary; an efficient, honest civil service, including well-organised, transparent tax administration, with a resultant high tax morality; and traditions of cooperation and civil responsibility at the level of local government and non-governmental organisations. By reducing transaction and information costs for private entrepreneurs, these institutions promote risk-taking and investment. A more complicated issue is whether these conditions favouring economic development include democratic government and institutions. While global evidence suggests that democracy favours economic growth over the long term, long-established democracies can also encounter problems of collective action by well-organised groups, which are aggressive in pursuing particularistic interests, thereby making it more difficult to translate the 'encompassing interest' of the society as a whole into decisions of the national government.[8] Needless to say, this characteristic of well-established democracies is not unique to advanced industrial societies, but may also be found in lower-income democratic societies such as India.

It is a premise of this volume that understanding these institutional and political underpinnings of economic development is essential to successful economic reform in developing countries. And such an understanding implies a reform effort that is broader, more multipronged, than before. Liberalising financial markets will not be fully successful unless there is an adequate framework of collateral and contract law, and a properly functioning judiciary to enforce these laws. The Central Government fiscal deficit cannot be reduced until public sector enterprises and state governments are also reformed, but in these areas, too, vested interests play an important role. Reformed public sector enterprises—whether operating under private or public ownership—will not function properly unless goods and labour markets are freed from a mountain of restrictive legislation and government controls, which are typically imposed to favour the interests of particular groups. Proper health and education services cannot be brought to the mass of a population unable to express its needs because of political and social controls exercised by dominant groups. No wave of a magic wand from the top level of national policymakers can transform the social and economic landscape; there is no substitute for painstaking, grass-roots efforts in reconstructing the fabric of public policies and institutions in a way that both meets the concerns of the particular groups perceiving themselves to be adversely affected by proposed reforms, and provides incentives for the society as a whole to build up its physical and human resources in a productive and equitable manner.

This, then, is the idea underlying the set of papers presented in this volume. They came about because of a programme financed by the United States Agency for International Development (USAID) and carried out by the Center for Institutional Reform and the

Informal Sector (IRIS) at the University of Maryland in College Park, Maryland, USA. USAID supported the commissioning of a number of papers by Indian scholars working both in India and abroad on a broad range of topics related to economic reform in India and which in all cases examine the institutional underpinnings of reform. The best of these papers were issued as IRIS/India Working Papers, and some of the best of these Working Papers are presented as chapters in this volume. They are grouped under five main headings: political economy of reform, fiscal reform, reforming public goods delivery, reform issues in agricultural parastatals and rural governance and reforming the industrial and financial structure. In each of these areas, the papers indicate that a major reform effort must still be sustained, and that this effort must deal not only with the well-known straightforward policy prescriptions such as lower fiscal deficits but also with serious institutional impediments to carrying out those policy prescriptions and therefore to achieving a more efficiently functioning and rapidly growing economy. The art of economic policy becomes then not only constructing the right package of policies in the sense of conventional economic theorising—that is, based on an economy's response to policies assuming properly functioning markets and rational individuals—but making sure that such a package also includes measures that bring about changes in institutions themselves, so that the economy's response to government policies in fact produces the desired outcome. Perhaps this can be seen, in broad conceptual terms, as an application of the Lipsey-Lancaster 'Theory of the Second-Best', in which a standard policy prescription on the assumption of perfect markets may not be the best policy in the presence of distortions, and is in any event highly unlikely to produce the theoretically predicted result. The relevant distortions—both those that can be quickly removed by policy changes and those deeply embedded in social and political institutions—are clearly set out in the papers in this volume, which are intended to help India meet the challenge of achieving a faster pace of economic and social development.

I POLITICAL ECONOMY OF REFORM

Government policies underlie much—although perhaps not all—of economic reform. In general, reform in a particular area entails changes in certain policies, and that in turn requires leaders to make decisions and see to it that the decisions are implemented by the organs of government. In a large, decentralised country such as India, government action is complicated not only by the diverse groups whose interests must be weighed in political decisions, but also by the federal structure of the government. The four chapters in this section explore the political economy of reform that pervades all the other topics dealt with in this volume. In particular, two chapters focus on the fiscal problem from the divergent standpoints of federal relations and electoral coalitions, respectively, and two others discuss the major issue of privatising state-owned enterprises, from both the standpoint of national policy and the perspective of centre–state relations.

A natural starting point in the study of political economy is fiscal policy, and it is natural in India to look at this subject in the context of both the Union (Central) Government and the state governments, to which important responsibilities have devolved. In 'Indian Fiscal Federalism: Political Economy and Issues for Reform', Kenneth Kletzer and Nirvikar Singh outline the complex pattern of fiscal, economic and political relationships that determine the structure of federal and state revenues, expenditures and intergovernmental transfers. The authors argue that the effort to control the Central Government deficit since 1991 has been unsuccessful mainly because the burgeoning deficits of the state governments have had to be covered largely by transfers from the Central Government. The ratio of state revenues to expenditures is especially low (43 per cent) compared to other large countries with federal systems. While there are legitimate reasons for such an imbalance, such as lower collection costs of federal revenues and the use of federal transfers as a means to reduce interstate inequalities, there are other causes that stem from political-economic factors. Among the latter, the authors discuss tax competition between central and state governments, as well as between state governments; they pay particular attention to the desires of key groups and individuals in the Central Government to determine the way expenditures are allocated in the states. Central Government decisionmakers, they hypothesise, find it useful to control state government expenditures in order to influence the outcome of national parliamentary elections, while state-level decisionmakers fail to cut expenditures because constituents argue for continued subsidies and other programmes that are financed wholly or partly from the centre. The authors argue that reforms are urgent, first, because coordination of tax systems between the centre and the states (as well as among states) is required for greater allocative efficiency, and the fiscal deficits of both the Central Government and the public sector as a whole are unsustainable. In addition to rationalising indirect taxes and broadening the overall tax base, they suggest reducing 'incentives for costly influence activities across levels of government'.

Another approach to analysing the political economy of fiscal policy is that of the political scientist who studies electoral systems and resulting ruling coalitions. Bhaskar Dutta, in 'Fragmented Legislatures and Electoral Systems: The Indian Experience', examines the impact of electoral laws on the stability of legislative coalitions. He concludes that a rule of proportional representation would have led to greater fragmentation in those cases where elections based on a plurality rule in fact produced a majority party, while, when such a rule fails to result in a majority party, proportional rule may lead to a more stable system. In turn, the stability of legislative coalitions has a significant impact upon economic policy. Dutta's evidence indicates that unstable coalition governments tend to be associated with higher expenditures, a smaller volume of non-tax revenues and higher fiscal deficits (or lower surpluses). This result provides an important reason why economists should be concerned about the electoral rules for choosing members of legislatures.

The last two chapters in this section explore aspects of privatisation of public enterprises, a major political-economic issue that lies at the heart of both fiscal reform and achievement of a more efficient, market-oriented economy. Anand Gupta, in 'The Political Economy of Privatisation in India', examines the ways in which privatisation has been advanced but also impeded, and the incentives that explain the slow progress of parastatal reform thus far. After enumerating the benefits of privatisation for market efficiency, investment and public finances, he points out that there have been relatively few cases of 'true complete privatisation', but a number of cases of incomplete and frustrated forms of this process: selling fractional equity to the private sector but retaining public sector control; putting public enterprises up for sale but either not going through with the sale, or selling but cancelling the sale later; closing down parastatals (none reported); and transferring management to the private sector but with enough public sector equity to continue effective government intervention. Why are politicians so reluctant to transfer public enterprises to the private sector? In

Gupta's view, this is due to several incentives: electoral support (assuming voters favourably regard continued public ownership); patronage (providing jobs and seats on governing boards for supporters); and resources that can be leaked from these enterprises to provide election finance. Gupta concludes that while declining budgetary support and increased competition in liberalised markets may put more pressure on public enterprises to operate more efficiently and even privatise, more needs to be done to reform the parastatal sector. His recommendations include building and strengthening the constituency for privatisation through dissemination of information about the state public enterprises and the advantages of privatisation; announcement of a properly structured and articulated privatisation policy; greater capacity building for enterprise management; and, after privatisation has occurred, careful evaluation of the impact of privatisation on efficiency, investment and public finances.

Leslie Armijo and Prem Shankar Jha, in 'Centre–State Relations in India and Brazil: Privatisation of Electricity and Banking', examine a number of cases where federal and state governments have been at odds on privatisation issues. Two cases—the electricity plant at Dabhol in Maharashtra state contracted for with the Enron Corporation of the United States, and the Banespa Bank in São Paulo, Brazil—are examined in detail, while privatisation in India's financial sector and Brazil's electricity sector are discussed more generally. The authors identify three sources of centre–state conflict: state leaders being ideologically opposed to privatisation, or some of its aspects, such as foreign investment; party differences that might create tactical advantages in an obstructionist position on the part of state leaders; and the belief by state leaders that 'the distribution of economic and/or political benefits between the centre and the state governments is unfair to them'. The authors conclude that ideology and politics have played a much smaller role—although occasionally a significant one—than real conflicts of interest with regard either to economic benefits, or political credit or blame.

II FISCAL REFORM

The impetus toward wide-ranging economic reforms stemmed from a balance-of-payments crisis in 1990–91, which led in turn to an

International Monetary Fund-supported adjustment programme that included major structural reforms designed to introduce greater market orientation into India's domestic and foreign trade. The immediate cause of India's balance-of-payment difficulties, however, was a large public sector deficit that had been worsening for several years, so that reduction of this deficit necessarily played a central role in the adjustment programme. The fiscal policy effort was complicated by structural reforms, some of which (for instance, lowering import and export taxes) might reduce government revenue, while others such as liberalising foreign trade restrictions and cutting subsidies might serve to strengthen the fiscal position. Greater difficulties were posed by a poorly conceived and administered tax system with overlapping and sometimes excessive taxes, an overly narrow tax base and well-entrenched traditions of tax evasion, and by the fact that the Central Government deficit stemmed to a large extent from deficits of state and local governments, deficits financed by transfers and loans from the Central Government, which itself had little ability to influence state and local finances. Thus, the conventional prescriptions for achieving a stronger fiscal position—rationalising the tax system, improving tax administration, cutting and prioritising government expenditures—are complicated by institutional factors including, as indicated by Kletzer and Singh (see Section I above), the two-way flow of political influence between central and state governments.

Starting from the revenue position of the Central Government, the need for wide-ranging tax reforms implies strengthening the income tax, discussed in 'Reforming Indian Income Tax Enforcement' by Dilip Mookherjee and Arindam Das-Gupta. The authors argue that despite reforms of the income tax schedule and tax base since 1991, 'relatively little effort has been made so far in improving the nature of the tax administration'. Large-scale tax evasion has led to a poor revenue performance compared with other developing countries, where income taxes amount to one-seventh of GDP, compared with one-ninth in India, and where, unlike in India, income tax revenue grows along with the economy. This sluggish revenue growth has resulted in inequity, inflationary pressures, compression of expenditures on essential infrastructure and social safety nets and reliance on indirect taxes (excise and sales taxes and customs) that are regressive and difficult to coordinate between central and state governments. The authors diagnose the weaknesses of the Indian income tax administration: a poor information system; poor allocation and organisation of manpower in the tax administration; an increase in workload with limited manpower that leads to a fall in time allotted to tax assessments; and the tendency to punish 'relatively technical violations' rather than serious tax evasion. This diagnosis is reinforced by the authors' review of international experience (principally selected countries in Latin America and Asia), which shows India to be relatively backward with regard to the diagnosed problem areas. Mookherjee and Das-Gupta admit that their proposed remedies—various improvements in collecting and processing tax-assessment information, better organisation of manpower, more aggressive tax scrutiny and prosecution efforts and greater penalties for tax evasion—would meet strong resistance from both those who pay income tax, who are mainly middle-class, and tax administration employees. They suggest overcoming this resistance by emphasising better income tax information and service *to* taxpayers; raising penalties for large evasions rather than minor offences, which should be favourable to all but the wealthiest taxpayers; and giving better salaries, work incentives and training to employees of the tax administration.

M. Govinda Rao examines the Indian fiscal problem from the perspective of the states' expenditure and revenue policies in 'Fiscal Adjustment and the Role of State Governments in India'. He argues that the fiscal problems of the states have become acute because, as the economy is liberalised, greater fiscal decentralisation is called for. At the same time, the widely perceived need for greater and more cost-effective outlays on health and education tends to increase pressures on state governments, where the primary responsibility for human resource development rests. This latter point is borne out by the fact that current expenditures have tended over the last decade to rise far more rapidly than capital expenditures, and somewhat faster than revenues as well. Rao sees the influence of special interest groups as an impediment to state fiscal reforms on both the revenue and the expenditure sides. With regard to the latter, one sees the influence of special interests in the growing explicit transfers and subsidies, and in wage increases of government employees growing faster than the economy, but perhaps even more in implicit subsidies, which are exemplified by the fall in user charges, the rising expenditures on quasi-public goods, price controls on urban goods and services that primarily benefit the better-off sections of the society and the poor and declining cost recoveries for social and economic services provided by the state governments (such as education, power and irrigation). At the same time, the intergovernmental transfer mechanism fails to change the high state-by-state correlation of per capita income and per capita level of government-provided social and economic services. On the revenue side, the overlapping sales and excise taxes imposed by the central and state governments, taxes on inputs and capital goods and the 'octroi' on interstate transactions are all highly distortionary and crying out for rationalisation, if not outright removal. Such tax reform would need to be combined with a compression of unproductive expenditures and the privatisation of loss-making public enterprises, but both these reforms would require resistance to pressures from special interests.

Tax administration is an important aspect of fiscal governance, and in a country where tax evasion is known to be substantial, tax amnesties become a significant issue. This topic is explored by Mookherjee and Das-Gupta in 'Tax Amnesties in India: An Empirical Evaluation'. They develop a theoretical model of the effect of amnesties on tax revenues, which includes the effects of amnesty-induced changes in the composition of 'white' and 'black' assets of taxpayers. Through this model, which is based on the Indian experience of repeated tax amnesties, it is evident that the possible short-run benefits from a tax amnesty—a one-time increase in revenues for the year it is taking place, and a higher level of revenues (based on more honest reporting) in the future—are offset by a number of negative effects. The latter include: a decline in future tax evasion penalties that might have been collected by the government; a fall on returns on assets, if returns on white assets are less than those on black ones; a fall in pre-amnesty income disclosures if the amnesty is anticipated (and given past history, Indian taxpayers have become used to a new amnesty every several years); the possible signalling role of the amnesty with regard to future government tax enforcement (the more recurrent the amnesties, the greater the expectation of weak ongoing tax enforcement); and the fall in revenues resulting from the diversion into amnesty reporting of white income disclosures that would have been made anyway. The authors conclude that a succession of tax amnesties, Indian-style, is a poor substitute for strong, credible, ongoing tax enforcement.

III REFORMING PUBLIC GOODS DELIVERY

Recent critiques of Indian economic performance have noted that health and literacy indicators in India compare poorly with those in other Asian countries that were at similar levels two or three decades ago, and even with those in some low-income African countries.[9] Interstate differences within India are also striking; to some extent these are correlated with per capita income, but some cases, such as Kerala, show that even in states with relatively low incomes, it is possible to provide primary health care and primary education to virtually the entire population. This, of course, raises interesting questions about the social and political reasons why an equally strong performance is not found in some other low-income states such as Uttar Pradesh and Bihar, to name two of the worst performers. Many of the same questions of public choice and private incentives arise in connection with the provision of physical infrastructure, whose inadequacy is now clearly impeding the continuation of the accelerated growth of output experienced since 1990. While this issue is not directly covered in the chapters in this volume, it represents a rich field of future research.

Some reasons for India's relatively poor performance with regard to health improvements are elucidated by Anil Deolalikar and Prem Vashishtha, in their chapter on 'The Health and Medical Sector in India: Potential Reforms and Problems'. In this chapter, they ask why India spends more on health, relative to its GDP, than do most other Asian countries, yet demonstrates lower levels of achievement in lowering infant mortality and raising life expectancy. Part of the problem, they argue, is the lack of equity and efficiency with which those health expenditures are carried out. First of all, Central Government spending tends to reinforce, rather than compensate for, inequalities among the state governments with regard to health-related outlays, as well as rural–urban differences in funds received. Second, the authors criticise the current emphasis on expensive secondary and tertiary care, and on medical training and research, rather than primary health care, such as immunisations, prenatal care and the communicable disease programme, as well as integrated child nutrition and health programmes. They note that India has a higher doctor–population ratio than other Asian countries but far fewer nurses. Another danger sign is that lowest-income groups spend nearly a quarter of their income on medical visits, while the richest-income groups spend only 3.5 per cent. In this connection, the lack of a health insurance system has serious consequences. Finally, they note that the pharmaceutical industry is geared to the needs of the urban middle class and, because of price controls, lacks incentives to produce sufficient quantities of 'essential drugs' that prevent or cure the most serious illnesses prevalent in the country. Deolalikar and Vashishtha indicate their belief that their proposed reforms would be strongly resisted by the medical establishment and pharmaceutical industry, respectively, leaving as a question for further investigation how this resistance might be dealt with as part of the reform process.

In some instances, opposition to social and economic reforms comes from the intended beneficiaries of such change. Mukesh Eswaran examines one example of this phenomenon in 'Fertility, Literacy and the Institution of Child Labour'. Eswaran shows how the institution of child labour can generate a poverty trap when fertility, as well as the decision to use children as a source of labour rather than educating them is driven by the need for old-age security. Poor education and health care contribute to the vicious circle, as high child mortality rates render education in children a risky investment and induce parents to have more uneducated children instead of fewer, educated children. The societal tolerance of the institution of child labour makes this trade-off possible. Based on a model developed in the paper, Eswaran suggests two complementary policies that would contribute to the eradication of child labour: the universalisation of access to health care services in order to reduce child mortality rates, and the legislation of compulsory education. The former would work by altering the risk–return trade-off in favour of educated children, and the latter by countering the reluctance of parents to educate daughters, who are regarded as less important than sons for old-age security. These policy recommendations are an excellent example of how policy needs to take into account the actual social institutions and the incentives perceived by households, whose 'rationality' may produce outcomes radically opposed to accepted value systems in high-income countries.

IV AGRICULTURAL PARASTATALS AND RURAL GOVERNANCE

In a country where agriculture is still the principal economic activity of the population, more than two-thirds of whom still live in rural areas, government intervention in agricultural production and marketing is necessarily a major political and economic issue, all the more so as such policies also affect the availability of foodstuffs for the urban population. The impetus toward economic reform in recent years has raised for India the same questions that have been debated for many years in other countries: What is the rationale of government intervention in the markets for agricultural products? Is such intervention justified by considerations of income security for farmers or food security of consumers? What is the impact of such intervention on the incentives to produce and thus on output? On the efficiency of distribution, and on exports and imports of agricultural output? If it is admitted that government intervention is in many respects costly and unnecessary, as an international consensus now concedes, how can beneficial government intervention be defined, and how can the current system be phased out with least harm to those currently benefiting from the system?

Ashok Gulati, Satu Kähkönen and Pradeep Sharma, in 'The Food Corporation of India: Successes and Failures in Indian Foodgrain Marketing', evaluate the role and performance of the Food Corporation of India (FCI) in Indian foodgrain marketing. The authors show that while FCI has succeeded in improving the overall availability of foodgrains, it has failed to target the foodgrain distribution to poor consumers and regions; its operations are economically inefficient; and it has not maintained buffer stocks at levels stipulated by the government. FCI's per-unit costs of operations have been substantially higher than those of private traders, leading to a sharply widening gap between costs and revenues that have been met by increasing government subsidies. The lack of accountability within FCI and the knowledge that the government will cover its losses have made such inefficiency possible; the failure to target the distribution of foodgrains to the poor makes these losses unjustifiable as well. The reform options proposed by the authors include the removal of FCI from its middleman role in domestic and foreign trade; the removal of zonal trade restrictions; a large reduction in FCI's grain stocking activities; and the replacement of the current Public Distribution System (PDS) by either a system of food stamps (in which case the FCI would have no more role in the PDS) or a procurement system (under which FCI would still supply grain to the PDS based on the calling of bids from private traders). It may be supposed that such reforms might be opposed by special interests such as employees of FCI and PDS, and those benefiting from PDS, but possibly a proper explanation of the benefits of these reforms could go a long way toward allaying their fears, as well as gaining the support of the general public.

The theme of inefficient government interference in markets for agricultural products is further elaborated upon in the chapter, 'Economic Reforms and Marketing Parastatals: The Case of the Cotton Corporation of India and the Maharashtra Federation' by Ashok Gulati and Sangeeta Shroff. The authors evaluate the Cotton Corporation of India (CCI) and Maharashtra Federation in terms of the stated objectives of these organisations: they have failed to reduce price instability, except to the extent that subsidies from Maharashtra state reduced price variability in some cases; they have a mixed record with regard to commercial viability, as the CCI became profitable after substantial losses up to the mid-1980s, while the Maharashtra Federation has continued over most years to be a losing operation; and they have no smaller marketing costs and margins than either private traders or cooperatives in Gujarat, implying that their operations did not result in a higher share of output for farmers. The authors conclude that the Monopoly Purchase Scheme is inefficient in serving the farmers' interests; that controls on internal and foreign trade of cotton (both imports and exports) should be abolished; and that the CCI's role should be limited to that of a marketing agency on commercial lines, undertaking price support operations as required. One would suppose that such reforms would gain the support of cotton producers and those engaging in cotton trading and distribution.

The agricultural policy issues discussed in the chapters on the Food Corporation of India and the Cotton Corporation of India must be seen against the background of social, political and economic institutions in rural areas that have slowed productivity growth and created apparent poverty traps for a substantial segment of the national population. Chandrika Gulati's chapter, 'Panchayati Raj in India: Problems and Prospects', is a groundbreaking attempt to tackle these institutional issues from the standpoint of a major political reform that is only in the process of being incorporated fully into Indian rural society. While Panchayati Raj (PR) is an institution that existed from ancient times in the form of village councils, the centralised rule of the British colonial government effectively destroyed it in its traditional form; and despite several ineffective attempts to revive it, PR was not meaningfully reestablished until the adoption of the 73rd Amendment to the Constitution. The wide interstate variances of success in establishing PR, and the generally slow progress that has been achieved, reflect political incentives such as the unwillingness of state governments to devolve their responsibilities to local councils, as well as deep-seated social institutions such as the difficulties in some regions of accepting low-caste and female participation in local governance. The linkage of local power with financial resources and the interaction between Central Government initiatives and grass-roots support are other issues dealt with in Gulati's study.

V REFORMING THE INDUSTRIAL AND FINANCIAL STRUCTURE

The post-Independence history of industrialisation in India can be regarded equally as a half-full or half-empty glass. On the one hand, India is a country with a large industrial sector and a wide range of goods produced, most of which have been developed since the 1940s; on the other hand, given India's size, variety of resources, manpower skills and entrepreneurship, it is to be wondered at that it has fallen so far behind a number of other Asian countries with regard to the extent and pace of industrialisation, and especially participation in world markets for manufactures. The reasons for India's relatively weak industrial performance until the early 1990s are well-known: a manufacturing sector hamstrung by price and investment controls, and severe import restrictions; an entrepreneurial class discouraged, and in part driven abroad, by (until recently) extremely high income tax rates, and at the same time induced to spend too much time in rent-seeking activities such as obtaining permits of every conceivable variety, rather than pursuing new commercial initiatives; parastatal enterprises that were run, in many cases, at a loss, and face, as private sector enterprises do, distorted price incentives because of controls over domestic and foreign trade; a largely nationalised financial sector whose credit policies were determined by the government on largely political criteria; labour policies that severely impede the growth and transformation of industry; and hostility toward foreign investment, even minority participation, in Indian manufacturing. A better formula for sluggish investment, poor foreign trade performance and increasingly backward technology would be difficult to find. Fortunately, the 1990s have seen a turnaround in these policies, as many price and investment controls have been eliminated, foreign trade restrictions eliminated or reduced, foreign investment liberalised and some parastatals privatised or put under new management.

Nevertheless, as noted at the beginning of the Introduction to this volume, a great deal remains to be done to complete this revolution. The chapters in this section address several areas in which continued reforms are needed: parastatal enterprises, reform of the financial sector and labour markets. These areas of reform are very closely related to each other. Heavy government involvement in both the industrial and financial sectors has led to an unproductive emphasis on rent-seeking activities on the part of both private entrepreneurs and public sector managers. A shift toward private ownership and management in manufacturing enterprises would not be meaningful unless the financial sector were also relieved of heavy-handed government direction of credits, thereby allowing loan decisions to be made on economic and financial rather than political grounds. Moreover, such a shift will not result in the long overdue allocation of resources from losing to profitable activities unless labour markets are freed from regulations and laws that prevent economically required labour mobility.

Pradeep Agrawal, in 'Regulation and Reform of the Financial Sector in India: An Analysis of the Underlying Incentives', shows how misconceived government policies can lead to weak institutions. While the nationalisation of the banking sector in 1969, and the government controls imposed on credit, interest rates and new entry were intended to improve credit access in the rural sector, as well as for small firms and the poor, the result has been an undynamic, largely insolvent banking sector that yields poor customer service and inefficient use of investible resources. The requirements for credits to be directed to government finance and priority sectors have had an especially pernicious effect, involving political influence and corruption as well as simply poor use of national savings. Agrawal supports the recommendations of the Narasimham Committee, i.e., dismantling barriers to entry and expansion of private banks, deregulating credit allocation and decontrolling interest rates, but suggests that these reforms should be taken further. Nevertheless, the experience of a number of other countries, which the author cites, suggests that the Indian authorities have been correct to reform gradually. Given this gradual approach thus far, moderate inflation, and the trade liberalisation already achieved, further liberalisation can be undertaken at a moderate pace without risk of a financial crisis.

The final two chapters of the volume deal with what may well be the weakest link in the Indian reform initiative, that is, labour markets. Extensive experience in developed as well as developing countries shows that the greater the labour market rigidities, resulting from either government policies or labour union pressures, the less easy it will be to develop a dynamic, flexible industrial sector. Mrinal Datta Chaudhuri, in 'Labour Markets as Social Institutions in India', develops the thesis that the efforts of unions in the organised sector have succeeded in establishing a legal regime, such as requirements for government permission before retrenching a worker, which make it difficult for industrial firms to respond quickly to market changes and technological progress. At the same time, public sector firms are further hampered by norms concerning labour use at the enterprise level. The net effect of these rigidities is to raise the effective labour cost facing Indian enterprises, which inhibits the growth of labour-intensive industries in a country whose comparative advantage clearly leans in that direction. In this way, as well as others, the failure to initiate labour market reforms inhibits the benefits derived from reforms in other areas, such as international trade and financial markets.

In 'Labour Policies, Employment and Worker Earnings: Indian and International Experiences', Pradeep Agrawal compares the Indian labour market policies with those in East Asia. He finds that in the latter region 'a peaceful industrial relations climate has been maintained' partly through compulsory cooling-off periods before a strike can be called and the use of voluntary and compulsory arbitration, and partly through the ability of firms to retrench workers (with compensation). He finds, further, that the widespread use of bonuses linked to productivity helps make workers more cooperative, responsible and motivated. By contrast, labour laws in India give organised sector workers what is tantamount to permanent employment after a brief probation period. Government permission to let workers go is rarely given. Public sector workers receive fixed annual wage increments unrelated to work performance. These laws result both in low productivity and high unemployment.

Agrawal recommends adoption of East Asian labour legislation; in addition to the points noted above, this would include laws limiting the number of unions per enterprise, which would make it easier to come to agreements than under the present system, where rivalries among a number of rival unions greatly complicate worker–management negotiations. It is implicit in Agrawal's analysis, that the linkage in India between labour unions and political parties make it unlikely that such reforms will take place without very strong leadership at the national level, supported by clear understanding by the public of what has been the economic cost to the country of tolerating the current labour regime.

The seriousness and complexity of economic reform challenges facing India are, of course, not only a reflection of the size and complexity of the country and its society, but also of the many decades over which distortions and poor economic incentives have been not only tolerated but in many instances actively sustained by government policies.

The variety of approaches to analysing the institutional problems inherent in economic reform were suggested by references to the literature near the beginning of this introductory essay. It is hoped that publishing these studies, which illustrate both the vastness of economic reform issues in India and the different methods of institutional analysis, will encourage further research and policy debate, which in turn will contribute to India's achieving its great, but so far only partially fulfilled, potential for economic progress.

NOTES

1. This phrase was coined by Michel Camdessus, Managing Director of the International Monetary Fund (IMF) in the late 1980s.
2. For discussion of the data and causes of output decline in former CMEA countries, see World Bank, 1996, *From Plan to Market: World Development Report*. Washington, DC: The World Bank; International Monetary Fund, 1992, *World Economic Outlook*, May, chap. 4; International Monetary Fund, 1995, *World Economic Outlook*, May, chap. 4; International Monetary Fund Research Department, 1995, *Staff Studies for the World Economic Outlook*, September, chap. 6.
3. See, for instance, Singh, M. 1996, 'India: The Unfinished Agenda of Economic Reforms'. 28th Jawaharlal Nehru Memorial Lecture, New Delhi, November.

See also International Monetary Fund, 1995, 'India: Economic Reform and Growth'. Occasional Paper 134, Washington, DC.

4. See Williamson, J. 1993, 'Democracy and the "Washington Consensus"', *World Development*, 21(8): 1329–1336. See also Rodrik, D. 1996, 'Understanding Economic Policy Reform', *Journal of Economic Literature*, 34(1): 9–41.
5. An excellent review of a number of the ideas associated with the new institutional economics is provided by Christopher Clague (Clague, C. 1997, 'The New Institutional Economics and Economic Development', in C. Clague (ed.), *Institutions and Economic Development*. Baltimore: Johns Hopkins University Press).
6. On the importance of institutions for economic growth, see Williamson, O. 1994, *Institutions and Economic Organisation: The Governance Perspective*. Washington, DC: The World Bank. See also Olson, M. 1996, 'Big Bills Left on the Sidewalk: Why Some Nations are Rich, and Others Poor', *The Journal of Economic Perspectives*, 10(2): 3–24.
7. See, for instance, Coleman, J. 1990, *Foundations of Social Theory*. Cambridge, Massachusetts: Harvard University Press.
8. For discussion of the effects of autocracy and democracy on economic development, see Olson, M. 1993, 'Dictatorship, Democracy and Development', *American Political Science Review*, 87(3): 567–76. See also Clague, C., P. Keefer, S. Knack and M. Olson, 1997, 'Democracy, Autocracy and the Institutions Supportive of Economic Growth', and Haggard, S. 1997, 'Democratic Institutions, Economic Policy and Development', in C. Clague (ed.), *Institutions and Economic Development*. Baltimore: Johns Hopkins University Press. On collective action problems, see Olson, M. 1965, *The Logic of Collective Action*. Cambridge, Massachusetts: Harvard University Press; and Olson, M. 1982, *The Rise and Decline of Nations*, New Haven: Yale University Press.
9. This point is developed in great depth by Jean Dreze and Amartya Sen (Dreze, J. and A. Sen, 1995, *India: Economic Development and Social Opportunity*. Delhi: Oxford University Press).

PART I

Political Economy of Reform

1

Indian Fiscal Federalism: Political Economy and Issues for Reform

Kenneth Kletzer and Nirvikar Singh

India is a federal state with a population larger than that of the United States and the European Union combined. Given India's size, it is not surprising that it is one of the most fiscally decentralised states, as measured by the proportion of government expenditure that occurs below the central level. The assignment of fiscal responsibilities to different levels of government has been determined by the country's political, social and economic history, as well as by its constitution and legal institutions. The institutional structure within which tax, transfer and public spending programmes are designed and implemented can be an important tool for, or a major impediment to, economic reform and development. Therefore, understanding how the fiscal federal structure works in India and the constraints given by its political economy are important inputs for analysing the likely effects of reform. Further, the reassignment of fiscal responsibility, respecting the legal, political and social environment, can create a fruitful area for institutional reform to promote growth and development.

A major policy issue since India's independence has been the division of authority for collecting revenues, and of responsibility for making public expenditures between the central, state and local governments. The Constitution of India recognised the political need for decentralisation by granting state governments a significant degree of fiscal autonomy in explicit provisions. It assigned specific tax instruments and autonomous responsibility for certain public spending programmes to the states. Political pressures for the decentralisation of fiscal authority arise from conflicts over the allocation of public resources across regions and social communities and the concern that concentrated political power at the federal level will benefit majority constituencies. Regional decentralisation of taxation and public spending may promote fairness and help protect minority interests in the distribution of public and private resources under majority rule. Even with constitutional mandates and a legal system that protects minority groups, the fiscal policies chosen by a federal government can favour some regions over others. Thus, public policy debate in India has questioned whether its system of fiscal federalism guards against a national majority choosing an allocation of public goods and distribution of tax burden that disfavours some regions or communities.

Studies of the economics of fiscal federalism in India have often been normative in nature, focusing on problems of allocative efficiency and the system of interjurisdictional transfers, but not modelling how politics and economics interact in the institutional setting of Indian federalism.[1] The goal of this chapter is to further such an investigation, with a framework for analysing how political forces influence the provision of public goods by different levels of government and the allocation of tax revenues across jurisdictions under different institutional structures. We discuss intergovernmental fiscal relations in a simple model in which public goods allocation at the federal and the state level is determined by majority voting.

The model is used to show how majority rule in a decentralised fiscal system leads to a division of tax revenues between the federal and state governments and an allocation of public expenditures between national and subnational public goods. A state government is identified with a particular local public goods spending plan that is chosen under majority rule by the median voter of the state. The federal government consists of a level of national public goods provision, and a set of interjurisdictional transfers which is chosen by a majority of the states, that is, by the median voter in a simple majority of states. The need for national policymakers to achieve a parliamentary majority leads to the possibility that a subset of states is favoured in the federal allocation of public resources. In this system, discretionary policymaking by national fiscal authorities chosen indirectly by a simple majority may conflict with social goals of fairness or equity in the distribution of public expenditures and tax burdens across regions or communities.

Further issues arise when authorities representing different jurisdictions can attempt to influence the policies chosen by other levels of government in the federation. The institutions of fiscal federalism determine how much discretion each level of government exercises and, therefore, the importance of influence activities in interjurisdictional fiscal relations. For example, when the Central Government has some discretion over intergovernmental transfers between the states and itself, state governments have incentives to try to influence the allocation of grants to favour their constituents. The Central Government might use matching grants to provide incentives to subnational levels to provide specific public goods or transfers. If the objectives or amounts of matching grants can be chosen by the national government, then the state governments will seek to have the formulae changed to the benefit of their jurisdictions. While these activities may have purely redistributive motives, they distort the allocation of resources so that efficiency and other social welfare objectives are adversely affected.

Institutional design can intensify or reduce rent-seeking, lobbying and similar unproductive influence activities. It is widely believed that opportunities for such activities are common in the different levels of government in India. Here, we only suggest that the system of fiscal federalism in India may give rise to undesirable efforts to influence transfers between jurisdictions. The same idea may apply to national government provision of public goods that have a subnational aspect—because the distribution of benefits to different regions can be chosen—and to taxes when the regional distribution of incidence varies with the tax instrument.

In our analysis, we show how influence activities at subnational levels of government can be incorporated into the political economy model of decentralised fiscal policies chosen through majority voting. One implication is that the stakes for state governments in influencing national public goods spending and the distribution of transfers from the federal government can be very large. Another is that a reduction in the degree of discretion available to the federal government over the allocation of common revenues across states might improve its ability to achieve overall social welfare objectives of distribution and efficiency. Although it reduces the ability of fiscal authorities to respond to changing circumstances, a fixed, well-defined assignment of tax authority, together with public spending responsibility and interjurisdictional transfers between the federal and state governments, reduces the capacity for counterproductive influence activities by lower levels of government.

This study proposes an approach to modelling the political economy of fiscal federalism in order to examine institutional reform when subnational public authorities engage in unproductive influence activities. At this stage, the model is just a starting point for identifying the importance of reform of the institutional structure in which fiscal assignments are made in a federation and is far from the point of application to real reform in India. However, the essential features of our model are based on the experience of federalism in India and rely on several observations about the allocation of federal revenues, as well as the assignment of fiscal authority and responsibilities in India. Before we detail our modelling strategy, we survey the elements of Indian fiscal federalism that are important for fiscal reform, with an emphasis on those that are germane to the assumptions we make in our model.

The remainder of the paper is organised as follows. In Section I, we provide an overview of several major issues and features of Indian fiscal federalism. This section begins with specific motivations for our analysis: the fiscal issues faced by the Indian government in its current process of overall economic reform. It ends by exploring three major issues around which our subsequent discussion is organised: tax competition among the state governments; tax competition between the centre and the states; and the fiscal imbalances between the centre and the states. Section II discusses the importance of these three issues in the political economy of fiscal federalism. Section III uses a median voter model of multijurisdictional fiscal policymaking to analyse the political economy of fiscal federalism more precisely. It focuses on the fiscal gap between the centre and the states, and the consequent determination of interjurisdictional transfers. Variants of the basic model are discussed, as well as their extension to incorporate influence activities. Section IV summarises and concludes the paper.

I THE CASE FOR REFORM OF THE FEDERAL FISCAL STRUCTURE

The Indian government has undertaken an extensive set of reforms since 1991.[2] These reforms have occurred at—and been partly motivated by—a time of government fiscal stringency. They have involved considerable scrutiny of the allocative role of the government in the Indian economy. This has particularly focused attention on the efficiency of government expenditures. India's fiscal federal structures are potentially important influences on this efficiency, and have received increased attention also in the reform period.

While substantial progress seems to have been made in the reforms, one major constraint faced by the government in its liberalisation attempts has been the fiscal deficit, which has increased to the point that some analyses suggest is unsustainable.[3] Attempts to control the Central Government deficit, however, have been relatively unsuccessful.[4] The Central Government deficit has continued to be in excess of 6 per cent of the Gross Domestic Product (GDP). Much of this deficit comes from statutory and discretionary transfers to the states from the centre. The states rely heavily on these transfers to cover their expenditures.

Therefore, the Central Government is unable independently to tackle the issue of the fiscal deficit.[5] The state governments must also play a role, but their own continued deficits indicate that they have not done so as yet. State governments point out that they are constitutionally obligated to make the lion's share of social expenditures, and that squeezing them will have dire consequences for the welfare of citizens. Clearly, the issue is one of some urgency, and understanding the political and institutional constraints and possibilities of the fiscal federal structure is vital. While this discussion does not model the fiscal deficits issue, it may be kept in mind as a motivating factor, in addition to the general attention to the government's role in a liberalised economy.

Revenue-sharing between Central and State Governments

A presentation of some basic facts regarding India's federal structure is essential to its analysis.[6] On average, India's subnational governments account for a little over half of total government spending (World Bank, 1988).[7] For 1987, the figure was 54.4 per cent (Rao, 1993).[8] Their revenue, on the other hand, was substantially lower as a fraction of total government revenue. The difference has been closed by Central Government revenue-sharing and other transfers. For 1987, the share of state government revenue in total government revenue was only 30.2 per cent, and the states financed only 43.4 per cent of their expenditure from their own revenues (excluding loans).[9]

Intergovernmental transfers are, of course, common in federal systems. The rationale for transfers is often based on fiscal capacity: the ability of the Central Government to raise revenue at lower collection costs and with smaller excess burdens. Stressed here is the dependence of that fiscal capacity on the particular institutional setting of fiscal policymaking. For example, one of the striking comparisons made by Rao (1993)[10] is how low the ratio of states' revenue to states' expenditure is for the Indian case, that is, 43.4 per cent. The only comparable figure is 44.6 per cent for Australia, which has a total population similar to one of the smaller Indian states. Figures for other larger federations are substantially higher: 88.1 per cent for the United States, and 67.4 per cent for Brazil. The Central Government also directly spends a greater proportion in these other federations: 69.1 per cent in the United States and 67 per cent in Brazil. India stands out as a large federation with a high degree of decentralisation of expenditure. This situation is consistent with India's size, but the high degree of centralisation of revenue collection in India is not. The result is what Rao (1993) calls a 'vertical fiscal imbalance'.[11] There is no automatic reason that this imbalance will be a problem. If it reflects differences in fiscal capacity, together with information differences that favour decentralisation of expenditures, there should be no problem at all. However, the political economy of transfers generated by this imbalance may be associated with inefficiencies.

The reduction of inequality is another possible reason for central transfers to lower-level governments: poor regions are able to raise less revenue per capita, and central transfers can play an equalising role. India stands out in this respect also, because of the wide range of per capita incomes, at least double from the richest state to the poorest.[12] In India, however, this equity objective has not been substantially achieved through Central Government transfers to the states, with some analyses suggesting that the overall effect of central transfers has been regressive.[13]

Why should such an outcome arise? Two possibilities suggest themselves, one involving the political economy of India's fiscal federalism, and the other the particular federal structure. First, the centre may be responding to political constraints and incentives that do not match the goals of equity or support their achievement.

Second, the centre, in its elaborate exercises to determine transfers to the states, incorporates features that reward resource mobilisation efforts by the states.[14] This incentive goal may easily conflict with the equity objective.

Institutions Governing Transfers

Two agencies partly govern central transfers to the states: the Planning Commission, which is permanently constituted as a part of the Central Government under the control of the Prime Minister; and the Finance Commission, which is constituted every five years as a quasi-independent body, advisory to the government.[15] The existence of the Finance Commission and its broad functions are mandated in the Indian Constitution, while the Planning Commission does not have such a constitutional status. The distinction between the responsibilities of the two bodies is partly based on differentiating between 'plan' and 'nonplan' expenditures, which notionally coincide, respectively, with 'developmental' and 'non-developmental' expenditures. Thus, transfers for different categories of expenditure have, in theory, been determined, or influenced, by the two separate bodies. This has given rise to problems of co-ordination of objectives, compounded by the ultimate fungibility of much of the transfers, which means that both Finance Commission and plan transfers are general purpose in practice.[16]

Plan transfers to the states have, to a considerable degree, been determined by formulae[17] based on factors such as state income, urbanisation and population, but they have also included expenditures completely earmarked for projects determined by the centre, as well as projects which the centre encourages by providing matching funds. Some of these latter two categories of transfers occur outside the formal planning framework, further complicating the system of transfers.

The large element of central discretion and control suggests the argument that the degree of fiscal decentralisation suggested by aggregate statistics is overstated. In other words, if state expenditures are to a large extent determined by central instructions, the issue of the vertical fiscal imbalance becomes less important. On the other hand, the state fiscal deficits and increases in their indebtedness imply the opposite. In other words, if the centre wishes to control the fiscal deficit, and states are running large deficits, they must be doing something beyond the centre's control.

While the Planning Commission's role is directing resources to their potentially best uses for economic growth and development, the Finance Commission's responsibility also touches on the issue of how those resources are raised through the tax system. In particular, it recommends how the proceeds of taxes, such as the national income tax, are to be shared between centre and states. Understanding these issues requires some description of the Indian tax system in a federal perspective.

Central and state responsibilities and rights, with regard to which level of government can levy a particular tax and how the taxes are to be shared, are described in the Indian Constitution.[18] The Constitution delineated these responsibilities in broad terms, leaving specifics to be determined by the Finance Commissions. Successive Commissions have made recommendations about specific issues of sharing revenues, according to their successive interpretations of the Constitution. The results, however, allow for considerable administrative discretion, and, in the view of some,[19] the system favours the centre at the expense of the states in terms of raising resources through taxation. In this view, the Central Government has not adequately used existing constitutional provisions for levying taxes exclusively for states' purposes, under Article 269. Finance Commissions have interpreted Articles 270, 271 and 272 as allowing the Central Government to collect some taxes in ways exempt from tax revenue-sharing, thus reducing the states' share of taxes. For example, the centre has used a long-lasting income tax surcharge that is exempt from sharing with the states, rather than merging such taxes into the basic income tax structure, the revenues of which must be shared between centre and states. A similar motivation is alleged with respect to newer taxes that are made the exclusive preserve of the centre: the gift tax, wealth tax on urban immovable property and tax on interest earnings on bank deposits.

The data are suggestive of these concerns. For example, between 1980–81 and 1987–88, income tax revenue grew by about 90 per cent: tax revenue-sharing formulas have assigned 85 per cent of this revenue to the states, although it is collected by the centre. On the other hand, corporation tax revenue, solely assigned to the centre, rose by about 170 per cent in the same period.[20] Other examples include customs duties and central excise duties, both 'belonging' solely to the centre, which also rose rapidly in this period. Nor should this be surprising: if the centre pays an effective 'tax' on some forms of revenues through revenue-sharing, it will shift its own tax effort in other directions, just as an individual shifts effort from higher-taxed to lower-taxed directions.

However, the analogy to the behaviour of an individual neglects the fact that the centre, in its competition with the state governments, is not in an adversarial position. The objectives of the centre will presumably include the welfare of its constituents in each state. However, there is the possibility—one that seems evident for the Indian case—that each government is composed of self-interested individuals.[21] This might lead to adversarial competition for the control of resources. This issue is touched on again in the discussion of tax competition between the centre and states later in this section.

To recapitulate, the Central Government may tend to circumvent the Finance Commission's intent in tax revenue-sharing, and it has a superior command over tax resources. In practice, as indicated by the vertical fiscal imbalance, the centre has not fully translated this superior command over resources into greater direct expenditures, partly because of the constitutional assignment of expenditure responsibilities between the centre and the states. Hence, resources have flowed to the states through other channels that allow the centre to exercise considerably more discretion than in the case of transfers determined by exogenous formulae.

In fact, discretionary transfers appear to have grown as a proportion of revenue-sharing with the states in recent years. These discretionary transfers tend to favour states with higher per capita incomes,[22] particularly for transfers from the Central Government that are allocated according to matching formulae, i.e., where the centre matches state expenditures for a particular project or category according to a pre-set rule. This favours richer states since they can more easily come up with their share, and may be one contributing factor in the growth of fiscal disparities among states in India.

Finally, state deficits have grown, and loans to states by the centre have grown correspondingly, representing another potential conversion of rule-based finance of the states' expenditure to discretion-based finance. Since states have not been able to raise adequate resources on their capital accounts, they have regularly borrowed from the centre. Loans are based on Central Government discretion, which we suggest is swayed by political considerations. This discretion can come about in two ways. First, the centre has the power to grant the loans. Furthermore, it has the power, which it has used in practice, to write off those loans as well. Thus, this particular institutional arrangement has had some pernicious political implications,[23] and the issue of loans is therefore an important one.

Tax Competition between Central and State Governments

The problem of tax competition between the centre and the states extends beyond tax revenue-sharing. There is also considerable overlap in the imposition of taxes, particularly indirect taxes. Excise taxes by the Central Government, sales taxes by states and even local taxes[24] by urban government bodies may fall on the same commodities. For each type of taxation, there are often multiple rates, and there is little evidence of tax coordination between centre and states.[25] Rate multiplicity is not just a problem across levels of government. States impose a wide variety of sales tax rates and exemptions leading to significant variation in the effective tax rates imposed on different sectors and activities. For example, the state of Gujarat at one time had twenty-two different sales tax rates.

There are some systematic economic analyses of the details of this complex Indian tax structure, in particular the work of Ahmad and Stern (1987, 1991),[26] on which we draw here. The Indian ratio of taxes to GDP rose to 17 per cent by the mid-1980s, which is high in comparison to the rest of South Asia.[27] There has also been a steady increase in the importance of indirect taxes in revenue collection since independence. Indirect tax revenues totalled 14 per cent of GDP in the same period, while direct tax revenues were only 2.7 per cent of GDP, the same proportion of GDP as in fiscal year 1950–51. Thus the growth of the ratio of tax revenue to GDP was due to growth in indirect tax revenue. The relative unimportance of direct tax revenue is illustrated by the fact that there are only about ten million registered personal income tax payers in a population of 900 million. Finally, since liberalisation of the trade regime, through reductions of tariff rates and the replacement of quantitative restrictions by tariffs, began in the mid-1980s, customs duties have increased in relative importance, although indirect taxes in total have not increased as a fraction of GDP.

As noted earlier in this section, the particular indirect taxes imposed in India have been heavily affected by the provisions of the Constitution. Under the Government of India Act of 1935, which formed the basis for the 1950 Constitution's assignment of fiscal rights and responsibilities, the provinces (precursors of present-day states) were granted jurisdiction over the taxation of final goods. This assignment was carried over to independent India, with the result that the Central Government increasingly relied on excise taxes on domestic production. This use of excise taxes by the centre in turn led to a cascading structure of indirect taxes, with very high effective tax rates that vary greatly across sectors. In the 1980s, this problem was finally beginning to be addressed by the adoption of a modified value-added tax system called MODVAT that allowed for rebates of some taxes under Central Government control.[28]

Ahmad and Stern (1987)[29] have conducted a detailed analysis of possible directions of tax reform in India, given the structure summarised above. They examine the balance, within indirect taxes, of excises, sales taxes and customs duties, using the concept of social marginal cost of revenue, which is simply the loss in social welfare from the marginal rupee raised from each source. Thus a balanced tax system would be one where these social marginal costs are equalised. They also compare the estimated social marginal costs for indirect taxes with those from some possible direct tax increases. Their analysis allows for differences in evasion and in administrative costs of collection. Their results support the view that a shift towards direct taxation would be desirable, because it would reduce the social costs of raising a given aggregate tax revenue. They also find that a move towards a uniform per-person subsidy for consumers, financed by indirect taxation, would increase welfare. The caveat they provide for this latter result is that of administrative feasibility, and this issue is not really addressed in their technical analysis. Nor does such an approach incorporate the political economy of centre–state fiscal relations and the resulting constraints on possible changes. Finally, this kind of analysis does not address how the tax revenues are shared. As our approach suggests, the issue of tax revenue-sharing must affect the question of how taxes are collected. Hence this topic will be further discussed in this section.

A review of the overall experience of tax revenue-sharing,[30] and the work of the Indian Finance Commissions indicates that after some sizeable shifts in practice in the first decades after independence, changes in revenue-sharing have been marginal. The Ninth Finance Commission was given a fairly broad charge in terms of the questions of federalism it was asked to address. This was a change in approach from what previous commissions were asked to do. In particular, it was asked to adopt a normative approach for assessing the receipts and expenditures of the centre as well as the states, and to assess the debt positions of the states. Furthermore, expenditures under the national five-year plans, previously excluded from Finance Commission scrutiny, were now included implicitly in the Ninth Commission's terms of reference.[31] While the softening of the artificial distinction between plan and nonplan accounts was a desirable reform, the recommendations did not depart significantly from those of previous commissions, and the issues before the Tenth Finance Commission were essentially the same as for its predecessor. Their report made further marginal recommendations for balancing the states' share of different taxes, but also suggested a radical alternative that may be adopted (note 20).

In general, however, despite the constitutional mandate of the Finance Commissions, the Central Government has been reluctant to adopt those recommendations of recent commissions that would provide it with no benefits. An example of this is the recommendation of the Eighth Finance Commission in 1984, that states be allowed to tax advertisements in newspapers and journals. This recommendation was never acted on.[32] The recent experience, therefore, suggests that a fresh look at these issues is worthwhile. Numerous detailed and practical suggestions for reforming some or all of the formulae used for revenue-sharing have been made.[33] However, as is the case for tax reform suggestions, these recommendations have been partial: they specify how taxes should be shared without examining how and from where they should be collected.

Tax Competition between States

We have focused so far on centre–state fiscal relations. The competition among the lower-level components of the federation provides another dimension of fiscal federalism. This includes the phenomenon of tax exporting—choosing taxes to shift tax burdens to nonresidents.[34] Rao (1993)[35] provides examples of this phenomenon for the Indian case, while Rao and Vaillancourt (1993)[36] conduct a quantitative analysis of the distortions associated with tax competition among states in India.[37] They find that the efficiency losses are quite large. Other aspects of such competition include regressivity and the proliferation of tax rates for different commodities alluded to earlier.

In the Indian case, the centre has not been able to coordinate state actions with respect to taxation. A provision preventing restraints on interstate commerce, as in the United States Constitution, could be used to rule out taxation of interstate trade. When such provisions are not built into a constitution, the requisite political coalition for a cooperative agreement in this respect may be more difficult to create ex post facto. It is not impossible, however, particularly if the centre can legislate such changes in the context of wider tax reforms that are seen to benefit the population-weighted majority of states.

Local Governments

When we realise that most of the Indian states have populations the size of European countries or greater, the weakness of local governments in India is striking. This is presumably a legacy of the historical evolution of the Indian union. For example, the administrative structure of districts and subdivisions at substate level developed to its present form during British rule, which placed an emphasis on a lean, hierarchical administration. The British did make some attempts towards strengthening local governments in larger cities, but these were tempered by the need for centralised control.

Post-independence India maintained this tendency in many respects, with local governments existing, but often starved of funds and any real autonomy. This is beginning to change with the passage and implementation of the 73rd and 74th Amendments to the Constitution, which give rural and urban local governments more expenditure responsibility, require states to hold regular elections to these local governments and mandate the appointment of state finance commissions to recommend state–local transfers.[38]

The decentralisation of expenditure authority to local governments appears to fit with the theoretical principles that guide the appropriate geographic or population scope of governments for different tasks.[39] However, concerns have been expressed about the implications of this change for the problem of the fiscal deficits of the states.[40] While local government reform must certainly not soften their budget constraints further, and they must be given incentives to raise more revenue on their own, there are positive aspects of the institutional reforms taking place. Replacing discretionary state–local transfers with rule-bound, transparent transfers governed by state finance commissions can reduce influence costs, as will be discussed later in the context of centre–state transfers. Furthermore, the political influence equation is somewhat different between state and local governments, compared to that between the centre and medium-sized or large states: with the exception of a few metropolitan cities, no single locality or district matters politically to the Central Government in the way a large entity such as a state can. This, too, should reduce the problem of soft budget constraints.

This overview has discussed three aspects of Indian fiscal federalism: the vertical fiscal imbalance between the centre and the states; tax competition between the centre and the states; and tax competition among the states themselves. An understanding of the operation of Indian fiscal federalism requires attention to the political and economic incentives of the different levels of government, and how they interact. Vertical fiscal relations are relevant to horizontal competition as well. Since we know that a benevolent, well-informed centre could resolve the problem, understanding why horizontal competition persists to such a great degree in the Indian fiscal system requires understanding the centre's incentives. Thus the next section will focus on the interaction of the centre with the states, rather than interactions among the states.

II POLITICAL ECONOMY OF FISCAL FEDERALISM

The picture of Indian fiscal federalism that emerges from the overview is one of inefficiencies in revenue collection and expenditure allocation, and an urgent problem of fiscal deficits. The inefficiencies in the tax structure are indicated by the various features of the tax system at different levels: cascading taxes; protectionist taxes; multiple and widely varying tax rates; absence of taxation of some sectors; and narrow tax bases. The results are a highly distortionary tax system and resulting inefficiencies. Many of these problems could and would exist in a unitary governmental system, but they appear to be exacerbated by the particular institutional structures of Indian federalism.

If all levels of government were benevolent and perfectly informed, it would be an easy matter to discuss optimal policies. Whatever the federal structure, the Central Government could use corrective taxes and subsidies for any positive or negative externalities that arose at lower levels of decisionmaking.[41] If we remove the assumption of perfect information, the problem becomes more interesting and complex, but again essentially straightforward: design the corrective policies to be incentive compatible, and that is all. The solution is essentially based purely on technical economic considerations of marginal benefits and costs. However, it is clear from the literature on Indian fiscal federalism that such solutions have been proposed in abundance. There are detailed analyses of formulae and outcomes for the work of the Planning and Finance Commissions over the last decades. The political and incentive issues are recognised, of course, but are not modelled systematically.

This discussion therefore begins with the premise that governments are made up of self-interested individuals[42] and that the government is subject to rent-seeking behaviour.[43] Government decisionmakers are in a position to create these rents through their policy choices. They cannot necessarily capture these rents directly, but it is often the case that they indirectly get a share through the competition of others for those rents. For example, a politician may not be able to directly take advantage of an import quota, but can allocate the quota to an industrialist in return for campaign contributions or to someone with kinship ties.

Government susceptibility to corruption is easily condemned. However, it is also possible that activities that come under the category of rent-seeking may inseparably have a positive role as well. Milgrom (1988) and Milgrom and Roberts (1988, 1990) bring this point out clearly in the context of behaviour in organisations.[44] They use the neutral term 'influence activities' instead of 'rent-seeking'. With respect to the design of institutions or organisations, if the benefits from such activities in conveying information for better resource allocation are relatively low, the central decisionmaker should be insulated from lower-level influence activities by not having discretion in such matters.

In examining Indian fiscal federalism, we have suggested that its development has been towards increasing discretionary control of resources by the centre. Part of this may reflect a divergence of objectives. If the centre wants a certain activity or project undertaken, it can earmark its transfer to the state for that purpose, or it can provide inducements through matching formulas. This is standard in discussions of fiscal federalism.[45] In the Indian case, however, the Central Government also sometimes effectively underwrites expenditures of the state governments that it does not control or direct. It does this through the granting of loans that are subsequently forgiven. What makes this method of providing resources superior to directly providing states with additional funds by allowing tax revenue-sharing of, say, income tax surcharges?

Several answers are possible. One is that different categories of expenditures, current and capital, require different sources of funds. Using tax revenue shares instead of loans may not be appropriate for capital expenditures. On the other hand, funds are fungible. There is no guarantee that a rupee raised by taxation will go for current expenditure, while a rupee raised by borrowing goes for capital expenditure, even if the borrowing is earmarked for investment, since the government can reallocate to current expenditure money that would have been spent on capital projects in the absence of the borrowing.

Another possibility is that a formulaic allocation of revenues might not serve the equity objectives of the Central Government, requiring further discretionary transfers. But we have observed that equity objectives did not appear to be met by discretionary transfers in practice. In fact, it is the formulaic transfers that have typically had some equity or equalising considerations built into them.

The remaining explanation is that the observed system of financing the state governments has given the centre the most discretion to achieve goals that are well-defined—and therefore fit the standard model of economic behaviour—but are determined by government decisionmakers' self-interest, rather than aggregate social welfare. This concept of self-interest does not exclude attention to the preferences of constituents. Government decisionmakers may trade off current gain against the possibility of future gain through reelection. Alternatively, government decisionmakers may pursue self-interest within the constraints imposed by the primary requirement of satisfying voters and winning reelection. This latter approach is taken in the following section.

Why should control over state governments in this manner matter for the central decisionmaker seeking to maximise long-run self-interest? We suggest that the states are the key political units for control of the Central Government. A cooperative state government in India can be very important in delivering a large fraction of its national parliamentary seats at the time of a general election. This is not a guarantee, but casual observation of Indian elections does suggest this as a possibility.

Two further issues remain. First, in the context of fiscal federalism, what is the analogue of the owner of a firm in the organisational setting as considered by Milgrom and Roberts?[46] The Central Government itself does not fulfil that role, since its interests lie in creating discretionary power and responding to influence activities. The closest analogue, instead, is the population of the country. How do the people collectively impose rules that prevent the kind of discretionary behaviour that may arise in the Indian case? Recall that such discretionary actions by the Central Government are not in themselves undesirable. Standard arguments in the fiscal federalism literature could justify them if the objectives of government were equity and externality correction that could not adequately be achieved by lower-level governments.

One can think of different solutions to this problem of imposition of collective will of the populace on its representatives. One is a rewriting of the Constitution, yet no Constitution can be detailed enough to completely rule out such behaviour, and achieving a constitutional change may be difficult. An alternative, more feasible route, is changing the rules that govern the interaction between the centre and states within the existing constitutional framework.

The second issue involves the behaviour of the state governments. The increasing discretionary aspects of the Central Government's transfers to the states imply increasing control of the centre over the expenditures of state governments. However, the states have been running deficits which have been covered by central loans and transfers, and they are perceived as being profligate in many ways.[47] The answer to this apparent contradiction lies in the state governments' responsiveness to influence activities from their own constituents, for example, farmers who receive subsidies, and their power in delivering votes to the centre. A possible prediction, therefore, would be that if power at the centre were to become more solidified than it has been recently, the centre would be able to squeeze state expenditures more successfully, shifting the focus of influence activities by various interest groups to the centre.[48]

The implications of the suggestions made in this section are as follows. A key implication is that any feasible reform must either work within the political constraints, or finesse them. Reforms that make everyone better off are obviously easiest to implement. The Central Government is moving towards a full-scale introduction of a value-added tax (VAT). This clearly has the potential to increase efficiency. It is less clear how those gains will be divided. To the extent that reforms can increase the size of the economy, the trade-off for central decisionmakers, in terms of different ways of achieving their self-interest, may also change. If they gain less from discretionary influence on state government expenditures and other, political, actions, they may be more willing to allow a reassignment of tax revenue rights that more closely aligns expenditures and revenues at the state level and provides better incentives for tax effort. In principle there is no constitutional problem with, for example, all direct taxes being collected and allocated by the centre and all domestic indirect taxes by the states. It could also be the case that a smaller vertical fiscal imbalance through such reassignments could be consistent with more efficient revenue raising without upsetting the Central Government's political control at the margin. Finally, once again it is noted that the urgency of the overall fiscal deficit exerts pressure to change the current fiscal federal structure.

The next section steps back from these more general thoughts on policy and reform to sketch a model that incorporates some of the above mentioned features of Indian fiscal federalism. It discusses how different layers of government may pursue self-interest within the context of also satisfying voters, and how two layers of government can interact in such a context. Even though it is far from capturing all the issues described in this section and the last, the model adds some insights to the political economy of Indian fiscal federalism.

III OUTLINE OF A MODEL

This section begins with a brief mention of related work. In terms of the median voter framework used in this study, the closest work is probably that of Persson and Tabellini (1992).[49] They examine alternative fiscal federal structures in the context of providing social insurance, and investigate methods of alleviating moral hazard problems in the provision of such insurance by different levels of government. The model in this study differs in the nature of the public goods being provided, and its attention to influence activities. Murty and Ray (1990) formally examine the problem of optimal commodity taxation in a federal system, comparing centralised and decentralised decisionmaking.[50] They use a standard social welfare framework, rather than being concerned with political economy aspects. Since they focus on tax coordination issues, their work is somewhat complementary to the model used here. Wildasin (1983, 1984) examines the welfare effects of intergovernment grants in situations where households may be mobile, and where local governments use distortionary taxes.[51] Again, his models highlight features that are complementary to those considered in this analysis. Constraints on policy reforms have been informally discussed but have not been dealt with in this model. An example of how this may be done in the context of commodity tax reform is the work of Kanbur and Myles (1993).[52] Finally, a static model is outlined, without intertemporal budget constraints. Velasco (1992) analyses fiscal deficits in a dynamic political economy model, though without layers of government.[53]

The model outlined here is an attempt to incorporate several features of Indian fiscal federalism in a formal framework.[54] This enables one to see more precisely the assumptions that underlie various informal arguments that have been made. In keeping with this focus, attention is restricted to two levels of government. The higher level is the centre, and the multiple jurisdictions under it are indexed by l to indicate the lower level. We may think of these as state governments. We assume there are L of these lower-level governments.

Basic Assumptions

Each government provides an amount of public goods. For the centre, this is denoted by G, and for lower-level government l it is G_l. There is also a single amount of private goods, and the amount of this in jurisdiction l is x_l. Household preferences over the three goods are identical up to a parameter, b, that measures the relative preference for public versus private goods. Two further assumptions are: first, the relative preference measured by b is for both public goods versus the private goods; and second, there is separability in the preferences of public versus private goods. Thus the household utility function is:

$$bU(G, G_l) + W(x_l).$$

Further restrictions on preferences are possible. Utility may be linear in private goods consumption, $bU(G, G_l) + x_l$, or it may be separable in the two public goods, $b[U(G) + V(G_l)] + W(x_l)$.

The preference parameter b has a cumulative distribution function $F_l\ (b)$, with support [0, 1]. The median of b in jurisdiction l is defined by $F_l\ (b) = 1/2$, and denoted by b_l^m. There is also a distribution of b at the national level, which is the average of the lower-level distributions. Specifically, if n_l is the number of individuals, households or voters in jurisdiction l, the national distribution of b is given by:

$$F(b) = \Sigma_{n_l} F_l\ (b)/\Sigma_{n_l} \quad (1)$$

This distribution is not of direct interest, since what matters to the Central Government is the median demand level for the public goods, rather than the median value of b at the national level.

Budget Constraints and Taxes

We assume that income per capita in jurisdiction l is given by I_l, exogenous and identical for everyone in that jurisdiction. However, it may differ across jurisdictions: there may be rich and poor states, for example. Both levels of government impose taxes on this income.[55] For simplicity, we assume these taxes are proportional to income, and that there is no deductibility of lower-level taxes. The respective tax rates for centre and lower levels are t and t_l. Unit costs of collecting the taxes are k and k_l respectively, so the tax revenues at the two levels are given by:

$$(2) \quad \begin{array}{ll} \text{Centre:} & (t - k)\Sigma\, I_l\, n_l \\ \text{State:} & (t_l - k_l)\, I_l\, n_l \end{array}$$

The budget constraint of an individual is given by:

(3) $$x_l = I_l - t_l I_l - t I_l$$

These collection costs can include losses due to bribery and corruption, though one has to be careful with this interpretation, since corruption in tax administration often means that less than the official taxes are paid by individuals. Here we are thinking of t and t_l as official tax rates, and the costs k and k_l are exogenous.

Government Expenditures

Governments use their tax revenues to finance the provision of public goods. The constant unit cost for the national public goods is c. This can include waste, administrative costs and corruption that may be involved in production. Similarly, the unit cost of the public goods produced in jurisdiction l is c_l. For the moment, we assume there are no intergovernment transfers. This is a static model, so there is no intertemporal reallocation possible by government, and current expenditure on public goods must be financed by current tax revenues. Hence the budget constraints are:

(4)
$$\text{Centre:} \quad cG = (t - k)\Sigma I_l n_l$$
$$\text{State:} \quad c_l G_l = (t_l - k_l) I_l n_l$$

Decisionmaking

Political objectives appropriate for a democracy are incorporated in the usual way, assuming that the government obeys the preferences of the median voter. The logic of this assumption is that a majority of voters will favour this over any other alternative, provided preferences are single-peaked so that alternatives (here the levels of the public goods) can be ordered in a unique way.[56] Single-peakedness is ensured by our assumptions about household preferences and budgets. Government decisionmakers may also seek monetary rewards. This is one of the possible reasons, along with power and prestige, that they wish to get reelected by pleasing the majority. We could think of this objective as being met through some share of the spending on public goods: some part of the unit cost of each level of public goods, exogenously determined, could be due to appropriation of funds by individuals in government. Therefore this second objective could be met by increasing the levels of the public goods. We assume that this objective is subordinate to doing what the median voter wants.[57]

Decisionmaking at the state level is straightforward, since everyone is identical up to the parameter b and faces identical taxes. The household with the median b also determines the median G_l . This value is determined as follows, assuming linear preferences for the private goods. Utility, incorporating the government budget constraint, is:

$$bU(G, G_l) + I_l - t_l I_l - t I_l = bU(G, G_l) + I_l - \frac{c_l G_l}{n_l} - k_l I_l - \frac{cGI_l}{\Sigma n_l I_l} - kI_l \tag{5}$$

The preferred level of the local public goods for this household is given by the first order condition:[58]

$$bU_2(G, G_l) - \frac{c_l}{n_l} = 0 \tag{6}$$

The subscript '2' indicates the derivative with respect to the second argument. Recall that b_l^m is the median b for this jurisdiction. Then, equation (6), with this value of b, implicitly defines the median level of the demand for the local public goods, G_l^m $(G, b_l^m, c_l/n_l)$, which will be chosen by the lower-level government. It depends on the level of the national public goods. If a higher G reduces the marginal utility of the lower-level public goods, i.e., the goods are weak substitutes, it will reduce G_l^m, making the two levels of government in competition with respect to their choices. If the two levels of public goods are complementary in individual utility, this is true of the interests of the two levels of government. These strategic considerations are within the constraints imposed by the need to satisfy the median voter.

Costs of tax collection do not enter the determination of the level of the local public goods in equation (6). However, this is just a consequence of the special, quasi-linear utility function. For example, if utility is separable, but not quasi-linear, the condition becomes:

$$bU_2(G, G_l) - W'(.)\frac{c_l}{n_l} = 0 \qquad (7)$$

and the additional derivative in the second term does depend on the costs of tax collection.

The key difference from the lower level in how the Central Government chooses G is that, since incomes vary across lower-level jurisdictions, there is no one-to-one correspondence between the preference parameter b and the demand for the national public goods. We illustrate this with an example where utility is separable in the public goods at the two levels.[59]

Example 1 We assume there are two states as the lower-level jurisdiction, each of size n. Income per capita in state 1 is 1 and in state 2 is 2. There are no collection costs for taxes. The unit costs of the public goods are $2n$ and n, respectively, at the national and state levels. This assumption is consistent with the national public goods having twice the size per unit, as it has to reach twice as many people (there are no economies of scale). The household utility function is $b(lnG + lnG_l) + x_l$. The distribution of b in each state is uniform on [0, 1], so the median b in each state is 1/2. Thus, the national distribution of b is also the same. At the state level, the first order condition is just $b/G_l - n/n = 0$. Substituting in the median value of 1/2, the equilibrium amount of G_l must be 1/2. For the national public goods, the general first order condition in this case is

$$bU_l(G, G_l) - \frac{cI_l}{\Sigma I_l n_l} = 0 \qquad (8)$$

Substituting in the particular values, for state 1 this reduces to $b/G - 2n/[n(1+2)] = 0$, so $G^d(b) = 3b/2$, where the superscript indicates that this is the demand of individual with preference parameter b, and not necessarily the outcome. Similarly, in state 2, the demand by individual b is $G^d(b) = 3b/4$. Individuals in the rich state demand less of the national public goods because, with a proportional tax on income, they have to pay more for it. To calculate the demand of the median person, we have to derive the distribution of demand levels, G^d. For state 1, the c.d.f. of G^d is $2G/3$, on the interval [0, 3/2]. For state 2, it is $4G/3$, on the interval [0, 3/4]. Since the states are of equal size, the national distribution of G^d is obtained by taking the simple average of these two functions. We obtain:

$$H(G) = \begin{cases} G & \text{on } [0, 3/4] \\ (1/2) + G/3 & \text{on } [3/4, 3/2] \end{cases}$$

Thus, the median of this distribution is $G = 1/2$, and this is chosen by the centre obeying median voter preferences. This level of G is optimal for individuals with $b = 1/3$ in state 1 and $b = 2/3$ in state 2, illustrating the lack of a one-to-one correspondence between the distributions of b at the state level or national level and the distribution of demands for G at the national level.

The example is particularly simple because the choices of public goods at the national and lower levels are independent. If this is not the case, the demand for G by individual b in state l is a function $G^d(G_l, b, s_l)$, where the last argument represents the cost share term. Now the distribution of demands for the national public goods depends on the levels of the state public goods. These levels, however, also depend on the level of the national public goods, as we saw earlier. That dependence did not matter in determining the median demand at the state level, because of the correspondence between the distributions of b and G_l. Here, however, the median demand for G can depend on the whole distribution of levels of state public goods. At the equilibrium, it must be true that the choices of the levels of government are consistent. In other words, the level of G chosen is the median of a distribution based on substituting each of the $G_l^m(G, b_l^m, c_l/n_l)$ into the function $G^d(G_l, b, s_l)$.[60]

In such cases, where there is interdependence of central and lower-level government choices, the issue of strategic behaviour becomes important. For example, one could think of the centre choosing G given the various lower-level choices and the equilibrium being a fixed point of the game. Alternatively, the centre could be able to pre-commit, knowing how the lower-level governments will respond to its choices. Why should either level of government care, since they always do what the median voter wants? A higher public expenditure at your level implies a greater cut for you as the political decisionmaker.

Representative Government

Political support at the centre depends not on direct elections, but on gaining a majority in parliament. Hence the Central Government may not be concerned with the median voter per se, but with achieving such a majority. The median voter logic still applies, in a modified form.

Example 2 In Example 1, let there be a third state, also of the same size, but with income level 1/2. Now all the demands must be recalculated, as the total income is $7n/2$. The demand for the national public goods in this poorest state is $G^d = 7b/2$, while the demands in the other two states are $7b/4$ and $7b/8$.[61] The distributions of demands in the states are now $2G/7$ on [0, 7/2], $4G/7$ on [0, 7/4], and $8G/7$ on [0, 7/8]. As before, we may construct the national distribution of demands for the national public goods:

$$H(G) = \begin{cases} 2G/3 & \text{on } [0, 7/8] \\ (1/3) + (2G/7) & \text{on } [7/8, 7/4] \\ (2/3) + (2G/21) & \text{on } [7/4, 7/2]. \end{cases}$$

If the Central Government directly cares about the national median voter, it chooses a level of 3/4, the median of this distribution. However, if the objective is to win support in a majority of constituencies, the optimal choice is different. To emphasise this, assume that each state is a single constituency. Then the level 3/4 is not optimal. For example, the level 4/5, which is greater, will be preferred by majorities in the two poorer constituencies or states, in a pairwise choice versus 3/4. In fact, the optimal choice here is $G = 7/8$, the preferred level for the median voter in the median constituency.

Representative democracy also has another consequence for fiscal federalism. Now the Central Government requires more information than it did in the case of direct democracy, where it had to know only the national median of demands for the centrally provided public goods. Here it must be able to rank constituencies in terms of demands for the public goods,[62] and then determine what the median voter in the median constituency would most prefer. This creates a role for state governments as providers of information, and possibly as implementers of the centrally desired level of the national public goods. Also, if the Central Government can not determine the optimal level of the national public goods, it may substitute spending by the relevant state government (where the median constituency may be located) as a way of gaining political support. This alternative would require the state and Central Governments to be complementary in terms of political support, as would be true if they were composed of the same or allied political parties. This logic provides an additional possible rationale for intergovernmental transfers.

Intergovernmental Transfers

The next step in modelling is to introduce the possibility of transfers between states or levels of government. Various positive reasons for such transfers can be enumerated. First, the Central Government may be relatively more effective or efficient at collecting tax revenues than the states. The standard reasons for this include tax coordination and the desire to avoid tax flight by mobile factors. What is also plausible in the Indian context is the fact that reasons such as the concentration of administrative talent at the centre can lead to greater ease in enforcing compliance at the centre. At the same time, this would not translate into higher expenditure directly by the centre for several possible reasons. The states may be able to deliver public goods at their level at lower unit costs than the centre. Furthermore, as suggested above, they may know individual preferences better than the centre does. In this model, for example, the centre may know only the aggregate distribution of preferences or public goods demands without knowing them at each lower-level jurisdiction. This pertains to possible central provision of lower-level public goods, and not to central provision of the national public goods. If the centre raised more revenue and simply spent it on a higher level of the national public goods, this would not achieve the desired pattern of public goods spending. This point is in addition to the political and informational reasons discussed in the previous paragraph.

While all the foregoing are standard reasons for intergovernmental transfers that can be included in this model without major changes, there are two additional ones that are not directly incorporated. First, the Central Government may wish to correct for interjurisdictional externalities or spillovers through the use of intergovernment transfers.[63] Second, it may wish to achieve redistribution on equity grounds, and can not do it effectively by direct transfers to individuals for informational or similar reasons.[64] While these considerations are not directly incorporated in this model, they may still be thought of as influencing the Central Government's need for transfers to lower-level governments.

Considering more formally the effects of introducing intergovernment transfers in the model outlined previously, let R_l be the amount transferred to jurisdiction *l*. The budget constraint for the lower-level government is now:

$$c_l G_l = (t_l - k_l)\, I_l\, n_l + R_l \qquad (9)$$

If the transfer is not tied to marginal spending on the local public goods, then this is a lump-sum grant.[65] For example, if utility is quasi-linear, there is no stimulative effect on consumption of the lower-level public goods. The effect of the transfer will be purely to raise private goods consumption, *ceteris paribus*. However, this ignores changes in the central budget constraint, which is now:

$$cG = (t - k)\Sigma\, I_l\, n_l - \Sigma\, R_l \qquad (10)$$

Again, with quasi-linear utility, the equilibrium amount of the national public goods is unchanged, but since the resulting tax rates are different, there is an effect on private consumption. In Example 1, with two states, the rich state is taxed more by the centre using a proportional tax. Assuming that the collection costs are unchanged, the net result of the transfers will be no change in public goods levels in any jurisdiction, but a possible redistribution from the rich state to the poor state.[66] Since total spending on public goods is unchanged, aggregate tax revenue, net of collection costs, is unchanged. However, if the Central Government can raise revenue more efficiently, shifting the tax burden to central taxes from state taxes has the effect of reducing the losses to individuals from the tax collection process. If the transfers are chosen appropriately as well, it is possible that all individuals could be better off than in the situation of no transfers.

Putting aside differences in tax collection costs, we now examine the implications of intergovernment transfers for political support in this model. So far, we have assumed that the Central Government chooses only G, and is driven by political competition to choose based on the preferences with respect to G of the median voter in the median state. Taxes, which finance expenditure, are uniquely determined by G when there are no intergovernment transfers. Thus the centre has a one-dimensional problem. Transfers add several dimensions to the centre's decision problem. We consider Example 2, with intergovernment transfers now allowed.

In general, net transfers per capita resulting from intergovernment grants, once changes in central taxation are allowed for, are:

$$\frac{R_l}{n_l} - \frac{I_l \Sigma R_l}{\Sigma I_l n_l} \tag{11}$$

In the example, with equal state population sizes, n, and per capita incomes of 1/2, 1 and 2, for states 1, 2 and 3 respectively, one obtains the following expressions for per capita net transfers: $(6R_1 - R_2 - R_3)/7n$, $(-2R_1 + 5R_2 - 2R_3)/7n$ and $(-4R_1 - 4R_2 + 3R_3)/7n$. These sum to zero, as net transfers must in this model. This implies two degrees of freedom for the centre: it can choose the R's to make one or two net transfers positive. If it is motivated by political support, it will choose the latter course of action, benefiting two states through intergovernment transfers at the expense of the third. Hence two of the above expressions will be positive, and the third negative. However, unlike in the choice of the level of the public goods, there is no natural ordering of states, so there are three different sets of policies[67] in this example that will satisfy the majority preference criterion, that is, any of the subsets of two states out of the three.

To illustrate the implied restrictions on the transfers, suppose that states 1 and 2 receive positive net transfers. The inequalities are $6R_1 - R_2 - R_3 > 0$, $-2R_1 + 5R_2 - 2R_3 > 0$ and $-4R_1 - 4R_2 + 3R_3 < 0$. In this case, it must be true that $4R_1 > R_3$, and that $2R_2 > R_3$. Thus transfers are weighted in favour of states 1 and 2 from a baseline defined by the income ratios ($4I_1 = I_3$, $2I_2 = I_3$). Also, to understand the relationship between R_1 and R_2, suppose that R_3 is zero. Then it must be true that $5/2R_2 > R_1 > 1/6R_2$. Similar inequalities can be derived for the other two cases (states 1 and 3 or states 2 and 3 receive positive net transfers).

A partial resolution of this indeterminacy, of the composition of the group that receives positive net transfers, can be obtained as follows. Recall that the best choice of G for the Central Government in this case is 7/8, the preferred level for the median voter in the middle income state. This is supported by majorities in the two poorer states, 1 and 2, against any lower alternative. It is supported by states 2 and 3 against any higher alternative expenditure level. Hence, since the middle-income state is always in the majority coalition for *G*, it may be reasonable to assume that the net transfer to state 2 will be positive, with either state 1 or state 3 joining it in this position.

A further resolution can be obtained by assuming that state 2 (or the legislator from this state) in this example has agenda-setting power, as a result of being the 'median state'. If it can choose combinations of transfers most favourable to it, then with state 1 on its side, it can set R_3 equal to zero, and make R_1 as close to $1/6R_2$ as possible. If it instead chooses to win over state 3, then it can set R_1 equal to zero, but must satisfy $5/2R_2 > R_3 > 3/4R_2$. The second inequality is less attractive for state 2. In essence, it is easier to 'buy off' the poorer state in this example. Of course this is not the only way to introduce agenda-setting into the model,[68] but our example helps to illustrate how the pattern of transfers may be affected by political considerations. To the extent that the outcome is not an efficient or equitable pattern, formulaic transfers may be preferable over discretionary ones. A further issue is that of influence costs, and that will be taken up later.

First, however, consider matching grants. In the discussion so far, it was assumed that intergovernment transfers are lump-sum, so that with quasi-linear individual utilities, there is no stimulative effect on local public goods consumption. Continuing with the quasi-linear, separable case, we note that the centre does have a way of stimulating lower-level public goods expenditure if it wishes. The reasons for wanting to do so could be, for example, spillovers across lower-level jurisdictions that are neglected by those lower-level governments. In this case, transfers may be in the form of matching grants, so that $R_l = a_l c_l G_l$. A matching grant of this form reduces the marginal cost of local public goods production, and therefore increases the equilibrium provision of local public goods.

To explore this more explicitly, suppose that collection costs are zero. Then the budget constraint (5) becomes, instead,

$$bU(G, G_l) + I_l - (t_l - t)\, t_l = bU(G, G_l) + I_l - \frac{c_l\,(1 - a_l)\, G_l}{n_l} - \frac{(cG + \Sigma\, a_l c_l G_l) I_l}{\Sigma n_l I_l} \qquad (12)$$

Now the first order condition for the choice of the local public goods is:

(13)
$$bU_2\,(G, G_l) - \frac{c_l\,(1 - a_l)}{n_l} - \frac{a_l c_l I_l}{\Sigma n_l I_l} = 0,$$

instead of equation (6). There are two additional terms, reflecting the direct subsidy, partly cancelled by the effect through the change in the central tax rate. It is clearly the case that G_j is increasing in a_l. It is now also decreasing in I_l, through the central tax rate effect, unlike the case of equation (6). In Example 2, the separability of U implies that this condition is independent of G, the level of the national public goods. Similarly, in the example, the level of the national public goods will be unaffected by the stimulative effect on local public goods levels.

The choice variables for the centre are now the matching rates as well as the level of G. In Example 2, the poorer state tends to benefit more for a given matching rate, because it pays the least in central taxes to finance the transfers. Hence, a uniform matching rate will definitely benefit the poorer state, and possibly the middle state as well. As in the case of lump sum transfers, it is possible to explore different combinations of matching rates: however the algebra is considerably more complicated in this case.

This model can be extended to one with a more general preference structure, in which preferences over national and local public goods are not separable and utility is not linear in the private good. In that case, transfers between jurisdictions will have additional effects caused by substitution in household preferences that can either support or hinder federal government objectives. This possibility will be reconsidered after influence activities are introduced into the framework.

Influence Activities

When the federal government designs transfer schemes to provide incentives for lower levels of government, the possibility arises that subnational authorities can engage in activities to try to influence the amounts of lump-sum transfers or the formulae that determine them. This can happen, as noted in earlier discussion, when the Central Government policymakers retain discretion over at least a portion of intergovernment transfers. Milgrom and Roberts' formulation of influence activities within an organisation can be applied to intergovernment transfers in a federation.[69] Discretion at the central level can give rise to unproductive redistributive activities by lower levels of government that can reduce or offset the gains from providing incentive schemes such as matching grant formulas. Suppose that the Central Government can select either the amounts of intergovernment transfers, R_l, or policy formula parameters, such as a_l. Because state or local government policymakers prefer receiving larger transfers from the Central Government so that they can provide higher levels of spending on state or local public goods, they will expend effort in general trying to change the federal policy. For example, the model can be extended to allow state fiscal authorities to expend effort e_l in jurisdiction l on activities that yield an increase in R_l. This can be costly, so also assume that the unit cost of producing the public goods, c_l, rises with e_l, perhaps because influence activities take attention away from the management of the state government. Each local or state jurisdiction will balance the costs with the benefits of these redistributive efforts at the margin to decide how much they engage in lobbying or other types of influence activities.

We also need to explain how efforts of the subnational public authorities influence the policy choices of the Central Government actors. We may assume that the federal authorities can be successfully swayed because they receive some benefit. The returns to the public officials could be monetary, although such gains might be obtained more easily in a direct fashion. The benefit could also be in the form of political support of various kinds. If the centre cares about the median voter in each jurisdiction, as well as at the national level, it may need to use state or other lower-level governments in this fashion, to please voters appropriately.

In the kinds of examples of intergovernment transfers that have previously been discussed, legislators of an agenda-setting state may be able to extract rents from the state that joins it in the winning coalition. While this may involve direct transfers, which have purely distributional effects, such transfers may be difficult to implement, and alternatives such as adjusting the level of the national public goods, which reduces efficiency, may also be used. Furthermore, there may not be a pure bidding process, and costly influence activities may be involved.

Finally, consider the case where there is substitution between national and state public goods in the preferences of the voters in each jurisdiction and where the utility function defined over these two goods differs across jurisdictions. That is, voter preferences are given by

$$bU^l(G, G_l) + W(x_l),$$

where the distribution over the characteristic b can vary across the states. $U^l(G, G_l)$ differs in functional form across states in a way so that the median voter in each state desires a different mix between national and state public goods. In general, federal authorities can choose different policy packages consisting of national public goods spending and a set of transfers to the states (along the lines discussed earlier regarding intergovernment transfers) that will meet the approval of a simple majority of the states' median voters. Different policy proposals that yield a parliamentary majority will necessarily attract a different collection of the states to the majority coalition.

It is assumed that federal authorities are self-interested, and either benefit from achieving a majority (which requires some more extensive modelling) or from payments from local authorities (a simple addition). In this case, the federal government decisionmakers do not have incentives to make generous transfers to the states that do not contribute to the winning coalition of states. In fact, they only need to make transfers to the states that form the majority coalition. This implies that the median voter in each state will want the state fiscal authorities to do whatever they can, up to the limit of marginal costs equalling marginal benefits, to get into the majority. The median voter of a state that forms part of the parliamentary majority achieves a more desired national and local public goods plan. The stakes for the states in this type of model can be quite large when, as in the case of India, intergovernmental transfers provide for a large share of state public expenditures.

This framework suggests that the costs of influence activities may outweigh the benefits of discretion in making transfers between the federal level and the states or across states through the federation. One solution is to remove such discretion by pre-committing to amounts or formulae. This restraint of discretion might lose some of the possible benefits of such transfers if, for example, it requires imposing uniformity where variation might be efficiency-enhancing.

One way to pre-commit that is less restrictive is to have the decisions delegated to another body that would not be as susceptible to influence. This is the significant potential role of the Finance Commissions in India, at the central level in the past, and now also in state–local fiscal transfers. We suggest that it may be beneficial to strengthen this role.

IV CONCLUSION

An overview and analysis of Indian fiscal federalism has been provided that stresses the interaction of political and economic factors in a particular institutional environment. A model has been sketched that may be extended to examine some of these factors in shaping Indian fiscal federalism and its consequences for resource allocation. The model proposes a systematic framework for analysing the interactions between the institutions of fiscal federalism and political decisionmaking, including strategic behaviour on the part of self-interested government decisionmakers. It incorporates the constraints imposed by a democratic polity through a median voter framework. Governments can still act in their own self-interest because they capture some of the revenues obtained through taxes or intergovernment transfers. In the context of intergovernment transfers, Section III indicates how there can be a trade-off between the cost of influence activities and the benefits of discretion in such a model. This helps to make more precise the kinds of issues raised in this overview of the Indian case.

Section III concludes with a discussion of the consequences of influence activities pursued between levels of government in a federation. These activities are motivated by the capacity of the federal government to make interjurisdictional transfers. Two essential features of the discussion are: (*a*) representative majority voting determines the fiscal policy of the federal government, and (*b*) federal fiscal authorities have some degree of discretion over public goods provision at the national level and transfers of federal revenues to the state or local governments.

There is a significant degree of discretion at the central level in India over both policy instruments and the share of tax revenues that accrue to the Central Government. The costs of discretionary policymaking at the centre of a fiscal federal system under representative majoritarian rule can be very large if the Central Government does not have an incentive to make transfers to states left out of the majority-forming coalition of states. This relates to concerns that Indian fiscal federalism may not promote national goals for equitable treatment of regions or communities. Discretionary policy making and consequent influence activities in the median voter model can reduce social welfare through adverse effects on allocative efficiency and the distribution of public resources. These costs of influence activities supplement concerns that, while discretion for policy-makers is important for allocative efficiency, it can come at the cost of encouraging rent-seeking.

A general note on reforms in India, based on the overview of India's tax and expenditure systems in a federal perspective in Sections I and II, concludes this discussion. There are several challenges to reforming India's federal structure of taxes and public expenditures. Coordination of tax systems among states and between the states and the Central Government is needed for improving allocative efficiency in the economy. However, tax reform will be difficult to negotiate because states have a constitutional right to levy sales taxes, allowing taxation of interstate trade. Base broadening should be a prominent goal of fiscal reform in India, although this too faces institutional impediments. For example, taxation of the service sector, the fastest growing part of the economy, is within the province of the states, as is taxation of agriculture. Rationalisation of indirect taxes and base-broadening of the overall tax structure are important and are receiving attention in policymaking. This analysis and discussion suggest that institutional reform should also include the reduction of incentives for costly influence activities across levels of government.

NOTES

This material in this chapter was originally prepared for a project exploring the institutional impediments to economic reforms in India, funded by USAID through the Center for Institutional Reform and the Informal Sector (IRIS) at the University of Maryland. Earlier versions were presented at conferences on Indian economic and institutional reform, sponsored by IRIS (final revision February 1998). The authors gratefully acknowledge the many helpful comments received on those occasions. Discussions with M. Govinda Rao and with Pritam Singh Kohli, and detailed comments by Satu Kähkönen on an earlier version of the paper were also most helpful. However, the views expressed here are our own and not those of any of these organisations or individuals.

1. Exceptions to this statement include Rao, Rao and Tulsidhar, and particularly, Rao and Sen (Rao, M. G. 1981, *Political Economy of Tax and Expenditure Determination: A Case Study of Four Indian States*, New Delhi: Allied Publishers; Rao, M. G. and V. B. Tulsidhar, 1991, 'Public Expenditure in India: Emerging Trends', Working Paper No. 5, New Delhi: National Institute of Public Finance and Policy; Rao, M. G. and T. K. Sen, 1993, 'Government Expenditure in India: Level Growth and Composition', [Processed.] New Delhi: National Institute of Public Finance and Policy). None of these papers attempts formal modelling. The authors began this task in a closely related paper: Kletzer, K. and N. Singh, 1997, 'The Political Economy of Indian Fiscal Federalism', in S. Mundle (ed.), *Public Finance: Policy Issues for India*. New Delhi: Oxford University Press.
2. See, for example, a summary of the experience of reform in the report on a conference held at the University of California, Berkeley (Kohli, I, 1993, *Economic Liberalisation in South Asia*, Symposium Rapportage at the Center for South Asia Studies, University of California, Berkeley.)
3. In particular, this is the conclusion of Buiter and Patel (Buiter, W. H. and U. R. Patel, 1997, 'Solvency and Fiscal Correction in India: An Analytical Discussion', in S. Mundle (ed.), *Public Finance: Policy Issues for India*, New Delhi: Oxford University Press).
4. For example, see the report by Jha, or subsequent coverage of the Central Government budget in Indian newspapers (Jha, P. S. 1994, 'Economy appears poised for leap forward', *India Abroad*, 28 January).
5. Rao and Narayana survey the role of sub-Central Government finances in the process of cutting the fiscal deficit in India (Rao, M. G. and M. R. Narayana, 1994, 'Fiscal Reforms and the Role of sub-Central Governments'. [Processed.] New Delhi: National Institute of Public Finance and Policy).
6. Rao and Chelliah, and Rao provide excellent surveys, so we do not attempt a comprehensive description (Rao, M. G. and R. J. Chelliah, 1990, 'Survey of Research on Fiscal Federalism in India', [Processed.] New Delhi: National Institute of Public Finance and Policy; Rao, M. G. 1993, 'Indian Fiscal Federalism from a Comparative Perspective', [Processed.] New Delhi: National Institute of Public Finance and Policy).
7. World Bank, 1988, *World Development Report*, New York: Oxford University Press.
8. Rao, 'Indian Fiscal Federalism.'
9. Ibid.
10. Ibid.
11. Ibid.
12. See, for example, Guhan (Guhan, S. 1988, 'Issues before the Ninth Finance Commission: On Closing the Pandora's Box', *Economic and Political Weekly*, 6 February) and Choudhury (Choudhury, U. D. R. 1992, 'Inter-State and Intra-State Variations in Economic Development and Standard of Living', *Economic and Political Weekly*, 5 December).

13. Toye and Rao give overviews of India's earlier experience (Toye, J. 1981, *Public Expenditure and Indian Development Policy*, Cambridge: Cambridge University Press; Rao, *Political Economy*). Guhan reaches the conclusion of regressivity of transfers (Guhan, S. 1989, 'The Norm and the Tilt: First Report of the Finance Commission', *Economic and Political Weekly*, 14 January). Rao and Das-Gupta, and Rao make clear that some components of central transfers have been equalising, while others have had the opposite effect. (Rao, M. G. and A. Das-Gupta, 1993, 'Inter-governmental Transfers as an Instrument to Alleviate Poverty'. [Processed.] New Delhi: National Institute of Public Finance and Policy; Rao, M. G. 1994, 'Intergovernment Transfers in India'. [Processed.] Paper presented at Conference on Fiscal Transfer Systems, Qingdao, China, 25–29 July). This point is taken up later in this chapter.
14. On encouraging resource mobilisation by the states, see Bajaj and Viswanathan, Viswanathan and Guhan (Bajaj, J. L. and R. Viswanathan, 1989, 'Financial Management in the States: Role of the Finance Commission', *Economic and Political Weekly*, 7 October; Viswanathan, R. 1990, 'Enforcing Fiscal Discipline: Ninth Finance Commission's Award', *Economic and Political Weekly*, 9 June; Guhan, S. 1988. 'Issues before the Ninth Finance Commission', and 1989. 'The Norm and the Tilt').
15. More specifically, the Finance Commission is constituted every five years with a charge to make recommendations that cover a period concurrent to the period of a five-year plan. Its membership includes academics as well as civil servants and politicians, but the government selects, and therefore to some extent controls, who serves on each commission.
16. See Rao, 'Indian Fiscal Federalism', 18, as well as Rao and Das-Gupta, 'Inter-governmental Transfers', and Rao, 'Intergovernment Transfers'. The latter states '... the absence of a clear and coordinated approach for distributing unconditional transfers to the states is a major weakness in the Indian federation' (p. 27).
17. For analyses of the formulae for plan transfers to states see Ramalingom and Kurup (Ramalingom, R. and K. N. Kurup, 1991, 'Plan Transfers to States: Revised Gadgil Formula, An Analysis', *Economic and Political Weekly*, 2 March) and Rao, 'Intergovernment Transfers'.
18. In particular, see Articles 268 to 293. Thakur has the full text of these articles (Thakur, R. 1989, *Finance Commissions and Centre–State Relations in India*, New Delhi: Deep & Deep Publications).
19. For example, see Panigrahi, D. D. 1985, *Centre–State Financial Relations in India*, New Delhi: Vikas Publishing.
20. These figures are derived from Table 5.5, World Bank, 1989, *India: Recent Developments and Medium-Term Issues*, Washington DC: The World Bank. Of course the evidence is only suggestive, since many other factors could have been at work. The Tenth Finance Commission (Finance Commission, 1994, Chapter 13) suggests that states receive a uniform share (29 per cent) of almost all federal revenue. This proposal seems eminently sensible. It would seem, however, to require a constitutional amendment to be implementable.
21. See, for example, Bardhan's seminal analysis (Bardhan, P. 1984, *The Political Economy of Development in India*, Oxford: Basil Blackwell).
22. See Chelliah, Rao and Sen, and Rao and Chelliah for overviews (Chelliah, R. J., M. G. Rao and T. K. Sen, 1992, 'Issues Before Tenth Finance Commission',

Economic and Political Weekly, 21 November; Rao, M. G., and R. J. Chelliah, 1990, 'Survey of Research on Fiscal Federalism in India'. [Processed.] New Delhi: National Institute of Public Finance and Policy). Rao and Das-Gupta in 'Inter-governmental Transfers', Table 8, report that specific purpose transfers from centre to states rose from 11.9 per cent of total transfers in 1975–76 to 18.3 per cent in 1988–89. Rao and Narayana in 'Fiscal Reforms' note that the capital of central public enterprises was also biased towards high income states. Rao in 'Intergovernment Transfers', Table 8, reports some striking figures. Looking at the seventh plan period, 1982–85, and at fourteen major states, divided into high, middle and low income groups, statutory transfers (shared taxes and Finance Commission grants) per capita were respectively, Rs 321, 439 and 472: hence these were equalising. However, nonplan loans were, respectively, Rs 722, 423 and 377 per capita: they particularly favoured the high income states as a group. Finally, central plan assistance including centrally sponsored schemes was, respectively, Rs 533, 227 and 287 per capita, again favouring high income states. Within each group and category there was an even greater variation, suggesting that discretion in central transfers was operating in non-obvious ways, perhaps based on political or economic importance in some dimension.

23. Two analogies come to mind. One is the practice, widespread in India now, of governments making loans to farmers and then 'forgiving' them at election time. The second is the existence of soft budget constraints for firms in the erstwhile socialist economies, and for public enterprises everywhere. Some figures on loans to states grouped by income were given in note 22.
24. In particular, there is the 'octroi', which is a tax on goods entering urban areas, imposed by urban local governments in several states. It falls disproportionately on capital and intermediate goods, and involves exporting of the tax burden to non-residents. Besides the distortionary effects of this tax, it is subject to criticism for its high collection costs and susceptibility to corruption.
25. Rao in 'Indian Fiscal Federalism' discusses tax competition in India in a comparative context.
26. Ahmad, E., and N. Stern, 1987, 'Alternative Sources of Government Revenue: Illustrations from India, 1979–80', in D. Newbery and N. Stern (eds), *The Theory of Taxation for Developing Countries*, New York: Oxford University Press.
27. For Pakistan, the comparable 1985 figure was 11.2 per cent, while it was only 7.2 per cent for Bangladesh. See note 26, p. 267.
28. Purohit surveys the experience with MODVAT in India, as well as comparing it with other countries' VAT schemes (Purohit, M. C. 1993, 'Adoption of Value Added Tax in India: Problems and Prospects', *Economic and Political Weekly*, 6 March).
29. See note 26.
30. See, for example Gurumurthi, S. 1993, 'Towards an Alternative System of Tax-Sharing', *Economic and Political Weekly*, 20 March.
31. See Chelliah et al., 'Issues Before Tenth Finance Commission', Rao and Chelliah, 'Research on Fiscal Federalism', Rao, M. G. 1990, 'Some Conceptual and Methodological Comments: Ninth Finance Commission's Award', *Economic and Political Weekly*, 9 June; and Chapter 10 of Thakur, R. 1989,

Finance Commissions and Centre–State Relations in India, New Delhi: Deep & Deep Publications.

32. Other examples of this kind of phenomenon may be found in Gurumurthi (see note 30).
33. These include questions of how to divide the states' share among them. This is as important and contentious as the division between the centre and the states, and it is where the greatest scope lies for variation, since there are so many possible characteristics of the states that can be used in devising formulae for determining shares. For example, see Singh, A. K. 1987, *Finance Commissions in India*, Allahabad: Chugh Publications; Gaur, A. K. 1988, *Federal Finance in India: Emerging Trends*, New Delhi: Deep & Deep Publications; Singh, B. P. 1988, *Fiscal Transfers: A Study of Finance Commissions in India*, Delhi: Amar Prakashan; Thakur, *Finance Commissions*; Chelliah et al., 'Issues Before Tenth Finance Commission'; and Gurumurthi, 'Alternative System of Tax-Sharing'.
34. See Wildasin for a comprehensive survey of the theoretical literature (Wildasin, D. E. 1986, *Urban Public Finance*, New York: Harwood Academic Publishers).
35. See Rao, 'Indian Fiscal Federalism'.
36. Rao, M. G., and F. Vaillancourt, 1993, 'Subnational Tax Disharmony in India: A Comparative Perspective', [Processed.] New Delhi: National Institute of Public Finance and Policy.
37. Ahmad and Stern's analysis is at a more aggregate level, and so does not look at interjurisdictional tax competition (see note 26).
38. Singh provides a detailed survey and evaluation of local government reform in India (Singh, N. 1997, 'Issues in Local Government Reform in India'. [Processed.] University of California at Santa Cruz). See also Datta, A. 1984, *Municipal Finances in India*, New Delhi: Indian Institute of Public Administration; and Jetha, N. 1992. 'Financing Urban Service in India: Selected Issues', [Processed.] World Bank.
39. A clear exposition of the theoretical principles on this topic is Olson, M. 1986, 'Toward a More General Theory of Governmental Structure', *American Economic Review*, 76(2): 120–25.
40. See, for example, The World Bank, 1995, *India: Recent Economic Developments and Prospects*, Washington, DC: The World Bank; and Shome, P. 1997, 'Economic Liberalisation, Fiscal Performance, and Tax Reform: Indian Experience and Cross-Country Comparisons', in S. Mundle (ed.), *Public Finance: Policy Issues for India*, New Delhi: Oxford University Press.
41. Again, Wildasin thoroughly covers this approach (see note 34).
42. This is, of course, the central tenet of the public choice approach.
43. The term is due to Krueger (Krueger, A. 1974, 'The Political Economy of the Rent Seeking Society', *American Economic Review*, 64: 291–303). Earlier analyses of similar behaviour include Tullock (Tullock, G. 1967, 'The Welfare Costs of Tariffs, Monopolies, and Theft', *Western Economic Journal*, 5: 224–232) and Olson (Olson, M. 1971, *The Logic of Collective Action*, Cambridge, Mass.: Harvard University Press).
44. Milgrom, P. 1988, 'Employment Contracts, Influence Activities, and Efficient Organisation Design', *Journal of Political Economy*, 96: 42–60; Milgrom, P.,

and J. Roberts, 1988, 'An Economic Approach to Influence Activities in Organisations', *American Journal of Sociology* (Supplement), 94: S154–S179; Milgrom, P., and J. Roberts, 1990, 'The Efficiency of Equity in Organisational Decision Processes', *American Economic Review* (Papers and Proceedings), 80: 154–159; Milgrom, P., and J. Roberts, 1990, 'Bargaining Costs, Influence Costs, and the Organisation of Economic Activity', in J. Alt and K. Shepsle (eds), *Perspectives on Positive Political Economy*, Cambridge: Cambridge University Press.

45. Oates, a significant early contributor to this literature, surveys this subject (Oates, W. 1991, 'Principles of Fiscal Federalism: A Survey of Recent Theoretical and Empirical Research', IRIS Working Paper No. 21, University of Maryland at College Park.)
46. See note 44 above.
47. See, for example, the article on this issue in *The Economist* magazine, 28 January 1994.
48. Note also that if we apply the logic of self-interest and rent-seeking to the state governments and their constituents, we may gain insight into the complex and distortionary tax systems at the state level, and the absence of strong or effective local governments in India. Clearly, more work needs to be done on this aspect.
49. Persson, T., and G. Tabellini, 1992, 'Federal Fiscal Constitutions, Part I: Risk Sharing and Moral Hazard', [Processed.] Harvard University and Institute for International Economic Studies, Stockholm.
50. Murty, M. N. and R. Ray, 1990, 'Fiscal Federalism and Optimal Commodity Taxes: A Comparison of Centralised and Decentralised Decisions'. Working Paper No. E/147/90, Institute of Economic Growth, Delhi.
51. Wildasin, D. E. 1983, 'The Welfare Effects of Intergovernment Grants in an Economy with Independent Jurisdictions', *Journal of Urban Economics*, 147–164; Wildasin, D. E. 1984, 'The Welfare Effects of Intergovernmental Grants in an Economy with Distortionary Local Taxes', *Journal of Public Economics*, 103–125.
52. Kanbur, S. M. R., and G. D. Myles, 1993, 'Policy Choice and Political Constraints', *European Journal of Political Economy*, 1–29.
53. Velasco, A. 1992, 'A Model of Fiscal Deficits and Delayed Fiscal Reforms', Research Report No. 92–06, C. V. Starr Centre for Applied Economics, New York University.
54. The authors build directly here on their closely related paper (see note 1).
55. Since the private goods is an aggregate, this tax is a composite of the usual income tax and various commodity taxes. The authors are restricting themselves to a closed economy, so there is no analogue in this model of customs duties, an important revenue source in India.
56. Calvert surveys the median voter approach (Calvert, R. L. 1986, *Models of Imperfect Information in Politics, Fundamentals of Pure and Applied Economics* 6, Chur, Switzerland: Harwood Academic Publishers). Lindbeck and Weibull develop a model of policy-motivated candidates or parties, where political competition converges on the mean preference (Lindbeck, A., and J. W. Weibull, 1993, 'A Model of Political Equilibrium in a Representative Democracy', *Journal of Public Economics*, 195–209). The insights of our model carry over to this alternative framework.

57. One can think of an alternative formulation, such as that of Appelbaum and Katz, where these two objectives are weighted in some way (Appelbaum, E., and E. Katz, 1987, 'Seeking Rents by Setting Rents: The Political Economy of Rent Seeking', *Economic Journal*, 97: 685–699). Their formulation assumes an exogenous probability of reelection (or reappointment) function, rather than adherence to the median voter's wishes. The authors will explore this specification in future work.
58. The authors assume that functions satisfy appropriate concavity properties so that first order conditions characterise unique interior optima.
59. The example is from Kletzer and Singh, discussing the more general case where there are interaction effects in the utility function (see note 1).
60. See Kletzer and Singh, Example 2, for an illustration (see note 1).
61. These expressions correct those used in Kletzer and Singh (see note 1), where the population was not adjusted in going from two states to three: the point of the example is unaffected, however. Note that Example 2 still assumes that the cost of the national public goods is 2n, as in Example 1: this introduces scale economies, but does not affect the point of the example.
62. Formally, the required ranking concept would be the first order stochastic dominance partial ordering.
63. This is the focus of Gordon, for example (Gordon, R. H. 1983, 'An Optimal Taxation Approach to Fiscal Federalism', *Quarterly Journal of Economics*, 98: 567–586).
64. General recent surveys of these kinds of issues may be found in Wildasin (see note 34 above) as well as in King, D. N. 1984, *Fiscal Tiers: The Economics of Multi-Level Government*, London: George Allen & Unwin.
65. This is also true even if the transfer is earmarked, unless the lower-level government happens to be at the resulting kink in its budget constraint: see King in note 64.
66. The net transfer to the poor state is $(2R_1/3) - (R_2/3)$, which is positive as long as the rich state is not heavily favoured in terms of the size of the direct transfer, i.e., $R_2 < 2R_1$.
67. Within each set there is further indeterminacy of the particular policy chosen. For example, vectors of transfers can be scaled up or down without affecting the majority coalition. This indeterminacy can presumably be removed by incorporating the tax collection costs, or other operating costs, in the appropriate way.
68. In particular, see Baron, D., and J. Ferejohn, 1989, 'Bargaining in Legislature', *American Political Science Review*, 83: 1181–1206; and Persson, T., G. Roland, and G. Tabellini, 1997, 'Comparative Politics and Public Finance', [Processed.] Harvard University and Institute for International Economic Studies, Stockholm. Other restrictions or approaches are also possible. For example, if transfers are constrained to be equal for states (for instance, based on population size), then the two poorer states receive positive net transfers.
69. See note 44.

2

Fragmented Legislatures and Electoral Systems: The Indian Experience

Bhaskar Dutta

The design of an appropriate electoral system is of fundamental importance in any democracy. However, the notion of what is appropriate is not straightforward since an electoral system has to balance multiple objectives. The problem of defining or selecting a suitable electoral system becomes more difficult in a parliamentary system because the different objec tives may then conflict with one another. For instance, since an electoral system is a mechanism which aggregates individual preferences in order to decide the winners of an election, it is natural to want the mechanism to be representative. This essentially means that the winners of the election reflect faithfully the positions and views of the electorate. Another goal or objective is the need to ensure that the elected legislature be conducive to the formation of stable governments. This requires that the legislature should not be too fragmented[1] since the presence of a large number of small parties reduces the chances of the existence of a single party commanding a simple majority of seats or the formation of stable ruling coalitions. Unfortunately, research on comparative electoral systems suggests that the more representative the system, the more fragmented it is likely to be.[2]

Fragmented legislatures can be costly because unstable coalitions or governments that are not likely to remain in power for an extended period of time are liable to introduce policy distortions. Such governments have short time-horizons. This has important implications for economic policy in general and budgetary policy in particular. If political power alternates rapidly and randomly between competing political parties or groups of parties, then each government will follow myopic policies since it assigns a low probability to being reelected. Hard policy options whose benefits flow after a long gestation lag are unlikely to be adopted by such a government. Instead, it may spend indiscriminately in order to satisfy the short-term needs of its support groups.

The second route through which the rapid turnover of governments may induce policy distortions is relevant in the case of coalition governments. The shorter the expected duration of such governments, the more difficult it will be for the members of the ruling coalition to agree on policies. Of course, the more heterogeneous the parties in the ruling coalition, the greater will be the lack of cooperation. Each party in the ruling coalition may then try to promote populist policies in order to exploit its own narrow interests. The most likely casualty of all this will be fiscal discipline since government expenditure will be excessive.

There has been some empirical verification of this hypothesis. For instance, Roubini and Sachs (1989) analyse the pattern of fiscal deficits in member countries of the Organisation for Economic Cooperation and Development (OECD). They find a clear tendency for larger deficits in countries characterised by a short average tenure of government and by the presence of many political parties in a ruling coalition.[3] Section II reports some results which show that the behaviour of state governments in India also conform to this pattern.

Conventional wisdom among political scientists suggests that plurality rule or the first-past-the-post system is most likely to produce majority parties. Indeed, the so-called Duverger's Law states that single-member district electoral systems in which winners are decided by simple plurality rule usually produce two-party systems.[4] However, plurality rule is characterised by a high degree of disproportionality between vote shares and seat shares, the number of seats won by bigger parties being unduly large compared to their vote shares. The use of the plurality rule encourages tyranny of the majority over the minority. For instance, an extreme form of violation of minority rights may occur if a particular group happens to be a minority in every constituency. In this case, the minority group may be denied any representation at all even though the group may command a sizeable following when its support is aggregated across constituencies.

In contrast, the family of Proportional Representation (PR) systems is more favourable to minority groups and small parties since the number of seats won by a party is close to its share of the overall votes. Of course, members within the class of PR systems also differ in the degree of proportionality. The specific PR formula influences the degree of proportionality. Another aspect of PR systems that is also relevant in this context is the district magnitude, that is, the average number of legislators elected per district. The smaller the district magnitude, the greater is the bias in favour of larger parties. Indeed, PR systems coincide with the plurality rule when each district has only a single member. Hence, the goal of representativeness would seem to suggest the use of PR systems with relatively large district magnitudes. Unfortunately, one drawback of PR systems is its tendency to promote fragmented legislatures.[5]

The electoral experience in India does not fit this general pattern. Despite the use of the plurality system, the Congress party occupied a dominant role along with a preponderance of a number of small parties up to 1967. The national elections of 1967 marked a watershed in Indian politics, with the Congress party's electoral support registering a sharp decline from 46 per cent in 1962 to 41 per cent in 1967. Its majority in parliament was reduced from 115 to barely twenty-five. Further setbacks followed for the Congress party in the elections to the state assemblies, with Opposition parties and coalitions coming to power in six major states. Subsequent state elections have witnessed an increasing tendency towards multipartyism or fragmentation, with a proliferation of small parties and Independent candidates. This fragmentation of legislatures has often resulted in loose and unstable coalitions. For instance, Brass (1968) points out that between the 1967 elections and July 1968, no less than eight governments were formed in the three states of Bihar, Uttar Pradesh and Punjab.[6]

This strongly suggests a need to examine why Duverger's Law has not been vindicated in India. A possible explanation is that while this law implicitly assumes that the distribution of electoral support for the various parties is uniform across constituencies, the Indian experience indicates that electoral support of the non-Congress parties (and certainly Independent candidates) is localised. It is easy to construct numerical examples[7] that show that under such conditions, legislatures elected under PR systems may be less fragmented than under the plurality rule.

This provides the motivation to compare the actual fractionalisation in state legislatures with the extent of fractionalisation that would have occurred in legislatures elected under PR systems. In order to do this, simulation exercises were conducted using the actual voting data of major states after 1967. Two parallel exercises were carried out. In the first exercise, which was done for four states and for a limited number of elections, the data used were the number of votes polled by each candidate in each constituency. In the other exercise, aggregate data on vote shares of different parties in all the elections conducted after 1967 in thirteen major states were used to calculate the hypothetical distribution of seats in the state assemblies if the electoral system was a member of the PR family. In particular, both exercises adopt the Droop quota to calculate the allotment of seats, and also assume that parties getting less than 5 per cent of the valid votes cast in all the constituencies put together are denied any representation in the state assembly.[8]

The hypothetical distributions of seats are compared with the actual distributions in terms of various characteristics of legislatures that have a bearing on the formation of stable ruling coalitions. One such characteristic is the well-known measure of fractionalisation, based on the Herfindahl-Hirschman index of industrial concentration, and introduced into political science literature by Rae (1967).[9] However, in Section I it is argued that this index of fractionalisation may not always be a very appropriate index of the impediments to the formation of stable coalitions. A new measure of stability of legislatures is suggested based on the idea that the larger the number of parties in a minimum winning coalition, the greater the degree of instability of the coalition.

Rae's index of fractionalisation as well as the measure of stability proposed here are related to the instability of coalitions through the possible adverse effects of multiparty competition.[10] However, as Brass (1968) points out, factionalism within the same party has been as disruptive as multiparty competition in many states in India.[11] Independents and individual party defectors, as well as cross-party alliances of factions have affected the stability of ruling coalitions. These groups are unlikely to have stable support bases in the electorate, and are hence unlikely to win seats in successive legislatures. The more stable the identity and relative strengths of different parties gaining representation in the legislature over time, the greater the party system stability (pss), a term coined by Dodd

(1976). Since a higher degree of party system stability is less likely to be associated with disruptions and threats to ruling coalitions, a comparison is also made of the degrees of pss associated with actual and hypothetical distributions of seats, using a measure of pss proposed by Dodd (1976).[12]

The simulation results indicate that PR systems do not necessarily result in legislatures that are more fragmented or that are likely to lead to more unstable coalitions, when the benchmark is the plurality system. The most likely pattern of representation under PR systems seems to be a few (up to three) relatively large parties winning the bulk of the seats.[13] In contrast, the actual distribution of seats under plurality rule has either seen one party winning a majority of seats or a relatively large number of smaller parties and Independent candidates gaining representation. This suggests that if the pattern of electoral support for parties prevents any single party from winning a majority of seats in the legislature, then the PR system is more likely to result in the formation of stable coalitions. In view of the increasing likelihood of 'hung' legislatures in India in the near future, this result is obviously of great topical interest.

The plan of the rest of this chapter is as follows. Section I discusses some methodological issues connected with fragmentation and stability of coalitions. Section II describes the result of regression exercises which show that unstable state governments in India have been guilty of fiscal indiscipline. Section III determines, with the help of an example, why PR systems may actually lead to the formation of more stable coalitions. Section IV describes the simulation exercise in greater detail and contains the main results, and conclusions are presented in Section V.

I FRAGMENTATION, PARTY SYSTEM STABILITY AND COALITIONAL STABILITY

A legislature is highly fragmented if a large number of parties gain representation, and if these parties are of relatively equal strength insofar as the number of seats captured by them is concerned. In the presence of a single, dominant party holding more than half the seats, the legislature is less fragmented since at most one party can approach the strength of the dominant party. In the absence of a majority party, a large number of equal-sized parties will bargain with each other to form ruling coalitions. This may lead to instability for a variety of reasons. The larger the number of parties, the greater are the number of possible ruling coalitions. This makes it more likely that a small party or party faction—or even a group of Independent candidates—can defect from one ruling coalition and form another majority coalition, a process that has been all too common in the Indian context. Indeed, Brass (1977) in his explanation of the duration of coalition governments in Indian states during the period 1952–1974 remarks that coalitions that contained independents and defectors were more unstable than those that did not.[14]

Moreover, a large number of small parties with representation in the legislature implies that ruling coalitions will also contain a relatively large number of parties. If the parties in the coalition have no ideological affinity, then the possibility of conflicts amongst parties increases with the number of members in the coalition.[15]

The most common measure of fractionalisation is a measure introduced by Rae (1967).[16] Rae's measure, which is based on the Herfindahl-Hirschman index of industrial concentration, is defined as:

$$F_R = 1 - \Sigma\, s_i^2 \qquad (1)$$

where the sum is taken over all parties gaining representation in the legislature, and s_i is the proportion of seats held by party i in the legislature. This index is sensitive to the number of parties gaining representation as well as the variance in the proportion of seats held by the parties. When one party captures all the seats, the index takes its minimum value of 0. The value of the index increases as more parties share the spoils.[17]

Although there are good reasons to believe that a higher degree of fragmentation will be associated with instability of ruling coalitions, several empirical studies find only a low correlation between F_R and the duration of coalition governments.[18] This may be partly because F_R does not reflect the specific characteristics of fractionalisation that influence cabinet instability. As previously noted, a fragmented legislature implies that any ruling coalition will consist of a relatively large number of parties, and that the larger the number of parties, the greater the likelihood of conflict between coalition partners. The instability arising due to the large number of parties in the ruling coalition is captured only indirectly by measures such as F_R.

This is the motivation for constructing a measure of stability that is defined directly in terms of the number of parties in a winning coalition. Borrowing terminology from game theory, a winning coalition may be defined as any group of parties that together command a simple majority of seats in the legislature. A coalition S is said to be a minimal winning coalition if S is a winning coalition and moreover no proper subset of S is a winning coalition. So, if S is a minimal winning coalition, then a defection by any member of S will result in the remainder ceasing to be a winning coalition. Hence, any member of S can bring about the collapse of the government by leaving the coalition.

Of course, this does not mean that all members of a minimal winning coalition are equally powerful. Suppose parties A, B and C have won thirty, eleven and eleven seats respectively in a 100-member legislature. Let the rest of the seats be held by parties D and E, who hold twenty-five and twenty-three seats, respectively. Now, A, B and C form a minimal winning coalition. Suppose that D is an extreme party (it could, for instance, be the Bharatiya Janata Party in India) with which no other party wants to form a coalition. In that case, B and C will have to think twice before breaking the coalition with A. This is because all possible majority coalitions must have A as a member since D is an 'outcast'. So, although A can break up with B and C and form a winning coalition with E, parties B and C must be members of a losing coalition if they leave A.

While it is reasonable to assume that parties would much rather be members of winning coalitions than of losing coalitions, parties do defect from ruling coalitions even if they have no immediate prospects of forming a new winning coalition. Hence, despite the possible asymmetries in the distribution of power within a winning coalition, it is implicitly assumed that all members of a minimal winning coalition are equally likely to disrupt the coalition. Assume moreover that the different coalitions do not differ in the extent of conflict between the members of each coalition.[19] Then, the instability of a minimal winning coalition becomes proportional to the number of parties in the coalition.

This idea is explored in Dutta (1996), who tries to explain the duration of various state governments. A party is said to be pivotal if it can defect from a majority coalition and convert it into a losing coalition. So, all members of a minimal winning coalition are pivotal. Of course, if a coalition is larger than the minimum needed for winning, then all its members need not be pivotal. Dutta shows that the larger the number of pivotal members of a ruling coalition, the smaller is the likely duration of the corresponding government.[20]

Of course, while this gives a criterion to judge the stability of one coalition, it does not indicate the stability of the legislature as a whole since different combinations of parties can form several winning coalitions. To address the issue of stability of the legislature, define Ω to be the class of permissible winning coalitions, where a coalition is defined to be permissible if it does not include two parties that will not form any alliance due to exogenous constraints. For example, if party A is considered to be too radical, then other parties may refuse to join any coalition containing A. In this case, a coalition is permissible only if it does not include party A. Now, define the *stability* of the legislature as the *reciprocal* of the *minimum* number of parties in some winning coalition in Ω. More formally, the measure is given by:

$$S_m = \min_{c \in \Omega}(1/|c|) \tag{2}$$

Here, $|c|$ denotes the *number* of parties in the coalition c. The following example illustrates the concept. Consider a legislature consisting of five parties, A, B, C, D, E, with the parties holding thirty, twenty-five, twenty-one, fourteen and ten seats, respectively. Since the legislature consists of 100 members, a winning coalition must hold at least fifty seats among them. Suppose that A and B will never form an alliance, so that no permissible coalition can contain A and B. Then, among the set of permissible coalitions, the set of minimal winning coalitions consists of {A,C}, {A,D,E}, {B,C,D} and {B,C,E}. Then, the value of S_m is 0.5 since {A,C} is the minimal winning coalition containing the smallest number of parties.

Notice that S_m overestimates the stability of the legislature since there is no guarantee that the coalition which minimises the number of parties will actually form.[21] For instance, in the example given above, the coalition {A,D,E} may form, whose stability in terms of our criterion is 0.33. The maximum value of the measure is 1, which happens when the legislature contains a majority coalition.

How closely are F_R and S_m related? As discussed in Section IV, the data on Indian state elections show that often the correlation between the two can be quite low. Example 1 is a hypothetical example that shows that at least in some cases, S_m may be a better indicator of stability than F_R.[22]

Example 1 Consider a 100-member state legislature, with distributions of seats in two elections as follows:

Distribution of Seats

Party	*A*	*B*	*C*	*D*	*E*	*F*	*G*	*H*	F_R	S_m
Period 1	51	10	10	10	5	5	5	4	.7008	1
Period 2	40	35	9	8	8	–	–	–	.6966	0.5

The fractionalisation index for period 1 is higher than that in period 2, although there is a majority party in period 1 and none in period 2. Despite the possibility of factionalism within the party resulting in defections from the majority party, there is overwhelming evidence to suggest that single party governments are more stable than coalition governments. Hence, S_m seems a better indicator of stability in this case.

Another characteristic of legislative systems that has a potentially important effect on stability is that of party system stability (pss). This represents the extent of continuity over time in the identity and relative strengths of parties.[23] An unstable party system exists when new parties are born each election, while some parties die out. This happens, for instance, when parties are created as a result of defections. Notice that this source of instability is quite different from those arising out of fragmented legislatures. Indeed, a high extent of party system instability arising due to defections from existing parties can lead to coalitional instability even when legislatures are not fragmented. That is why the impact of PR systems on pss is also studied.

Following Dodd (1976),[24] the following measure is used to represent pss:

(3) $$PS_t = \Sigma_i \, |L_{i,t} - L_{i,(t-1)}|$$

Here, $L_{i,t}$ is the proportion of seats held by party *i* in period *t*, while $L_{i,(t-1)}$ is the proportion of seats held by party *i* in period $(t - 1)$. The sum is taken over all parties *i* which hold at least one seat in either period *t* or period $(t - 1)$. So, the formation of a new party or the disintegration of an old party increases the value of the index. Notice, however, that PS_t may be very high even in a two-party legislature if there are huge swings in the proportion of seats held by the two parties. This happened, for instance, in many Indian states in 1977, when the Janata party emerged as a major force, and the Congress was decimated. So PS_t was very high in 1977 in these states because of the swings in party representation. However, this kind of increase in PS_t is not always a source of instability.

The convention of measuring each Independent candidate as a 'party' in his or her own right has been followed. This has the desirable property of accentuating the effect of Independent candidates on the instability indicator. Estimates of pss are presented in Section IV.

II UNSTABLE COALITIONS AND FISCAL POLICIES

This section examines whether unstable coalition governments in the different states in India are guilty of fiscal indiscipline.[25] Of course, fiscal indiscipline is only one source of policy distortion associated with coalition governments. It is, however, an important indicator of the kind of governance associated with different political institutions. Governments that practise fiscal discipline are more likely to adopt policies which bring long-term benefits even if they are politically costly in the short run.[26]

In order to mitigate the effects of the states' dependence on the centre as far as possible, variables such as revenue expenditure, own tax revenue, own non-tax revenue and surplus (or deficit) in the revenue budget are the focus of this discussion. In order to neutralise the effects of factors such as size of population and state income, all the variables of interest are deflated by the state domestic product (SDP). Denoted by E, T, N and S are the ratios of revenue expenditure, own tax revenue, own non-tax revenue and surplus in the revenue budget, respectively, to the SDP. Data on these variables is used for each of the twenty-six financial years between 1967–68 and 1992–93.

A ruling coalition is defined as unstable if it contains at least two pivotal members. Since the main purpose is to analyse whether unstable ruling coalitions have any effect on the levels of E, T, N and S, a proxy needs to be determined for the type of government in a state in each financial year. Since there have been many instances in which the type of government has changed midway through the year, the following procedure was adopted. A dummy variable, denoted as *c*, was used to represent the presence or absence of unstable ruling coalitions during any year in any particular state. The variable *c* is defined to take the value of 1 if there was an unstable coalition (that is, one with at least two pivotal parties) for at least two months of the relevant (financial) year and relevant state, and 0 otherwise. Of course, the cut-off mark of two months is necessarily arbitrary.

There are some states that have not had any experience of coalition governments. Some of the other states have had coalition governments on a few occasions. Due to insufficient variation in the values of the explanatory variable, the impact of coalition governments on fiscal policy cannot be estimated separately for these states.[27] However, the states of Bihar, Punjab and Uttar Pradesh are of particular interest because they have experienced both unstable coalition governments and single-party (or stable coalition) governments in several years.[28] Separate regressions were run for each of these states, using some version of equation (4).[29]

The basic equation estimated on the pooled data was:

$$y = \alpha + \beta \ln t + \gamma c \tag{4}$$

where *y* denotes the values of the dependent variable (E, T, N or S), *t* represents time and *c* is the dummy for type of government. An alternative specification (used for S) was:

$$S = \alpha + \beta_1 t + \beta_2 t^2 + \gamma c \tag{4'}$$

Tables 2.1 and 2.3 describe the regression results for the three individual states. The strongest corroboration of the basic hypothesis is provided by Bihar. Unstable coalition governments have incurred a significantly higher revenue expenditure. Most interestingly, the more unstable the ruling coalition (that is, the larger the number of pivotal parties) the greater is the proclivity for excessive expenditure. Table 2.1 also shows that unstable coalitions collect a smaller volume of non-tax revenues. The strength of the relationship between unstable ruling coalitions and fiscal indiscipline is strong enough to carry over to the case of *S*; it turns out that unstable ruling coalitions also have a lower surplus (or larger deficit) in their revenue budgets. Notice, however, that unstable coalitions do not have lower tax effort.

The results for Uttar Pradesh are qualitatively similar to that of Bihar, the only difference being that the index of instability of ruling coalitions has no significant influence on any of the fiscal variables. Thus, unstable coalitions have higher revenue expenditure, collect a smaller volume of non-tax revenues, and have a lower surplus in the revenue budget. However, Punjab follows a somewhat different pattern. Here, tax effort is significantly higher, although the revenue surplus is lower under unstable ruling coalitions.

These results indicate some of the economic costs associated with unstable coalition governments in Indian states. Of course, these are the costs that are easily quantifiable. There are many other policy distortions likely to be introduced by coalition governments that cannot be so easily verified.

III PLURALITY RULE, PR SYSTEMS AND FRACTIONALISATION

This section presents a few examples to illustrate why the conventional wisdom regarding the supposed bias of the plurality rule in favour of large parties is true only when the distribution of electoral support for various parties is of the 'right kind'.

The particular member of the PR family that will now be compared to the plurality rule in the rest of this chapter is the largest remainders formula using the Droop quota. As in all quota systems, the first step is to calculate the quota of votes that entitles a party to a seat. A party gets as many seats as it has quotas of votes. Any seats that remain after all full quotas are exhausted are given to those parties having the largest numbers of unused votes. The Droop quota divides the total number of valid votes by the number of seats plus one. So, it is represented by

$$Q_D = V/(n+1) \tag{5}$$

where Q_D is the Droop quota, V is the total number of valid votes cast, and n is the number of seats to be allotted.

The next example shows that there can be distributions of electoral support under which the plurality rule produces a legislature that is more fragmented than that produced by PR with the Droop quota.

Example 2 Consider a ten-member legislature with distribution of vote shares as indicated in the following table. Party A is a 'big' party getting a sizeable number of votes in each constituency, while each party I_j (for j = 1–10) is a small, 'localised' party (or Independent candidate) getting votes only in constituency j. The total number of valid votes in each constituency is 100.

Constituency	1	2	3	4	5	6	7	8	9	10
A's vote share	48	48	48	48	48	49	49	49	49	49
I_j's vote share	52	52	52	52	52	51	51	51	51	51

Then, under plurality rule, party A is denied any seats at all since I_j wins the seat from constituency j. What if the PR system with the Droop quota is employed? In this example, Q_D = 91. So, party A gets five seats, while parties I_1 to I_5 get one seat each.

While this example is contrived, the distribution of votes does have some similarity to the actual electoral situation in India. Consider, for example, the large number of Independent candidates who get elected in many elections. A sizeable number of seats is also captured by small parties, each with very localised support. On the other hand, the bigger national parties such as the Congress party have some support in each constituency, although they may not get enough votes to score over the smaller parties and Independent candidates in several constituencies. Under these circumstances, there is no a priori reason to rule out the possibility that these bigger parties may do better under a PR system. Of course, if the bigger parties actually do better under the PR system, then it also raises the possibility that the extent of fractionalisation may be lower under the PR system.

The next section reports on simulation results that use the following modification of the Droop quota. This modification specifies that a party has to win at least 5 per cent of the total valid votes cast in the state election in order to get any representation in the state legislature. The seats are then allocated according to the Droop quota among the parties satisfying the 5 per cent requirement. Obviously, this works against the smaller parties and Independent candidates. In particular, it prevents the Independent candidates from getting any representation at all since no Independent candidate wins 5 per cent of the seats on his own. Going back to Example 2, if the number of constituencies in the legislature is eleven instead of ten, then party I_j would have to secure at least fifty-five votes to win a seat. Thus, an extra constituency along with the same distribution of electoral support would mean that party A would win all the eleven seats.

This example is not at all far-fetched: in the 1972 elections in the state of Andhra Pradesh, the Congress secured 52.3 per cent of the total valid votes polled. The Communist Party of India (CPI) with 6 per cent of the votes was the only other party to capture more than 5 per cent of the votes. Independent candidates secured 32.2 per cent of the votes, and won as many as 57 seats in a house of 287.[30]

IV THE SIMULATION RESULTS

This section briefly discusses the methodology and assumptions underlying the simulation exercise, then compares the actual and simulated values of F_R, S_m and PS_t, the latter set of values being those associated with the state legislatures estimated by the simulation exercise.

As noted earlier, two parallel simulation exercises were conducted. The first exercise uses the aggregate vote shares of different parties in each state; it is assumed that each state is a district by itself. This assumption on the district magnitude was made because the actual votes polled by the different parties in the individual constituencies were not available for all the states and for all elections since 1967. However, detailed constituency-level data were available for four states. These constitute the inputs of the second simulation exercise. Here, groups of geographically contiguous constituencies are being defined as the district. In most cases, the administrative unit of a district constitutes the electoral district. In a few cases, there are very few constituencies in the administrative district. In such cases, constituencies in two contiguous administrative districts make up the electoral district.

Once the electoral district has been specified, the party lists are constructed. For the large parties such as the Congress, which put up candidates in all constituencies in a district, the party list is taken to be the set of candidates nominated for these constituencies. Parties that did not contest all the constituencies have been assumed as submitting incomplete lists. In particular, it is assumed that each Independent candidate is a separate party with a 'list' consisting of a single candidate. The number of votes polled by each party in a district is taken to be the sum of the actual votes polled by the candidates in the party list. Parties that get less than 5 per cent of the total votes polled in the district are eliminated. Finally, the PR system using the Droop quota is used to allocate seats within each district to the parties.

It is worth mentioning at this stage that the construction of the party list in this way is problematic if a group of parties have formed electoral alliances. In the presence of electoral alliances, the procedure outlined cannot be used to derive the seat allocation among the individual parties making up the alliance. Suppose, for instance that parties A and B have formed an electoral alliance and have come to a compromise on the pattern of seats to be contested by each party. Then, the combined party list can be derived, and the actual distribution of votes will yield the total number of seats captured jointly by the two parties. But since the candidates on the list cannot be ordered, there is no method by which the seats can be allocated between parties A and B. In view of this problem, the states of West Bengal and Kerala have been omitted from the analysis since these are states that have had electoral alliances in most of the elections since 1967.

Some implicit assumptions are being made in these simulation exercises. First, it is assumed that the behaviour of parties would not have changed even if the electoral system were some member of the PR family instead of the plurality rule. In other words, it is assumed that the parties would have put up the same set of candidates in each district even if the electoral system had been some PR system. This might not be an outrageous assumption for the larger parties that contested in almost all the constituencies in a district, but the behaviour of the smaller parties would certainly have changed. For instance, there would have been more alliances at the stage of announcing party lists if India had actually used a PR system. Certainly the Independent candidates would not have contested the elections since they would not have any chance of winning representation given the 5 per cent cut-off mark. Also, parties would not have submitted incomplete lists since an additional candidate on the party list would typically gather some extra votes.

In a discussion of the principal results, let us first examine the patterns in the index of fractionalisation (F_R). The difference between the actual and simulated values of F_R is shown in Table 2.4.

A striking feature of the table is that the actual values are not necessarily lower than the simulated values. For instance, the actual fractionalisation in 1967 was higher than the simulated value in all states except Maharashtra in the legislatures produced by the 1967 elections. In other words, proportional rule with the 5 per cent cut-off provision will not necessarily result in a more fragmented legislature.

Can something more be said about the pattern of differences between the actual and simulated values? Reading Table 2.4 in conjunction with Table 2.7, which gives the pattern of state governments, a weak pattern is discernible. States that have had coalition governments are generally the states where actual fractionalisation has been higher than the simulated levels of fractionalisation. However, Uttar Pradesh is a clear counter-example to this since although it has experienced coalition governments throughout the period, its actual level of fractionalisation has been lower than the simulated values.

In a comparison of levels of stability as measured by S_m, a specification of the set of permissible coalitions is necessary. It is assumed here that the SSP, BJS (and its later reincarnation, the BJP), CPI(M), Swatantra and the Congress (O) would not form an alliance with the Congress. This specification is chosen because these are the national parties that have never joined a coalition government with the Congress in any state. Hence, a permissible coalition cannot contain the Congress along with any of these parties.

Table 2.5 shows the difference between the actual and simulated values of S_m. As in the case of fractionalisation, there is no reason to believe that plurality rule leads to a higher degree of stability in comparison to proportional rule. In several states and at different points of time, the simulated value of S_m has been higher than the actual value.[31] Indeed, Table 2.5 exhibits a clear pattern. The actual level of S_m is higher than the simulated level only in legislatures that had a majority party under the plurality rule, and where the use of the proportional rule would have resulted in the absence of a majority party. Correspondingly, in legislatures where the value of S_m was low under the plurality rule, the proportional rule would have produced a more stable legislature. This is because legislatures with a low value of S_m have a relatively large number of parties even in the smallest permissible winning coalition. This implies the presence of several small parties. The proportional rule with the

5 per cent cut-off mark essentially eliminates the smaller parties, thereby producing a higher level of stability according to S_m.

Turning to a comparison of the levels of party system stability (pss), Table 2.6 shows clearly that proportional rule improves party system stability since the actual values of PS_t are generally higher than the simulated values.[32] One reason for this is that the larger the number of Independent members in the legislature, the higher the value of PS_t. More generally, it is the smaller parties and splinter groups whose fortunes fluctuate more wildly under the plurality rule. Moreover, this tendency increases the value of PS_t. On the other hand, Independent candidates are completely eliminated, while the number of small parties is greatly reduced under the proportional rule with the 5 per cent cut-off mark. This explains why the plurality rule results in more instability, according to PS_t.

Finally, Table 2.8 reports the values of F_R derived from the second simulation exercise, where the inputs of the simulation exercise are the constituency-level data. The results are similar to those of the first exercise. In particular, note that there is no appreciable change in the levels of F_R according to the two exercises. Since the two exercises differ in district magnitude, this goes against the hypothesis that the larger the district magnitude, the more favourable it is to small parties.

V CONCLUSION

There is strong evidence suggesting that unstable coalition governments in India have introduced policy distortions. Since unstable ruling coalitions are more likely to be produced by fragmented legislatures, the main focus of this chapter has been on the effects of the electoral system on different aspects of legislative stability. In order to examine this, a comparison is made of the values of different parameters of legislative stability in thirteen major Indian states under two alternative scenarios. The first scenario is the actual legislatures in these states from 1967. The second scenario looks at the legislatures that would have been produced by proportional rule with the stipulation that a party has to get at least 5 per cent of the total votes cast in order to win any seats.

The principal conclusion which emerges is that the proportional rule does not necessarily lead to a greater degree of instability or fractionalisation. The crucial variable is the distribution of electoral support for the various parties. In cases where plurality rule has produced a majority party, the introduction of proportional rule may lead to greater fragmentation. In particular, proportional rule may result in the absence of majority parties. However, in situations where the plurality rule itself results in the presence of a relatively large number of small parties and Independent candidates, proportional rule may lead to a more stable system. This is of great topical interest in India today since the state legislatures as well as the national parliament are becoming increasingly fragmented under plurality rule.

Table 2.1
Regression Results (Bihar)

Dependent Variable	*Constant*	*Explanatory Variables*			*p(T)*	$\bar{R}^2$
		ln t	*t*	*c*		
S	2.85	– 0.60		– 3.18*		0.53
		(1.77)		(5.28)		
E	– 0.47	5.51*		4.86*		0.85
		(11.94)		(5.92)		
E	– 1.98	5.88*			0.86*	0.77
		(9.08)			(3.94)	
ln T	1.07	0.16*		0.05		0.74
		(8.23)		(1.54)		
ln N	– 0.05		0.06*	– 0.30*		0.81
			(9.33)	(2.90)		

Notes: *indicates that coefficient is significant at the .01 level.
p(T) represents the number of pivotal members in a coalition.
Source: Tables constructed by author on the basis of actual electoral data. Data supplied by the Centre for Study of Developing Societies.

Table 2.2
Regression Results (Uttar Pradesh)

Dependent Variable	*Constant*	*Explanatory Variables*			R^2
		ln t	*t*	*c*	
E	2.35	4.27*		2.72*	0.87
		(12.91)		(4.43)	
ln T	0.94	0.26*		0.05	0.79
		(9.88)		(1.08)	
S	1.95		– 0.10*	– 1.27**	0.52
			(3.47)	(2.68)	
ln N	0.87		– 0.02*	– 0.13**	0.42
			(4.30)	(2.01)	

Notes: *indicates that coefficient is significant at the .01 level.
**indicates significance at the .05 level.
Source: Tables constructed by author on the basis of actual electoral data. Data supplied by the Centre for Study of Developing Societies.

Table 2.3
Regression Results (Punjab)

Dependent Variable	*Constant*	*Explanatory Variables*			R^2
		ln t	*t*	*c*	
E	2.76	3.65*		2.84	0.58
		(4.59)		(1.57)	
ln T	1.40	0.23*		0.14*	0.85
		(8.89)		(2.33)	
S	3.34		– 0.20	– 1.85*	0.52
			(5.18)	(2.27)	

Notes: *indicates that coefficient is significant at the .01 level.
Source: Tables constructed by author on the basis of actual electoral data. Data supplied by the Centre for Study of Developing Societies.

Table 2.4
Difference in Values of Actual and Simulated F_R

	I	*II*	*III*	*IV*	*V*	*VI*	*VII*	*VIII*
Assam	0.281	−0.089	0.094	−0.002	0.407	0.045		
Bihar	0.062	0.074	−0.059	−0.020	−0.053	−0.067	−0.085	
Orissa	0.025	0.011	0.046	−0.067	−0.216	−0.122	−0.171	
UP	0.235	−0.017	−0.047	−0.177	−0.201	−0.074	−0.003	−0.116
Punjab	0.091	0.188	−0.021	−0.003	−0.005	−0.022	−0.200	
Haryana	0.238	−0.009	0.046	−0.188	0.142	−0.072	−0.063	
MP	0.059	−0.120	−0.076	−0.102	−0.148	−0.090		
Rajasthan	0.098	−0.178	−0.086	−0.133	0.004	0.027		
TN	0.041	−0.055	0.087	0.280	0.279	−0.155	−0.203	
Maharashtra	−0.142	0.020	0.077	−0.077	0.038	0.029		
Gujarat	0.044	−0.244	0.057	−0.180	−0.216	0.017		
Karnataka	0.244	−0.041	−0.087	0.099	0.028	−0.233		
Andhra	0.114	0.229	−0.039	−0.003	0.000	0.063		

Notes: A positive value means that the actual fractionalisation is higher than the simulated fractionalisation.
Source: Tables constructed by author on the basis of actual electoral data. Data supplied by the Centre for Study of Developing Societies.

Table 2.5
Difference in Actual and Simulated Values of S_m
(District Magnitude = Entire State)

	I	*II*	*III*	*IV*	*V*	*VI*	*VII*	*VIII*
Assam	0	0	0	0	0	0.5	0	
Bihar	−0.167	−0.167	0.667	0	0.5	0	−0.167	
Orissa	0	−0.167	0	0	0	0	0	
UP	−0.667	0	0.5	0	0	0	0	0.5
Punjab	−0.5	−0.667	0	0.5	0	0.5	0	
Haryana	0	0	0	0	−0.5	0	0.5	
MP	0	0	0	0	0	0	0	
Rajasthan	−0.75	0	0	0	0	0	0	
TN	0.5	0	0.5	0.5	0.5	0.5	0	
Maharashtra	0	0	0	0	0	0	0	
Gujarat	0	0	−0.333	0	0	0	0	
Karnataka	0	0	0.5	0	0	0	0	
Andhra	0	0	0.5	0	0	0	0	

Notes: A positive value means that the actual stability is higher than the simulated stability.
Source: Tables constructed by author on the basis of actual electoral data. Data supplied by the Centre for Study of Developing Societies.

Table 2.6
Difference in Actual and Simulated Values of Pss
(District Magnitude = Entire State)

	I	*II*	*III*	*IV*	*V*	*VI*	*VII*
Assam	0.521	0.860	0.384	−0.151	0.317	0.000	
Bihar	0.245	0.406	0.201	0.327	−0.222	−0.047	
Orissa	0.293	0.086	0.395	0.469	−0.395	0.585	
UP	−0.112	0.174	0.532	0.551	−0.099	0.449	0.293
Punjab	−0.102	0.538	0.744	0.427	0.479	0.500	
Haryana	−0.025	0.160	1.185	0.167	0.722	0.878	
MP	0.331	0.277	0.525	0.069	0.900	0.000	
Rajasthan	0.554	0.345	0.340	−0.020	0.440	0.000	
Tamil Nadu	−0.376	−0.004	−0.179	0.197	0.573	0.577	
Maharashtra	−0.019	0.217	−0.003	−0.135	−0.080	0.000	
Gujarat	−0.411	0.676	0.133	0.363	0.560	0.000	
Karnataka	−0.046	0.022	0.460	0.272	0.357	0.000	
Andhra	0.278	0.268	−0.473	0.143	0.803	0.000	

Notes: A positive value means that the actual Pss is higher.
Source: Tables constructed by author on the basis of actual electoral data. Data supplied by the Centre for Study of Developing Societies.

Table 2.7
Pattern of State Governments

	I	*II*	*III*	*IV*	*V*	*VI*	*VII*	*VIII*
Assam	M	M	C	M	M	M		
Bihar	C	C	M	M	M	M	C	
Orissa	C	C	M, PR	M, PR	M	M	C	
UP	C	C	C	C	C	C	C	C
Punjab	C	C	M	C	M, PR	PR	M	
Haryana	C	C	M	M	C	C	M	
MP	C	M	M	M	M, PR	M	M	
Rajasthan	M	M	M	M	M	M	C	
TN	M	M	M	M	M	C	M	
Maharashtra	M	M	M	C	M	M	M	
Gujarat	C	M, PR	C	M	M	C	C	
Karnataka	M, PR	M	M	M	M	M		
Andhra	M	M, PR	M	M	M	M		

Notes: C denotes the formation of a coalition government at least for some time during the period; M represents a majority government (although one majority government may have been replaced by another), PR stands for President's rule.
Source: Tables constructed by author on the basis of actual electoral data. Data supplied by the Centre for Study of Developing Societies.

Table 2.8
Values of F_R Under Proportional Rule
(Input = Constituency-level data)

State	*Uttar Pradesh*			*State*	*Bihar*		
Year	Sim(S)	Actual(A)	S–A	Year	Sim(S)	Actual(A)	S–A
1974	0.689	0.657	0.032	1972	0.727	0.683	0.045
1977	0.481	0.301	0.180	1977	0.524	0.528	– 0.004
1985	0.609	0.556	0.053	1985	0.648	0.608	0.041
1989	0.688	0.692	– 0.004	1990	0.688	0.786	– 0.098
1991	0.763	0.654	0.109				
		Punjab				*Gujarat*	
Year	Sim(S)	Actual(A)	S–A	Year	Sim(S)	Actual(A)	S–A
1972	0.585	0.534	0.050	1972	0.507	0.296	0.211
1977	0.671	0.679	– 0.008	1985	0.511	0.320	0.191
1985	0.547	0.533	0.014	1990	0.665	0.683	– 0.018
1992	0.585	0.436	0.149				

Notes: The electoral district is taken to be one or two administrative districts.
Source: Tables constructed by author on the basis of actual electoral data. Data supplied by the Centre for Study of Developing Societies.

NOTES

The author is most grateful to the Centre for the Study of Developing Societies for making available the data used in this paper, to Sanghamitra Das, B. Ramaswami and E. Sreedharan for most useful comments on earlier drafts of the paper and to the Center for Institutional Reform and the Informal Sector (IRIS), University of Maryland, for financial support. This chapter was first published as an IRIS Working Paper in December 1996.

1. Political scientists use the term *fractionalisation* rather than *fragmentation*. This discussion uses the two terms interchangeably.
2. See, for instance, the classic work of Rae (1967) or Lijphart (1990): Rae, D. 1967, *The Political Consequences of Electoral Laws*, New Haven: Yale University Press; Lijphart, A. 1990, 'The Political Consequences of Electoral Laws', *American Political Science Review*, 84: 487–96.
3. Roubini, N., and J. Sachs, 1989, 'Political and Economic Determinants of Budget Deficits in the Industrial Democracies', *European Economic Review*, 33: 903–938.
4. Duverger (1951) made this assertion on the basis of an observed empirical regularity. See also Palfrey (1986), who gives a mathematical proof of Duverger's Law. Duverger, M. 1951, *Political Parties*, London: Methuen and Co.; Palfrey, T.

1986, 'A Mathematical Proof of Duverger's Law', in P. C. Ordeshook (ed.), *Models of Strategic Choice*, Ann Arbor: University of Michigan Press.

5. Using data on national elections in industrialised countries which have had a long history of elections, Blais and Carty (1987) study the impact of electoral formulae on the creation of majority governments. They report that the probability of a one-party majority system is close to zero in PR systems, and increases by 40 per cent in simple plurality systems. Blais, A. and R. K. Carty, 1987, 'The Impact of Electoral Formulae on the Creation of Majority Governments', *Electoral Studies*. Vol. 6: 207–216.
6. Brass, P. R. 1968, 'Coalition Politics in North India', *American Political Science Review*. Vol. 62, 1968: 1174–1191.
7. One such example is constructed in Section III.
8. Further assumptions are discussed in Section V.
9. Rae, *Political Consequences of Electoral Laws.*
10. Ibid.
11. Brass, 'Coalition Politics'.
12. Dodd, L. C. 1976, *Coalitions in Parliamentary Government*, Princeton: Princeton University Press.
13. An exception was the election to Andhra Pradesh in which no party other than the Congress won 5 per cent of the votes.
14. Brass, P. R. 1977, 'Party Systems and Government Stability in the Indian States', *American Political Science Review*. Vol. 71: 1384–1405.
15. See Dodd, *Coalitions*, for a different explanation of why greater fragmentation may lead to instability.
16. Rae, *Political Consequences of Electoral Laws.*
17. A second index of fractionalisation is based on the Theil measure of entropy, and was first proposed by Kesselman (1966) and Wildgren (1971): Kesselman, M. 1966, 'French Local Politics: A Statistical Examination of Grass Roots Consensus', *American Political Science Review*, Vol. 60, No. 4: 963–973; Wildgren, J. K. 1971, 'The Measurement of Hyperfractionalisation', *Comparative Political Studies*. Vol. 4: 233–243.
18. See, for instance, Brass, 'Party Systems'.
19. This is an extremely strong assumption. One coalition may consist of parties with similar ideologies, whereas another coalition may contain opportunistic parties who have joined the coalition simply to share the spoils of power. Obviously, the first coalition is likely to be more stable. But it is fair to say that the vast majority of ruling coalitions in India fall in the second category.
20. Dutta, B. 1996, 'Coalition Governments and Policy Distortions: The Indian Experience' (mimeo). New Delhi: Indian Statistical Institute.
21. Since it is difficult to predict which minimal coalition will form, one possibility is to modify S_m by taking the reciprocal of the average number of parties in the set of minimal winning coalitions. In subsequent work, these alternative measures of stability will be used as explanatory variables for the duration of coalition governments in India.
22. The reader should keep in mind that while S_m is an indicator of stability, F_R is an indicator of instability. In other words, a higher value of S_m indicates greater stability, while a higher value of F_R represents a more unstable situation.

23. Dodd, *Coalitions*.
24. Ibid.
25. An early contribution on the impact of political factors on fiscal policies of different state governments is Rao, M. Govinda, 1979, 'Political Stability and Taxation in India', *Public Finance*. Vol. 34, No. 1: 114–128.
26. See Dutta, 'Coalition Governments,' for a discussion of the problems in analysing fiscal indiscipline of state governments in India since state governments have less than complete control over their resources. This section depends heavily upon Dutta.
27. In the case of Kerala, there was a converse problem since there were only a few years in which Kerala had a government with only one pivotal party!
28. Orissa is another state which has had some experience of coalition governments. However, the explanatory power of the regression equation for Orissa is very poor. A possible explanation for this is that the Jan Congress–Swatantra government which was in power for almost four years between 1967 and 1971 provided very stable governance.
29. Dutta, 'Coalition Governments,' also reports results for another exercise in which data for all the fifteen major states over twenty-six years was pooled. This exercise also corroborates the hypothesis that unstable coalition governments have a higher proportion of revenue expenditure to state domestic product, as well as a lower proportion of non-tax revenue to state domestic product.
30. Under this simulation exercise, the Congress and the CPI would win 257 and thirty seats respectively, whereas actually they won 218 and seven seats.
31. The reader is reminded that a higher value of S_m indicates greater stability.
32. Note that a higher value of PS_t denotes a lower degree of party system stability.

3

The Political Economy of Privatisation in India*

Anand Gupta

India has a huge public sector. It consists of nearly 1,300 enterprises, owned and managed by the Central Government, state and union territory governments and local governments in the country. These enterprises manage, according to the World Bank (1994), as much as 55 per cent of the economy's (excluding households') capital stock and account for one-fourth of nonagricultural Gross Domestic Product (GDP).[1] They dominate many sectors of the economy: surface irrigation; water supply in rural and urban areas; railways; river transport; ports; postal services; telecommunications; mining (including hydrocarbons and coal); one-third of registered manufacturing (particularly steel, petrochemicals, capital goods, pharmaceuticals and fertiliser); power generation and distribution; oil and gas production and marketing; air transport; one-third of bus transport; storage; and banking and insurance.

Although there are differences in the performance of individual public enterprises, most public enterprises are overstaffed[2] and suffer from other operational inefficiencies. It is not merely public enterprises such as Bihar State Electricity Board, Uttar Pradesh Road Transport Corporation, Indian Iron and Steel Company, Scooters India Limited, Heavy Engineering Corporation, National Textiles Corporation, Fertiliser Corporation of India and Hindustan Fertilisers Corporation that are inefficient. Even seemingly well-positioned public enterprises are also operating inefficiently. A study (Gupta 1988)[3] has shown that Rashtriya Chemicals and

*This paper was first published in the *Economic and Political Weekly*, vol. 31, no. 39, 1996

Fertilisers, which is considered by many to be one of India's better-run public enterprises, has performed poorly: its pretax profits relative to its net worth ranged between 2.1 per cent and 10.2 per cent during the period 1978–1986, which is much lower than what the Government of India (GOI) effectively paid for the resources that it borrowed to invest in it, with inefficiency in the use of inputs (e.g., gas and power) being a major factor responsible for this outcome. Similarly, the GOI's National Thermal Power Corporation, which received a rating of excellent for achieving its output target in 1991–92, in effect did poorly in that year: output indeed went up, but the use of material inputs rose even faster.[4]

Public enterprises have been a major contributor to India's huge public sector deficit, that is, the deficit of all public entities in the country, including the central, state, union territory and local governments, departmental and nondepartmental public enterprises and public entities such as the Oil Coordination Committee. According to a recent estimate, the deficit of public enterprises in the energy sector alone adds up to over 4 per cent of GDP.[5] The public enterprises' deficits have added to the country's current large stock of domestic and external public debt, which in turn results in massive annual liabilities on account of interest payments. The interest payments of the GOI alone, which has financed much of the investment in the country's public enterprises, and the losses that many of them have incurred, through borrowings on its account, add up to about 5 per cent of GDP. Indeed, the GOI's interest payments currently eat up as much as about 45 per cent of its total current receipts,[6] up from 39.1 per cent in 1990–91 and 26.8 per cent in 1985–86.

What is more distressing is the phenomenon of many public enterprises in India reporting losses despite being overprotected. This means that these enterprises' operational inefficiencies are so huge that they exceed the benefits resulting from the substantial protection that they enjoy and, as a consequence, they incur losses. With protection levels coming down, with competition increasing, and with many qualified people leaving public enterprises because of substantially better opportunities available in the private sector,[7] the public enterprises' financial performance may worsen.

Many people vehemently disagree with the view that most of India's public enterprises operate inefficiently. G. V. Ramakrishna, currently heading the GOI's Disinvestment Commission and a former member of India's Planning Commission, for example, is reported to have claimed that thinking of all public enterprises as inefficient and unprofitable is fallacious, and to substantiate his claim, he is reported to have said that over 131 healthy public enterprises, including those in the infrastructure sector, are making annual profits of about Rs 80 billion.[8] Two points need to be raised here. First, what is the source of these profits? Is it efficiency in the use of inputs, or protection and/or monopoly or administered pricing? Further, how do the profits compare with what the government effectively paid for the resources that it borrowed to invest in the public enterprises in question? If one evaluates the performance of India's public enterprises in this manner, one will discover that most of them are operating inefficiently, as the study on Rashtriya Chemicals and Fertilisers, referred to previously, illustrates.

Why are public enterprises in India so inefficient? The answer lies in the environment in which public enterprises in India operate, and in the effect this environment has on the public enterprise managers' incentives to develop new, better and less expensive products, develop new markets, minimise capital and current costs and maximise profits. Iyer (1991) provides a graphic account of the unhealthily close and dysfunctional network of formal and informal links and relationships between the government and public enterprises, as well as some of the other components of the environment in which public enterprises in India operate.[9] Descriptions that illustrate this environment include the government's deep involvement in the actual management of public enterprises, with the concerned administrative ministries' tendency to function as if they were a kind of supermanagement on top of the Board of Directors;[10] the Parliament's involvement in public enterprises' affairs in several ways, including through numerous questions and enquiries ranging from questions of overall performance and policy issues to the minutest details of day-to-day functioning; and expansion of the horizon of Article 12 of the Constitution to treat even industrial, manufacturing and commercial public enterprises as 'state' and thereby subject them to the various obligations that go with such a treatment.

Some people believe that the performance of India's public enterprises can be substantially improved. They assert that what India urgently needs is the putting in place of a programme of public enterprise reform that, among other things, will have to include reform in government at both the political and bureaucratic levels.

An objective assessment of the situation, however, suggests that public enterprise reform is not a realistic goal in India.

A recent study has documented public enterprise reforms that a number of countries have put in place, have aimed at and the problems that they have faced.[11] The reforms aimed to expose public enterprises to domestic and external competition and level the playing field by eliminating easy access to credit from both the budget and the banking system; by freeing public enterprise managers from non-commercial goals and government interference in day-to-day decisionmaking; and by developing institutional mechanisms, such as contract plans (or Memorandums of Understanding [MOUs]) and performance evaluation systems to hold managers accountable for results. In response to these reforms, some public enterprises have indeed performed better, but three problems persist.

First, the reforms are technically and politically difficult to implement. Often, well-designed programmes have fallen short in implementation.

Second, performance does improve when the full reform package is put in place, but the necessary steps are numerous and hard to coordinate, and entire reform programmes have seldom been enacted. For instance, governments often discontinue budgetary support but continue to guarantee borrowings from banks, and pay and employment reforms have yielded little without increased managerial autonomy and accountability.

The third and most important problem of public enterprise reform is sustainability. Faced with a financial crisis or pushed by external forces, a government may initiate fundamental and far-reaching reforms in public enterprises that give managers the mandate and the power to run their enterprises in a commercial manner. As the reforms are put in place, economic and financial performance does improve, but as the crisis fades or the external pressure weakens, government ownership facilitates the revival of non-commercial objectives, which in turn often leads to renewed poor performance.

India's experience with public enterprise reform is no different from that of other countries. Indeed, India's biggest failure in its economic reforms programme is that there has not been a single transformation in public enterprises. There have been some marginal changes in such things as wage conditions and managerial autonomy, but these are very limited. Even if something significant does happen, the chances are that it will not sustain.

It therefore appears that privatisation is the only way out. Yet privatisation has not made much headway in India. Why? This discussion attempts to answer this important question and in doing so, explores the political economy aspects of the privatisation process in India. To be specific, it explores the incentives that influence the behaviour of India's politicians and policymakers while dealing with the privatisation issue in the country.

This chapter is divided into five sections. Section I provides an idea of how properly designed and implemented privatisations may benefit India. Section II describes India's privatisation experience and paves the way for Section III which explores the incentives that influence the behaviour of India's politicians and policymakers while dealing with the privatisation issue in the country. Finally, Section IV presents some concluding remarks.

I BENEFITS FROM PRIVATISATION

Privatisation, if designed and implemented properly, may benefit India in several ways. First, it will improve the environment in which public enterprises operate and thereby strengthen their managers' incentives to be efficient, which in turn can contribute to making the Indian economy substantially more efficient, as can be seen from the available evidence on privatisations in India. The Government of Andhra Pradesh's Allwyn Nissan Limited (ANL), which incurred losses from the very beginning in 1985, has done substantially better after its privatisation in 1988. The market share of the company, renamed as Mahindra Nissan Allwyn Limited (MNAL), after privatisation rose from 17 per cent before privatisation to 21 per cent at the end of 1990–91 in the fiercely competitive light commercial vehicle market; the company made an entry into the export market and improved its status from being a loss-making company to a net profit-making one in 1990–91.[12] The Board for Industrial and Financial Reconstruction has recently approved MNAL's merger with Mahindra and Mahindra Limited.[13] The merger is expected to enable Mahindra and Mahindra make substantially more efficient use of MNAL's plant and equipment and of its dealership and other infrastructure.

Bajaj (1994) has documented the privatisation of the Government of Uttar Pradesh's Auto Tractors Limited (ATL) which was established in Pratapgarh, a backward district of Uttar Pradesh, for manufacturing tractors and diesel engines.[14] With ATL's losses accumulating to Rs 479.4 million at the end of 1989–90 and there being no evidence of its being able to operate profitably, it was decided in November 1990 to close the plant down. The company was shortly thereafter converted into a joint venture with Sipani Automobiles Limited (SAL), with SAL taking over the possession of the plant in March 1991. SAL has concentrated on the production of engines. It produced 1,249 engines in 1991–92 and 1,541 in 1992–93 (more recent information on this is not readily available), against 273 in 1988–89 and 267 in 1989–90, and it has already started making a net profit.

Incidentally, Bajaj (1994) has reported that with ATL located in a backward district, a posting as its chief executive was not considered an important position by senior civil servants.[15] The result was that most of the time the civil servants posted to ATL were trying to get out of the district. Politicians used the public enterprise as a source of patronage to enhance their influence by distributing jobs and favours. In this way they were seeking to maximise their influence rather than improve the performance of the enterprise. The interest of the enterprise was far removed from their mind.

No other privatisation in India has been documented. But some studies[16] have compared public enterprises' performance before and after privatisation in a number of countries. These studies show considerable efficiency gains that have resulted from privatisation.

Second, privatisation may create conditions for substantial additional investment and, especially if privatisation is accompanied by labour market reforms, conditions for the generation of a large number of productive employment opportunities, which in turn may contribute to removing poverty. According to a study, privatisation revived a near-dead textile company in Niger, which now operates profitably at close to full capacity with a larger work force.[17] The company exports much of its production and has won a large domestic market share against imports.

Third, consumers may also gain from privatisation. A study that examined the welfare consequences of selling selected public enterprises in Chile, Malaysia, Mexico and the United Kingdom found that quite apart from any benefits from improved service, consumers for the most part gained or remained unaffected by privatisation.[18] In the five cases in which consumers did lose, the generally small losses were attributable mostly to prices moving closer to their scarcity values. The study concluded, for example, that consumers in Chile were unaffected by the sale of ENERSIS, the sole electricity distributor in Santiago. Paying consumers were better off, but this gain was balanced by losses to those who had hitherto been getting the electricity free through illegal connections. This means that if only those who had previously been paying for electricity had been considered legitimate consumers, the way it should have been, the study would have shown substantial increases in consumer welfare. These findings are especially relevant for the Indian situation, given the substantial losses that public entities in the power sector suffer because of illegal connections.

Fourth, given the environment in which public enterprises in India currently operate, they can spread their sickness even to efficient private enterprises in sectors in which both public and private enterprises coexist. Thus, a sick mill belonging to National Textiles Corporation, a GOI enterprise, directed by the government to keep on running to keep its workers employed and to keep on selling its fabrics at a heavily subsidised price, can easily drive an efficient private sector mill producing comparable fabrics out of business. One can imagine what may happen to private investors currently planning to enter India's power sector if loss-making state electricity boards continue to operate. Privatisation can be of major help in addressing this problem and thereby allowing the Indian economy to fully realise the potential benefits from the policy of industrial liberalisation that has been put in place.

Fifth, privatisation can be of help in reforming public intervention. India suffers from excessive public intervention, with public ownership and management of hundreds of enterprises being one form of public intervention. These enterprises are engaged in innumerable activities: manufacturing steel; building ships; generating, transmitting and distributing electric power; running domestic and international airlines; exploring, producing and refining oil; operating domestic and international telecommunications networks; running hotels; manufacturing polyester film; making condoms; producing fruit pulp and juice; running banks as well as life and general insurance and electronic entertainment businesses; and many more. Privatisation will result in the correction of such distortions and allow the government to concentrate on things it has failed to do but that it alone can do. As the recent outbreak of pneumonic plague in Surat and its rapid spread to other parts of India has highlighted, the government has failed to effectively intervene in the country's public health sector—and, as *The Times of India* commented in a January 2, 1995 lead editorial, 'a dirty country cannot be globalised'.[19] And public health is not the only example of the failure of public intervention in India. There are many examples such as protection of the environment, provision of primary education and maintenance of law and order.

Finally, privatisation can be of major help in reducing India's huge public sector deficit. This can happen in three ways. To begin with, the proceeds from the sale of public enterprises can be used to finance the public sector deficit or, in case the proceeds exceed the deficit, to reduce the outstanding public debt, both domestic and external.[20] This in turn will reduce the burden of interest payments and thereby the deficit.

Another way in which privatisation can be of major help in reducing India's public sector deficit is by substantially reducing, if not totally eliminating, the public enterprises' various demands on the country's public sector finances. These demands, which add up to substantial amounts, include demands for budgetary support to loss-making public enterprises, on the grounds that this will enable the concerned public enterprises to restart and produce goods. Consider, for example, the additional budgetary support of Rs 1.1 billion that the GOI recently approved for the sick units of Fertilisers Corporation of India (FCI) and Hindustan Fertilisers Corporation (HFC), both GOI enterprises. The GOI's Minister for Chemicals and Fertilisers is reported to have claimed that the additional budgetary support will enable FCI and HFC factories to restart and produce urea.[21] That amounts to saying that every sick enterprise in the world can produce goods if subsidised. But that is no reason to provide budgetary support to a sick enterprise. The same money could be used much more productively elsewhere. The Minister's game plan was simply to throw good money after bad with a view to serve his political interests. Privatisation will do away with all this nonsense and thereby help to reduce the deficit.

There is still another way in which privatisation can be of major help in reducing India's public sector deficit. Public enterprises in India have built and acquired enormous assets over the last five decades, running into trillions of rupees. With privatisation helping put these enormous assets to substantially more productive uses, direct and indirect tax revenues from privatised firms can be expected to exceed by a wide margin the revenues from taxes and dividends currently received from public enterprises. The following two examples illustrate how this can happen. Malaysia sold a government sports lottery in 1985. By 1989 the revenues generated through levies on the privatised lottery were three times greater, in real terms, than the revenue from the former public enterprise.[22] In Chile the net annual receipts from ENERSIS, the sole electricity distributor in Santiago, declined after privatisation because the government no longer received dividends on its equity, but tax revenue increased as performance gradually improved.[23]

II INDIA'S PRIVATISATION EXPERIENCE

India's privatisation experience can be discussed under six headings: selling a public enterprise's fractional equity, with the controlling ownership and management continuing to remain in the public sector; putting up a public enterprise for sale, with the intention of transferring its control and management to the private sector, but the sale not going through; putting up a public enterprise for sale, with the sale going through, but scuttling the entire deal later; winding up a public enterprise; transferring the control and management of a public enterprise to the private sector, but with a substantial proportion of the equity, enough for managerial intervention, continuing to remain in the public sector; and complete privatisation, or what Bhagwati and Srinivasan (1993)[24] call true privatisation, under which the control and management of a public enterprise is transferred to the private sector, although some public sector equity holding, without managerial intervention, may continue.

Selling Fractional Equity, with Controlling Ownership and Management Continuing to Remain in Public Sector

Beginning in July 1991, the GOI put in place a programme to sell a part of its equity held in selected central public enterprises. *The*

Economic Survey 1996–97 (Government of India 1997) provides year and public enterprise details of the equity sold during the period July 1, 1991 to March 31, 1996.[25] Three issues emerge from a study of these data. First, of the 246 non-departmental central public enterprises (CPEs), only forty CPEs' equity was sold during this period. Second, the quantity of equity that was sold was not significant: in nineteen of the CPEs in question, the equity sold added up to less than 10 percentage points; in seven, between 10 and 20 percentage points; in six, between 20 and 30 percentage points; in six, between 30 and 40 percentage points; and in two, between 40 and 50 percentage points. Finally, the controlling ownership and management of all the forty CPEs continued to remain with the GOI.

In addition, most of the equity that has been sold so far has been sold only to public entities in the financial sector, with the Unit Trust of India alone, for example, accounting for 69.4 per cent of the total sales in 1991–92. This was done, as the Minister of Finance put it in response to a calling attention motion in the Rajya Sabha, 'as it was the government's intention to ensure that the benefits accrued to public sector institutions rather than private entities in the event of the sales taking place at an underpriced level'.[26]

Putting up a Public Enterprise for Sale, but with the Sale not going through

A review of the available material suggests many cases of public enterprises that were put up for privatisation, but which could not be privatised. Examples are Indian Iron and Steel Company, Scooters India Limited and Great Eastern Hotel.

The Indian Iron and Steel Company (IISCO), a subsidiary of the Steel Authority of India Limited (SAIL), a GOI enterprise, had accumulated losses of Rs 8.9 billion as of March 31, 1994 against its paid-up capital of Rs 3.9 billion; it thus had a negative net worth of Rs 5 billion at the end of 1993–94. According to a GOI diagnosis in 1991, IISCO's problems included technological obsolescence, ageing plant and equipment, outmoded operational practices and overmanning.[27]

With the IISCO management not able to raise the resources required for turning the company around on its own, and with the GOI also not in a position to provide the required resources through budgetary support, the GOI decided to privatise the company, and even found a buyer, Mukund Limited. But as IISCO, which earlier used to be in the private sector, was acquired by the GOI under two acts of the Parliament (i.e., The Indian Iron and Steel Company (Taking Over of Management) Act of 1972 and The Indian Iron and Steel Company (Acquisition of Shares) Act of 1976), parliamentary approval was necessary for the privatisation to be put in place. Two bills to repeal these acts and thereby to seek the Parliament's approval for IISCO's privatisation were listed for introduction in the Lok Sabha on December 23, 1993 but given the vehement protest of the Left Front and other opposition members of the Lok Sabha, they had to be referred to a parliamentary committee. The GOI's Minister of State for Steel sought the support of the Parliamentary Consultative Committee for Privatisation of the Indian Iron and Steel Company, but his fervent appeal did not receive any favourable response.

In March 1994, IISCO's case was referred to the GOI's Board for Industrial and Financial Reconstruction (BIFR). The BIFR, set up in 1987 to implement the Sick Industrial Companies (Special Provisions) Act of 1985, appointed the Industrial Development Bank of India (IDBI) as the operating agency. The IDBI received a plan for the revival of IISCO. The plan, submitted by SAIL, was contingent on the GOI's Ministry of Steel providing a budgetary support of Rs 11 billion for reviving IISCO. But the GOI rejected the possibility of providing any budgetary support for turning around the ailing Burnpur (West Bengal)-based IISCO. Given India's political economy, this certainly was a bold decision—some people had argued that the then ruling Congress Party at the Centre had no alternative but to provide the budgetary support in question, because in case it did not, it would lose West Bengal in the 1996 general elections.

At one time it appeared that IISCO would almost certainly be privatised, with Mukund Limited, which earlier had offered to take over IISCO, buying it.[28] But this didn't happen. At another time it appeared that IISCO would be modernised jointly with Tyazpromexport (TPE), a Russian company, with TPE financing its part of the deal with money from the Russian government's rupee–rouble account. But the Russian government refused to release the money from this account and as a consequence the plan to modernise IISCO jointly with TPE had to be abandoned.

As things currently stand, SAIL has proposed a Rs 5 billion revamp of IISCO, possibly with low-interest funds from the Steel Development Fund. But the GOI's Disinvestment Commission has recommended the privatisation of IISCO. The GOI will make the final decision, depending on what its Ministers of Finance and Steel recommend.[29]

Scooters India Limited (SIL), a GOI enterprise, was incorporated as a public limited company in 1972 and started commercial production in 1975. It has two units located at Lucknow and New Delhi, with the Lucknow unit manufacturing two-wheelers and three-wheelers and the New Delhi unit, which is under lease, manufacturing electrical ceiling fans. SIL has performed very poorly. Its accumulated losses amounted to Rs 4.8 billion on March 31, 1994 against its paid-up capital of Rs 78.1 million; it thus had a negative net worth of Rs 4.7 billion at the end of 1993–94, up from Rs 2.5 billion at the end of 1990–91 and Rs 0.7 billion at the end of 1985–86. According to a GOI study (1991), SIL continued to be in bad shape because of: (*a*) outdated plant and machinery, (*b*) excessive manpower, (*c*) poor marketing and servicing network, and (*d*) inability to compete in a highly competitive market.[30]

The GOI decided in 1987 to sell the Lucknow unit to Bajaj Auto Limited, a major scooter producer in the private sector, but the decision could not be implemented because SIL's 3,125 employees opposed the GOI's privatisation move as it was feared that it might result in a retrenchment of 1,625 employees.[31]

In May 1992, SIL was referred to the BIFR. A package for its rehabilitation and restructuring has recently been approved.[32] Complete details of the package are not available, but there is reason to believe that the package involves writing off of SIL's liabilities (interest and excise duty payable, and loan repayment) and voluntary retirement of workers. A joint management committee to oversee implementation of the package has also been set up.

The Great Eastern Hotel, a Government of West Bengal (GOWB) enterprise, is over 150 years old, and is located in Calcutta. In 1994 the Communist Party of India (Marxist) (CPI[M])-led GOWB decided to privatise the hotel and transfer the control and management to Accor Asia Pacific, a subsidiary of Accor SA of France, which planned to convert it into a 250-room five-star hotel at a cost of about Rs 950 million. Accor agreed to buy the hotel on the condition that it would be allowed to retrench all of its 640 employees.

The GOWB responded to this by offering the employees thirty-six to forty months' salary, apart from provident fund and gratuity dues. But four labour unions, including those affiliated with the Centre of Indian Trade Unions and the Indian National Trade Union Congress, rejected the GOWB's offer.

Jyoti Basu, Chief Minister of GOWB, had announced that the hotel would have to be closed if it was not privatised, given that the GOWB did not have the funds to subsidise it. But the CITU leaders are reported to have impressed upon the Chief Minister that the privatisation of the Great Eastern Hotel just before the elections would not be politically wise. According to them, the Congress Party could use this as a weapon against the CPI(M), especially when the CPI(M) had opposed the privatisation of Bailadila mines.[33] This suggests that the issue of privatising the Great Eastern Hotel may be revived when the political climate improves.

Putting up a Public Enterprise for Sale, with the Sale going through, but Scuttling the Entire Deal Later[34]

There has been at least one such case of this type: the sale of the Government of Uttar Pradesh's UP State Cement Corporation Limited (UPSCCL). The UPSCCL had accumulated losses of Rs 1.6 billion as of March 31, 1990 against its net worth of Rs 0.7 billion; it thus had a negative net worth of Rs 0.9 billion at the end of 1989–90. The UPSCCL's problems included inherent defects in plant design, inadequacy of trained technical personnel, poor maintenance, overmanning and recurring labour problems, low capacity utilisation and high cost of production.

Considering the mounting losses, the Government of Uttar Pradesh (GOUP) decided in April 1990 to privatise UPSCCL. It found a buyer, Dalmia Industries. In February 1991 the GOUP and Dalmia Industries entered into a joint venture agreement which provided, among other things, for: (*a*) the GOUP transferring 51 per cent of UPSCCL's equity to Dalmia Industries, with the balance of 49 per cent remaining with the GOUP, (*b*) the joint venture taking over all the employees of UPSCCL, and (*c*) Dalmia Industries taking over the management of UPSCCL. The decision to transfer the equity and hand over the management was opposed by the UPSCCL's employees. A petition was filed in the Allahabad

High Court, which prohibited the GOUP from converting UPSCCL into a private corporation. The GOUP responded to this by transferring only 49 per cent of the equity, with the stipulation that another 2 per cent of the equity would be transferred after the Court's decision. The GOUP also handed over the UPSCCL's management to Dalmia Industries. But as there was labour unrest, the transfer of management could take place only with the help of the police. The police had to resort to gunfire to control the workers, as a result of which nine workers died.

After some time, a number of employee labour unions filed a petition, stating that as the interests of workers had already been safeguarded by specific provisions in the agreement which guaranteed that no worker would be retrenched and that service conditions would not be changed to their detriment, the petition earlier filed by them may be dismissed.

The events, however, took a dramatic turn. There was a change in government in Uttar Pradesh; the new government decided to cancel the agreement with Dalmia Industries and resumed the equity shares transferred to it through an ordinance issued on October 11, 1991.

There has been a further deterioration in the UPSCCL's financial situation, with its accumulated losses on March 31, 1994 adding up to over four times its net worth. More recent information on its financial situation is not readily available.

Winding up a Public Enterprise

As part of the country's economic reforms programme, the Sick Industrial Companies Act of 1985 was amended in December 1991 to bring public enterprises under the purview of the Board for Industrial and Financial Reconstruction (BIFR). Consequently, up to the end of 1996, 145 cases of sick public enterprises were registered with the BIFR. The BIFR recommended winding up in twenty-four of these cases.[35] The public enterprises the BIFR has recommended for winding up include: National Textiles Corporation (NTC) (Gujarat), NTC (Madhya Pradesh), NTC (Uttar Pradesh), NTC (West Bengal), British India Corporation, Cawnpore Textiles, Elgin Mills, Mandya National Paper Mills and National Bicycle Corporation.

But none of these public enterprises has been wound up so far. Indeed, the government seems to have abandoned, at least for the time being, even the idea of shutting down public enterprises. The GOI's Minister of Industry is reported to have announced that whenever the BIFR ordered the winding up of a sick public enterprise, the GOI did not accept the order as 'final'. According to him, no stones would be left unturned to restructure, revive and strengthen public enterprises and the route of winding up would be adopted only as the last resort.[36]

Partially Transferring the Control of a Public Enterprise to the Private Sector

There have been cases of public enterprises whose control and management has been transferred to the private sector, but a substantial proportion of their equity, enough for managerial intervention, has continued to remain in the public sector. The case of Maruti Udyog Limited (MUL) is an excellent example of this kind of privatisation experience in India.

Until mid-1992, MUL was a public enterprise, with the GOI holding 60 per cent of its equity and Suzuki Motor Corporation (SMC) of Japan holding the remaining 40 per cent. Currently, SMC holds 50 per cent of MUL's equity, with the GOI holding 49.74 per cent and MUL employees the remaining 0.26 per cent. This allows the GOI to effectively intervene in decisionmaking at MUL. One can argue that this is not necessarily a bad thing, provided the intervention is in MUL's commercial interest. And this is where the difficulty lies.

Consider, for example, the GOI's stand on the issue of MUL's proposed expansion and modernisation programme involving an investment of Rs 23.7 billion. MUL wants to modernise and expand in order to withstand the increased competition resulting from the opening up of India's passenger car sector while tightening the grip on its market share. The GOI wants MUL to finance the expansion and modernisation programme through borrowings and internal accruals, while SMC wants to use these routes as well as equity through an increase in the paid-up capital. Responding to a question on SMC's objection to financing MUL's expansion and modernisation programme only through borrowings and internal accruals, SMC President Osamu Suzuki said, 'There will have to be a balance between borrowing, equity and internal accruals. If anybody suggests that borrowings and internal accruals can be enough, he does not know business. Maybe some people in India are happy with the impasse. Maybe some car manufacturers are behind it as they resent Maruti's monopoly'.[37]

And what is the GOI's objection to raising part of the required resources through equity? The answer is simple: the GOI wants to retain its equity holding at the current level of 49.74 per cent, and in order to be able to do that it will have to expend a substantial amount of money, which it cannot afford to do. It cannot expend the money largely because of its current difficult fiscal situation, but also because of the perverse signals that this will send out to all those who were denied budgetary support for the programmes that they had supported (e.g., programme for IISCO's revival)—they will argue that if the GOI can manage to find resources for investing in MUL's equity, it must find resources for, say, IISCO's revival as well.

The bottom line is that while MUL is no longer a public enterprise, the GOI's current actions are being guided much less by commercial rationality than by its desire not to dilute its current 49.74 per cent equity stake, so that it may continue to control MUL and effectively intervene in its affairs.[38] The irony is that all this is being allowed to happen despite the noise that the GOI has made in recent years about getting out of non-core areas.

Complete or True Privatisation

Finally, India's privatisation experience also includes cases of complete or true privatisation, under which the control and management of a public enterprise is transferred to the private sector, although some public sector equity holding, without managerial intervention, may continue. Indeed, a careful review of the available evidence, including the results of a recent survey in *The Economic Times* on how fourteen state governments have dealt with the privatisation issue, clearly suggests many cases of complete or true privatisation in India.[39] The public enterprises that have been completely or truly privatised in India include ACC Babcock, Allwyn Nissan Limited, Auto Tractors Limited, East Coast Breweries and Distilleries Limited, Goa Telecommunications Limited, Goa Time Movers, Haryana Breweries

Limited, Hindustan Allwyn Limited's Refrigeration Division, Orissa Mining Corporation's Charge Chrome Plant and Rajasthan State Tanneries. Information on the total value of the public enterprises that have been completely or truly privatised so far is not available, but there is reason to believe that it is not significant.[40]

The foregoing discussion reveals the variety of ways in which India's politicians and policymakers behave when it comes to dealing with the issue of privatisation in the country. But why do they behave the way they do? To be specific, why doesn't the percentage of equity of the central public enterprises that the GOI has sold during the last several years add up to much? Why didn't the GOI privatise the ailing Indian Iron and Steel Company, when it had announced its decision to do so and had even found a buyer in Mukund Limited? Why didn't the GOI privatise the ailing Scooters India Limited, when it had announced its decision to do so and had even found a buyer in Bajaj Auto Limited? Why didn't the Government of West Bengal privatise the ailing Great Eastern Hotel when it had announced its decision to do so and had even found a buyer in Accor Asia Pacific, a subsidiary of Accor SA of France? Why did the Government of Uttar Pradesh scuttle the deal involving the privatisation of UP State Cement Corporation Limited? Why haven't the public enterprises which have been recommended for winding up by the BIFR been wound up so far? Why is the GOI insisting that it must continue to control Maruti Udyog and effectively intervene in its affairs even though Maruti is no longer a public enterprise? And so on.

The following section presents a framework developed for addressing these issues. The framework explores the incentives that influence the behaviour of India's politicians and policymakers while dealing with the privatisation issue in the country.

III INCENTIVES INFLUENCING THE BEHAVIOUR OF INDIA'S POLITICIANS AND POLICYMAKERS

While India's politicians and policymakers have generally opposed privatisation, they have also allowed the privatisation of certain public enterprises. Politicians or policymakers may oppose privatisation on ideological grounds—privatisation is a bad thing; public enterprises can be reformed. Politicians or policymakers may resist privatisation also because they perceive privatisation as something which is not in their self-interest. Politicians or policymakers may perceive the privatisation of a given public enterprise as damaging, directly or indirectly, the chances of their election or reelection if that privatisation is likely to affect adversely one or more of the following interest groups: the public enterprise's employees, input suppliers, output dealers and customers accustomed to subsidised output. Further, to the extent that a public enterprise can be used as a milch cow or as a source of patronage, or as both, its privatisation may be perceived by politicians or policymakers as a development which is not in their self-interest.

On the other hand, when politicians or policymakers allow the privatisation of a given public enterprise, they may do so, one may argue, because of one or more of the following considerations: ideological grounds (privatisation is good; it will benefit the economy in several ways), pressure from well-informed voters and an increasingly difficult public finance situation.

A careful review of the available evidence and discussions with knowledgeable people suggest that Indian politicians' and policymakers' opposition to privatisation has been influenced much less by ideological considerations than by considerations of self-interest. Indeed, the considerations of self-interest seem to have been so pervasive and overwhelming that these considerations largely explain why the percentage of central public enterprises' equity that the GOI has sold over the last several years does not add up to much; why the GOI did not privatise Indian Iron and Steel Company and Scooters India Limited; why the Government of West Bengal did not privatise Great Eastern Hotel; why the Government of Uttar Pradesh scuttled the deal involving the privatisation of UP State Cement Corporation Limited;[41] why the public enterprises which the BIFR has recommended for winding up have not been wound up so far; and why the GOI is insisting that it must continue to control Maruti Udyog Limited and effectively intervene in its affairs even though Maruti is no longer a public enterprise. The last subsection of this chapter describes in some detail how India's politicians and policymakers use public enterprises to serve their self-interests.

But this is not all. The increasingly difficult public finance situation has begun putting pressure on Indian politicians and policymakers to behave differently. They have begun to realise that many sick public enterprises will have to be privatised to release scarce resources for more pressing public purposes and/or for some populist schemes that they had announced in their election manifestos. It is this recognition that may have triggered all the moves that have been made for complete or true privatisation in India. Also, it is this recognition that may ultimately compel the GOI to proceed with the privatisation of Indian Iron and Steel Company.

But a given privatisation move may not necessarily turn into a complete or true privatisation. Much depends on how the process of transition from a privatisation move to a complete or true privatisation is managed. Given that most public enterprises in India are grossly overstaffed, a major consideration here relates to the employment implications of privatisation. In the Haryana Breweries privatisation case, the employment issue was handled by the buyer (Shaw Wallace and Company) and the seller (Government of Haryana) entering into an agreement which clearly stipulated that 'there will not be any retrenchment or downward revision of pay scale of existing workmen or employees'.[42] Similarly, in the Allwyn Nissan Limited (ANL) privatisation case, the employment issue was handled by the buyer (Mahindra and Mahindra Limited) and the seller (Government of Andhra Pradesh) entering into an agreement under which the buyer undertook to 'protect the rights and service conditions of the employees on the payroll of ANL, abide by the written commitments of the present management to them and not envisage any reduction in the overall workforce'.[43] But in the GOI's Scooters India Limited case, the privatisation move did not succeed, as the employees opposed the move on the grounds that it might result in retrenchment of roughly half the employees.[44]

But all this does not necessarily suggest that in order for a privatisation move to succeed, the buyer must agree to employ all the workers. In the Government of Uttar Pradesh's Auto Tractors Limited (ATL) case, privatisation was not opposed even though the buyer (Sipani Automobiles Limited) had made it clear that while preference would be given to the ATL employees, it would employ only as many workers as it considered necessary. One may ask how such an outcome was managed. The answer lies in the fact that once it became evident that it would not be possible to operate ATL profitably, the Government of Uttar Pradesh (GOUP) decided to close the plant, retrench all of its about 1,230 employees and pay them the compensation and benefits that they were entitled to, totalling about Rs 50 million, and it was only after all this had been done that the GOUP started exploring the options available to it, including that of privatisation, rather than exploring the privatisation option while continuing to operate the plant.[45]

IV WHERE DO WE GO FROM HERE?

One may argue that although the progress on the privatisation front so far has not been very encouraging, the momentum will pick up as time goes on, given the incentives for privatisation that will result from pressures that are building up.

First, the screw of budgetary support to finance public enterprise investments and losses is gradually being tightened—witness, for example, the developments on the IISCO front. This reflects India's public finance situation which continues to be bad. 'There is', as Little (1996) has put it, 'a time-bomb ticking away, since borrowing is at unsustainably high levels. India is heading for another crisis'.[46]

Second, the mechanisms which earlier served to protect public enterprises from the workings of competitive markets are now eliminated to a large extent and as a consequence public enterprises are experiencing difficulties in responding to the new environment—witness, for example, the exodus of qualified people from Bharat Electricals Limited, National Thermal Power Corporation, Indian Airlines and others. This, combined with the gradual hardening of the budget as well as the reforms in the financial sector, may have the effect of substantially weakening the public enterprise employees' opposition to privatisation; indeed, some of them may even start openly demanding privatisation.

While there is merit in this argument, it will not be in India's interests to passively wait for the above two pressures to work themselves out and thereby create the incentives for privatisation.

Something more should be done—something that may make privatisation happen in India before India is driven to the wall again. A major initiative for turning India toward privatisation should be launched. Its work programme will have four components, with the first component guided by the urgency of building and strengthening a constituency for privatisation in India. This will be considerably aided by the widest possible dissemination of information about the various benefits—benefits not just on the public finance front, but on the efficiency and other fronts as well—that properly designed and implemented privatisations may bring to the Indian people. The people will have to be convinced that, given the extremely high opportunity costs, India cannot afford public sector misadventures in areas such as running hotels, manufacturing polyester film, making condoms and producing fruit pulp and juice that properly belong to the private sector.

The second component of the work programme will address the issue of formulating a privatisation policy for India. This is important, for once the necessary climate conducive to privatisation has been created, it will be highly desirable to follow this up as soon as possible with the announcement of a properly structured and articulated privatisation policy. The policy will need to clearly address at least the following issues: Why privatise? What should be privatised? India cannot afford to limit its privatisation programme to certain sick public enterprises only; most of the other public enterprises (sick as well as non-sick) also will have to be privatised. When should an enterprise be privatised? Which organisation will serve as the nodal agency for privatisation and what will be its composition, powers and responsibilities? What are the institutional mechanisms that will be put in place to gain public enterprise employees' support for privatisation? What is the role that India would like foreign investors to play in its privatisation programme?

The third component of the work programme will address the issue of capacity building for managing privatisations in India. Privatisation is a difficult process; it involves reconciling the government's political objectives and the business needs of a given public enterprise with the need to interest private investors in the enterprise and to generate efficiencies.[47] It will therefore be absolutely necessary to come up with training programmes designed to equip selected public enterprise managers and government officials in India with the knowledge and skills required for managing the various components of the privatisation process.

Finally, the proposed initiative will address the issue of evaluating India's post-privatisation experiences. This will involve rigorous work on estimating the impact of privatisation on efficiency and investment, on public finances and balance of payments, on employment, on management practices and strategies and on managers' skills, attitudes and behaviour. Evaluations of post-privatisation experiences along these lines may generate ideas that may help India maximise the gains from privatisation.

India's Politicians' and Policymakers' use of Public Enterprises[48] The internal rate of return that the business of politics generates in India is pretty high. Politicians therefore want to get elected and reelected. This explains the cut-throat competition for votes that one witnesses—votes for getting elected or reelected, for example, as an MLA (Member of [a State] Legislative Assembly) or an MP (Member of Parliament) and for getting elected or reelected and then surviving as a Chief Minister or as Prime Minister. And it is here that public enterprises, which elected politicians use as milch cattle, come in handy: access to the public enterprises' resources helps politicians in getting votes. This can happen in a variety of ways.

First, public enterprises can be used to create and provide jobs, often at wages or salaries higher than the market rates, to those who directly or indirectly help a politician in getting votes; in India it is much easier to create a job in a public enterprise than in a government department. This explains to a large extent the phenomenon of gross overstaffing and the resulting inefficiency in public enterprises. To illustrate: the cost of producing sugar in the Government of Bihar's sugar mills recently ranged between Rs 9 and 245 per kilogram. Six of the mills that were closed in 1992 were operating so inefficiently that their closure enabled the Government of Bihar, even with the employees continuing to be paid their wages or salaries, to reduce its budgetary support in financing their losses by Rs 70 million a year.[49]

Second, public enterprises can be used as parking places for selected members of a rival group within a political party, or for such other people whose support may be critical for the continued survival of, say, a Chief Minister. These people can be nominated or appointed as chairpersons or as members of the management boards of selected public enterprises. This is a standard practice in India, with the recent appointments to the boards of Gujarat's public enterprises being an example: the Gujarat Chief Minister is reported to have appointed supporters of one of his political rivals as chairpersons of Gujarat's public enterprises such as Gujarat Industrial Development Corporation and Gujarat State Export Corporation.[50]

Finally, public enterprises can also be milched through leakages in, for instance, their spending under various heads, both current and capital. Thus, plant facilities and machinery required for implementing a public enterprise's investment projects, especially projects of a public enterprise operating in a regime of administered (cost-plus) pricing, may be acquired at inflated prices, with at least a part of the difference between the market price and the actual price charged to the public enterprise directly or indirectly accruing to an elected politician. And the resources so acquired can be used for facilitating the engineering of political defections, for financing the huge reelection expenses and for many other purposes.

Given this state of affairs, no wonder most politicians and policy-makers oppose privatisation of public enterprises, especially at a time when, thanks to the economic reforms that have been put in place, some of the opportunities for rent-seeking that they used to thrive on have disappeared.

NOTES

1. The World Bank, 1994, *India: Recent Economic Developments and Prospects.* Report Number 12940-IN. Washington, DC: The World Bank.
2. Officials of Coal India Limited (CIL), a GOI enterprise, are reported to have said that under the national coal wage agreement, CIL is obliged to provide employment to the dependants of workers, irrespective of the vacancies, after the death of a worker while in service and after the termination of service of a worker on medical grounds after the age of 58. As a result of these provisions, CIL had to provide employment to over 62,000 people who are redundant ('Liberalisation Pulls Coal India Out of Red', *The Times of India* (Ahmedabad edition), 23 August 1995). Available information suggests substantial overstaffing in many other public enterprises as well. A recent study reveals overstaffing of 19–80 per cent in telecommunications, of 91 per cent in Bombay Port (container section) and of more than 33 per cent in steel, chemicals and textiles (Banerji, A. and R. H. Sabot. 1994, 'Wage Distortions, Overmanning, and Reform in Developing Country Public Enterprises', Background paper, Policy Research Department, The World Bank. Washington, DC: The World Bank).
3. Gupta, A. P. 1988, 'Financial Performance of Public Enterprises in India: A Case Study of Rashtriya Chemicals and Fertilisers Limited', *India: Review of Public Enterprises*, Report Number 7294-IN. Washington, DC: The World Bank.
4. The World Bank, 1995, *Bureaucrats in Business: The Economics and Politics of Government Ownership*, New York: Oxford University Press.
5. Gupta, A. P. 1992, 'India: Resources for Financing Energy Sector Investments', Background Paper prepared for *India: Energy Sector Review*, Washington, DC: The World Bank.
6. Even this figure of 45 per cent understates the GOI's true interest liability as interest payments are calculated on a cash basis rather than on an accrual basis.
7. At least 100 senior personnel from Bharat Heavy Electricals Limited, a GOI enterprise, are reported to have jumped the fence to join its MNC competitor,

Asea Brown Boveri ('MOUs to be Linked with Performance of CMDs', *The Times of India* (Ahmedabad edition), 12 January 1995). Similarly, National Thermal Power Corporation, another GOI enterprise, is facing an exodus of its top brass ('NTPC Faces Exodus of Top Brass', *The Economic Times* (Ahmedabad edition), 1 December 1995).

8. 'Govt. to Set Up Regulatory Bodies in Core Sectors', *The Times of India* (Ahmedabad edition), 13 January 1995.
9. Iyer, R. R. 1991, *A Grammar of Public Enterprises: Exercises in Clarification*, Jaipur: Rawat Publications.
10. Air India, a GOI enterprise, is reported to have sought the Ministry of Civil Aviation's final clearance for chartering an aircraft for a wedding in the air ('Jeweller's Son to Tie Nuptial Knot in Sky', *The Times of India* (Ahmedabad edition), 6 October 1994). Why couldn't Air India's management decide the matter on its own? Then HMT Limited, another GOI enterprise, is reported to have sought the government's permission to file suits against TUSRC of Iran to recover expenditure incurred and damages for failing to honour contractual obligations; it has also sought the government's approval to file a suit against a customer in Africa for overdue amounts on supplies ('HMT Seeks Rs 354-Cr Govt Aid for Revival', *The Economic Times* (Ahmedabad edition), 16 October 1995). Why couldn't the HMT management make decisions on the issues involved on its own and go ahead with their implementation without seeking the government's permission or approval?
11. Kikeri, S., J. Nellis and M. Shirley, 1994, 'Privatization: Lessons from Market Economies', *The World Bank Research Observer*, 9(2): 241–272.
12. Reddy, Y. V. 1992, *Public Enterprise Reform and Privatisation*, Bombay: Himalaya Publishing House.
13. 'BIFR Approves MNAL's Merger with Mahindra & Mahindra', *The Economic Times*, 4 August 1994.
14. Bajaj, J. L. 1994, 'Divesting State Ownership: A Tale of Two Companies', *Economic and Political Weekly*, 28 August.
15. Ibid.
16. Megginson, W. L., R. C. Nash, and M. van Randenborgh, 1994, 'The Financial and Operating Performance of Newly Privatized Firms: An International Empirical Analysis', *The Journal of Finance*, 49(2): 403–452.
17. See note 11.
18. Galal, A., L. Jones, P. Tandon and I. Vogelsang, 1994, *Welfare Consequences of Selling Public Enterprises: Case Studies from Chile, Malaysia, Mexico and the United Kingdom*, New York: Oxford University Press.
19. 'More of the Same', *The Times of India* (Ahmedabad edition), 2 January 1995.
20. The proceeds from the sale of public enterprises should be treated as a financing (below-the-line) item, not as a receipt (above-the-line) item. A major advantage of such a treatment is that it eliminates all possible incentives to reduce a given public sector deficit with no fiscal correction or a relatively small one (Gupta, A. P. 1993, 'Reforming Deficit Measurement: The Indian Case', *Economic and Political Weekly*, 20 February and 26 February. See also Gupta, A. P. and D. M. Levy, 1993, 'Rent-Seeking Data Manipulation'. [Unpublished paper]; and United Nations Development Programme. 1993, *Human Development Report 1993*, New Delhi: Oxford University Press.)

21. 'Non-Plan Aid Released to Ease Urea Shortage', *The Times of India* (Ahmedabad edition), 20 November 1994.
22. See note 18.
23. Ibid.
24. Bhagwati, J. and T. N. Srinivasan, 1993, *India's Economic Reforms*, New Delhi: Government of India, Ministry of Finance.
25. Government of India. 1997, *Economic Survey 1996–97*, New Delhi: Government of India.
26. 'Disinvestment: Manmohan Denies Impropriety Charge', *The Times of India* (Ahmedabad edition), 7 August 1993.
27. Government of India. 1991, *Monograph on the Performance Status of Central Public Sector Enterprises.* Vol. 2. New Delhi: Government of India.
28. 'Mukund to Bid Again for IISCO', *The Economic Times* (Ahmedabad edition), 1 December 1995.
29. 'IISCO Staff Seeks Revival Package', *The Times of India* (New Delhi edition), 15 April 1998.
30. See note 27.
31. Pendse, D. R. 1991, 'Planning for Privatisation in India: Preparatory Measures', in Geeta Gouri (ed.), *Privatisation and Public Enterprise: The Asian Pacific Experience*, New Delhi: Oxford and IBH Publishing Company Private Limited. Pendse cites 'Scooters India Workers to Resist Takeover', *Business Standard* (Calcutta edition), 8 March 1988.
32. 'Rehabilitation Package for 12 PSUs Finalised', *The Economic Times* (Ahmedabad edition), 12 September 1995.
33. 'Unions Win Over Basu on Privatising Great Eastern', *The Times of India* (Ahmedabad edition), 22 August 1995.
34. This subsection draws heavily on material in Bajaj (see note 14).
35. Of the remaining 121 cases of public enterprises registered with the BIFR, twenty-eight were dismissed as non-maintainable, thirty-six were approved for revival, four were declared as no longer sick and fifty-three were pending for disposal.
36. 'Ministry Wants Review of Disinvestment Limit', *The Times of India* (Ahmedabad edition), 21 October 1995.
37. 'Suzuki Chief Lambasts Govt for Inaction', *The Times of India* (Ahmedabad edition), 15 December 1995.
38. Press reports suggest that the GOI has finally won the battle, with the SMC agreeing to financing the Maruti's proposed expansion and modernisation programme through debt and internal accruals ('Suzuki Not to Increase Stake in Maruti Udyog: Expansion Proposal's Chances Brighten', *The Economic Times* (Ahmedabad edition), 6 July 1996).
39. 'Privatisation: End of the Beginning', *The Economic Times* (Ahmedabad edition), 17 February 1996.
40. The sale value of 76 per cent equity of ACC Babcock amounted to US$ 16.5 million (EPW Research Foundation. 'Opportunities in Power Sector', *Economic and Political Weekly*, 29 July 1995), that of 51 per cent equity of Haryana Breweries Limited to Rs 75 million ('SWC Takes Over Haryana Breweries', *The Economic Times* (Ahmedabad edition), 19 July 1994) and that of 74 per cent equity of Auto Tractors Limited to Rs 55.5 million (Bajaj 1994, see note 14).

41. The death of nine workers in the wake of transfer of the UP State Cement Corporation Limited's (UPSCCL's) management to Dalmia Industries added a new dimension to the issue. The Bharatiya Janata Party (BJP) took this up as one of the election issues and announced that it would scuttle the UPSCCL's privatisation if it came to power. The BJP won the elections and accordingly the agreement with Dalmia Industries was cancelled. If the elections had been held some time later, things probably would have been different.
42. Malik, R. S. 'No Retrenchment', Letter to the editor, *The Economic Times*, 26 July 1994. Malik was corresponding as Commissioner and Secretary, Department of Industry, Government of Haryana.
43. See note 12.
44. See note 31.
45. See note 14.
46. Little, I. M. D. 'India's Economic Reforms,' *The Economic Times* (Ahmedabad edition), 1 April 1996.
47. Donaldson, D. J. 1995, *Privatization: Principles and Practice*, Washington, DC: International Finance Corporation.
48. This section draws heavily on material in Gupta, A. P. 1996, 'Privatisation and India's Economic Reforms', IRIS-India Working Paper 15, College Park, Maryland: Center for Institutional Reform and the Informal Sector, University of Maryland.
49. Singh, L. 1993, 'Reforms in Financing of Investments in Bihar's Public Enterprise Sector', Note Prepared for Presentation at the Indian Institute of Management Programme on 'Restructuring of India's Economy', 13–17 December, Ahmedabad.
50. 'CM Weans Away Solanki's Flank with Plum Posts', *The Economic Times* (Ahmedabad edition), 6 January 1994.

4

Centre–State Relations in India and Brazil: Privatisation of Electricity and Banking*

Leslie Elliott Armijo and Prem Shankar Jha

Privatisation, or the transfer of economic activities from public sector ownership to private investors, has become increasingly popular over the past decade and a half in both industrialised and developing countries. Politicians at all levels, from the central government to state and municipal elected authorities, in the 1980s and 1990s have come to embrace many of the hopes of the new global pro-market ideology of competition and private entrepreneurship as the road to economic prosperity. This shift toward economic liberalisation has encompassed even traditionally socialist, or at least heavily state interventionist, countries such as India, most dramatically under the leadership of Prime Minister P. V. Narasimha Rao (1991–1996). Privatisation and other market-oriented economic reforms also in the 1990s have come to the top of the economic agenda in other large developing countries that have been significantly more pro-capitalist and pro-foreign investment than India, yet whose actual practices over decades also have led to the development of a large state-owned productive sector. Brazil, for example, had talked a great deal about privatisation since the mid-1980s, but only began to make noticeable changes under Presidents Fernando Collor de Mello (1990–1992), Itamar Franco (1993–1994), and now Fernando Henrique Cardoso (inaugurated 1995).

Where countries are large, federal entities, with significant ownership of public enterprises at both the central and state government

*This paper was first published in the *Revista de Economia Politica*, vol. 17, no. 3, 1997.

levels, as well as the politics and economics of centre–state relations, often complicate the process of privatisation. Furthermore, if the nature of national political competition is opening up—as in India from the mid-1980s because of the end of Congress Party hegemony or in Brazil because of redemocratisation and the important changes in electoral rules in the mid-1980s—privatisation can become an even more complex affair. This discussion uses four focused case studies to explore the question: When and why do state governments oppose (or support) privatisation programmes initiated by the central government? We examine privatisation initiatives in the 1990s of the federal governments of India and Brazil in the fields of electricity and finance, and the varying responses of the state governments in each country's major industrial state and financial capital, respectively, Maharashtra and São Paulo. As of June 1996, electricity privatisation in the Indian state of Maharashtra had been highly contentious; but planned, incremental privatisation of banking seemed likely to be less divisive. In São Paulo, by contrast, planned electricity privatisation looked as if it would be fairly straightforward, but banking privatisation had caused a large and very public political battle between the state governor and the national government.

What explains these divergent outcomes? We hypothesise that three important reasons may lead state governments to oppose federal-level initiatives to privatise: (*a*) economic ideas and beliefs of state level politicians, (*b*) partisan politics, that may cause state politicians to oppose central government initiatives simply because the two levels of government represent different political parties or coalitions, and (*c*) the expected distribution of benefits and costs between the state and central governments. Frustrated central government liberalisers tend to assume that state leaders who oppose their plans either are obscurantists (reason *a*) or opportunists (reason *b*). In fact, our case studies suggest that most politicians are pragmatists. Often a greater willingness by the centre to respect the perceptions and distributions of costs and benefits *as experienced by the state government* (reason *c*) can help to resolve these conflicts.

In the four cases examined here we define 'privatisation' broadly, so that it includes both sale to private owners of historically state-owned enterprises and allowing new private sector entrants into sectors which previously had been legally off-limits to them. Thus, for example, privatisation of electricity could mean either selling off a public sector firm to private owners or, for the first time, allowing a private investor to build a 'greenfield' electricity plant to compete with existing public sector firms.

I CENTRE–STATE RELATIONS IN INDIA AND BRAZIL

What was the context of centre–state economic relations in India and Brazil in the early 1990s? First, each country had a history of activist central government intervention in both regulation and direct production. Both state governments and the private business sector often had resented the heavy hand of the centre in guiding national economic development according to centrally mandated priorities.

Since its first Five-Year Plan in the early 1950s, India officially had been a socialist country.[1] Of course, since India was also a democracy, the Central Government could not compel the private sector to follow its plan. However, since many sectors were nationalised—including banking, power generation and distribution, most capital goods production and production of many intermediate goods, such as steel—the Central Government had many levers to encourage private businesses to comply with central planners' preferences. In addition, India developed an extensive framework for licensing of private enterprise. An entrepreneur not only needed a government permit to open a new factory, but also could not alter the production mix in even relatively minor ways (shifting from the production of, for example, ceiling fans to standing fans) without new government licenses. Owners also could not open new plants or close existing ones (even if they were unprofitable) without getting the agreement of several government agencies. Indians called this the 'permit-license raj'. Finally, not only were some sectors of production reserved to state-owned enterprises, other entire sectors, such as the production of cotton cloth and clothes, were legally reserved for small businesses and labour-intensive production processes, as a means of guaranteeing employment.

Brazilian rhetoric and reality since the 1950s had given greater scope to private business, including multinational investors. Nonetheless, the central government's control of investment was very substantial.[2] Central government investment priorities were enforced through differential exchange rates, taxes and credit subsidies for different kinds of production. For example, even though approximately half of the financial sector, whether measured by loans or deposits, remained privately owned (unlike in India), the ministers of finance and planning had a large influence on the patterns of national investment. The state-owned enterprise sector, by some measures, was as large as India's, although only a very few sectors (including electricity, telecommunications, air transport and armaments production) were declared entirely off-limits to private business. The public sector's share in gross fixed capital formation was about 34 per cent in both Brazil (in 1979) and India (in 1980).[3]

Second, in India and Brazil both the nation and individual states experienced greater political competitiveness in the late 1980s and 1990s than they had in previous decades. In India, this was due to the end of the Nehru/Gandhi political dynasty's lock on national leadership, as well as the debilitation of the Congress Party which, after more than four decades, could no longer credibly bill itself as the party of the victorious struggle for independence. As opposition parties won more state governments, they became increasingly concerned about receiving what they believed to be their fair share of public resources, and more likely to suspect that their political opponents in New Delhi might be withholding revenues for partisan purposes. In Brazil, redemocratisation in the early 1980s exposed the weaknesses of the country's fractured political party system, leading to intense competition between a plethora of mostly regionally based, personalistic new political parties. In both national cases, one consequence of these larger political changes was to intensify the potential for politically and electorally motivated conflicts between the central government politicians and state politicians (many of whom, of course, aspired to a national stage).

II CENTRE–STATE BARGAINING OVER PRIVATISATION IN INDIA

The context of centre–state relations in India is in the process of shifting rather dramatically as Indian states, long quite tightly managed by planners in New Delhi, gain significantly greater economic decision powers at the state level. At the national level, a primary motivation for privatisation appears to be the desire for achieving improvements in performance in the sectors to be liberalised. The relations between the centre and the state governments, however, are influenced by both economic efficiency considerations and by politicians' search for electoral advantage. In addition, state-level leaders, quite naturally, find themselves more absorbed by the consequences of a given development within their own home state than at the national level.

Privatisation of Electricity: Enron and the Dabhol Generation Plant

From the late 1980s it had been apparent to the government of Prime Minister Rajiv Gandhi (1984–1989) that the resources at the command of the central and state governments, both from domestic savings and foreign aid, were simply not sufficient to meet the need for additional power-generating capacity in the country. So in 1986 Rajiv Gandhi opened the power sector to the Indian private sector. To the government's surprise, in the next 5 years it did not receive a single proposal from the private sector for the setting up of a power plant. The most important reason was the state governments' monopoly over power distribution. Paradoxically, this monopoly weakened the state governments' capacity to set profitable rates for electricity, and to recover even the subsidised payments from the consumers, especially in the agricultural sector. In 1992, when the average cost of power generation in India was Rs 1.17 per unit, the average recovery from the agricultural sector, which consumed 26 per cent of the total power generated, was a mere Rs 0.17 per unit.[4] As a result, the loss incurred on the supply of power to agriculture was Rs 83,846.6 million (US$ 2.67 billion) in 1993–94.[5] As the state governments showed little inclination to court disfavour with the powerful farm lobby by raising power tariffs, their capacity to pay for the power they consumed became more and more open to question. As a result, private investors did not feel that investment in power was safe.

By 1992, it had become clear that the country was set to encounter a huge power crisis a few years down the line. In the late 1980s, a total of 26,090 megawatts (MW) of power generating capacity had been added to existing capacity in the country.[6] Even this was 759 MW short of the target. The next two years of structural adjustment saw the annual addition to capacity fall to 2,904 MW.[7] For the Eighth Five-Year Plan (1992–97), the Central Electricity Authority estimated the need for an additional 38,000 MW of generating capacity. But this was scaled down to a mere 19,000 MW, as it became clear that the state simply could not raise the money.[8] As a result, the Ministry of Energy estimated that the peak power shortage in the country could rise from 16 to 20 per cent in the early 1990s to 27 per cent by 1997–98.[9]

Private investment in power projects was therefore essential. This was the sense of urgency that drove the Narasimha Rao government to send out a high-powered delegation to talk to power generating companies around the world. The end product of that initiative was that the Central Government signed memoranda of understanding with various foreign firms for eight large power projects. These were to be directly negotiated deals, where the accent was to be on speed. They therefore came to be known as 'fast track' projects. Their secondary purpose was to break the ground for the negotiation of other private power projects in the future. The agreement negotiated with the United States-based Enron Corporation to build a new plant at Dabhol in southern Maharashtra state was the first and largest of these projects.

Enron had first proposed a 2,000 MW power plant to be built in a single phase, but the World Bank, which acted as a consultant to the Indian government, pointed out that the western Indian grid, into which the power would have to be fed, could not take such a large input. Enron therefore agreed to implement the project in two phases, of 695 MW and 1,400 MW, respectively, to run on natural gas. The gas itself would be piped into Bombay (in 1996 renamed Mumbai, a name employed henceforth), the capital of Maharashtra, from the Middle East or brought in as liquefied natural gas in ships. Breaking the project up into two phases raised costs in a number of ways. Much of the infrastructure for the second phase, including port facilities and a road to link the port to the power plant, could not be divided and had to be built in the first phase. In addition, a regassification plant for the liquefied natural gas was also included in the first phase. As a result, when the first estimates of project costs for the first phase came out—pegged at $ 1.3 million per MW of capacity—they caused eyebrows to be raised all over the country. This was higher than the going rate for coal-based plants being sanctioned at the time, which was in the neighbourhood of $ 1.05 million.[10] Gas-based power plants, the critics pointed out, should cost around 40 per cent less than coal-based ones.[11]

There were some sound reasons for the higher capital cost in the first phase. One that got almost completely overlooked until the project was on the verge of being cancelled was that the Dabhol estimate was for December 1997, that is, 4 years after the reference projects being used to criticise it. But neither Enron nor the Maharashtra government, then under Chief Minister Sharad Pawar of the Congress Party, made any attempt to explain the reasons for the higher apparent capital cost. As a result, the impression gelled in the country that Enron had taken India for a ride. Many observers quickly assumed that this was because Enron had paid a kickback to the Congress Party in Maharashtra. Nonetheless the contract was signed and Enron began work on the Dabhol project in 1994.

State elections got underway in early 1995. The major challenge to the Congress Party in Maharashtra came from a coalition of the Bharatiya Janata Party (BJP), a national force in Indian politics since the mid-1980s, and the Shiv Sena, a strong regional party. Their main campaign themes were, first, an appeal to rightist Hindu nationalism via an attack on India's pervasive and decades-old affirmative action preferences for Muslims and the lower castes and, second, criticism of the long-ruling Congress Party for being corrupt. When the BJP–Shiv Sena coalition took office in March, its promise to cancel the Enron deal became an albatross around its neck, as the state's new leaders began to understand the seriousness of the power shortages they would have to confront. At this point, a respected news daily published a leaked version of the contract that had been negotiated by the Central Government—but signed by the Sharad Pawar administration in Maharashtra—and Enron. In an analysis of the agreement, Kirit Parikh, a well-known economist, claimed, on the basis of a comparison with an almost identical power plant set up in Hong Kong, that the project cost was 15 to 20 per cent too high.[12] Parikh also pointed out that the terms of the power purchase agreement were unnecessarily loaded against the Maharashtra government. More specifically, since the Maharashtra State Electricity Board was committed to buying 86 per cent of the power generated by the plant, to fulfil this commitment it would have to give preference to Enron during off-peak hours over its own power plants, which were lower-cost producers. Both these observations turned out to be only partly correct. But they were sufficient to force the government to announce that it would review the Enron project before deciding whether it should be allowed to continue.

International reactions were predictably negative. The first was a statement from the United States Department of Energy that it viewed with 'deep concern' the attempts to reopen the Enron deal after it had been finalised. The statement expressed the fear that this would affect other projects that were also in the pipeline.[13] The American decision aroused the latent xenophobia of a large section of the Indian middle class, and was therefore received with undisguised glee by the BJP. Western governments learned their lesson from this and decided virtually unanimously to refrain from any public statements. They also advised large corporations from making public statements. But the Japanese suffered from no such inhibitions. The Japanese Consul-General in Mumbai minced no words and said bluntly that the decision would impede future investment in India, because it showed that 'State governments are unreliable'.[14]

The Central Government, led by Congress Party Prime Minister P. V. Narasimha Rao in New Delhi, had embarked upon a project of significant economic liberalisation in 1991, in which new foreign investment flows figured prominently; Rao's economic team therefore was quite worried. The centre was also fully aware that if the power crisis in Maharashtra became more acute, it would be as severely affected as the four other large states linked together in the western electricity grid. In fact by July 1995 power breakdowns, which had been utterly unknown in Mumbai, were occurring every three months.[15] The Rao government therefore had every conceivable reason for stepping in and preventing the cancellation of the project. Within the cabinet in New Delhi, the energy minister, N. K. P. Salve, argued strongly in favour of stepping in and taking over the project. He was supported by the former chief minister of Maharashtra who had signed the deal, Sharad Pawar of the Congress Party. But they were overruled by other colleagues and the prime minister, who pointed out that they would play straight into the BJP's hands, and enable it to reinforce the impression, already strong in the public, that the Congress Party was trying to hide its misdeeds.[16] The prime minister, therefore, wisely decided to stay out of this fight, at least in public.

Fissures were already appearing within the BJP–Shiv Sena coalition. The BJP was mainly interested in discrediting the Congress

Party with charges of corruption, paving the way for it to come to power at the national level. But the Shiv Sena (and some in the Maharashtra BJP) wanted to prove to the electorate that they were the party of efficient, honest government in Maharashtra state. Shiv Sena head Bal Thackeray, the power behind the throne in the new government, and the new Maharashtra Chief Minister, Manohar Joshi, therefore tried to keep their criticisms narrowly focused on the issue of the allegedly high cost of the project. However, the national BJP and their allies in the Indian religious right kept public interest and press coverage of the corruption issue high. For example, an enterprising researcher discovered that Linda Powers, an Enron representative testifying before the United States Congress, had stated that Enron had spent $ 20 million in educating Indian officials about the details of world class contract negotiations and the legal frameworks necessary to attract global capital, a novelty in this country that for decades had been quite closed to foreign investment.[17] In fact, Powers was trying to convince the United States Congress to allocate more funds for overseas technical assistance, so that private multinationals wouldn't have to spend their own money. Taken out of context, however, the $ 20 million spent on 'education' sounded to the Indian public precisely like an admission by Enron that it had paid bribes to the Sharad Pawar government.[18]

After much internal bickering within the new Maharashtra government, along with quiet discussions with Enron, a commitment for renegotiation of the project was made in early November 1995. Not incidentally, an opinion poll commissioned by the *Times of India* in nine Indian cities had, in the meantime, shown that even in Mumbai, which had been exposed the most to the BJP and Shiv Sena's pre-election propaganda, 55 per cent of the respondents wanted the project to be saved, that is, renegotiated. The Shiv Sena's uneasiness grew as it realised that in Dabhol itself the loss of jobs was causing a backlash against the project's cancellation.[19] Two weeks after constitution of the new negotiating committee, there was a new deal, in most important respects one not terribly different from its predecessor, but one which enabled both the Joshi administration in Maharashtra and the Enron Corporation to claim that they each had bettered the terms for their side.

What were the real issues in this conflict that made the front pages of Indian newspapers almost daily during more than four months? At first it seemed, at least from the perspective of Central

Government technocrats and, of course, worried foreign investors, as though the BJP–Shiv Sena coalition had allowed its fanatic fringe of ideological zealots to take control of public policymaking. There also was the issue of the national ambitions of the BJP, which would be served by embarrassing the Congress Party, even at the cost of leaving Maharashtra without sufficient electricity. If either of these explanations were really important, however, it is hard to credit what seems like the extraordinary passivity of leading Maharashtrian governing coalition members, especially Joshi and Thackeray, in letting the dispute drag on for months before being settled.

The true problems with the original 'fast track' contract, essentially negotiated between New Delhi bureaucrats and Enron, were more mundane, and had to do with the distribution of both economic and political costs and benefits from the project between the Central Government and the new Maharashtrian incumbents. The core of the many complaints from the Maharashtrian BJP–Shiv Sena coalition about costs was that in its anxiety to attract foreign investment in power, the Central Government had announced early in 1992 that it would guarantee a 16 per cent return on the equity capital invested in power projects. As several economists quickly pointed out, this gave the investors every incentive to pad their capital costs as much as they could. The dissatisfaction rose another notch when the states realised that the basis of calculating the returns was so generous that any halfway efficient plant could earn far higher returns. In particular the basis for calculation of the power tariff was the capital cost incurred when the plant was operating at only 68.5 per cent of capacity. However, all private sector projects were confident of running at 80 and even 90 per cent of capacity. This would raise their returns to 25 per cent and even more. The chairman of one Indian private company which made a bid to enter the power generation field reported that the low plant load factor ensured that his company would earn up to a 33 per cent return on its equity capital.[20] Nearly all the state government's complaints stemmed from the fact that while the decision on returns was made exclusively by the centre, the state electricity boards and therefore eventually the state governments would have to do the paying.

In fact, the essentially non-partisan and non-ideological core of this legitimate complaint on the part of the state government was underscored by the fact that the new opposition-led state government in Maharashtra was not the only state government to complain.

In the state of Orissa, the newly elected government also wanted to renegotiate their 'fast track' power plant, the Ib valley project, which had been negotiated during the 1990s by the then Janata Dal Party state government in collaboration with the Congress Party Central Government of Prime Minister Rao. The newly elected chief minister, who happened to be from the Congress Party, made allegations identical to those made by the BJP–Shiv Sena government in Maharashtra, and demanded a renegotiation of the project to bring its cost down. AES, the foreign investor, agreed and recast the project, increasing its size in the process. The solution for the renegotiated Enron project in Maharashtra also included increasing the overall size of the project and implementing both phases jointly, thus significantly lowering its per unit cost. Moreover, Enron agreed to sell 30 per cent of its equity (an increase of 20 per cent over the original 10 per cent) to the state government, thus sharing with it what were expected to be ample profits.

A second real issue was that the state government didn't want to be burdened with implementing policies that could be expected to be politically unpopular with one of its key constituencies: farmers. A publicly trumpeted concern of the Joshi government had been worry over possible environmental damage that might be caused by the project. Interviews conducted by one of this paper's authors in Mumbai suggested that the genuinely sensitive issue camouflaged as environmental concern had to do with purchases, from a myriad of small farmers, of land needed for the project. By the time the project was cancelled, a group of farmers already had gone to court to sue the state government over the amount of compensation they had been offered. The state government believed that, if Enron itself bought the land rather than having the Maharashtra government act as intermediary, farmers would be more likely to negotiate a fair price, since they could not threaten to withdraw their votes from the multinational. However, a 1970 law passed by the Central Government that was intended to protect small farmers had forbidden the sale of agricultural land for non-agricultural uses above a token amount—except to the state government. That this too was a concern not limited to Maharashtra became apparent when the newly elected chief minister of the state of Karnataka, Deve Gowda, passed an amendment to the Karnataka Land Reform Act raising the ceiling on the sale of agricultural land for non-agricultural purposes from 5 to 100 hectares. In doing so he simply ignored the objections of the Central Government that this violated the 1970 Land Reform Model Act, and would require the President of India's assent to become law. His justification, given to the press, was that with a raging power famine in the state, twelve power projects awaiting clearance, and a 300 kilometre superhighway to build, he simply could not wait for the centre's assent.[21] Once Deve Gowda had broken the ice, it became easier for the Maharashtra government to avoid the political onus of having to negotiate with farmers by also simply deciding to ignore the 1970 law.

Liberalisation of Banking and Finance: A Bone of Contention to be?

Finance in India has been primarily a national, rather than a state-level, arena of government activity. Nonetheless, major changes in the financial sector have powerful effects in Maharashtra, and especially in Mumbai, because financial activity is heavily concentrated there. Any political conflicts that erupt over privatisation of banks and financial institutions are certain to be extremely important in Maharashtra. Through mid-1996 there had been significant, although incremental, progress in financial liberalisation, with virtually all initiatives originating with the Central Government in New Delhi. Some of these regulatory changes had been controversial, as had some of the responses of financial markets to such changes. Interest groups with a strong presence in Mumbai, including stockbrokers, unionized bank clerks and unions of financial institution officers at the Industrial Development Bank of India (IDBI) and the Reserve Bank of India (RBI) expressed clear policy preferences on various aspects of financial liberalisation, and had considerable success in enlisting media support. Nonetheless, through mid-1996, the state government of Maharashtra, under Congress Party Chief Minister Sharad Pawar in the early 1990s as well as under BJP–Shiv Sena Chief Minister Joshi in 1995 and 1996, kept a very low profile on the issue of financial reforms.

This section argues that two circumstances have kept banking and financial regulatory policies off the agenda of centre–state conflicts thus far. First, when a major financial scandal roiled Mumbai and the country as a whole in 1992–1993, the state government was of the same political party as the Central Government, whose inadequate and anachronistic oversight procedures were widely blamed for permitting the misdeeds that caused the financial market crash and scandal. Second, the process of incremental financial reform clearly advantages some social groups, particularly internationally competitive private industry and new financial entrepreneurs, while disadvantaging others, especially unionized employees of public sector banks and financial institutions. Since the effects in Maharashtra of gradual liberalisation are bound to antagonise some politically important groups while pleasing others, there are no clear benefits to local political parties, even if they are in opposition to the Central Government, that might come from politicising the issues. If the issues of financial liberalisation become more politicised, then politicians may be forced to take sides.

Moreover, since most of the Maharashtrian and Mumbai business communities, and most professional economists, expect gradual financial deregulation to stimulate economic growth in both the state as a whole and its capital city, it is in the interest of politicians to paint the issue as one of technical, uninteresting and apolitical 'modernisation', rather than as a zero-sum game between winners and losers. However, should centrally directed financial reform begin to move in a direction that promises to drain resources or wealth from Maharashtra in order to redistribute them elsewhere in India, then one might expect centre–state conflicts over banking privatisation to increase. In fact, though, market-oriented economic reform generally gives advantages to the strongest competitors. Thus Maharashtra state, already India's financial centre, is likely to prosper from it.

In India, virtually all of the financial reforms proposed thus far involve deregulation (for example, of interest rates, which is not privatisation per se), lowering barriers to entry by private firms into sectors previously reserved for public sector banks (privatisation of the sector), and/or sales of minority shares in 100 per cent government-owned banks (partial privatisation of the firm). The remainder of this section briefly reviews the reform process to date.

Through the late 1980s the overwhelming majority of India's entire financial sector, from commercial banking to long-term industrial credit to the insurance industry, was owned and run by the Central Government.[22] After years of prodding and scolding by scholars and some members of the business community, the new government of Prime Minister P. V. Narasimha Rao decided to get serious about banking reform by setting up an expert commission, composed primarily of the heads of India's major banks and financial institutions, all in the public sector, to issue recommendations.[23] Its principal recommendations included, first, privatisation of the banking sector by liberalising entry and, second, deregulation, particularly in the areas of interest rate controls, high requirements for banks to invest in low-yielding government securities and high requirements for banks to make loans, frequently subsidised, to targeted groups such as farmers or small businesses ('priority sector credit'). In addition, the two private-sector members of the Narasimham Committee, both well-known academic economists with private consulting experience, strongly urged abolition of the banking department of the Ministry of Finance, which long had exercised centralised control over staff recruitment, remuneration and other personnel policies.

The short-term response to the Narasimham Committee report was a nation-wide strike in early 1992, involving not only clerks in the nationalised commercial banks, but also the bank officers' (middle management) unions in both the country's premiere development bank, the IDBI, and in the central bank, the RBI. Their fears were of job losses due to both increased competition and computerisation. This strike action alone would not have deterred the Rao government from pushing ahead with deregulation. After all, many of the biggest public sector commercial banks, although not the State Bank of India (SBI), the granddaddy of them all, were bankrupt, although the general public was blissfully unaware of this fact.[24]

Then, in April 1992, India's largest-ever financial scandal exploded. The illegal trades and short-term liquidity problems of a single brash young investor caused investors and financial institutions, including several leading public sector banks, to lose $ 1.2 billion. The huge public outcry, in which commentator after commentator linked financial deregulation to illicit profiteering, stopped banking reform in its tracks for a year, and limited it to slow, technical, and non-controversial reforms for several years thereafter.[25] In this case, the political explosion was national, as Congress Party Prime Minister Rao was attacked in parliament both from the BJP on the political right (for inadequate regulatory oversight and the presumed corruption of public sector banks taking disallowed types of risks with depositors' funds) and the National Front–Left Front on the left (for selling out to national and, especially, foreign finance capital).

After that, the financial reformers in the Central Government trod carefully. Some militant unionists in the IDBI, who had feared job losses resulting from competition from private sector investment banks ('merchant banks') were mollified when New Delhi awarded the IDBI the job of setting up India's first nation-wide, computerised stock trading system, the National Stock Exchange (NSE). In 1991 the Central Government had decided to cease budget subsidies to the IDBI, while for the first time allowing the institution to float corporate debt instruments in local financial markets; by early 1996 the IDBI was meeting as much as 40 per cent of its investment needs through market borrowing. In July 1995 the IDBI sold its first equity to the public, in India's largest ever initial public offering, worth Rs 21.8 billion, or about US$ 69 million.[26] The state government chose to remain on the sidelines for all of these issues, despite the fact that the IDBI headquarters and overwhelming majority of its employees were located in Mumbai.

In 1994 the RBI (the nation's central bank and the principal regulatory authority) decided to license new private banks. This change, too, was implemented in a very cautious manner. Previously, the only private banks were foreign banks whose agencies predated the 1969 bank nationalisation decreed by Prime Minister Indira Gandhi, and those private banks too small to have qualified for nationalisation then or in two subsequent waves in the early 1980s. Of around a hundred applications received, the RBI by the end of 1995 had agreed to extend only five or six licenses, of which three were to public sector financial institutions—the IDBI, the Industrial Credit and Investment Corporation of India (ICICI), and the joint public–private Housing Development Finance Corporation of India (HDFC).[27]

The more politically challenging reform tasks have not yet been tackled including, for example, abolishing the banking department of the Ministry of Finance and instead giving control of hiring, promotion and other personnel matters to bank presidents and their senior associates themselves. The following predictions can be made, however. If bank and other financial institution unions feel their jobs or perquisites threatened by liberalisation and privatisation, they will not be shy about taking to the streets, linking their particular troubles with other groups' related worries about virtually any aspect of economic liberalisation (whether logically connected to bank privatisation or not), and forging alliances with vote-seeking politicians and political parties. Within Maharashtra, the BJP–Shiv Sena government will continue to be split; the Shiv Sena, on the whole, is more concerned with the Maharashtrian economy (within which the private financial sector is a very important player, particularly in Mumbai), while the Bharatiya Janata Party, an aspirant to national power, might find it more convenient to take up the unions' cause—as long as the BJP is not currently governing at the centre. While financial sector privatisation and liberalisation thus far has proceeded very quietly and without great fanfare or political opposition, the future potential for the arena to become politicised remains very real, particularly so long as the centre and Maharashtra are governed by politicians of different parties. In April 1996 Narasimha Rao's Congress Party lost the national election. In June, after an abortive attempt by the BJP to form a national government, the centre–left coalition of the National Front–Left Front (now renamed the United Front) formed a new national government under Prime Minister Deve Gowda, the pro-liberalisation former chief minister of Karnataka.

III CENTRE–STATE BARGAINING OVER PRIVATISATION IN BRAZIL

In Brazil, in contrast to India, most state enterprises in infrastructure sectors were considered to have been reasonably efficient through the 1970s.[28] However, central government finances deteriorated rapidly from about 1979, and were exacerbated by the Latin American debt crisis, which hit Brazil in late 1982.[29] Thereafter, public sector investment spending dropped off sharply. The gradual return to democracy—which officially occurred in 1985, but may with equal reason be dated from the free elections for state governors and big city mayors in 1982—meant much larger expenditures at the state level as well, as incumbents appointed by the military spent large sums of public and quasi-public monies on their election campaigns. Finally, Brazil's new democratic constitution of 1988 transferred a large chunk of federally collected tax revenues back to the state level (from whence they had been grabbed during the military regime installed in 1964), but without also transferring spending responsibilities back to state governors. For all of these reasons, the overriding impulse to rapid privatisation at the federal level in

Brazil has been fiscal, with considerations of improved efficiency and access to modern technology coming only second.

In contrast to India, in Brazil financial sector liberalisation and privatisation has progressed further than electricity privatisation, which has been planned but thus far for the most part is yet to be implemented. The centre–state political conflicts over bank privatisation thus are more acute, while those that may later appear in the electricity sector thus far remain latent.

Privatisation of Public Sector Banks in Brazil: The Banespa Saga

Generalising very broadly, the division of labour that evolved in Brazil's financial sector after the far-reaching liberalising financial reforms of the newly installed military regime in 1964–1967 was that the more lucrative corners of the financial markets were left to the private financial sector, while public sector banks supplied those financial services that private banks shunned, particularly subsidised agricultural and residential housing credit, and long-term financing of all types. The country's largest commercial bank was the federally owned Banco do Brasil, whose background and current activities make it quite similar to the State Bank of India. (Both institutions, for example, date from the nineteenth century and once served as both commercial banks and national monetary authorities.) State governments also had state-level public commercial banks, which often doubled as industrial and agricultural development banks. Several of the bigger states had more than one. Banespa, the Banco do Estado de São Paulo (State Bank of São Paulo) consistently has been one of Brazil's top ten banks. If one looks only at commercial, investment ('merchant') and development banks, the public and private sector each have approximately half the financial sector, whether measured by loans, assets or net worth. If the state savings bank system (which accepts term deposits and funds mainly residential mortgage and construction lending, as well as municipal water and sewerage projects) is included, the public banks have a slightly larger share of deposits.

During the 1970s and 1980s Brazil's good economic growth, very high inflation, and the unique peculiarities of its financial legislation allowed commercial banks to expand greatly.[30] By 1989, for example, financial services, by one measure, accounted for an astonishing

26 per cent of the gross national product. In 1994, 18 per cent of banks' earnings were due simply to their ability to profit from the inflation that harmed the rest of society. The end in mid-1994 to what by the 1990s had become four-digit annual inflation was essential for Brazil's economy, but very bad news for most banks and financial institutions. By 1995, their share of GDP had plummeted to only 6 per cent, and inflationary earnings contributed less than 1 per cent to their gross profits.[31] Not surprisingly, many Brazilian banks found themselves in serious trouble. Even the venerable Banco do Brasil, which in 1985 held 24 per cent of all bank deposits in Brazil,[32] announced a deficit of over $ 4 billion in early 1996, requiring the Banco Central (BC) to come up with a new cash infusion of $ 8 billion. Not including the federal aid to the Banco do Brasil, by one estimate the central government had spent about $ 10 billion on rescues of five private sector banks through March 1996, approximately equal to the $ 9.5 billion received from all privatisations up to that point.[33]

The problems of the public sector banks owned by individual state governments, however, were of a different order. Although most of them, excepting São Paulo's Banespa, were fairly small, their poor financial health went well beyond unwise dependence on inflationary earnings. As noted, the return of democracy and competitive elections in the 1980s had encouraged governors in virtually every state and from every political party to lean on these banks to give loans for political purposes, either directly to the state government or in the form of unscrutinised, unsecured, low-interest loans to large campaign donors. The ill health, for example, of Banerj, the state bank of Rio de Janeiro, one of Brazil's largest and most important states, had been an open secret in financial circles since the early 1980s. In the early 1990s, under Presidents Collor and Franco, two or three state-level public banks owned by small, weak states such as tiny Rio Grande do Norte had been 'intervened' by the BC and subsequently closed, over the loud but ineffectual protests of their comparatively powerless governors and congressional delegations. A related problem was the growing indebtedness of many state treasuries to the federal government, in some cases because of de facto bailouts of state-level banks by the BC, and in other cases due to other debts. By mid-1991 the total debt of state and municipal governments to the centre was about $ 57 billion, of which the three wealthy south-eastern states of São Paulo, Minas

Gerais, and Rio de Janeiro owed 53 per cent.[34] Given the federal government's own debt problems, by the 1990s this situation had become unsustainable.

On July 1, 1994 then finance minister Fernando Henrique Cardoso inaugurated Brazil's seventh major stabilisation programme since the return to civilian, democratic national government in early 1985. Dubbed the 'Plano Real', this stabilisation programme, like many of its predecessors, involved a new currency, de-indexation, a temporary wage and price freeze, and solemn promises of cuts to the federal government budget. It differed from the failed previous plans in that it used a 'currency anchor' to the US dollar that supposedly would force Brazil to adjust, as the domestic tradables sector would have to cut prices to compete with now fairly free imported goods. The Plano Real resembled Argentina's successful, though draconian, 'currency board' system, then in place for almost three years, and, despite some opt-out clauses in Brazil's version, was rather similar to the pre-World War I gold standard. On the strength of the Plano Real, Cardoso was elected president in October 1994, running at the head of a broad and heterogeneous coalition. The president's own small reform party, the Partido da Social Democracia Brasileira (PSDB), also elected several governors on Cardoso's coattails, including Marcelo Alencar in Rio de Janeiro and Mário Covas in São Paulo, all of whom were to take office on January 1, 1995.

On December 30, 1994 governors-elect Alencar and Covas received phone calls from Pedro Malan, then president of the BC but tapped as Cardoso's incoming finance minister, informing them that the new administration would announce BC intervention on the following day in the management of both Banerj and Banespa.[35] Malan explained that one reason the intervention—which included an indefinite freeze of the deposits of all bank stockholders and direct day-to-day oversight by the BC—was scheduled for December 31 was that this would enable the new governors to distance themselves from the federal government's decision, should this prove politically convenient. The subsequent reactions of the two PSDB governors hardly could have been more different.

Within his first month in office, Rio Governor Marcelo Alencar announced his full support for the process of recapitalisation and then privatisation of Banerj, and contracted with the private financial consulting firm, Bonzano, Simonsen, to implement the project. He also announced planned privatisation of ten other state-level public firms owned by the Rio de Janeiro government. Soon thereafter he convinced the state legislative assembly to grant him the blanket authority to privatise whatever public enterprises his administration saw fit to sell. By these moves Alencar staked out positions very different from his two predecessors, both members of the PDT (Partido Democrática Trabalhista, or Democratic Workers' Party) party headed by perennial presidential candidate, veteran campaigner against the military, and Rio governor from 1982–1988, Leonel Brizola. Brizola, a long-time leftist, was a strong opponent of selling 'the nation's patrimony'. For example, during the Collor administration, Brizola had organised and personally led a demonstration in front of the Rio de Janeiro stock exchange on the day of the public auction for the controlling stake in what was then Brazil's largest privatisation, the sale of the federal steel mill and conglomerate, Usiminas, which ultimately raised $ 1.5 billion. Despite the strength of the PDT and other left parties in the city and state of Rio, not to mention his own membership in the moderately left PSDB, Alencar bit the bullet and decided to take the lead on privatisation. One benefit for Alencar was that the BC agreed to advance to the Rio government the expected proceeds for the privatisation of Banerj (planned for 1997) and other enterprises to be sold, thus enabling Rio to pay off its debt to Brasília.

Mario Covas in São Paulo, on the other hand, despite a pro forma declaration of total support for President Cardoso's economic and political agenda, immediately went on the offensive, vowing that Banespa would never be privatised. The battle had been joined. In fact, Covas' views were in complete agreement with those of his two predecessors, Governors Orestes Quércia (1982–1988) and Luís Antônio Fleury (1988–1994), both of the Brazilian Democratic Movement Party (PMDB), since 1985 the largest single party in Brazil. The PMDB had supplied the president in 1985–1990, José Sarney, but had been only one of many very loosely allied parties that sometimes voted with the government but other times did not, during the presidencies of Fernando Collor and Itamar Franco in the early 1990s.

During all of 1995 Covas fought with President Cardoso, and especially finance minister Malan, over Banespa, both publicly and behind the scenes. The Cardoso administration, hoping for a political settlement, refrained from using its legal authority to go one step further than intervention and declare Banespa federal property, forfeited because it was technically bankrupt with a debt to the Banco Central of $ 9.7 billion when Covas took office, but up to $ 15 billion by December 1995, due mainly to very high interest rates resulting from the Plano Real. In the final month of 1995 a provisional solution was announced. The federal senate agreed to extend a $ 7.5 billion twenty-year loan to São Paulo; the other $ 7.5 billion would be paid off by the transfer to the federal government of São Paulo's three major airports plus its state-owned railroad, Fepasa, all of which later would be privatised and the proceeds kept by the national treasury. In return, Banespa would not be privatised, but rather would be returned, recapitalised, to the government of São Paulo.

Nonetheless, the conflict dragged on, despite the supposed deal. While various ostensibly minor points were being negotiated, Banespa's debt to the BC, being carried at market rates of interest, mounted from $ 15 billion to $ 18 billion. In April 1996 Alencar and Covas, along with other PSDB heavyweights from around the country, appeared with the president in Brasília, announcing that henceforth they would be more supportive of the president, who had recently met several defeats in getting congress to pass the necessary enabling legislation for his overall economic reform and liberalisation programme. In early May the state attorney general of São Paulo announced he was freezing the assets of the two former governors, Quercia and Fleury, along with 107 former Banespa administrators, pending an investigation into Banespa's losses between 1989 and 1994, widely believed to have resulted from politicised lending practices during the 1980s.[36] In May Covas went public with a complaint that the BC was discriminating against Banespa which, in his view, had received less favourable treatment than the private banks Econômico and Nacional.[37] Covas was particularly incensed over the additional $ 3 billion in interest obligations that had accumulated between December 1995 and May 1996. Meanwhile, the finance minister and others in Brasília felt that they could not be flexible—or perhaps even reasonable—with the *paulistas* for fear of setting a precedent that other states with bankrupt financial institutions would insist on copying. As of September 1996 the exact details of the settlement had yet to be worked out; what was certain was that Banespa would not be privatised in the near future.[38]

Although Banespa was not sold, the central government did not necessarily lose out. Unlike the Indian situation, increasing efficiency in Brazil's financial sector was not the central government's main goal. The years of high and highly variable inflation had made Brazilian banks among the most agile in the world. The major impetus for privatisation, from Brasília's viewpoint, was to get the states to pay off their debts to the central government—and, of course, to make it institutionally more difficult for them to rack up further debt. If the debt of São Paulo to the centre could be taken care of, and better yet if the state government could be credibly warned off of using Banespa for politically-motivated lending in the future, then a substantial portion of President Cardoso's goals would have been realised.

Still, an intriguing puzzle remains. What explains the different behaviour of the two PSDB governors, Alencar of Rio de Janeiro and Covas of São Paulo? Among those knowledgeable persons interviewed for this project in late May 1996, opinions as to Covas' motivations were divided. One prominent economic journalist with extensive contacts with Covas' campaign and administration was of the opinion that the rift was largely personal. He suggested that Covas, himself a senior PSDB politician, had been offended that he was not consulted in advance about the Cardoso team's plans, but only informed when the decision already had been made. Interviewees generally agreed that Covas long had been a believer in a strong state presence in production and infrastructure. However, this description applied with equal force to a great many of Brazil's politicians, including President Cardoso.

The following additional considerations, which did not apply in Rio de Janeiro, seem to explain Covas' determined opposition to privatisation, despite his close political ties to President Cardoso. First, the state of São Paulo, out of twenty-six states plus the federal district, alone was responsible for 35 per cent of Brazil's gross national product. São Paulo was not to be trifled with, even by a president who himself was a paulista. In addition, although the federal government had the legal right to simply take over Banespa and privatise it whether or not the state government assented, Covas possessed two specific bargaining chips not enjoyed by Alencar. Banespa's debt of $ 18 billion to the Banco Central was many times that of Banerj. Were the Cardoso administration to have carried out its full legal mandate of summarily assuming ownership of Banespa, the state government would have been justified in declaring the entire debt quits, to the fatal disadvantage of the federal government. Furthermore, São Paulo had two state banks, Banespa and A Nossa Caixa, the state-level savings bank. Had the federal government legally snatched Banespa, the state government immediately could have transferred its lucrative banking business to its other state-level public bank, A Nossa Caixa, thus certainly provoking the precipitous and irredeemable crash of Banespa. As one informant put it, both the federal and state governments thus possessed 'an atomic bomb', creating a stalemate and forcing both sides to bargain.

Moreover, the debt position of São Paulo state was perhaps even more desperate than that of the federal government, despite the state's high growth and good reputation in international markets. As of May 1995 the state's total domestic and foreign debt totalled $ 68 billion.[39] This fact, of course, might explain Covas' hardball bargaining over the distribution of costs with the BC, but hardly his refusal to privatise Banespa. For that, we must understand the distribution of political benefits and costs as they looked from the viewpoint of the state government. Unlike Banerj, Banespa had an excellent reputation in its state, not only with small depositors, but also with the business and farming communities, and with politicians throughout the state, particularly in the hinterlands, which were less well-served by the big private banks whose business concentrated in São Paulo City. Covas, like his predecessors Fleury and Quercia, must have realised that the politician who sold Banespa might never be elected to anything in São Paulo again. Furthermore, the consensus among policy-influential paulistas, even those generally sympathetic to Cardoso's reform efforts, was that São Paulo needed a commercial and development bank. In the words of a senior policymaker in the state government, 'Once Banespa has been cleaned up financially, what's the point of selling it? After all, it wasn't Mário Covas who created Banespa's problem; it was Quércia and Fleury'.[40]

From the viewpoint of the federal government, of course, the crucial points clearly were, first, that if it let Banespa off the hook, many other states would demand equally favourable treatment, and second, that there was no mechanism to prevent future Quércias or Fleurys from using the bank to make huge quantities of questionable loans. Then, in the name of the national interest (not to mention maintaining a winning legislative coalition in congress), the Banco Central, under orders from the president, would be obliged to rescue the bank again. There was, however, one additional factor that helped tip the equation in Covas' favour: given Banespa's large size and the special expectations its customers and the state and municipal governments had of it, could a buyer be found? Surely it would be foolhardy to try to sell the bank so long as the state government opposed that route. On most points, therefore, the national government was obliged to yield. Governor Covas had succeeded in preventing the sale of Banespa.

President Cardoso and Finance Minister Malan clearly had hoped that the impending sale of a giant like Banespa would send a positive signal to international investors, but that plan had fallen through. The federal government needed São Paulo's help on too many other urgent matters—notably a package of liberalising economic reforms, from removing legal barriers to foreign direct investment to social security reform—some of which required a two-thirds majority in order to push through a constitutional amendment. Because the Cardoso administration had not managed to convince Covas that privatising Banespa would be in São Paulo's interest, as opposed to the interests of the country as a whole, the president's persuasion had fallen on deaf ears.

Electricity Privatisation in Brazil: Peaceful thus Far

In many ways the status of privatisation in Brazil's power sector, as of mid-1996, resembled privatisation of India's financial sector: in both cases, the central government had moved ahead with a national plan that would deeply affect conditions in the country's major financial and industrial state, but thus far, progress had been only incremental. Furthermore, although privatisation in the sector could be expected to have important repercussions for the state, thus far the state government had not chosen to engage in public battle with the central government over the terms and conditions of privatisation. Whatever hard political battles actually might result were still ahead. In another way, however, electricity privatisation in Brazil resembled bank privatisation in Brazil: in both cases, and in sharp contrast to India, the major public sector firms, whether majority owned by the federal or state governments, were actually joint public–private ventures, with controlling interest (usually but not always 51 per cent) maintained by the government, but with large numbers of minority shareholders, or even large blocs of shares, held by multinational corporations. (A Japanese consortium, for example, long had held about 20 per cent of the federal steel company, Usiminas, privatised in 1991.) Privatisation of the power sector would not mean simply allowing private firms, including multinationals, to enter: in Brazil, it would mean outright sale of the controlling interest. Furthermore, and unlike earlier privatisations in Brazil, the buyers for power firms, or of the concessions to construct new plants, were likely to be multinational corporations, not local Brazilian companies.

Before the 1950s, virtually all of Brazil's electric power sector was in private and, overwhelmingly, foreign hands. From the 1950s, the Brazilian government gradually bought out the foreign investors. Through the mid-1980s, Brazil's electricity sector expanded rapidly and was considered by most observers to be generally efficient. However, due to the debt crisis and other macroeconomic problems, new public sector investment had virtually ceased from the early 1980s on. By the later years of the decade, brownouts and other indications of underinvestment had begun to annoy residential and especially business consumers, making them more receptive to privatisation.

In 1993 through 1995, accordingly, Brazil's national congress passed a series of laws constructing the legal framework for electricity privatisation, ranging from permission in 1993 for private industrial firms to build generating plants for their own use to 1995 legislation mandating competitive bidding for all new power concessions (that is, for the rights to build or operate a power plant or transmission or distribution grid). In late 1995, the Cardoso administration announced plans to privatise the entire electricity sector, worth, according to one (high) estimate by the United States Department of Commerce, up to $ 120 billion.[41] Up to mid-1996, there had been virtually no public outcry against either privatisation per se—or, more surprisingly, against sale of the sector to foreigners.

Total installed generating capacity as of March 1996 was about 24,700 MW,[42] including the Itaipú plant jointly owned with Paraguay. Itaipú itself enjoys a generating capacity of over 12,500 MW, making it the world's largest hydroelectric facility. Brazil has estimated additional capacity needs of 2,500 to 3,500 MW annually for the next ten years.[43] At present the federal government through its holding company, Electrobrás, owns about three-quarters of the generating capacity, which often is located hundreds of kilometres from its ultimate users, as over 60 per cent of total electricity comes from renewable resources such as hydroelectric power and ethanol. States and a few municipalities own the remainder. The Cardoso administration hopes to sell, either directly or through enlisting the state governments, virtually all of electricity generation. Transmission facilities are in federal hands. Due to the need for national planning and coordination among geographic areas, the tentative plan is for the federal government to remain dominant in transmission. Distribution, presently about 70 per cent owned by state and local governments, also is slated for virtual full privatisation. It is at this level that any future political problems are likely to appear. Of possibly great significance is the fact that in 1993 utilities, for the first time in decades, were permitted to charge differential rates to customers in different parts of the country. Prior to that, federal fiat had made all electricity rates artificially equal, irrespective of actual costs. Brazil's average cost to the consumer in 1993 was about 5 cents (US) per kilowatt hour, as compared to 6.5 cents in the United States,[44] 4.4 cents in India, 8.7 cents in Chile and 9.9 cents in Argentina, both of which recently have privatised electricity.[45] Since Brazilian utility managers thus far have been cautious about exercising this newly acquired right, the ultimate politics of electricity rates is not yet clear.

Electricity privatisation for the most part remains notional only. Only two firms, both state-level companies engaged primarily in distribution, have been sold thus far. The first, Ecelsa, sold in 1995, is located in the small state of Espírito Santo, interestingly governed by the Workers' Party, or PT, the furthest left of any of Brazil's major political parties. Ecelsa sold for $ 500 million. The second was the huge generation and distribution firm based in Rio de Janeiro, known as 'the Light'. Along with his enthusiasm for eventual privatisation of Banerj, Rio de Janeiro Governor Marcelo Alencar pushed forward with this sale, accomplished in May 1996. The selling price for the 58 per cent of the stock offered was $ 2.2 billion, making it Brazil's largest single privatisation to date, and bringing the total privatisations thus far, under all administrations, to a total of $ 11.6 billion.[46] The French state-owned power firm Eletricité de France (EDF), in consortium with two private American firms, Houston Industry and AES, took just over 34 per cent of the stock, giving it the controlling interest.

In São Paulo, meanwhile, Governor Covas had given rhetorical support to privatising his three state-level electricity firms, the largest of which, Eletropaulo, is a true giant, distributing about a third of all power in the country. Plans are (slowly) underway to break it up into four more manageable firms, to facilitate the job of finding buyers. Only time would tell whether electricity privatisation would remain a largely technical issue to be dealt with by the relevant central and state government 'experts', or, instead, would become another source of overt conflict between Brasília and São Paulo.

IV CONCLUSION

The lessons for national governments that wish to privatise, thus, are relatively straightforward. First, the leftist ideology and beliefs of particular politicians may be a factor in shaping politicians' attitudes toward privatisation, but it is unlikely to be the most crucial one. Jyoti Basu, the long-serving Communist Party Chief Minister of the Indian state of West Bengal, in the early 1990s found it advantageous to shed his historic anticapitalist position and court foreign direct investment in his state, and has done so with enthusiasm and success. Former Rio Governor Brizola in 1991 got national attention from demonstrating at the auction of Usiminas against 'entreguismo', but was remarkably quiet about the even larger sale of the Light in mid-1996, perhaps because the current governor, Marcello Alencar, had managed to make it popular. Successful democratic politicians are pragmatists. The opposition of Maharashtra Chief Minister Manohar Joshi to the power plant deal with Enron, or of São Paulo Governor Mário Covas to privatisation of Banespa, cannot credibly be explained mainly by the allegedly socialist or nationalist beliefs of these politicians.

Second, the overall political context, and particularly whether or not central and state government politicians are close political allies, does have an impact, but probably a smaller one than outside observers initially might expect to find. Thus, in 1995 the political party differences between the BJP–Shiv Sena government in Maharashtra and the Congress Party coalition in the centre undoubtedly heightened tension in India. Within the governing coalition in

Maharashtra, the more belligerent attitude of the state-level BJP than the Shiv Sena toward the Enron deal clearly resulted from the national aspirations of the BJP, which the Shiv Sena did not share. Similarly, the fact that the newly elected Congress Party government of Orissa had replaced a Janata Dal Party predecessor may have contributed to that state's decision to criticise the power plant contract it had inherited. On the other hand, the political alliance between President Cardoso and Governor Covas, also in 1995, did little to mute the genuine conflict of interests in Brazil over the disposition of Banespa. That is, reasons of political rivalry may have caused state governments to *initiate* opposition to the privatisation plans of a political competitor, but political party affiliation did not *prevent* conflicts in either country. Centre–state disagreements also, of course, are more likely if the state leader in question disposes of useful bargaining resources vis-à-vis the centre, as the different responses of Rio's Marcello Alencar and São Paulo's Mário Covas to the proposed sale of their state-level banks made clear. Covas, like Joshi in Maharashtra, was the elected leader of a very powerful state, whose cooperation the central government needed across a broad range of issues. Therefore, neither Covas nor Joshi had much to fear from publicly battling the central government over privatisation.

Third, and most significantly, this discussion has shown that centre–state disagreements over privatisation generally erupt when there are real conflicts of interest at stake. In some cases these may be primarily political, as when the state government fears being blamed for an unpopular policy that causes hardship to some constituents. Fear of being punished by constituents appears to have been important in arousing São Paulo Governor Covas' opposition to sale of Banespa, for example, and is likely to be a primary reason that the Joshi government, or any successor in Maharashtra, might oppose rapid financial sector privatisation, especially if it went so far as to attempt outright sale of the public sector commercial banks. In other cases, the distribution of economic benefits between the centre and state appears to the state government either to be unfair, or not the best deal that it could get with hard bargaining. This motive clearly was important both in the Enron and Banespa cases. Both the Rao and Cardoso central governments legitimately can be faulted for being more attuned to the ramifications of these two large projects as nationally useful symbols for would-be foreign investors than the central governments were to possible excessive costs, monetary (as in Maharashtra) or political (as in São Paulo) at the state level. The future privatisation of most of Brazil's electrical power sector, for example, will go more smoothly to the extent that both central and state governments are involved in shaping the terms of any proposed deals.

Centre–state conflicts in our cases seem not to be due primarily to state leaders' personal piques, ideological obscurantism or even political opportunism, but rather to have arisen from genuine, and ultimately negotiable, conflicts of interests. More competitive national political environments, as in both India and Brazil from the early 1980s, gave state leaders the resources and opportunity to express legitimate dissatisfactions through a democratic if occasionally bumpy process, leading men like Joshi and Covas to active participation in bargaining with both the central government and potential private investors. All in all, these are hopeful findings, suggesting that mutually beneficial compromises between central and state government interests often exist, if only negotiators seek them out. These findings bode well for the future of both centre–state relations and the gradual process of national economic liberalisation in both countries.

NOTES

An earlier version of the material in this chapter appeared in *Revista de Economia Politica* (São Paulo, Brazil), Vol. 17, No. 3 (67), July–September 1997, pp. 120–142. We thank the editors for permission to publish in India as well. The authors wish to thank the United States Agency for International Development and the Institutional Reform and Informal Sector (IRIS) India Project for financial support, Professor Alvaro Antônio Zini for facilitating one author's trip to Brazil and numerous interviewees in both countries. We alone bear responsibility for errors.

1. For overviews of the economic role of the Indian government see Encarnation, D. J. 1989, *Dislodging Multinationals: India's Strategy in Comparative Perspective*, Ithaca: Cornell University Press; and Armijo, L. E. 1997, 'The Business Environment in India: Democratic Integrity and Financial Molasses', in R. Bingham and E. W. Hill (eds), *Government and Business Finance: Global Perspectives on Economic Development*, Newark: CUPR Press of Rutgers University.
2. For an overview of the economic role of Brazil's government, see Malan, P. and R. Bonelli, 1990, 'Brazil 1950–1980: Three Decades of Growth-Oriented Economic Policies', Working Paper for INPES/IPEA, March, Rio de Janeiro;

or Lamounier, B. and E. L. Bacha, 1993, 'Redemocratization and the Impasse of Economic Reform in Brazil', Paper prepared for Overseas Development Council Conference on Interactions between Redemocratization and Market-Oriented Reforms in Latin America and Eastern Europe, April, Washington, DC.

3. Figures on the public share in gross fixed capital formation (GFCF) for India are from Short. Short's percentage for Brazil, 22.8 per cent, however, is taken from Brazil's national accounts, which include state-owned enterprise (SOE) investment with private sector investment. The estimate for Brazil cited here, therefore, comes from Trebat and includes investment by federal government 'direct administration', plus large SOEs owned by the central government. Short, R. P. 1984, 'The Role of Public Enterprise: An International Statistical Comparison', in R. Floyd, C. S. Gray and R. P. Short (eds), *Public Enterprise in Mixed Economics,* Washington, DC: International Monetary Fund; Trebat, T. J. 1983, *Brazil's State-Owned Enterprises: A Case Study of the State as Entrepreneur*, Cambridge: Cambridge University Press.
4. Figures provided to the authors by the Ministry of Finance, New Delhi.
5. Centre for Monitoring the Indian Economy, 1995, *India's Energy Sector*, Bombay: Centre for Monitoring the Indian Economy, 14 July (hereafter CMIE). Even this figure is a gross underestimate, because the base price of Rs 1.18 per unit is arrived at by taking the book value of power plant equipment, and not its replacement value.
6. Ibid., 2.
7. Ibid.
8. CMIE 1995, 12.
9. This figure was given by the Minister for Energy, N. K. P. Salve, in an oral presentation at an economic editors' conference in New Delhi, September 1995.
10. This was the average rate used for the calculations of the cost of thermal power plants in the Eighth Plan estimates. Coal-based power projects cleared by the Central Electricity Authority in 1993 cost Rs 3.25 million per MW ($ 0.103 million). See CMIE, 1995, *India's Energy Sector*, Bombay: CMIE.
11. Ibid., 24.
12. *Times of India*, 1 April 1995.
13. Reported in the *New York Times* and *International Herald Tribune*, as well as virtually all Indian newspapers in early May 1995.
14. *Times of India*, 29 August 1995.
15. In 1995 there were breakdowns on 19 April, in mid-July, and on 16 November. In other words, three major power failures occurred even as the Enron project was being cancelled.
16. This information is from off-the-record discussions with a senior member of the central government cabinet. Energy Minister Salve later made several strong statements in parliament and to the press.
17. Testimony given by Linda Powers before the Committee on Appropriations, Subcommittee on Foreign Operations, of the United States House of Representatives, 31 January 1995. This evidence was given three months before the Dabhol power plant ran into trouble.
18. See, for example, the letter to the managing director, Dabhol Power Company, from Ravindra Mahajan of the Swadeshi Jagaran Manch, dated 14 July 1995. Copy provided by the Dabhol Power Company.

19. *India Business Intelligence*, 30 August 1995.
20. This information is from a conversation with K. L. Chugh, Chairman of ITC, in November 1994. ITC was contemplating setting up a 300 MW coal-based plant at the time. Differences within the company eventually made it shelve its plans.
21. Perhaps not coincidentally, Deve Gowda became India's prime minister as the leader of a coalition of leftist parties in June 1996, after the Congress Party lost April's general parliamentary elections, and the BJP, which had emerged as the single largest party, proved unable to attract any coalition partners.
22. The major exceptions were the stock exchanges and a very few commercial banks, including local branches of foreign banks, which were private, and small state-level financial and development corporations run by state governments but which, in any case, received most of their funds (which they reloaned to smaller firms) from nationally constituted institutions.
23. The chairperson of the expert commission was former governor of the Reserve Bank of India, M. Narasimham, who was no relation to the prime minister.
24. In late 1991, for example, non-performing assets comprised about 40 per cent of the loan portfolios of the nationalised commercial banks (that is, all public sector commercial banks except the SBI). See Srinivasa-Raghavan, T. C. A. 1995, 'Now for the hard part: The second phase of the bank reform process could be more problematic', *Business World* (Bombay), 13–26 December, 104–116.
25. On the stock and banking scam, see Kabra, K. N. 1992, *Financial Sector Scam: Fruits of Liberalisation*, New Delhi: Sehyong Prakashan; and Murthy, R. C. 1995, *The Fall of Angels*, New Delhi: Indus (an imprint of HarperCollins India).
26. 'India's development bank: Seeking direction', *The Economist*, 2 March 1996, 69.
27. This information is from an R. C. Murthy interview, Bombay, 29 December 1995.
28. See Trebat, *Brazil's State-Owned Enterprises*; and Afonso, J. R. R. and S. Dain, 1987, 'O Setor Publico e as Financas Publicas na America Latina: O Caso do Brasil'. Paper presented at Coloquio Franco-Latinoamericano sobre Finanzas Publicas y Desarrollo, IIAP–IEI/UFRJ–CEPAL, Rio de Janeiro, November.
29. See Fishlow, A. 1989, 'A Tale of Two Presidents: The Political Economy of Crisis Management', in A. Stepan (ed.), *Democratizing Brasil: Problems of Transition and Consolidation*, New York: Oxford University Press.
30. See Zini, Jr., A. A. 1992, 'Monetary Reform, State Intervention, and the Collor Plan', in A. A. Zini (ed.), *The Market and the State in Economic Development in the 1990s*, UK, n.p.: Elsevier Science Publishers B.V.
31. 'De olho no porquinho', *Veja*, 15 November 1995, 32–37.
32. Baer, W. 1995, *The Brazilian Economy: Growth and Development*, 4th ed., New York: Praeger, 256.
33. Rosenblatt, A. 1996, 'Special Report: Brazil', *IEEE Spectrum*, June, 21–42.
34. 'Estados que mais devem são os do Sudeste', *Jornal do Brasil*, 3 September 1991.
35. The information in the next several paragraphs, except where noted, comes from several interviews done by one of the authors in São Paulo in late May 1996. Interviewees included three well-known economic journalists, a senior economic policymaker and his top aide in the São Paulo state government, a former

director of both the Banco Central and Banco do Brasil now employed as a private financial consultant and a federal minister in the Cardoso government.

36. See 'Quércia's assets frozen', *Gazeta Mercantil International*, 6 May 1996, 3. Quércia and Fleury, naturally, claimed they were victims of a political vendetta. All of our informants, however, insisted that the attorney general was not acting under Covas' orders and, furthermore, that the investigation was fully justified.
37. Rosa, A. C. 1996, 'Covas cobra solução do Banco Central', *Estado de São Paulo*, 22 May.
38. Note: The writing of this chapter was completed in September 1996. As this book went to press (1998) there were new developments. In December 1997 Brazil's finance ministry signed an agreement with the government of the state of São Paulo, in which the federal government would purchase a controlling interest in Banespa and two other state companies in exchange for financing of US$ 53.5 billion (Rs 1,680.1 billion) of São Paulo state's debt to the federal government. Brazil's federal government would then privatise the bank. Seeing that Banespa's shares—49 per cent of which traded on the São Paulo Stock Exchange—had increased in price more than 600 per cent in 1997 under federal government stewardship of the bank seems to have convinced the state government that going ahead with privatisation, expected by Brazilian financial markets from mid-1997, might not be such a bad idea. The considerable autonomy of the state government vis-á-vis the central government described in this case, however, remained unchanged. See Wheatley, J. 1997, 'Way cleared for Banespa sale', *Financial Times*, 29 December.
39. This figure is from an interview with senior economic journalist CM, 22 May 1996.
40. From an off-the-record interview with CL, São Paulo, 3 May 1996.
41. Rosenblatt, 'Special Report: Brazil', 22.
42. Ventura Filho, A. 'Utilities for sale', in Rosenblatt, 'Special Report: Brazil', 30.
43. Ibid., 33.
44. Ibid., 33.
45. 'Draining power', *India Today*, 30 November 1995, 73.
46. Castellani, M. and M. Magnavita, 1996, 'Investimento na Light será de US$ 200 milhões', *Estado de São Paulo*, 22 May.

PART II

Fiscal Reform

5

Reforming Indian Income Tax Enforcement

Arindam Das-Gupta and Dilip Mookherjee

Large-scale evasion of income taxes is a well-known characteristic of the Indian economy and the principal cause of a substantial underground economy.[1] Apart from making the tax system inequitable, tax evasion increases fiscal pressure on the government, which in turn leads to inflationary deficit financing and inadequate expenditure on essential infrastructure and social safety nets. These pressures also limit the scope of reduction in import tariffs and indirect taxes.

Since 1991, Indian tax reforms have dealt primarily with reform of rates of tax and, to a lesser extent, with widening the base of taxes. Relatively little effort has been made to initiate improvements in tax administration or strengthen enforcement of existing tax rules in order to curb evasion. Yet, as the experience of other developing countries suggests, tax reform that is not accompanied by suitable changes in tax administration is usually ineffective. In light of this, an examination of the nature of income tax enforcement and directions for its reform is necessary.[2]

The purpose of this chapter is to examine Indian income tax enforcement and suggest measures that can lead to its improvement. These suggestions draw upon a number of studies of Indian income tax administration, as well as international experience.

In broad terms, tax enforcement covers a range of activities all of which contribute to the ability of the government to ensure that taxes due to it, according to the prevailing law, are indeed collected. Logically, the first step is to designate a body to whom the task of collecting the tax is delegated: the tax administration. Specifying the legal authority of the tax administration to undertake various activities needed to collect taxes from those required to pay taxes is the next step. Legal powers of a tax administration range from the prosaic—such as the power to design tax forms—to the controversial and coercive power to enter and search dwellings of private individuals. These powers determine the extent to which it is feasible for a tax administration to set up an adequate information system to ascertain taxes due from various individuals (or other legal entities); to assess and collect these taxes; and to penalise those not complying with their tax obligations. The legal basis for Indian income tax administration and enforcement is laid out in the Income Tax Act, 1961. The powers specified in this Act are comprehensive and broadly in accordance with powers delegated to tax administrations in other countries.[3]

The actual use of powers by the Indian Income Tax Department (ITD), however, is far from adequate. The internal organisation of the department and the structure of delegated powers is perceived to hinder effective administration. The information system is outmoded and grossly inadequate. Assessment and tax collection are carried out inefficiently, and are plagued with mounting arrears. Penalties are frequently watered down through various forms of amnesties, are imposed on very few tax offenders and that only after protracted delays owing to penalty and court procedures. On the other hand, tax procedures are cumbersome and impose substantial compliance costs on taxpayers. Such harassment is allegedly aggravated by widespread corruption within the ITD. In consequence, the contribution of the Indian income tax to government revenue has deteriorated over the past twenty-five years and tax compliance has declined steadily. There is therefore a need for drastic reform of income tax administration in India.

The rest of this chapter is organised as follows. In Section I, problems with the Indian income tax and its administration are examined in greater detail. The section begins by comparing the performance of the Indian income tax with other countries to assess the seriousness of the problem in its proper perspective. It then discusses proximate causes for the poor and deteriorating performance of Indian income tax revenues, and argues that tax evasion is the major cause. This leads to an examination of the proximate causes for falling tax compliance since the mid-1960s. The section closes with an examination of the major problems encountered in enforcement of the income tax by the ITD. Section II describes recent experiences of other developing countries with administering income taxes and in reforming their tax administrations. Finally, Section III concludes with an assessment of lessons for Indian policymakers, drawing on reforms suggested by studies of the Indian context as well as international experience.

I DIMENSIONS OF THE PROBLEM

This section attempts to substantiate the following broad hypotheses: (*a*) the performance of the income tax in India has been poor by international standards and has been deteriorating over the past three decades, (*b*) compliance with the personal income tax has steadily worsened over this period, (*c*) the two principal tools of enforcement in India—search and seizure activity, and prosecution of tax offenders—have been ineffective in influencing levels of tax evasion, and (*d*) problems with the internal organisation of the Indian tax administration render it unable to cope with a steadily increasing workload.

International Comparison

Is the problem with income tax collection in India really serious in comparison with other countries at a comparable level of development? Table 5.1 presents basic cross-country statistics on tax efforts in the late 1980s. For countries with per capita income below US$ 360, tax revenue formed about one-seventh of their Gross Domestic Product (GDP) in the late 1980s. In contrast, in countries with per capita income between $ 1,620 and $ 6,000, tax revenues amounted to one-fifth of their GDP, while in countries with per capita incomes exceeding $ 6,000 it amounted to one-third of their GDP. Income taxes accounted respectively for about 3.5 per cent, 6.8 per cent and 11 per cent of their GDP for these three groups.[4] Correspondingly, developing countries tend to rely more on indirect taxes, particularly on foreign trade. Trade taxes, largely import duties, accounted for 5.3 per cent, 3.12 per cent and 0.72 per cent of their GDP, respectively, for the three groups.

India, with a per capita income below $360, belongs to the first group of countries. Its performance is distinctly poorer than the average for this group, with total tax revenue forming about one-ninth of the GDP. India's performance with respect to collection of income taxes is especially weak, with income taxes generating about 18 per cent of all tax revenues, compared to a group average of 25 per cent. This causes a stronger reliance on domestic indirect taxes.

In absolute terms, the performance of Indian income tax collections appears especially poor. For instance, the personal income tax generated about Rs 50 billion in 1989–90, which was less than the entire amount spent on the fertiliser subsidy that year.[5] The number of income tax assessees in 1989–90 was approximately 5.2 million, forming less than 0.6 per cent of the total population.[6]

From the cross-sectional evidence in Table 5.1 as well as from the experience of many developing countries, it is evident that the process of economic development is usually associated with growth in the relative contribution of personal income taxes to revenue. This results from a variety of factors, such as a widening of the taxpayer population, increase in personal incomes and improvements in administration and enforcement technology. The Indian experience runs counter to this general pattern: the contribution of income taxes has diminished over the past two decades despite economic growth. Over the period 1970–90 the share of Indian income tax revenues in total central tax revenue fell from 14.7 per cent to 9.7 per cent. The proportion of personal income tax in non-agricultural GDP[7] fell from 2.17 per cent to 1.89 per cent.[8] Not only is the standard of income tax collection in India low by international standards, it appears to be deteriorating in recent decades.

The implications of the falling capacity to collect income tax are serious. The government is forced to rely increasingly on excise, sales and customs duties, as well as administered price hikes for public-sector products. These taxes are regressive and inflationary. They create problems of coordination of indirect taxes between the central and state governments. The resulting cascading effects distort relative prices, besides encouraging excessive vertical integration. Imports are discouraged by the high levels of tariffs and spending on essential infrastructure and social services is restricted.

Direct taxes are inherently less regressive—being related more closely to the ability of taxpayers to pay—and less distortionary.

Proximate Causes of Declining Tax Revenues

What were the principal causes of this deterioration? The fact that agricultural income is exempt from the central income tax under the Indian Constitution, the high exemption limit of the income tax and falling tax rates can all be ruled out as possible explanations. Figure 5.1 reveals that the share of agriculture in GDP declined substantially between 1965 and 1992. Moreover, the ratio of income taxes to non-agricultural GDP displayed a falling trend over this period.[9] Since the income tax exemption limit is about three and a half times per capita income, only a small fraction of the population not engaged in agriculture is actually subject to the tax. However, Figure 5.2 shows that the ratio of the exemption limit to per capita income fell substantially, from about 6.5 in 1965 to 3.5 in 1992. Hence, while the exclusion of agricultural income and the high exemption limit contribute to the low *level* of income tax revenues relative to non-agricultural GDP, they cannot explain the deteriorating *trend*. Finally, Figure 5.2 reveals that the average effective tax rate increased over this period, despite reductions in top marginal rates.

Falling compliance appears to be the principal cause for deteriorating income tax collections during this period. Das-Gupta, Lahiri and Mookherjee (1995) (hereafter DLM) have examined the time series behaviour of an aggregate index of compliance with the personal income tax.[10] This compliance index measures the fraction of taxes due that were actually collected.[11] The compliance index is displayed in Figure 5.3. While subject to considerable year-to-year fluctuations, the index followed a secular downward trend. In particular, the level of compliance in 1991 was less than half that in 1965.

It is interesting to contrast the downward trend in tax compliance with the upward trend in income tax revenues. Even after adjusting for inflation, revenues increased sharply, especially since 1985–86. This revenue growth has masked the fall in compliance levels. Put another way, the growth in revenue is below what ought to have been achieved, given the growth in non-agricultural GDP and in tax rates during this period.

Proximate Causes of Deteriorating Compliance

Possible explanations for the decline in tax compliance were analysed in DLM. These include macroeconomic variables (non-agricultural GDP and inflation), tax structure (marginal tax rates and the exemption limit) and enforcement efforts of the ITD (search and seizure activity, quantity and quality of assessments, penalties and prosecutions). Besides these variables, the effects of tax amnesties are examined in Das-Gupta and Mookherjee (1995).[12]

The conclusions of these papers throw some light on the causes of falling compliance. Variables with statistically significant negative effects on tax revenues and compliance include tax rates, the exemption limit, audit intensities and tax amnesties. Since the exemption limit declined during the past decade, it could not have contributed to declining compliance, especially since 1980. The candidates for explaining deteriorating tax compliance can therefore be narrowed down to the rise in tax rates, the fall in audit intensities and the repeated offering of amnesties.

The evidence suggests that marginal tax rates exercised a significant negative effect on compliance, but not on revenues. In other words, the fall in compliance tended to be neutralised by the direct effect of changing the tax rate: the evidence in favour of a backward-bending Laffer curve in India is not compelling. Simply reducing tax rates may therefore not lead to a major change in tax revenues. Moreover, this factor cannot be an important explanation for the declining performance of income tax revenues.

Audit intensities turn out to be the only dimension of the ITD enforcement effort that exercised a significant effect on compliance. Consequently, one factor contributing to the fall in compliance has been the declining fraction of taxpayers coming under scrutiny assessment, combined with the reduction in time devoted to individual scrutiny assessments, especially since the mid-1970s.[13] Prosecution effort (measured by number of prosecutions launched against tax evasion, or success with respect to convictions obtained or compounding of tax offences) had no appreciable impact on tax compliance. Search and seizure (measured by value of assets seized in searches), the principal tool of the ITD in collecting information about taxpayer assets, had a statistically significant positive effect on compliance, but the magnitude of this effect was negligible.

Tax amnesties in 1965–66, 1980–81, 1985–87 and 1991–92 had negative effects on compliance and revenue.[14] The direct receipts from the amnesty were substantially outweighed by a number of induced effects on filing behaviour, and on penalties collected during non-amnesty years. Moreover, repeated amnesties signal the weak ability of the government to enforce the income tax. The only exception to this pattern was the 1975 amnesty, which exercised a positive impact on compliance and revenues. This amnesty, however, coincided with an internal emergency characterised by stronger enforcement of laws and curtailed civil liberties, and the positive compliance effects observed in 1975 could be owed to this rather than to the amnesty.

One other important variable identified by DLM in explaining year-to-year fluctuations in compliance and revenues was the inflation rate. Higher inflation tended to reduce compliance and revenues, both via its indirect effect on effective tax rates (owing to lack of indexation of tax brackets), as well as directly (by inducing taxpayers to delay tax payments or to shift white assets into black). However, since there have been no noticeable trends in inflation over the past three decades, it cannot be viewed as a cause of the secular decline in compliance.

Table 5.2 reports estimates of the extent to which revenues would have increased in any given year with a switch of the policy that year to the corresponding 'best practice' policy over the period 1965–92, based on the importance of different explanatory variables identified by DLM.[15] Limiting attention to past best practice is a natural way to incorporate possible administrative and political constraints on policy reforms. The estimates suggest that in the early 1990s, one could expect a revenue increase of the order of 30 per cent by reforming tax structure, in particular by reducing marginal tax rates to the level of the mid-1960s. The only reform in enforcement policy with a significant potential impact on revenues (of the order of 40 per cent) would be in audit policy, involving an increase in the frequency of audits and extent of time devoted per audit. Stepping up search and seizure activity or prosecution effort, the principal tools of enforcement policy of the ITD during the past few decades, would yield negligible revenue additions.

Problems with Income Tax Administration in India

Table 5.2 indicates that the revenue improvements possible from reform of conventional policy tools are modest in relation to the magnitude of tax evasion estimated by Acharya and Associates (1985) or Virmani (1986).[16] Hence policymakers should examine the possibility of reforming the institutional setting of income tax administration in India. The need for administrative reform is also highlighted by the limited deterrent effect of the two principal tools of enforcement policy, namely, searches and prosecution activity.

In a descriptive study of the ITD, Das-Gupta, Mookherjee and Panta (1992) (hereafter DMP) reported serious problems with the administration of the income tax in India.[17] The study was based on a field survey of five income tax ranges and interviews with officers of the ITD. It examined the information system, methods of record-keeping, manpower allocation policies, target-setting methods, performance incentive systems and appeals, penalty and prosecution policies. Major problems were identified in each of these different aspects of ITD functioning, and will be described in further detail.

The information system of the ITD appears to be outdated and out of line with contemporary requirements. Computerisation of operations or data on taxpayers is practically non-existent, while taxpayer record-keeping is primitive and tamper-prone. There is no functioning system of taxpayer identification numbers; the system of tax withholding is grossly inadequate. While a system of third-party reporting exists on paper, percolation of information to assessing officers is slow. Consequently, audit operations fail to utilise available information concerning transactions of taxpayers.

Manpower resources of the ITD grew substantially more slowly than its workload. However, DMP found no evidence that this was due to improved efficiency in the utilisation of manpower. The ITD appeared to pay limited attention to the rational allocation and deployment of manpower across different units of the ITD, and to the design of effective systems of planning and evaluation, audit selection, work targeting and employee incentives. In particular, the ITD displayed little awareness of the effects of these systems on revenues and taxpayer compliance. For instance, it reacted to a growing workload by stressing the disposal of pending assessments and collection of tax arrears, while allowing the quantity and quality of scrutiny assessments to deteriorate sharply. In simulations of alternative manpower deployment strategies, Das-Gupta and Mookherjee (1995) find substantial scope for improving the revenue productivity of manpower devoted to assessment.[18]

In penalty and prosecution activity, DMP identified a similar tendency to emphasise quantity over effectiveness. Penalties and prosecutions have increasingly been oriented towards the punishment of relatively technical violations (such as failure to deposit tax deducted at source, or failure to pay advance tax). The consequence is that relatively less effort has been devoted to penalising tax evasion.

On these grounds, therefore, it may be argued that weaknesses in administration represent a principal cause of the poor performance of income taxes in India. These administrative weaknesses have atrophied especially with the sharp growth in workload, arising in turn from the increasing number of taxpayers. It is therefore appropriate to turn to the experience of other countries in the area of income tax administration.

II INTERNATIONAL EXPERIENCE

In recent times tax reforms have been carried out in several countries in what appears to be a world-wide movement toward modern tax systems. India is therefore in the happy position of being able to draw upon international experience in planning its own reforms. The purpose of this section is twofold. First, the experience of selected countries is used to assess the importance of effective administrative reforms in successful tax reform. Second, the experience with detailed administrative reforms in these countries is used to identify choices that might be considered seriously in designing administrative reforms in India.

A brief description of the countries reviewed and their experiences is appropriate at this point to explain the reason for their selection. Mexico undertook a complete overhaul of its tax administration as part of the economic reforms initiated in the late 1980s. Besides modernisation of administrative systems, tax enforcement was stepped up greatly. Tax performance in Mexico improved markedly thereafter. Spain completely overhauled its tax information system by introducing comprehensive computerisation, but took few measures to increase the severity of tax enforcement. It too realised significant gains and cost economies, though these gains were perhaps less spectacular than those of Mexico. The Philippines has undertaken extensive income tax reform during the past twenty years but has paid less attention to administrative reform. Improvement in tax revenue realisation has been sporadic over the period. In contrast to most other countries, Singapore's income tax retains several traditional features such as the absence of self-assessment or withholding taxes and, until recently, field audits. However, it has one of the most automated tax systems in the world, and has a record of successful prosecution of a small number of high-profile tax evaders. Its persistence with outmoded tax provisions has not prevented a satisfactory tax performance, owing largely to its advanced administrative systems.[19] The importance of improved administration in successful tax reform is, therefore, supported by the experience of these countries. Additional support for this position can be found from the experience of many other countries as well. For example, Indonesia's income tax has not fared well despite drastic tax simplification and base broadening, due mainly to slow implementation of administrative reform.[20] On the other hand, countries such as Colombia, Costa Rica, Ecuador and Jamaica achieved substantial gains from comprehensive reforms which included administrative reforms.[21]

One lesson that appears warranted is the importance of political will in initiating successful reform. The fiscal crises in such countries as Argentina, Bolivia, Colombia and Peru during the 1980s resulted in the election of governments with a mandate to carry out economic reforms. This enabled reforms such as the successful overhaul of tax systems, which had not been possible with the weak governments that had prevailed earlier. With respect to specific areas of administrative reform, the most far-reaching changes were achieved in modernising the tax information system. This involved large-scale computerisation and use of modern information-processing technology, besides organisational reforms intended to enable effective utilisation of information. In contrast, increased levels of auditing and stepped-up prosecution activity did not appear to have been widespread. Following computerisation, reforms in the organisational structure of tax administration and of employee incentives formed a second major initiative in many countries. These will be reviewed in greater detail.

Overall Perspective

Many countries, particularly in Latin America, witnessed significant reforms in tax administration during the 1980s. Silvani (1990) characterised the 1980s as the 'winning decade for tax administration'.[22] The motivating factor for these reforms was the onset of fiscal crises during the early 1980s. Foreign borrowing could no longer be relied upon to overcome fiscal problems; neither could inflation, which was already prevailing at a high level in most of these countries. The initial reaction of many countries was to introduce reforms in tax law to encourage investment, index for inflation and broaden the tax base. These reforms were largely unsuccessful in substantially increasing revenues. Consequently, during the 1980s, significant changes in tax administration were introduced in many Latin American countries. Similar reforms were initiated in other countries for a variety of reasons. Spain and Portugal embarked on ambitious tax modernisation programmes to enable them to catch up with the rest of the European Community. The end of the Marcos era in the Philippines heralded many economic reforms, including tax reform, although administrative reform was less thoroughgoing. Indonesian reforms were motivated by falling petroleum prices, causing deteriorating terms of trade and declining capital inflows in the early 1980s, leading to a perception that non-oil revenues needed a boost.

Most successful reform initiatives were associated with strong political support from the highest levels. Such support was necessary to overcome inertia within the administration and resistance from adversely affected taxpayers, and to make available necessary finances and leadership. The political will resulted from the need for elected governments to successfully resolve ongoing fiscal crises to ensure a continuation of their mandates.

A careful quantitative assessment of the results of reform in different countries is not available. Two basic indicators are, however, presented in Table 5.3 for countries that have successfully overhauled their administrations (as well as for Indonesia and the Philippines). Singapore's atypical performance reflects, in part, a deliberate reduction in its tax burden, as well as a wage hike for tax employees. Though its real tax revenue declined in 1985 and 1986, tax buoyancies with respect to GDP increased from 1.44 during

1980–85 to 1.5 during 1986–1992.[23] Overall, the figures suggest that appreciable gains can be achieved by reforming administration.

Specific Reforms

International experience with five specific components of administrative reform are now described in more detail: information system; organisational structure; auditing; tax collection; and treatment of offenders. The review is selective and concentrates on aspects of relevance to the Indian situation.

The Information System The major components of a tax information system include subsystems dealing with the identification of potential taxpayers, ascertainment of their tax dues from their own records and from the records of third parties, monitoring the progress of tax proceedings with particular taxpayers and keeping track of tax collections. Several other subsystems, ranging from those that facilitate internal control of operations to those that permit tax officers and taxpayers to make informed decisions are also important. From the point of view of Indian reform, three reform trends have been significant. The first is computerisation of the information system, which usually starts with basic taxpayer identification, construction of taxpayer master files and current accounts and then proceeds to an overhaul of systems for tax filing, record keeping and retrieval, and cross-matching. A second initiative involves strengthening of withholding systems. Introduction of presumptive taxes forms a third reform that can compensate for weaknesses in the information system.

The most important reform initiative has undoubtedly been computerisation, which brings with it several unique benefits, such as: (*a*) a tamper-proof, readily accessible and updatable information base on the identity of taxpayers, their payment records and third party information, (*b*) cross-matching of information from different sources concerning the activities of any taxpayer, (*c*) efficient collection and tax recovery operations, (*d*) sophisticated audit selection programmes and enhanced information on taxpayer activities that is speedily available to tax auditors during audits, (*e*) less corruption owing to reduced scope for person-to-person contact between officials and taxpayers and reduced auditor discretion over conduct of audits, (*f*) improved taxpayer information and assistance services, and (*g*) a comprehensive information base for managerial planning and supervision.

Virtually all comprehensive computerisation programmes have included the following components: a system of nationwide taxpayer identification numbers and identity cards; a Taxpayer Master File (listing all potential taxpayers, with identifying information); a Taxpayer Current Account (containing a record of tax-related transactions); and a Tax Data Base, used in audits, taxpayer assistance and management control. The development of these components represents the natural first stage of a computerisation programme. These were successfully introduced over a period of about thirty months or less by many Latin American countries, usually with external assistance from the Inter-American Tax Conference (CIAT) and the Inter-American Development Bank (IDB).[24] Countries such as Mexico and Spain achieved even more comprehensive computerisation within a relatively short span of time: 1988–93 for Mexico and 1984–91 for Spain.[25]

The returns on investment in information technology appear to have been realised fairly quickly; indeed, virtually no country witnessed any disruption in its revenue collections during the transition period. Virtually all the CIAT–IDB-assisted programmes in Latin America realised immediate benefits, especially with respect to collections and recovery operations. In countries for which data on costs of these investments are available,[26] the investments were invariably below 1 per cent of average yearly tax revenues. The absolute cost of computerisation was below US$ 10 million, with the exception of Spain and Mexico. The total Mexican investment has been estimated at about US$ 18 million, as against an annual revenue of US$ 26,197 million in 1989.

Computerisation brings with it the need for complementary legal reform. This includes changes in filing requirements and filing processes, and treatment of signatures in electronically filed returns and tax demand notices. In addition, the issue of taxpayer rights to privacy and security must also be dealt with. Mexico has introduced a number of innovations designed to track transactions of small taxpayers, including the mandatory use of sales registers that track sales in retail establishments, of invoices that carry taxpayer identification numbers of both buyer and seller and the use of industry association affiliations to register small businesses. It should also be noted that virtually all the countries surveyed have a system of nationwide taxpayer identification numbers that has been in place for several decades. The only exception is the Philippines, which is still consolidating its taxpayer identification system.

An important component of the information-cum-tax-collection system is withholding of tax at source. Withholding from wages, or pay-as-you-earn (PAYE) systems, interest and dividends are an important source of revenue for most countries studied. An exception to this is Singapore. The Philippines has compensated for its relative lack of success with computerisation by a major extension of withholding taxes. This was facilitated by a move away from global income taxation to schedular taxation, which involves separate tax schedules for different sources of income in order to reduce the complexity of administering the tax. Creditable withholding taxes on bank deposit interest, dividends and royalties at a flat rate of 15 per cent and on money market interest at a flat rate of 35 per cent were introduced in the late 1970s. These were soon followed by an expanded withholding system, under which all persons making payments to residents were required to withhold taxes at rates ranging between 2.5 and 35 per cent, and a progressive (10 and 20 per cent) final withholding tax on property sales. To encourage compliance, a number of penalty provisions were introduced in 1979 and subsequently strengthened in 1987. To circumvent bank secrecy laws, central bank auditors monitor compliance with interest withholding requirements by commercial banks. The overall results of these reforms have been striking: the share of withholding taxes in total revenue collections increased from 7.8 per cent during 1972–81, to 16.2 per cent during 1982–85 and 19.7 per cent during 1986–91. In 1990 and 1991, collections from withholding taxes amounted to about 3.5 per cent of the GDP, exceeding those from income and corporation taxes combined. This experience contrasts with that of India, where a 1991 measure to introduce withholding from bank interest had to be withdrawn after one year.

In order to deal with hard-to-tax groups (such as retailers, professionals or other service-sector categories) whose incomes are hard to measure, presumptive taxes have been used in various countries. The most well-known example is the tax on real assets introduced in Mexico, Colombia and Argentina during the late 1980s. In Mexico, for instance, this is levied at 2 per cent of the gross inflation-adjusted assets of a company, principally aimed at reducing tax evasion based on 'innovative' accounting methods. It is a minimum tax, refundable to companies in years of above-normal profit declarations. This tax has been the most controversial of all the Mexican tax reforms of the past decade, with numerous court cases filed—suggesting that the tax has exercised considerable bite. Revenue returns have been of the order of 0.3 per cent of the GDP.[27]

Organisational Restructuring The experience of other countries suggests that Indian tax administrators can consider five potential sets of organisational changes: increasing functional specialisation; reducing regional decentralisation; awarding greater autonomy to the tax administration; altering manpower allocation systems; and reforming employee compensation policies. These will be elaborated upon.

There has been a general trend amongst the CIAT countries towards adopting a functional structure for tax administration, with different departments specialising in different functions (such as assessment; collections and recovery; information processing; taxpayer assistance; and penalties and prosecutions). This is also true of the three Asian countries examined. Indeed, it is difficult to visualise effective computerisation of operations if a tax administration is not organised along functional lines. There has also been a trend toward unifying administration of direct taxes, indirect taxes and customs duties. These stand in direct contrast to the organisation of the Indian system, where different functions tend to be simultaneously carried out by local units in isolation from one another, and where different taxes tend to be administered by different bodies.

Unlike Indian administration, certain functions such as planning, evaluation and taxpayer assistance are explicitly recognised by building them into the organisational structures of tax administrations in many countries. For instance, the Philippines created a management information system in 1981, and instituted a practice of creating and implementing long-range plans for improvements in selected areas. This facilitated the phased introduction of major pieces of tax reform (such as the Modified Gross Income Tax), based on feedback from different quarters, over a period of some five or six years. Spain has an advanced computer-based planning and evaluation function, making available continuously updated statistics on collections and audits classified in various ways (for instance, by taxes, regions or functions), projecting future revenues and monitoring progress towards achievement of different target goals. Computers are also actively employed in providing assistance to taxpayers, with respect to providing answers to taxpayer queries and assistance with preparation of tax returns. Computer-based taxpayer assistance is also provided in Chile, Colombia, Canada and Portugal.

Another distinctive feature of the Indian administration is the high degree of decentralisation of tax to local units, with relatively little sharing of overhead staff functions, limited supervision from higher levels and granting of substantial discretion to local officials. In contrast, the trend in many countries is to increase the degree of centralised control and resource-sharing. This makes it difficult for local officers to tamper with records, besides allowing centralisation of audit selection and manpower allocation. For instance, Spain and the Philippines have created regional offices that act as an intermediate level of the tax administration hierarchy. These regional offices have special branches for collection, assessment and administration. Taxpayer records and other sensitive information are usually stored at central information processing departments, and are electronically accessible to the entire administration. In contrast, taxpayer files are stored in single paper copy at local offices in India, causing limited and delayed access to other offices.

Greater autonomy of the tax administration is important if the administration is to retain the flexibility to respond to administrative problems quickly and effectively. Autonomy over salary levels, incentive systems, training and procurement has been increased in varying degrees in a number of countries, such as Argentina, Colombia, Ghana, Peru and Singapore. An important dimension of autonomy concerns the budget of the tax administration. In several countries this is linked to revenues collected. For example, the Internal Revenue Authority of Singapore is an independent statutory corporation whose income consists of agency fees paid to it by the government of Singapore. The fee is linked to tax collections achieved, relative to a pre-decided target. A second dimension of autonomy pertains to personnel policy. In Peru and Singapore, extensive autonomy over employment conditions, including the hiring and firing of employees, has existed since the early 1990s. Peru's tax administration utilised its powers to drastically reduce staff strength and increase salary levels on a merit basis. Singapore revised wages in line with market wages, a measure that was made possible by the fact that tax officials are not part of the civil service. The degree of autonomy in Spain, on the other hand, has been limited by the constraints imposed by the civil service of which the tax administration forms a part. In India, by contrast, almost all items of expenditure, and not just the overall budget, require approval by officials outside the tax administration. Furthermore, tax officers form part of the civil service, thereby restricting the scope for introducing wage and employment conditions appropriate to the particular needs of tax administration.

The previous section noted how the increasing ratio of workload to manpower in India has caused significant dilution of the frequency and quality of taxpayer audits. Other countries have also witnessed significant growth in workload, without significantly increasing manpower allocated to audit operations. Most important, this problem was successfully confronted without reducing the effectiveness of audit operations. The Mexican tax administration, for instance, reduced its staff strength by over 20 per cent between 1988 and 1991, despite an over 20 per cent increase in the number of taxpayers, and an 80 per cent increase in the fraction of taxpayers audited. During the same time there were impressive gains in the yield of individual audits. In Spain the number of taxpayers more than doubled between 1981 and 1992, but the number of tax inspectors and subinspectors employed increased only 11 per cent. In the Philippines the number of taxpayers increased 12 per cent between 1976 and 1988, but total employment was almost stationary during this period. By and large this was made possible by the increasing computerisation of operations, which allows for automation of routine tasks. The task of manpower management is greatly facilitated by granting the tax administration autonomy over manpower recruitment and deployment decisions.

A final area of organisational reform concerns compensation of tax administration employees. Some countries such as Mexico and Peru have recently introduced flexible hiring and firing policies, with use of incentive systems offering substantial rewards to tax officials based on revenue collections. These appear to have exercised a significant impact in curbing corruption and increasing revenues. Spanish tax administration employees, on the other hand, are part of the general civil service whose salary levels are not comparable with the private sector and rely little on positive incentives. Reliance is placed instead on a sophisticated system of decentralising decisions and evaluating the performance of individual cost or budgetary centres. The tax administration in Singapore also relies on non-monetary incentives for employees, besides revising wages upwards quite substantially to bring them in line with market wages. Employees of the tax administration in the Philippines are part of the general civil service, where incentives are provided by systems of promotion. Similar to Indian practice, work targets are assigned in detailed quantitative terms, and success of individual employees and departments in meeting centrally laid down targets are monitored and used in performance evaluations. Salary levels are periodically upgraded. Overall, the system is believed to be characterised by a great deal of corruption and low work incentives. In the Indian context, where official corruption is alleged to be more akin to the Philippines and (pre-reform) Mexico, a system of positive incentives would appear to be appropriate. It may be argued, however, that the more fundamental reform involves granting autonomy to the tax administration, whose budget is linked to its performance; the self-interest of the administrators themselves can then be subsequently relied upon to reform employee incentives without external direction.

Auditing The following three dimensions of audit policy are important: the types of audits carried out; selection of which taxpayers to audit; and the number of audits of different kinds carried out by an auditor on a yearly basis. Most countries conduct two or more types of audits of differing intensity. In systems with a high degree of computerisation such as Canada, Singapore or the United States, mechanical checking of returns for arithmetical and prima facie correctness (or pre-auditing) is usually performed automatically. Cases selected thereafter for audit can be subjected either to a desk audit, or a more comprehensive field audit (as in Singapore). The former type of audit is useful in detecting questionable tax deduction claims, while the latter is appropriate for the detection of tax evasion. For a small number of serious fraud cases, tax investigations conducted by specialised teams are often used (e.g., in the Philippines, Singapore and the United States).

In order to maximise the number of returns to be audited, selection of cases is best performed at the national level so that uniform criteria are applied to all taxpayers. Furthermore, criteria can be designed to facilitate computerised selection of returns as in Canada,

Mexico, Singapore, Spain and the United States. These criteria reflect past experience of characteristics of audited taxpayers whose reported income deviated substantially from the income subsequently assessed.

In most countries studied, the number of audits carried out per year by a single auditor was less than thirty, implying an average of about ten days per audit. Audit proportions run above 10 per cent in Chile and Portugal, between 2 per cent and 10 per cent in Argentina, Costa Rica, El Salvador, Guatemala and Mexico and less than 2 per cent in Ecuador, Spain, Panama and the Philippines. Typically countries auditing a larger fraction of taxpayers (such as Chile and Portugal) have less intensive audits.

It is instructive to compare these with Indian practice. The standards of auditing in India have been significantly diluted by the growing workload over the past two decades.[28] The fraction of taxpayers audited in India fell from about 60 per cent in the early 1970s to below 3 per cent in the 1990s. This, however, masks trends in audit intensity, since the definition of a scrutiny assessment (the Indian term for an audit) has been progressively strengthened since the 1960s. For instance, an assessing officer carried out almost 400 scrutiny assessments a year in the early 1980s, compared to a little over a 100 by the late 1980s. With respect to the audit frequencies expressed as a proportion of the total taxpayer population, Indian practice does not seem out of line with international practice.

The major discrepancies arise with respect to the quality of audits. With each assessing officer carrying out a hundred audits a year, an average of three days were spent per audit. Moreover, only a small fraction (about 20 per cent on the average) of the time of tax inspectors is spent on field enquiries, so the audits are overwhelmingly desk audits.

Moreover, the decision of which taxpayers to select for audit is predominantly delegated to the relevant assessing officers, with little oversight exercised by any centralised body. The officers are often issued general guidelines by the ITD concerning which taxpayers to select, but these tend to be designed without much thought to consequent effects on taxpayer reporting incentives, and also leave substantial room for subjective judgements and discretion on the part of the assessing officers. There was also little evidence that assessing officers utilised information available concerning transactions of taxpayers with the ITD, or any other systematic procedure.

Another practice in India that contrasts markedly with other countries is the extensive reliance on search and seizure operations by its tax investigation unit. In none of the countries studied was there a strong reliance on search and seizure activity either as a tool for gathering information or for initiating prosecution for tax offences.

The scope for substantive reforms in auditing practice is illustrated by the experience of Mexico. Prior to 1988 the auditing system was not substantially dissimilar from the current Indian practice. Since 1988 a variety of measures were introduced to reduce corruption, and motivate auditors in a positive manner. These include reliance on pre-programmed 'laptop' audits, which substantially reduced the scope for auditor discretion; a system of bonuses based on additional revenues collected, amounting on the average to about 130 per cent of the overall wage bill; induced attrition of corrupt officials; and increased job rotation. Vigilance activities were also stepped up: for example, auditors are subjected to polygraph tests, and an audit which yields no additional revenues can be closed only by an official from a different department. Second, the audit selection system is now based on a computerised information base; selections are decided by the programming departments of local offices, on the basis of criteria issued by the central office. Third, large taxpayers are required to be inspected by private auditors, just as in the case of financial statements; the returns are filed electronically, and the third party auditor is held partly responsible for irregularities or improper disclosures in the return. This has freed audit manpower resources within the tax administration to turn their efforts away from large taxpayers to middle-sized and small taxpayers.

In Spain, improvements in auditing have been achieved through an enhanced information base, especially with the development of 'expert systems' software allowing identification of taxpayers according to the intersection of different criteria relating to transactions and assets. A national data base is also used to identify potential non-filers. Taxpayers are selected for audit at local offices based on criteria laid down by the central office; the latter also lays down targets in terms of the number of audits to be carried out, and revenues expected to be realised. However, there is no system of financial incentives for auditors, or other mechanisms to insure auditor responsibility. For instance, additional tax demands made by auditors are frequently appealed by taxpayers and subsequently overturned, and the tax auditor has little responsibility beyond issuing the original demand. Not surprisingly, levels of tax evasion appear to be quite high: it is estimated that about 68 per cent of income was concealed under the personal income tax in 1992, with special concentration in construction, restaurant and transport sectors. In these respects, the Spanish situation is similar to that in India, despite the deployment of a sophisticated computer system. That contrasted with Mexico serves to highlight the importance of offering positive incentives to inspectors.

Tax Collection The main point of interest is the extensive privatisation of tax return filing and tax collection operations through commercial banks. The degree of privatisation varies, but the feature itself is common to most CIAT countries, as well as the Philippines and Singapore.[29] While tax collection is also carried out through banks in India, the system is poorly designed and cumbersome in contrast to the systems prevailing in other countries studied. Reform of the Indian collection system along the lines of systems in Mexico or Colombia could greatly increase its efficiency.

Appeals, Penalties and Prosecution It is worth considering the striking reforms achieved by Mexico in these areas, and contrasting the resulting system in Mexico to that currently prevailing in India.

The Mexican reforms were designed to encourage incentives for voluntary settlement by taxpayers and to strengthen prosecution of large tax offenders. First, an 'autocorrection' facility was introduced to reduce frivolous or strategic penalty litigation whereby penalty rates are reduced by half (from 100 per cent to 50 per cent) if the taxpayer complies with the additional demands made by the tax inspector. As many as 70 per cent of all additional demand cases are now settled in this fashion, serving to reduce the pressure on the appeals and court system. Second, the appeals procedure allows only one level of appeals, and is now time-bound. The incentive to delay payments via frivolous appeals have also been reduced by introducing inflation adjustments to penalties, as well as liability rules where taxpayers must compensate the tax administration for legal expenses incurred if the appeal is overturned. Finally the administration increased prosecution efforts markedly, with special concentration on large offences. More than 500 tax evasion prosecution cases have been launched since 1988, with over 200 people given jail sentences (in contrast to only three prosecutions in the entire history of the system prior to 1988).

The Indian system involves excessive delays, even by the already low standards of countries such as Spain and the Philippines. Appeals are not time-bound and ex parte hearings are not allowed. Various amnesty and settlement programmes dilute the deterrent effect of penalties, as does the fact that many prosecutions are launched against tax offences of a technical nature which do not involve large-scale tax evasion. The discretion allowed to tax officials and settlement authorities over terms of settlement and the granting of immunity stand in sharp contrast to the formula-bound autocorrection approach used in Mexico.

In conclusion, the experience of many developing countries illustrates the wide range of reforms that could be considered by the Indian tax administration. Their experience also suggests that such a reform process is logistically feasible over a five to eight year horizon. Financing costs have tended to be low in relation to annual revenues, and revenue returns have usually been realised fairly quickly without any major disruptions. Nevertheless, serious reforms require political will at the highest level within the tax administration, as well as in the government. The following section attempts to summarise some lessons that Indian policymakers could learn from the experience of other countries.

III LESSONS FOR INDIAN POLICY

The first point that needs emphasis is that continuation of current administrative and enforcement practices cannot lead to dramatic improvements in the performance of the income tax in India. This is evident from Table 5.2, which demonstrated the possibility of at most 60 to 70 per cent revenue increases from switching to best practice levels of these policies over the period 1965–92.[30] However, almost half of this improvement would result from increases in assessment efficiency, reflecting a return to the audit frequencies of the 1960s. Changes in tax structure would yield less by comparison. Furthermore, even if both tax structure and tax administration reforms are carried out to the levels of best practice since 1965, the order of gains is insufficient to restore the performance of the Indian income tax to the level of other developing countries.[31]

Consequently, reform of income tax administration must be more thoroughgoing if income taxes are to significantly increase their contribution to revenue. Areas requiring reform have already been identified in preceding sections, and are now summarised.

The first main area is the information system. Necessary reform measures include computerisation, introduction of a nationwide system of taxpayer identification numbers, current accounts and taxpayer master files; a major extension of the withholding system; improved methods of cross-matching of information from different sources; and a special drive to track down non-filers.[32] The second area involves organisational restructuring, where the government could consider the following reform measures that appear to have been effective in other developing countries: increased tax administration autonomy over salary levels, hiring and firing of employees, procurement and privatisation of select operations; increased functional specialisation, and increased centralisation, in order to reduce discretion of local officials and to improve sharing of overhead resources; the creation of new units for long-term planning and evaluation; and taxpayer services. The third main area where reforms are necessary is auditing. There is a need to enhance the quality of audits by allowing auditors more time to carry them out, for instance by reducing quantitative norms. Audit selection procedures which make effective use of available information need to be introduced. Most importantly, improvements in auditor incentives and monitoring need to be introduced to reduce corruption. A fourth possible area of reform concerns ways of improving the effectiveness of current manpower resources of the tax administration to cope with the large workload. This may involve the introduction of rational manpower allocation plans designed to increase revenues without increasing total employment, and improved training and infrastructural facilities. Finally, appeals, penalties and prosecution activities should close off loopholes exploited by large-scale tax evaders, emphasise formula-based voluntary settlement and engage in selective but intensive prosecution launched against large tax evaders.

A gradual programme of modernisation of the tax administration can be introduced in a phased manner. The transition requires careful management to limit resistance from entrenched interests. To be implemented successfully, the reforms therefore have to be sequenced appropriately. Two main sources of resistance can be expected: affected taxpayers, and employees of the tax administration. Elements of the reform programme that would appeal to these two groups should be given strong emphasis at the outset. The experience of other countries suggests that with a few notable exceptions, greater emphasis has been given to improvements in the information system within the tax administration, rather than heightened activities of audits and prosecutions. This may have been partly to avoid strenuous opposition from middle-class taxpayers.

In a similar fashion, the Indian reforms could also limit resistance from taxpayers by initially focusing on computerisation, and improvements in taxpayer services. The culture of acquiring information concerning tax offences via brute force can be replaced by a less visible but more comprehensive method based on extended third-party reporting and withholding. The number and geographical spread of collection centres for tax returns could be enhanced, special offices dealing with taxpayer enquiries could be opened and processing of refunds could be speedier and offered on an automated, impersonal basis.

The support of internal employees could be sought by including programmes of salary enhancements, improved work facilities, flexible work targeting systems, positive reward-based incentive schemes, less frequent transfers and improved training (especially with respect to computer-based tasks). These changes will necessitate granting a certain degree of autonomy to the tax administration. DMP report that their interviews with assessing officers revealed a positive attitude towards a reform package which included these elements.

Improvements in audit systems could be brought about by redesigned manpower allocation schemes, which are unlikely to meet with much resistance from employees. For instance, an important component of the intensity of audits of specific groups of taxpayers (defined by occupation, region or scale of reported income) is the amount of manpower allocated to their assessment. Das-Gupta and Mookherjee (1995)[33] show that manpower allocation norms have a strong impact on revenues collected, owing to induced effects on audit frequencies and therefore on taxpayer incentives to disclose income. For instance, the current practice of organising taxpayers into wards and circles, based on size of reported income, has the effect of lowering audit frequencies for wards (corresponding to low-income disclosures) relative to circles (corresponding to high-income disclosures). This increases the incentive for a high-income taxpayer to disclose little, in order to be included in a ward where the likelihood of audit is low. This perverse effect can be avoided by allocating more manpower to circles, or better still, abolishing the ward–circle distinction altogether.

Reforms in penalties and prosecution policies are also essential, and are likely to be unpopular. However, they are likely to reduce harassment of middle-class taxpayers if oriented towards punishment of large-scale tax evasion rather than small-scale technical offences. Of course, the closing of various loopholes exploited by large tax evaders will meet with political resistance, and in this one respect the government has to stand firm. Increased autonomy of the tax administration (for example, at least analogous to that offered to the Reserve Bank of India), is a possible method of increasing the distance between officials responsible for initiating prosecutions, and channels of political influence.

These reforms would necessitate a shift in the fundamental orientation of the Indian tax administration away from relatively technical objectives such as clearance of pending assessments, better tax recovery percentages and prosecution of technical offences, toward raising additional revenues, and detecting and punishing tax evasion.

This gives rise to the fundamental question: is there the requisite political will to enact such reforms in India? In many countries with weak, democratically elected governments (such as Argentina, Bolivia, Colombia or Peru), such a will has nevertheless been forthcoming, owing to a severe fiscal crisis, and election of a new government with a clear mandate to carry out deep-seated structural economic reforms. This opportunity was clearly present in India in 1991, when the current government took over. The likelihood of enacting such reforms have progressively weakened ever since.

Figure 5.1
Share of Agricultural GDP in Total

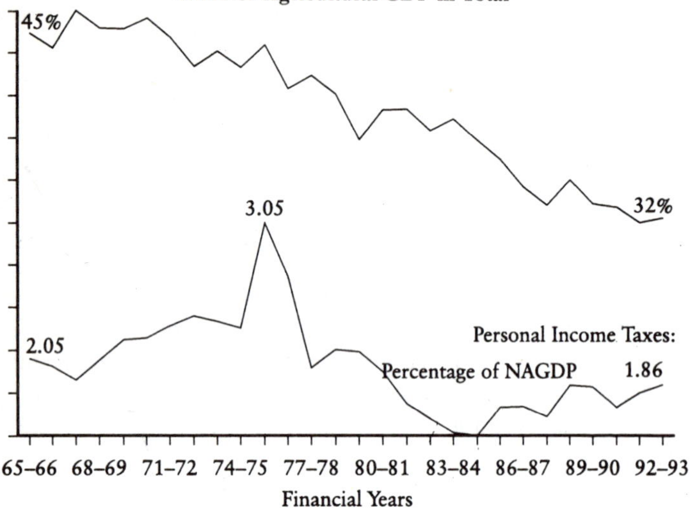

Notes: NAGDP: Non-agricultural GDP.
Source: Authors' calculations.[34]

Figure 5.2
Exemption Limit to Per Capita NNP Ratio

Notes: NNP: Net National Product.
Source: Authors' calculations.[35]

Figure 5.3
Percentage of Income Tax Revenues

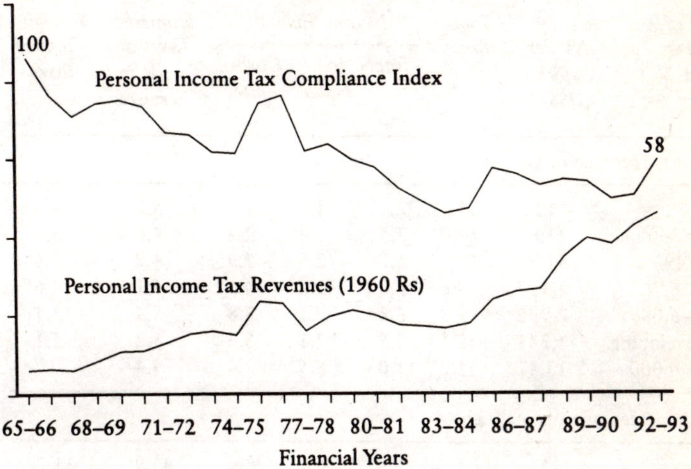

Source: Authors' calculations.[36]

Table 5.1

Tax Structure and Per Capita Income

Range of GNP Per Capita (US$)	*Average GNP Per Capita (US$)*	*Total Taxes*	*Income Taxes*			*Domestic Taxes on Goods and Services*	*Foreign Trade Taxes*	*Other Taxes*
			Total	*Indi-vidual*	*Corp-orate*			
(a) As a percentage of GDP								
India	311	11.3	2.1	1.0	1.1	5.2	4.0	0.1
Below 360	239	14.0	3.5	1.4	2.2	4.6	5.3	0.7
360–749	517	19.7	5.7	2.5	2.9	4.7	7.6	1.5
750–1,619	1,127	18.6	6.0	2.2	4.1	6.1	4.6	1.9
1,620–6,000	2,996	19.8	6.8	2.1	3.8	5.4	3.1	4.7
All Developing	1,241	18.1	5.5	2.1	3.3	5.2	5.1	2.2
Above 6,000	13,477	31.2	11.0	8.5	2.4	9.4	0.7	10.1
(b) As a percentage of total taxes								
India	311	100	18.4	8.7	9.6	45.8	35.1	0.6
Below 360	239	100	24.7	9.7	15.6	32.5	37.8	5.0
360–749	517	100	29.2	12.9	14.9	24.1	38.6	7.7
750–1,619	1,127	100	32.1	11.7	21.9	32.5	24.9	10.4
1,620–6,000	2,996	100	34.4	10.8	19.2	27.3	15.8	24.0
All Developing	1,241	100	30.5	11.5	18.2	28.9	28.4	12.2
Above 6,000	13,477	100	35.1	27.1	7.6	30.2	2.3	32.4

Source: Burgess and Stern (1992).[37]

Table 5.2

Income Tax Revenue Improvements Possible with Best Practice Tax and Enforcement Policies (Percentage of Income Tax Revenue)

Financial Year	*Income Tax Revenue (% of NAGDP)*	*Exemption Limit*	*Marginal Tax Rates*	*Search and Seizure*	*Assessment Efficiency*	*Total*	*Revenue with Best Practice (% of NAGDP)*
1965–66	2.05	41.6	0.0	11.2	2.2	55.0	3.17
1966–67	1.99	40.4	5.3	16.5	0.0	62.2	3.23
1967–68	1.89	37.4	10.6	14.6	2.1	64.7	3.11
1968–69	2.03	36.6	11.2	28.1	22.4	98.2	4.03
1969–70	2.19	34.2	12.7	14.5	27.7	89.2	4.14
1970–71	2.20	31.6	12.6	13.3	28.8	86.2	4.09
1971–72	2.29	14.3	23.4	10.9	33.0	81.4	4.15
1972–73	2.36	10.8	26.1	10.3	26.8	73.9	4.10
1973–74	2.32	3.6	31.3	9.7	20.2	64.9	3.82
1974–75	2.27	2.7	29.4	5.3	23.8	61.2	3.66
1975–76	3.05	16.4	31.9	4.5	24.1	76.9	5.39
1976–77	2.65	16.4	20.5	5.3	23.5	65.7	4.39
1977–78	1.98	25.4	23.8	12.9	27.2	89.3	3.74
1978–79	2.11	23.5	24.8	12.1	16.0	76.3	3.73
1979–80	2.10	19.1	30.1	7.5	12.3	69.0	3.55
1980–81	1.95	12.9	25.2	6.2	13.5	57.8	3.08
1981–82	1.71	29.8	27.2	4.9	15.8	77.8	3.04
1982–83	1.60	25.2	35.6	5.5	16.0	82.3	2.92
1983–84	1.50	19.4	38.3	5.9	24.0	87.7	2.81
1984–85	1.48	15.1	32.1	6.6	37.2	91.0	2.83
1985–86	1.69	21.7	19.6	5.2	40.2	86.7	3.15
1986–87	1.69	17.3	19.6	2.9	39.2	79.0	3.02
1987–88	1.62	12.6	21.5	1.2	42.1	77.3	2.87
1988–89	1.85	8.4	26.0	1.3	43.5	79.1	3.31
1989–90	1.84	5.2	28.3	2.1	39.1	74.6	3.21
1990–91	1.69	0.0	29.7	0.5	39.7	69.9	2.87
1991–92	1.80	3.5	31.7	1.7	40.0	76.9	3.18
1992–93	1.86	10.8	18.0	0.0	33.9	62.7	3.02

Notes: NAGDP: Non-agricultural GDP.
Source: Das-Gupta, Lahiri and Mookherjee (1995).[38]

Table 5.3

Tax Collection Costs and Revenues

Country	*Collection Costs (Per cent of Revenues)*		*Revenues (Per cent of GDP)*	
	1980	1989	1980	1989
Colombia	1.11	0.68	8.4	9.9
Costa Rica	1.15	0.99	12.8	15.0
Ecuador	1.43	0.66	12.8	16.0
Indonesia	NA	NA	22.8	16.0
			(6.6)	(9.2)
Jamaica	NA	1.83	24.8	31.4
Mexico	1.11	0.22	15.3	18.6
Philippines	0.98	0.79	12.5	13.2
Spain	NA	NA	13.6	23.2
Singapore	0.69*	0.80*	17.5	16.9

Notes: 1. Indonesia: Non-Oil Tax Revenue in Parentheses.
2. *1984 and 1990.
Source: Country studies cited in the text.

NOTES

Support from the Center for Institutional Reform and the Informal Sector (IRIS) at the University of Maryland, and the National Institute of Public Finance and Policy, New Delhi, is gratefully acknowledged. Revisions were carried out while Das-Gupta was a Fulbright Research Scholar at Rutgers University. Support from the Fulbright Foundation and the hospitality of Rutgers University are also gratefully acknowledged. The authors are grateful to participants in IRIS seminars held in New Delhi in March and December 1994 for comments on an earlier version of this material (revised March 1995). Finally, the authors thank Satu Kähkönen for her valuable and detailed comments on an earlier draft.

1. For example, Acharya and Associates (1985) estimated the size of the underground economy at 18 per cent of the Gross National Product (GNP) and income evading tax at 186 per cent and 243 per cent of income assessed to tax in 1975–76 and 1980–81 respectively. Virmani obtains an even higher estimate for 1975–76. Acharya, S. and Associates, 1985, *Aspects of the Black Economy in India,* New Delhi: National Institute of Public Finance and Policy; Virmani, A. 1986, 'Measuring Income Tax Incentives Under Evasion: Effective Marginal and Average Rate Schedules', Discussion Paper No. DRD 187, Development Research Department, Washington, DC: The World Bank.

2. See, for example, the studies reported in Bird, R. M. and M. Casanegra de Jantscher, 1992, *Improving Tax Administration in Developing Countries*, Washington, DC: International Monetary Fund.
3. See, for example, Organisation for Economic Cooperation and Development (OECD), 1990, *Taxpayers' Rights and Obligations*, Paris: Organisation for Economic Cooperation and Development; and Hussey, W. M. and D. C. Lubick, 1992, *Basic World Tax Code and Commentary*, Arlington: Tax Analysts.
4. The disparity is more pronounced if social security taxes are included in total tax revenue.
5. See Government of India, 1993, *Indian Economic Statistics (Public Finance), 1991–92*, New Delhi: Ministry of Finance.
6. See Government of India, 1993, *Report of the Comptroller and Auditor General of India: Revenue Receipts—Direct Taxes, 1991–92*, New Delhi: Ministry of Finance.
7. The potential base of the Indian income tax corresponds roughly to personal income from non-agricultural sources, since agricultural income is exempt under the Indian Constitution. Of course, this base is eroded by the exclusion of various incomes for 'merit good' or other less praiseworthy reasons. Since data on personal income from non-agriculture are not available, and non-agricultural GDP is closely correlated with non-agricultural personal income (the correlation coefficient between GDP and personal income for 1960–92 was 0.9987), the former is usually taken as a proxy for the potential base of the income tax.
8. See Government of India, 1991, *Interim Report*, Tax Reforms Committee (TRC). New Delhi: Ministry of Finance.
9. The average ratio for 1960–61 to 1974–75 was 2.18 per cent, compared to 1.78 per cent for the period 1977–78 to 1992–93. The peak was achieved during 1975–76 amid the internal emergency, a period of curtailed civil liberties and harsh police measures.
10. Das-Gupta, A., R. Lahiri and D. Mookherjee, 1995, 'Income Tax Compliance in India: An Empirical Analysis', revised (mimeo), New Brunswick: Rutgers University (hereafter DLM).
11. The compliance index is the ratio of actual income tax collections to the product of non-agricultural GDP (a proxy for the tax base) and the average effective tax rate (computed by averaging the effective tax rate across different income groups). The level of this index is subject to a number of biases, but it is less likely that year-to-year fluctuations are similarly affected. This was confirmed by examining how the index was modified with respect to treatment of deductions, and arrears or exclusion of registered firms for years for which data concerning these variables were available. Indeed, the index is biased upward if black income is not fully reflected in measured non-agricultural GDP. The reader is invited to consult DLM for additional details.
12. Das-Gupta, A. and D. Mookherjee, 1995, 'Tax Amnesties in India: An Empirical Evaluation', Department of Economics (mimeo), Boston: Boston University.
13. Time series of these variables are reported in Das-Gupta, A., D. Mookherjee, and D. P. Panta, 1992, 'Income Tax Enforcement in India: A Preliminary Analysis', Report submitted to the Tax Reforms Committee, Government of India, New Delhi: National Institute of Public Finance and Policy (hereafter DMP).

14. An amnesty during the 1975–77 emergency did have a positive effect on revenues. As pointed out earlier, this was an exceptional period.
15. The estimates in Table 5.2 should be treated with caution and viewed as illustrative, for a variety of reasons. For one, independent switches of assessment policy and search and seizure policy to their respective best practice levels may not be feasible in any one year, given the manpower and budgetary resource constraints on the ITD. The presence of such constraints would, however, reduce the revenue gains possible from changes in conventional enforcement policy, thus strengthening our qualitative conclusion. For another, the estimates are based on coefficient estimates reported in DLM, which are sensitive to changes in the specification of statistical equations. However, the qualitative nature of the results are less sensitive to specification changes.
16. See note 1.
17. DMP, 'Income Tax Enforcement'.
18. Das-Gupta, A. and D. Mookherjee, 1995, 'Manpower Productivity and Organization in Tax Assessment' (mimeo), New Brunswick: Rutgers University.
19. The country studies are based on: (Mexico) Mookherjee, D. 1994. 'Reforms in Income Tax Enforcement in Mexico' (mimeo), New Delhi: Indian Statistical Institute; (Spain) Mookherjee, D. 1994, 'Income Tax Enforcement in Spain' (mimeo), New Delhi: Indian Statistical Institute; (Philippines) Das-Gupta, A. 1994, 'Reforming Income Taxes and Administration in the Philippines' (mimeo), New Delhi: National Institute of Public Finance and Policy; (Singapore) Das-Gupta, A. 1994, 'The Administration of Internal Taxes in Singapore' (mimeo), New Brunswick: Rutgers University.
20. See Gillis, M. 1990, 'Micro- and Macroeconomics of Tax Reform: Indonesia', in R. M. Bird and O. Oldman (eds), *Taxation in Developing Countries*, 4th ed., Baltimore: Johns Hopkins University Press; and Nasution, A. 1994, 'Recent Experience in Tax System Reform with Special Reference to the Impact on Income Distribution and Poverty: The Case of Indonesia' (mimeo), Bangkok: Economic and Social Commission for Asia and the Pacific.
21. See Mookherjee, D. 1994, 'Recent Trends in Income Tax Administration in the CIAT Countries' (mimeo), New Delhi: Indian Statistical Institute.
22. Silvani, C. 1990, 'General Rapporteur's Report' (report presented at the CIAT Technical Conference, Madrid, October 1990).
23. Das-Gupta, 'Taxes in Singapore'.
24. The list of countries includes Costa Rica, the Dominican Republic, Ecuador, El Salvador, Guatemala, Honduras, Panama, Suriname and Uruguay.
25. Besides the basic components mentioned, Mexico has computerised data entry from filed returns; information on sales and purchases by businesses and financial deposits; and has a system for cross-matching these deposits. It has also automated tax collection, issue of notices to delinquents, tax refunds and audit selection. In addition to having computerised all subsystems that the Mexicans have, Spain is also able to utilise information on luxury expenditures by taxpayers, identify nonfilers and provide computerised assistance to taxpayers. The computer database is also utilised more extensively for managerial control in Spain. Essentially the same level of computerisation as in Spain is present in Singapore. However, Singapore also has automated return filing and tax payment systems.

26. These countries are Costa Rica, Chile, El Salvador, Spain, Guatemala and Portugal.
27. For a comprehensive review of presumptive taxation see, for example, Tanzi, V. and M. Casanegra de Jantscher, 1987, 'Presumptive Income Taxation: Administrative, Efficiency and Equity Aspects', Working Paper WP/87/54, Fiscal Affairs Department, Washington, DC: International Monetary Fund.
28. Furthermore, selection of cases for audit is unscientific or largely discretionary: See DMP.
29. Some countries such as Mexico have also privatised information-processing functions and the printing and distribution of tax forms.
30. Further details of these estimates are available in DLM.
31. Furthermore, the tax structure identified by the regression as best practice from the point of view of revenues (the 1965–66 structure) involved high tax rates which are undesirable on other grounds.
32. The research of Virmani, 'Measuring Income Tax Incentives Under Evasion', suggests that non-filing comprises the bulk of the tax evasion problem in India.
33. Das-Gupta and Mookherjee, 1995, 'Manpower Productivity and Organization in Tax Assessment' (mimeo), New Brunswick: Rutgers University.
34. These calculations draw heavily on Das-Gupta, A. and D. Mookherjee, 1998. *Incentives and Institutional Reform in Tax Enforcement, An Analysis of Developing Country Experience*, Ch. 3–4, New Delhi: Oxford University Press.
35. Ibid.
36. Ibid.
37. Burgess, R. and N. Stern, 1992, 'Taxation and Development', Development Economics Research Programme, STICERD, DEP No. 42, London: London School of Economics. The figures are based on three-year averages for years closest to 1987 for which data were available. GDP per capita is measured in 1987 US dollars for the year 1987. The sample included eighty-two countries.
38. See note 10.

6

Fiscal Adjustment and the Role of State Governments in India

M. Govinda Rao

State governments play an important role in both directing and regulating economic activities in the Indian federation. In 1991–92, the share of state governments in aggregate expenditures was more than 55 per cent. About 85 per cent of spending was on social services such as education, health and social security and welfare payments and almost 60 per cent of spending was on economic services such as agricultural development and extension, irrigation, industrial promotion and roads. The share of state governments in raising taxes was about 43 per cent of the total and they collected almost 55 per cent of the total domestic trade taxes. Therefore, the method of raising revenues and the level and composition of spending by the state governments can have important consequences on the efficiency of resource allocation.

In a liberalised economic environment, state governments will have to play a relatively more important role than in the past. Previously, although planning was implemented in the context of a mixed economy, it necessitated centralisation of economic power. However, as the economy is liberalised, a greater degree of fiscal decentralisation becomes necessary. Significant increase in the outlay on human resource development and its cost-effective spending is critical to improve the overall productivity in the economy, and the primary responsibility for human resource development rests with the state governments. Further, with the 73rd and 74th Constitutional Amendments enabling substates to decentralise and specifying the powers and functions of rural and urban local governments, the state governments will have to substantially augment their resources.

While the expenditure commitments of the state governments are likely to increase, they are faced with a relatively hard budget constraint. They do not have independent borrowing powers; the volume of their borrowing is determined by the Union Ministry of Finance and the Planning Commission in consultation with the Reserve Bank of India. Given that the Central Government itself is faced with a difficult fiscal situation, the prospect of obtaining a larger share of central revenues than in the past by way of transfers does not appear to be bright either. Therefore, unless the state governments undertake steps to improve their fiscal management, and adopt innovative methods to contain unproductive expenditures and raise revenues, a fiscal adjustment programme cannot be brought to successful fruition.

In this chapter, an attempt is made to identify the problem areas in states' revenue and expenditure policies and to suggest policy changes needed to improve fiscal management in the states. Section I analyses fiscal imbalances in the states and brings out their difficult fiscal situation. In Section II, the problem is evaluated in terms of the inability of the state governments to contain their fast-growing current expenditures and the consequent displacement of capital expenditures, particularly on infrastructural sectors. In Section III, the adverse efficiency consequences of raising revenues from tax and non-tax sources is highlighted. Section IV indicates the directions for reform at the state level.

I FISCAL IMBALANCES OF THE STATE GOVERNMENTS

The acute budgetary difficulties and the continuous deterioration in the states' financial position is brought out in Tables 6.1 and 6.2. During the 1970s, although the growth of the states' own revenues lagged behind the growth of their current expenditures, the buoyancy in Central Government transfers helped to balance their current accounts. However, in the 1980s, the growth of current expenditures accelerated and the transfers from the Central Government decelerated. Consequently, the current budgetary position of the state governments deteriorated from a surplus of 1.2 per cent of Gross Domestic Product (GDP) in the mid-1970s to a deficit of about 1 per cent of GDP in 1990–91 and remained at that level thereafter. In absolute terms, the current account deficits of the state governments in 1994–95 amounted to Rs 83.6 billion.

The principal cause of states' budgetary problems has been the high and accelerating growth of current expenditures. In particular, in the 1980s, the current expenditures, on an average, grew 17.6 per cent per year—almost two percentage points higher than the growth of revenues. Of course, even in the 1970s, current expenditures increased at 16.6 per cent, but as already discussed, that was possible because the transfers from the Central Government increased at almost 20 per cent per year. With increasing pressure on the Centre's own finances in the latter part of the 1980s, the growth of Central Government transfers failed to keep pace with growing current expenditures. Consequently, a deficit emerged in the current account in 1986–87 and widened thereafter. At the same time, with the effective implementation of the 'overdraft regulation scheme'—the scheme to restrict states' power to borrow from the Reserve Bank of India for ways-and-means purposes since 1985—the states had to accommodate increasing current expenditures by displacing capital expenditures. Thus, the growth of capital expenditures decelerated from about 20 per cent in the 1970s to just 9.6 per cent in the 1980s, and as a proportion of GDP it declined from 3.9 per cent in 1980–81 to 1.2 per cent in 1992–93.

It is important to note that the states' current budgetary deficits or governmental dissavings have grown steadily in the 1980s in spite of tax revenues registering a growth rate of about 16 per cent per year, up from the 14.8 per cent seen in the previous decade. This was possible because the economy grew at an average rate of 5.3 per cent during this period, much higher than the 3.5 per cent recorded in the previous decade. The non-tax revenues, however, grew only 12 per cent per year during the 1980s and even this was possibly due to very high increases in the taxation of natural resources by way of cess on coal, which was exported to non-residents to a significant extent.[1] The revenues from user charges and returns from public undertakings by way of interest and dividend receipts were virtually stagnant in real terms.

The high and increasing current budgetary deficits of the state governments necessitated a larger volume of borrowing. At the same time, borrowed funds were increasingly employed to finance current expenditures. Even capital expenditures on specific projects were not used to create either direct revenue-yielding assets or infrastructural facilities. Consequently, debt servicing and repayment liabilities had to be met by incurring more loans. Thus, the outstanding liabilities of the state governments, which were Rs 216 billion in March 1980, increased by about seven times in fourteen years to reach Rs 1548 billion in March 1994. As a proportion of the GDP, the indebtedness of the state governments increased from 17.6 per cent in 1980–81 to 19.3 per cent in 1994–95. Even after the finance commissions tried to mitigate the hardship of the state governments by periodically rescheduling and writing off of the states' loans, the repayment liability in 1993–94 amounted to Rs 50.9 billion; this formed 21.3 per cent of their capital receipts during the year.

Thus, the state governments face an explosive cycle of current expenditure growth and are in the throes of a debt trap. At the same time, the tax revenues of the state governments have grown fairly rapidly and it may be difficult to achieve much more acceleration. Therefore, fiscal imbalances have to be phased out mainly by compressing expenditures. If eliminating current budgetary deficits in the year 2000 is taken as the target, and if the revenues continue to increase at the current rate, the growth of current expenditures will have to be decelerated by 2.6 percentage points to 14 per cent per year. In fact, growth of expenditures other than interest payments will have to be brought down to 12.5 per cent. Alternatively, if the current trend in expenditures continues, the revenue receipts of the state governments will have to increase at over 17.5 per cent per year, an increase of more than two percentage points. This is by no means an easy task. Fiscal correction at the state level, therefore, will have to examine the usefulness of every item of expenditure and revenue and take corrective measures to eliminate unproductive expenditures. At the same time, it is important to ensure that the revenues are raised in the least distortionary manner.

Special interest group politics, however, is an obstacle in achieving the fiscal correction. In fact, the budgetary difficulties of the state governments, to a large extent, are due to the influence of special interest groups on the fiscal decisions of the state governments. As these groups compete to gain from the benefits of expenditure policies, a more-than-proportionate allocation of public expenditures is incurred on quasi-public goods which enhances the share of current expenditures in the total. Thus, in the 1970s, current expenditures increased at a fast rate; this was facilitated by the buoyancy in central transfers. But the trend continued even when the budget constraint hardened in the 1980s: current expenditures simply displaced capital expenditures. At the same time, as public services could not be priced at economic rates, revenue from user charges continued to stagnate. Uneconomic pricing along with inefficient operation resulted in poor returns from the large investments in public enterprises. While the implementation of reforms is an extremely difficult task owing to the influence of interest groups, fiscal correction is nevertheless imperative. However, it is important to ensure that the revenues are raised in the least distortionary manner.

II STATE GOVERNMENT EXPENDITURES: MAJOR ISSUES

The economic implications of expenditure growth are clearly seen when the government expenditure trends are analysed by classifying them into economic and functional categories broadly on the lines indicated in the United Nations Manual (1958).[2] The analysis in terms of economic categories helps to identify whether the expenditure growth was due to fast increases in government consumption expenditures, or transfer payments to the private sector, or increased capital formation. Expenditure analysis of functional categories helps to identify the relative importance of general administration; social services like education, health, housing, social security and welfare and economic services like agricultural and industrial promotion, and building of physical infrastructures in aggregate expenditures.

It may be seen from Table 6.3 that since the mid-1970s, the growth of current expenditures has been high; this has accelerated further in the 1980s. Per capita current expenditures at constant prices in the latter half of the 1970s grew at 6 per cent per year and accelerated to 6.8 per cent during the 1980s even as per capita aggregate expenditures decelerated from 6.3 per cent to 5.2 per cent during the same period. In fact, in the 1980s, per capita capital expenditures actually declined to 1.2 per cent per year.

Among the various items of current expenditure in the 1980s, interest payments, transfers and subsidies grew at the fastest rate

(8.3 per cent) followed by compensation to employees (7.4 per cent). A major reason for the growth of transfers and subsidies is the strong influence exerted by the farm lobby and consequently, subsidies for irrigation and spending on rural development schemes. The expenditures on wages and salaries increased due to increases in employment as well as wage rates. The net employment grew at about 3.6 per cent per year[3] and the increase in emoluments per employee in constant prices, on an average, was about 3.8 per cent per year. Partly, this shows the ability of the government employees to secure wage increases faster than the economic growth. The influence of these interest groups in expenditure decisions appears to be stronger in the 1980s than in the 1970s.

The implicit subsidies due to the influence of special interest groups is much larger than the explicit subsidies mentioned above. As each interest group competes to enhance its benefits from public services and minimise tax payments, its share of total expenditures on quasi-public goods increases, and direct payments from the beneficiaries by way of user charges tends to decline. In the case of state governments, as shown in Table 6.6, the subsidies implicit in the provision of social and economic services in 1987–88 amounted to Rs 275 billion or 8.3 per cent of the GDP. These subsidies grew at over 18 per cent per year in nominal terms during the decade 1978–88.[4]

In contrast, expenditures on the maintenance of assets and capital formation grew at low rates. As shown in Table 6.4, per capita expenditure in the 1980s on net government maintenance grew at only 2.7 per cent and the growth of per capita capital expenditures was just 1.5 per cent. It is further seen from Table 6.3 that the negative growth of capital expenditures in this period was mainly due to the decline in allocations to physical infrastructures such as roads, irrigation works and industrial infrastructure under economic services (– 0.3 per cent), and school and hospital buildings under social services (– 2.7 per cent) as well as net loans given to public enterprises (– 3.1 per cent) including electricity boards and road transport corporations.

Table 6.3 shows that expenditure on interest payments registered the fastest growth during the 1980s. This was caused by a phenomenal increase in states' indebtedness as well as increases in effective rate of interest on states' borrowing. Indebtedness of the state governments in nominal terms increased at an average of about 16 per cent per year from the 1980s on; the average rate of interest on their borrowing increased from 6.1 per cent in 1981–82 to 11.7 per cent in 1991–92.

Expenditures on social services such as education, health, housing, social security and welfare continued to increase at a high rate even as the budget constraints of the states tightened, particularly after the mid-1980s when the overdraft regulation scheme was introduced. A large part of the growth in expenditures must be attributed to fast increases in the unit cost of providing the services rather than the quantity or quality of the services provided. Wages and salaries constitute over 80 per cent of expenditures on social services and much of the increase in these expenditures was due to an increase in wage rates. The analysis of per capita education expenditures, for example, shows that the growth of per capita expenditure (constant prices) increased at 6.6 per cent per year during the latter half of the 1980s and of this, 3.5 percentage points were attributable to the real increase in the per-employee salary alone.

However, in spite of recording very high growth rates during the last decade, the level of expenditures on social services continued to be low. Expenditures on education in 1990–91, for example, were less than 3.5 per cent of the GDP. This compares poorly with the average levels prevailing in the developing countries, that is, 4.1 per cent.[5] At the same time, of the total expenditure on education, the share of primary education was just about 40 per cent. Moreover, since 1991–92, the effect of deceleration in central transfers to states and attempted expenditure compression by the states themselves has been to reduce the share of social services expenditure in the total expenditures.[6] Similarly, as a ratio of the GDP, expenditure on medical and public health was less than 1.5 per cent, housing and urban development was just about 0.3 per cent and the amount spent on social security and welfare was 0.8 per cent. The Constitution assigns a predominant role to the states in the provision of these services, and satisfactory provision of these services calls for substantial increase in the outlay on them.

The problem is not merely one of low levels of expenditure on social and economic infrastructures but also their uneven spread. The study by Rao and Sen (1993) has shown that generally per capita expenditures are highest in the states with high per capita incomes. The interstate variations in per capita expenditure levels were particularly significant in social and economic services. However, this cannot be attributed to their better tax efforts. The failure of the intergovernmental transfer mechanism to offset the fiscal disabilities of the states with low tax bases is the principal reason for the skewed distribution of per capita expenditures among the states. It is also seen that expenditure levels are high in the states where the physical levels of services are high (Rao and Sen, 1993).[7]

The uneven distribution of expenditures clearly indicates unequal access to physical and social infrastructure. This, in turn, results in uneven flow of private investments and accentuates inequalities in the standards of living in different regions. The issue is particularly relevant when the transition is attempted from a self-reliant planned development strategy to a market economy with important roles assigned to both domestic and foreign investments. Besides the economic reasons, hindering less-developed regions' efforts to provide certain minimum standards of social and physical infrastructures may not be politically acceptable. This calls for reforms in the intergovernmental transfer system to make them purposive and targeted in offsetting the fiscal disabilities of the less developed states.

III STATE GOVERNMENT REVENUES: MAJOR ISSUES

Tax Revenue

The revenues of the state governments show an interesting trend as may be seen from Table 6.5. The tax revenues of the state governments grew fairly rapidly, at 16.1 per cent per year during the 1980s. The growth performance was particularly impressive in the case of indirect taxes such as sales tax and state excise duties. In contrast, direct taxes, particularly the revenue from land and agricultural income tax, was not buoyant. This is due to the fact that none of the state governments levy taxes on agricultural incomes except the incomes received from plantations. The exemption of agricultural incomes from personal income taxation continues to be a major avenue of tax evasion and avoidance. The tax can be evaded simply by misclassifying the non-agricultural incomes as agricultural incomes.[8] Thus, increases in revenue productivity of the state tax system have to come about mainly by reforming the agricultural taxes.

The indirect taxes which contribute over 85 per cent of the revenues of the state governments have grown fairly rapidly during the 1980s. At the same time, states' indirect taxes have been a source of inefficiency and relative price distortions. In particular, the sales taxes levied by the states are characterised by a narrow base and complicated structures. The taxation of inputs and capital goods enhances unintended changes in the relative prices. The taxation of interstate transactions impedes the free flow of interstate trade, distorts resource allocation across states and causes interregional inequity. These issues will be discussed further in some detail.[9]

A salient feature of the states' sales tax system is its narrow base. The Constitution allows the state governments to levy the sales tax only on goods; they cannot levy taxes on services. In addition, the states have found it administratively convenient to levy the sales tax predominantly at the first point of sale and therefore, the value added in all subsequent stages is excluded from the tax base. For these reasons, the states' narrow tax base requires them to levy the tax at high rates in order to collect a given amount of revenue. The levy of pre-retail sales taxes, in addition, causes cascading and distorts relative prices of different commodities.

Allocative distortions are compounded by the taxation of inputs and capital goods. For reasons of revenue, states levy taxes on inputs and capital goods alike, although some of them levy the tax at concessional rates or relieve a part of the tax paid on inputs. In a closed economy where the prices, by and large, are marked up over the average cost, cascading taxes increase the prices more than the tax element. They also alter the relative prices in unintended ways. Further, such a tax system makes it difficult to completely relieve the tax on exports.

Another serious shortcoming of the sales tax system is its complicated nature. Although the tax is levied predominantly at the first point of sale, on some commodities the tax is levied at the last point, or at multiple points. Excessive rate differentiation across commodities made by the states for equity reasons has caused severe problems of classification, tax avoidance and litigation. The interstate competition to attract trade has further added to rate differentiation. This has, in addition, imparted irrationality to the rate structures.[10] At present, the number of tax rate categories varies from six in Orissa to twenty-one in Bihar and Gujarat.

Another serious problem arising from the prevailing sales tax system is the interstate tax exportation. The taxation of interstate sales at the rate of 4 per cent has virtually segregated the states' economies into different tariff zones and substantially reduced the gains accruing from an integrated common market. The taxation of inputs and capital goods under the states' Sales Tax Acts has accentuated this phenomenon. Even in cases where the tax system allows setoff of the tax paid on inputs, in some states the relief is limited to the goods sold within the state. Thus, interstate sales and even branch transfers carry the burden of input taxes as well. Besides being a source of inefficiency, the taxation of residents in the consuming states by the producing states has resulted in perverse resource flows. Trade and industry has tried to avoid the interstate sales tax through branch transfers, and there has been considerable pressure on the Central Government by the state governments to levy the tax on such branch transfers. So far, the Central Government has avoided such a short-sighted policy. Surely, tax evasion cannot be condoned, but it is necessary that the tax itself should not be undesirable or unreasonable.

Both for reasons of allocative efficiency and interregional equity, interstate sales tax should be abolished. The economic gains from a federation—better integration of the country and rational resource allocation—cannot be realised unless such barriers to interstate trade are removed.

An even more serious barrier to the interregional movement of goods than the interstate sales tax is the levy of 'octroi' or the tax on the entry of goods into a local area for consumption, use or sale. The Constitution allows the state governments to levy such a tax and in a number of states, this source of revenue is the mainstay of the urban local body finances. The levy of octroi which is in the nature of an import duty into the local body jurisdiction has segregated the country into several tariff zones. The allocative distortions from this tax have not been measured, but it is agreed that the distortions could be considerable.

Non-tax Revenues

The non-tax revenues of the states mainly consist of user charges on services rendered and interest receipts from the loans given to the rest of the economy along with profits and dividends from their investments.

An important feature of the state finances is the poor and declining cost recoveries on social and economic services provided by the state governments. It may be seen from Table 6.6 that the recovery rate on social services in 1987–88 was just 2.8 per cent of the cost of these services. In the category of higher education, the cost recovery as a proportion of the cost of providing the service declined from 6.7 per cent in 1977–78 to 1.7 per cent in 1987–88. Even in commercial sectors such as irrigation and power, the cost recovery was less than 30 per cent of the cost of providing the service. The study by Rao and Mundle (1992) shows that the cost recovery as a proportion of the cost of delivering the service declined in every sector during the decade, 1978–88 and for social and economic services taken together, the decline was from 22 to 14 per cent. Consequently, the implicit subsidies in the provision of these services increased significantly and as these were poorly targeted, they benefited better-off sections and regions disproportionally.[11]

Another reason for the stagnancy in non-tax revenues is the poor financial performance of the public enterprises managed by the state governments. The electricity boards incurred a loss of 12.6 per cent of the capital invested; investments in these in 1992–93 amounted to Rs 62 billion. Similarly, net losses of the road transport corporations in 1992–93 amounted to Rs 3.6 billion, or 9.4 per cent of the capital investments. In addition, there were 829 state-level enterprises in 1989–90.

Compared to the normative return of Rs 1.75 billion reckoned by the Ninth Finance Commission, these enterprises yielded a dividend of just Rs 480 million. The number of state-level enterprises by March 31, 1992 had gone up to 875, but their financial performance continued to remain as dismal as before.[12] Overall improvement in the non-tax revenues cannot be brought about unless the state-level enterprises are professionally managed, which would vest them with sufficient autonomy and ensure accountability. It is also important that user charges at proper rates should be levied on social and economic services. The pricing of the services at less than their average cost (and implicit subsidies arising from it) can be justified only if the social benefits of the services are larger than the private benefits or if it has a high redistributive content.

Uneconomic pricing of many of the commercial activities of the state governments has not only resulted in the implicit subsidies accruing to better-off sections of society, it has constrained the government from using its resources to make adequate investments in critical sectors such as education, health, power, roads and irrigation and embankment works. In the power sector where there is a perennial excess demand situation, the response of the government has been to invite foreign investors by assuring them a guaranteed rate of return on their investments. In the absence of economic pricing of power, this could entail sizeable budgetary support.

IV CONCLUSION

The fiscal adjustment process initiated in 1991 at the instance of the International Monetary Fund has been largely confined to the Central Government. Perhaps non-involvement of the state governments has been guided by the belief that, in effect, they do not have independent borrowing powers, and that the Central Government can effectively control stabilisation policies.

Such a strategy, however, may have serious consequences on the efficiency in resource allocation. In the Indian context, while the Central Government can effectively control the volume of fiscal deficits of the state governments, it cannot prevent the latter from running deficits in their current accounts. The influence of special interest groups on public expenditure policies results in very high increases in current expenditures; the hard budget constraints faced by the state governments only cause the displacement of expenditures on physical infrastructure.

There is a serious problem of growing fiscal imbalance at the state level in terms of excess of current expenditure over current revenues. This, on the one hand, is attributed to the growth of current expenditures, particularly in wages and salaries, interest payments, transfers and subsidies, and on the other, to the inability of the state governments to levy proper user charges and get economic returns on their investments. At the same time, the tax system, although reasonably productive in terms of revenue performance, has been a source of inefficiency and inequity. The sales tax, in particular, has altered relative prices in unintended ways, caused distortions in the production structure, impeded free flow of trade across the country and led to inequitable resource flows from the less-developed to more-developed regions.

Therefore, reforms in both tax and expenditure policies at the state level are extremely important for the successful implementation of the fiscal adjustment programme in India. Unless unproductive expenditures are compressed, attempts at stabilisation may themselves be sources of allocative distortion and may work against structural adjustment. Similarly, reforming the sales tax system is essential to imparting competitiveness to Indian manufactures. This should be done by broadening the base, reducing the rate, lessening rate differentiation, simplifying the tax structure, getting rid of the taxes on inputs and capital goods and removing the taxes on interstate transactions. It is also important to privatise loss-making public enterprises as most of them do not serve any social purpose, but are merely used by various special interest groups for their own benefit. Even if some public enterprises make profits, there is no reason why they should be run by the state governments unless they have a clear comparative advantage in terms of social benefits.

Table 6.1

Growth of States' Revenues and Expenditures (Per cent per year)

Item of Revenue/Expenditure	*1974–75 to 1980–81*	*1980–81 to 1991–92*	*1974–75 to 1991–92*
States' Revenue Receipts			
Own Tax Revenue	14.8	16.1	15.7
Non-Tax Revenue	11.8	12.7	12.4
Total	14.2	15.5	15.1
Central Transfers to States	20.0	15.4	16.9
Total Revenue Receipts	16.8	15.6	15.9
States' Expenditures			
Current Expenditure	16.6	17.6	17.3
Capital Expenditure	19.9	9.6	12.6
Total Expenditure	17.4	15.8	16.3

Notes: Growth rates have been calculated by employing the Kinked Exponential Model (Boyce, 1986).[14] Figures for 1991–92 are revised estimates.

Source: Indian Economic Statistics/Public Finance Statistics, Ministry of Finance, Government of India (relevant years).

Table 6.2

State's Budgetary Deficits

Year	*States' Revenue Deficits (Rs Million)*	*States' Fiscal Deficit (Rs Million)*		*States' Revenue Deficit as Percentage of GDP*	*States' Fiscal Deficit as Percentage of GDP*		*Aggregate Fiscal Deficit (Rs Million)*		*Aggregate Fiscal Deficit as Percentage of GDP*	
		Gross	*Net*		*Gross*	*Net*	*Gross*	*Net*	*Gross*	*Net*
1980–81	+ 14,850	37,130	17,150	+ 1.1	2.7	1.3	104,480	72,590	7.7	5.3
1985–86	+ 6,540	75,120	47,990	+ 0.2	2.9	1.8	236,210	153,070	9.0	5.8
1990–91	53,090	187,870	145,320	1.0	3.5	2.7	534,410	395,010	10.0	7.4
1991–92	56,510	189,000	157,460	0.9	3.1	2.6	458,520	341,500	7.4	5.5
1992–93	51,140	208,920	157,700	0.7	3.0	2.2	521,440	422,030	7.4	6.0
1993–94 (RE)	60,550	233,120	182,420	0.8	2.9	2.3	714,560	576,920	9.0	7.2
1994–95 (BE)	83,650	297,380	231,460	0.9	3.2	2.5	709,650	589,010	7.8	6.4

Notes: Estimated on the basis of implicit GDP estimates derived by fiscal deficit/GDP ratio of Centre at 6 per cent.
RE: Revised Estimates; BE: Budget Estimates; + Indicates surplus.
Source: Annual Report 1993–94, Reserve Bank of India, Bombay.

Table 6.3

Growth of Government Expenditures by Functional Categories in 1981–82 Prices: All Selected States (Per cent per year)

	Current Expenditure			*Capital Expenditure*			*Total Expenditure*		
	1974–75 to 1981–82	*1981–82 to 1990–91*	*1974–75 to 1990–91*	*1974–75 to 1981–82*	*1981–82 to 1990–91*	*1974–75 to 1990–91*	*1974–75 to 1981–82*	*1981–82 to 1990–91*	*1974–75 to 1990–91*
Administrative Services	3.5	8.0	6.1	11.3	2.8	6.2	3.7	7.9	6.2
Interest Payments	3.6	11.7	8.3				3.6	11.7	8.3
Social Services	6.0	6.4	6.3	9.0	– 2.7	5.6	6.2	6.3	6.2
Economic Services	8.0	5.3	6.4	6.2	– 0.3	2.3	7.3	3.6	5.1
Net Loans and Advances				8.9	– 3.1	1.7	8.9	– 3.1	1.7
Total Expenditure	6.0	6.8	6.5	7.6	– 1.2	2.3	6.3	5.2	5.6

Source: Rao and Sen (1993).[15]

Table 6.4

Growth Per Capita of State Government Expenditures by Economic Categories at Constant Prices (Per cent per year)

Expenditure Items: Economic Categories	*1974–75 to 1981–82*	*1981–82 to 1989–90*	*1974–75 to 1989–90*
Consumption Expenditure			
Compensation to Employees	5.86	7.37	6.32
Net Government Maintenance	8.39	2.72	5.25
Total	5.88	6.22	6.86
Transfers			
Subsidies	34.70	6.02	18.16
Transfer to Local Bodies	1.71	7.43	4.80
Other Transfers	6.70	8.48	7.67
Total	7.69	8.35	8.85
Total Current	6.38	7.15	6.89
Gross Fixed Capital Formation	9.25	4.55	6.65
Financial Outlay	3.01	4.84	4.01
Total Capital Transfers and Advances			
Local Bodies	9.68	1.95	5.38
Others	8.78	– 2.06	2.71
Total	8.76	– 1.20	3.19
Total Capital Expenditure	8.35	1.49	4.54

Source: Rao and Ṣen (1993).[16]

Table 6.5

Growth of State's Revenue (Per cent per year)

Item of Revenue	*1974–75 to 1980–81*	*1980–81 to 1991–92*	*1974–75 to 1991–92*
Land Revenue and Agricultural Taxes	7.8	12.2	9.8
Stamps and registration	15.2	16.8	15.9
Sales Taxes	15.0	16.0	15.7
Taxes on Transport	14.5	14.9	14.7
State Excise Duties	14.8	17.0	16.2
Other Taxes	13.0	14.5	13.8
Total Taxes of the State Governments	14.8	16.1	15.7
Non-Tax Revenues	11.8	12.1	12.4
Total States' Own Revenues	14.2	15.5	15.1

Notes: Growth rates have been calculated by employing the Kinked Exponential Model (Boyce, 1986).[17] Figures for 1991–92 are revised estimates.

Source: Indian Economic Statistics/Public Finance Statistics, Ministry of Finance, Government of India (relevant years).

Table 6.6

Subsidies in Major States

	1987–88 Subsidies (Rs million)	*Per cent of Total*	*Recovery Rate (Per cent)*
Social Services			
Education:	83,090	30.3	1.4
Higher Education	19,940	7.3	1.7
Medical and Public Health	25,910	9.4	2.7
Water Supply, Sanitation, etc.	21,110	7.7	5.9
Other Social Services	15,280	5.6	5.6
Total Social Services	145,390	52.9	2.8
Economic Services			
Agriculture and Allied Activities	40,650	14.8	28.6
Irrigation	47,050	17.1	20.6
Power and Energy	16,330	6.0	26.5
Industry and Minerals	7,050	2.6	28.4
Transport and Communication	17,450	6.4	12.7
Other Economic Services	710	0.2	
Total Economic Services	129,240	47.2	24.6
Total Subsidy	274,630	100.0	14.4

Source: Rao and Mundle (1992).[18]

NOTES

Financial assistance from the Center for Institutional Reform and the Informal Sector (IRIS), University of Maryland, is gratefully acknowledged. Thanks are also due to Dr. Satu Kähkönen for detailed comments on the earlier draft of this material.

1. The royalties on all major minerals are determined by the Central Government. The state governments levied a cess on the royalties, ostensibly to develop the regions surrounding the coal mines. In 1992, however, the Supreme Court of India ruled that the levy of cess is not according to the provisions of the Constitution.
2. The United Nations, 1958, *A Manual on Economic and Functional Classification of Government Budget*, New York: The United Nations.
3. Rao, M. G. 1992, 'Proposals for State Level Budgetary Reforms', *Economic and Political Weekly*, 2 February.
4. Rao, M. G. and S. Mundle, 1992, 'An Analysis of Changes in State Government Subsidies: 1977–87', in A. Bagchi, J. L. Bajaj and W. A. Byrd (eds), *State Finances in India*, New Delhi: Vikas Publishing House.

5. The estimate relates to 1987. See United Nations Educational, Scientific and Cultural Organisation (UNESCO), 1989, *Statistical Year Book*, Paris: UNESCO.
6. Gupta, S. P. and A. K. Sarkar, 1994, 'Fiscal Correction and Human Resource Development', *Economic and Political Weekly*, 26 March.
7. Rao, M. G. and T. K. Sen, 1993, 'Government Expenditure in India—Level, Growth and Composition' (mimeo), New Delhi: National Institute of Public Finance and Policy.
8. It is not uncommon to see a large number of rich individuals owning farmhouses in the vicinity of metropolitan areas as a tax management strategy.
9. For a detailed analysis of the problems with domestic trade taxes in India, see National Institute of Public Finance and Policy, A. Bagchi (team leader), 1994, 'Reform of Domestic Trade Taxes in India: Issues and Options'. New Delhi: National Institute of Public Finance and Policy. See also Rao, M. G. and F. Vaillancourt, 1994, 'Interstate Tax Disharmony in India: A Comparative Perspective', *Publius: The Journal of Federalism*, 24(4): 99–114.
10. In Punjab, for example, motor cars are taxed at a lower rate than food grains.
11. See note 4.
12. Shankar, T. L., R. K. Mishra and R. Nandagopal, 1994, 'State Level Public Expenditure in India', *Economic and Political Weekly*, 27 August.
13. Even as a redistributional device, making direct transfers to targeted groups is preferable to general subsidisation arising from the pricing policy.
14. Boyce, J. K. 1986, 'Kinked Exponential Models for Growth Rate Estimation', *Oxford Bulletin of Economics and Statistics*, 48(4).
15. See note 7.
16. Ibid.
17. See note 14.
18. See note 4.

7

Tax Amnesties in India: An Empirical Evaluation

Arindam Das-Gupta and Dilip Mookherjee

Failure to impose sufficiently high penalties for tax offences is often cited as a cause of widespread tax evasion, especially in developing countries. This view obtains support from the theoretical analyses of Becker (1968), and Allingham and Sandmo (1972), which predict that tax evasion is unambiguously reduced by higher penalties, thereby suggesting that enforcement policies should optimally involve the use of maximal penalties.[1] In practice, penalties for most offences tend to be non-maximal.[2] Indeed, a common practice in many countries is to offer amnesties for past offences in an effort to encourage voluntary disclosure of past tax evasion. Amnesties have been used by both developed and developing countries in recent years. For instance, during the 1980s, tax amnesty programmes have been employed in more than half the states in the United States, as well as Belgium, France, Ireland and Italy. Among developing countries, they have been employed in Argentina, Bolivia, Chile, Colombia, Ecuador, Panama, Peru, Mexico and the Philippines more than once in the recent past.

India has also offered a large number of amnesty programmes in past decades: in 1951, 1965, 1975, 1980, 1985, 1986 and in 1991. Since 1975, therefore, they have been offered frequently and predictably: once every five or six years. Section I of the paper discusses the nature of these programmes in greater detail. These amnesties have formed part of a general climate of weakening enforcement of the Indian income tax. Other manifestations include a lower intensity of prosecution effort for tax evasion, and the introduction of various forms of out-of-court settlement for evaded income taxes due from large taxpayers.[3]

The purpose of this chapter is to provide empirical estimates of the revenue effects of various temporary amnesty schemes offered in India since 1965. The approach used follows the theoretical framework laid out in a companion paper by Das-Gupta and Mookherjee (1995), which examines the role of amnesty programmes in allowing taxpayers to launder previously undisclosed (black) assets. Section II of the chapter provides a broad summary of the main results of this approach. These results stand in contrast to a number of prevailing views concerning the usefulness of temporary amnesty schemes. The differences stem from the indirect revenue effects that arise from the effects of the amnesty on filing behaviour and on subsequent collections from penalties. Being spread out over a number of years both preceding and following the amnesty year, these indirect effects tend to be less visible than the direct collections from the amnesty. The indirect effects are, however, typically adverse, and can outweigh the direct effects.

Empirical results pertaining to the revenue effects of the amnesties are presented in Section III. Utilising aggregate data for the period 1965–66 to 1992–93, these effects are estimated after controlling for other important influences on aggregate income tax revenues. The temporal specification of dummy variables used to capture the effect of amnesties draws on the theoretical predictions described in Section II.

Based on the resulting estimates, a number of broad conclusions concerning the effect of amnesties in India emerge. The three amnesties that took place before the mid-1980s were arguably unanticipated by taxpayers. Of these, only the 1975 amnesty lead to significant revenue gains, of the order of 25 per cent of annual revenues. The 1965 and 1980 amnesties had negative overall effects on revenues, even during the amnesty year itself.[4]

Following 1980, amnesties have been periodic and therefore anticipated. Their indirect revenue effects were adverse, and outweighed direct amnesty receipts. Nevertheless, the overall revenue effects of amnesty programmes from 1980 onwards have been small relative to aggregate income tax revenues, with estimated effects frequently turning out to be statistically insignificant.

The results of these effects provide support for the hypothesis that negative indirect compliance effects or falling penalty collections can overwhelm the direct receipts from amnesties. This is particularly true when amnesties are offered at predictable intervals. In light of this, and the fact that the revenue impact of amnesties appears to be shrinking progressively, Indian tax administrators would be well advised to resort to alternative methods for improving enforcement of the income tax.

I TAX AMNESTIES IN INDIA

This section describes the main features of various amnesty schemes offered in India since 1950, excluding permanent amnesties,[5] and serves to provide background information for the analysis of later sections.

Voluntary disclosure schemes were offered during the years 1951, 1965 (two schemes), 1975, 1985 (extended to 1986) and 1991. These schemes provided taxpayers immunity from penalty and prosecution in exchange for disclosures of income that had evaded tax in the past. In 1980 the government introduced a Bearer Bond Scheme. Funds used for their purchase were promised immunity from investigation or prosecution. The bonds had a maturity period of ten years, with a cumulative interest of 20 per cent payable at the end of the period. Government sales of these bonds are not reflected in income tax revenue receipts, unlike other amnesties. The invested amount was not subject to income, wealth or gift taxes. Bagchi (1981) calculates that the interest rate was below market rates by almost exactly enough to cancel out the tax benefits, so there was no implicit subsidy on these bonds for the average taxpayer.[6] Table 7.1 describes the main features of the various non-permanent amnesty schemes between 1951 and 1986; complete details of the 1991 amnesty are not as yet available.

The objective of the government in introducing these amnesty schemes appears to have been to curb tax evasion and to enable taxpayers to disclose their hitherto unreported (black) assets. As the report of the Comptroller and Auditor General on the 1985 amnesty scheme stated:

> To induce the tax-payers to respond and declare larger incomes, the Government further adopted a lenient and sympathetic approach as regards the penal proceedings and offered amnesty to repentant tax-payers to reform themselves and to declare their true income/wealth...Salient features of the Scheme were—Sole objective of curbing tax evasion and unearthing the considerable amount of black money that is vitiating the nation's economy—No probe to be made into past assessments and immunity afforded from interest, penalty and prosecution on true and full disclosures of income or wealth and prompt payment of tax—No undue benefit to repentant tax-payer vis-à-vis honest tax-payer...
>
> Controller and Auditor General, 1990[7]

The stated objectives do not include notions of signalling future enforcement resolve, or the need to provide benefits of insurance or consumption smoothing to taxpayers, objectives stressed by a number of amnesties in other countries, as well as most existing theoretical treatments.[8] The scheme amounted to an admission by the government of its failure to curb tax evasion in the past, and constituted an attempt to provide taxpayers with the opportunity to launder their black assets into white.

It is evident from Table 7.1 that amnesty receipts have formed a shrinking fraction of revenue receipts, falling from about a fifth of total revenues in the 1960s and 1970s to one-tenth or less during the 1980s. In this sense, the direct returns from the amnesties have been quite meagre in comparison with the massive estimates of black money or tax evasion of Acharya and Associates (1985) or Virmani (1986).[9] Due to the poor response, many government committees have advised against their use, starting with the 1958–59 Direct Taxes Administrative Enquiry (Tyagi) Committee, the 1971 Direct Taxes Enquiry (Wanchoo) Committee and going on to Acharya and Associates (1985).[10] Nevertheless, the government continues to use amnesty schemes, for instance in 1991 when four schemes were announced: three aimed at domestic evaders, and one designed to attract foreign capital inflows.[11] Revenue estimates for the 1991 schemes are not currently available.

Of the various amnesties offered, the 1975 scheme coincided with the declaration of an internal Emergency, and was associated with a curtailment of civil liberties, stepped up search activity and an increase in the rate of conviction for tax offences. Given the ten year gap between this and the previous amnesty, it appears reasonable to suppose that the 1975 amnesty was unanticipated. It may also have been interpreted as a prelude to stepped-up enforcement.

The 1965 amnesty was unlikely to have been anticipated, with just one amnesty scheme previously offered in 1951. There is no reason to suppose that the 1980 amnesty was anticipated either, given the unusual circumstances of the previous one. The end of the Emergency in 1977 was followed by a significant dilution of standards of enforcement. This suggests that the introduction of the 1980 amnesty induced taxpayers to associate the standards with weak enforcement resolve and therefore expect amnesties to be introduced periodically. A policy of repeated amnesties could be favoured by a government that gave more importance to short-term revenue gains from amnesty disclosures than to long-term revenue losses. These expectations came to be realised, of course, with amnesties offered in 1985–86 and again in 1991.[12]

The empirical modelling therefore proceeds under the assumption that the 1965, 1975 and 1980 amnesties were unanticipated. Moreover, it is supposed that the introduction of the 1965 and 1975 amnesties did not lead any fresh amnesties to be anticipated in the future, whereas the 1980 amnesty did lead to such an expectation. Consequently, the 1985–86 and 1991 amnesties are assumed to have been anticipated.

One additional feature of these amnesties deserves to be noted: the tax rate applicable to disclosures was typically below the maximum marginal tax rate on ordinary income disclosures prevailing at the time. In 1965, the maximum marginal rate was 65 per cent, with an additional surcharge of around 2 per cent. The amnesty tax rate of 60 per cent was therefore lower than this rate. In 1975, the top marginal tax rate was 77 per cent, substantially higher than the maximum rate of 60 per cent applied to assets declared in the amnesty. For taxpayers whose disclosures were large enough to fall in the highest income bracket, therefore, these amnesties amounted to allowing a concessional tax rate, relative to taxes liable for earlier—or even contemporaneous—disclosures. Moreover, the 1980 Bearer Bond Scheme effectively amounted to a zero effective tax rate on the amounts disclosed.[13] Finally, the 1985–86 amnesty levied tax at the usual rates, but waived interest on the delayed payment. This was tantamount to allowing a concessional tax rate.[14] Consequences of these concessions are discussed later in this chapter.

II THEORETICAL FRAMEWORK

This section outlines a framework for analysing the effects of a temporary amnesty on inducing voluntary disclosure of black assets in order to increase government revenues, the stated objective of the Indian amnesty schemes. The main conceptual elements necessary to evaluate the disclosure and revenue effects of amnesties are introduced. This is followed by a summary of predictions concerning these effects that will prove useful in interpreting the empirical results. The theory is developed formally in a companion paper by Das-Gupta and Mookherjee (1995).[15]

Black assets represent accumulation of past incomes that were not voluntarily disclosed by a taxpayer, nor discovered by tax authorities. These assets are typically invested in the underground economy where sources of investable funds are not usually investigated, such as construction, real estate purchases or moviemaking. Consequently, the growth of these sectors is related to the accumulation of black assets among citizens. In contrast, white assets are those invested in 'legal' sectors, such as deposits with financial institutions, or shares held in legal companies. The fact that the two kinds of assets are invested in different sectors has two important implications. First, incomes from white assets are easier to monitor by tax authorities. Second, the rates of return on black and white assets typically differ, owing to limited mobility of assets between the two sectors. While empirical evidence on relative rates of return are not available, casual evidence suggests that rates of return are substantially higher in the black sector, although they are accompanied by higher levels of risk.

Incentives for voluntary disclosure of incomes depend on the probability of undisclosed income being discovered by tax authorities, and the level of penalties imposed for tax evasion. Unlike white incomes, citizens usually have no incentive to voluntarily disclose black assets or incomes from these assets in the normal course. The reason is that the authorities would impose penalties on these disclosures, as they are tantamount to admission of past tax evasion. Penalties differ little from those that would be imposed if the assets were not to be disclosed, and were discovered by the tax authorities instead. The citizen therefore has no incentive to disclose black assets as this would simply increase the likelihood of incurring penalties for past tax evasion.[16]

An amnesty lowers the penalty rate on voluntary disclosures of black assets, relative to the penalties imposed for discovery of these assets by tax authorities. This promotes the citizen's incentives to voluntarily disclose these assets. The disclosure decision trades off the certainty of having to pay the amnesty fine rate (consequent on participating in the amnesty), with the probability of having these assets discovered later by the tax authorities and having to incur higher penalties (consequent on not participating).

If the taxpayer participates in the amnesty, black assets disclosed will thereafter be converted into white assets. In other words, the amnesty serves as a device for the taxpayer to launder black assets into white. Owing to the intrinsic differences between white and black assets described above, this will have an impact on income flows and tax compliance in the future. To the extent that rates of return on white assets are lower than they are on black assets, income flows accruing to the citizen in the future will be diminished. Moreover, since income from white assets are more easily detected by tax authorities, tax compliance in the future is likely to be enhanced.

The idea of encouraging voluntary disclosures of black assets via a temporary amnesty may appear sensible on the grounds that it would increase revenues directly (in the form of the taxes and penalties owed on the declared assets) during the amnesty as well as in later years by switching income flows of citizens from black to white, thus promoting greater compliance. Stella (1990), for instance, suggests that an amnesty may even be a necessary precondition for the success of a programme of stepped-up enforcement aimed particularly at discovery of undisclosed white incomes.[17]

Countering these beneficial effects is the possible adverse impact on tax compliance in pre-amnesty years, if the amnesty happens to have been anticipated by citizens. In such instances, they will be induced to engage in a form of intertemporal substitution with respect to their voluntary disclosures: disclose less in pre-amnesty years, so as to accumulate more black assets, which are subsequently disclosed in the amnesty. This will generate an adverse revenue impact in years immediately preceding an amnesty that is correctly anticipated. Part of the revenue gains accruing in the form of receipts from the amnesty will thus tend to be illusory, and will be mirrored by revenue losses in pre-amnesty years. This forms the basis of the view that amnesties are more effective when they are not anticipated in advance by citizens, and when they do not lead further amnesties to be expected in the future. Stella (1990) argues that for this reason amnesties ought to be used sparingly—perhaps on a once-and-for-all basis—otherwise the government will find it hard to credibly commit to not offering additional amnesties in the future.[18]

Nevertheless, a detailed examination of the preceding arguments suggests that they are simplistic and ignore a number of additional compliance and revenue effects of temporary amnesties. These supplementary effects are typically indirect and less visible compared to the direct effects outlined above. Moreover, they usually run in an opposite direction to the direct effects and under fairly natural conditions can overwhelm the latter.

The main issue is the incentive of a citizen with black assets to participate in an amnesty. As explained above, the main motive is to avoid incurring higher penalties if these assets are not disclosed in the amnesty and are discovered later by tax authorities. The amnesty penalty rate f applicable to the tax due on these assets must therefore be low enough to induce participation, relative to the probability q that they will be subsequently discovered (in the absence of disclosure) and be subject to a higher penalty rate. Assume that monetary penalties are imposed rather than prosecution or imprisonment: this is a realistic assumption in the current Indian context.[19]

It follows from this consideration that *there is an adverse effect of participation in the amnesty: the government will forego the revenues that it would have earned from penalties in the future had the citizen not participated in the amnesty, and if black assets were subsequently discovered*. In other words, the increased revenues from the amnesty disclosures will be followed by a subsequent decline in additional collections from penalties, compounding or settlement fees.

How do these two opposite effects on revenues compare with one another? Consider first the case where the pre-tax rates of return on black and white assets are the same and the citizen is risk-neutral. This assumption implies that participation in the amnesty does not affect the stream of total income accruing to the citizen, before taxes and penalties are accounted for. Then the citizen participates in the amnesty only in the expectation of lowering total expected tax and penalty payments to the government. The consequence must be that total expected receipts of the government must fall in the long run. This may appear counterintuitive in circumstances where discovery of black assets is especially unlikely, as that would suggest that the expected reduction in subsequent penalty collections—following amnesty participation—will be small. What such an argument overlooks is that in such circumstances the amnesty fine rate f must be concomitantly lower in order to induce participation in the amnesty.

Now suppose that the expected rate of return on black assets exceeds that on white assets. Then amnesty participation must incur an additional loss to the taxpayer, arising from a reduction in total pre-tax income that is the result of switching assets from black to white. To induce participation, the amnesty rate must be even smaller, thereby reducing the total revenue effect of the amnesty even further.

A third additional consideration arises when the amnesty is a sale, in the sense that the effective tax rate on these disclosures is less than the tax rate applicable to normal white income disclosures (i.e., the amnesty fine rate f is negative). It has been noted in the preceding section that this appears to have been the case for most Indian amnesties. This creates an incentive for habitual filers to misfile, in the following sense: instead of declaring their white income in the customary fashion in the amnesty year, they declare it as 'previously undisclosed' income in the amnesty in order to avail of the concessional tax rate. Since the source of amnesty disclosures are not investigated by the tax authorities, such misfiling behaviour is difficult to detect. The consequence is a net reduction in total voluntary collections during the amnesty year. Some amnesties which are sales prohibit such diversions explicitly, but the Indian amnesties have been somewhat ambiguous in this regard and do not appear to have successfully deterred such cases of misfiling.[20] Consequently, some of the receipts of an amnesty may actually represent diversions from taxes that would have been voluntarily paid in the absence of the amnesty.

Why might a government ever want to allow an amnesty to be a sale, i.e., offer concessions on the tax liability, over and above immunity from penalties and prosecution? The main motive may be to ensure that participation in the amnesty is not too limited, which would make it appear to have failed. It can be shown that habitual non-filers of income tax will participate in an amnesty only if it is a sale. In other words, an amnesty which is not a sale will only attract habitual filers of the income tax who by their very nature are unlikely to have accumulated much black assets. In order to widen participation to include non-filers, an amnesty must therefore be a sale. The cost of this is the direct reduction in amnesty revenues from filers who would have participated in the amnesty in any case, in addition to the revenue losses arising from misfiling by habitual filers.

The preceding arguments indicate why the direct receipts from an amnesty may provide only a very limited perspective on their aggregate revenue effects. Note that the arguments apply to amnesties that are unanticipated. Indeed, such an amnesty may appear to be a success, judging by the direct receipts, as well as by the boost to voluntarily filed taxes in years following the amnesty owing to the induced asset laundering. The losses resulting from reduced penalties will only appear in the future and will typically not be identified as a cost attributable to the amnesty. Losses due to misfiling during the amnesty year also cannot be identified, unless all other factors that help determine the level of tax revenues are explicitly controlled for. An econometric analysis that carefully controls for other determining influences and examines the revenue effects in a number of years following the amnesty is required in order to estimate the indirect effects and contrast them with the direct revenue receipts. This is the objective of the following section.

Some qualifications to the preceding results need to be noted concerning the adverse revenue effects of unanticipated amnesties. First, if rates of return on black assets are lower than on white assets, the asset-laundering effect of an amnesty may increase revenues. Second, if taxpayers are risk-averse, then the amnesty has the feature of offering insurance to taxpayers against the risk of their black assets being discovered later. The government could conceivably increase the amnesty fine rate in order to capture the associated risk premium, without jeopardising participation. Third, if imprisonment rather than monetary penalties results in the event of discovery of black assets by tax authorities, then an amnesty may result in an increase in total revenues owing to an effective conversion of non-pecuniary into pecuniary penalties. Amnesties may also lead to a savings in the cost of prosecuting offenders who would have been detected and prosecuted in the absence of amnesty participation.

How is the analysis modified when an amnesty is anticipated? Somewhat contrary to conventional wisdom, anticipation of an amnesty may have a less adverse impact on revenue than an unanticipated amnesty. Citizens do indeed engage in intertemporal substitution with respect to their payments to the government when they anticipate the amnesty; they accumulate black assets faster in pre-amnesty years and then disclose them in the amnesty. The effect of this is to switch their asset portfolios in favour of black assets in pre-amnesty years. If black rates of return are higher than white rates, the effect of the amnesty is to increase the before-tax total income of the taxpayer. Some of this increase can be appropriated by the government in the form of a higher tax rate imposed on assets disclosed in the amnesty. As a consequence, it is conceivable that an amnesty that is anticipated generates a favourable effect on aggregate revenues, whereas it would have an unfavourable effect if it were unanticipated. Nevertheless, this can happen only if white incomes that are not reported in pre-amnesty years in anticipation of an amnesty are sufficiently large relative to total black assets. Furthermore, it can be shown that an anticipated amnesty will have a negative overall revenue effect if the probability q of discovery of black assets by tax authorities is small, even if the proportion of white assets switched prior to an amnesty is substantial relative to black assets.

Predicted Amnesty Effects

This section concludes with a summary of predictions concerning the timing of revenue effects of amnesties that are, respectively, unanticipated and anticipated. These will be useful in setting up the dynamic specification of the revenue regressions in the following section and in interpreting the empirical results.

For an amnesty that is unanticipated:

1. Prepaid taxes at the amnesty date increase by the amount of amnesty receipts, or by less if the amnesty induces some taxpayers to misfile. With sufficient misfiling, they may even fall.
2. Prepaid taxes following the amnesty also increase.
3. Additional collections from penalties decrease at both amnesty and post-amnesty dates, because of the laundering of black assets that would otherwise have been subject to penalties or settlement fees on discovery.
4. Consequently, total collections—the sum of prepaid taxes and additional collections from penalties—increase by less than direct amnesty receipts at the amnesty date and may even fall owing to misfiling. At later dates, also, total collections increase less than do prepaid taxes, and could conceivably decrease.
5. If the pre-tax gross return (not adjusted for risk of discovery) on black assets is not lower than that on white assets, the overall revenue effect aggregated across the amnesty and post-amnesty dates is negative.

For an amnesty that is anticipated, we would expect the same results to hold as with an unanticipated amnesty, both during and after the amnesty. In addition:

1. Prepaid collections in pre-amnesty years fall. Additional collections rise, but the effect on aggregate collections in pre-amnesty years cannot be predicted.[21]
2. The overall revenue effect, aggregated across all dates, is expected to be negative.[22]

These results are illustrated in Figures 7.1 and 7.2, for the case where there are long lags involved in collecting penalties associated with tax offences discovered in any year and minimal losses due to misfiling. They assume that all other factors are unchanging over the period under consideration, so that revenues would be stationary in the absence of the amnesty. For an unanticipated amnesty, therefore, revenues are not affected in pre-amnesty years. With some—but not excessive—misfiling, and delayed penalties or settlements of tax evasion cases, revenues increase in the amnesty year, but by less than the direct amnesty receipts. Revenues also increase immediately following the amnesty, owing to the switch from black to white assets by taxpayers, which promotes compliance. They fall eventually, however, as the reduced penalties and settlement fees reflect the lower stock of black assets. For an anticipated amnesty, there is the additional effect of a drop in pre-amnesty revenues owing to the intertemporal substitution in compliance.

These figures also depict a situation where the introduction of the amnesty does not signal information to taxpayers concerning the future enforcement resolve of the government. Such signalling effects could either serve to step compliance up or down following the amnesty, depending on the precise context. In the Indian context, it may be expected that the 1975 amnesty served to signal tougher enforcement in the years ahead, while the others had the opposite effect. Accordingly, one would expect the amnesty year and post-amnesty effects of the 1975 amnesty to be higher than depicted in Figures 7.1 and 7.2, and lower for all the others.

III EMPIRICAL ANALYSIS

This section presents estimates of the revenue effects of various amnesties in India since 1965, after controlling for other determinants of income tax revenues.[23] The estimates are based on yearly data for income tax revenues for the period spanning financial years 1965–66 to 1992–93. Unfortunately, a breakdown of revenues between prepaid taxes and additional collections from penalties is not available for most of this period. This prevents us from being able to test some of the detailed predictions described at the end of the previous section, in which effects on prepaid taxes differ qualitatively from those on additional collections. No information is available concerning the length of lags in collecting penalties associated with tax offences. Consequently, the collection figures in any given year correspond to the sum of prepaid taxes for that year and additional collections associated with tax evasion in a number of previous years.

The revenue effects of various amnesties are estimated by the coefficients of various variables corresponding to pre-amnesty, amnesty and post-amnesty years. As explained in Section I, the 1965–66, 1975–76 and 1980–81 amnesties are treated as unanticipated amnesties, unlike the subsequent ones. Accordingly, for these three amnesties we do not have any dummies corresponding to pre-amnesty years and instead have one dummy for the amnesty year effect and another for post-amnesty effects. With the 1985–87 and 1991–92 amnesties being treated as anticipated, pre-amnesty effects also have to be incorporated for these. Since following 1980–81 successive amnesties were spaced only five years apart, the periods 1981–82 to 1984–85 and 1987–88 to 1990–91 can be viewed as combining the post-amnesty effects of the preceding amnesty and the pre-amnesty effects of the succeeding one. Consequently, in one specification used below, we simply include a composite dummy variable for the interamnesty years 1981–82 to 1984–85 and 1987–88 to 1990–91. In the other, less parsimonious, specification we treat the two years following an amnesty as embodying a post-amnesty effect and the subsequent two years a (possibly distinct) pre-amnesty effect in anticipation of the next one.

In estimating the effects of the amnesties, the following influences on tax revenues are controlled for: non-agricultural gross domestic product (NAGDP); the inflation rate (INFL); the effective marginal income tax rate averaged across different income groups (AMTR); the exemption limit for incomes (EXEM) below the taxable minimum; and two indicators of enforcement effort: the value of assets seized during search and seizure operations (SEIZ), and an index of assessment activity (ASS).[24] Other potentially important variables such as prosecutions in tax evasion cases or the conviction success rates for the Income Tax Department, turn out to be jointly statistically insignificant.[25]

The dummy variable approach is subject to certain shortcomings. First, the method itself imputes the entire effect of all influences on tax revenues to amnesties, apart from variables explicitly controlled for. To the extent that variations in enforcement effort are not adequately captured by the variables included in the regression, they could simply reflect an omitted variable bias.[26] For instance, the effects attributed to the 1975–76 amnesty could simply reflect the effect of introduction of the internal Emergency, which signalled stronger enforcement resolve. A second problem stems from the fact that assessments and revenue collections for any one year arise partially out of taxes filed for earlier years. This can lead to bias in the estimation of temporal effects of amnesty schemes.[27]

Moreover, the theory says little about the number of years that the pre-amnesty anticipation and post-amnesty laundering effects persist. Given the shortness of the time series used, there is a need to use as parsimonious a specification as is permitted by the data, in order to improve the accuracy of the estimates and hypothesis tests. This creates the need to experiment with different specifications of the temporal structure for these effects. In this respect a general-to-specific methodology was adopted: starting with the most unrestricted specification permitted by the data, successive restrictions were tested, in order to arrive at the most parsimonious specification available, i.e., where further simplifying restrictions are rejected.

The completely unrestricted specification (referred to as specification U) allowed for distinct two-period pre- and post-amnesty effects, and for different amnesties to have disparate effects. The most parsimonious specification (referred to as specification P) uses a single dummy for all interamnesty years following 1980, thereby assuming that the revenue effect was equal across all these years. In addition, the amnesty year effects of the 1985–86 and the 1991–92 amnesties are also assumed to be equal.[28] Coefficient estimates corresponding to both specifications are reported in Table 7.2. For each specification we report the results of level and first-difference (Engle-Granger) regressions.[29] Fortunately, the results do not vary much between these specifications, suggesting that inferences concerning significant influences do not spuriously arise from a common time trend.

Empirical Results

Table 7.2 presents estimated coefficients for both parsimonious (P) and unrestricted (U) specifications. All variables are measured in logs, so the coefficients have an elasticity interpretation. In particular, the coefficient of any dummy variable can be interpreted as the percentage change in revenues that can be attributed to the corresponding period. The special circumstances of the 1980 amnesty need to be kept in mind in interpreting these coefficients: the direct revenue receipts from this amnesty are not included in the revenue series used, unlike other amnesties. Hence the coefficient for 1980 represents only the indirect effects of that amnesty during the amnesty year. Government receipts from the Bearer Bond Scheme must be added to the indirect revenue effect implied by the coefficient to obtain the total effect of the 1980 amnesty. Table 7.3 presents absolute revenue effects associated with different amnesties, with the 1980 estimate adjusted to reflect direct effects of the Bearer Bond Scheme.[30]

Up to and including the 1980 amnesty, relevant amnesty and post-amnesty year effects are statistically significant (except for the post-1975 period) and numerically sizeable. Indeed, the 1965 amnesty is estimated to have reduced revenues by as much as 30–40 per cent during amnesty and post-amnesty years, which appears implausibly large. The 1975 amnesty is estimated, on the other hand, to have increased revenues by about 30 per cent during the amnesty year, with negligible after-effects. The indirect effects of the 1980 amnesty during the amnesty year are estimated to have reduced revenues by 15 per cent, exceeding the direct yield from the Bearer Bond Scheme and resulting in a net reduction of about 5 per cent of annual revenues. With the exception of 1975, therefore, indirect effects associated with amnesties served to substantially reduce revenues even during the amnesty year. While this may be attributed partly to induced misfiling, it is plausible that the 1965–66 and 1980–81 amnesties also played a role in signalling the weak enforcement resolve of the government. The opposite was the case with the 1975–76 amnesty, as it coincided with the onset of the Emergency, causing revenue increases in 1975–76 to exceed the direct receipts from the amnesty.

Following 1980, when amnesties every five years came to be anticipated, interamnesty years were associated with a drop of the order of 10 per cent a year. These possibly reflect intertemporal substitution effects, as well as reduced collections from penalties and settlement fees owing to declaration of black assets in previous amnesties. Nevertheless, the revenue effects are less significant during this period. Moreover, the 1985–87 and 1991–92 amnesties appear to have had insignificant revenue effects during amnesty years. The negative indirect effects during interamnesty years definitely overshadowed whatever meagre revenues were yielded directly by these amnesties.

One additional benefit of an amnesty is that it may induce a reduction in the incidence of non-filing behaviour, by drawing more individuals into the tax net. The effect of the Indian amnesties on increasing the total number of filers can be estimated by regressing the number of income tax assessees on amnesty dummies, after controlling for some basic features of the tax structure and tax base (INFL, NAGDP, AMTR and EXEM).[31] The sample period was identical to that of the regressions reported above. The four economic variables were significant and had the expected signs in both level and first difference (Engle-Granger) specifications, except for EXEM which proved to be insignificant in the first-difference specification.[32] None of the amnesty dummy variables was significant with the exception of the 1975 amnesty, which may simply be picking up an Emergency effect. Hence there is also no evidence that the amnesties served to reduce non-filing behaviour.

IV CONCLUSION

The empirical results corroborate what one may expect from theory: that the indirect effects of amnesties—arising from reduced collections from penalties, misfiling and intertemporal substitution—are adverse and can significantly overwhelm the positive direct effects. The negative effects are less visible, being spread out both before and after the amnesty. Only the 1975 amnesty appears to have exerted a significant positive effect on revenues, which may simply represent the effect of the state of Emergency that prevailed during the same period. All other amnesties exerted a negative overall effect. Moreover, amnesties appeared to be increasingly insignificant after 1980. It is hard to avoid the conclusion that since 1980, amnesty programmes have run into negative or diminishing returns.

Most amnesties appeared to have been sales, in the sense of offering a concession over the tax normally levied on white income disclosures. This may have resulted in misfiling of white incomes in the amnesty, causing additional revenue losses. Other forms of misfiling include disclosure of black assets recently discovered by tax authorities and disclosure in the name of children, spouses and fictitious entities in order to lower the tax liability during the amnesty.[33] The only possible justification for such low rates may have been to attract habitual non-filers to participate in the amnesty.[34] Nevertheless, there was also no evidence to suggest that amnesty programmes served to draw non-filers into the tax net. If the government must persist with amnesty programmes in the future, it should perhaps reconsider whether to continue to design them as sales.

Table 7.1
Temporary Amnesties in India

Year	*Authority for the Scheme*	*Tax Rate*	*Duration*	*Number of Cases ('000)*	*Income Disclosed (Rs crore)*	*Revenue Yield (Rs crore)*	*Yield as % of Year's Revenues*
1951	n.a.	n.a.	May–Oct. 1951	20.9	70.2	10.89	
1965	Finance Act 1965	60 %	March–May	2.0	52.18	30.8	18.5†
1965	Finance Act (no.2) 1965	n.a.	Aug 1965–March 1966	114.2	145	19.45	
1975	Voluntary Disclosure Act 1976	25–60 %	Oct 1975	245.6	746.07	249	20.5
1980	Special Bearer Bond Scheme 1981	*	*		400	160*	10.6*
1985–1986	Finance Act 1985	**	Nov 1985–March 1987	1539.9	2940.37	388.03	7.2

Notes: *See text for explanation.
**Subject to normal tax rates, but waivers of interest granted.
†Aggregate of the two 1965 schemes.
Source: CAG (1990).

Table 7.2
Coefficient Estimates

Variable	*Specification P*		*Specification U*	
	Level	*First Diff.*	*Level*	*First Diff.*
1965	– 0.36*	– 0.38*	– 0.61*	– 0.53*
1996–97	– 0.27*	– 0.29*	– 0.45*	– 0.40*
1975	0.30*	0.27*	0.25*	0.27*
1976–77	0.04	0.05	– 0.01*	0.03?
1980	– 0.18*	– 0.15*	– 0.16*	– 0.16*
1981–82	– 0.15*	– 0.11?	– 0.04	– 0.08*
1983–84	– 0.15*	– 0.11?	– 0.00	– 0.07+
1985–86	– 0.11?	– 0.04	0.06	0.02
1987–88	– 0.15*	– 0.11?	– 0.00	– 0.07+
1989–90	– 0.15*	– 0.11?	– 0.07	– 0.10*
1991	– 0.11?	– 0.04	0.11	0.01
1992	– 0.15*	– 0.11?	– 0.07	– 0.14*
NAGDP	0.84*	0.89+	0.55*	0.70*
INFL	– 0.91*	– 1.00*	– 1.48*	– 1.11*
ASS	0.59*	0.67*	1.00+	0.88*
SEIZ	0.03+	0.03*	0.06*	0.05*
EXEM	– 0.59*	– 0.48*	– 0.69+	– 0.55*
AMTR	– 0.65*	– 0.49*	– 0.80+	– 0.70*
Error Correction	– 0.96*		– 1.99*	
R^2	.99	.93	.99	.99
R–	.98	.84	.99	.99
SEE	0.05	0.04	0.03	0.01
d_w	2.10	1.57	2.76	1.90
3 Period Forecast F	2.20	1.56	4.37	135.9

Notes: *Denotes significant at 1 %, + at 5 %, and ? At 10 %.

Table 7.3
Estimated Revenue Effects of Amnesties (in crores of 1960 Rupees)

Year	*Model P*	*Model U*	*Amnesty Receipts*	*Total Revenues*
1965	– 119	– 144	38	206
1966	– 86	– 103	0	210
1967	– 84	– 101	0	205
1975	105	106	90	438
1976	18	11	0	431
1977	14	9	0	439
1980*	– 21	– 22	43	433
1981	– 35	– 28	0	357
1982	– 34	– 28	0	352
1983	– 34	– 25	0	345
1984	– 35	– 26	0	362
1985	– 6	8	34	442
1986	– 7	9	32	470
1987	– 47	– 34	0	478
1988	– 57	– 42	0	586
1989	– 63	– 66	0	650
1990	– 61	– 64	0	627
1991	– 10	7	n.a.	691
1992	– 71	– 110	n.a.	734

Notes: *Imputed revenue from Bearer Bond Scheme, allocated to 1980.

Figure 7.1
Predicted Revenue Impact of an Unanticipated Amnesty

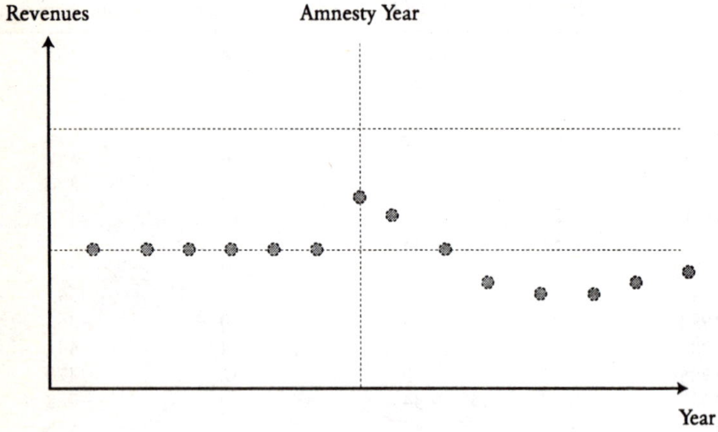

Figure 7.2
Predicted Revenue Impact of an Anticipated Amnesty

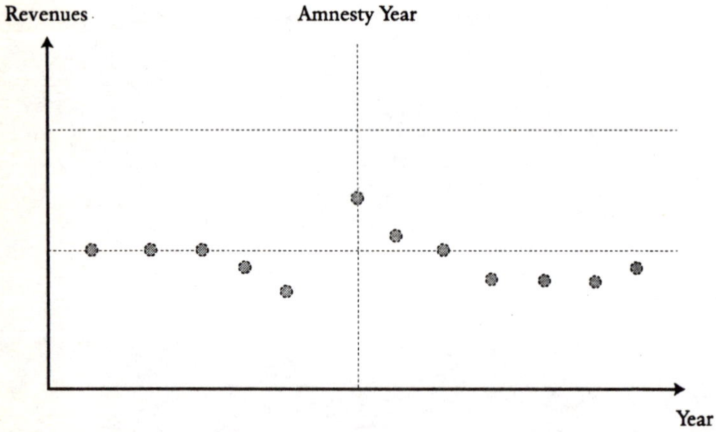

NOTES

This chapter forms part of a research project on reforms in Indian Income Tax Enforcement which was funded by a grant from the Center for Institutional Reform and the Informal Sector (IRIS) at the University of Maryland. The authors are grateful to the National Institute of Public Finance and Policy, New Delhi, for hosting this project, and to Dr. Amaresh Bagchi for his continued support and inspiration. We also thank Arbind Modi, Radhika Lahiri and Prabal Ray Chaudhuri for advice and assistance at various stages of this project, and to Satu Kähkönen for detailed comments on an earlier draft of this paper.

1. Becker, G. S. 1968, 'Crime and Punishment: An Economic Approach', *Journal of Political Economy*, 76(2): 169–217; Allingham, M. and A. Sandmo, 1972, 'Income Tax Evasion: A Theoretical Analysis', *Journal of Public Economics*, 1(3): 322–338.
2. A large literature has subsequently explored modifications of the Becker-Allingham-Sandmo model to explain why optimal penalties may be non-maximal. Explanations range from heterogeneity and risk-aversion of offenders and the likelihood of mistaken convictions, to the infeasibility of graduating monitoring effort with the seriousness of the offence, prosecution costs that rise with the penalty and the impact of the penalty level on the likelihood of conviction. See Andreoni, J. 1991, 'Reasonable Doubt and the Optimal Magnitude of Fines: Should the Penalty Fit the Crime?' *Rand Journal of Economics*, 22(3): 385–395; Bolton, P. 1986, 'The Principle of Maximum Deterrence Revisited' (mimeo), Cambridge, Massachusetts: Harvard University Department of Economics; Malik, A. S. 1990, 'Avoidance, Screening and Optimum Enforcement', *Rand Journal of Economics*, 21(3): 341–353; Mookherjee, D. 1989, 'The Economics of Enforcement' (mimeo), New Delhi: Indian Statistical Institute; Mookherjee, D. and I. P. L. Png, 1992, 'Monitoring vis-à-vis Investigation in Enforcement of Law', *American Economic Review*, 82(3): 556–565; Mookherjee, D. and I. P. L. Png, 1994, 'Marginal Deterrence in Enforcement of Law,' *Journal of Political Economy*, 102(5): 1039–1066; Polinsky, M. and S. Shavell, 1979, 'The Optimal Trade-Off Between the Probability and Magnitude of Fines', *American Economic Review*, 69(5): 880–891; Polinsky, M. and S. Shavell, 1993, 'Enforcement Costs and the Optimal Magnitude and Probability of Fines', *Journal of Law and Economics*, 35(1): 133–148; Shavell, S. 1991, 'Specific versus General Enforcement of Law', *Journal of Political Economy*, 99(5): 1088–1108; Stigler, G. L. 1970, 'The Optimal Enforcement of Laws', *Journal of Political Economy*, 78(3): 526–536; Wilde, L. 1992, 'Criminal Choice, Nonmonetary Sanctions and Marginal Deterrence: A Normative Analysis', *International Review of Law and Economics*, 12(3): 333–344.
3. See Das-Gupta, Mookherjee and Panta for further details (Das-Gupta, A., D. Mookherjee and D. P. Panta, 1992, 'Income Tax Enforcement in India: A Preliminary Analysis' [report], New Delhi: National Institute of Public Finance and Policy).
4. The increase in revenues in 1975 may have reflected the effects of tightened enforcement during the internal Emergency that was declared in the country,

rather than the effect of the amnesty per se: it is not possible to disentangle amnesty effects from the impact of the Emergency itself.

5. India has a number of legal provisions that resemble a permanent tax amnesty in many respects. Examples are the Settlement Commission allowing for out-of-court settlement of penalties due and immunity from prosecution if past evasion is voluntarily disclosed; explanation 5 to Section 271(1)(c) of the Income Tax Act for voluntary disclosures during search and seizure operations; and Sections 220(2A) and 273(1) of the Income Tax Act providing respectively for waiver or reduction of interest, and a once-in-a-lifetime amnesty from prosecution.
6. Bagchi, A. 1981, 'Special Bearer Bonds: A Retrospect', *Economic and Political Weekly*, 16 June.
7. Comptroller and Auditor General (CAG), 1990, *Report of the Comptroller and Auditor General of India*, Report for the year ended 31 March 1989, Amnesty Scheme (1985), No. 7, p. v. New Delhi: Government of India.
8. For a review of literature concerning amnesties, see Das-Gupta, A. and D. Mookherjee, 1995, 'A Theory of Tax Amnesties as an Asset Laundering Device' (mimeo), Boston: Boston University.
9. Acharya, S. and Associates, 1985, *Aspects of the Black Economy in India*. New Delhi: National Institute of Public Finance and Policy; Virmani, A. 1986, 'Measuring Income Tax Incentives Under Evasion: Effective Marginal and Average Rate Schedules', Discussion Paper No. DRD187, Development Research Department. Washington, DC: The World Bank.
10. Acharya, S. and Associates, *Aspects of the Black Economy in India*.
11. The latter permitted remittance in foreign exchange to any person in India with immunity from all direct tax and exchange control regulations. Of the others, one involved deposits with the National Housing Bank, one amended Section 273A of the Income Tax Act to provide an additional opportunity to declare undisclosed income and Gold Bonds were put on sale with the sources of funds for their purchase being granted immunity from investigation.
12. The 1985–86 amnesty was, however, introduced amid the 'raid-raj' of Finance Minister V. P. Singh, and may therefore have signalled temporarily stronger enforcement resolve.
13. Bagchi's calculation indicates that the tax on income from these bonds was effectively equal to the loss from the deviation below market interest rates. In other words, the disclosures themselves invited no tax, though subsequent income from the disclosed assets implicitly paid tax at the usual rate (see note 6).
14. The CAG Report on the 1985–86 amnesty scheme described the offer of blanket waivers of interest on past tax obligations, which amounted to a substantial revenue loss of Rs 4712 million, against an overall gain of Rs 4588 million from income and wealth tax amnesty combined (see note 7).
15. See note 8.
16. The discussion here abstracts from the possibility of a taxpayer resorting to a permanent amnesty when discovery of black assets by tax authorities is imminent.
17. Additional advantages flow from reducing the size of the underground economy, if the social rate of return is higher in the white than in the black sector.

18. Stella, P. 1990, 'Do Tax Amnesties Work?' *APTIRC Bulletin*, February: 40–43, Amsterdam: International Bureau of Fiscal Documentation, Asian and Pacific Taxes and Investment Research Centre.
19. See Das-Gupta et al., for evidence of negligible prosecution effort with respect to tax evasion offences, particularly in recent years. Discovery of tax offences are penalised more frequently by out-of-court settlements, which essentially involve the payment of compounding fees or settlement fees (see note 3).
20. See, for instance, the list of irregularities reported by the CAG report on the 1985–86 Amnesty Scheme (see note 7). It reveals that the rate of tax levied on amnesty income disclosures amounted to only 13 per cent!
21. The overall effect depends on the lags involved in levying penalties applicable to black asset discoveries in pre-amnesty years. In the absence of any lags, total collections will rise, while with sufficient delays in collecting penalties, they will fall.
22. This is based on the following assumptions: black assets do not earn a lower pre-tax rate of return than white assets, the probability of tax authorities discovering black assets is low and the aggregate stock of black assets is large relative to white income switched to nondisclosure in anticipation of an amnesty.
23. For related empirical estimates of amnesty programmes in various state governments in the United States, see Alm and Beck (Alm, J. and W. Beck, 1993, 'Tax Amnesties and Compliance in the Long Run: A Time Series Analysis', *National Tax Journal*, 46(1): 53–60) and Dubin, Graetz and Wilde (Dubin, J., M. Graetz and L. Wilde, 1992, 'State Income Tax Amnesties: Causes', *Quarterly Journal of Economics*, 107(3): 1057–1070). The former test the hypothesis that the 1985 Colorado amnesty had no effect on the level or trend of tax collections, using time series data. The latter use a pooled cross-section time series data set for different states to infer that amnesties did have a positive impact on revenue growth rates.
24. This index is provided by the work disposal rate, i.e., the rate at which currently pending assessments are disposed of. This rate has increased steadily in the last fifteen or twenty years, following the steep growth of the workload of the income tax department, relative to available manpower. The consequence has been a declining quality of scrutiny assessments. The upward movement of the work disposal rate is also negatively and strongly correlated with the decline in the fraction of taxpayers audited under the scrutiny assessment scheme. It therefore proxies for both the quality and frequency of income tax audits.
25. The reader is referred to Das-Gupta, Lahiri and Mookherjee for details of the definition and construction of these variables (Das-Gupta, A., R. Lahiri and D. Mookherjee, 1995, 'Income Tax Compliance in India: An Empirical Analysis' [revised mimeo], New Brunswick: Rutgers University).
26. Nevertheless, the non-amnesty variables included in the regression by themselves explain over 90 per cent of year-to-year variations in revenues.
27. No significant lagged variable influences have been detected, however, except those captured in a dynamic error correction effect.
28. The homogeneity restrictions embodied in the parsimonious specification were not rejected by the data at 5 per cent significance level, whereas any further simplifying assumptions were rejected. In particular, the hypothesis that pre- and post-amnesty effects lasted only one year was rejected.

29. With the exception of the inflation rate, all non-amnesty variables exhibit strong time trends. In particular, they fail Dickey-Fuller stationarity tests. However, it is well known that such tests are not very powerful for a series as short as ours. The results are therefore reported for both level regressions and first-difference regressions including a dynamic error correction effect. The regressions happen to pass standard co-integration tests.
30. These are calculated on the basis of the first-difference regression coefficients.
31. Note that NAGDP is the product of per capita non-agricultural income and total population, so that the effects of both rising taxable income and rising population are incorporated.
32. These results are not reported in the text. The R^2 was 0.98 for the level regression and 0.76 for the first-difference regression.
33. Some corroborating information is provided by the CAG Report (see note 7), which pointed out certain 'deficiencies' in its framing and implementation. It drew attention to a number of cases of acceptance of disclosures, despite evasion already having been detected by the income tax department. Tax on many disclosures was also sought to be avoided by making the disclosures in the names of 'ladies, minors and benamis' and by declaring disproportionate income in one year.
34. The analysis of Virmani (*Measuring Income Tax Incentives Under Evasion*, see note 9) suggests that this forms a significant component of the tax evasion problem in India.

PART III

Reforming Public Goods Delivery

8

The Health and Medical Sector in India: Potential Reforms and Problems

Anil B. Deolalikar and Prem S. Vashishtha

The economic reforms undertaken in India since 1991 have not yet touched the health sector in any meaningful way. However, if increasing efficiency and equity in the economy is an important objective of the economic reforms being implemented, the government will have to address problems in the health sector. A number of recent studies have convincingly demonstrated the large productivity losses associated with poor health in such varied developing country settings as Sierra Leone, Sri Lanka, India and the Philippines.[1] The income losses for agricultural households and the self-employed may be even greater, as these households cannot avail themselves of sick leave that is normally available to salaried employees. The effects of chronic infections and morbidity on children are even worse, since they are more lasting. Infections severely reduce the absorption of nutrients in the body, thereby causing malnutrition. Malnutrition affects cognitive development and schooling performance adversely, both of which in turn depress future economic productivity. All of these effects have been well documented in the literature.[2]

The gains from improved health can be quite substantial. A pioneering study by Ram and Schultz (1979) concluded that declines in mortality in India during the 1960s—achieved largely via an impressive malaria eradication programme—accounted for almost one-third of the increase in aggregate productivity in Indian agriculture.[3] Other studies undertaken at the micro level hint at yet larger pecuniary returns from improved health. Thus, even from a purely economic perspective, health improvements deserve to be high on the list of policy goals.

Role of Primary Health Services in Improving Health

Given the obvious importance of health improvements, a logical question is: what interventions are most likely to improve health outcomes? Inadequate public provision of curative and preventive health services, such as immunisations and prenatal care, is generally thought to be an important factor contributing to poor health status and high mortality rates in developing countries. Indeed, the remarkable performance of countries like Sri Lanka, China and the Indian state of Kerala in achieving low morbidity and mortality rates in spite of their relatively low per capita incomes is attributed largely to their success in expanding the breadth and improving the quality of primary health services.

However, the mere provision of primary health services is generally not sufficient to assure improved health outcomes. For the health care system to have a real impact on health status, individuals need to utilise the health services provided by the public or the private sector. Gish et al. (1988) and Gish (1989), among others, have argued that an average of three to four annual contacts per capita with the health services is adequate in achieving basic preventive health care goals.[4] For instance, this level of contact with mothers and children assures a high level of immunisation of the child population and proper monitoring of pregnancies and deliveries.

Health Situation in India

Available estimates suggest an impressive reduction in mortality in India during the last three decades. For instance, the infant mortality rate (IMR) fell by almost 40 per cent between 1965 and 1992: from 150 infant deaths per 1,000 live births to 79 (World Bank 1994).[5] Yet India has significantly higher infant and maternal mortality rates than other low-income Asian countries such as Vietnam,

Sri Lanka, China and Indonesia. Further, the relative decline in the infant mortality rate during the last twenty-five years has been much smaller in India than in these countries.[6]

The average infant mortality rate for India is somewhat misleading in view of the wide mortality variations across regions and between rural and urban areas. The infant mortality rate in the urban areas of the country was estimated at sixty-one per 1,000 live births in 1988, compared to the estimate of 102 in the rural areas in 1988 (Ministry of Health and Family Welfare 1990). Similarly, the infant mortality rate varies enormously across states, from a low of twenty-eight in Kerala to a high of 123 in Uttar Pradesh (Ministry of Health and Family Welfare 1990).[7]

Health Expenditure Levels and Trends

Expenditure on health is not only surprisingly high in India (relative to other countries at similar income levels) but has been increasing over time. For instance, Table 8.1 shows that aggregate health expenditure (by states and the Central Government) in India was 4.3 per cent of GNP in 1987, higher than that of any other country in Asia with the sole exception of South Korea. Nearly 60 per cent of this was private health expenditure, with the remaining share being largely government health expenditure (35.6 per cent) and insurance (4.4 per cent).

Further, government (central plus state) health expenditure per capita has been increasing in real terms secularly since 1974–78. In constant 1988–89 prices, per capita government health spending increased from Rs 40.53 in 1974–78 to Rs 75.06 in 1986–90, an annualised increase of 5.3 per cent. Since per capita GNP was not growing nearly as fast during this period, government health spending as a proportion of GNP increased from 1.3 per cent to 1.9 per cent during this period.

Is India getting its money's worth in the health sector? Unfortunately, the answer to this question is a resounding no. India's health achievements are not even remotely comparable to those achieved by countries whose governments spend significantly smaller amounts on health relative to their GNPs, such as China and Sri Lanka. The way in which government funds are spent on the health sector in India probably has much to do with the low returns that the government has obtained. The evidence that will be presented clearly suggests that there is considerable inefficiency (and inequity) in the utilisation of government health resources in India.

The remainder of this chapter addresses some of the problems associated with the distribution of public and private spending on health in the country.

Regional Distribution of Government Health Expenditure

Interstate Differences. Government health expenditures are unevenly distributed across states. In 1986–89, for instance, Bihar and Uttar Pradesh spent less than Rs 45 per person on health, while Gujarat, Tamil Nadu and Rajasthan spent more than Rs 90 per person.[8] The reason for the inequitable interstate distribution in government health expenditures has to do with the nature of public financing of health care in India. Because the bulk of public spending on health is undertaken by the states, there is a strong positive correlation between state government health expenditures and state domestic products. Governments in high-income states are able to spend more on health because of their greater revenue collection. But what makes the distribution worse is that Central Government contributions to state health spending are based on matching grant formulas that reward states that are already spending more on the health sector. Thus, instead of compensating for interstate differentials in health spending, the Central Government reinforces them.

Analysis of health expenditure data compiled by Tulasidhar (1992) for fifteen states over four time periods (1974–78, 1978–82, 1982–86 and 1986–89) reveals an inverse association between infant mortality rates (IMRs) and per capita state government health expenditure (Figure 8.1).[9] There is no doubt that this inverse association reflects the impact of additional government health spending on health improvements and infant mortality reduction. However, it also reflects the fact that states that have higher infant mortality rates continue to spend less on health activities despite the fact that the marginal impact of government health spending on infant mortality reduction is greatest for states that have high IMRs and low levels of government health spending. For instance, regression of infant mortality rates on state government health expenditure data reported in Table 8.2 results in the estimation of the following equation:

$$IMR_{it} = \underset{(4.5)}{227.66} - \underset{(3.6)}{3.512}^{*}\ GHLTEXP_{it} + \underset{(2.8)}{0.021}\ ^{*}(GHLTEXP)^{2}_{it},$$

where IMR_{it} is the infant mortality rate in state i at time t and GHLTEXP is per capita government health expenditure (in constant 1988–89 rupees). (Numbers in parentheses are absolute values of t-statistics.)

The above results suggest that an additional rupee of government health expenditure reduces the IMR by 2.67 for a state spending Rs 20 per capita on health (and having an IMR of 166), while the corresponding reduction in IMR for a state spending Rs 100 per capita on health (and enjoying an IMR of 86) is only 1.4. Thus, an additional rupee of public health expenditure saves more infant lives if it is targeted to high-IMR states that have low government health expenditures per capita. Such targeting increases the overall internal efficiency of government health expenditure.

Rural–Urban Differences. In addition to the interstate differences, there are major rural–urban disparities in access to health services. While it is difficult to allocate government expenditures separately by rural and urban areas, Rao, Kahn and Prasad (1987) have calculated that in 1983, 41.1 per cent of state government health spending in India was concentrated in urban areas, where 23.3 per cent of the population lived.[10] Only 18.6 per cent of state government health funding was directed to rural areas, while 40.3 per cent of expenditure was not apportionable to either rural or urban areas. The targeting of Central Government health expenditure to rural areas was even worse; less than 1 per cent of central health spending was targeted to rural areas and 55 per cent was allocated to urban areas. Thus, 44 per cent of the overall (central and state) government health and family welfare expenditure benefited 23.3 per cent of the population (i.e., the urban population) in 1983, which meant that each urban resident received 2.3 times the public health resources available to each rural resident.

A recent detailed study of government health and family welfare (H&FW) expenditures at the district and municipality levels for four states—Gujarat, Tamil Nadu, West Bengal and Uttar Pradesh—found that average H&FW expenditures per capita in urban municipalities in 1990–91 and 1991–92 were 2.5 times the corresponding expenditures at the district level.[11] The highest degree of 'urban bias' in the allocation of resources to health was found in Tamil Nadu and the lowest in Gujarat. Of course, to the extent that government H&FW expenditures are dominated by expenditure on urban-based hospitals, many of which are also used by rural patients, the extent of urban bias in government health expenditure may be overstated. Yet the reason patients in the rural areas visit urban hospitals is because those areas lack decent medical care opportunities.

There is some evidence, however, that the distribution of government health expenditures appears to be shifting toward the rural sector. Tulasidhar (1992) reports that, with the exception of Andhra Pradesh and Tamil Nadu, most States spent between 20 and 30 per cent of their health budgets on rural health facilities in 1988–89.[12] If one looks at disaggregated budgetary data, expenditure on primary health centres (PHCs) and rural dispensaries as a percentage of the medical relief budget increased in nine out of ten states for which time-series data are available. The increase in the allocation of PHCs has been quite pronounced since 1982. Again, since infant mortality rates are much higher in the rural areas than in the urban areas, it is likely that targeting government health expenditure to rural areas will raise the internal efficiency of government health spending.

Functional Distribution of Government Health Expenditures

Labour Input Mix. There appears to be a serious distortion in the labour input mix found in the Indian health delivery system. After South Korea and China, India has the largest supply of physicians per capita in Asia (Griffin 1992).[13] In the mid-1980s, for instance, India had 389 physicians per million population, compared to 346 for Malaysia, 156 for Thailand, 149 for the Philippines, and 102.9 for Indonesia.[14] On the other hand, India had only fifteen nurses, midwives and medical assistants per million population in the mid-1980s, compared to 159 for Malaysia, 145 for Thailand, 104 for the Philippines and 231 for Indonesia.[15] This makes India's ratio of nurses to physicians and of non-physician personnel (nurses, midwives and health assistants) to physicians among the lowest in Asia. These low ratios reflect the Indian health delivery system's heavy emphasis on secondary rather than primary health care, and raise the question of efficient use of labour inputs in the health sector, since physicians tend to cost significantly more to train and to utilise (and offer more sophisticated services) than other health personnel.

Primary, Secondary and Tertiary Care. There is also strong evidence that the distribution of central and state government health spending among primary, secondary and tertiary care is highly distorted towards secondary and tertiary care in India. As noted earlier, while India spends a larger proportion of the total government expenditure on health than many other countries in Asia, some 71 per cent of the total health budget is spent on secondary and tertiary hospitals.[16] This means that primary health clinics, which form the backbone of rural health services, and public health programmes receive less than one-third of the total health resources.

The picture at lower administrative levels is no different. The survey of government health expenditures at the district level in the four states referred to earlier found that public health accounted for only 24.3 per cent of non-capital health expenditure (excluding expenditure on family welfare). In the municipalities surveyed, public health expenditure accounted for an even smaller share (15.1 per cent) of current health expenditure.[17]

This functional distribution of health expenditure is inequitable, since primary health centres and public health activities generally serve a larger number of people, many of whom are poor, while secondary and tertiary hospitals cater to a much smaller population that is typically better off. The distribution of health expenditure is also allocatively inefficient for two reasons. First, the cost of curative health services per additional life saved can often be up to eight times greater than that of preventive services, such as maternal and child health (MCH) care, and up to twenty times greater than the cost of communicable disease control programmes.[18] Second, economic theory suggests that governments should subsidise activities of a public goods nature, such as communicable disease control programmes, for which there is typically low private willingness to pay, and should not subsidise activities of a private-goods nature, especially for middle- and high-income patients, such as curative care in hospitals. Admittedly, hospitals are a necessary part of referral systems and are bound to cost more than health centres because they treat the most difficult cases; however, the existing allocation of health resources between hospitals and primary health care in India is too unbalanced.

In India, the large allocation to secondary/tertiary care hospitals has resulted in an extraordinary large amount of expenditure per government hospital bed, particularly when compared to other low- and middle-income countries. While cost-accounting data on government hospitals are hard to come by, it is possible to obtain a rough estimate of expenditure per government hospital bed by multiplying total government health spending by the fraction going to hospitals and dividing the result by the number of government hospital beds. No doubt this is a crude estimate. To the extent that hospitals provide outpatient care, the figure derived above will overstate the actual expenditure per inpatient day. The figure is also overstated by the common practice of including medical training and research expenses in government hospital expenditure in many countries. But since these practices are common to most countries in Asia, a cross-country comparison of average government expenditure per hospital bed is not entirely groundless. Figures obtained this way for twelve Asian countries are reported in Table 8.3. The data in this table make India appear more like a low-mortality, high-income country (for example, South Korea) in terms of its expenditure on the hospital sector. With the exception of South Korea and Malaysia, India has the highest absolute expenditure per government hospital bed (US$ 6,650) among Asian countries. This means that India spends a staggering 23 times its per capita income to support each government hospital bed every year—significantly more than even South Korea and Malaysia.

Private Medical Expenditure

Because government health spending is tilted in favour of the non-poor, the poor have to spend proportionately more on their own for their medical needs. Using data from a national probability sample health survey (called MISH) conducted in 1990,[19] annualised household medical expenditures (extrapolated from a two-week recall period) were calculated for different income groups. The results, which are reported in Table 8.4, show that the lowest-income group (those earning less than Rs 12,500 per year) spends an astounding 24.1 per cent of its annual income on medical visits. On the other hand, the highest-income group (those earning more than Rs 56,000 per year) spends merely 3.4 per cent of its income on medical visits. These are obviously rough estimates, since they are based on two-week recall data on reported illnesses. However, they underscore the fact that because of the virtual absence of health insurance that would cover routine or catastrophic illnesses, it is especially the poor who have to rely on their own limited resources for coping with unanticipated health problems.[20]

Utilisation of Medical Services

Table 8.5, which presents information on the choice of providers by income group from the MISH household survey, shows that over one-half of the sampled individuals reporting an illness obtained care from hospitals and nursing homes—facilities that are supposed to provide inpatient care. Since it is virtually impossible that such a large proportion of illnesses require inpatient care, it follows that most individuals obtain outpatient care from facilities that are primarily intended for inpatient care. This in turn implies that the referral system, in which an individual first visits a PHC or private clinic and is then referred to successively higher levels of care, is not working. This may indicate that individuals have little faith in the ability of the grass-roots outpatient facilities to help them with their medical problems. Indeed, Table 8.5 suggests that only 4–12 per cent of treated illness episodes are treated at primary health centres, depending upon rural/urban residence and income class.

Another surprising result that emerges from an examination of Table 8.5 is that the poor appear to rely less on primary health centres than the non-poor. For example, only 8.0 per cent of rural individuals in the low-income group, but 11.7 per cent of high-income individuals experiencing an illness episode sought treatment from a PHC. The low rates of utilisation of PHCs, especially by the poor, should be a matter of concern, since the PHCs are primarily supposed to serve low-income individuals and households.

Price of Medical Services

The true price of medical services has been calculated from the MISH household survey by purging both the (disease-specific) complexity and the (consumer-chosen) quality effects from observed amounts paid by individuals for each illness episode. Much of the previous work on medical care demand has confounded the price, quality and disease-specific variations. These prices are shown by rural/urban areas of the entire country in Table 8.6 and by state in Table 8.7.[21]

There are two observations that emerge from an examination of Table 8.6. First, as one would expect, medical care prices are significantly lower at government than at private facilities. As can be seen from Table 8.6, care at private clinics costs 26 per cent more than at PHCs for urban residents and 37 per cent more for rural residents. The difference between prices charged by private and government hospitals is even greater; private hospitals and nursing homes cost 40 per cent more for rural residents and 53 per cent more for urban residents.

Second, after adjusting for cost-of-living differences, medical services from all types of health providers, including government facilities, are significantly more expensive for rural than for urban residents. Table 8.6 indicates that rural residents, on average, pay 44 per cent more than their urban counterparts for services obtained from PHCs.[22] Among inpatient facilities, the rural–urban price differential is larger for government institutions (36 per cent) than for private hospitals and nursing establishments (25 per cent). Higher medical care prices in the rural areas probably reflect the inadequate supply and relative shortage of medical services and health care providers in these areas.

The average—rural and urban—prices of care from five types of health providers vary substantially across states.[23] Table 8.7, which presents the average prices of medical care in eighteen major states, shows that prices charged by all health providers, whether public or private, appear to be unusually low in Kashmir and Himachal Pradesh; lower than average in Gujarat, Haryana and Kerala; above average in Bihar and Rajasthan; and very high in Andhra Pradesh and Assam.

What accounts for the variation in medical-care prices across states? To answer this question, the medical care prices constructed and reported in Table 8.7 were regressed on certain state-level variables that reflect the availability of medical facilities and medical infrastructure. The regression results (reported in Table 8.8) indicated a strong negative effect of state government (recurrent) health expenditures per capita on the prices charged by most types of health care providers (with the single exception being medical care prices at private clinics), with an additional rupee spent in recurrent health activities and programmes by the government being associated with reductions of Rs 0.69, Rs 0.93 and Rs 0.72 in medical care prices at government hospitals, private hospitals and PHCs, respectively. The empirical results also showed an inverse—although, for the most part, statistically insignificant—association between the per capita income of a state and medical care prices in that state. Finally, the results indicated that, controlling for population size, a larger supply of medical facilities (the number of hospital beds and the number of primary health centres and sub-centres) in a state was associated with lower medical care prices, although this relationship too was not statistically significant owing to the small size of the sample. All these results clearly imply that medical infrastructure, government health expenditures and the general standard of living in a community all serve to reduce the real cost of medical care for consumers. Conversely, consumers face higher prices for medical services in states that have poor medical infrastructure, low levels of government spending on health and low per capita incomes.

Role of the Pharmaceuticals Industry

The pharmaceuticals industry can play an important role in preserving and improving the health of a nation. However, two conditions are necessary for it to be effective: first, its products have to be easily available and affordably priced, and, second, its product mix must match the disease pattern of the population. How does the Indian pharmaceutical industry perform on these two counts?

The Indian pharmaceuticals industry is one of the most advanced among less-developed countries.[24] India also ranks as the largest producer of pharmaceutical products in the developing world, after Brazil. A total of over 15,000 branded drugs are produced in India, and imports constitute only 7.8 per cent of total production. In addition, multipurpose plants that manufacture drugs are themselves being exported by Indian manufacturers.[25]

Although the Indian pharmaceuticals industry is the second largest in the developing world, the per capita consumption of drugs in India is small. A committee of the Indian Parliament estimated that the average annual per capita consumption of modern drugs in 1975 was merely Rs 6 (or about 1.7 per cent of per capita income) and that only 20 per cent of the Indian population used these drugs.[26] The small size of the Indian market in pharmaceuticals is the result of low incomes, combined with an unequal distribution of income and of health opportunities.

Further, the product mix of the Indian pharmaceuticals industry is ill-suited to the disease profile in India. This can be seen by comparing the distribution of Indian pharmaceuticals sales by therapeutic groups (reported in Table 8.9) with the disease pattern in the country (presented in Table 8.10). The most prevalent diseases in India are primarily parasitic (filariasis, malaria, dysentery). Leprosy and tuberculosis also are very common, the latter being a major killer. In contrast, cancer and heart disease are so uncommon as to not even figure in the distribution shown in Table 8.10. But the distribution of pharmaceutical sales by therapeutic groups indicates that vitamins, cough and cold preparations and tonics and health restorers constitute 22 per cent of the total pharmaceutical sales in India. Anti-tuberculosis drugs have a market share that is equal to that of antacids and smaller than that of cardiovascular drugs. Agarwal (1978) reveals other interesting details about the Indian pharmaceuticals industry: '...Although malaria is a major disease in India, primaquine and triethoprim are not produced locally at all and imports of chloroquine exceed local production...For many important drugs, installed capacities are far below licensed capacities. The actual utilisation of the installed capacity is still less—only 12 per cent for anti-leprosy drugs and 14 per cent for thiacetazone [an anti-tuberculosis drug]'.[27]

There are two reasons for the inadequate production of essential drugs. First, the market for pharmaceuticals is largely made up of the urban middle class. The vast majority of the rural poor are simply beyond the reach of modern drugs. Hence, the pharmaceuticals industry responds to the ailments of the middle class, such as general fatigue, headaches and constipation, rather than to the diseases afflicting the poor, such as leprosy, tuberculosis and filariasis.[28]

Another reason for the inadequate production of 'essential' drugs is related to past government policy. Until very recently, essential drugs were subject to strict price controls by the Indian government. This reduced the incentives for their production by the private sector. As part of the industrial deregulation that has occurred since 1991, the government has relaxed many of the strictest bureaucratic controls on the pharmaceuticals industry, but it may take some time to undo the damage of past policies on this sector.

Integrated Child Health/Nutrition Programmes

Closely related to health—particularly child health—is the issue of child nutrition. There is general consensus in the medical literature that high rates of neonatal and infant mortality and poor child health owes much to undernutrition among infants, children and pregnant and lactating mothers.[29] Because of the strong complementarities between good health and good nutrition, especially among children and pregnant women, there is often a strong case for integrated health/nutrition programmes targeted to these groups.[30]

Integrated Child Development Services In India, a national programme that is directly targeted to child health and welfare is the Integrated Child Development Services (ICDS) programme. Initiated in 1975, it has expanded rapidly and covers more than 1,300 blocks of approximately 100,000 population each.[31] It is 'integrated' in that it aims to improve the nutrition and health of children 0–6 years of age by simultaneously providing supplementary feeding, immunisation and curative medical care to children and pregnant and lactating women, and health and nutrition education to mothers. However, the primary emphasis in the ICDS programme is on providing meals. ICDS is sponsored by the Central Government but administered by the states. There is cost sharing between the Central Government and the states. The backbone of the ICDS is the *anganwadi*, which is a community centre where children and mothers gather to avail themselves of ICDS services. While in principle there is both programme as well as area targeting of ICDS benefits, in practice nutritional screening is rarely done to determine eligibility for supplementary feeding. Virtually all of the targeting of benefits is achieved via location of ICDS projects in tribal areas and rural areas with a heavy concentration of scheduled (backward) caste households, where malnutrition problems are generally most severe.[32]

While there are a large number of evaluation studies on the ICDS, most of these have looked at specific ICDS projects, and not at the programme as a whole. The following appear to be the main conclusions of these studies.[33]

1. The impact on child nutritional status varies widely from one ICDS project to another. As such, it is difficult to generalise from the successes or failures of individual ICDS projects.
2. The coverage of children under 3 years of age in supplementary feeding and immunisation efforts is low, since such children typically need to be brought to the anganwadi by a parent. The coverage of pregnant and lactating women is even lower. Thus, ICDS fails to prevent many preventable child deaths, such as those that occur in early infancy and those that are attributable to poor maternal health.
3. Although supplementary feeding is often uneven because of erratic food supplies received by the anganwadi centre, it attracts mothers and children to the centre where they can then avail themselves of other important services of the package.
4. There is little community participation in the ICDS programme. Hence, ICDS is viewed by potential beneficiaries more as a government centre than as a community centre.
5. Although coverage of rural areas has been increasing rapidly, the ICDS, like the PDS, has a strong urban bias.[34]
6. Although it is supposed to be a supplementary feeding programme for undernourished pre-school children, in practice the ICDS provides a replacement noonday meal to all pre-school children who come to an ICDS centre. The lack of targeting in the programme, as well as its tendency to make beneficiaries dependent on food assistance for extended periods, limits its coverage of the truly needy and its sustainability over the long run.

Despite these shortcomings, Subbarao (1988) concludes that '... ICDS is a well-conceived programme reflecting a bold and innovative approach; many of its observed ills can be removed by effective implementation; and the observed failure in eliciting community participation is not peculiar to ICDS but evident in other welfare programmes such as the IRDP [Integrated Rural Development Programme]'.[35]

Tamil Nadu Integrated Nutrition Project In contrast, the Tamil Nadu Integrated Nutrition Project (TINP), initiated in 1980 by the

Government of Tamil Nadu with financial assistance from the World Bank, has been one of the most successful nutrition intervention programmes in India and in the world.[36] TINP is area, age and need targeted. It is confined to the rural areas of six districts in Tamil Nadu that have the lowest caloric consumption in the state.[37] Only children 6–36 months of age, who account for 90 per cent of the pre-school deaths in the state, and pregnant and lactating women are eligible to participate in the project.[38] Further targeting is achieved by monitoring the weights of all children 6–36 months old in the project villages, and enrolling only those children whose weight gain over a certain period falls below standard in a 90-day supplementation programme that includes daily feeding and counselling of mothers. Since the children are on the supplementation programme only for the duration of time their weight gain is below standard, the project is basically seen as a short-term intervention that seeks to reduce long-term dependence of beneficiaries on public assistance.

Often a problem with child supplementation programmes is that parents reduce a child's allocation at home since they view the supplementation as a substitute for home consumption. TINP avoids this problem by serving snacks made from wheat to a population that often does not consider food not containing rice to be a meal. Community participation is achieved in the project by enlisting women in the project villages to assist in the preparation of the food supplement.

TINP links the delivery of health and nutrition services. Children who do not respond to the nutrition supplementation are provided with health services, which include check-ups and referrals, treatment of diarrhoea, deworming and immunisation. These services are also available to pregnant and lactating women. In addition, the programme includes intensive counselling of mothers in nutrition and hygiene education.

Evaluation studies of the TINP have indicated dramatic effects. Berg (1987) notes:

> '...by late 1986 preliminary findings...pointed toward a 53 per cent decline in serious and severe malnutrition, down to 8 per cent of all children between 7 months and 5 years old. Given what was happening to the economy during this period,[39] there is fairly strong evidence that without TINP malnutrition rates would have

> been from 14 to at least 18 per cent. (In the untreated area studied in 1986 serious and severe malnutrition was more than 20 per cent.) . . . Children between ages 4 and 5 who had been through the programme were a significant 1.75 kilograms (or 3.9 pounds) heavier than children from control villages. That the weight advantage was maintained two years after the children completed the programme indicates the longer-run effects'.[40]

Dapice (1987) has estimated the annual recurrent cost of the TINP in 1986–87 to be approximately Rs 10 per person (not beneficiary) living in the target area.[41] In contrast, Tamil Nadu's portion of the ICDS programme costs approximately Rs 22 per capita per year. The difference in cost arises almost entirely from the fact that the ICDS is a mass feeding programme, while the TINP is a highly selective supplementary feeding programme.

How do the benefits of the two programmes compare? Although there are several conceptual difficulties in arriving at an accurate figure, Dapice (1987) estimates that the TINP has reduced severe malnutrition among children 6–36 months old by twice as much as the ICDS in Tamil Nadu.[42] Given the effectiveness of the TINP, can it be afforded by a poor country, such as India? According to Dapice (1987), expenditure on TINP constitutes less than 0.5 per cent of Tamil Nadu's GDP, 2.5 per cent of recurring state revenues, and 12 per cent of the total state government expenditure on social and community services.[43] These are relatively modest costs for a programme that has reduced serious and severe malnutrition and related health problems among pre-school children by over 50 per cent.

Potential Reforms and Constraints

The main problem with the health sector in India is the distribution of government health resources—across states, between rural and urban areas, among different levels of health care (primary, secondary and tertiary) and between preventive and curative care programmes. For once, the total volume of resources is not a major constraint. Indeed, as argued earlier, India spends considerably more on health (as a percentage of its GNP) than most other countries in Asia. In addition, government health spending constitutes about a third of total spending on health, which implies that government health projects and programmes can leverage relatively high levels of private expenditure to achieve goals in the health sector. It is unlikely, therefore, that the quantity of resources devoted to health is a major constraint to improving health conditions in the country.

This chapter has focused on some of the major issues that need to be addressed. Better targeting of government health expenditure to poorer states that have high infant mortality rates will not only improve equity but also raise the internal efficiency of health expenditure. However, there is a built-in mechanism that will make it difficult to achieve redistribution of government health spending. The vast bulk of government health spending in India is undertaken by the states, and richer states that have low IMRs are simply able to spend more on health programmes. What could change is the manner in which the Central Government allocates its health grants to the states. Currently, Central Government spending reinforces—rather than compensates for—inequalities in state government health spending. There is a need to change the formula or basis on which states receive central funding for health programmes.

But perhaps the greatest failing of the Indian health care system is its strong bias in favour of secondary/tertiary care and medical training/research. This has been achieved at the expense of primary health care, communicable disease programmes and integrated child nutrition/health programmes, although there is some evidence to suggest that the emphasis on preventive and primary care grew in the 1980s. Some of this bias can be traced to the recommendations of the Health Survey and Planning Committee, headed by Sir Joseph Bhore, appointed by the Government of India in 1943. The Bhore Committee included its comprehensive recommendations in a long-term health plan for the country that could be implemented in a time period of thirty to forty years. Although many of the Bhore Committee's numerical targets, in terms of access to health services, have not been realised even as of yet, it is instructive to examine the Committee's basic recommendations for the health sector, since these probably guided much of health policy in the early days.

Among the Bhore Committee recommendations were: (*a*) elimination of the licentiate medical training course, with focus on a single 5-year instruction programme to train a 'basic' physician, (*b*) hospital-based health services, with all preventive, curative and rehabilitative services flowing from hospitals and (*c*) a system of referral (vertical) services from lower to higher-level units for complete health care and supervision.

Verma (1986) has summarised the effects of these recommendations on the development of the Indian medical system:

> Rise of specialties was the natural outcome of creation and expansion of teaching hospitals and the Bhore Committee recommendations. With this was linked the demand for more sophisticated technology with consequent straining of resources for the basic levels. More and more resources were spent on development of prestigious advanced treatment centres than on general promotive and preventive measures which only helped the few and neglected the many. This also led to greater attraction for hospital jobs which in turn led to a serious competition for such jobs. Acquisition of post-graduate degrees became sine qua non for hospital appointments...The 'basic' doctor produced by such institutions, therefore, remained more patient- than community-oriented.... Such postgraduates were hardly suitable for rural areas where even primary health care was not available.[44]

There is a good deal of evidence to suggest that a number of adult health problems have their origins in chronically poor health and undernutrition in childhood. Because of the strong synergies between child/maternal nutrition and health, integrated health/nutrition programmes targeted to vulnerable groups such as children and pregnant/lactating women are much more effective than traditional health interventions alone. Unfortunately, although India boasts of one of the most successful child nutrition/health interventions in the world—the Tamil Nadu Integrated Nutrition Programme—such programmes are generally underfunded in the country.

There is some evidence that the new health policy, formed in the aftermath of the Alma Alta Declaration, has attempted to reverse some of the bias in favour of curative interventions since 1982. However, unless deep-rooted changes in the medical curriculum, funding of medical education and structure of the pharmaceuticals industry take place, it will be difficult to reverse the strong bias toward secondary/tertiary curative care in the Indian medical system. It is likely that the well-established medical community in India will strongly resist any major changes in health-sector reform.

Table 8.1

Aggregate Health Expenditure as a Percentage of GNP in Selected Asian Countries, Latest Year

Country	*Total Health Expenditure*	*Government Health Exp.*	*Year*
Bangladesh	1.7	0.7	1987
China	4.0	0.8	1987
India	4.3	1.6	1987
Indonesia	2.4	0.9	1986
Korea	5.1	0.6	1987
Malaysia	3.5	2.7	1987
Myanmar	3.2	1.1	1986
Nepal	1.4	0.8	1987
Philippines	2.4	0.6	1987
Sri Lanka	2.3	1.3	1986
Thailand	3.8	1.1	1987

Source: Griffin (1992),[45] (see note 13).

Table 8.2

Per Capita Expenditure on Health Sector, by State, 1974–78 to 1986–89

State	*Total Government Health Expenditure Per Capita in Constant 1988–89 Rupees (Four-year Averages)*			
	1974–78	*1978–82*	*1982–86*	*1986–89*
Andhra Pradesh	35.18	46.22	56.52	63.73
Assam	30.14	41.92	58.14	73.34
Bihar	17.76	26.77	31.70	38.21
Gujarat	43.29	53.67	70.02	92.95
Haryana	39.43	56.58	80.41	84.98
Karnataka	39.51	46.46	64.05	67.94
Kerala	57.34	72.15	82.62	86.74
Madhya Pradesh	32.53	42.41	58.06	71.76
Maharashtra	53.12	65.65	81.32	87.92
Orissa	31.19	44.05	55.87	66.24
Punjab	46.85	59.39	69.70	84.22
Rajasthan	49.46	68.50	103.04	100.78
Tamil Nadu	42.49	51.12	105.51	95.62
Uttar Pradesh	21.56	28.73	38.00	45.82
West Bengal	47.36	56.62	61.90	60.23
All fifteen states	36.43	46.87	62.65	68.91

Source: Tulasidhar (1992),[46] (see note 8).

Table 8.3

Expenditure on Government Hospital Beds, Most Recent Year (estimated)

Country	*Expenditure Per bed (US$)*	*Multiple of Annual Per Capita Income Per bed*
Bangladesh	2,661	17
China	665	2
India	6,650	23
Indonesia	5,882	12
Korea	27,881	12
Malaysia	13,474	7
Myanmar	1,122	6
Nepal	3,371	22
Philippines	2,658	5
Sri Lanka	1,508	4
Thailand	4,270	5

Source: Griffin (1992),[47] (see note 13).

Table 8.4

Annual Household Medical Expenditure, by Income Class, India, 1990

Income Class	*Annual Household Income (Rs)*	*Annual Household Medical Expenditure*	
		in Rupees	*as Per Cent of Annual Income*
Less than Rs 12,500 Per Annum	8,429.45	1,621.23	24.14
Rs 12,501–Rs 56,000 Per Annum	29,295.49	1,946.00	7.57
More than Rs 56,000 Per Annum	76,554.07	2,327.53	3.40

Source: Author's Calculations.

Table 8.5

Choice of Providers, by Income Class, India, 1990

Provider	*Urban*				*Rural*			
	Income Class			*All*	*Income Class*			*All*
	Low	*Middle*	*High*		*Low*	*Middle*	*High*	
Government Hospital	37.3	31.8	23.8	33.6	32.3	26.3	16.7	30.4
Private Hospital/ Nursing Home	19.9	21.3	25.6	20.9	21.5	20.8	19.5	21.3
PHC	4.5	7.3	5.0	6.1	8.0	8.2	11.7	8.1
Private Clinic	22.8	21.9	28.9	22.5	20.3	23.1	39.4	21.3
Medical Shop	12.8	14.2	13.0	13.6	9.5	14.2	10.1	10.9
Others	2.8	3.6	3.8	3.3	8.4	7.5	2.6	8.1
Total	100.0	100.0	100.0	100.0	100.0	100.0	100.0	100.0

Source: Author's Calculations from MISH raw data tapes.

Table 8.6

Computed Prices of Medical Care, by Provider, India, 1990

Sector	*Government Hospitals*	*Private Hospitals*	*PHCs*	*Private Clinics*	*Others*
Urban	92.44	141.23	93.80	117.99	90.74
Rural	126.11	176.62	135.12	185.27	122.49
All	118.15	168.25	125.02	169.45	115.01

Notes: All prices represent the cost of a single visit and include all costs (e.g., fees, drugs, surgical procedures, etc.). The prices are purged of variations associated with quality of care and type of disease/ailment. They are also deflated for cost-of-living differences across states and across rural/urban areas.
Source: Author's Calculations from MISH raw data tapes.

Table 8.7

Computed Prices of Medical Care, by Provider and by State, 1990

State	*Gov't Hospitals*	*Private Hospitals*	*PHCs*	*Private Clinics*	*Others*
Andhra Pradesh	169.07	240.34	125.92	379.69	229.45
Assam	146.61	261.84	215.99	302.11	213.12
Bihar	125.55	188.22	131.76	154.43	83.68
Gujarat	144.18	86.84	96.66	83.16	
Haryana	93.85	88.89	111.97	70.19	63.20
Himachal Pradesh	121.93	145.48	70.67	44.66	36.90
Jammu & Kashmir	73.04	47.18	55.95		82.06
Karnataka	148.27	172.69		90.47	140.98
Kerala	137.79	94.95		59.61	97.82
Madhya Pradesh	107.92	162.29	63.69	138.70	165.53
Maharashtra	91.49	159.93	111.69	98.07	93.82
Meghalaya	61.00	236.94	80.75	161.13	63.45
Orissa	114.80	258.63	120.27	144.99	82.37
Punjab	167.32	189.16	119.09	89.77	113.68
Rajasthan	187.41	174.97		120.12	83.13
Tamil Nadu	54.11	123.55	75.27	106.48	66.68
Uttar Pradesh	72.80	102.71	76.49	86.68	79.62
W. Bengal	191.60	217.61	129.73	224.45	114.27

Notes: All prices represent the cost of a single visit and include all costs (e.g., fees, drugs, surgical procedures, etc.). The prices are purged of variations associated with quality of care and type of disease/ailment. They are also deflated for cost of living differences across states and across rural/urban areas.
Source: Author's Calculations from MISH raw data tapes.

Table 8.8

Regression Analysis of State-level and Provider-Specific Computer Prices of Medical Care, India, 1990

State-level Independent Variables	*Price charged at:*									
	Gov't Hospitals		*Private Hospitals*		*PHCs*		*Private Clinics*		*Other Providers*	
	Parameter	*T-ratio*	*Parameter*	*T-ratio*	*Parameter*	*T-ratio*	*Parameter*	*T-ratio*	*Parameter*	*T-ratio*
Per capita State Government Expenditure on Health 1986–87	– 0.685	– 2.127	– 0.930	– 2.075	– 0.717	– 2.418	0.517	0.55	– 0.803	– 2.06
Per Capita Net State Domestic Product (1980 prices), 1988–89	– 0.005	– 0.311	– 0.040	– 1.682	– 0.009	– 0.507	– 0.071	– 1.417	– 0.029	– 1.369
No. of Hospital Beds in State, 1990	0.000	– 0.209	– 0.001	– 1.493	0.000	0.243	– 0.002	– 1.067	0.000	– 0.553
No. of PHCs and Sub-centres in State, 1990	– 0.007	– 0.742	– 0.026	– 1.92	– 0.003	– 0.311	– 0.049	– 1.749	– 0.016	– 1.386
State Population, 1991	0.597	0.366	3.710	1.633	– 0.268	– 0.142	8.380	1.761	2.250	1.13
Intercept	215.253	3.447	385.257	4.436	205.805	3.521	340.449	1.869	259.747	3.415
R-squared	0.282		0.392		0.400		0.354		0.340	
No. of Observations	18		18		15		18		17	
F-Ratio	0.940		1.540		0.382		0.321		0.399	

Notes: Ordinary least squares on state-level data, using health-care prices reported in Table 8.1.
Source: Author's Calculations from MISH raw data tapes.

Table 8.9

Market Share of Some Theraputic Drugs Groups, India, 1985

Drug Group	*Sales (Rs Million)*	*Per cent of Total Market*
Systemic Antibiotics	2490.2	21.15
Vitamins, Tonics, Mineral Supplements	1877.8	15.95
Cough and Cold Mixtures, Nasal Decongestants	554	4.70
Antiparasatic	467.8	3.97
Analgesics	442.9	3.76
Antacids	381.7	3.64
Anti-inflamatory and anti-rheumatic	530.6	4.50
Anti-tuberculosis	303.9	2.50
Enzymes	246.9	2.10
Sex Hormones	236.1	2.00

Source: Bal, 1986.[48]

,Table 8.10

Cases and Deaths Reported due to Various Diseases, India, 1973–74

Disease	*No. of Cases*	*No. of Deaths*
Filariasis	20,000,000	·1,360,000
Dysentery	3,800,000	2,114
Leprosy	3,200,000	?
Influenza	1,643,142	101
Malaria	1,300,000	?
Gastroenteritis	799,199	3,514
Tuberculosis	340,052	5,530
Whooping Cough	198,094	304
Enteric Fever	190,997	1,343
Infectious Hepatitis	99,816	948
Gonococcal Infection	90,544	55
Syphilis	60,606	42
Measles	56,521	149
Tetanus	52,535	3,291
Chickenpox	34,067	30
Cholera	17,000	3,600
Rabies	14,187	151
Diptheria	11,437	444
Meningococcal Infection	11,052	283
Poliomyelitis	6,435	143
Dengue and Haemorrhagic Fever	3,792	1,728
Encephalitis	?	1,728

Source: Central Drug Research Institute, 1976.[49]

Figure 8.1

Infant Mortality Rates and Per Capita Real Health Expenditures, Indian States, 1974–78 to 1986–89

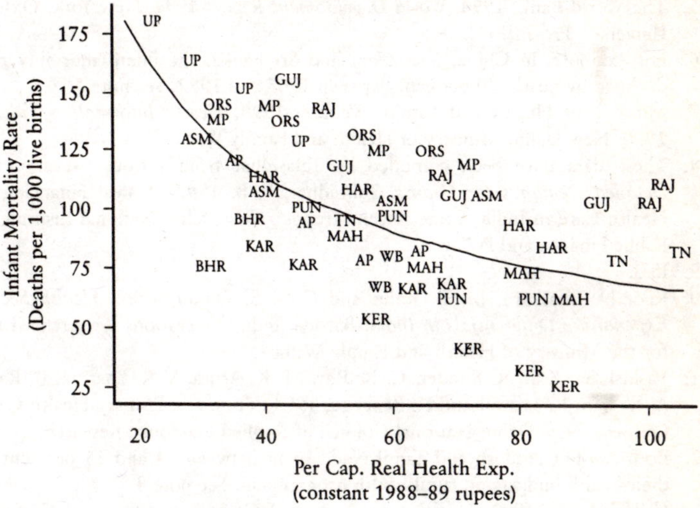

NOTES

1. Strauss, J. 1986, 'Does Better Nutrition Raise Farm Productivity'? *Journal of Political Economy*, 94(2): 297–320; Deolalikar, A. B. 1988, 'Nutrition and Labour Productivity in Agriculture: Wage Equation and Farm Production Function Estimates for Rural India', *The Review of Economics and Statistics*, 70(3): 406–413; Sah, D. E. and H. Alderman, 1988, 'The Effect of Human Capital on Wages, and the Determinants of Labour Supply in a Developing Country', *Journal of Development Economics*, 29(2): 157–183; Haddad, L. and H. Bouis, 1991, 'The Impact of Nutritional Status on Agricultural Productivity: Wage Evidence from the Philippines', *Oxford Bulletin of Economics and Statistics*, 53(1): 45–68.
2. Martorell, R. and T. J. Ho, 1984, 'Malnutrition, Morbidity, and Mortality', in W. H. Mosely and L. C. Chen (eds), *Child Survival Strategies for Research*, Cambridge: Cambridge University Press; Behrman, J. R. and A. B. Deolalikar, 1988, 'Health and Nutrition', in H. Chenery and T. N. Srinivasan (eds), *Handbook of Development Economics*, Vol. 1. North Holland: Elsevier Science Publishers B. V.
3. Ram, R. and T. W. Schultz, 1979, 'Life Span, Health, Savings and Productivity', *Economic Development and Cultural Change*, 27(3): 399–421.

4. Gish, O., R. Malik and P. Sudharto, 1988, 'Who Gets What? Utilisation of Health Services in Indonesia', *International Journal of Health Planning and Management*, 3: 185–196; Gish, O. 1989, 'Some Links Between Successful Implementation of Primary Health Care Interventions and the Overall Utilisation of Health Services', *Social Science and Medicine*, 30(4): 401–05.
5. The World Bank, 1994, *World Development Report 1994*, New York: Oxford University Press.
6. For example, in China, Viet Nam and Sri Lanka, the infant mortality rate declined by nearly 70 per cent between 1965 and 1992. See note 5.
7. Ministry of Health and Family Welfare, 1990, *Health Information India—1990*, New Delhi: Ministry of Health and Family Welfare.
8. These data have been compiled by Tulasidhar from various issues of the *Detailed Demands for Grants*, Tulasidhar, V. B. 1992, 'States' Financing of Health Care in India: Some Recent Trends', New Delhi: National Institute of Public Finance and Policy.
9. Ibid.
10. Rao, N. Bhaskara, M. E. Kahn and C. V. S. Prasad, 1987, *Health Sector Expenditure Differentials in India*, Baroda, India: Operations Research Group for the Ministry of Health and Family Welfare.
11. Vashishtha, P. S., R. Sunder, C. R. Ray, M. K. Arora, V. K. Sharma, B. Ram, A. K. Jain, R. Jaiswal and K. Banerjee, 1994, 'Survey of Primary Health Care' (mimeo), New Delhi: National Council of Applied Economic Research.
12. Both Andhra Pradesh and Tamil Nadu spent between 14 and 15 per cent of their health budgets on rural health programmes. See note 8.
13. Griffin, C. C. 1992, *Health Care in Asia: A Comparative Study of Cost and Financing*, World Bank Regional and Sectoral Studies, Washington, DC: The World Bank.
14. In comparison, the United States had 2,381 physicians, and Austria 4,348 physicians per million population in 1990. See note 5.
15. See note 13.
16. See note 13.
17. See note 11.
18. De Ferranti, D. 1985, 'Paying for Health Services in Developing Countries: An Overview', World Bank Staff Working Paper No. 721 (mimeo), Washington, DC: The World Bank.
19. This survey, called the Medical Module of the All-India Market Information Survey of Households (MISH), was conducted by the National Council of Applied Economic Research (NCAER) in 1990. The survey obtained information on illness episodes that had occurred among individuals in 18,102 households in the two weeks preceding the survey. Respondents were asked to select among a list of nine possible symptoms that were associated with their illness. In addition, information on how and where the illness was treated, the cost of treatment (by various components such as fees, drugs, surgery, and transport) and the distance to the health provider was also obtained. Individuals in a total of 18,102 households residing in twenty-one states and union territories of the country were canvassed between May and July of 1990. A multistage stratified random sampling design was used to select the sample households.

20. The Employees State Insurance Scheme (ESIS) only covers government employees and salaried workers in the organised sector, who typically belong to middle- and high-income groups.
21. For a detailed explanation of how the prices were derived, see Deolalikar, A. B. and P. S. Vashishtha, 1992, 'The Utilization of Government and Private Health Services in India' report prepared under the Options Aid Project; AID Contract No. DPE-3035-C-00-0053-00; The Futures Group Project No. 5100.54, August, New Delhi: National Council of Applied Economic Research.
22. Note that these price comparisons refer to prices that are purged of quality; the quality-unadjusted expenditures per illness episode either do not vary significantly across rural and urban areas or are higher in the urban areas. However, once there is control for the fact that urban residents, who typically have higher incomes and better education, pay more for higher quality services, the true price of medical services facing rural residents is in fact higher.
23. Average prices could not be calculated for smaller states due to an insufficient number of observations over which to compute means.
24. Agarwal, A. 1978, *Drugs and the Third World*, London: Earthscan Publications.
25. Ibid.
26. Government of India, 1975, 'Report of the Committee on Drugs and Pharmaceutical Industry' (mimeo), New Delhi: Government of India, Ministry of Petroleum and Chemicals.
27. See note 24.
28. Admittedly, these are observations based on casual empiricism. There are no household or medical surveys conducted in India that throw light on the distribution of diseases or symptoms by income group.
29. See note 2.
30. Berg, A. 1987, *Malnutrition: What Can Be Done? Lessons from the World Bank Experience*, Baltimore: Johns Hopkins Press.
31. Dapice, D. 1987, 'A Cost Study of ICDS and TINP', World Bank Consultant Report (mimeo), Washington, DC: The World Bank.
32. Subbarao, K. 1988, 'Improving Nutrition in India: Policies, Programs and Impact' (mimeo), Washington, DC: The World Bank.
33. Ibid.
34. See note 31.
35. See note 32.
36. See note 30.
37. These districts alone represented a population of 17.2 million, Berg, *Malnutrition*, 17.
38. For more details on the TINP, see notes 30 and 31, as well as Martorell, R. 1987, 'Impact Evaluation of the Tamil Nadu Integrated Nutrition Project', World Bank Consultant Report (mimeo), Washington, DC: The World Bank.
39. Tamil Nadu had gone through a bad drought and severe economic difficulties during this period.
40. Berg, *Malnutrition*, 19–25.
41. Dapice, 'A Cost Study', 5–7.
42. Ibid.
43. Ibid.

44. Verma, O. P. 1986, 'Forty Years after the Bhore Committee', *Indian Journal of Public Health*, 30(1): 7–14. This quotation is from page 10.
45. See note 13, 51.
46. See note 8, 39.
47. See note 13, 74.
48. Bal. 1986, 2009.
49. Central Drug Research Institute, 1976, 7–8.

9

Fertility, Literacy and the Institution of Child Labour*

Mukesh Eswaran

Child labour is an institution that is prevalent in many developing countries, but one that is particularly entrenched in South Asia. The evidence indicates that child labour renders the lot of the poor somewhat more tolerable to them than it would be otherwise. Nevertheless, the institution has some serious long-term consequences. As long as parents find it worthwhile to have their children work for a substantial number of hours each day either inside or outside the home, the children's education inevitably suffers. Apart from perpetuating an uneducated labour force, the institution also renders a reduction in fertility less likely. This chapter examines these issues in an old-age security model for fertility,[1] in which the opportunity cost of child labour is taken to be foregone education. It is demonstrated here that when the institution of child labour is legal and is deemed socially acceptable, risk-averse parents would tend to trade off the education of children in favour of greater fertility in order to ensure a more secure old age.

In many cultures, such as those of South Asia, old age in the absence of surviving children is an extremely undesirable prospect. Fertility is strongly motivated by the desire to ensure that at least one child (usually male) survives to adulthood. From the point of view of this pension motive, educated and uneducated children may both be desirable assets. However, the education of children not only requires expenditures on the part of parents but typically also requires parents to forgo much of the economic contribution of children, whether at home or in formal labour markets. In an environment in which child mortality is significant, the expected return on education will be low and parents would tend not to educate their children, as observed by Rodgers and Standing (1981).[2] Furthermore—and this is the focus of attention in this paper—educated children are also riskier assets, since the possibility of premature death exposes parents to the risk that their investment in the education of their children may not pay off in terms of old-age support. Consequently, in developing countries in which child mortality rates are still significant, parents would tend to prefer many uneducated children to a few educated ones. Risk considerations would generate such an outcome even when the private rate of parents' expected return on the education of their children substantially exceeds the return on having uneducated children. Child mortality, in other words, induces a trade-off between the quantity and quality of children when the institution of child labour is deemed socially acceptable.

It is child and young adult mortality rather than infant mortality that is relevant here, since parents swiftly compensate for infant fatalities by having additional children. More precisely, the emphasis here is on children who survive early childhood but fail to survive long enough to provide old-age security to their parents. It is possible to obtain a rough idea of the magnitude of this probability for developing countries. Using mortality tables, Murray, Yang, and Qiao (1992, Table 2–6) have computed that for India over the period 1970–83, the proportion of 15 year old males (females) who failed to survive until they were 60 was 32.8 per cent (29.4 per cent).[3] In other words, during 1970–83 approximately one out of every three male children in India who lived long enough to be able to go through school died before providing old-age security for his parents for the entire length of their retirement.[4] The above source also reveals considerable variation in these proportions across the Indian states: the above proportion for males (females) goes from a maximum of 39.0 per cent in Orissa (37.4 per cent also in Orissa) to a minimum of 20.7 per cent in Punjab (16.4 per cent in Kerala). These are state-wide averages, covering urban and rural areas. One would expect the relevant proportions for rural areas to be higher than these averages because of the limited availability of rural health care facilities.

If adults had alternative means of handling the risk of facing old age without income support, they would be inclined to invest in their children's education (provided the return on this investment is sufficiently high). However, when access to capital markets is very limited and one's surviving offspring are the only means available for smoothing consumption over one's lifetime, the poor are essentially forced to trade off quality of children in favour of quantity. Child labour facilitates this trade-off by relieving the need to drastically curtail current consumption in order to increase family size.

This chapter considers a scenario where education offers attractive private returns but parents can neither save for their retirement nor borrow against the future earnings of their children because they lack access to capital markets. It is shown that even if education is completely subsidized by the state, parents who are themselves educated are more likely to educate their children than are uneducated parents. This is because educated adults have a higher present income, and the diminishing marginal current utility of income implied by risk-aversion renders them more amenable to taking the risk of educating a child than are uneducated parents who earn a lower income. Thus, the institution of child labour, by facilitating risk-diversification for parents in the face of child mortality, is a poverty trap. This may partly explain why, despite significant returns on education and a substantial increase in the availability of schools in a developing country such as India, progress in literacy rates is excruciatingly slow.

It is well known that the inability of the poor in developing countries to borrow leads to the generation and perpetuation of class structure. Unequal access to capital has been shown to lead to class structure in production organisations.[5] In addition, by facilitating consumption-smoothing and risk absorption, access to consumption credit can promote the adoption of risky, but profitable, crops such as the high-yielding varieties that spearheaded the Green Revolution.[6] In this chapter, it is seen that lack of access to credit markets leads the poor to perpetuate poverty in yet another—and possibly the most pernicious—manner: it forces them to bear children and leave them illiterate in order to facilitate the bearing of yet more children.

Finally, this chapter discusses some policy implications that follow from the analysis. First, it is argued that government expenditures devoted to the delivery of health care targetted to the reduction of child mortality rates can have substantial payoffs for society by rendering the risk–return combination for educated children more attractive than that for uneducated ones. Second, it is argued that the enforcement of compulsory education that is subsidised for one generation by the state could render the education of children completely compatible with the self-interest of parents in subsequent generations, thus permanently eliminating the equilibrium in which children are borne but are deprived of an education. These two policies are complementary, since the former by itself could not counter the reluctance of parents to educate their daughters in many developing countries (such as India) where the old-age security system relies only on support from sons.

Cain (1981) was the first to suggest that in developing countries the demand for children is motivated by parents' desire to counter the risk of being left without old-age support; that is, parents view children as insurance against contingencies in old age when insurance markets are unavailable.[7] Appelbaum and Katz (1991) have provided a formal model of the demand for children in the absence of capital and insurance markets, when this demand is motivated by risk and insurance considerations.[8] The focus of their attention is the risk arising from uncertainty in the incomes of parents and children; child mortality is not explicitly addressed. In a paper investigating the relationship between child mortality and fertility, Sah (1991) has demonstrated with an elegant model that, consistent with empirical observations, the fertility of risk-averse parents can decline as child mortality rates decline.[9] Eswaran (1995) has theoretically examined circumstances under which reductions in child mortality rates can induce demographic transitions in developing countries.[10] In none of these studies, however, is the institution of child labour a serious consideration. One of the contributions of this chapter is the point that the viability of the institution of child labour in developing countries is intimately related to the prevalence of high child mortality rates.

The economic contribution of child labour and its role in determining fertility in developing countries is empirically well-documented.[11] In his study on the economic activities of children in the village of Char Gopal (Bangladesh), Cain (1977: 40) concludes that high fertility is rational for parents on the basis of the economic contribution of children. He estimates that 'male children become net producers by age 12, compensate for their cumulative consumption by age 15, and compensate for their own and one sister's cumulative consumption by age 22'.[12] Assessing the economic contribution of children in the Nepalese and Javanese peasant societies, Nag, White and Peet (1978) concluded that the contribution was substantial in terms of the household economy and also in terms of support for elderly parents.[13] Examining data from six villages in the Marathwada region of Maharashtra, India, Nadkarni (1976) has corroborated Mamdani's (1972) thesis that poor households in India find their family labour to be an asset and definitely not a surplus.[14]

Rosenzweig and Evenson (1977) empirically tested the importance of children's earnings on fertility at an aggregate level. Using district-level data for 189 districts of rural India in 1961, they sought to explain variations in fertility, child labour force participation and school enrollment. They found that the wage rate of children significantly increased fertility and decreased enrollment in schools.[15]

The rest of the chapter is organised as follows: Section I briefly describes some of the salient aspects of child labour in India, drawing from the voluminous literature on the subject (but citing only a representative sample of references); Section II spells out the model used to investigate the impact of child labour on fertility and literacy; Section III presents some results generated from the model; and Section IV discusses the policy implications of these results. Concluding observations are made in Section V.

I A CASE IN POINT: CHILD LABOUR IN INDIA

Child labour is a very pervasive phenomenon in India. Estimates of the number of child workers vary, depending on the source. The official estimate of this number in 1983 was 17.4 million children below the age of 15 years. By including child labourers who work but are not paid, the Operations Research Group of Baroda arrived at an estimate of 44 million child workers.[16] About 86 per cent of the child labour in the country is engaged in family labour alongside parents in the agricultural sector. Of the remaining, part is in family enterprise such as handicrafts, where the children assist their parents. The rest of the child labour is hired out to entrepreneurs and restaurants, for example. Some of the industrial activities in which child labour is pervasive are in the manufacture of carpets, matches, glassware and bangles, *bidis* (local cigarettes) and brassware.

Work consumes a substantial fraction of the time of child labourers. A study of child labour in different occupations in Greater Bombay was undertaken by the National Institute of Public Cooperation and Child Development. Singh, Kaura and Khan found that child labourers worked daily for an average of 8.5 hours in service establishments, 9 hours in garages and construction work, 11–12 hours in restaurants and 8 hours in domestic work.[17] In view of this, it is not surprising that their academic achievements are stunted. For example, in a study of child labour in metropolitan Delhi, Nangia found that 33 per cent of his sample were illiterate, and 43 per cent were literate but had not even attained primary level education. Only 20 per cent of the sample had completed primary education, and 2 per cent had completed middle-level education.[18] This finding regarding the poor educational attainments of child labourers is replicated in numerous studies. At an aggregate level in 1981, around 51.7 per cent of the 158.8 million children in the age group 6–14 years did not attend school, despite the universal availability of neighbourhood schools.[19]

Child mortality rates are strongly correlated inversely with family income levels (World Development Report 1993).[20] Since child labourers hail from poor families, their experience with child mortality is unusually high. For example, in the study of Nangia previously alluded to, one-third of the child workers in the sample had lost brothers and two-thirds had lost sisters. This also reflects the well-known fact that the mortality rates of female children in India are significantly higher than those of male children.[21]

The contribution of child labour income to the family income, typically, is quite substantial. In a micro level study of child labour in four districts of the state of Tamil Nadu in 1986–87, Sumangala and Nagarajan found the following distribution of the contribution of child labour income to the family income in their sample of 400 child workers and their families. In 15.25 per cent of the families the contribution was up to 10 per cent of family income; in 41.5 per cent of the families between 11–20 per cent; in 23.73 per cent of the families between 21–30 per cent; in 12.5 per cent of the families between 31–40 per cent; in 4.75 per cent of the families between 41–50 per cent; in 1.25 per cent of the families between 51–60 per cent; in 0.75 per cent of the families between 60–70 per cent; and in 0.25 per cent of the families the contribution was above 71 per cent.[22] This distribution is consistent with those found in several other studies conducted in other parts of India.

Not only do child workers contribute substantially to family income, their role in holding the family above the poverty line is significant. For example, in a study of child labour in the urban informal sector of the city of Patiala in the mid-1980s, Sharma and Mittar found the following incidence of poverty in their sample.[23] The percentage of households below the poverty line when child labour income is included (excluded) was 22.2 per cent (77.8 per cent) for households of three to four persons; 58.7 per cent (85.3 per cent) for five to six persons; 64.0 per cent (75.8 per cent) for seven to eight persons; and 69.7 per cent (87.9 per cent) for nine persons and above. A significant proportion of the families with child labourers, therefore, manage to stay above the poverty line by means of income derived from child labour. The authors also find that there seems to be a positive relationship between the size of the family and the proportion of families below the poverty line, a relationship that is stronger if the income from child labour is excluded.

Female child labourers typically tend to hail from families that are poorer than those from which male child labourers come. This is seen, for example, in a study conducted in the 1980s by Patil of 600 child workers in the city of Bangalore. The male (female) child labourers' share of the family income, 4.82 per cent (1.64 per cent) contributed nothing to the family income, 23.64 per cent (9.01 per cent) had a share up to 10 per cent; 28.24 per cent (22.13 per cent) had a share between 11 and 25 per cent; 17.99 per cent (32.78 per cent) had a share between 26 and 50 per cent; 17.16 per cent (22.95 per cent) had a share of more than 50 per cent but less than 100 per cent; 5.64 per cent (9.01 per cent) had a share of 100 per cent; 2.51 per cent (3.28 per cent) had no idea of their contribution.[24] The contribution of female child labourers is higher than that of their male counterparts in the upper end of the distribution. Thus the share of family income attributable to female child workers is higher than that attributable to male child workers. As Patil points out, this is so because more of the female child workers come from poorer families than do male child workers.

Child workers typically come from large families. A recent study of child labour in the carpet-producing belt in the state of Uttar Pradesh in India confirms this. It was found that of the working children sampled, none came from families of one to three persons; 14 per cent came from families of four to six persons; 65 per cent came from families of seven to ten persons; the remaining 21 per cent came from families exceeding ten persons.[25] As mentioned previously, at an aggregate level, Rosenzweig and Evenson find a positive correlation between fertility and the child wage rate in rural India of 1961.[26]

There is considerable legislation in India intended, in principle, to protect the interests of child workers.[27] Indeed, the Constitution of India bans child labour and promises compulsory education for all children. In reality, however, enforcement has been all but nonexistent, and in 1986, in enacting the Child Labour (Prohibition and Regulation) Act, the Government of India conceded that child labour cannot be abolished in the current stage of the country's development. In this piece of legislation, the government sought, rather, to institute regulations intended to ensure that children are not exploited and to improve their conditions of work. Furthermore, although there is legislation allowing for the possibility of local bodies implementing compulsory education, it does not require education to be compulsory. Indeed, the procedure prescribed for implementing compulsory education is such that it cannot withstand the opposition of the parents of child labourers, should they find that their vested interest is in having their children work.

In summary, child labourers in India tend to come from large, poor families to whom the income from child labour represents a significant contribution. Child labourers are poorly educated, if at all, and these children typically experience high mortality rates. Legislation regarding child labour and compulsory education, while on the books, are perceived to be unenforceable.

II THE MODEL

In this section, a simple model is set out in which parents' choices regarding fertility and the education of their children in the presence of child mortality are endogenously determined in terms of the pension motive. The model is a simplified version of the framework set out recently in Eswaran (1995), but to which the possibilities of child labour and education are added.[28]

Each agent (assumed sexless but referred to as 'he') is assumed to live for three periods. In the first period, the person is a child. In the second period of his life, the person earns an income by working. In this period, the person is bound by altruism to take care of his parents by transferring some of his income to them. In the second period, the agent also makes fertility decisions. In the third period, the agent is in retirement and lives on the income he receives from his surviving children.

The preferences attributed to a generation t adult, $t = 0, 1, 2, \ldots$, are assumed to be represented by the additive utility function:

(1) $$U(c_3^{t-1}, c_2^t, c_3^t) = u(c_3^{t-1}) + u(c_2^t) + u(c_3^t).$$

where c_i^t denotes the consumption of an agent of generation t in period i, $i = 1, 2, 3$, of his life. The von Neuman-Morgenstern utility function $u(.)$ is assumed to be strictly concave: all agents are risk-averse. The first term on the right hand side of (1) captures, as in Zhang and Nishimura (1993), the altruism of an adult towards his elderly parent: it represents the utility that an adult receives from seeing his parent consume c_3^{t-1} in his retirement.[29] This is also the utility the parent gets from his consumption in his last period. Note that while altruism towards parents is captured in these preferences, altruism towards children is not. This is a simplification, but one that is appropriate to invoke when considering the old-age security motive for having children.

The cost of raising n children, $B(n)$, is assumed to be given exogenously by a non-decreasing, convex function:[30]

(2) $$B(n) = B_1 n^{\theta},\ B_1 > 0,\ \theta \geq 1.$$

An essential feature of the model is the fact that not all the children an agent has will live to be adults. It is assumed that infants who die are swiftly and costlessly replaced. Denote by q the probability that a child who has survived early childhood will live to be a working adult. (This will subsequently be referred to as the *survival probability*.) The survival probability is taken to be exogenous and independent of the parent's income. Moreover, it will be assumed that the probabilities of different children dying before reaching adulthood are statistically independent. Then the probability, $p(q; n, m)$, that m of n children will survive to adulthood is given by the binomial probability.[31]

In the model that is constructed here, it is presumed that there are no capital markets. As in Neher (1971), children are the only capital goods available, and so all saving is done through them.[32] This is a very appropriate assumption to make for a substantial fraction of the population of many present-day LDCs.

All parents are dependent in their old age on income transfers from their children. It is assumed that the fallback utility of a person who in retirement is childless is $\bar{u}$.This is the utility of surviving by such means as living off the commons, living with distant relatives or living on alms. Clearly, this fallback utility is deemed so low that having children is viewed almost as a necessity in this society.

In the first period of a person's life, the person is a child who is either sent to school to receive an education or is put to work at home or outside the home. In the second period, the person is an adult, earning an income that depends on whether or not he was schooled in the first period. Apart from making fertility decisions (how many children to have), the adult also makes schooling decisions (how many of the children, if any, are to be sent to school and how many put to work). In the third period, the agent is in retirement, and lives on the income he receives from his surviving children, if any.

The maintained assumption that children are the only avenue for savings implies that the education of children, if undertaken at all, must be entirely self-financed by curtailing current consumption. Even if education is provided free of charge by the state, as is assumed to be the case here, parents cannot borrow money to compensate for the child labour income foregone by sending the child to school.

The decision to educate a child will clearly depend on the extent to which a child can augment the family income.[33] Even if they deem education for their children to be worthwhile, there is no presumption that parents will choose to educate all of them. The likelihood of girls being educated in many developing countries is less than that of boys. Even among boys, it is fairly common for only some of them to be schooled while others in the same family are not. Suppose that of the n^t children an adult of generation t chooses to have, he educates n^t_e and leaves unschooled the remaining $n^t_u \equiv n^t - n^t_e$. Denote by m^t_e and m^t_u, respectively, the number of schooled and unschooled children who survive until adulthood;[34] these are the children who will provide old-age support for the parent. From the point of view of a parent making decisions in his period 2, of course, these numbers are random variables.

The incomes of an unschooled adult, a schooled adult and of a child are denoted by y_u, y_e and y_c, respectively, all exogenously given, with $y_e > y_u > y_c$. It is assumed that the income generated by a child's labour, y_c, is the same irrespective of whether the child works inside or outside the home. The assumption that the various incomes are assumed to be exogenous implies that the analysis is one of partial equilibrium. As will be seen, the analysis underlying the results obtained here is robust, and thus very little is to be gained by conducting a general equilibrium analysis in which these incomes are endogenous.

In setting out an agent's optimization problem, a natural assumption will be invoked to simplify the problem while retaining the primary focus of attention, which is the pension motive as a determinant of choices regarding fertility and schooling. It will be assumed here that each surviving offspring is required to hand over a positive fraction α of his period 2 income to his parent, where α is exogenously determined by social and cultural traditions.[35] Since the filial obligations of a generation $t + 1$ adult are prespecified, a generation t adult does not have to condition his choices on his expectations of his children's fertility. Severance from the past and the endogenous choices of the future implies that the optimization problem confronting an adult is not generation-dependent; the model has no inherent dynamics. (Hence the time superscript will be dropped subsequently.) Since the incomes of schooled and unschooled adults are different, however, these two types of agents (denoted by e and u subscripts) will need to be distinguished.

Under the assumptions made above, an adult of type i $\{e, u\}$ solves:

$$\max_{n,\, ne} u[(1-\alpha)y_i - B(n) + (n - n_e)\, y_c] + p(q, n_u, 0)\, p(q, n_e, 0)$$

(3)

$$\bar{u} + \sum_{\substack{m_u, m_e \\ m_u + m_e > 0}} p(q; n_u, m_u)\, p(q; n_e, m_e)\, u[\alpha(m_u y_u + m_e y_e)].$$

The first term in the objective function in (3) represents the current period utility of the adult making the decisions: this is the utility derived from current consumption, given by total income (inclusive of child labour income) less the transfer to one's parent and the cost of rearing one's children. The second term represents the expected utility of the adult in retirement when none of his children survive to adulthood. The last term represents the adult's expected utility in retirement from income transfers received from his surviving children. On invoking the assumption that an adult transfers a fixed proportion of his period 2 income to his parent, the utility derived by the adult from his parent's consumption reduces to an additive constant independent of the adult's control and, hence, has been dropped.

III RESULTS

The fertility rate, the number of children to educate and the number to leave unschooled are all discrete choice variables here. If these were treated as continuous variables, the risk to a parent arising from child mortality would be entirely eliminated, for one could infer with certainty that exactly a proportion q of one's children will survive. (Child mortality could then merely be seen as increasing the effective cost of raising a child to survive into adulthood.) The elimination of the risk associated with child mortality is inappropriate here, since this risk is modelled here as an essential determinant of fertility and of educational choices. However, the discreteness of the choice variables renders difficult the derivation of analytic solutions. Nevertheless, we present below some analytic results and make some plausible inferences based on numerical simulations.

For very low survival probabilities, an adult would not have any children since the expected return from the consumption-smoothing service children may provide is too low to warrant the cost. When the only motive for having children is the pension motive, as is the case in the model under consideration, the survival probabilities have to be sufficiently large in order for fertility to be positive. Denote by q_i^u (q_i^e) the minimal survival probability required to induce an adult of type i $\{e, u\}$ to have one uneducated (educated) child. It is a simple matter to discern how these probabilities change with various parameters. At probability q_i^u (q_i^e), the adult is indifferent between having one uneducated (educated) child and having none. Thus the probability q^u_i is determined by the condition:

$$\text{(4)} \qquad u[(1-\alpha)y_i - B(1) + y_c] + qu(\alpha y_u) + (1-q)\bar{u} = u[(1-\alpha)y_i] + \bar{u}.$$

Likewise, the probability q^e_i is determined by the condition:

$$\text{(5)} \qquad u[(1-\alpha)y_i - B(1)] + qu(\alpha\, y_e) + (1-q)\bar{u} = \bar{u}[(1-\alpha)y_i] + \bar{u}.$$

Some properties of the probabilities of $q^u{}_i$ and q^e_i are recorded in the following propositions.[36]

Proposition 1: The smallest survival probability at which an adult will have one uneducated child is (*a*) decreasing in the child labour income, y_c, (*b*) decreasing in the uneducated worker's income, y_u, (*c*) increasing in the fallback utility in childless retirement $\bar{u}$, and (*d*) lower for an educated parent than for an uneducated one.

Parts (*a*) and (*b*) of the above proposition follow from the fact that higher incomes of a child labourer and of an uneducated worker both increase the parent's rate of return on an uneducated child for a given survival probability—the former by lowering costs and the latter by increasing the pension benefits. Part (*c*) follows from the fact that if the fallback utility without children in retirement is higher, an adult would require a higher expected return on children in order to be induced into having a child for pension purposes. Finally, part (*d*) follows from the fact that educated adults, by assumption, are currently earning higher incomes than are uneducated ones and, given risk-aversion, their marginal utility of current consumption is lower. Thus the desire for consumption-smoothing renders educated adults more willing to take the chance of having a child.

The analogue of Proposition 1 for a child who is educated is the following.

Proposition 2: The smallest survival probability at which an adult will have one educated child is (*a*) decreasing in the educated worker's income, y_e, (*b*) increasing in the fallback utility in childless retirement $\bar{u}$, and (*c*) lower for an educated parent than for an uneducated one.

The intuition for the above proposition is similar to that of Proposition 1. An important implication of part (*c*) of Proposition 2 is that educated (rich) parents are better able to take advantage of the high returns of children's education than are uneducated parents. The greater risk that the education of a child exposes parents to is a poverty trap: it discourages the poor from educating their children. This result underlines the point that economic development in the sense of higher per capita incomes would automatically reduce the incidence of child labour. The reason is not that richer people do not need the income from child labour: higher incomes increase a parent's demand for consumption-smoothing, and this could be satisfied merely by having more uneducated children. Rather, the reason for this result here is that, as they get richer, adults are better able to handle the risk of losing the investment in their children's education. This result is analogous to one derived in Eswaran and Kotwal (1989), where it was shown that rich landlords were more apt to adopt the riskier but more productive HYV technologies during the Green Revolution, since they were better able to smooth consumption than were poor farmers.[37]

The above discussion compares the probabilities q_i^u and q_i^e for parents of different incomes. It is not possible, however, to order q_i^u and q_i^e for the same adult; if the income of an educated child is so high that it more than compensates for the increased risk that educating children exposes parents to, adults may opt to have and educate a child at lower survival probabilities than they would have in an uneducated one. By rearranging (4) and (5), it is easily seen that for an adult of type i $\{e, u\}$, $q_i^u < q_i^e$ provided y_e is not too high relative to y_u. Since one rarely observes the return on education to be so high as to directly induce parents to have children and educate them, it is reasonable to assume that $q_i^u < q_i^e$ is the valid scenario.

For values of survival probabilities larger than that required to induce an adult to have one child, parents may opt to have more children. An increase in the survival probability not only increases the expected return on a child but also impinges on the risk parents face of being left childless in retirement. When the survival probability increases to sufficiently high levels, the reduction in risk may induce parents to actually reduce their fertility.[38] More relevant to the discussion here, however, is the interaction between fertility and the education of children. Given the discreteness of the choice variables, the precise mix of educated and uneducated children a parent would find it optimal to have cannot be determined analytically.

It is clear that a parent will either educate all children or educate none when the survival probability of children approaches unity.

In this limit, all risk arising from child mortality ceases, and the decision to educate children or to leave them uneducated is determined entirely by the relative rates of return. This is not the case, however, for intermediate values of the survival probability, as will be seen in the numerical results presented below. For given values of the survival probability, y_c and y_u, the mix is likely to tilt in favour of educated children the higher the value of y_e. Of course, if y_e is not high enough to induce parents to educate their children when $q = 1$, they will certainly not educate any when $q < 1$ since in the latter scenario education entails risk in addition to having lower expected returns.

In what follows, the sub-utility function appearing in (1) is assumed to be logarithmic:

(6) $$u(c_i^t) = \ln(c_i^t),\ i = 1, 2, 3;\ t = 0, 1, 2, \ldots.$$

This function is particularly appropriate since it severely penalises very low levels of consumption, a feature that is important to the phenomenon being investigated.

Figure 9.1 displays the optimal fertility and schooling choices of uneducated parents (lower panel) and of educated parents (upper panel) as a function of the survival probability, q. (The parameter values are indicated at the bottom of the figure.) The two types of parents are distinguished here simply by their incomes. These incomes, in turn, impinge on their demands for consumption-smoothing and on their ability to bear risk. As q increases beyond about 0.6 in the figure, uneducated parents start reducing the number of children they have. However, they do not educate their children until q reaches about 0.95, at which point one schooled child is the optimal choice of these parents. The broad features of the choices made by educated parents, shown in the upper panel of Figure 9.1, are different in some essential ways from those made by uneducated parents. Since the former earn higher incomes, they necessarily will have more (or at least as many) children in a world where no borrowing is possible.[39] As the survival probability increases beyond 0.26, educated parents also begin to have fewer children; as q approaches 0.6 they begin educating some of them; before q reaches 0.65, all the children of educated parents are educated.

Observe that the greater tendency exhibited by richer, educated parents to opt for the riskier asset (educated children) arises despite the fact that the logarithmic sub-utility function (6) exhibits increasing absolute risk aversion. Here, as in Eswaran and Kotwal (1989), the consumption-smoothing behaviour of risk-averse agents is driven only by the concavity of the von Neuman-Morgenstern utility function.[40]

Figure 9.1 also shows that fertility begins its decline at lower levels of survival probability for educated (rich) parents than for uneducated (poor) ones. This is because the former, earning a higher income, can have more children and thus more effectively protect themselves against the prospect of being left without support in old age. In other words, the prospect of facing retirement without surviving children ceases to be threatening at lower levels of survival probabilities for educated parents than for unschooled ones.

Since the type of economy being assumed here is one in which children are the only form of savings, it would not be surprising if rates of return on children are negative;[41] agents desiring consumption-smoothing would accept negative rates of return when that is the only option available. (This rate of return will depend, of course, on the survival probability q.) If the parameter in (2) is unity, the expected marginal rate of return on a child would be independent of the number of children there are in the family—although it will depend on whether the child is educated or not. However, when greater than one, the expected marginal rate of return for each type of child will decline with family size, since the marginal cost of a child is increasing in the number of children.

Denote by $r_e(n)$ and $r_u(n)$ the marginal rate of return to the parent on the nth child when the child is educated and uneducated, respectively. Denote by r_s the rate of return to the parent on the child's schooling.[42] For the parameter values indicated at the bottom of Figure 9.1, these rates of return to the parent for the very first child turn out to be given by $r_u(1) = 1.2\,q - 1$ and $r_e(1) = 1.4\,q - 1$. The parental rate of return on the schooling of children is given by $r_s = 1.6\,q - 1$. Thus the return to parents of their children's schooling becomes positive at survival probability 0.625. From Figure 9.1 it is seen that, despite the fact that the parental return of an educated child exceeds the return of an uneducated one for all positive survival probabilities, uneducated parents opt for the education of their children only when the survival probability reaches 0.95; at lower values of q, they would rather have more uneducated children than fewer educated ones. This is because the education of children would call for a drastic reduction in fertility, since the labour income of the children has to be relinquished. And this reduction in fertility would be unpalatable from the point of view of old-age security. Educated parents, on the other hand, begin to educate their children even before the expected return on schooling becomes positive, though they will not necessarily educate all their children for survival probabilities less than one.

These results may explain why parents may not opt to educate their children even when the private return on education is very high. When the survival probability is slightly below 0.95 in the above example, the parental return on the education of their children is 52 per cent. In contrast, the true private rate of return on education is a staggering 660 per cent in this case.[43] Thus, even when the rate of return on education is substantial, the institution of child labour generates a poverty trap. This is seen to be true here when the expenses of education are assumed to be borne entirely by the state. Were parents to incur school expenses, the argument made here would apply with greater force. In his survey of returns on education in over sixty countries, Psacharopoulos reports that the private rate of return on education in Asia as a whole is 31 per cent, 15 per cent and 18 per cent for primary, secondary and higher education, respectively.[44]

In India, since Independence, schools have been made available within each village. Despite this, the attendance rate of children is appallingly low. In aggregate, only 44.5 per cent of the male children and 32.3 per cent of the female children within the ages of 5–9 years were attending school in 1985–86. Furthermore, the combined dropout rate for male and female children from primary school was 47.6 per cent and 64.4 per cent for children in middle school.[45] Thus not only is it difficult to persuade parents to send their children to school in the first place, it is also difficult for schools to retain a large proportion of the children who do begin schooling.[46]

Investment in the education of girls is frequently considered a waste, particularly in South Asia. For example, according to the 1981 Census of India, the male and female literacy rates in the country were 40.8 per cent and 18.0 per cent, respectively, in rural areas, and 65.9 per cent and 47.8 per cent, respectively, in urban areas. In the same year, of children in the school-going ages of 6–14, the number attending school was 47.9 million boys and 28.7 million for girls. It is easy to see why this arises in the South Asian context: old age security is largely provided by male children and hardly at all by female children. In terms of the above model, the parameter for daughters is either zero or close to it; so the parental return on schooling is negative. Even if parents have no aversion to receiving financial help in old age from their daughters, the incentive to invest in the education of daughters would be diluted if, for whatever reason, the labour market discriminates against women, that is, if for equal education levels, y_e is lower for women than for men.

It must be noted, however, that there are several other important avenues that are not modelled here through which education impinges on fertility and schooling decisions. For example, educated parents are better able to recognise the life-threatening illnesses of their children and are able to take timely steps to avert disaster. Education also brings home the importance of hygiene and of balanced nutrition. All these effectively increase a child's survival probability (which in the model is taken as exogenous to individuals). In other words, educated parents have the added advantage of being able to better protect their investment in children than uneducated parents. This reinforces the result that educated parents tend to educate their children.[47]

In the model of this chapter, the higher income accruing to educated adults cannot be invested in riskless, non-human assets which can be liquidated in retirement. Were this possible, a higher income in the working period would automatically translate into a higher fallback utility of childless retirement, $\bar{u}$. As income increases, agents will increase the number of children they have if the rate of return on children is high enough to compensate for the higher risk they entail than do the non-human assets. As the return on children decreases in the number of children, there will be a point beyond which all additional income will be invested in the non-human assets and in the education of children. Thus, ultimately higher incomes will not translate into commensurate increases in fertility rates but, rather, into higher education levels of children. If income levels determine the access an agent has to capital markets—a scenario that is very plausible in developing countries—it is entirely possible that fertility would, in fact, decline with income.[48] This could well be an important route through which economic development leads to a lower population rate of growth, rationalizing the belief that 'the most effective contraceptive is development'.[49] Neher (1971)[50] has argued that the emergence of capital markets would lead to a decline in the steady-state population of a primitive economy, since children and savings accounts would be perceived as substitutes.[51]

Figure 9.2 displays the number of children parents find it optimal to have and the number they send to school as a function of the income generated by child labour. Since child labour helps defray some or all of the costs of having children, parents of course opt to have more children and educate a smaller proportion of them as the child labour income increases. More interestingly, the figure shows that for educated parents to completely cease from educating any of their children, the child labour income must be much higher than that required to persuade uneducated parents to withdraw all their children from school. This is consistent with the empirical fact that there is a greater preponderance of child labour in the families of uneducated parents than those of educated ones.

A higher income for child labour is not necessarily in the interest of children. To the extent that parents are driven to settle for short-term gains and a more secure retirement, the institution of child labour militates against the long-run interests of children.[52] From Figure 9.2 we see that, when the child labour income is not excessively high, educated parents choose to curtail their fertility and to educate their children. Thus, enforced compulsory education for one generation would tend to induce a permanent transition to an equilibrium in which children are *voluntarily* educated in all subsequent generations.[53]

Developed countries have recently started contemplating a ban on the imports of the products which use child labour in developing countries. Such a ban, by lowering the return to child labour, may encourage parents to send their children to school. However, such a measure would affect only those industries in which the demand for child labour is derived from export markets; the proportion of such industries may be quite small. If this is so, the elimination of export markets for some industries would result, most likely, in merely reallocating the existing child labourers among the industries serving only domestic markets, and the reduction in child labour earnings may be marginal. Furthermore, in the short run this measure would make the lot of children worse; fertility would adjust only in the future. Thus, before implementing a ban on the imports of products produced with child labour, the developed countries should ensure that the developing countries' governments have in place some income-supplementing scheme for families with child labourers.[54] If not, a ban of this sort would hurt the very children it is intended to protect.

IV TWO POLICY RECOMMENDATIONS

The results of the simple model of fertility and schooling choices in a less developed country analyzed above suggest that governments can play an important role in alleviating the problem of child labour. Two clear policy implications emerge.

Universalising and Improving the Health Care Delivery System

Investment in health care is an important input into the determination of the mortality rates of children who are potentially capable of providing old-age support for their parents. This is particularly so since a large proportion of deaths between the ages of 15 and 60 years are health-related. For example, Table 2–14 in Murray, Yang and Qiao reveals that in 1986, of the Indian males (females) who died between the ages of 15 and 60 years, 80 per cent (84 per cent) died of communicable, reproductive and non-communicable diseases; the rest died due to injuries.[55] Thus there is considerable scope for reducing mortality rates in the relevant age groups by improving access to medical intervention.

A decline in mortality rates has important consequences for the incidence of child labour. Since, for a given fertility, more children are expected to survive to adulthood when mortality rates fall, parents need have fewer children to protect themselves against a retirement without any surviving children. Since current consumption thus is not excessively constrained by a large number of children, the need for parents to have their children augment the family income is diminished. Thus parents would be more disposed to send their children to school.

There is, however, a further effect of declining child mortality rates on the institution of child labour. We have seen that, at high levels of mortality rates, in terms of old-age security, unschooled children are deemed better assets than schooled ones, whereas the opposite is true at low mortality rates. Lower mortality rates alter the risk–return combination in favour of educated children and, hence, would lower the incidence of child labour. This suggests that efforts on the part of government through increased public expenditure on health care to reduce mortality rates would contribute to an increase in the population's literacy level.

It has been demonstrated in Eswaran that at reasonably high levels of survival probabilities, fertility rates can fall more rapidly than mortality rates, so that a society's population rate of growth can decline when mortality rates decline.[56] Thus an increase in public expenditure directed at lowering child mortality rates in countries like India with high population growth rates would reduce the population growth rate and also effect a transition to a more literate population. It has certainly been recognised by policymakers that, empirically, reductions in fertility are closely linked to reductions in child mortality rates. For example, this was explicitly recognised in India after the Third Five-Year Plan and, in subsequent plans, family planning programmes have been linked to maternal and child health care programmes.[57] The point being made here, however, is that the benefits of reducing child mortality go well beyond the fact that it induces reductions in fertility.

The Enforcement of Compulsory Education

It was argued previously that by making educated children a better asset than uneducated ones, a policy intended to decrease child mortality will contribute to a decline in the incidence of child labour. Such a policy, however, is not likely to completely eliminate the institution of child labour in the cultural setting of countries like India. As mentioned earlier, old-age security for parents comes from male children in Indian and some other cultures. Thus, even if the expected return to parents on the education of sons is substantial, that on the education of daughters will likely be perceived to be considerably lower. It is unlikely, therefore, that daughters would be educated to the same degree as sons. A policy of compulsory education—which will be politically acceptable only when mortality rates are sufficiently low—would address this problem.

Girls of school-going ages are frequently prevented from attending school because they are required to help around the house, while their brothers are sent to school. In effect, given the cultural norm of reliance only on sons in old age, the institution of child labour (within or outside the home) presses daughters into service to subsidise the education of sons, in alignment with their parents' self-interest.[58] Legislating compulsory education and enforcing it would have an additional benefit, apart from lowering fertility rates and generating a more educated labour force: it would go a long way towards reducing discrimination against girls.

There is also a very direct (and well-understood) benefit that society derives from the education of girls in terms of lower fertility. There is strong empirical evidence that educated mothers not only have fewer children, but also experience lower child mortality rates.[59] The effect of fathers' education on these variables is much less important. There are many persuasive reasons for this: for example, marriages are later for educated women, opportunity costs of having children are higher and more effective measures are taken against life-threatening illnesses of children. It is ironic that a cultural bias in terms of old-age security militates against the education of the sex that matters more in the determination of fertility.

Demographers have argued that the demographic transition in the developed countries was hastened by compulsory education.[60] In fact, Weiner (1991) has argued that a ban on child labour is enforceable only when education becomes compulsory.[61] The reason is persuasive: it is considerably more difficult to verify that no agricultural or industrial enterprise is secretly employing children than to verify whether all the children in a neighbourhood are attending the local schools. Historically, child labour has been in existence in almost all the now-developed countries; sooner or later, however, this institution was rendered illegal.[62]

As an inducement to parents to educate their children, the subsidisation of schooling would clearly be appropriate. If the subsidy extends so far as to compensate parents for the entire child labour income they forgo by educating their children, getting children into school would be a relatively easy task, but the burden on the public purse may be prohibitive. Subsidisation to a partial extent may be feasible. Alternatively, the government could offer free education only for, say, the first two children of a couple, in order to encourage them to restrict fertility. This incentive scheme would work, however, only if parents perceive education to be essential for *all* their children. For reasons already discussed, this is likely to be so only when the mortality rates are low.

It must be noted that the expenditure of an education subsidy need be incurred by the state for a maximum of twelve years or so. It was seen in the previous section that, for sufficiently high survival probabilities, it is in the self-interest of educated parents to educate their children. Thus, if one generation of children is put through school, the higher incomes of this generation as adults would keep the momentum going. In other words, a once-and-for-all schooling subsidy could potentially move the economy permanently from an equilibrium of minimal literacy to one that has an educated labour force.

V CONCLUSION

This chapter has considered the incentives of adults to have and to educate children in an environment characterised by significant child mortality and by an absence of capital markets. It has been argued that, in the presence of high mortality rates, the institution of child labour renders uneducated children a better risk than educated ones from the point of view of old-age security. Consequently, even if the private return to parents on their children's education is substantial, they would opt for not educating children because this avenue affords better risk-diversification. Policies intended to reduce child mortality rates (a worthy goal in itself) will have the beneficial effect of undermining the institution of child labour by enhancing the value parents put on their children's education. These policies, however, need to be complemented by the legislation of compulsory education—especially in countries like India—to ensure that parents, driven by the pension motive, do not discriminate against daughters in the investment of education.

In his treatise on child labour in India, Weiner (1991) infers that poverty has little to do with the mass illiteracy that prevails in India. He argues that, rather, it is the 'belief system of the state bureaucracy' that is a more relevant explanatory factor. This belief system, which he avers is widely subscribed to, views education as a means for maintaining a distinction between classes; universal education is seen as a threat since it would blur these distinctions and result in social upheaval.[63] Without disputing the possibility that there may be some truth in Weiner's (1991) sociological theory, this chapter may be seen as offering an alternative view. It has been argued here that there are sound economic reasons, rooted in poverty, for the perpetuation of illiteracy in developing countries, particularly India. Consequently, there are sound economic policies that could contribute to the eradication of the institution of child labour.

Figure 9.1

Fertility and Schooling Decisions as Functions of the Survival Probability of Children. (Parameter values: $\alpha = 0.2$, $y_c = 2$, $y_u = 12$, $y_e = 28$, $B_1 = 4$, $\theta = 1.1$, $\bar{u} = -5$)

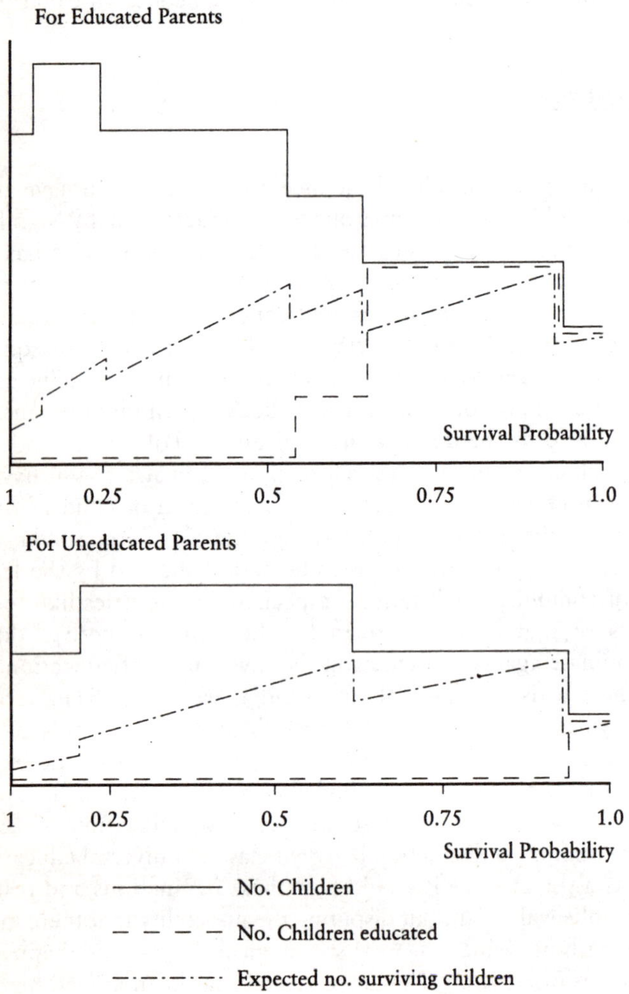

Figure 9.2

Fertility and Schooling Decisions as Functions of the Child Labour Income.
(Parameter values: $\alpha = 0.2$, $y_u = 12$, $y_e = 28$, $B_1 = 4$, $\theta = 1.1$, $\bar{u} = -5$, $q = 0.9$)

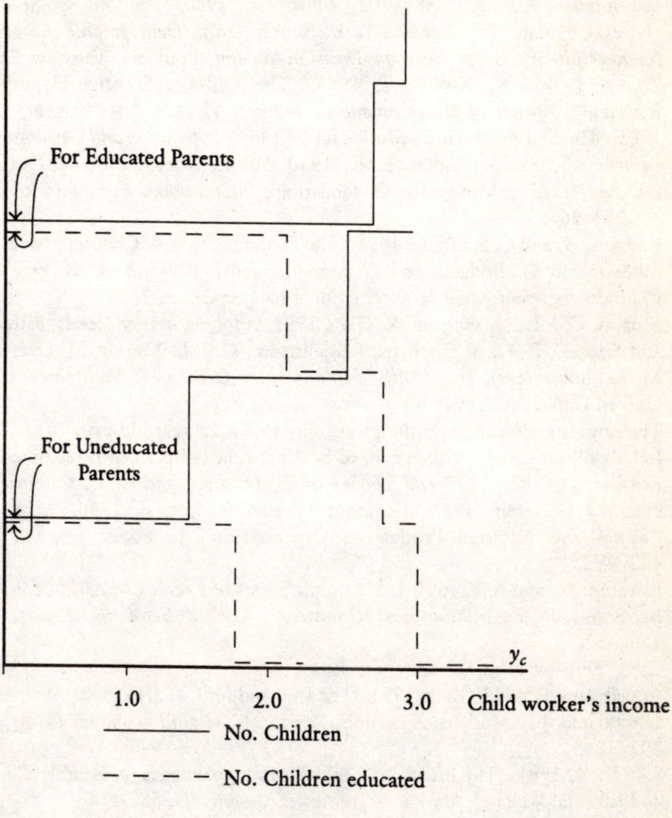

NOTES

*The research for this chapter was made possible through the support provided by the United States Agency for International Development to the Center for Institutional Reform and the Informal Sector (IRIS) and administered by the Office of Economic and Institutional Reform, Center for Economic Growth, Bureau for Global Programs, Field Support and Research, and was completed in June 1996. The author is grateful to Jonathan Kesselman and Bharat Ramaswamy for useful comments on an earlier draft, and to Hashmat Khan for research assistance.

1. Standard references for the analysis of the old-age security motive for having children are Neher; Cain; Willis; Zhang and Nishimura; and Nugent. An empirical verification of the hypothesis is provided in Jensen. Neher, P. A. 1971, 'Peasants, Procreation, and Pensions', *American Economic Review*, June, 380–89; Cain, M. 1983, 'Fertility as an Adjustment to Risk', *Population and Development Review*, 9, 688–702; Willis, R. J. 1980, 'The Old Age Security Hypotheses and Population', T. K. Burch (ed.), *Demographic Behavior: Interdisciplinary Perspectives on Decision-Making*, Boulder: Westview Press; Zhang, J. and K. Nishimura, 1993, 'The Old-Age Security Hypothesis Revisited', *Journal of Development Economics*, 41, 191–201; Nugent, J. B. 1985, 'The Old Age Security Motive for Fertility', *Population and Development Review*, 11, 75–98; Jensen, E. R. 1990, 'An Econometric Analysis of the Old-Age Security Motive for Childbearing', *International Economic Review*, 31, 953–968.
2. Rodgers, G. and G. Standing, 1981, 'The Economic Role of Children: Issues for Analysis', in G. Rodgers and G. Standing (eds), *Child Work, Poverty and Underdevelopment*, Geneva: International Labour Office, 26.
3. Murray, C. J. L., G. Yang and X. Qiao, 1992, 'Adult Mortality: Levels, Patterns, and Causes', R. G. A. Feachem, T. Kjellstrom, C. J. L. Murray, M. Over and M. A. Phillips (eds), *The Health of Adults in the Developing World*, New York: Oxford University Press.
4. The same source computes the probability that a 15 year old male (female) in India will not survive until age 40 to be 8 per cent (10 per cent). See note 3.
5. Roemer, J. 1982, *A General Theory of Exploitation and Class*, Cambridge: Harvard University Press; Eswaran, M. and A. Kotwal, 1986, 'Access to Capital and Agrarian Production Organisation', *Economic Journal*, 96, 482–498.
6. Eswaran, M. and A. Kotwal, 1989, 'Implications of Credit Constraints for Risk Behaviour in Less Developed Countries', *Oxford Economic Papers*, 42, 473–482.
7. Cain, 'Fertility as an Adjustment to Risk'.
8. Appelbaum, E. and E. Katz, 1991, 'The Demand for Children in the Absence of Capital and Risk Markets: A Portfolio Approach', *Oxford Economic Papers*, 43, 292–304.
9. Sah, R. K. 1991, 'The Effects of Child Mortality Changes on Fertility Choice and Parental Welfare', *Journal of Political Economy*, 99, 582–606.
10. Eswaran, M. 1995, 'One Explanation for the Demographic Transition in Developing Countries', University of British Columbia Discussion Paper No. 95–43.
11. For a survey of this literature, see Dinesh, B. M. 1988, *Economic Activities of Children: Dimensions, Causes and Consequences*. Delhi: Daya Publishing House.
12. Cain, Mead, 1977, 'Village Fertility Study', Report No. 3, *The Economic Activities of Children*, Dacca: Bangladesh Institute of Development Studies, 40. For an alternative view on the economic contribution of children, see Mueller, E. 1976, 'The Economic Value of Children in Peasant Agriculture' in R. Ridker (ed.), *Population and Development: A Search for Selective Interventions*, Baltimore: Johns Hopkins Press.

13. Nag, M., B. N. F. White and R. C. Peet, 1978, 'An Anthropological Approach to the Study of the Economic Value of Children in Java and Nepal', *Current Anthropology*, 19, 293–301.
14. Nadkarni, M. V. 1976, 'Over population and the Rural Poor', *Economic and Political Weekly*, August, 11, 31–33; Mamdani, M. 1973, 'The Myth of Population Control', *Monthly Review Press*, New York.
15. Rosenzweig, M. R. and R. Evenson, 1977, 'Fertility, Schooling, and the Economic Contribution of Children in Rural India: An Econometric Analysis', *Econometrica*, 45, 1065–1079. The next section outlines the evidence from India in somewhat greater detail.
16. Weiner, M. 1991, *The Child and the State in India*. Princeton: Princeton University Press.
17. Singh, M., V. D. Kaura and S. A. Khan, 1980, *Working Children in Bombay*, New Delhi: National Institute of Public Cooperation and Child Development, 63.
18. Nangia, P. 1987, *Child Labour: Cause-Effect Syndrome*, New Delhi: Janak Publishers, 166–68.
19. See note 16, chap. 5.
20. The World Bank, 1993, *The World Development Report 1993*, New York: Oxford University Press.
21. See note 18.
22. Sumangala, M. and B. S. Nagarajan, 1993, *Economics of Child Labour and Fertility*, Delhi: B. R. Publishing Corporation, 121.
23. The poverty line was computed by assuming that the income level ensures a minimum consumption of 2,383 calories per person. Sharma, B. K. and V. Mittar, 1990, *Child Labour and Urban Informal Sector*, New Delhi: Deep & Deep Publications, 109.
24. Patil, B. R. 1988, *Working Children in Urban India*, Bangalore: Indian Institute of Management, 141.
25. Vijayagopalan, S. 1993, *Child Labour in the Carpet Industry: A Status Report*, New Delhi: National Council of Applied Economic Research, 18.
26. See note 15.
27. The history of this legislation is comprehensively traced and documented in Weiner, chap. 16. See note 16.
28. See note 10.
29. Zhang and Nishimura, 'The Old-Age Security Hypothesis Revisited'.
30. Increasing returns to scale in raising a family may introduce a nonconcavity in the objective function in (3) following and thus is assumed away here. However, the nature of the results is not expected to change if this assumption is dropped.
31. More formally,

$$p(q; n,m) = \frac{n!}{m!(n-m)!} \quad q^m(1-q)^{n-m}.$$

32. Neher, 'Peasants, Procreation, and Pensions'.

33. This presumes that children are not given an education on a part-time basis—in the evenings, for example. While this is possible in principle, the present approach has the virtue of underlining the fact that losing an education is most frequently the opportunity cost of child labour.
34. It is assumed here, for simplicity, that the survival probabilities of educated and uneducated children are the same. One might expect that, in reality, greater parental care may be directed towards the educated children in order to protect their investment.
35. Neher, 'Peasants, Procreation, and Pensions', makes the assumption that consumption levels of all people in the extended family are determined by an exogenous rule he calls the 'share-alike ethic', in which all members of the family receive an equal share of the income. However, Neher's model is not equipped to deal adequately with the effects of child mortality on fertility and educational choices.
36. Proofs of these comparative static propositions are omitted because they are readily derived by totally differentiating expressions (4) and (5), respectively. The last parts of Propositions 1 and 2, following, invoke the strict concavity of the von Neuman-Morgenstern utility function implied by risk-aversion.
37. See note 6.
38. See notes 9 and 10.
39. This result will be tempered by other considerations, as later discussed.
40. See note 6.
41. Cain, 'Fertility as an Adjustment to Risk', forcibly makes the point that empirical studies arguing that bearing children is irrational in developing countries, when rates of return on children are negative, are misguided since parents choose a 'safety first' strategy for having children.
42. The expected marginal rate of return to the parent on the *n*th child is given by

$$r_u(n)\ \alpha\, q\, y_u / [B(n) - B(n-1) + y_c] - 1,$$

if the child is uneducated, and by

$$r_e(n)\ \alpha\, q\, y_e / [B(n) - B(n-1)] - 1,$$

if the child is educated. The denominators of the first terms on the right-hand sides of these expressions are the respective increases in cost incurred by the parent in raising a family with an additional child; the numerators are the revenues the parent expects to receive next period as pension from the child. The parental rate of return on a child's education is given by:

$$r_s\ \alpha q\, (y_e - y_u) / y_c - 1,$$

since once a child is born, by losing the child's labour income the parent receives a fraction of the expected increase in the adult earnings of the child.
43. The true private rate of return on a child's education is the return accruing to the parent plus that accruing to the child, and is given by:

$$q\, (y_e - y_u) / y_c - 1.$$

This is the private as opposed to the social rate of return, since education is assumed to be fully subsidised and so the cost to the state of providing the education is not factored in.

44. Psacharopoulos, G. 1985, 'Returns to Education: A Further International Update and Implications', *The Journal of Human Resources*, 20, 583–604.
45. Kumar, S. 1993, 'Child Labour and Education', in B. P. Singh and S. Mahanty (eds), *Children at Work*, Delhi: B. R. Publishing.
46. Of course, nonattendance in schools certainly cannot be entirely attributed to the riskiness of the investment. One reason often given by parents for not sending their children to school is the perceived irrelevance of education to earning a living.
47. Child labourers are exposed to higher mortality rates than other children, partly because of their greater expenditure of energy without a compensating increase in nutrition and partly because the work itself is frequently of a hazardous nature. This, through the pension motive, would reinforce the tendency of the poor to increase fertility, further entrenching the vicious circle of poverty and high fertility.
48. The same outcome would obtain if one invokes the standard argument that the opportunity cost of children is increasing in the income of the mother because of the time required for childbearing and childrearing.
49. This is the manner in which Chenais summarises the view of people who see growth in income as a precursor of the demographic transition. Chenais, J. C. 1992, *The Demographic Transition*, trans. E. and P. Kreager, Oxford: Clarendon Press.
50. Neher, 'Peasants, Procreation, and Pensions'.
51. This has been explicitly modelled recently by Zhang and Nishimura, 'The Old-Age Security Hypothesis Revisited'.
52. It might be argued that following a wage increase for child labour, if parents opt not to educate the child, it is because they are better off by doing so; when the child becomes an adult, he can do the same with respect to his own children. Thus the child must also be better off in terms of lifetime utility when child labour income rises. This, indeed, is so in the partial equilibrium model. The fact that increased participation in child labour and the increased number of children brought forth has enormous general equilibrium consequences is not captured here. In particular, the privately rational higher fertility would lower the wage rate of labour if there is a fixed factor such as land (see Eswaran, 'One Explanation', for an analysis). If, in addition, the source of demand for child labour dries up in the future, the current generation of children will be rendered unambiguously worse off.
53. One possibility not modelled here is that children are useful for performing household chores, which releases time for parents to engage in income-earning activities outside the home. This possibility would temper but not eliminate the effect on educational choice of a reduction in the labour income accruing to children.
54. This would be particularly relevant, for example, to the carpet industry of India alluded to previously, where the demand derives essentially from export markets. Child labour is especially deemed to be appropriate for the highly valued hand-knotted carpets, since the nimbleness of children's fingers, as opposed to

those of adults, enables them to make more knots per unit area (which increases the value of the carpets).

55. See note 3.
56. See note 10.
57. Srinivasan, K. 1995, *Regulating Reproduction in India's Population*. New Delhi: Sage Publications.
58. Nadkarni, in his survey of six villages in the Marathwada region of Maharashtra, India, found that the proportion of children who were prevented from attending school for the purpose of looking after their younger siblings and for doing household chores was 28.1 per cent for boys and 58.6 per cent for girls. Similar evidence can be found for Nepal in Nag, White, and Peet. See notes 13 and 14.
59. See, for example, *The World Development Report 1994*, and the references cited therein. (The World Bank, 1994, *The World Development Report 1994*, New York: Oxford University Press.)
60. Caldwell, J. C. 1982, *Theory of Fertility Decline*, New York: Academic Press.
61. See note 16, chap. 6.
62. Ibid.
63. See note 16.

PART IV

Agricultural Parastatals and Rural Governance

10

The Food Corporation of India: Successes and Failures in Indian Foodgrain Marketing

Ashok Gulati, Satu Kähkönen and Pradeep Sharma

Man cannot be too serious about eating, for food is the force that binds the society together.

Confucius

Given that about two-thirds of India's population earn their income from agriculture and that an Indian household spends an average of 30 per cent of its budget on foodgrains, the structure and efficiency of Indian foodgrain marketing is not inconsequential for the Indian economy.[1] Foodgrain marketing consists of all activities in the movement of foodgrains from producers to consumers.[2] These activities include the purchase, storage, transportation, distribution and processing of foodgrains. These marketing arrangements structure incentives to produce and trade foodgrains and, thereby, guide the economic activity within the agricultural sector. Hence, their structure and efficiency warrants a detailed analysis.

Government intervenes in foodgrain markets in India not only indirectly through pricing and other regulative policies, but also directly as a buyer and seller of foodgrains. India has dual foodgrain markets: a government-controlled public market and an open, private market. About half of the marketed surplus of foodgrains is channelled through the public market and the other half through the private one. However, while the private market is comprised of a large number of private traders competing with each other, the public market is controlled by one agency, the Food Corporation of India (FCI).

The FCI is a parastatal foodgrain marketing agency that represents the government in Indian foodgrain markets. It purchases, stores, transports and distributes foodgrains throughout the country. It procures rice and wheat from farmers at prices stipulated by the government. These foodgrains are then sold to consumers at subsidised prices through the public distribution system. In addition to these marketing activities, Indian imports of foodgrains are canalised through FCI. FCI is the largest agricultural parastatal in India in terms of turnover, the value of commodities and the significance of commodities in the Indian consumption basket. It also has the largest number of employees of all agricultural parastatals in India.

FCI was established to achieve the following objectives: (*a*) to provide price support to producers, (*b*) to distribute foodgrains at subsidised prices to the poor through the public distribution system, and (*c*) to ensure national food security by carrying buffer stocks. Its operation has been facilitated by various government policies such as concessional credit and transport, budget support and freedom from movement controls.

The purpose of this chapter is to evaluate the role and performance of FCI in Indian foodgrain marketing. Specifically, it aims to assess whether the Food Corporation of India has reached its objectives, and to evaluate the economic efficiency of its operations. Operations are considered to be efficient if they ensure high returns to producers at a low unit cost of distribution. Further, a marketing system is considered to be efficient if it stabilises producer and consumer prices and producer incomes, in addition to encouraging production. Given India's recent economic reforms and gradual liberalisation of the agricultural sector, this study also attempts to assess how the role of the Food Corporation of India would change if controls on agriculture were lifted.

This chapter shows that while FCI has reached some of its objectives, it has failed to target the distribution of foodgrains to poor people and regions, make its operations economically efficient and maintain buffer stocks at levels stipulated by the government. In particular, it is shown that while FCI has succeeded in improving the overall availability of foodgrains in India, it has failed to cover its costs by its revenues. The gap between its costs and revenues has been sharply widening over the years, leading to spiralling governmental subsidies. This financial imbalance is largely due to the high cost of its operations. Specifically, per-unit distribution costs of FCI have been excessive compared to those of private traders. The lack of accountability within FCI and the knowledge that the government will cover its costs, if necessary, have made inefficient operations possible.

Following this introduction, Section I discusses the emergence and the role of FCI in Indian foodgrain marketing. Section II reviews the objectives of the FCI and examines whether these objectives have been achieved. The economic appraisal of the FCI is carried out in Section III. Finally, Section IV contains a few concluding remarks and reform options.

I FOODGRAIN MARKETING AND FCI

The government began controlling foodgrain marketing in India in 1939 at the outbreak of the Second World War. The controls escalated, however, only after the Bengal Famine in 1943. The committee that was set up to explore the reasons for the famine concluded that the famine was due to the failure of the foodgrain distribution system, not due to a shortage of foodgrains in India as a whole. Because foodgrain markets across the country were not integrated, foodgrains from surplus areas failed to move to Bengal and prevent the famine. To correct this market failure, government intervened in foodgrain marketing.

The Department of Food under the Ministry of Agriculture was assigned to manage the Indian food economy. Its main functions were to import and procure foodgrains from farmers for public distribution, maintain central reserves, control and regulate prices of foodgrains and construct and hire storage facilities. Rationing and controls on the interstate movement of foodgrains were also introduced.

In 1952 the government announced a gradual relaxation of movement controls as the foodgrain supply situation improved. After approximately two years, rationing was drastically reduced and the interstate movement of wheat was restored. Procurement was abolished first for wheat and later for rice. With increased production and lower rationing commitments, the government was left with sizeable stocks of foodgrains, which it released to the market. Due to strict monetary controls and enhanced crop prospects, this caused a sharp decline in foodgrain prices between 1953–54. By 1954, rationing was completely abolished. Trade in foodgrains was free again.

By the middle of 1955, however, foodgrain prices started rising and government controls on foodgrain trade reemerged. Population growth and rising incomes led to a gradual rise in the demand for foodgrains. In 1957, the government set up a committee to analyse foodgrain marketing and suggest new food policies.

The committee recommended state trading of foodgrains. specifically, the committee advised the government to establish a Foodgrains Stabilisation Organisation. This organisation would not only take over some of the tasks of the Department of Food but operate as a trader in foodgrain markets.

Government intervention was deemed necessary on two counts: (*a*) to ensure the efficiency and integration of foodgrain markets—that is, to ensure the availability of foodgrains across markets over time, and the stability of foodgrain prices avoiding large differences between (i) producer and consumer prices, and (ii) prices across markets, and (*b*) to counterbalance speculative activities of private traders.[3] The premise was that Indian foodgrain markets are inefficient and disintegrated. Private traders were considered to be primarily responsible for this inefficiency and price variability. They were viewed as profiteers that held speculative stocks to earn above-normal profits. It was believed that their speculative activities could be countered only by either holding large stocks or imports in the public sector. It was held that, unlike private traders, a public sector agency would act in the social interest. It was also recognised that market prices of foodgrains are bound to fluctuate since the supply of foodgrains depends heavily on monsoon conditions, and the aggregate demand for foodgrains in India, where about 40 per cent of the population live below the poverty line, is price inelastic.[4] Given the price inelasticity of demand, an increase in food prices, *ceteris paribus*, would erode the real income of population, and particularly that of the poor who spend a major share of their income on food. Also, fluctuations in prices would affect adversely the long-term investment and production decisions of producers and lead to a sub-optimal allocation of resources.[5]

Therefore, it was concluded that government intervention as a trader in foodgrain markets was warranted.

However, previous studies of Lele (1971) and Moore, Johl and Khusro (1973) on Indian foodgrain marketing have found that Indian open foodgrain markets are efficient and integrated.[6] The intermarket price correlations are high and price differences between markets do not exceed transportation costs. According to these studies, storage activities of private traders are normal: traders respond to off-season price rises in order to make profits, which is a normal trading activity. Further, because the number of traders is large, it is unlikely that they could collude to earn above-normal profits. If market prices were found to be weakly correlated, it was not due to any inherent weakness in the marketing system, but due to infrastructural bottlenecks such as the lack of roads. This implies that government intervention cannot be justified on the grounds that Indian private foodgrain markets are inefficient and disintegrated. However, other goals such as the food security of low-income consumers may warrant it.

In 1965, the government set up FCI to act as a state trader and to implement the food policy designed by the Central Government.[7] FCI was set up under the Food Corporation of India Act (1964) as the sole agency of the Central Government that would purchase, store, transport and distribute foodgrains.[8] Until the late 1970s, FCI handled all cereals, including coarse cereals. Since 1980 FCI has confined its operations to rice and wheat. It does, however, distribute levy sugar in some states and imported sugar through the public distribution system. Imports of rice and wheat are also canalised through FCI. Private traders are not allowed to import foodgrains. Under the Essential Commodities Act, private traders and millers are also prohibited from carrying stocks of foodgrains beyond a stipulated limit.[9]

Even though the specific duties of FCI have changed over time, its main objectives, which reflect the rationale behind government intervention, have remained the same. They are as follows: (*a*) provision of price support to farmers by procuring foodgrains at a support price, (*b*) distribution of foodgrains at subsidised prices to the poor, and (*c*) maintenance of buffer stocks to ensure national food security.

Has FCI achieved these objectives and has it been commercially viable? The next two sections attempt to answer these questions.

II HAS FCI ACHIEVED ITS OBJECTIVES? ANALYSIS OF BENEFITS

This section explores whether FCI has reached its objectives: providing price support to producers, protecting the poor by distributing foodgrains through the public distribution system and guaranteeing national food security. FCI, like all public agencies, has been saddled with social and political objectives in addition to economic ones. This has complicated its management. It also complicates the assessment of its performance.

Price Support to Producers

The first objective of FCI is to provide price support to producers of foodgrains. It does that by procuring foodgrains for the public distribution system and buffer stocks. Producers are obligated to sell a share of their production to FCI; the size of the share depends on the state, region and holding size.

These foodgrains are procured at a support price, at which FCI guarantees to buy all foodgrains from producers.[10] The support price aims to encourage foodgrain production by guaranteeing a remunerative price to producers. It acts thus as an insurance and incentive.

Government announces support prices for foodgrains annually. The Commission for Agricultural Costs and Prices (CACP) advises the Central Government in setting the prices. Its recommendations are based on the following criteria: cost of production, changes in input prices, trends in domestic open market and international prices, demand and supply, estimated effect of changes in the support price on the industrial cost structure and cost of living, inter-crop price parity, input–output price parity and parity prices paid and received by farmers. However, CACP has not explicitly stated: (*a*) the relative importance of each of these criteria, (*b*) how each of these is expressed as a quantitative indicator, and (*c*) whether the relative importance of some of these criteria has changed over time.[11]

The support price is normally less than the open market price. The support price sets the floor for the open market price, the ceiling being set by the demand and supply.

Comparing support prices with open market prices reveals that in most years they have been close. This implies that in the absence of support price policy, open market prices would have fallen below support levels, at least in surplus states, since by reducing the availability of foodgrains in open markets, procurement raises the open market price.

To minimise the difference between the support and open market price, the government imposed zonal movement restrictions on foodgrains when the difference between the support and open market price was large. These restrictions limited the movement of foodgrains between states by private traders. A zone could either be comprised of a single state or a group of contiguous states. These restrictions enabled the government to bottle up supplies in surplus states and procure foodgrains in those states at a lower price than that which would have prevailed had traders been allowed to transfer the grain. This ensured sufficient procurement for the public distribution system and buffer stocks. Though formally withdrawn in 1977, zonal restrictions keep recurring in one form or another. As will be discussed later, these restrictions have increased the interregional variation in foodgrain prices and impinged on farmers' incentives to produce.

Has the procurement of foodgrains at a support price benefited producers? Specifically, has it provided: (*a*) income insurance, and (*b*) incentives for expanded production?

Impact of Procurement on Producer Income. Whether producers gain or lose from procurement in terms of income depends on whether the weighted average of the support price and open market price is higher or lower than the price that would have prevailed in the absence of procurement. If it is higher, producers gain from government intervention. If the weighted price is lower, producers lose.

Previous studies on the impact of procurement on producers' income, as exemplified by Dantwala (1967), Subbarao (1979), Hayami, Subbarao and Otsuka (1982) and Chetty and Srinivasan (1990), indicate that the weighted average of the support and open market price has been higher than the open market price would have been without government intervention.[12] Hence, procurement has helped producers. Dantwala (1967: 9) argues that

> whenever there is procurement by the government, open market prices go up steeply and disproportionately to the quantum

> withdrawn by the government from the open market. As such it would be reasonable to hold that the weighted average price received by the producer for the total sales (to the government and in the open market) is no less than what he would have received in the absence of procurement.[13]

Dantwala states that there is such a large difference in price elasticities of low-income and high-income consumers that a reduction in the open market supply of foodgrains due to procurement may not lead to a commensurate reduction in the open market demand.

These studies, however, can be criticised on several counts. Lieberman and Ahluwalia (1990), Narayana, Parikh and Srinivasan (1991) and Schiff (1994), for example, have challenged the conjecture that procurement increases the weighted average producer price for five reasons.[14]

First, the calculation of the weighted average price depends on weights which are not independent of prices. Dantwala's argument may hold when the gap between the support and open market price is small. If the gap were large, to avoid income loss, producers would sell less to the government and more in the open market than if the gap were small. In this situation, however, the government is likely to impose movement restrictions from surplus to deficit states to prevent further open market sales. This might neutralise gains to producers.

Second, consumers, like producers, try to circumvent procurement if the difference between the support and open market price is large. High-income consumers may try to get their supplies from the subsidised market, while low-income consumers may try to sell their share of subsidised supplies in the open market at high prices. This could change the welfare implications.

Third, all producers do not have the same opportunity to sell in the open market because procurement shares differ.[15] The impact of procurement on producers is thus bound to vary.

Fourth, procurement operations are regionally concentrated. Figure 10.1 depicts the procurement shares of different states for rice and wheat in 1989–90 to 1991–92. For example, in 1988–90 the states of Punjab, Haryana and Uttar Pradesh contributed almost the entire wheat procurement, although they generated only 69 per cent of total wheat production. Similarly, these states contributed 63 per cent of rice procurement, while their share of total rice production was only 23 per cent.

Finally, all these studies use domestic open market prices, not world prices, to work out income gains/losses. This may be appropriate given that the focus is on the effects of procurement, and foreign trade in foodgrains has not been free in India. However, since free trade would have been and is an option to the Government of India, the income effect is assessed next using a free trade scenario as a reference.

Producers of foodgrains would have been better off under free trade than with government procurement in trade autarky. This can be shown by estimating nominal protection coefficients for rice and wheat, at both official and shadow exchange rates. The results obtained are presented in Table 10.1. The results indicate that foodgrains, rather than being net subsidised, have been net taxed.[16] The degree of taxation (disprotection) is more on rice than on wheat. Also, if the shadow exchange rate, instead of the official one, is used, the degree of taxation goes up. Since the weighted average price falls between the support price and open market price and farmers are taxed even at the open market price, it is evident that although the weighted average price may be higher than the open market price prevailing in a no-procurement situation in trade autarky, it is surely less than the free-trade price.

To summarise, the evidence regarding the impact of procurement on producer income is mixed. Several studies indicate that farmers have gained from procurement but these studies have a number of shortcomings. In any case, farmers would have been better off under free trade than with procurement.

Impact of Procurement on Foodgrain Production. While the support price policy has augmented the production of rice and wheat, it has failed to provide incentives to growers of coarse cereals. Tyagi (1990) shows that in many years, open market prices of coarse cereals have fallen below the support level.[17] FCI finds it uneconomic to procure them since they are grown by small farmers with small marketed surpluses and with a much larger geographical spread than rice or wheat.

Controls through levy on millers in rice markets have led to other incentive problems. Field visits have revealed that rent-seeking is rampant in the rice mill sector. Under-reporting of paddy stocks, sale of substandard rice to FCI and the evasion of levy are common. Further, since FCI officials do not follow any scientific method in measuring the quality of foodgrains, quality cuts are imposed arbitrarily.[18] All these malpractices undermine farmers' incentives.

Zonal movement restrictions have also adversely affected farmers' incentives to produce foodgrains. Krishna (1965), Subbarao (1978) and Krishna and Chhibber (1983) indicate that zonal restrictions have increased the interregional variation in foodgrain prices and distorted production decisions.[19] In bad crop years, prices of foodgrains in deficit areas have gone up, whereas prices in surplus areas have declined. Low prices in surplus regions have driven out economic cultivation, while high prices in deficit regions have encouraged uneconomic cultivation. In addition to being inefficient, this has had deleterious effects on long-term production prospects. Farmers in surplus areas have switched from foodgrains to other crops where no zonal restrictions exist. In recent years farmers have been shifting acreage from wheat to mustard in almost all major wheat-growing areas. Also, paddy cultivators in Andhra Pradesh have been switching from paddy to sugar cane production.

In short, procurement has had a mixed effect on foodgrain production. While procurement has had a beneficial effect on the production of rice and wheat, movement restrictions have countered these. Further, procurement has failed to promote the production of coarse cereals.

Public Distribution System: Consumer Benefits

The second objective of FCI is to distribute foodgrains, especially to the poor, at subsidised prices through the Public Distribution System (PDS).[20] PDS was established in 1939 with three objectives: (*a*) to ensure the availability of foodgrains to low-income consumers, (*b*) to stabilise consumer prices of foodgrains by supplying foodgrains at below open market prices, and (*c*) to ensure equality in foodgrain availability and consumption.[21]

PDS is a generic name given to various schemes under which FCI distributes foodgrains at concessional prices. These schemes include: (*a*) Fair Price Shops, (*b*) employment programmes, (*c*) the Integrated Tribal Development Programme (ITDP), and (*d*) the Revamped PDS (RPDS). PDS supplies are supplemental; the aim is not to meet total requirements of all households. The open market is expected to be the primary source of supplies for households.

There is a large network of Fair Price Shops through which central and state governments supply essential commodities at subsidised prices to consumers.[22] The Central Government supplies seven items through these stores: wheat, rice, sugar, kerosene oil, coking coal, imported edible oil and controlled cloth. State governments are free to supply any other items as long as they bear the cost. Many state governments run their own PDS schemes which further subsidise foodgrains issued to them by the Central Government.[23]

The supply of foodgrains through employment programmes has been an important feature of PDS since 1978 when the Food-for-Work program was launched. The Food-for-Work programme was later replaced by the National Rural Employment Programme (NREP) and the Rural Labour Employment Guarantee Programme (RLEGP). These two were eventually merged into one programme, called Jawahar Rojgar Yojana (JRY).

The Integrated Tribal Development Programme (ITDP) was launched in 1985 to supply concessional foodgrains to people in tribal areas at prices even lower than general PDS rates. It served a population of 57 million. Since June 1992, ITDP has been a part of the Revamped PDS.

The Revamped PDS (RPDS) was established in January 1992. Under RPDS, rice and wheat prices are kept lower and allocations higher than under PDS. Since RPDS serves primarily tribal populations, it was merged with the Integrated Tribal Development Programme (ITDP) in June 1992.

The rationale for public distribution rests on the fact that open market prices of foodgrains are bound to fluctuate—because the supply of foodgrains depends heavily on monsoon conditions—and these fluctuations hurt consumers. Given the price inelasticity of foodgrain demand, an increase in food prices would erode the real income of population and, in particular, that of the poor who spend a major share of their income on food. Public distribution of foodgrains at affordable and stable prices is seen as an efficient way to prevent malnourishment and starvation.

FCI and state governments run PDS. FCI procures foodgrains from farmers for the central pool which is then sold to state governments. The Central Government determines the interstate allocation of foodgrains. Its decision, though not clearly defined, appears to be based on the demand of state governments, the state's foodgrain production, the state's past allocation from PDS and the financial capacity of the state.

FCI sells foodgrains from the central pool to state governments at central issue prices.[24] These prices are below open market prices and vary according to the type and quality of foodgrains.[25] They are fixed by the Central Government and based on the support price and expenses incurred by FCI in the procurement, storage, transportation and distribution of foodgrains.[26] States' use of rice and wheat from the central pool is influenced, among other things, by the difference between the issue and open market price. The higher the issue price relative to the open market price, the lower the off-take and vice versa.

The role of PDS in total purchases of rice and wheat in India is relatively small. PDS supplies only about 13 per cent of all wheat and 17 per cent of all rice consumed in Indian rural areas and 19 per cent of both rice and wheat consumed in urban areas.[27] This implies that both the rich and the poor depend heavily on open markets for foodgrains.

Whether PDS has achieved its objectives—that is, ensured: (*a*) the availability of foodgrains to low-income people, (*b*) the stability of consumer prices, and (*c*) the equity in foodgrain distribution—is assessed next.

Foodgrain Availability to Low-Income People Has PDS improved the availability of foodgrains to the poor? It turns out that PDS has helped to manage droughts and improve the overall availability of foodgrains, though the availability of subsidised foodgrains has varied across states.

Since 1965, the net availability of foodgrains—defined as the total domestic production, net imports and depletion in stocks—has considerably improved in India, largely due to increased domestic production. Figure 10.2 graphs the net availability of rice and wheat between 1964–90. The net availability of wheat grew at a rate of 4.2 per cent per year and that of rice at 2.6 per cent per year over 1964–90, while the population grew at a rate of 2.0 per cent per year over the same period. Hence, the per capita availability of rice and wheat has improved. Unless income distribution has worsened, it can be asserted that the poor have also benefited from the improved per capita availability of foodgrains.

The quantity of foodgrains distributed through PDS has also increased since 1965. The average combined annual distribution of rice and wheat per capita increased from about 17 kg in 1973–74 to about 22 kg in 1988–89. Although the average distribution of wheat declined from about 11 kg to 10 kg over that period, the increase in the average distribution of rice from 6 kg to 12 kg more than compensated for the decline. However, these amounts are not sufficient to satisfy the needs of the poor: PDS would have to supply at least 67 kg per capita of rice and wheat combined per year to households living below the poverty line to meet 50 per cent of their consumption needs.[28] Foodgrains have been primarily distributed through government-run Fair Price Shops and since 1978 through employment programmes.

Further, the availability of foodgrains through PDS has varied from state to state. In some states, foodgrains distributed through PDS form a substantial portion of per capita foodgrain consumption, whereas in others PDS plays only a minor role. Table 10.2 reports the shares of per capita public distribution of rice and wheat in total per capita consumption of rice and wheat for different states at two points in time, 1973–74 and 1988–89. For example, over half of the rice and wheat consumption in Kerala and Maharashtra in 1973–74 was contributed by PDS. However, in both states the degree of dependence on PDS supplies has decreased over time.

The major achievement of PDS, however, has been the successful management of foodgrain availability during drought years. Buffer stocks, which will be discussed later in more detail, have guaranteed the availability of foodgrains in drought years so that famines have been avoided.[29]

Stability of Consumer Prices The second objective of PDS is to stabilise consumer prices of foodgrains. The presumption is that the distribution of foodgrains through PDS, by reducing the demand for foodgrains in open markets, relieves pressure on open market prices. This objective, however, has not been achieved.

The impact of PDS on price stability has been marginal. The role of PDS in containing inflation has been limited because PDS supplies account for no more than 15 or 16 per cent of total foodgrain consumption. Parikh (1994), in fact, reports that open market prices have not been lower in areas where PDS does not operate than in those areas where it does.[30] In general, between 1966–90, real prices of foodgrains declined and the variability in nominal rice and wheat prices also decreased.[31] These declines were consistent with increases in the total availability of rice and wheat over the same period.[32] However, between 1990–91 and 1994–95, real prices of foodgrains went up. Use of PDS declined due to the narrow gap between the open market and issue price. FCI, instead of selling surplus foodgrains at the open market, decided to store surplus grain in buffer stocks. This reduced the availability of foodgrains in open markets and pushed up prices.

Equity in Distribution Have PDS supplies been targeted successfully to the poor; that is, have PDS supplies been distributed to those states and rural areas where the bulk of the poor live? The answer to this question turns out to be negative: the targeting of PDS supplies to the poor has failed.

PDS supplies have not been targeted to states with high poverty levels. This can be seen from Table 10.3 which documents the relationship between the state-wide distribution of PDS supplies and poverty. Bihar, Madhya Pradesh, Rajasthan, Orissa and Uttar Pradesh combined obtained less than 16 per cent of rice and wheat distributed through PDS, although over half of the Indian poor live in these states. The correlation between the share of obtained PDS supplies and the share of population living below the poverty line across states is as low as 0.25.

Further, PDS purchases per capita are higher in urban areas than in the rural areas where most of the poor live. The correlation between the share of obtained PDS supplies and the share of urban population is high (0.56), implying that there is an urban bias in PDS. Table 10.4 documents the per capita quantities of foodgrains purchased in urban and rural areas. It indicates that urban bias holds for both rice and wheat. Kerala stands apart with a significant rural bias. The rural bias is also present in Andhra Pradesh.

Several previous studies—such as Krishna (1967), Gupta (1977), National Commission on Agriculture (1975), Gulati and Krishnan (1975), Vyas and Bandyopadhyay (1975), Government of India, Ministry of Finance (1979), George (1985), Suryanarayana (1985), Pinstrup-Andersen (1988), Bapna (1990) and Tyagi (1990)—also claim that there is an urban bias in PDS in most states.[33] A contrary view can be found in Ahluwalia (1990) and Dev and Suryanarayana (1991).[34] Their results, however, may be biased since they are based on a survey conducted in a drought year.[35] In a drought year, PDS supplies to rural areas increase which may bias results.

Ahluwalia (1990) reports that the poorest 40 per cent of the Indian population consumes only 40–50 per cent of foodgrains sold through PDS, while the richest 40 per cent of the population gets

30–35 per cent.[36] Bapna (1990) argues that the poor have not been able to take full advantage of PDS because of lack of income, the location of Fair Price Shops and the uncertainty of supplies.[37] Further, according to Ahluwalia (1990), about one-third of the rice and wheat supplied through PDS leaks to the open market before reaching customers; the quantities supplied to PDS are considerably higher than the quantities sold.[38]

Parikh (1994) observes that the subsidy for the bottom 20 per cent of Indian households is on average Rs 2.08 per capita per month.[39] Sharma (1994) estimates the income effect of PDS across rural and urban income groups. He finds that even the highest income effect for the bottom 20 per cent of rural households was no more than 1.35 per cent for rice and 0.30 per cent for wheat.[40] Applying these percentages to the per capita national income of Rs 2,962 in 1986–87 (in current prices) gives a per capita annual subsidy of Rs 40 for rice and Rs 9 for wheat, or a total subsidy of Rs 4.08 per capita per month. In short, benefits provided by PDS to the poor are very small.

National Food Security through Buffer Stocks

The third and final objective of FCI is to ensure national food security by maintaining buffer stocks. There are three kinds of public stocks in India: operational stocks to feed PDS, buffer stocks to provide food security against droughts, and baseline stocks.[41] Buffer stocks have been maintained in India since the mid-1970s. It turns out that these buffer stocks have either been too low, in which case food security has been jeopardised, or too high—which has been costly and inflationary—compared to the norms.

Storage is a normal trading activity. However, motives for private and public storage differ. Private traders store in order to make profit from off-season price increases. They make their storage decisions by matching the expected changes in prices with storage costs. By contrast, public storage aims to reduce off-season price increases.

The basic idea behind maintaining a buffer stock is to smooth fluctuations in price and availability by accumulating stocks during bountiful years and depleting them when there are shortages. This activity is supposed to help both producers and consumers. It helps producers in surplus years, because if buffer stocks were not kept, producers would suffer losses due to falling prices. It helps consumers, because in the absence of buffer stocks, the availability of foodgrains in drought years would decline and raise consumer prices.

Buffer stocks are also kept for political reasons. They reduce the reliance on imports at the time of shortages. India's large size and grain requirements have also been considerations in the building of buffer stocks.

Keeping buffer stocks is not the only, or necessarily the best, method to stabilise foodgrain prices and availability. Stabilisation can be achieved also by trade, that is, by exporting foodgrains in surplus years and importing them in drought years. The decision to store or trade should be based on the comparison of the cost of storage with the gains from exporting now and importing at a later date.

The Government of India has stipulated the minimum level of buffer stocks to be held at different points in time during a year.[42] The appropriate level of buffer stocks depends on what objectives the government wants to achieve. In general, the greater the desired price stability, the greater quantities the government needs to hold in storage.

In eleven out of the past fifteen years the size of actual buffer stocks in India has deviated from the stipulated norm by over 20 per cent. These deviations are shown in Figure 10.3. In most years, actual stocks have been much below the norm indicating that FCI did not provide desired food security to the nation. Also, there were years when FCI was holding much bigger stocks than desirable, indicating FCI's insensitivity to the high costs of storage.

To summarise, it has been shown that FCI's performance has been mixed; it has succeeded in reaching some of its objectives, while failing to reach others. FCI's procurement of foodgrains has not necessarily benefited producers of foodgrains. The evidence regarding the impact of procurement on producer income is mixed. It turns out that free domestic and foreign trade in foodgrains would have benefited producers more than the procurement system. Further, since FCI operations concentrate on rice and wheat and neglect coarse cereals, benefits from procurement, if any, have fallen primarily on rice and wheat producers. Consumers have benefited from FCI operations since the overall availability of foodgrains has improved. The per capita availability of foodgrains under PDS, even in remote areas, has increased over time. But quantities distributed through PDS remain small compared to total consumption and, therefore, their impact on price stability and income transfer has been marginal. Hence, it cannot be deduced that increased availability of foodgrains is the result of PDS. Further, PDS has operated as a universal food subsidy scheme and has failed to target the distribution of foodgrains to the poor people and regions. Buffer stocks maintained by FCI to stabilise the availability and prices of foodgrains have been either too low or too high compared to stipulated norms. While too-low buffer stocks are jeopardising national food security, carrying too-high stocks is costly and inflationary.

At what cost have these objectives been achieved or attempted? It is examined next whether the operations of FCI have been commercially viable.

III ECONOMIC EFFICIENCY OF FCI

FCI was established on the premise that it operates as a commercial company competing with private traders. It was expected to gain a sizeable share of the market simply because of its large size and financial strength. The assumption was that the sheer volume of FCI operations would allow it to take advantage of economies of scale and keep its operational costs down. This was expected to keep it viable and competitive in an environment where its purchase and selling prices are beyond its control.

It will be shown in this chapter that FCI has been operating inefficiently. Economic efficiency means here that revenues of FCI cover its costs, and that costs of FCI are comparable to those of private traders. FCI would not have been able to operate without a government subsidy: the cost of its operations has far exceeded its revenues. Operational costs of FCI have been much higher than those incurred by private traders even though, unlike private traders, FCI enjoys concessional freight and credit rates and is free from credit controls, movement restrictions and restrictions imposed by the Essential Commodities Act.

The Economic Cost and Consumer Subsidy

To assess the economic efficiency of FCI operations, it is first examined whether FCI has been able to cover the economic cost of its operations with its revenues. The per unit (that is, per quintal) economic cost of FCI operations consists of the support price, per unit procurement and distribution costs. FCI's revenues are measured by the average sales realisation. The average sales realisation is the weighted average of centrai issue prices at which FCI has sold foodgrains to state governments. Since central issue prices are fixed by the Central Government, FCI has no control over the average sales realisation. If the average sales realisation falls short of the economic cost, the Central Government reimburses the difference to FCI as a consumer subsidy. FCI also incurs costs by carrying buffer stocks. These costs are, however, fully reimbursed by the Central Government. Hence, the total subsidy, if any, to FCI is comprised of the consumer subsidy and the cost of carrying buffer stocks.

It turns out that the average sales realisation of FCI has not covered the economic cost of its operation from 1968–1993. The ratios of the average sales realisation to the economic cost for rice and wheat are depicted in Figure 10.4 and reported in Table 10.5. Figure 10.4 shows that these ratios have been sharply declining over the years.

The fact that the average sales realisation of FCI has fallen short of its economic cost means that FCI has not been able to operate without a government subsidy. Since the economic cost per unit has increased at a higher rate than the average sales realisation, the gap between costs and revenues has been widening over time, and the subsidy has been increasing correspondingly. The consumer subsidy for rice, as a per cent of the unit price of rice, increased from about 20 per cent in 1980–81 to about 31 per cent in 1992–93. For wheat, the rise was from about 34 per cent to 82 per cent over the same period. The cost of carrying buffer stocks also increased substantially over the period. Why has this discrepancy between costs and revenues happened and persisted? Has the government's price setting or FCI's internal cost control failed?

In the case of rice, price setting has been a problem: since 1980 FCI has sold rice at a lower price than it was procured. The average sales realisation for rice covered the support price at which FCI procured rice until 1978–79, but not beyond. By contrast, the average sales realisation for wheat has covered the support price all the time.

In addition, the economic cost of FCI operations has risen sharply. Table 10.5 shows how economic costs of rice and wheat have evolved over time. Both in the case of rice and wheat, the economic cost has risen at an average annual real rate of about 7 per cent.

Economic costs of rice and wheat have risen at a higher rate than corresponding support prices, implying that per unit procurement and distribution costs have ballooned. Figure 10.5 displays the ratios of economic costs of rice and wheat to their respective support prices. The economic cost of wheat has been 80–90 per cent higher than the support price of wheat. Per unit procurement and distribution costs for wheat were thus almost as high as the support price. The economic cost of rice has been lower than the cost of wheat because rice is purchased directly from millers.

Have per unit procurement and distribution costs of FCI been excessive compared to those of private traders? It is possible that FCI has failed to cover its costs with revenues, not because its costs have been excessive, but simply because it has been obligated to sell foodgrains at less than the open market price. To find out whether its costs are comparable to those of private traders, the economic costs of FCI operations are compared to revenues measured at wholesale prices that FCI would have obtained had it sold foodgrains in open markets. The wholesale price, like the economic cost, is formed after all expenses are incurred and traders have earned their profit.

It turns out that FCI's wheat procurement and distribution costs have been excessive. Even if FCI had sold wheat at wholesale prices, FCI would have needed a subsidy to continue its operations. At the all-India level, costs FCI incurred in procuring and distributing wheat have been substantially higher than its revenues would have been at wholesale prices. Figure 10.6 presents ratios of economic costs of rice and wheat to respective wholesale prices. Since aggregation subsumes interstate differences, economic costs and wholesale prices are also compared at the state level. Also at the state level, the economic cost of wheat has been higher than the wholesale price, notably in surplus states. The economic cost of rice, however, has exceeded the wholesale price only in surplus states.

Instead of economies of scale, FCI has faced diseconomies of scale. The principle of economies of scale suggests that as the size of operation increases, the unit cost of operation declines and reaches an optimal point. However, in the case of FCI, the relationship between the size and cost of operation has been the opposite.

Which costs have been excessive, procurement costs, or distribution costs, or both? These costs and how they have evolved over time are examined next.

Procurement Costs

Procurement costs of FCI have been higher than procurement costs of private traders. Procurement costs can be divided into two groups: obligatory and non-obligatory costs. Obligatory costs are incurred by both FCI and private traders. They form about 70 per cent of total procurement costs. Non-obligatory costs in turn are controlled by FCI.[43]

Obligatory costs of FCI have been higher than those of private traders. Obligatory costs include: (*a*) mandi charges, (*b*) sales/purchase tax, and (*c*) the cost of gunnybags. Mandi charges account for about 6 per cent of the support price.[44] Sales/purchase tax rates vary from state to state. In Punjab, Haryana and Uttar Pradesh this tax is levied at the rate of 4 per cent of the support price on rice, paddy, and wheat. High mandi charges and sales taxes have induced private traders to bypass the mandi system and buy foodgrains directly from farmers.[45] The cost of gunnybags accounts for the major share of obligatory expenses: about 25 per cent of the total procurement cost of wheat, 63 per cent of rice and 45 per cent of paddy. For private traders this cost is generally smaller than for FCI because: (*a*) private traders recycle a bag three or four times, whereas FCI disposes it after one use, and (*b*) FCI moves foodgrains by rail, which involves multiple handling, many times by a hook, and hence requires a sturdy bagging. Private traders move foodgrains mostly by road in which case an inferior bagging is adequate. These practices have kept obligatory costs of private traders low.

Distribution Costs

Distribution costs of FCI have also been excessive compared to distribution costs of private traders. They form a major share of the economic cost of FCI and they have drawn much attention and criticism because some of them are controllable.

Distribution costs include interest, freight and storage charges, handling expenses, storage and transit shortages, and administrative expenses. These costs compare to those of private traders as follows.

Interest Charges FCI's per unit interest charges are lower than those of private traders because FCI is getting concessional credit through a consortium of Indian commercial banks to finance its operations.[46] By contrast, borrowing against foodgrains is difficult for private traders. Until 1982–83 the interest rate applicable to FCI was about seven percentage points lower than the rate applicable to private traders. After that the difference has narrowed down. Since October 1994, the interest rate applicable to FCI has been about five to six percentage points lower than the market rate.[47] Interest charges account currently for about one-third of distribution costs.

Freight Charges Freight charges of FCI are lower than those of private traders because FCI moves its grains by rail at subsidised freight rates.[48] Foodgrains in India are transported either by trucks or railways. Between regions, FCI transports more than 90 per cent of rice and wheat by railways. About 40 per cent of FCI's intra-regional transportation is also done by rail.[49] Freight charges account for about one-fourth of FCI's distribution costs.

Private traders prefer to move foodgrains by road, even though it is almost twice as expensive as rail on long routes. This is due to several factors: trucks provide door-to-door service and save the cost of local cartage. Trucks also take less time than railways. Physical losses and pilferage from trucks is less than from railways. Further, trucks are more easily available than railway wagons, especially during a busy season. Finally, since trucks provide door-to-door service, the amount of handling is less than by railways. As a result, even inferior packaging is adequate. In short, even though railway freights appear to be lower than those of trucks, if other aspects of service are taken into account, the freight differential goes down.

Storage Charges FCI storage charges are higher than those of private traders.[50] Storage charges are incurred while moving grains for the distribution through PDS and for buffer stocks.

Storage charges of FCI have risen over time due to poor capacity utilisation and rising establishment costs. FCI constructs and hires godowns to store foodgrains.[51] The average cost of storage is higher for FCI-owned godowns than for the hired ones. For example, in 1992–93 the rate per quintal per month was Rs 1.90 for FCI-owned godowns, whereas the rent for a hired godown was between Rs 1.07 and Rs 1.14.[52] These rates are for the average capacity utilised. In 1992–93, the average capacity utilisation rate of FCI-owned and hired godowns was only 53 per cent.

Handling Charges Handling charges are about the same for FCI and private traders. They refer to costs incurred in the handling of grains at mandis, ports, and rail depots.[53] In 1992–93, handling expenses formed about 10 per cent of distribution expenses.

Storage and Transit Shortages Transit and storage shortages of FCI are higher than those of private traders. Transit shortages occur due to missing wagons, natural calamities, theft, and pilferage. Storage losses occur due to the loss of weight, infestation, deterioration of stocks, and theft. About 3–4 per cent of foodgrains procured by FCI is lost, the loss being largest for rice/paddy.

Transit shortages are higher than storage shortages. The fact that railways accept foodgrains on a 'said-to-contain' basis facilitates leakages. Further, railways do not issue receipts for foodgrains received because they are reluctant to bear losses. The dispatching and receiving centres also receive foodgrains on an estimated basis which makes theft easy. Also, since foodgrains are not weighed at any stage during transportation, storage losses can easily be classified as transit losses.

Interestingly, the major share of shortages takes place in eastern states such as Bihar, Orissa, West Bengal and Assam. The high storage losses of rice in the northern states are also intriguing. In 1987–88, storage losses of rice in Punjab, Haryana and Uttar Pradesh formed about 67 per cent of the total storage losses of rice. A report by the Bureau of Industrial Costs and Prices (BICP) suggests that in these states FCI officials collude with rice millers and do not obtain full levy quota of rice from the mill.[54] The resulting shortage is reported as a storage loss.

Administrative Expenses Compared to private traders, the administrative expenses of FCI are high. Administrative expenses of FCI have shown a sharp increase over the past few years. FCI staff has increased at a higher rate than the volume of its operations.[55] In 1990, FCI had a staff of 69,398 employees; if casual workers were included, the number was close to 100,000. These expenses account for over 11 per cent of the distribution costs.

What Explains the High Cost Structure of the Food Corporation of India?

Why has the high cost structure of FCI persisted and what has made leakages possible? To examine this question, one must distinguish between policies beyond the control of FCI and FCI's own inefficient practices.

First, the government has not provided incentives for FCI to operate as a commercial enterprise. FCI has no control over the pricing of foodgrains it procures and distributes: the Central Government fixes its purchase and sales prices over time and space. Since, in addition, FCI's losses are automatically covered (and profits taken) by the Central Government, FCI has no incentive to control its costs. Whether foodgrains reach their destination or not, in time or not, in correct quantities or not, has hardly any significance for the FCI. By contrast, delays are costly to private traders. Delayed arrival of grains at the terminal market means higher costs, in terms of interest payments, to a trader.

Second, some management practices within FCI have contributed to the high and rising cost structure and made leakages possible. Officials are not held responsible for poor management decisions that cause losses to FCI and they are not made accountable for reaching specific government-defined goals. As noted earlier, grain shortages in storage, which are made possible by poor management, are conveniently categorised as transit losses. The actual size of FCI's stocks is unknown because no physical inventory of stocks has been done. Stocks are recorded in the books of FCI on the basis of a sample stocktaking. As a result, actual stocks and foodgrain losses are difficult to estimate.

Third, the sheer size of FCI, in terms of activities and geographical spread, has made cost control difficult. The supervision of activities has become increasingly difficult as FCI has expanded. Many of FCI's activities could be contracted out to private agencies at a low cost. For example, FCI was made responsible for carrying and managing buffer stocks and constructing needed storage capacity. Whether this task is suitable to FCI has never been questioned or reviewed. As a consequence, FCI has substantially expanded its storage capacity at a high cost, while warehousing corporations, which have specialised in storage, could have stored grains at a lower cost than FCI.

Finally, the fact that FCI has not only economic but also social and political objectives has further complicated its management.

IV CONCLUSION AND REFORM OPTIONS

This chapter examined the role and performance of the Food Corporation of India in Indian foodgrain marketing. In particular, it explored whether FCI has reached its objectives: provision of price support to farmers, distribution of foodgrains to the poor through PDS and maintenance of buffer stock to ensure national food security. Also, the performance of FCI was evaluated by assessing the economic cost of FCI operations. The analysis resulted in several interesting insights into the performance of FCI.

The main conclusion of the chapter is that while there have been some benefits from FCI operations to both producers and consumers, there have also been significant costs that would warrant a reform of FCI. FCI has been successful in improving the overall availability of foodgrains in India. It has, however, failed in some respects. First, FCI has been unable to cover its costs by revenues. The gap between its revenues and costs has been increasing over time. As a result, the subsidy to FCI has been mounting at an alarming rate. The fiscal imbalance of FCI reflects partly a pricing problem: since 1980 the central issue price of rice has been lower than the support price. The main reason for the fiscal imbalance, however, is that the cost of FCI operations—in particular, FCI's distribution costs—have been excessive compared to those of private traders.

Second, FCI has been ineffective in distributing foodgrains through PDS to pooi consumers and regions. The distribution of foodgrains across states reveals a bias in favour of states with a high urban population and against states with a high incidence of poverty. Also, a large share of foodgrains leaks from PDS to the non-poor. Leakages are bound to occur when there are dual markets and prices. Dual markets create incentives for individuals to try to circumvent procurement and controls, and siphon off commodities from the controlled market to the open one where prices are higher. Third, buffer stocks FCI has managed have either been substantially lower or higher than the prescribed norms. Too-low stocks have jeopardised national food security, whereas too-high stocks have been costly and inflationary.

The solution to these problems requires reconsideration of the role of FCI in the Indian foodgrain marketing system. Should its tasks remain unchanged or should it concentrate on just one or two activities, if any, and target the support to the poor? These questions should be considered in the context of other reforms in the agricultural sector in India.

The recent liberalisation of the Indian economy is slowly extending to Indian agriculture. The Central Government has announced the withdrawal of all Central Government controls on the movement of foodgrains within the country, although some movement controls imposed by state governments still exist. Exports of rice and wheat have also been recently decanalised. As a result, Indian agriculture is poised for a big jump. The logical extension of these reforms would be the elimination of any levies and controls on domestic and foreign trade.

Given these reforms and the findings of this chapter, the role of FCI in the following areas needs to be reevaluated. First, the canalising role of FCI has disappeared. If there are no restrictions on imports and exports, there is no need for a government agency to act as a middleman. Second, the role of FCI in ensuring the availability of foodgrains to the poor through PDS would need to be reconsidered. Given the targeting problems of PDS, Bhagwati and Srinivasan (1993) have suggested that it be replaced either by: (*a*) food stamps, or (*b*) the calling of bids. Either of these suggestions, if implemented, would significantly change the role of FCI.[56]

If PDS were revised to operate on the calling of bids basis, procurement by FCI would not be necessary. In the bids system, the private sector supplies foodgrains. The government invites bids from private traders to supply foodgrains at a specified time to a specified location. The contract is granted for the lowest price bidder. To minimise rent-seeking opportunities inherent in this kind of a system, the process of call, receipt, opening and acceptance of bids needs to be made as transparent and open as possible.

For the calling of bids system to work efficiently, private traders would need to be allowed to store foodgrains without limit and trade in futures markets both domestically and internationally. This would necessitate removing foodgrains from the Essential Commodities Act.

If PDS were replaced by a food stamps system, there would be no need for FCI to procure and distribute foodgrains. In the food stamps system, holders of food stamps buy commodities from open markets. Food stamps with a fixed money value are distributed to people below a specified income level.

A precondition to the success of the food stamps system is the availability of foodgrains in open markets, especially in remote and otherwise difficult areas. The misuse of stamps could be reduced by having only coarse varieties of grains in the scheme. The erosion in the real value of stamps could be corrected by indexing their money value to food prices.

The government, however, seems to be leaning towards targeting PDS on specific areas, instead of replacing it. As mentioned earlier, it launched in 1992 the Revamped Public Distribution System (RPDS) in 1,775 backward blocks of the country. In the Central Government budget of 1995–96, the Finance Minister announced that RPDS will be increased to 2,275 blocks. This would amount to a rising food subsidy bill, unless the government withdrew the general PDS from other blocks or increased central issue prices significantly elsewhere. To contain the food subsidy bill, the government may want to consider imposing an upper limit for state subsidies that depends on the state's poverty level. The subsidy over and above this limit would be met out of the state government's budget. Increasing states' own fiscal responsibility in food management would ensure that states do not launch populist schemes and make the Central Government bear the fiscal burden. An alternative, which could be tried out in the short run, would be to impose a ceiling on the quantity of grains sold below cost. States could purchase the rest of their requirements from either FCI at its economic cost or from the open market.[57]

Third, the government may want to reassess the amount of buffer stocks needed to ensure national food security, and the role of FCI in this regard. It appears that placing greater reliance on imports and exports would be more efficient than storing huge quantities of foodgrains with FCI.[58] Managers of Indian food policy, however, have been reluctant to rely on foreign trade. They have argued that India gets a low price as an exporter but has to import at a high price when it enters the market. This happens typically when a parastatal goes to the world market with its bulk demand (or supply), and the entire world knows about it. Decanalisation of exports and imports, however, takes care of this concern.

Finally, in case the government wants to retain FCI, it should consider reorganising its management to reinforce commercial operation. One option would be to introduce performance agreements to managers and employees of FCI. These agreements would increase the accountability of managers and employees and focus operations by clarifying performance expectations and the roles, responsibilities and rewards of all those involved. Alternatively, government could contract to private providers the responsibility for managing the operations of FCI. This would increase the autonomy of the management and reduce the risks of political interference in FCI's operations.

This analysis reveals that India does not require a public agency of the size and type that FCI is today. If FCI is to survive, it should start reforming itself without delay.

Table 10.1
Nominal Protection Coefficients of Wheat and Rice

Year	*Wheat*				*Rice*			
	SupportPrice		*WholesalePrice*		*SupportPrice*		*WholesalePrice*	
	OER	*SER*	*OER*	*SER*	*OER*	*SER*	*OER*	*SER*
1980–81	0.70	0.59	0.75	0.63	0.40	0.34	0.50	0.41
1981–82	0.72	0.59	0.81	0.67	0.59	0.49	0.74	0.61
1982–83	0.84	0.69	0.87	0.72	0.74	0.62	1.07	0.89
1983–84	0.84	0.69	0.88	0.72	0.73	0.61	0.99	0.82
1984–85	0.76	0.63	0.77	0.64	0.76	0.64	0.91	0.76
1985–86	0.79	0.65	0.81	0.67	0.85	0.70	1.03	0.86
1986–87	0.96	0.80	1.01	0.84	0.84	0.70	1.05	0.87
1987–88	1.04	0.85	1.16	0.84	0.63	0.52	0.90	0.75
1988–89	0.76	0.62	0.86	0.71	0.51	0.42	0.73	0.61
1989–90	0.56	0.46	0.67	0.55	0.59	0.48	0.69	0.58
1990–91	0.71	0.58	0.73	0.60	0.53	0.44	0.58	0.49
Average	0.79	0.65	0.85	0.69	0.65	0.54	0.84	0.70

Notes: OER = official exchange rate and SER = shadow exchange rate (taken as 20 per cent higher than OER).
Source: Authors' Calculations.

Table 10.2
Statewise Dependence on PDS for Consumption of Wheat and Rice

States	*Wheat*				*Rice*			
	1973–74		*1988–89*		*1973–74*		*1988–89*	
	PDS	*Per Cent*	*PDS*	*Per Cent*	*PDS*	*Per Cent*	*PDS*	*Per Cent*
Andhra Pradesh	2.73	30.74	2.36	26.22	5.10	3.80	14.10	11.43
Assam	9.19	59.37	9.91	57.35	6.80	5.14	20.70	15.83
Bihar	7.10	12.40	9.05	12.65	0.45	0.49	0.70	0.81
Gujarat	15.38	22.37	19.27	29.20	2.70	13.99	8.70	32.46
Haryana	12.40	9.49	7.16	6.15	1.00	11.24	1.60	10.74
Himachal Pradesh	10.28	12.17	16.43	16.80	1.90	5.65	12.90	23.89
Karnataka	5.35	52.45	5.37	28.56	3.80	5.45	13.60	19.24
Kerala	10.96	130.48	6.86	58.93	34.80	40.09	52.50	50.68
Madhya Pradesh	3.15	3.35	5.76	5.99	2.94	7.30	3.80	9.31
Maharashtra	24.53	59.25	15.41	27.97	5.50	29.26	9.20	26.44
Orissa	4.84	20.17	7.76	25.95	6.71	4.95	8.25	6.13
Punjab	15.49	13.18	4.06	3.93	0.63	7.95	0.21	1.70
Rajasthan	8.53	8.64	21.75	15.88	0.00	0.00	0.33	6.11
Tamil Nadu	3.43	142.92	4.05	45.51	5.45	4.30	31.23	28.16
Uttar Pradesh	4.77	4.46	4.45	4.02	2.52	7.75	2.72	9.61
West Bengal	25.81	50.49	14.95	39.55	13.71	17.58	11.24	10.96
All India	11.16	21.53	10.14	16.97	6.06	9.39	11.60	18.07

Notes: Figures under 'PDS' are the per capita quantities (kgs per year) distributed under PDS (including roller flour mills). The 'per cent' indicates the share of PDS in consumption.
Source: Sharma (1994).[59]

Table 10.3
Statewise Public Distribution and Shares in Poverty

State	*Share of State in All-India*	
	PDS 1990	*Poverty 1987–88*
Andhra Pradesh	8.81	8.23
Assam	4.04	2.23
Bihar	2.92	14.16
Gujarat	6.03	3.08
Haryana	0.20	0.76
Himachal Pradesh	0.64	0.19
Karnataka	5.71	5.74
Kerala	11.58	2.06
Madhya Pradesh	2.89	9.47
Maharashtra	10.75	9.01
Orissa	2.62	5.69
Punjab	0.07	0.58
Rajasthan	3.97	4.19
Tamil Nadu	11.23	7.44
Uttar Pradesh	3.21	18.86
West Bengal	10.09	7.30
Others	15.22	1.01
Total	100.00	100.00

Source: For PDS, *Bulletin on Food Statistics* (various issues); for poverty estimates, Planning Commission.

Table 10.4
Rural-Urban Distribution of PDS Purchases (Per Month), 1986–87

State	*Rice per cap. (kg)*		*Wheat per cap. (kg)*	
	Rural	*Urban*	*Rural*	*Urban*
Andhra Pradesh	7.43	6.27	0.03	0.74
Assam	1.98	9.32	0.10	0.06
Bihar	0.04	0.05	0.09	0.79
Gujarat	2.08	1.73	2.51	3.54
Haryana	0.13	0.47	0.00	0.00
Himachal Pradesh	4.78	21.42	1.48	2.56
Karnataka	2.00	4.85	0.60	1.54
Kerala	21.78	14.61	2.04	1.96
Madhya Pradesh	0.31	1.13	0.38	1.09
Maharashtra	1.00	3.08	1.70	3.71
Orissa	0.06	0.11	0.06	0.87
Punjab	0.00	0.46	0.15	0.02
Rajasthan	0.06	0.36	3.31	1.03
Tamil Nadu	2.85	4.56	0.25	1.19
Uttar Pradesh	0.20	0.46	0.21	0.57
West Bengal	1.58	5.97	1.42	6.80
All India	1.83	3.51	0.66	2.43

Notes: Based on information from the Report of the NSS 42nd Round on Utilization of Public Distribution Systems (1986–87).
Source: Sharma (1994).[60]

Table 10.5
Indicators of Economic Efficiency of FCI: Wheat

Year	*Support Price Wheat (Rs/Qt)*	*Economic Cost Wheat (Rs/Qt)*	*Average Sales Realisation Wheat (Rs/Qt)*	*Wholesale Price Wheat (Rs/Qt)*
1968–69	76.00	85.81	75.28	73.37
1969–70	76.00	80.58	77.99	75.57
1970–71	76.00	80.62	78.95	71.66
1971–72	76.00	91.20	78.80	67.87
1972–73	76.00	98.13	79.98	75.17
1973–74	76.00	111.66	81.94	85.95
1974–75	105.00	169.58	130.32	139.81
1975–76	105.00	161.57	130.45	110.56
1976–77	105.00	154.20	126.07	102.49
1977–78	110.00	149.10	124.53	109.52
1978–79	112.50	157.37	126.55	110.19
1979–80	115.00	157.44	129.23	112.63
1980–81	117.00	169.92	129.71	127.46
1981–82	130.00	203.48	149.75	144.42
1982–83	142.00	219.94	164.54	155.03
1983–84	151.00	233.48	184.41	157.56
1984–85	152.00	239.44	175.98	150.17
1985–86	157.00	246.31	176.74	165.15
1986–87	162.00	273.20	188.27	173.14
1987–88	166.00	274.74	191.94	192.84
1988–89	173.00	295.98	203.00	212.76
1989–90	183.00	306.33	199.43	213.64
1990–91	215.00	358.50	239.95	248.67
1991–92	225.00	390.79	251.68	295.26
1992–93	275.00	504.10	279.36	320.00
Growth Rates:				
1971–93	5.22	6.78	5.26	6.08
1981–93	5.72	7.18	5.12	7.01

Notes: Information on procurement incidentals from 1968–69 to 1975–76 is derived as the cost of purchase minus the support price.
Source: Data from Food Corporation of India and BICP Report.

Table 10.6
Indicators of Economic Efficiency: Rice

Year	*Support Price Rice (Rs/Qt)*	*Economic Cost of Rice (Rs/Qt)*	*Average Sales Realisation Rice (Rs/Qt)*	*Wholesale Price of Rice (Rs/Qt)*
1968–69	81.85	101.47	99.22	112.53
1969–70	83.64	114.39	108.89	115.71
1970–71	84.59	110.84	111.96	112.67
1971–72	85.10	112.43	114.20	121.50
1972–73	90.87	111.10	112.66	139.52
1973–74	114.30	128.19	126.52	185.30
1974–75	120.00	153.92	159.11	218.23
1975–76	122.33	154.55	156.17	173.69
1976–77	123.09	156.26	155.02	178.46
1977–78	128.30	155.10	152.94	169.14
1978–79	138.33	169.33	151.19	172.56
1979–80	157.19	173.65	155.67	204.65
1980–81	171.50	193.32	159.29	220.17
1981–82	190.97	223.72	180.78	244.57
1982–83	202.06	249.11	195.76	287.97
1983–84	216.87	275.63	208.95	297.69
1984–85	228.47	298.81	223.94	284.73
1985–86	240.52	305.26	227.92	301.06
1986–87	242.64	318.68	238.21	327.88
1987–88	249.55	327.58	246.63	367.85
1988–89	265.17	369.68	262.39	385.12
1989–90	305.79	418.55	294.32	414.30
1990–91	342.11	457.52	330.02	463.52
1991–92	390.93	497.04	365.58	476.70
1992–93	457.08	585.27	442.40	511.00
Growth Rates:				
1971–93	7.08	7.43	5.45	6.31
1981–93	7.11	8.14	7.23	6.64

Notes: Information on procurement incidentals from 1968–69 to 1975–76 is derived as cost of purchase minus procurement price.
Source: Data from Food Corporation of India and BICP Report.

Figure 10.1

States' Share in Total Wheat and Rice Procurement from 1989–90 to 1991–92

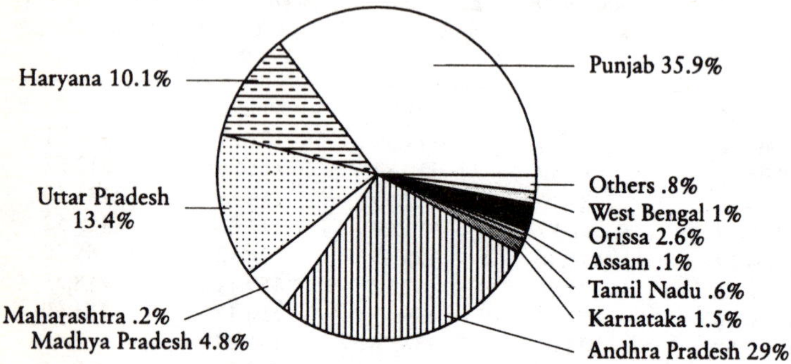

Share of states in all-India wheat procurement

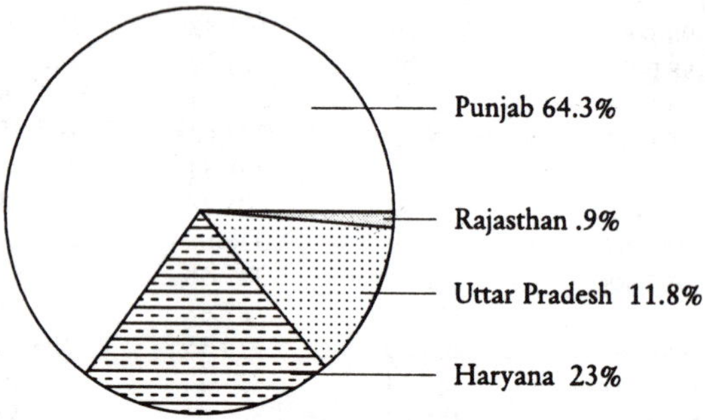

Share of states in all-India rice procurement

Source: Data from *Bulletin on Food Statistics* (various issues)

Figure 10.2
Net Availability of Wheat and Rice in 1964–1990 (thousand tons)

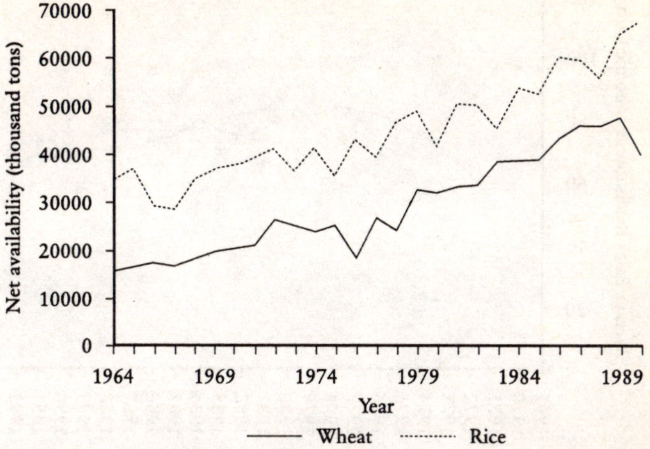

Notes: Net availability = total domestic production + net imports + depletion in stocks.
Source: Data from Food Corporation of India and BICP Report.

Figure 10.3
Deviation of Buffer Stocks from Norms (as of January 1)

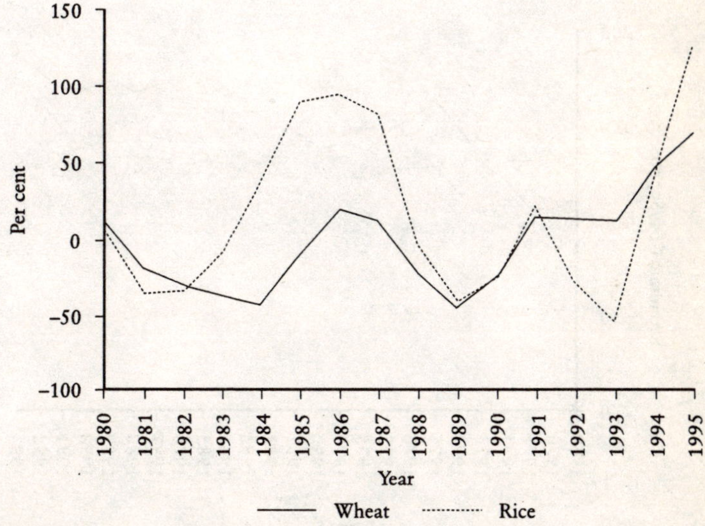

Source: Data from Economic Survey, 1994–95.

Figure 10.4
Average Sales Realisation to Economic Cost

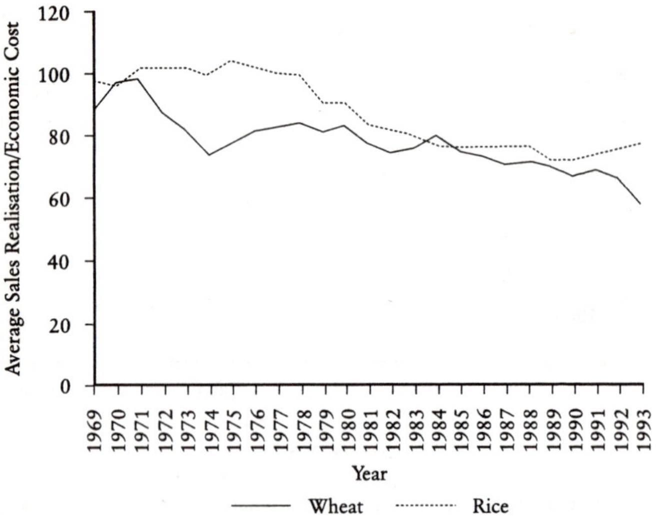

Source: Data from Food Corporation of India and BICP Report.

Figure 10.5
Economic Cost to Support Price

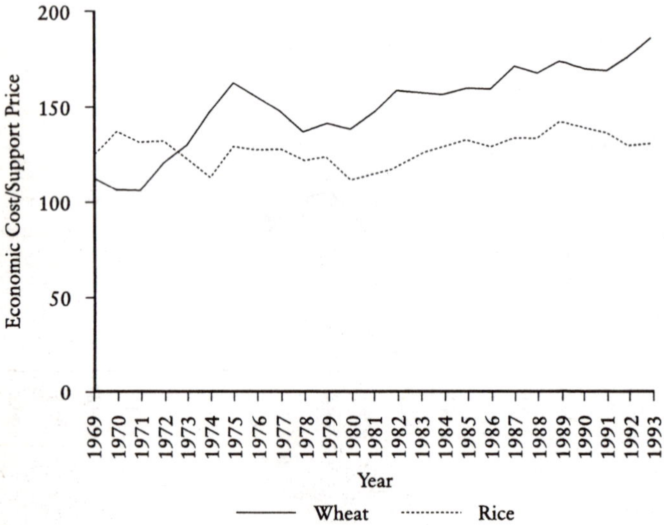

Source: Data from Food Corporation of India and BICP Report.

Figure 10.6
Economic Cost to Wholesale Price

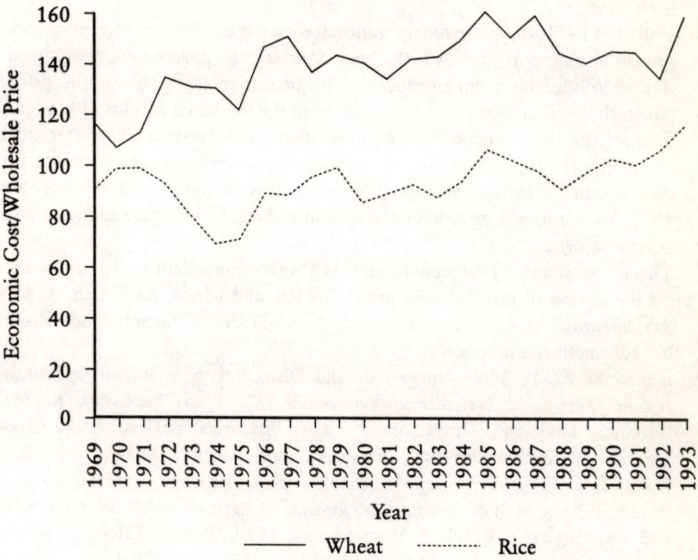

Source: Data from Food Corporation of India and BICP Report.

NOTES

1. Tata Services Limited, 1992, 'Statistical Outline of India 1992–93'.
2. Foodgrains refer to rice, wheat and coarse cereals.
3. Sharma, P. 1994, 'Government Intervention in Foodgrain Economy: Case of Rice and Wheat', (mimeo), Indian Economic Service.
4. Radhakrishna and Ravi report price elasticities of cereals, based on cross-section National Sample Survey (NSS) data, to be – 0.43 and – 0.20 for rural and urban groups, respectively.
5. Kahlon, A. S. and D. S. Tayagi, 1983, *Agricultural Price Policy in India*, New Delhi: Allied Publishers.
6. Lele, U. 1971, *Foodgrain Marketing in India: Private Performance and Public Policy*, Ithaca: Cornell University Press; Moore, J., S. S. Johl and A. M. Khusro, 1973, *Indian Foodgrain Marketing*, New Delhi: Prentice Hall of India.
7. In 1965, the Commission of Agricultural Costs and Prices (CACP) was also established to advise the government on agricultural pricing policy.
8. FCI functions under the supervision of the Departments of Food and Civil Supplies of the Ministry of Agriculture. General management, superintendence and direction of FCI vests in the Board of Directors. For its operations, FCI has

divided the country into five zones that are further subdivided into regions, districts, storage centres and storage godowns.

9. A violation of this act can lead to a conviction ranging from a fine to imprisonment.
10. Until 1971–72, the government announced separate support and procurement prices. The support price was the price at which the government guaranteed to buy all foodgrains from producers. The procurement price was the price at which the government purchased a share of the marketed surplus of foodgrains to meet the requirements of the public distribution system and buffer stocks. The support price was aimed at a producer, whereas the procurement price served other purposes of food policy, such as national food security. Since 1972–73, a uniform price has been announced that is both the support and procurement price.
11. This leaves scope for subjectivity in CACP's recommendations. For a discussion on the setting of procurement prices for rice and wheat, see Gulati, A. 1987, *Agricultural Price Policy in India*, New Delhi: Concept; and Sharma, 'Government Intervention'.
12. Dantwala, M. L. 1967, 'Incentives and Disincentives in Indian Agriculture', *Indian Journal of Agricultural Economics*, 22: 1–25; Subbarao, K. 1979, 'Producer Levy, Evasion and Income Loss: Empirical Evidence from Coastal District of Andhra Pradesh', *Economic and Political Weekly*, 24 March; Hayami, Y., K. Subbarao and K. Otsuka, 1982, 'Efficiency and Equity in the Producer Levy of India', *American Journal of Agricultural Economics*, 64(4): 655–63; Chetty, V. K. and P. V. Srinivasan, 1990, 'Welfare Effects of Selected Foodgrain Policies in India', *Agricultural Economics*, (4): 179–92.
13. Dantwala, 'Incentives and Disincentives'.
14. Lieberman, S. S. and D. Ahluwalia, 1990, 'Review of GOI Agricultural Product Market Interventions', (mimeo), New Delhi: The World Bank; Narayana, N. S. S., K. S. Parikh and T. N. Srinivasan, 1991, *Agricultural Growth and Redistribution of Income: Policy Analysis with a General Equilibrium Model of India*, New Delhi: Allied Publishers; and Schiff, M. 1994, 'The Impact of Two-Tier Producer and Consumption Food Pricing in India', *The World Bank Economic Review*, 8(1).
15. Lieberman and Ahluwalia, 'GOI Agricultural Product Market Interventions'; and Krishna, R. and A. Chhibber, 1983, 'Policy Modelling of a Dual Grain Market: The Case of Wheat in India', Research Report 38, International Food Policy Research Institute, Washington, DC, May.
16. The nominal protection coefficients are estimated here only for rice and wheat, but results are valid for foodgrains as a whole. Sharma has shown that coarse cereals (sorghum and maize) received neither high nor low incentives (Sharma, P. 1994, 'Effective Incentives in India's Agriculture: Case of Coarse Cereals', *Journal of Indian School of Political Economy*, July–September).
17. Tyagi, D. S. 1990, *Managing India's Food Economy: Problems and Alternatives*. New Delhi: Sage Publications.
18. For further details, see Garg, V. K. 1980, *State in Foodgrain Trade in India*. New Delhi: Vision Books; and Bureau of Industrial Costs and Prices (BICP). 1990, 'Report on the Operations of the Food Corporation of India'. New Delhi: Government of India.

19. Krishna, R. 1967, 'Government Operations in Foodgrains', *Economic and Political Weekly*, 16 September; Subbarao, 'Producer Levy, Evasion and Income Loss'; Krishna and Chhibber, 'Policy Modelling of a Dual Grain Market'.
20. FCI documents do not list the protection of the poor as a goal of PDS. However, several official statements found in five-year plan documents since the Fourth Plan would confirm that protecting the poor by supplying foodgrains at subsidised prices was an underlying goal of PDS. The Seventh Plan wanted PDS to be 'a stable and permanent feature of our strategy to control prices, reduce fluctuations in them and achieve an equitable distribution of essential consumer goods'. In particular, it suggested extending PDS to rural, unserved and inaccessible areas so that it becomes supplementary to poverty alleviation programmes. The Eighth Plan aimed to target food supplies exclusively to the poor to reduce food subsidies.
21. About the evolution of PDS, see Gupta, A. 1977, 'Public Distribution of Foodgrains in India', Centre for Management in Agriculture. Ahmedabad: Indian Institute of Management; Chopra, R. N. 1981, *Evolution of Food Policy in India*. New Delhi: Macmillan; George, P. S. 1985, 'Some Aspects of Procurement and Distribution of Foodgrains in India'. Working Paper on Food Subsidies No. 1, International Food Policy Research Institute, Washington, DC; and Bapna, S. L. 1990, 'Food Security Through PDS: The Indian Experience', in D. S. Tyagi and V. S. Vyas (eds), *Increasing Access to Food: The Asian Experience*. New Delhi: Sage Publications.
22. There were 358,490 fair price shops in operation in 1990 compared to 102,000 shops in 1965. The number of persons per shop declined from 8,000 to 2,334 during that period. Most of these shops are in rural areas.
23. For example, in Andhra Pradesh the state government bears annually a subsidy of over Rs 16 billion to maintain its Rs 2 per kg rice distribution scheme. Tamil Nadu is another state with a large state-run food subsidy programme.
24. The central issue price is different from the state issue price. The state issue price is obtained after state government has added to the central issue price transport and handling expenses and deducted the state subsidy, if any. Adding dealers' margins to the state issue price gives the retail issue price at which consumers get their supplies from PDS.
25. For example, separate prices are issued for common, fine and superfine rice.
26. Issue prices of wheat are adjusted more readily to changes in costs than issue prices of rice (Sharma, 'Government Intervention'). There may be an unwritten policy to provide rice at lower prices than wheat, since the majority of the country's poor are rice eaters.
27. The NSS Report of the 42nd Round on the Utilisation of Public Distribution System (1986–87).
28. Report of the Committee of Ministers on National Policy on Public Distribution System, Government of India, Ministry of Civil Supplies, Consumer Affairs and Public Distribution, July 1993.
29. Droughts reduce the supply of foodgrains and increase the demand for public distribution. The reduced supply raises open market prices. As a result, the gap between the open market and issue price widens, causing an increased demand pressure on PDS. This leads to a sharp depletion in stocks and/or imports. The

role of imports has decreased and the depletion of stocks increased since 1965 as a means to satisfy the demand. For example, in the drought year 1987, stock depletion contributed about 74 per cent of total PDS supplies of wheat. In previous drought years, the contribution of stocks had been only about 30–40 per cent.

30. Parikh, K. 1994, 'Who Gets How Much from PDS: How Effectively Does it Reach the Poor?', *Sarvekshana*.
31. Lieberman and Ahluwalia, 'GOI Agricultural Product Market Interventions'.
32. Sharma, 'Government Intervention'.
33. Krishna, 'Government Operations in Foodgrains'; Gupta, 'Public Distribution of Foodgrains in India'; National Commission on Agriculture. 1975, 'Interim Report on Agricultural Price Policy'. New Delhi: Government of India; Gulati, I. S. and T. N. Krishnan. 1975, 'Public Distribution and Procurement of Foodgrains: A Proposal', *Economic and Political Weekly*, 24 May; Vyas, V. S. and S. C. Bandyopadhyay. 1975, 'National Food Policy in the Framework of National Food Budget', *Economic and Political Weekly*, 10 March; Ministry of Finance. 1979, 'Report of the Committee on Controls and Subsidies'. New Delhi: Government of India; George, 'Some Aspects of Procurement and Distribution of Foodgrains in India'; Suryanarayana, G. 1985, *Public Distribution in India*. New Delhi: Chugh; Pinstrup-Anderson, P. 1988, *Food Subsidies in Developing Countries: Costs, Benefits, and Policy Options*. Baltimore and London: Johns Hopkins University Press; Bapna, 'Food Security'; and Tyagi, *Managing India's Food Economy*.
34. Ahluwalia, D. 1990, 'Public Distribution of Food in India: Issues and Evidence', (mimeo); Dev, M. and M. H. Suryanarayana. 1991. 'Is PDS Urban Biased and Pro-Rich?', *Economic and Political Weekly*, 12 October.
35. See note 27.
36. Ahluwalia, 'Public Distribution of Food'.
37. Bapna, 'Food Security'.
38. See note 36. For example, nearly half of the procured rice is of the superfine variety. However, such rice is rarely available in fair price shops.
39. Parikh, 'Who Gets How Much from PDS'.
40. Sharma, 'Government Intervention'.
41. The difference between these stocks is only conceptual; they are not physically distinct.
42. Each year on January 1 the stocks should be as follows: 7.7 million tons of wheat and 7.7 million tons of rice. Krishna and Chhibber, 'Policy Modelling of a Dual Grain Market', criticise these targets observing that they have been 'usually inoperative as ex ante goals' and 'sometimes the committees simply rationalised actual stocks as desirable'.
43. Non-obligatory costs include storage and interest, mandi labour, forwarding, internal movement and establishment charges. Of these, FCI reimburses storage, interest and establishment charges to state agencies.
44. Mandi charges include the market fee, the commission of a kutcha arhatia, the market cess and auction fee.
45. Neelakantan, J. 1989, 'Procurement, Buffer Stocks and Distribution of Foodgrains in India' (mimeo). Indian Institute of Management, Ahmedabad; Randhawa, N. S. 1993, 'Globalisation of Agriculture and Implications for Domestic Market and External Trade', (mimeo).

46. The cash credit limits are fixed periodically by the Reserve Bank of India. The funds are arranged by a consortium of commercial banks and channellised through the State Bank of India against hypothecation of stocks. In a good year, FCI's demand for credit goes up and vice versa. This credit is preemptive in a sense that it gets precedence over other credit. Thereby, it reduces funds available for other lending. Since this credit is supplied at a concessional rate, it is being cross-subsidised by other credit.
47. FCI is also exempt from selective credit controls and the Essential Commodities Act, which apply to private traders.
48. In 1988–89, Indian railways incurred a loss of Rs 1.31 billion for carrying foodgrains for FCI.
49. Interestingly, the total quantity of foodgrains moved by rail as a percentage of the quantity purchased by FCI has always exceeded 100. In 1989–90, this percentage was 109 for the purchases and 141 for the sales of foodgrains. This implies that some stocks are moved multiple times between storage godowns.
50. Storage charges incurred by FCI-owned godowns are comprised of establishment costs, stores and spares consumed, depreciation charges, repair and maintenance charges, insurance and taxes. In the case of hired godowns, the storage cost equals the rent paid.
51. In August 1993, FCI had a total storage capacity of about 22 million tons of which about 20 million tons was covered and the rest was of cover-and-plinth (CAP) type. Of the covered storage, 12 million tons was owned by FCI. The rest was hired from the Central Warehouse Corporation (CWC), the State Warehousing Corporation (SWC) and state governments.
52. Garg, *State in Foodgrain Trade in India*.
53. Handling costs incurred during procurement operations are included in procurement costs. The remaining handling costs are treated as distribution costs.
54. See 'Report on the Operations of the Food Corporation of India', note 18.
55. See note 52.
56. Bhagwati, J. and T. N. Srinivasan. 1993, *India's Economic Reforms*. New Delhi: Government of India, Ministry of Finance.
57. Government of India. 1994, *Economic Survey 1993–1994*. New Delhi: Government of India, Ministry of Finance.
58. Krishna and Chhibber, 'Policy Modelling of a Dual Grain Market', using a simulation model, show that the cost of wheat operations could be cut down by 30–35 per cent by allowing exports and cutting buffer stocks down to one-fourth of the level in 1979. Those buffer stocks would be large enough to meet the foodgrain requirements of a bad year.
59. Sharma, 'Government Intervention'.
60. Ibid.

11

Economic Reforms and Agricultural Parastatals: The Case of the Cotton Corporation of India and the Maharashtra Federation

Ashok Gulati and Sangeeta Shroff

The crisis of 1991 compelled Indian policymakers to usher in a two-pronged economic reform—stabilisation of the macroeconomic situation, and structural adjustment in selected sectors. One hallmark of the economic reform was that the Indian economy would be gradually exposed to world markets and foreign capital. This was to lead to globalisation of the Indian economy. The process started with the industrial sector, and gradually spread to other sectors, including agriculture.

In the case of agriculture, there was an additional economic event that would lead to its globalisation: the signing of General Agreement on Tariffs and Trade (GATT) under the Uruguay Round. The commitments under the Uruguay Round specify that all non-tariff barriers be converted into tariffs, that tariffs be reduced gradually, that subsidies in agriculture as measured by the Aggregate Measure of Support (AMS) be reduced and that countries give minimum access to imports from other countries starting at a level equal to 3 per cent of domestic consumption eventually increasing to 5 per cent. Although there have been several loopholes in the GATT agreement, which can delay globalisation of agriculture, the overall direction seems to be toward opening up agricultural sectors around the world.

The liberalisation of agriculture and successful implementation of economic reforms thus calls for removal of impediments to better allocation of resources: among crops, among regions and among agriculture and other sectors. This also involves assessment of different government interventions in both the agricultural input as well as product markets. For example, when extending the structural adjustment programme to agriculture, what should be the role of marketing parastatals such as the Food Corporation of India (FCI), the Cotton Corporation of India (CCI), the Maharashtra Federation (MF), the Jute Corporation of India (JCI) and other marketing boards created by the government for providing necessary support to the farmers, protecting consumers, supplying industry with raw materials and building stocks to stabilise prices?

What would happen to agricultural marketing parastatals in India in the liberalised economic environment that is likely to emerge in the years to come? The issue is important as these parastatals were created under the highly regulated economic regimes of the mid-1960s or early 1970s. There was a basic disbelief in the efficient functioning of agricultural markets; traders were viewed as hoarders and exploiters of the farmers as well as consumers. The marketing parastatals were created to remove the deficiencies of agricultural markets, give an assured price to the cultivator and charge a stable and low price to the consumer. To achieve these objectives, the parastatals controlled procurement and stocking operations. Sometimes imports and exports were also channelised through them.

These parastatals have now operated for over two decades and have been functioning with government support in the form of such things as cheap credit, concessional transport, budget support and monopsonistic support. These policies are, however, not in tune with the liberalised atmosphere that has set in since 1991. There has been a sea change in the objective conditions, be it the production of agricultural commodities, development of marketing infrastructure or above all in the belief of the private sector in agricultural marketing. The time has now come to evaluate the performance of these parastatals in terms of whether they have been able to achieve the objectives set for them, and at what cost they have carried out their operations. Can the private sector attain the same objectives as the parastatals at lower economic costs? What changes are required to make the parastatals compatible with liberalised marketing rules and conditions? These questions are the subject matter of this study; the marketing parastatals considered are the Cotton Corporation of India and the Maharashtra Federation, and the commodity is cotton.

Cotton is one of the major cash crops in the country and the Indian textile industry, perhaps the largest industry in India, is predominantly cotton-based. The trade-offs between exporting raw material or exporting the processed product become acute. There are several forms of government interventions in marketing: in the state of Maharashtra, a monopsonistic government agency buys all the raw cotton; in Gujarat there are cooperative marketing societies, and in other states there is the public sector agency, namely the Cotton Corporation of India, which buys raw cotton in the regulated markets in competition with private traders. Each of the interventions were justified by perceived inefficiencies prevailing in the markets, and aimed to correct the inefficiencies. This study assesses the success of these interventions in achieving the tasks set out for them as well as the cost of the intervention compared to the benefits achieved.

This study is a continuation of a similar study on the Food Corporation of India, the largest agricultural marketing parastatal in India.[1]

The evolution of the CCI and the Maharashtra Federation is covered in Section I. An evaluation of these parastatals in terms of their objectives, and how far they could be achieved with the support of the government, is covered in Section II. Section III examines the level and behaviour of the cost of operations of the two parastatals and attempts to discover any economies or diseconomies of scale in their operations, as well as how their costs compare with those of cooperatives and private trade in cotton marketing. Finally, Section IV spells out some reform options that could help these parastatals become compatible with the new environment without incurring undue expense.

I EVOLUTION OF THE COTTON CORPORATION OF INDIA AND THE MAHARASHTRA FEDERATION

With independence and partition, nearly 40 per cent of the area's cotton production went to Pakistan, whereas almost all (97 per cent) of the textile industry remained in India. The country thus had to depend upon imports of raw cotton in order to meet the requirements of the textile industry, which had a large organised sector. Cotton is also important to the handloom sector, and it was in this context that the CCI was created in July 1970 as a public sector organisation that would import cotton to meet the requirements of the textile industry. The CCI was solely responsible for importing raw cotton with the idea that centralised purchases would be more economical and useful from the point of view of speedy contracting and economical shipments. The canalised system, it was thought, would also prevent any loss of foreign exchange through over-invoicing of imports and under-invoicing of exports.

In the field of domestic trade, however, its operations were limited: it worked as an agent to purchase cotton for National Textiles Corporation (NTC) mills and other mills, if required, and also at times to perform price support operations. However, in 1978–79, the role of the corporation underwent a change. Due to a technological breakthrough in the late 1970s, leading to the introduction of new high-yielding varieties of long staple cotton, the country became self-sufficient and the need to import cotton was no longer felt. In fact, over the years, India became a net exporter of cotton. Cotton imports, which have now diminished or disappeared, are currently placed under open general licence (OGL); the role of the corporation is thus confined only to domestic operations. Besides meeting the needs of NTC and other mills, the CCI also performs price support operations. Further, it participates in open auctions in the regulated markets and also exports cotton up to the export quota allotted to it by the government from time to time.

Soon after setting up the CCI in 1970, a scheme of monopoly purchase of raw cotton was introduced by the state of Maharashtra, which came into effect on August 1, 1972. The scheme aimed at eliminating middlemen and securing for the growers the full advantage of the terminal price. The Minister for Cooperation noted that this effort to set up monopoly machinery was not a duplicated function of the CCI, as the CCI was set up in 1970 mainly to import cotton.

The notable feature of the Maharashtra State Cooperative Cotton Grower's Marketing Federation (henceforth referred to as the Maharashtra Federation) was that it ensured a guaranteed price to the growers that would remain the same throughout the season.

It also gave a bonus in case the scheme made a profit due to the final price being greater than the guaranteed price. This bonus accounted for 75 per cent of the profits (if any) while 25 per cent was credited to the Price Fluctuation Fund (PFF). The PFF was created so that in years of losses, the guaranteed price could be ensured to the growers from this fund. In case there was no balance in this fund, the growers were ensured the guaranteed price by contributions from the state government.

Overall, it appears that the main issues on which state intervention in cotton marketing was introduced were:

1. initially significant imports to meet the needs of the industry and the possibility of deriving greater economies of scale by entrusting the job to a single entity;
2. instability in the price of cotton with post-harvest prices rising higher than warranted by carrying costs; and
3. the premise that farmers were deprived of their due share in the terminal price as they were exploited by traders, which was possible as farmers had poor stocking capacity and were often in urgent need of cash.

State intervention, it was thought, could be a remedy for the inefficiencies prevailing in the marketing of cotton by private trade. Further, public sector organizations could also take up programmes to enhance yield, promote scientific cultivation practices and enable cultivation of new high-yielding varieties by providing the necessary market support.

The state agencies account for only about 25 per cent of the total cotton produced, indicating that private trade is still dominant in the cotton marketing scene. However, in the case of the Maharashtra scheme, its influence is nearly complete within the state as by legislation no other channel can function in which the farmer can sell his produce. The influence of the CCI is limited to the rest of the country where it competes with private trade for the purchase of cotton.

The CCI and the Maharashtra Federation have been in existence for about two and a half decades. Perhaps an assessment of their operations would be a useful lesson in policymaking. This is attempted in the ensuing sections, which examine:

1. the extent to which state intervention has succeeded in reducing price instability through canalising imports of cotton and by the state's purchase and sale operations in the domestic market;

2. the cost of operations of these parastatals, as the magnitude of marketing costs incurred by them would indicate their commercial viability and operational efficiency; and
3. the efficiency in the marketing operations of these parastatals vis-á-vis that of other marketing agents such as private trade and cooperatives.

In the light of the above analysis, some reform options are suggested whereby these parastatals can be more productive to society.

II AN EVALUATION OF OPERATIONS

Cotton is mainly a rain-fed crop in the major areas where it is cultivated, and rainfall can affect cotton output favourably or otherwise and hence cause fluctuations in prices. These fluctuations in prices make it difficult for the producers as well as consumers (textile mills) to plan their business activities. The price fluctuations within a year are also significant as the cotton harvest is spread over a considerable period of time and decisions on imports and exports are based on estimates of cotton output for the year. Again there is often considerable variation in the crop output estimates made by trade and government agencies. Due to intra-year price variations it was felt that benefits of higher prices in the lean season accrued largely to traders and not the farmers. The state intervention, therefore, was expected to reduce intra-year as well as inter-year price variations.

Inter-Year Price Variability

The CCI was set up in 1970 and the Maharashtra Federation was instituted in 1972. We may take 1970–71 as the cutoff point for comparison of the price variability in the period when the two state agencies were operating and the period when these agencies did not function. By taking the coefficient of variation as the measure of variability in the prices, we have provided a comparison of price variability in the two periods in Table 11.1. The second period is subdivided further into subperiods.

If one considers inter-year variations as shown in Table 11.1, there is no clear evidence that this variation has decreased with the emergence of the CCI and the Maharashtra Federation. The coefficient of variation in cotton prices was higher during the 1970s than during the 1960s. During the 1980s, it did show some decline, but it is difficult to attribute this result to the activities of the CCI or the Maharashtra Federation. A number of factors, especially a substantial improvement in the production of cotton, helped to stabilise prices as imports became an unimportant source of supply for the Indian textile industry by the early 1980s.

Price Variability in Domestic and World Markets of Cotton

The price variability may also be seen from another angle, that of international price instability. A comparison of the coefficient of variation (CV) in Indian prices with the CV of international prices (Table 11.2) reveals that price variability in the Indian markets is greater than in the international markets. In other words, Indian farmers and consumers faced greater variability in cotton prices than the international consumers and producers despite the fact that Indian markets were insulated from the outside market forces partly to achieve the opposite results.

Thus when one looks at the reduction in price variability over time or relative to world prices or even in the inter-year price variability of cotton compared to other cash crops,[2] the intervention at the national level does not appear to have succeeded in the case of cotton.

Inter-Year Price Variability and the Maharashtra Federation

The purchase operations of the Maharashtra Federation seem to have helped stabilise inter-seasonal prices, albeit with the help of subsidies from the state government. The variability in the price of *kapas* in Maharashtra relative to other regulated markets in the country for similar varieties, for the period 1972–73 to 1985–86, as measured by coefficient of variation, is summarised in Table 11.3.

The estimates of coefficient of variation were lower in the case of Maharashtra than in the case of other markets in other states, which one can ascribe to the functioning of the Maharashtra Federation.

It may be pointed out here that the monopoly procurement scheme aimed to stabilise the prices received by the cotton growers in Maharashtra from year to year by virtue of its Price Fluctuation Fund. This fund had been wiped out, however, and showed a negative balance; the guaranteed price was often ensured to the growers by means of subsidies received by the state government. The inter-seasonal prices have thus been stabilised with the help of subventions received by the state government and not by the Price Fluctuation Fund alone.

Intra-Year Price Variability

The market intervention, in principle, can reduce variability either by providing competition to the traders or by price regulation. However, the empirical evidence on this score is often mixed, which is presented in Table 11.4.

Except for Abohar and Raichur, the results indicate that the intra-year variation in raw cotton prices declined with the entry of the CCI. In the case of Maharashtra, since the guaranteed price is fixed and remains the same throughout the season, the problem of intra-seasonal variation in prices does not arise.

Meeting the Needs of Public Sector Mills

One of the objectives of the CCI was to meet the raw cotton needs of the public sector textile mills. In keeping with this objective, the CCI made large purchases of cotton to meet the demands of NTC mills and other institutional buyers. However, the NTC often did not honour its commitments and the CCI was left with unsold stocks purchased at the beginning of the year when prices were higher. Carrying stocks resulted in carrying charges mainly in the form of interest and insurance charges. As the NTC did not keep its commitments, from the 1978–79 season on it no longer placed indents with the CCI. Thereafter, the CCI has offered quantities to the NTC at ruling prices, depending upon how much is available with the CCI. The special role of the CCI as a supplier of raw material to NTC mills, therefore, has been significantly reduced since its original conception.

III OPERATIONS OF THE CCI AND THE MAHARASHTRA FEDERATION: AT WHAT COST?

Although the mandates of the two state agencies have varied over time, their prime objectives have been to bring about stability in cotton prices and ensure that the farmers receive a better share in the final sale price (which is the mill price, or export price in the case of cotton) by eliminating the middlemen who have always been accused of operating on higher-than-warranted margins.

It is therefore important to examine whether these objectives were pursued with efficiency, i.e., whether the costs of operations of these parastatals were kept at the lowest minimum feasible, or at least lower than other marketing agents such as private trade. There are several indicators of the operational efficiency and commercial viability of these parastatals. The profit and loss accounts of the two parastatals, for instance, provide an idea of their commercial viability, and may also throw some light on their operational efficiency. Similarly trends in the ratio of average sales realisation to economic costs of operations can also be an indicator of overall efficiency/commercial viability in operations. The trends in the per-unit real costs (adjusted for inflation) of the agencies can be examined in order to understand if there has been any improvement in the operational efficiency of the agencies. Further, if the trends in real unit costs of operation are related to the size of operation it would also give an idea of whether the parastatals have economies of scale or not. Analysis of marketing costs incurred by these agencies also enlightens us as to whether these agencies are performing their operations within reasonable costs.

Profits and Losses: Commercial Viability of the CCI and the Maharashtra Federation

The annual reports of the CCI for various years reveal that the CCI earned profits only in fourteen out of twenty-five years of its existence: in the first ten years of its existence (1970–1980) it made profits in six years; in the next ten years (1980–1990) there were profits only in three years. From 1990–91 on the corporation made profits for the next five years (Table 11.5).

Profits or losses as a percentage of gross receipts over the twenty-five year period are shown in Figure 11.1. It is calculated as a percentage of gross receipts so that the inflationary impact on the two variables—profits or losses and gross receipts—is cancelled out. The figure shows that the highest profit percentage crosses (+) 9 in 1975–76 while the highest loss percentage touches (–) 9 in 1981–82. Since 1988–89, the CCI has been making continuous profits and also paying taxes on its profits.

On the other hand, it is a bit difficult to define the very concept of profit or loss in case of the Maharashtra Federation (MF). This is because of the Price Fluctuation Fund (PFF). Even if the MF makes profits on its current operations, i.e., earns more than the cost of purchases plus other marketing costs, it can still show a negative balance in the PFF due to its accumulated losses. Under the pricing scheme of cotton in Maharashtra, the federation cannot use the entire amount of profits to offset accumulated losses; only 25 per cent can be credited to the PFF while the balance is given to the cultivators as a bonus. Thus to examine the profit and loss situation of the federation, one should look at both variables, i.e., the amount credited to the PFF and the balance in the PFF (Table 11.6). In Figure 11.2 we have shown the balance in the PFF as a percentage of gross receipts. From Figure 11.2 it is clear that the huge losses that the MF incurred during the mid-1980s could not be settled even after a decade. It is still reeling under the negative balance of the PFF to the tune of Rs 1,440 million in 1993–94. The Maharashtra Federation would have had to wind up its operations had the state government not come to its rescue by a contribution of Rs 2,836.7 million. Thus overall, the operations of the MF have not been commercially viable without support from the state government.

There were several reasons for the losses but the primary reason perhaps was improper grading of cotton by the federation. Cotton of inferior quality had often been graded as superior quality. This interesting fact was revealed by the High Level Committee on Monopoly Cotton Procurement Scheme (April 1987) which went into the reasons behind the losses of the scheme in the 1985–86 season. Further, the disputes relating to grading of cotton, which were settled by the Wandha Committee, went in favour of farmers. As a result, the federation had to pay the farmers high guaranteed prices for superior quality cotton. But the federation could not recover the high prices while selling it in the market. The years of 1984–85 and 1985–86 were also years of a bumper crop of cotton in Maharashtra as well as in the country. The MF was strained by paying unduly high guaranteed prices but received low sale prices, resulting in a net loss of Rs 770 million in 1984–85 and Rs 3,080 million in 1985–86. These losses could not be recovered from the PFF or even the Capital Formation Fund (where growers contributed 1 to 3 per cent of the guaranteed price) and the state government had to come to the rescue of the Maharashtra Federation to fulfil its commitment of paying the guaranteed price to the growers. The government contribution to the scheme was Rs 514 million in 1984–85 and Rs 2,836.7 million in 1985–86. A decade later, i.e., for the seasons 1994–95 and 1995–96, the same story is likely to be repeated and the scheme is expected to take heavy losses with delayed payments to farmers. While the accounts for these years are not yet settled, the scheme was holding 1.9 million bales of cotton (as of May 1996). These stocks are obviously going to attract heavy carrying costs and this is going to further weaken the commercial viability of the scheme if stocks are not sold at remunerative prices.

The commercial viability was further weakened by the inflow of cotton into Maharashtra, as the guaranteed price in Maharashtra was higher than that prevailing in neighbouring markets. In this case, the state government not only subsidised the Maharashtra farmers but also those who smuggled cotton into the state. Outflow of cotton had its own problems as growers avoided contributing to the PFF and also repaying cooperative dues. The financial burden of the scheme thus was aggravated.

As a result of the huge subsidies injected by the state government, the share of the grower in the sale receipts of the federation was often very high. For example, the share of the grower which was 93.2 per cent and 115.8 per cent of gross receipts of the federation in 1984–85 and 1985–86 respectively, would have been 83.2 per cent and 74.2 per cent respectively without the government subsidy. Thus paying the farmers a high share of the terminal price by depending on government subsidies is hardly a sign of efficient marketing by state agencies.

It is also important to note that the losses incurred by the parastatals are underestimated as the two organizations received preferential treatment in export quotas. Indian cotton prices are often below world prices and the nominal protection coefficient for cotton is estimated to be less than unity in most of the years under exportable hypothesis, especially when foreign exchange was shadow priced at 20 per cent higher than the official price up to 1992 (Figure 11.3).[3] This clearly indicates that exports are a lucrative area of marketing. Since 1978 India has turned out to be a net exporter of cotton, and export quotas are allocated by the government mostly in favour of the CCI and the MF (more than 80 per cent). These export quotas and subsequent profits on these exports helped to contain overall losses of the parastatals, or losses would have been much higher. Also the MF received concessional credit at 13.5 per cent against the market rate of 16 to 18 per cent. Hence at least up to 1985–86 the losses are underestimated.

The above analysis reveals that the two parastatals made huge losses up to the mid-1980s. Since then the CCI has turned the tables and emerged as a commercially viable organisation while the Maharashtra Federation continues to reel under losses in its operations.

Real Per-unit Costs of Operations: The Question of Economies of Scale

It would be interesting to examine how the per-unit costs of operation of the two parastatals have behaved over time. To eliminate the impact of inflation we have converted the costs at constant prices by using General Wholesale Price Index (1981–82 = 100). If they are related to the scale of operations, they can throw interesting light on whether the parastatals are enjoying economies of scale or not. This could help in deciding the optimum scale of their operations. The resulting estimates are presented in Figures 11.4 and 11.5.

Looking at the CCI's real per-unit cost of marketing at 1981–82 prices, the pattern seems to be that of an inverted 'V'. This indicates that up to a scale of, say, 1.2 million bales, the CCI experienced diseconomies of scale as the real per-unit cost of marketing increased up to that level. Thereafter, it declined, meaning that it started experiencing economies of scale in marketing. In the case of the Maharashtra Federation, however, one finds strong diseconomies of scale. The cluster of plots is neatly arranged in an ascending order, which speaks of high statistical significance.

It may be interesting to analyse why there are strong diseconomies of scale in the operations of the MF. Two components of marketing costs seem to be contributing the most. One is the high interest burden, especially on unsold stocks, and the other is rising salaries and other benefits (per bale) of the staff in the Maharashtra Federation. There have been years, especially in mid-1980s, when the MF ended up procuring significantly more than even the production of cotton in Maharashtra due to its high guaranteed price. These stocks could not be disposed of and they led to interest cost on the capital tied up in these stocks. This leads to diseconomies of scale.

The Structure of Marketing Costs

Marketing costs of the CCI and the MF are basically comprised of ginning and pressing charges, interest on working capital that is required to buy cotton, insurance of stocks and many other miscellaneous expenses. We have seen the behaviour of total marketing costs (in real terms on a per-bale basis) with respect to the scale of operation. But how much do they account for as part of the selling price? The data in Table 11.7 show that the CCI's marketing costs in relative terms had been quite low (5.14 per cent) during the first five years of its operation. Very soon, these caught up with the cost levels of the Maharashtra Federation, especially during 1980–81 to 1984–85. During this period both the parastatals had heavy losses and became the subject of severe criticism. Thereafter, the CCI made reasonable improvements. It reduced its marketing costs in the later periods which did not happen with respect to the MF, which remained saddled with a high cost structure of about 15.7 per cent of its selling price.

As mentioned earlier, the interest cost was the dominant cost, especially in the case of the CCI where at times it formed 62 per cent of the total cost during the five year period from 1980–81 to 1984–85. In the absence of any reliable crop estimates, the CCI used to play safe and import a great deal of cotton. If domestic production turned out to be satisfactory, imported cotton was difficult to unload on a profitable basis as domestic prices in most of the years were below import parity price. Mills often backed out of their commitments and the CCI was saddled with stocks.

Are Marketing Costs of Parastatals Comparable to Those of Private Trade or Other Marketing Cooperatives?

A number of micro level studies on marketing costs and margins in cotton trading conducted over time in different parts of the country showed mixed results. While some studies supported the view that farmers were exploited by private traders, others indicated that middlemen work on narrow margins (less than 15 per cent). The main conclusions of past studies on the marketing of cotton follow.

Khandevale (1971), Shroff (1989), Singh (1989), et al. and Rao's (1985) studies supported the view that farmers' share in the terminal market price was low (below 85 per cent),[4] while those of Dantwala (1937) as well as Pavaskar and Radhakrishnan (1970) revealed that farmers in fact received more than 85 per cent share in the terminal market price.[5] The study by Hosmani and others (1984) found that the share of farmers in the terminal market price of cotton is higher in cooperatives than in private trade.[6]

While the marketing costs and margins of private traders are around 15 per cent, this study on marketing costs and margins showed that the parastatals operated on similar costs and margins. However, there is one difference: private trade makes profits and prospers within the same marketing margins, while parastatals have often gone into losses; the MF is still running a negative balance in the PFF. If the state exchequer has to finance these losses, it is neither good economics nor commendable commercial policy.

Further, in many cotton-growing states, there are several cooperatives functioning. Gujarat is one of the leading states in this direction. The Gujarat State Cooperative Marketing Federation operates in Gujarat in competition with private traders. The annual reports of the Gujarat Federation indicate that the farmers' share in the selling price of the cooperative was 90 per cent, which is quite high compared to that of the CCI or private trade. The Gujarat Federation has no history of losses, while all marketing costs are kept to the minimum. Further it also paid a 6 per cent dividend to the Gujarat government on its investment in share capital. The track record speaks quite well for the commercial viability of the Gujarat Federation as well as for its economic efficiency. Perhaps this achievement is possible due to minimum political interference and also competition with private trade.

What is the conclusion with respect to efficiency in the operations of the CCI and the MF? That they are no better placed in terms of giving a higher share of their receipts to the farmers than private trade or the Gujarat Federation. Also, the price received by the farmer in Maharashtra has not always been more than the price received in other states. In Gujarat, for instance, the wholesale price has exceeded the final price in Maharashtra often by more than 15 per cent during the period 1974–75 to 1991–92. Whenever the MF or the CCI tried to give a higher price to the farmer they were saddled with larger stocks, raising the interest burden, thereby dragging them into the red. The MF is still accumulating losses, while the CCI has turned the corner since the late 1980s, thanks to the favourable treatment received from the government in allocation of export quotas.

IV LESSONS FOR REFORMS

With the opening up of the Indian economy, the economic policies pertaining to marketing and trade would obviously be different from those followed in a regulated economy. Even in a small sector like cotton, new options have emerged—from a chronic deficit situation, India emerged largely with a surplus of cotton in the 1980s and 1990s. Therefore imposing controls on exports and following autarkic policies would not be appropriate in the new framework cut out for the Indian economy. The fact that in most years, domestic prices of cotton are observed to be lower than their international prices (nominal protection coefficient being less than unity), indicates there is scope for exporting cotton, which will benefit the interests of the farmers. Under the GATT commitments, parastatals cannot be given preferential treatment in the allocation of export quotas. In fact all quantitative controls on exports must be gradually eliminated. This implies that the scope of covering the losses of marketing parastatals such as the CCI and the MF through preferential allocation of export quotas would be restricted.

The evolution of state intervention in order to reduce price instability, meet the needs of public sector textile mills and improve the cotton producer's share in the final price had its limitations and in fact was not really successful. This leads to two important questions. First, should the monopoly procurement scheme for cotton in Maharashtra be abolished? And second, what should be the role of the CCI in the changed scenario of economic policies for the 1990s and beyond?

To recapitulate the major findings of this study: the price variation in cotton in Maharashtra was found to be lower than in other neighbouring states but at the cost of subsidies from the exchequer; the analysis also showed that price instability was higher in domestic markets than in international ones. This suggests that insulating Indian farmers or consumers from world markets by canalisation of imports and export controls did not lead to higher price stability.

Further, the cooperatives in Gujarat have perhaps been more successful in getting a better share of the final price of the product to the farmer than the Maharashtra Federation or even the CCI. There appear to be strong diseconomies of scale in the operation of the federation indicating that size is no advantage. The study also showed that the CCI's role first as a canalizing agent and then as a supplier of cotton to the public sector mills has diminished or disappeared. The CCI's operations are more on a commercial basis. However, it benefits from the export quotas allocated by the government. Hence true efficiency of the corporation can not be easily assessed. The CCI's efforts to improve productivity in cotton cultivation and processing are important initiatives. If the input improvement programmes are commercially viable, there would not be any objection to the CCI reorienting its activities from marketing to productivity enhancement. But if it demands subsidies in the name of productivity improvement, it would raise questions regarding the need to undertake such activities, which are already being done by research institutions under the Indian Council of Agricultural Research.

These results suggest that in the cotton sector, government policies both at the central and state level would have to undergo major changes. In the first place, the monopoly procurement scheme of cotton should be abolished. It is not justified on any rational economic grounds. It does not pay higher prices to farmers without subsidies, it does not allow integration of the national cotton market, it leads to 'smuggling' of cotton from/to neighbouring states, breeds corruption at the borders and insulates the domestic cotton sector from the world markets, leading to domestic prices being lower than international prices. This amounts to 'taxation' of cotton peasantry. If cotton prices are to be controlled in order to safeguard the interests of the textile industry, or for weavers, it does not make economic sense to do so at the cost of the Indian cotton cultivator.

The main recommendations relating to the cotton sector indicate that:

1. While imports of cotton are under open general licence (OGL), there are restrictions on exports in the form of export quotas allocated by the government and also minimum export prices. Export of cotton needs to be freed from these controls and made less erratic than it is at present, so that India can emerge as a reliable source of cotton in the world market.
2. Cotton trade should be brought out of the purview of Essential Commodities Act which means that stocking limits for traders will be eliminated. Selective credit controls on cotton trade should be abolished; futures trading is a better option than price controls.
3. The monopoly purchase scheme is inefficient in serving farmers' interests. The state purchase scheme should be run in competition with private trade.
4. The CCI's role should be to act purely as a marketing agency on commercial lines. It would have to continue to undertake price support operations depending on the government's policy in this regard. But surely, with changes in cotton marketing rules in domestic and external markets, the role, size and contribution of the CCI must shrink in the years to come.

The study has not addressed the problems relating to the textile sector. However, the need to support handlooms and provide cheap cloth for the poor should not be met by providing disincentives to the cotton sector. Doing so only distorts the allocation of resources in this sector in favour of other enterprises, which may not be the best use of productive resources in the economy.

Table 11.1
Inter-year Price Variability in Cotton

Period	*Coefficient of Variation (per cent) in Cotton Price (Raw Cotton, WPI)*
Pre-CCI and Maharashtra Federation	
1960–61 to 1969–70	19.09
Post-CCI and Maharashtra Federation	
1970–71 to 1979–80	25.83
1980–81 to 1989–90	22.23

Notes: WPI stands for wholesale price index.
Source: Gulati, et al. (1996).[7]

Table 11.2
Variation in Domestic and International Cotton Prices
(coefficient of variation, per cent)

Period	*International Prices*		*Indian Cotton Raw (WPI)*
	Orleans/Texas CIF N Europe	*California CIF N Europe*	
1965–70	12.97	11.66	14.61
1971–80	9.09	8.30	25.83
1981–93	8.16	7.62	38.14

Notes: The International prices are August–July for the period up to 1979–80 and November–February for the later years. In the case of Indian prices, the year is April–March in all cases.
CIF N Europe stands for cost, insurance and freight, North Europe; and WPI for wholesale price index.
Source: Authors' Calculations.

Table 11.3
Variation in Cotton Prices in Maharashtra vis-à-vis Other States (CV in per cent)

Variety	*Market*	*Price of Kapas in Coefficient of Variation*	*Selected markets Standard Deviation*
1. H-4	Maharashtra	15.7	74.4
	Bhainsa, AP	24.6	116.9
	Adilabad, AP	21.0	102.3
	Khandwa, MP	18.2	88.8
2. G-6	Maharashtra	25.3	95.9
	Bhainsa, AP	28.1	115.3
3. AK-277 and 235	Maharashtra	26.0	99.3
	Adilabad, AP	27.4	109.2
4. L-147	Maharashtra	20.7	86.5
	Adilabad, AP	23.2	101.6
5. Laxmi	Maharashtra	22.0	93.0
	Hubli, Karnataka	23.0	78.7
6. MUC-5	Maharashtra	17.0	77.1
	Tirupur	19.5	101.6

Source: Shroff (1989).[8]

Table 11.4
Variation in Monthly Prices of Raw Cotton

Market	*Coefficient of Variation in Monthly Prices of Raw Cotton*
1. Abohar (Punjab)	Remained High Even After the Entry of CCI
2. Buranpur (MP)	Decreased After CCI Entry
Khandwa (MP)	Decreased After CCI Entry
3. Bodeli (Gujarat)	Decreased After CCI Entry
4. Raichur (Karnataka)	No Major Change
5. Adoni (AP)	Lower for Varalaxmi Variety which is Purchased by CCI than Mungari which the CCI Does not Buy
6. Bhainsa (AP)	Lower for H-4 Variety which the CCI Buys than G-6 which it Does not Buy
7. Tirupur (Tamil Nadu)	Lower for CCI Purchased Kapas than Otherwise

Source: Shroff (1989).[9]

Table 11.5

Marketing Operations of Cotton Corporation of India

	Units	1970–71	1971–72	1972–73	1973–74	1974–75	1975–76	1976–77	1977–78	1978–79	1979–80	1980–81	1981–82
Bales Purchased	Lakhs	0.11	5.17	3.86	3.10	0.33	1.46	5.35	6.67	10.36	11.14	11.83	10.55
Value of Purchases	Rs Crores	1.03	48.28	48.16	55.13	4.81	26.82	119.89	136.58	189.90	216.38	316.73	258.25
Opening Stock	Lakh Bales	0.00	0.06	4.34	2.51	1.78	0.95	0.05	1.58	2.76	7.76	5.13	3.12
Value of Opening Stock	Rs Crores	0.00	0.45	40.32	26.02	22.73	9.71	2.32	27.66	44.06	127.31	94.58	92.68
Bales Purchased + Opening Stock	Lakhs	0.11	5.23	8.20	5.61	2.11	2.41	5.40	8.25	13.12	18.90	16.96	13.67
I) Value of Purchases + Opening Stock	Rs Crore	1.03	48.73	88.48	81.15	27.54	36.53	122.21	164.24	234.05	343.69	411.31	350.93
II) Total Marketing Costs	Rs Crore	0.05	3.22	6.90	5.96	1.41	3.32	12.65	25.24	35.47	61.92	66.87	67.37
a) Ginning & Pressing	Rs Crore	0.00	1.65	1.87	1.60	0.13	0.88	3.58	5.13	7.76	9.35	11.94	12.40
b) Salaries + Other Benefits	Rs Crore	0.01	0.09	0.25	0.52	0.31	0.36	0.24	0.70	1.00	1.33	1.81	1.84
c) Interest	Rs Crore	0.01	0.60	2.73	1.79	0.43	0.82	5.27	14.27	20.04	34.62	40.77	43.09
d) Rent Insurance & Bank Charges	Rs Crore	0.01	0.34	0.85	0.85	0.36	0.38	2.06	2.04	2.87	4.07	4.26	4.38
e) Other Costs	Rs Crore	0.02	0.54	1.20	1.20	0.18	0.88	1.52	3.10	3.00	12.55	8.07	5.66
III) Gross Total Receipts	Rs Crore	1.09	51.13	101.90	90.58	31.24	44.01	136.74	182.88	259.03	390.24	478.78	383.35
Purchases + Expenses + Opening stock (I + II)	Rs Crore	1.08	51.95	95.38	87.11	28.95	39.85	134.86	189.48	269.52	405.61	478.68	418.30
Profits	Rs Crore	0.01	− 0.82	6.52	3.47	2.29	4.16	1.88	− 6.60	− 9.59	− 15.37	0.10	− 34.95
Profits as % of Gross Receipts	Per cent	0.92	− 1.60	6.40	3.83	7.33	9.45	1.37	− 3.61	− 3.69	− 3.94	0.02	− 9.12
Share of Farmer in CCIs Gross Receipts	Per cent	94.5	95	86.8	89.5	88	83	89	89.8	80	88	86	91

(Table 11.5 contd.)

(Table 11.5 contd.)

	Units	1982–83	1983–84	1984–85	1985–86	1986–87	1987–88	1988–89	1989–90	1990–91	1991–92	1992–93	1993–94	1994–95
Bales Purchased	Lakhs	9.71	5.25	6.69	15.74	8.23	6.48	4.36	10.10	12.11	11.23	9.62	9.39	7.61
Value of Purchases	Rs Crores	218.09	161.37	187.27	378.96	213.37	297.81	192.30	450.41	540.29	764.89	555.58	643.27	966.85
Opening Stock	Lakh Bales	6.30	3.90	0.39	1.79	6.96	0.31	0.28	1.88	4.30	3.24	4.28	5.73	2.41
Value of Opening Stock	Rs Crores	142.49	53.10	14.68	43.70	111.35	7.20	12.35	89.43	230.54	165.82	254.14	282.72	165.69
Bales Purchased + Opening Stock	Lakhs	16.01	9.15	7.08	17.53	15.19	6.79	4.64	11.98	16.41	14.47	13.90	15.12	10.02
I) Value of Purchases + Opening Stock	Rs Crore	360.58	244.47	201.95	422.60	324.72	315.01	204.65	539.84	770.83	930.71	809.72	925.99	1132.54
II) Total Marketing Costs	Rs Crore	72.20	48.91	43.35	78.63	65.77	57.55	25.06	61.72	94.52	104.40	116.40	150.81	78.17
a) Ginning & Pressing	Rs Crore	10.90	6.28	8.22	24.32	11.68	9.87	6.46	17.54	23.53	27.07	24.46	28.02	23.54
b) Salaries + Other Benefits	Rs Crore	2.00	2.47	2.55	2.59	3.36	3.35	2.17	5.60	5.24	6.00	6.77	7.94	13.12
c) Interest	Rs Crore	45.82	32.36	24.83	35.69	30.99	21.68	9.67	18.73	22.40	23.47	30,02	22.59	7.70
d) Rent Insurance & Bank Charges	Rs Crore	4.73	2.56	2.79	6.38	4.55	4.18	2.03	5.35	8.48	8.12	5.94	7.31	5.73
e) Other Costs	Rs Crore	8.75	5.24	4.96	9.65	15.19	18.47	4.73	14.50	34.87	39.74	49.21	84.95	28.06
III) Gross Total Receipts	Rs Crore	400.95	281.76	233.78	482.56	390.29	359.96	237.96	625.61	923.70	1061.00	955.97	1113.01	1239.10
Purchases + Expenses + Opening stock (I + II)	Rs Crore	432.78	293.38	245.30	501.23	390.49	362.56	229.71	601.56	865.35	1034.47	926.12	1076.80	1210.77
Profits	Per cent	–31.83	–11.62	–11.52	–18.67	–0.20	–2.60	8.25	24.05	58.35	26.53	29.85	36.21	28.33
Profits as % of Gross Receipt		–7.94	–4.12	–4.93	–3.87	–0.05	–0.72	3.47	3.84	6.32	2.50	3.12	3.25	2.29
Share of Farmer in CCIs Gross Receipts	Per cent	90	86.7	86.3	87.5	83	82.2	86	86	83.4	87.7	84.7	83.20	91.40

Notes: Item III includes seed and other income: Item II includes purchase tax (1% of purchase), selling and distribution expenses rates and taxes, legal and professional fees, tax on profits.

Source: Cotton Corporation of India (Annual Reports of different years).

Table 11.6
Operations of Maharashtra Federation in Cotton Marketing

Item	*Units*	*1972–73*	*1973–74*	*1974–75*	*1975–76*	*1976–77*	*1977–78*	*1978–79*	*1979–80*	*1980–81*	*1981–82*
Bales Pressed	Lakhs	11.48	1.88	17.66	8.20	8.14	1.54	9.74	17.36	12.61	14.84
I. Gross Total Receipts	Rs Crore	173.71	40.62	329.18	174.32	231.72	37.54	201.14	402.29	403.11	406.20
II. Total Marketing Costs	Rs Crore	19.73	4.90	57.54	21.32	20.94	4.79	31.49	58.34	57.08	69.22
a. Ginning Charges	Rs Crore	3.99	0.83	8.82	4.55	4.63	1.00	6.13	11.01	9.11	11.36
b. Pressing Charges	Rs Crore	3.13	0.56	5.88	2.70	2.68	0.55	3.49	7.17	5.58	6.75
c. Bank Interest	Rs Crore	3.32	0.68	13.34	2.01	2.19	1.02	8.96	16.32	16.36	23.13
d. Insurance	Rs Crore	1.95	0.71	5.26	1.49	1.64	0.38	2.65	4.65	4.25	4.83
e. Chief Agent's Commission	Rs Crore	4.00	0.89	7.25	3.78	5.19	0.84	4.80	6.28	7.03	8.09
f. Other expenses	Rs Crore	3.34	1.23	16.99	6.79	4.61	1.00	5.44	12.91	14.75	15.06
IIIa. Payments to Cultivator	Rs Crore	148.92	32.93	292.28	143.00	185.76	32.30	173.95	347.19	343.44	382.16
(1) at Guaranteed Price	Rs Crore	133.67	24.95	291.63	113.10	110.75	25.64	171.24	339.56	326.96	385.26
(2) as Bonus	Rs Crore	15.25	7.96	3.28	29.90	75.01	6.66	2.71	7.63	19.72	0.73
(3) less Contribution to CFF	Rs Crore	0.00	0.00	2.63	0.00	0.00	0.00	0.00	0.00	3.24	3.83
IIIb. Payments to Cultivator Net of Government Contribution	Rs Crore	148.92	32.93	279.43	143.00	185.76	32.30	173.95	347.19	343.44	371.88
I Va. Payments to Cultivators As % of Gross Receipts	%	85.73	81.07	88.79	82.03	80.17	86.04	86.48	86.30	85.20	93.62
IVb. Government Contributións	Rs Crore	0.00	0.00	12.85	0.00	0.00	0.00	0.00	0.00	0.00	10.28
IVc. Net Payments to Cultivators as % of Gross Receipts	%	85.73	81.07	84.89	82.03	80.17	86.04	86.48	86.30	85.20	91.10
Va. Amount Credited to PFF	Rs Crore	5.05	2.75	– 19.98	9.97	25.00	0.39	– 4.96	– 3.20	– 0.10	– 47.08
Vb. Balance in PFF	Rs Crore	5.05	7.80	– 12.18	– 2.21	22.79	23.18	18.22	15.02	14.92	– 32.16
Vc. Balance in PFF as % Gross Receipts	Per cent	2.91	19.20	– 3.70	– 1.27	9.84	61.75	9.06	3.73	3.70	– 7.88
VI. Kapas Value at Final Price	Rs Crore	153.96	35.72	271.64	153.00	210.78	32.75	169.65	343.95	346.63	339.00
Marketing Cost as % of I	%	11.36	12.06	17.48	12.23	9.04	12.76	15.66	14.50	14.16	16.96

(Table 11.6 contd.)

(*Table 11.6 contd.*)

Item	*Units*	*1982–83*	*1983–84*	*1984–85*	*1985–86*	*1986–87*	*1987–88*	*1988–89*	*1989–90*	*1990–91*	*1991–92*	*1992–93*	*1993–94*
Bales Pressed	Lakhs	18.18	7.69	17.85	29.88	12.48	12.58	11.77	20.92	13.55	10.69	19.94	13.36
I. Gross Total Receipts	Rs Crore	503.58	285.93	512.29	682.26	493.70	605.87	519.73	949.86	766.35	712.84	1101.22	1104.48
II. Total Marketing Costs	Rs Crore	81.72	44.00	97.08	174.50	69.26	73.40	77.92	145.70	97.18	115.15	200.17	139.23
a. Ginning Charges	Rs Crore	15.06	7.39	16.34	31.53	14.38	13.88	13.81	28.27	20.72	18.17	39.62	28.16
b. Pressing Charges	Rs Crore	8.88	4.21	11.76	18.06	7.43	7.35	7.50	16.09	12.01	11.07	22.47	16.57
c. Bank Interest	Rs Crore	21.91	10.63	33.27	68.53	16.19	12.74	13.72	44.26	14.63	24.42	48.70	17.94
d. Insurance	Rs Crore	5.64	2.51	5.88	11.36	3.55	5.54	4.40	8.61	4.99	5.27	9.80	6.43
e. Chief Agent's Commission	Rs Crore	7.94	9.78	9.84	11.83	11.50	15.90	17.10	18.46	20.86	30.19	34.08	32.29
f. Other expenses	Rs Crore	22.29	9.48	19.99	33.19	16.21	17.99	21.39	30.01	23.97	26.03	45.50	37.84
IIIa. Payments to Cultivator	Rs Crore	430.38	230.90	477.61	790.22	388.89	468.30	402.97	747.32	603.90	537.50	860.53	917.18
(1) at Guaranteed Price	Rs Crore	438.82	224.14	492.38	814.65	323.15	318.03	325.66	659.36	483.49	405.30	839.95	651.84
(2) as Bonus	Rs Crore	4.53	13.33	0.00	0.00	75.43	159.77	87.01	107.76	154.36	144.31	45.78	284.84
(3) less Contribution to CFF	Rs Crore	12.97	6.55	14.28	24.43	9.69	9.50	9.70	19.80	13.90	12.10	25.20	19.50
IIIb. Payments to Cultivator Net of Government Contribution	Rs Crore	421.75	230.90	426.21	506.55	388.89	468.30	402.97	747.32	603.90	537.50	860.53	917.18
IVa. Payments to Cultivators as % of Gross Receipts	%	85.46	80.75	93.23	115.82	78.77	77.29	77.53	78.68	78.80	75.40	78.14	83.04
IVb. Government Contributions	Rs Crore	8.63	0.00	51.40	283.67	0.00	0.00	0.00	0.00	0.00	0.00	0.00	0.00
IVc. Net Payments to Cultivators as % of Gross Receipts	%	83.75	80.75	83.20	74.25	78.77	77.29	77.53	78.68	78.80	75.40	78.14	83.04
Va. Amount Credited to PFF	Rs Crore	– 21.60	4.44	– 77.17	– 308.10	25.21	53.62	29.00	35.20	51.45	48.10	15.26	31.65
Vb. Balance in PFF	Rs Crore	– 53.76	– 49.32	– 126.49	– 434.59	– 409.19	– 355.56	– 326.56	– 290.60	– 239.18	– 191.08	– 175.82	– 144.17
Vc. Balance in PFF as % Gross Receipts	Per cent	– 10.68	– 17.25	– 24.69	– 63.70	– 82.88	– 58.69	– 62.83	– 30.59	– 31.21	– 26.81	– 15.97	– 13.05
VI. Kapas Value at Final Price	Rs Crore	423.86	241.93	415.21	507.76	424.44	532.47	441.81	804.26	669.17	597.69	901.00	968.20
Marketing Cost as % of I	%	16.23	15.39	18.95	25.58	14.03	12.11	14.99	15.34	12.68	16.15	18.18	12.61

Source: Maharashtra Federation, Government of Maharashtra.

Table 11.7
Marketing Costs and Selling Price

Year	*Marketing CCI*	*Cost as Per Cent of Selling Price MSCGCMF*
Average for		
1970–71 to 1974–75	5.64	13.99
1975–76 to 1979–80	11.94	12.80
1980–81 to 1984–85	16.92	16.10
1985–86 to 1989–90	13.68	16.20
1990–91 to 1992–93	10.73	15.70

Source: Gulati, et al. (1996).[10]

Figure 11.1
Profits of CCI as % of Gross Receipts

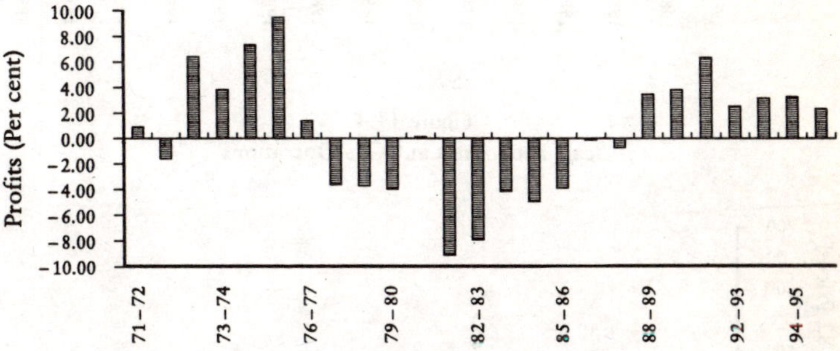

Figure 11.2
Balance in PFF as % of Gross Receipt Maharashtra Federation

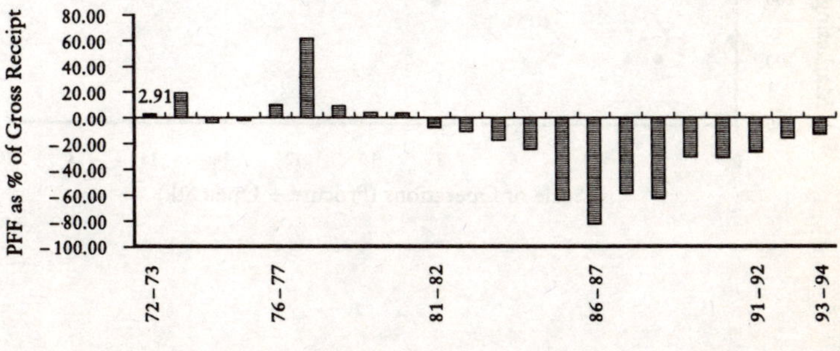

Figure 11.3
NPCs of Cotton under Exportable Hypothesis (SER)

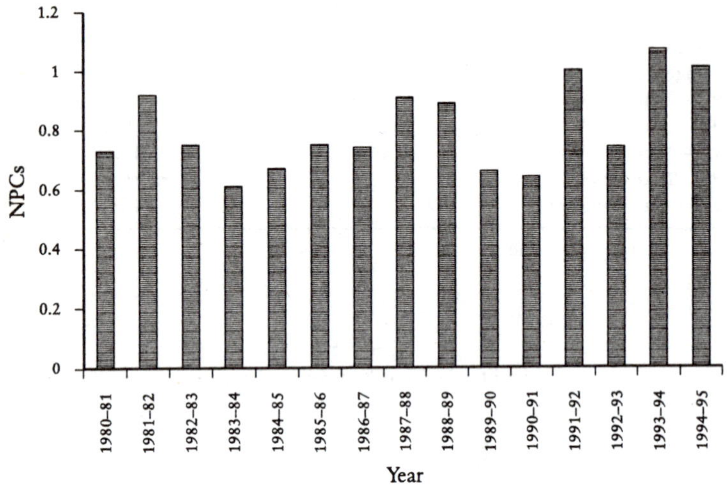

Figure 11.4
Scale Economies in CCI's Operations

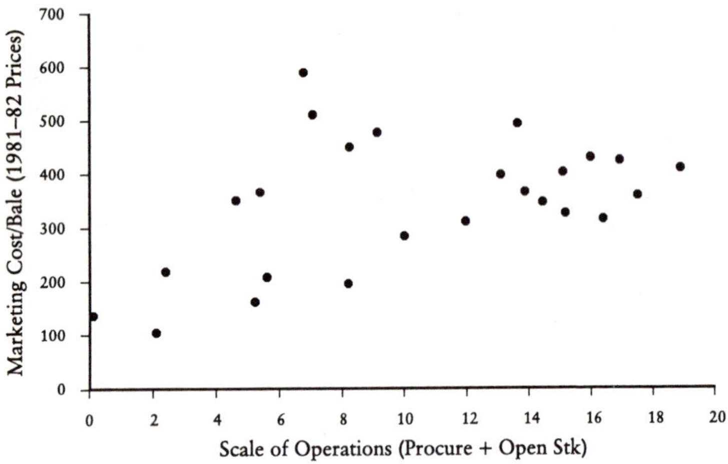

Figure 11.5
Diseconomies of Scale in Operations: Maharashtra Federation

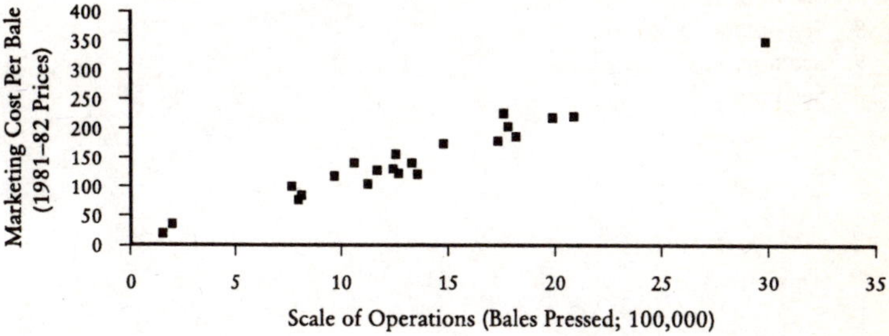

NOTES

The material in this chapter was first presented at the conference on 'Agriculture and Rural Reform: Institutions and Economic Policy', organised jointly by the Indian Institute of Management, Calcutta and the Center for Institutional Reform and the Informal Sector (IRIS), University of Maryland, in January 1997.

1. Gulati, A., S. Kähkönen and P. K. Sharma, 1995, 'Economic Reforms and Foodgrain Marketing in India: Case of Food Corporation of India', National Council of Applied Economic Research (NCAER)–IRIS Collaborative Study, NCAER.
2. Gulati, A., S. Bhide, S. Bhagat and S. Shroff, 1996, 'Economic Reforms and Agricultural Parastatals: The Case of Cotton Corporation of India and Maharashtra Federation', IRIS-India Working Paper No. 19, IRIS, University of Maryland, College Park.
3. Ibid.
4. Khandevale, S. V. 1971, *Economics of Cultivation and Marketing of Cotton in Vidarbha*. Nagpur: Suvichar Prakashan Mandal; Shroff, S. 1989, 'State Intervention in Cotton Marketing in India: Role and Efficiency of the Maharashtra State Cooperative Cotton Growers' Marketing Federation and the Cotton Corporation of India', unpublished Ph.D. thesis, Gokhale Institute of Politics and Economics, Pune; Singh, I. J., K. Chaudhry and R. C. Goel, 1979, 'Dynamics of Cotton Production and Marketing in Haryana', Haryana Agricultural University; Prabhakar Rao, J. V. 1985, *Marketing Efficiency in Agricultural Products: A Case Study of Cotton in Guntur District in Andhra Pradesh*. Bombay: Himalaya Publishing House.
5. Dantwala, M. L. 1937, *Marketing of Raw Cotton in India*. Bombay: Longmans and Green and Co. Ltd.; Pavaskar, M. G. and Radhakrishna, R. 1970, *Cost of Marketing Cotton*. Bombay: University of Bombay.

6. Hosmani, S. B. and Others, 1984, 'An Economic Analysis of Production and Marketing of Cotton—A Case Study of Small Farmers in Karnataka', Department of Agricultural Economics, Dharwad University.
7. See note 1.
8. See note 4.
9. See note 4.
10. See note 2.

12

Panchayati Raj in India: Problems and Prospects

Chandrika Gulati

PANCHAYATI RAJ: TOWARD DECENTRALISATION OF POLITICAL AND ECONOMIC POWER

Decentralisation, Democracy and Development

How do governments establish and sustain political and economic institutions that effectively decentralise decisionmaking processes? Vital to effective federalism and democracy, successful decentralisation promotes regional development and effectively transmits local voices to higher authorities. Decisionmaking at the local level, based on familiarity with local needs, problems and issues, enables efficient use of local resources and increases the likelihood of successful implementation of economic policies. In sum, local decisionmaking promotes democratic participation 'due to immediacy of its actions and the ease of access to its working compared to remote and complex national centres many of which are considered hostile to the local'.[1]

Five decades of Indian democracy and federalism have failed to create an environment conducive to effective participation of the majority of Indian citizens in decisionmaking processes. The 'top-down' approach to economic development has given the mass of the population a passive role in the process of development planning, in contrast with the Gandhian philosophy of non-violent social structure, which was based on self-sufficient villages sustained by cottage industry.[2] Perhaps as a result, 'trickle-down' development strategies in India neglected agriculture and rural development in favour of public sector development in heavy industry, which was believed to benefit indirectly economically and socially deprived rural groups. Moreover, Indian planners believed that the largely illiterate rural population was not able to perceive its problems, nor to comprehend the complexities of policymaking.

Thus, villagers have had no role in the formulation and implementation of those economic policies that concern them most. Perhaps in part as a result, Indian villages have remained far behind in economic development. In spite of decades of centralised planning and implementation of several anti-poverty programmes, one-third of the Indian population still lives in deprivation.[3]

Panchayati Raj

The 73rd Amendment (1993) to the Indian Constitution grants constitutional status to Panchayati Raj (PR), an institutional arrangement supporting decentralisation of power and responsibility to local levels through elective bodies at the village, intermediate block and district levels. PR is a system of government linking the Gram Sabha (village assembly) to the Lok Sabha (Lower House of the Union Parliament).[4] It is a mechanism for decentralising political power by enabling local participation in planning and implementation of local development programmes. PR is based on faith in the power and capability of people to self-govern.

PR supports the economic liberalisation programmes being implemented by the Government of India that give rights of management of resources to user groups. Endowing local citizens with local responsibilities reduces excessive and unresponsive intervention from higher levels of the state. PR does not mean shirking responsibilities to look after those who can not help themselves or 'get rid of obligations to commitment to social and distributive justice made forty years ago'.[5] Rather, it is a 'process, not a consummation,' a process of 'all people coming together with a mandate from the constitution or legislation to discuss and decide how they should develop themselves'.[6]

Several attempts in the past to securely establish grassroots democratic institutions in India have not been successful. Bestowing constitutional authority on Panchayati Raj is the most aggressive action taken thus far, since it stipulates conditions that must be implemented by all states: reservation of seats for women, scheduled castes and scheduled tribes; mandatory elections through state-level machinery; local responsibility for local development, including project design and implementation; and financial assistance. However, in designing their own legislation to implement Panchayati Raj institutions (PRI), the states' interpretations of the 73rd Amendment have been broad. Further, the fate of PR may be tied to issues of federalism at the centre/state level. Devolution of administrative responsibilities and financing (for state-level projects, including PRI) from the centre to the states are sensitive issues that will affect the states' implementation of PRI. For example, the PRI can effectively discharge responsibilities only when requisite resources and power are made available to them from the state. States, however, will part with their money and authority only when they receive less interference and more financial support from the centre.

Plan of the Study

This study is a modest attempt to understand the dynamics of decentralisation and evolution of PR in India. The structure of the study is as follows: Section I traces the evolution of PR in India from ancient times to the present. Elements of the 73rd Amendment granting statutory recognition to PR and related provisions in state enactments are examined in Section II. Section III presents an overview of the implementation process of Panchayati Raj enactments, empowerment of local bodies and subsequent problems in the states of Uttar Pradesh (UP), Punjab and Karnataka. Section IV assesses the impact of PR on disadvantaged social groups, especially women, and also summarises the broad issues and conclusions arising from the findings of this study.

I EVOLUTION OF PANCHAYATI RAJ IN INDIA

Historical Background

From ancient times, up to the advent of British rule, village councils were responsible for important decisions pertaining to communities.

The system of panchayats, an effective force of social control, was destroyed by the centralised rule and revenue collection policies imposed by the British colonial regime.

With Mahatma Gandhi's backing, the reestablishment of PR became integrated with the struggle for Indian independence. Gandhi believed that 'true democracy can not be worked by twenty men sitting at the centre. It has to be worked from below by the people of every village'.[7] The village, in his plan, would be governed by the panchayat (five persons annually elected by all adults in the village), which would serve in executive, legislative and judicial roles. Rather than a pyramidal government structure, he envisioned a democratic India composed of innumerable villages with 'ever widening, never ascending circles'. Through guidance received from the panchayats, the national leadership would be responsive to the needs and priorities of villagers. This arrangement would permit assessment of local needs and resources as well as planning that arose from below rather than being imposed from above.[8]

In spite of this history and Gandhi's vision, the first draft of the constitution did not even contain a reference to PR.[9] Early leaders of independent India, influenced by British bureaucratic structures, relied on a centralised system for development planning and denied the village, through PRI, a role in the formulation and implementation of development plans. Anti-poverty programmes and special provisions to lift economically and socially deprived populations were designed and administered by the Central Government and resulted in benefiting only a meagre percentage of the targeted populations.

From the years following independence to 1993, several attempts were made to reintroduce PRI. Highlights of these efforts are described in the following subsection of this chapter. Eventually, in 1993, the 73rd Amendment to the Constitution granted constitutional recognition to PR.

The Nehruvian Era

The first prominent rural development programme integrating local participation and economic policy was the Community Development Programme (CDP). Launched in 1952, the CDP initiated fifty-five projects throughout the country. Its objective was to improve welfare though a community-based approach that motivated people to help themselves. The government provided general guidance, as well as technical and financial assistance to local groups. Development blocks, created as the basic units of administration below the district level, were guided by the district administration and headed by a block development officer, assisted by subject specialists. Advisory committees were established in blocks and in the districts, so that the people might participate in local planning and implementation. Village panchayats motivated people to participate in community-based development activities. State governments were assigned the responsibility for overall guidance, subject to review of the Central Government.

Initially, there was great enthusiasm for the programme. The CDP ignited a developmental and cooperative spirit in rural areas. However, the euphoria over the devolution of power began to peter out with increasing bureaucratisation and malpractice. Officers at higher levels were loath to work under the direction of local representatives. State leadership also was not favourably disposed to competition from the nascent local leadership. The achievements of CDP remained, therefore, below expectations.

In 1957, the Balwant Rai Mehta Committee (BRMC) was established to identify problems with the CDP. Remedies suggested by the BRMC stressed local initiative and administrative decentralisation—for instance, advocating that public participation in community works be organised through statutory representative bodies.[10] Placed under the administrative authority of elected representatives, this new experiment in rural development relied on a democratic approach to form a partnership between elected representatives and government officials.[11] Authority and responsibility were allocated in a three-tier system based on the village, the block, and the district. The Panchayat Samiti (PS), at the block level—the focal point of decentralisation—was responsible for development pertaining to agriculture, minor irrigation, primary education and certain other local concerns. Village-level panchayats performed functions such as maintenance of roads, provision of water supply, sanitation, health and education. Above the Panchayat Samiti, at the district level, was the Zilla Parishad (ZP), which coordinated functions of Panchayat Samitis. The three bodies were integrated in a symbiotic relationship in which the lower body was represented in the higher body, and the higher body in the lower.

The Central Government directed the states to adopt PR and adapt it to local requirements. Rajasthan was the first state to inaugurate PR according to the BRMC model. By 1959 almost all states in India had initiated different patterns of PR. In these initial years, PRI succeeded in establishing schools and constructing roads, primary health centres and minor irrigation works.[12]

Nevertheless, despite the popularity accompanying its establishment, PR diminished in importance. Powers and functions originally devolved to local bodies were snatched away. Programmes launched by the central and state governments bypassed the CDP and panchayat bodies. Local feudalistic interests, fearing ascendancy of the lower classes, began obstructing the functioning of PRI. In many states, elections to panchayat bodies were not held for years. Financial resources of PRI were drastically curtailed. Eventually, by the time Indira Gandhi came to power, PR had practically ceased to exist except in a few states like Maharashtra and Gujarat.

Revival Attempts by the Janata Party

Under the directive of the Janata Party government, the Asoka Mehta Committee (AMC) was created to analyse PRI. The AMC reported that PR had contributed substantially to the processes of democratic politicisation among rural people, but remained weak as an agent of rural development.[13] It concluded that for the extension of democratic development to the grassroots level, it was imperative to strengthen PRI. The report focused on panchayats as political bodies serving as vehicles of development, suggesting a two-tier system: the district and the mandal (an administrative unit between village panchayat and block Samiti). The report favoured additional devolution of functions, empowerment, better financial support and representation of weaker segments of the population in PR bodies.

The BRMC had identified the block as the key unit of development, since it was large enough for functions that the village panchayat could not perform, yet small enough to attract the interest and services of residents. However, among structural changes, the AMC assigned the central role to the ZP as the first unit of decentralisation under popular supervision below the state level. The district was considered the unit of planning since the 'emerging scenario of dynamics of development necessitate that the technical expertise of a high order be made available below the state to sustain the momentum of rural development'.[14]

West Bengal followed the AMC recommendations in modified form, while Karnataka and Andhra Pradesh amended existing legislation or introduced new acts to implement the AMC report. Nevertheless, the unstable Janata government was unable to rejuvenate the PRI, which continued to stagnate or decline. The central and state governments began to withdraw legal authority, as well as financial and administrative support, from the PRIs. In Tamil Nadu, Bihar and UP, elections to panchayats were not held for years. Large rural development and poverty alleviation programmes were assigned to district administrations or newly-created field agencies. The District Rural Development Agency (DRDA) was established in every state at the district level to implement poverty eradication programmes sponsored by the Central Government with the collaboration of state governments. PRIs were accorded a minimal role in these projects and, while continuing to exist, made little impact on rural backwardness.

True to the prediction of the AMC, the predominance of socially and economically privileged people in rural society led to the growth of oligarchic forces barring weaker sections from participation in Panchayats. These forces dominated village panchayats, as moneylenders, rich farmers and local bureaucrats colluded to protect the interests of the rural elite. Rural local institutions were influenced by caste considerations and suffered from corruption, inefficiency and political interference.

From Rajiv to Rao: The Resurrection of PR

Although bold experiments with PR were already underway in some states like Karnataka, it was Rajiv Gandhi who initiated the process of resurrection of PR through constitutional change. Assuming office in 1984, he proposed a constitutional amendment to place PR elections on the same legal footing as elections to the Lok Sabha and the state assembly.[15] To address the popular revival of the Panchayati Raj, numerous committees were established to analyse the institutional arrangements and implications of PRI.[16] A PR bill introduced in May 1989 passed in the Lok Sabha, but was defeated in Rajya Sabha by two votes ostensibly for two reasons: states feared the Central Government would bypass them and deal directly with local bodies; and the PR bill imposed a uniform pattern on the states irrespective of their local geographical and historical needs.

In September 1991, the Rao government introduced a remodeled scheme for PRI, which was adopted as the 1992 Constitution (73rd) Amendment Act on 24 April, 1993.[17] The amendment provides for discretion by the state governments to design PRI within broad parametres of a three-tier system (village, intermediate block/taluk and district level).[18] Other provisions include reservation of seats and offices for scheduled castes and tribes in proportion to their population (including reservation of one-third of the seats for women); fixed five year tenure of panchayats; provision of an independent election commission for superintendence, direction and control of the electoral process; and establishment of a state-level finance commission ensuring adequate financial resources and listing of functions for panchayats.

In addition, the 74th Amendment to the Constitution grants constitutional status to urban local bodies. Together panchayats and municipalities make local administration the third tier of governance. The 74th Amendment also has provisions for a District Planning Committee (DPC) to act as a link between urban and local bodies by consolidating plans prepared by panchayats and municipalities into a draft plan for the entire district.

It has thus taken approximately half a century to re-create an organisational structure of PR in India. Still, the 73rd Amendment Act has raised as many doubts as it has attempted to resolve. While most of the states have passed PR Acts in consonance with 73rd Amendment, the success of PRI in decentralising decisionmaking and economic power depends on numerous factors. To understand this, it is worthwhile to study provisions of the 73rd Amendment and the corresponding provisions of state-level PR Acts in the states of Karnataka, UP and Punjab.

II PANCHAYATI RAJ: THE 73RD AMENDMENT AND ITS AFTERMATH

Does the 73rd Amendment really create a third tier of Indian federal polity? Are PRI truly local self-governing institutions? By conferring constitutional status on PRI, the 73rd Amendment attempts to ground them in an encompassing legal framework. However, the whole of the PR system has not been placed on a firm constitutional basis. The provisions of the act, along with Article 246[19] of the Indian Constitution, leave ample scope for the states to fiddle with PR in their partisan political interests. Thus, whether local bodies will be mere secondary administrative arms of the state governments or become autonomous units remains to be seen.

Constitutional Provisions Relating to Panchayats

Article 243B provides for the establishment of panchayats in every state at the village, intermediate and district levels.[20] The article provides for state discretion regarding the composition of panchayats, provided that all seats in a panchayat are to be filled by members directly elected from their territorial constituencies in the panchayat area. The state may grant representation to members of state legislatures and members of Parliament in panchayats at the intermediate and district levels. The state can also assign representation of a lower-level chairperson to the level immediately higher. Thus, a chairperson of a village panchayat may be given representation in the intermediate-level panchayat (in the absence of an intermediate-level panchayat, such representation would be at the district level). In village- level panchayats, the election of the chairperson may be decided by the state legislature. Intermediate- and district-level panchayat chairpersons are chosen by the elected members.

Structural changes in the social composition of panchayats are sought through mandatory provision of reservations for weaker sections of the population. Seats for scheduled castes (SCs) and scheduled tribes (STs) are reserved in proportion to their population. One-third of the total number of seats at every level (including the number of seats reserved for SCs and STs) have been reserved for women. The reserved seats, including offices of chairpersons, are allotted by rotation to different constituencies in a panchayat area. Further reservations for backward classes (BC) may be granted by state legislatures for membership of panchayats and chairpersons at any level.

The tenure of panchayats is five years, although this may be shortened in accordance with state legislation. Panchayat elections take place through state-level election machinery before expiry of the previous round, thus ensuring continued existence of the system. If a panchayat is dissolved prior to the end of a five year term, elections will be held within six months from the date of dissolution. Article 243(K) vests preparation and supervision of all elections to panchayats to the state election commission.

The authorities and responsibilities of panchayats are not explicitly defined within the provisions of the Amendment Act. Article 243G confers on state legislatures the authority to endow powers to panchayats at various levels to enable them to function as self-governing institutions. Power may be assigned to appropriate levels relating to the planning and implementation of economic development and social justice programmes such as agriculture, primary and secondary education, health and sanitation, rural housing, drinking water and social forestry.[21]

State legislatures are empowered to make provisions for the financing of panchayats. They may authorise panchayats to levy, collect and appropriate local taxes, duties, tolls and fees. They may also transfer to panchayats taxes, duties, tolls and fees levied and collected by state governments. To review the financial positions of the panchayats, the Amendment establishes a State Finance Commission (SFC),[22] whose responsibilities include making recommendations governing the distribution of tax revenue between the state and panchayats, deciding appropriate taxes, duties and fees collected and appropriated by panchayats, deciding on grants-in-aid from the Consolidated Fund of the State to the panchayats and suggesting measures to improve the financial position of panchayats.

The 73rd Amendment: A Critical Appraisal

Provisions for Social Change Reservation of panchayat seats for the weaker sections of the population is intended to reduce the local power of economically affluent groups. The state Acts have provided for reservation of the seats for SCs and STs in the various tiers of panchayats. Bihar, UP, Rajasthan, Himachal Pradesh and many other states additionally guarantee reservation for the backward classes (BC). The UP Act stipulates that such reservation should not exceed 27 per cent. Karnataka provides for reservation in all tiers for SC (minimum 15 per cent) and ST (minimum 3 per cent) in proportion to the population, and one-third reservation for BC. In Punjab there are no STs; reservation for SCs exists proportionate to total seats; one seat is reserved for BCs when they constitute 20 per cent of population. Bihar and Tamil Nadu (TN) have provided for substantial reservation for Other Backward Classes (OBC), 40 per cent and 50 per cent respectively, in their Panchayat Acts (although this has dragged them into legal battles).[23]

Dependence of PR on States The 73rd Amendment and the state-level PR Acts raise as many questions as they attempt to resolve. Is the whole exercise faithful to the idea of grassroots democracy? Will mere inclusion in the Constitution guarantee the success of PRI? The concept of PR as a local self-governing institution serves its purpose only when the various tiers enjoy freedom to chart their own course of development unfettered by preferences and choices of upper-level legislators, ministers, bureaucrats and the socially powerful. They must be free from political strings and have a statutory right to a share in the revenues of the state.

However, PRIs continue to depend on the discretion of state governments for assignment of functions, powers and finances. States may or may not grant sufficient power to panchayats to enable them to function as instruments of local self-government. Surprisingly, although planning for socioeconomic development has been entrusted to local bodies, they have not been given a substantial role in programme implementation. Only schemes of economic development and social justice (listed in the 11th Schedule) have been entrusted to them; however, the 11th schedule is not binding on the states. Further, some of the responsibilities listed are also subject to central and state authority, which may lead to arbitrary intervention by the centre and state. A mandatory list of responsibilities identifying the exclusive functions and finances of local jurisdiction would be needed to ensure the inviolability of panchayats.

Some of the responsibilities assigned to panchayats (such as education and health) require an investment greater than panchayats can acquire from tax collection and state-level transfers.[24] Take the case of the minor irrigation projects entrusted to the Gram Panchayat in UP and the block-level Panchayat Samiti in Punjab. Minor irrigation requires irrigation of 2,000 hectares of land and an investment of nearly Rs 100 million. Neither the requisite money nor the technical knowhow is available at this level for managing irrigation projects of this magnitude. In fact, village and block panchayats do not have the capacity for creating irrigation facilities beyond 200 hectares.

If the panchayats are dependent on states for their financial needs, their autonomy will be diluted. Programmes, in general, will not be prioritised by need, but by financial constraints. Further, the issue of adequate finances from the states to panchayats is related to the crucial question of balancing centre–state fiscal relations. Direct central disbursement of funds to districts (bypassing the state level) has caused conflict in centre–state relations. The states tend to transfer to the panchayats the financial crunch imposed on them from the centre.

Distribution of Functions among the Tiers There is no direction in the 73rd Amendment relating to the distribution of powers and functions among the tiers, and the states have, in general, also failed to designate clear guidelines in this respect.[25] Maharashtra, Himachal Pradesh, Andhra Pradesh and Madhya Pradesh have drawn up their own lists of panchayat functions; others have faithfully incorporated the twenty-nine subjects suggested in the 11th Schedule.[26] In Gujarat, West Bengal, Orissa and Kerala, attempts have been made to categorise functions as obligatory duties and discretionary activities (which are undertaken subject to availability of funds). Along with subjects drawn from the 11th Schedule, panchayats usually have additional responsibilities such as writing annual plans and budgets, collecting essential statistics, organising relief in natural calamities and promoting unity and harmony in society.

Some attempts have been made to distinguish responsibilities among the tiers. The village-level gram panchayats (GPs) primarily perform municipal functions, provide for local amenities, implement poverty alleviation schemes and take care of agricultural and allied activities; the block-level Panchayat Samitis (PSs)—in some states called Kshetra Panchayats (KPs)—handle minor irrigation, rural housing, industry, roads and welfare of weaker sections; and the district-level Zilla Parishads (ZPs) handle non-conventional energy, minor forest produce and soil conservation, as well as planning and coordination of PSs' activities.

Panchayats as Institutions of Self-government Article 243 defines panchayats as institutions of rural self-government. Local self-governance requires free election of local representatives who are empowered to make decisions regarding local welfare, design and implement local public programmes, manage local revenue collection and appropriation and maintain law and order. The suggested responsibilities of the PRI stipulated in the 11th schedule concern issues primarily relating to economic development and do not include maintenance of law and order—a key factor of self-governance.

The Amendment and PR Acts have only devolved functions from higher levels of government, not provided genuine local self-government.[27] Article 243G leaves to the discretion of state legislatures the endowment of the status of self-governing institutions on PRI; this means states may or may not recognise them as such. Most state acts do not describe panchayats as autonomous bodies or as institutions of local self-government. For example, the Andhra Pradesh PR Act (1994) recognises the Gram Panchayat as 'the body constituted for local administration of a village under the Act'. The Karnataka Act defines the GP as 'gram panchayat established under the Act'. The objective of the three-tier PR system in Karnataka with elected bodies at gram taluk, and district levels is 'greater participation of people and more effective implementation of programmes'.[28]

Inherent in the definition of self-government is autonomy. The Amendment is silent on the question of control, power of dissolution and suspension of panchayats. An examination of the state acts reveal that in almost all states the governments reserve for themselves considerable scope for intervention in the functioning of PRI. In most states an officer is authorised by the state government to inspect all books, proceedings and records of panchayats on behalf of the state government. If the government (or prescribed authority) determines that a panchayat exhibits substandard performance, abuses power or is unable to implement orders of the state government, the panchayat may be dissolved. The state government also retains the power to take ad hoc administrative measures to carry on the business of panchayats. The governments retain powers to issue directives and suspend resolutions of panchayats. The scope for state government intervention establishes a framework that may result in panchayats becoming organs of state power, rather than of the promotion of grass-roots democracy.

For example, under the Kerala Panchayat Act, the state may suspend panchayat resolutions, dissolve panchayat systems and remove any panchayat members (including the chairman). Similarly, in Karnataka, the state retains supervisory power and control over all three levels of PRI. It may suspend panchayat resolutions, issue directives, transfer officials and exercise the power of supersession. In Punjab, the Director of Panchayats may cancel any resolution passed by panchayats which in his opinion is not in conformity with provisions of the Act. In case of default in performance of duty, the Director reassigns duties at his discretion.

Control over administrative appointments and disbursement of salaries is an important tool ensuring efficient implementation of panchayat programmes. However, the 73rd Amendment does not define parameters regarding control over appointments or autonomy of the panchayat administrative staff. Intervention from upper levels is bound to interfere with the functioning of the panchayat administrative staff. This potential problem was identified in 1963 by the Santhanam Committee, which recommended that all PRI should have control over their staffs, whether appointed by the panchayat or placed at their disposal by state governments. In UP, provisions permit appointments of the Gram Sewak (Secretary of Panchayat) by the state government. The Gram Sewak performs duties outlined by the state authority rather than functioning under the guidance of the GP. The state authority reserves the right to transfer staff from one panchayat to another within a district, in some cases across districts. In the intermediate tier, Kshetra Panchayat (KP), the Khand Vikas Adhikari (Block Development Officer) has administrative control over employees. This arrangement is bound to politicise panchayats instead of making them responsive to the local population.

The AMC recommended induction into Zilla Parishads of nominees from larger municipalities, persons with special interest in rural development and university social science teachers. It opposed inclusion of MPs (Members of Parliament) and MLAs (Members of the Legislative Assembly) in local bodies on grounds that this would hinder the growth of local leadership. The 73rd Amendment did not recognise this argument and has incorporated MPs and MLAs with voting rights in panchayat bodies. This inclusion bluntly deviates from the objective of local leadership growth, since MPs and MLAs will use their substantial clout to influence voting behaviour at local levels (not to mention the effects of party politics on local elections). The covert objective appears to be control and supervision from above. Andhra Pradesh, Assam, Bihar, Haryana, Karnataka, Punjab, Uttar Pradesh, Tamil Nadu and West Bengal provide for representation of MPs, MLAs and members of Legislative Councils (where they exist) in panchayats at the intermediate and district levels. Gujarat and Rajasthan give no representation to MPs, though MLAs are granted the status of permanent invitees without voting rights. In Punjab, voting rights are granted to all members irrespective of whether they are elected or not.

If the local participatory process ended at election of panchayat representatives, then the PR system would remain incomplete. It is only when the people can observe and discuss policy and programme implementation that grassroots democracy is established. The sovereignty of the local electorate and the accountability of the elected body is expressed through the Grama Sabha (GS).[29] But the 73rd Amendment leaves the role of the GS, the backbone of participatory democracy, to the whims of the state assembly. Legislative enactments of the states have diminished the role to merely a recommendatory body, with provision to hold meetings two to four times a year. For example, the Andhra Pradesh Panchayat Act (1994, Section 6) stipulates that 'the GP shall give due consideration to the suggestions, if any, of GS'. Similarly, the Karnataka Act (Section 3{3}) states, 'The GP shall give due consideration to recommendations and suggestions of GS'.

In various provisions of state and adult education enactments, the GS is authorised to submit recommendations on such matters as the annual accounts of the GP and adult education, and to report on development projects undertaken by panchayats and other proposed projects. It can also discuss any matter submitted by the PS, the ZP or the Deputy Commissioner. However, its recommendations are not binding. In UP, the GS is a recommendatory body to the GP for suggestions on annual statements of accounts, administration of the previous year, development programmes of previous and current years and promotion of unity and harmony in the village. It is also responsible for mobilising voluntary labour and contributions for family welfare programmes, identification of beneficiaries for various programmes and rendering assistance in implementation of development schemes.

The 73rd Amendment makes no mention of a judicial role for panchayats, although such a role has been of historical importance. Earlier, some states (e.g., Rajasthan) provided for Nyay (judicial) panchayats over a cluster of GPs to adjudicate in civil and criminal cases and impose minor fines. UP provides for establishment of a Nyay Panchayat whose members are appointed out of the GP by the prescribed authority. In Punjab, under the new provisions, GP is assigned responsibilities of civil, revenue and criminal courts. Nevertheless, in most of the states the existing Nyay Panchayats are defunct, and there has been no attempt to revive them.

Though the 73rd Amendment is a worthy starting point, there are numerous loose ends. It is too early to predict how it will fare in due course. States still hold enormous power to manoeuvre and manipulate panchayats, and there is a lurking fear that panchayats will be divided along party lines similar to state assemblies or at the Union Legislature. Acquiring sufficient autonomy may remain a mirage for the local bodies.

III PANCHAYATI RAJ: A CRITICAL LOOK AT IMPLEMENTATION

Once the election process is completed in all tiers there will be 3.5 million representatives participating in the democratic process: 200,000 panchayats, 8,500 panchayat Samitis and 400 Zila panchayats in the country.[30] Panchayat elections have been completed in almost all states.[31] Table 12.1 illustrates the progress of PR elections. Now, the important task remaining in most states is the transfer of authority, power and resources to the PRIs. How the states of Karnataka, Punjab, and Uttar Pradesh have proceeded in this next stage is examined next.

Uttar Pradesh (UP)

Legislative and Governmental Actions 80 per cent of the population of UP, the most populous state of India, resides in rural areas. Of its labour force, 73 per cent is engaged in the primary sector. The state has a low level of literacy of 42 per cent, according to the 1991 Census.

UP is one of the states that has pioneered entrusting the responsibilities of governance and development functions to village bodies. The UP PR Act (1947) established self-government in rural areas through three bodies: Gaon Sabha (all adult village members), Gaon Panchayat (executive body of the Sabha) and Panchayati Adalat (regional court system). Following the BRMC recommendations, the Kshetra Samiti (similar to the block- or taluk-level panchayats referred to earlier) and Parishad Adhiniya Acts (1961) adopted a three-tier PR system decentralising powers at district, block and village level. The UP PR Act (1994) conforms with the stipulations of the 73rd Amendment and replaces the earlier PR Acts. Elections to all tiers of panchayats were held in April 1995 after repeated postponement barring hill districts owing to ongoing agitation for separate statehood. Today, there are sixty-six Zila Panchayats (ZP), 901 Kshetra Panchayats (KP), and 58,605 Gram Panchayats (GP) in UP.[32]

The UP government has decided to entrust panchayats with local responsibilities for economic development and socioeconomic justice. The Construction of Village Pavement and Drains is one government-sponsored scheme implemented entirely by the Gram Panchayats with partial contributions from their own financial resources.[33] The Act of 1947 also enables panchayats to use surplus funds for investment in rural industry (Panchayat Udyog). This scheme has created employment opportunities for rural artisans and unskilled labourers with the use of local resources. Goods for local consumption are produced including agricultural tools, handloom textiles, furniture, toys and wooden carts. At present there are ninety-one Panchayat Udyogs in the state.

Activities pertaining to thirty-two state departments will be transferred to panchayats. The state government provides 90 per cent of the funds for construction of panchayat bhawan (administrative buildings). Recognising that training is an important component for success of PR, the annual plan (1995–96) proposes an outlay of Rs 1 million for training 4,300 panchayat office holders. To improve efficiency of panchayats, the state awards additional funds (for use in public welfare works) on the basis of outstanding performance of Gram Sabhas in the district.

Implementation: Achievements and Problems Although it is too early to evaluate PR in UP, field visits reveal that most of these schemes are encumbered by the state bureaucracy, and the actual devolution of authority remains to be seen. For example, the Zila Parishad has not had any significant role in developmental activities. Departmental heads have resisted transferring authority to panchayats and continue to run development departments on their own. For example, the DRDA[34] retains its powerful role in local development. The Jawahar Rojgar Yojna (JRY) and Integrated Rural Development Programme (IRDP), administered by DRDA, have not been handed over to the authority of the panchayats. It absorbs a large number of resources, otherwise earmarked for poverty alleviation programmes that should be administered by the PRI. It is this author's impression that bureaucrats who are expected to support PRI have no faith in them, nor are they ready to part with their powers.[35]

In UP, planning functions have not percolated down to the elected bodies at lower levels. Decentralisation of the planning process at district levels began in 1982–83, following recommendations of the Braham Dutt committee. The objective was to reduce inter- and intra-district disparities in development by providing development opportunities to all districts. Planning was divided into two sectors: state and district. Plans for district development were administered by the district; plans for state development were administered by the state. Of the plan outlay, 30 per cent was earmarked for distribution among districts and determined by a formula considering factors such as population, percentage of weaker sections and level of backwardness.[36] Extra points were given to districts for their efforts and accomplishments in national and small savings.

The apex planning body at the district level is the District Planning and Monitoring Committee (DPMC).[37] The other body is the District Plan Coordination and Implementation Committee (DPCIC).[38] Plans are prepared by DPCIC with consideration of district guidelines and outlays allocated by the state government. They are finalised and implemented by the DPMC. However, until present, the majority of plan outlays for sectoral programmes have been absorbed by existing programmes. No untied funds have been available at the district level for implementation of new innovative projects. From 1989–1990 until present, with the exception of plan outlays (mostly tied funds), discretionary funding for district-level employment generation programmes has been sparse.

Decentralised planning has thus not achieved the desired results due to inadequate resources and the lack of broad-based participation. The result is that proper assessment of local development needs cannot be made. Since the constitutional amendment mandates PRI participation in multi-level planning, it is necessary to restructure planning bodies at the district level. So far there is no involvement of the lower levels in planning. Further, involvement of panchayat bodies from the GP and upwards requires expertise and training, which has yet to take place. As far as implementation is concerned, the GPs are severely constrained due to lack of resources as well as obstructions by all levels of the state bureaucracy.

Field visits revealed that GPs are starved of funds and face numerous problems in implementing PR. For example, the village of Sitapur in the Haridwar district received only Rs 20,000 to administer JRY. This meagre amount, the Panchayat Pradhan (chairperson) felt, was grossly inadequate even to clean the drains. Further, he stated, the injunction in JRY stipulating that contractors could not be hired impaired panchayat work, since the wage rate stipulated by government was lower than the market rate. Funding for the poverty alleviation schemes had not yet reached the panchayats. The funding awards were highly publicised by the government, hence people were not willing to voluntarily contribute efforts (Shramdan) for community works, since they believed that the panchayat was filching all the money.

Problems galore were evident in the implementation of PR. There were reports of bureaucratic interference by officers at various levels, corruption and bribes (suvidha shulk or convenience tax, as the phrase is termed). For example, programme beneficiaries identified by the panchayat must be endorsed by the office of the District Magistrate (DM). The file has to physically move from bottom upwards through the ranks, with each officer demanding suvidha shulk! Due to similar activity, loans sanctioned by the government never reach the targeted beneficiaries in the full amount. Another example is a village that was facing an acute water shortage. After a great deal of paperwork and pressure on higher authorities, one tube well was finally approved for the village. In the meantime, due to the intervention of the local MLA, the installation location was shifted to another village.[39]

In the past, the panchayats have undertaken construction activities, tree planting and drain cleaning; however, continuation is becoming increasingly difficult due to financial constraints. There are hardly any locally derived revenues to support panchayats.[40] For example, one panchayat has installed twenty-six tube lights to electrify the village streets but has no money for maintenance work on the lights. The linesmen of the electricity department demand bribes, and if the work is to be done, payment has to be made. The village faces an acute shortage of water in the humid months, but the panchayat is helpless. The maintenance of water works is the responsibility of UP Jal Nigam (Water Corporation) and the panchayat has been unable to fund repairs due to lack of resources. Panchayats have no administrative staff of their own. Employees of state departments demand bribes for petty works. Since the payment of salaries to these employees is not under the authority of panchayats, the latter is unable to exert pressure to induce the former to perform their duties. The scenario is the same for schools.

There is little panchayat control over officials at the village level. Panchayats can lodge complaints against lower-level officials but have no recourse for action. The police authorities do not comply with the directives of panchayat, only those of the DM. For example, one panchayat knew that the Patwari (officer of revenue administration) was charging Rs 100 instead of Rs 10 as authorised for a copy of a land record but could not take any action. Panchayats can technically prevent illegal encroachments on public land and property,[41] but once they report the matter it takes about six months before the necessary authorisation comes to stop it. In regard to allotment of agricultural land to the landless and house sites to the shelterless, bureaucratic interference occurs again.

At the ZP level, practical difficulties prevent speedy implementation of PR. Not only the bureaucracy—local MLAs and MPs of the area—but even elected members of panchayats create hurdles. The Additional Chief Officer (ACO) expressed concerns that pork-barreling by the ZP members has prevented appropriate distribution of development grants—everyone wants development funds directed to his region irrespective of local requirements. Committees could not be created due to conflicts among elected members. Caste discrimination is prevalent. Elected members of weaker sections are snubbed to the advantage of the stronger ones. For example, two members were fighting over the location of a tube well, and eventually agreed to install it equidistant from the two villages. However, following installation, the village of the weaker panchayat was prevented from using the tube well.

Decisions are sometimes based on power maintenance of particular persons or groups. The authority of the ZP Adhyaksha (head of the panchayat) has been misused in many instances. A female ACO was removed from the post by a woman Pradhan in the district,

Muzzafarnagar, because she did not want the academic and professional superiority of the ACO to prevent her own husband (de facto head) from holding on to power in the panchayat. This particular ACO recounted an instance in the village Khanpur (Muzzafarnagar district), where a makeshift bridge connecting parts of the village and the village with the town was destroyed by the monsoons. The plight of the villagers induced this ACO to construct a costly new bridge. The upper-caste members of panchayat opposed and filed a case against her. The woman chairperson, in a subdued tone, expressed that she herself favoured a bridge. However, she was overruled by her husband and the upper-caste males who feared that their own hegemony over village affairs was under threat.

No monetary stipend is given to Gram Panchayati members for attending and conducting meetings or undertaking panchayat work. Government authorities feel that the development of the village is a sufficient incentive for local initiative in establishing PRI. Here is reason enough for one to understand why so many villagers have complained of the complacency of panchayat members and have charged them with usurping people's money. Travel allowance is paid for attending ZP meetings at 3 paise/kilometer, an inadequate recompense for the monetary and time costs incurred with travel. ZP Adhyakshas receive allowances since they are considered Class II employees of the government of UP. They are also entitled to an orderly and a car. GP Pradhans resent that the fact that the ZP Adhyakshas are entitled to a number of benefits while elected heads at GP level are not. At the Kshetra Panchayat level, if the relations of the Block Development Officer (BDO) and Pramukh (chairperson) are cordial, then the latter may be assigned a car. In many districts there is a visible struggle to allocate promised vehicles.

Punjab

Backdrop and the Process of Change Punjab, the most prosperous state of India, is primarily an agrarian economy with 71 per cent of its population residing in rural areas; 56 per cent of its labour force is engaged in the primary sector. The literacy rate in Punjab is 58.5 per cent. The state has lowest incidence of poverty in the country, but a decade of militancy (1982–1992) crippled the socioeconomic life of

Punjab. As peace returned to the state, the political environment became more responsive to development.

The Punjab Panchayat Act (1952) was the first attempt to reintroduce PRI. In conformity with recommendations of the BRMC, the PR was revamped in 1961 with the Punjab Panchayat Samiti and Zila Parishad Act. The new three-tiered structure is comprised of Gram Panchayat (village), Panchayat Samiti (block) and Zila Parishad (district). District Boards created earlier were abolished. Gram Panchayats continued to operate; the Panchayat Samiti and the Zila Parishad were suspended and eventually taken over by government officials. After 1978, there were no elections for Panchayat Samiti and Zila Parishad in the state.

The Punjab PR Act (1994) revived PRI in the state: 12,400 villages have 1,591 Gram Panchayats (GP), 136 Panchayat Samitis (PS) and fourteen Zila Parishads (ZP).[42] Elections were held in September 1994 for Panchayat Samitis and Zila Parishads. Earlier elections to Gram Panchayats were held in 1993 (they were due in 1988). In a number of panchayats, members were chosen by consensus.

Panchayats in Punjab are entrusted with developmental functions by the central and state governments. The ZPs are responsible for implementation of various schemes under the JRY and Unnat Gram Developed Village Scheme (UGS) of the state government. The JRY is a joint centre–state scheme funded in the proportion of 80:20. The central government contribution is released directly to the districts. The districts reserve 20 per cent for block and village works managed at the district level and the remaining is transferred to gram panchayats. This ensures that a large number of local citizens participate in the programme, and employment opportunities are provided to at least one member per family. The targeted finances for JRY in Punjab in 1995–96 add up to Rs 250 million. This is expected to generate 2.95 million man-days of employment.[43] These numbers, however, are not enough to assess the impact of the schemes since there has been a significant amount of corruption and misuse of funds by the bureaucracy and recipients.[44] For example, capital subsidies (20–50 per cent) to farmers and matching loans from banks under IRDP have induced a number of fictitious transactions.

Gram Panchayats are expected to implement other centrally sponsored schemes such as TRYSEM (Training of Rural Youth for Self Employment) and DWACRA (Development of Women and Children in Rural Areas), drinking water schemes and the state-sponsored

UGS. The Mahila Mandal scheme, organised in 11,500 villages, targets women's welfare through skill training in income-generating activities such as durry (carpet) making, preparing washing soaps, and making leather purses, pullovers, garments and embroidered articles. The mandals are engaged in additional activities in family welfare and work to eradicate social evils (dowry and drinking). An outlay of Rs 3.5 million has been proposed for this scheme for the year 1995–96.

For promoting rural development with panchayat involvement and local resources, the state government offers matching grants. Under this scheme, the government provides partial assistance to panchayats and the balance is met by the concerned panchayat's own resources. Rs 6 million is expected to benefit 400 panchayats in 1995–96. The state government also provides financial assistance to panchayats for each to construct a panchayat ghar (building), where panchayat meetings and dissemination activities occur; 8,731 panchayat ghars have been completed (1992–93 figures). In 1995–96, construction of 750 panchayat ghars at an outlay of Rs 3 million has been proposed.

An interest subsidy to banks for providing loans to PRIs is a state government scheme to provide low-interest (or no-interest[45]) loans to panchayats to fund development projects. These loans can be used to construct shopping complexes, bank buildings and residential quarters; to reclaim and develop *shamlat* lands; and to invest in other potential assets which will diversify (and increase) their revenue resources.

In 1991, the UGS of the state government was created to improve rural sanitation. In this scheme, pavement of streets, construction of drains, disposal of sewage water and other activities are the management responsibility of the village. The total cost of the works depends on the village size. The village panchayat is required to provide a 25 per cent cash contribution and a voluntary labour force. In 1995–96, 4,000 villages are expected to participate in the scheme. Funding sources for UGS are Plan Funds and the Marketing Board and Rural Development Funds. Rs 1 billion is expected to be generated in 1995–96.

Assessment In spite of state legislation and elections in 1994 organising PRI, the state government has failed to devolve power to PRIs. Planning functions have not percolated down to the lower levels.

ZPs have no autonomy and operate as government agencies for implementation of different rural development schemes. The panchayats have little in the way of discretionary funds for undertaking development schemes on their own. A few panchayats have managed to maintain programmes like veterinary dispensaries and libraries. A larger chunk of the ZP budget is allocated to outlays for establishment functions, contingency expenditures and electricity and telephone charges.[46] They levy hardly any taxes and cannot survive without central and state financial support. The provisions in the PR Act stipulate that PR bodies will monitor the functioning of twenty-seven departments at the district level; however, Zila Parishad meetings conducted once in three months have concluded without transacting any business.[47]

It will take some time before the full impact of PR is felt in Punjab. Though Punjab has progressed faster than other Indian states and the incidence of poverty is not as great, the poor do constitute 8 per cent of the population and consist of mostly small and marginal farmers, agricultural labourers and rural artisans. Strengthening PRI with adequate financial resources would contribute to the development and social harmony of these populations.

Karnataka

Background Prior to the 73rd Amendment, a reasonably well-functioning PR was in place in Karnataka. Since the constitutional amendment, grass-roots institutions empowering local populations have been weakened. Karnataka still constitutes one of the few states where grass-roots institutions have been strengthened.

Karnataka in its present form was established in 1956. Sixty-nine per cent of its population lives in more than 27,000 rural villages. Three-fifths of its labour force participates in the agrarian sector. The state reported a 47 per cent literacy rate in 1990–91. It is an example of one of the few states where grass-roots democracy has been successful.

The Village Panchayats and Local Boards Act, passed in 1959, followed the BRMC recommendations for PRI. Major restructuring of PRI on the Asoka Mehta model occurred again in 1987, following a second Act passed in 1983. The Act created an institutional arrangement for planning and management at local levels. It reserved 20 per cent of the seats for BCs and 25 per cent for women. The authority of local elected representatives was recognised by officials. PRIs performed well in diversified sectors of development: health, education and poverty alleviation. During five years of functioning (1987–92) the Mandal Panchayat and Zila Parishads successfully strengthened local democratic development processes.

With changes in state-level political leadership, the new government began dissolving the powers of PRI towards the end of 1991. In the meantime, the Karnataka PR Act, 1993, was adopted, which was a step backwards since it provided for administrators to take over responsibilities of elected representatives. The Government of Karnataka appointed the Nayak Committee to review controversial provisions of this Act.[48] Accordingly, the Act was amended in March 1994. It has made CEO, EO and other officials of ZP and TP subservient to the general powers of superintendence and control given to these bodies' chairpersons, who have now been designated executive heads. The Act has differentiated functions (although there is also overlap) for the three tiers based on the principle that what is appropriate at a certain level should be implemented at that level, not a higher one.

There are 5,641 Gram Panchayats (GP), 175 Taluk Panchayats (TP) and twenty Zila Parishads (ZP) in Karnataka. Elections to GPs were held in December 1993 for 78,426 members. Elections to GPs and ZPs were held in March 1995 for 3,340 and 919 members respectively.

In 1995–96, Rs 6.2 billion was allocated by the state for equitable distribution among districts.[49] Panchayats also receive allocations from the centre. IRDP, a centrally sponsored scheme, is implemented in all ZPs. Its objective is to elevate people from poverty by providing income-generating activities and developing an infrastructure for better utilisation of assets provided to beneficiaries under the scheme; 85,000 beneficiaries were covered as of December 1994. By 1995–96, the coverage is expected to go up to 107,000 including the SC and ST populations. Under JRY, 21.5 million mandays of employment were generated by end of December 1994. Under the 'Million Wells' scheme, a sub-component of JRY, irrigation wells free of cost are being provided to poor SC/ST farmers and freed bonded labourers. Several agricultural schemes will be transferred to panchayats. The government is going to launch a massive programme directed by local panchayats for construction of low-cost rural housing which will minimise leakage, ensure quality construction and generate employment in rural areas.

Karnataka, introducing district decentralised planning in the last decade, has built a proper relationship between PRI and the state government officials between 1987 and 1992. However, it received a setback as panchayats were dissolved. Between 1992 and 1995, there was more or less a standstill, waiting for panchayats to be installed. Hence, the district plans were designed by the district officials, secretaries to the state government and department heads. An attempt is now being made to decentralise planning by incorporating village and intermediate-level plans into the district plans. It will take a long time before bottom-up planning is established. For this purpose, planning and finance officers are provided at ZP and TP levels.

Assessment PR bodies continue to be conduits for centre- and state-sponsored rural development programmes for which money is allocated directly to the districts. Allocations for the lower tiers are routed through the ZP. Interviews with members of GPs in Karnataka stressed the fact that the eagerness of state-level authorities to enable village panchayats to become independent entities has yet to be seen. For example, the GP budget and development plan, 1994–95, was prepared by administrators and submitted to the TPs. Since elections to Taluk and Zila Panchayats were held later, the authorities of these bodies were controlled by state officials. Decentralisation to local authorities to assess local planning needs did not occur, since the state retained authority when elections were delayed. Further, in spite of GP elections, power was not fully transferred to the duly constituted panchayats; rather, administrators of the former Mandal Panchayats continued to use their political influence in daily business.

Panchayat members were disappointed with the amount of financial assistance from the state. Many of the funds are tied, so there is little flexibility to accommodate local needs. For example, grants for construction of water tanks were available, but not for borewells. Subsequently, water tanks have been built and the scheme appears successful on paper—but there is no water in the tanks!

Areas of the Mangalore district which are not heavily rain-fed remain without water.

IV CONCLUSION

Panchayati bodies constituted after the 73rd Amendment are still in their infancy and have experienced a variety of teething problems. In states such as Maharashtra, Gujarat, Karnataka and West Bengal, district-level panchayats are managing projects and are participating in decentralised planning activities. The same is not true with Punjab, UP and other states where the GPs and the intermediate panchayats are not involved in multi-level planning. They lack both expertise and resources. In terms of project implementation, a few successful GPs and block panchayats tend to be the ones adjacent to towns with higher levels of education.

This section assesses several areas of panchayat performance and evolution: financial resources; administrative oversight and accountability; and representation of social groups. A final sub-section offers some general comments.

Financial Resources

Panchayats at all levels identify the lack of state financial support as a primary problem. The massive responsibilities now entrusted to panchayats require adequate finances. For example, the government of Madhya Pradesh has given to panchayats full control of eight departments: rural development, school education, agriculture, fisheries, health, engineering, social welfare and women and children, all of which require financing commensurate with their needs. At present, the bulk of revenue for local bodies is composed of shared taxes and grants from states. Their own revenues through tax and non-tax revenues are inadequate to provide basic minimum services. Most good sources of revenue, such as sales tax, excise and motor vehicle tax, are under the authority of state governments. Stagnant and inelastic sources of revenue (except for octroi in some states) are assigned to local bodies.[50] To solve this problem, the states may have to give up some of their own sources of revenue in favour of PRI.

The central allocation of finances to local bodies has been improved. In the Eighth Plan, allocation for rural development programmes has risen to Rs 300 million. The states must transfer 36 per cent of their 1994–1995 plan outlays to the sub-state level planning bodies. Out of this, 30 per cent will be given to PR in lump sum grants for such specific areas as water supply, roads, electricity and education in rural areas. Five per cent of it will be untied to fund programmes special to the needs of the local areas. The final 1 per cent is for poverty alleviation or employment-generation activities planned and funded at the village level. Under centrally sponsored schemes such as JRY, Employment Assurance Scheme and IRDP, funds are allocated directly to districts to facilitate poverty alleviation programmes. Other centrally sponsored schemes that are entrusted to panchayats are the National Social Assistance Programme, Provision of Nutritious Meals for Children, Rural Group Insurance Scheme (including old age pensions) and wasteland development.

The 10th Finance Commission of India has recommended a statewide allocation totaling Rs 43.8 billion to PRI from 1995 to 2000. Direct central assistance to panchayats (bypassing states) raises two important points. First, is such a move not politically motivated? At present, the states' share in central revenue is only 29 per cent.[51] With an added tier of governance, an additional burden is imposed on states that they may not be able to manage with their meager resources. If the central aid goes directly to PRI, the financial autonomy of states is further diluted. There is an apparent paradox in the Central Government policy regarding devolution of more authority to the grass-roots level while further centralising tax revenues at the expense of states and also directly allocating funds under various centrally sponsored schemes to the local bodies. Curiously, panchayat members were pleased that at least central assistance reaches them, while the state flow of funds is delayed or stopped for a variety of reasons.

Are panchayat resources sufficient for their requirements? Given the argument that PR is simply a transfer of function from states to panchayats, funds earmarked for the intended areas of PR responsibility could also be transferred in the same direction. Simultaneously, the cost of establishing and maintaining panchayats would have to be added and transferred. This cost, pertaining to village level bodies alone, is estimated at not less than Rs 5 billion per year.[52] The cost of holding five yearly elections for panchayats is an additional burden on the state exchequer. Raising their own resources may impose an additional heavy tax burden on the rural poor.

Public health and family welfare are among the important functions of panchayats. Experiences from Chile illustrate that transference of responsibility for public health from Central Government to municipalities has resulted in a substantial improvement of coverage.[53] In India, an improvement in health care delivery is possible under PR, since it has the potential to return 80 per cent of health and illness care to the people.[54] Grassroots health care requires trained community health and paramedical workers. However, a meagre Rs 30 per capita per year is allocated for rural health out of Rs 120 per capita per year for public sector health.[55] For panchayats to establish themselves as the third tier of the fiscal federal system, they must have independent sources for revenue and an efficient fiscal administration. The allocation of taxes and fees for panchayats does not add to their financial strength, especially when the demand for the taxed goods is inelastic, the tax rate and fees are uneconomical and the rate of revenue recovery is poor.

The role of panchayats in rural development has always been recognised. The First Five-Year Plan stressed that the success of rural development largely depended upon an active unit in the village, which represented the community as a whole. It was the 'village panchayat which could be the foundation of administrative structure for national development'.[56] Poverty alleviation programmes launched by the government from time to time had marginal impact on the lives of rural poor since people's representatives at lower levels were not involved in local planning. The programme approach ignored the local needs and sociopolitical and economic constraints. Article 243 ZD of the 73rd amendment attempts to initiate a participatory planning process at local governmental levels to accommodate the needs of the community.

The experience of Grameen Banks in Bangladesh and the Chinese experience of farmers managing 25 per cent of irrigation by themselves affirms that given necessary inputs, infrastructural support and empowerment, users are likely to take better care of scarce resources and increase productivity compared to plan implementation on their behalf. In West Bengal, where panchayats have a firm role in finance allocation for various poverty alleviation programmes, there is better targetting of resources. As the poor themselves constitute panchayats, they are able to appreciate problems and set priorities accordingly.

Multilevel planning which starts at the bottom and moves upwards is essential to accommodate local variations in requirements and resource endowments. However, so far PRIs have not been assigned any effective role in planning. Decentralised planning in some states takes the form of planning at district levels which is more or less consolidation of sectoral department plans. District planning bodies such as District Planning Boards (DPB) in Punjab are responsible for planning. With plan formulation entrusted to panchayats, redefining the role of district planning bodies is essential to prevent confusion and political meddling in plan formulation. This is because the chairperson of DPB is a cabinet minister, e.g., in Punjab, and the vice chairperson is a minister of state. Among other members there are a few MLAs and a few sarpanchas. There thus remains little room for local initiative in planning departments: rural development, school education, agriculture, fisheries, health, engineering departments, social welfare, women and children.

Administrative Oversight and Accountability

Administrative control over panchayat personnel at all levels rests, in most states, with state officials. This authority needs to be vested in panchayats, in order to improve efficiency and accountability of local personnel to panchayats. In Madhya Pradesh provisions for creating a group of class II officers to head block panchayats and 450 posts to manage Janpad panchayats are being made. Panchayats would be empowered to transfer officers in these department and also sub-contract doctors for three years. Where such direct control is not given, coordination between panchayats and departments would be of utmost importance as the role of government officials in planning and implementation of development projects cannot be totally ruled out. Enlisting their cooperation while maintaining control over them will not be an easy task.

The enormous money, power and staff made available to underprivileged sections may have a corrupting influence. It is essential that panchayats are made accountable to the Gram Sabha rather than the state government. There were reports in the Kalloli village, Belgaum district, Karnataka, that villagers had auctioned all thirty-two panchayat seats. A total of Rs 450,000 was collected in which each general seat fetched Rs 20,000. Reserved seats were auctioned for Rs 10,000.[57] It is important to ensure that GS is not hijacked by a handful of power brokers. Experience from Punjab reveals that transparency in transactions is of utmost significance. There have been instances of fictitious transactions, such as GS meetings held only on paper, and signatures obtained and approval of GS budget and development plans without meetings ever been held.[58] Rules pertaining to business conduct also need modification. For example, there is a rule in UP that a GP meeting can be adjourned for lack of a quorum, but the rule is relaxed for a second such meeting. This rule has been conveniently used by some Pradhans (chairpersons) to promote their own interests. The result is that in a UP village there is neither GS Raj nor PR. It has an unmasked Pradhan Raj or his coterie's Raj.[59]

There may not be complete austerity and transparency in transactions, once all panchayats are properly functioning. However, one can expect a reasonable amount of monitoring as people will now have access to officials in their vicinity. Earlier in the centralised decisionmaking and implementing system, the pilferer was unseen. Even if it was known, ordinary citizens could not bring about the corrective action at the higher levels of government. In fact, the impact of such control could be enormous in direct monitoring, as the experience from Kaladeh GP near Bhim in Rajasthan demonstrates. This GP was sanctioned Rs 1.2 million for the Apna Gaon Apna Kaam (Own Village Own Work) scheme. The objective was to promote people's responsibility and involvement in development of their own area, while avoiding bureaucratic interference. However, BDO and Gram Sevak made discretionary decisions without consulting villagers involved with the projects. Subsequently, there were apprehensions regarding misuse of funds and fraud. Schools, dispensaries, small dams and community structures existed only on paper. Under the influence of Mazdoor Kissan Shakti Sangthan, a voluntary organisation, the people pressured the government to enforce local officials' accountability to them. The Chief Minister (Shekhawat) was forced to announce in the state assembly that photocopies of records of local works would be provided by local functionaries to the residents of that panchayat area.[60]

Representation of Social Groups

The Indian rural society is characterised by caste, sectional, ethnic and feudal-class discrimination, which has, in some cases, led to violence in the PRIs.[61] It is pertinent that PRIs continue their role as vehicles of social change in rural life. Table 12.2 indicates the impact of reservation on the social composition of panchayats. In Karnataka, for example, nearly 13 per cent of SCs, 6 per cent of STs and 33 per cent of BCs occupy positions in panchayats. A study conducted by the Institute of Social Services (ISS) revealed that the reservation policy has a positive impact on social change at lower levels in Karnataka, where panchayati leadership is no longer the prerogative of only the dominant communities. The hold of the two major communities, Lingayats and Vokkaligas, has loosened at lower levels and their overall share in panchayats has been reduced to 17.6 per cent and 14.4 per cent respectively. Also, the significant rise of the BCs in 1996 Parliamentary elections will hopefully permeate to lower levels.

Representation of Women

While the Constitution of India guarantees equal rights to both men and women in all spheres of life, the status of women, especially rural women, is not very impressive, even after decades of democracy. In the countryside, women perform several roles in both domestic and income-generating activities: bearing and rearing children, managing the household (cleaning house, cooking, collecting firewood for fuel), tending livestock and participating in farming activities either as family labour or as a breadwinner. Despite the wide spectrum of functions women perform, they are subjected to exploitation at all levels, with little or no say in decisionmaking at home, not even decisions regarding their own reproductive systems. Women are denied positions of authority in polity and society, and tend not to recognise their own rights, since tradition-based constraints dissuade them from availing themselves of educational opportunities and participating in public life.

These general observations are borne out by qualitative measurements that reveal serious shortfalls in literacy and workforce participation.[62] The adult literacy rate of women is relatively low (i.e., 36 per cent compared with 64 per cent for males). Earned income of women in 1996 was 39 per cent of the total, compared with 61 per cent for males. Only 29 per cent of Indian women are engaged in economically gainful activities, 90 per cent of which are in the primary sector.[63]

Greater political empowerment of women has the potential to improve the development of half the country's population.[64] The representation of women even in the national Parliament is an insignificant 7 per cent and the record in the state parliaments is not significantly better (Tables 12.3 and 12.4). These data indicate that through normal political processes, women may not be empowered; proactive state action may be required. The 73rd Amendment to the Constitution, by providing for 33 per cent representation by women in local bodies, may lay the legal foundations to empower women. A large number of women have been elected to panchayats, nearly 40 per cent in Karnataka, 34 per cent in West Bengal and 26 per cent in Punjab (See Table 12.5).

Nevertheless, male-dominated rural institutions have not been keen to alter the power structure in favour of women or accept them as chairpersons of their panchayats. Women are still not accustomed to the authority of their new political roles outside their households. While male members of panchayats sit on a high pedestal, women, even women sarpanchas (chairpersons), sit on the ground, and many still hold onto their veils. One incident, not uncommon, narrated by a secretary of the AIPP illuminates problems caused by women's traditional social norms: 'In a certain village, when male members of a panchayat visit a female sarpancha in her house, she draws a charpoy (bed), makes them comfortable and positions herself behind them in a corner. She is essentially a mute spectator of decisions to be made at the next meeting of the panchayat'.

Provision of the one-third reservation for women is frequently misused by the powerful for promoting their own self-interest. The ruling elite support Panchayati candidacy for women in their own families. These women, unable to assert their authority in policymaking, are only a proxy used to carry out the wishes of male elders. This arrangement reinforces the low status of women by diminishing their role in the political process and discounting their interests in welfare and community development, and perpetuates the powerful hold of the rural elite in local government.

In the northern Indian states of Bihar, UP and Rajasthan, the fear of sexual exploitation keeps many women from venturing alone into new arenas or assuming leadership roles. In the Dhar district of Madhya Pradesh, women panchas (members) and sarpanchas (chairpersons) have been exploited.[65] Even in Karnataka, during elections to Gram Panchayats in December 1993, there were incidences of women being abducted and forced to withdraw their nominations.[66]

Field visits to villages of the Haridwar and Dehradun districts in UP found that villagers believed that women were elected to panchayats only because of the constitutional injunction. The women, due to the political environment and household duties, were willing neither to contest elections nor to accept leadership positions. For example, in the village of Sitapur, in the Bahadarabad block, there are four women in the fourteen members of the Gram Panchayat, including the Pradhan. These women are not comfortable in the midst of male colleagues and seldom attend meetings. If they attend, they come with their veils on, sit silently, sign the register and leave. We questioned the person we believed to be the Pradhan, and he explained the problems and difficulties in PRI. When we inquired how long he had held the position, he told us nonchalantly that it was not he, but his wife, who was the Pradhan. Upon my request she came out, and sat in a corner with her face partially covered from male visitors. Upon my repeated queries, she told me she had no spare time for 'all this' since she had to cook, care for the children, tend the cattle, draw milk, make uple (a type of fuel made with cow dung) and much more. She did not talk in the meetings because nobody posed questions to her. She felt uncomfortable with our questions, and took leave of us. When I asked her husband, 'Why don't you let her take charge of the panchayat?' he replied that his wife was not educated enough to follow intricacies of panchayat work, financial accounting and tedious policy questions. Further, she might be implicated if anything went wrong. Moreover, he did not think it proper for ladies of the house to go about meeting officers in the higher-ups, deal with employees or get the drains cleaned.

In another village, I was told the woman Pradhan had floated a resolution to the effect that 'my husband would be my advisor'. It could not be passed; however, as things stand today the woman Pradhan is nothing but a pawn. The Additional Chief Officer of the district insisted for a long time on the attendance of only genuine panchayat members in ZP meetings. Eventually, however, he had to allow proxy members for women to participate in the deliberations. He said that he could handle the rowdy, rustic, untrained and sometimes physically aggressive elected members, but could a woman resist their pressure?

One need not, however, lose hope. In Karnataka, interviews with members of the panchayats in the Mangalore district revealed that initially women were hesitant to participate in politics, considering such debates dirty and dreadful. Once they become members, even if under pressure from male members of the family, they begin to more assertively exert their authority. Although to some extent they may be carrying out the wishes of their male elders, they have become fully conscious of the power and authority they possess.

The Committee on Status of Women recommended in 1976 the establishment of an all-women village level panchayat to manage welfare and development programmes for women and children. This institutional arrangement assists in breaking down inhibitions of women who are socially not attuned to working with men. Involvement in development activities displays women's potential for managing political institutions. The Manjerai panchayat, the first all-women panchayat, was established in the 1980's in Tehsil Idapur, Maharashtra. Similar panchayat arrangements followed in other states.[67] Today, Maharashtra has nine exclusively all-women panchayats. All-women panchayats in various states have, for example, provided safe drinking water, controlled alcoholism,[68] established informal schools, encouraged girls to attend school, demonstrated outside the houses of husbands who abuse wives and established a women's bank that provides credit to men and women to establish small-scale businesses.

The problems faced by women are part of a social transition. Increasing awareness among women through education and economic independence is vital to this process, which has been greatly helped by total literacy missions. Mahila Samakhya (Women Education) programmes aim at education for women's empowerment, organises women into groups, trains them for contesting open and reserved seats and makes them more articulate in political bodies. Economic independence is equally vital in redefining the role of women in asserting their identity, and giving them greater say in the decisionmaking process.[69] When the voice of nearly one million women is heard in the local bodies, it will definitely influence rural power equations. Eventual empowerment of women, harnessing their creative abilities and giving them new responsibilities to shoulder, is one important promise of the PR.

General Conclusions

It has taken almost half a century and a constitutional amendment to reestablish the Panchayati Raj system, which establishes democratic participation while supporting economic development (through local planning, implementation and management) and stimulating social change by focusing on empowerment of women, scheduled castes and scheduled tribes. Whether the panchayats fulfill their role as self-governing instutions will depend on several key factors: political will of the centre and state leadership, the positive attitude of bureaucrats, adequate financial resources and autonomy, and training and education for panchayat members.

The political will to sustain PR institutions is crucial, and means, inter alia, allowing panchayats to continue in office until the expiration of their terms—not dissolving them, as has been done in several states, in some cases without holding new elections. State governments must also be willing to share power with the local bodies.

Establishing appropriate attitudes of bureaucrats from central and state agencies is crucial to ensure responsiveness to the desires of elected panchayats. Transparent coordination among parastatal bodies such as water authorities, electricity boards and housing boards is essential.

Without financial autonomy, devolution of power and responsibility to panchayats will be futile. Presently, panchayats do not have adequate access to capital for funding needed infrastructure investments and welfare improvement. The Central Government should award funds directly to panchayats for these purposes.

Vast numbers of rural people entering political bodies for the first time need education and training with regard to their participatory rights and authorities, as well as local policy implications and economic issues. Many of these individuals have had no formal education, are ignorant of the intricacies of politics and administration and are in danger of simply being manipulated by the ruling elite, although they are technically holders of the seats themselves.

A final comment is that the villagers now empowered by the Constitution must themselves demand that power, if they do not wish to remain passive partners in the political process. In some regions, the panchayat has continued its traditional role of moral authority in the village, and in this case its role is now strengthened through formal constitutional authority. Vigilance and assertion of rights by the mass of the population is vital to retain the grant of constitutional power that has been given.

Table 12.1
Progress of Panchayat Election in the States and Union Territories

	Last Election Held for			
State/UT	*GP*	*PS*	*ZP*	*Elections Due*
Andhra Pradesh	1995	1995	1995	NO
Arunachal Pradesh	9/92	9/92	9/92	NO
Assam	1992	1992	1992	Due
Bihar	1978	1979	1980	Due
Goa	1991			Due for ZP
Gujarat	1995	1995	1995	NO
Harayana	1994	1994	1994	NO
Himachal Pradesh	1995	1995	1995	NO
Jammu & Kashmir	*Not Ratified u/a 370 of Constitution*			
Karnataka	12/93	3/95	3/95	NO
Kerala	1995	1995	1995	NO
Madhya Pradesh	1994	1994	1994	NO
Maharashtra		2/92	2/92	NO
Manipur	9/91			Due for ZP
Meghalaya	*Part IX of the Constitution Not Applicable*			
Mizoram	*Part IX of the Constitution Not Applicable*			
Nagaland	*Part IX of the Constitution Not Applicable*			
Punjab	1/93	9/94	9/94	NO
Rajasthan	1995	1995	1995	NO
Sikkim	1993		1993	NO
Tamil Nadu	1996	1996	1996	NO
Tripura	1994	1994	1994	NO
Uttar Pradesh	1995	1995	1995	NO*
West Bengal	1993	1993	11/93	NO
Andaman & Nicobar	1995	1995	1995	NO
Chandigarh	1983			Due for GP & ZP
Dadra & Nagar Haveli	1995	1995	1995	NO
Delhi				
Daman & Diu	1995		1995	NO
Lakshadweep				Due for GP & ZP
Pondicherry				Due for GP & ZP

Notes: *Elections to PRIs in the Hill districts are yet to be held.
Source: Ministry of Rural Areas and Employment, 1996.

Table 12.2

Social Composition of Members and Chairpersons in the Elected Panchayats Including SCs, STs, BCs, in Some States

State	*Year of Election*	*Total Number of Members*			*Number of SC Members*			*Number of ST Members*			*Number of BC Members*		
		GP	PS	ZP	GP	PS	ZP	GP	PS	ZP	GP	PS	ZP
Arunachal	1992	5,733	1,205	77 (1)	(NA)	(NA)	(NA)	5,733	1,205	77 (11)	(NA)	(NA)	(NA)
Pradesh		(NA)			(NA)	(NA)	(NA)	(NA)	(78)		(NA)	(NA)	(NA)
Haryana	1994	54,159	2,415	303	11,793	519	64 (3)	(NA)	(NA)	(NA)			
				(16)	(1,199)	(21)		(NA)	(NA)	(NA)			
Himachal	1992	14,223	1,225		3,016	195	(NA)	697	60 (14)	(NA)	(NA)	(NA)	(NA)
Pradesh					(590)	(14)	(NA)	(278)		(NA)	(NA)	(NA)	(NA)
Karnataka	1993 & 95	78,426	3,340	919	10,539	601	165 (4)	6,878	169	47	28,275	1,117	306(7)
				(NA)	(1,029)	(32)		(297)	(9)	(1)	(1,874)	(58)	
Madhya	1994	443,429		945	64,997	1,345	143 (5)	132,638	2,780	267	75,410	1,541	164(8)
Pradesh				(45)	(4,530)	(41)		(9,050)	(92)	(10)	(5,389)	(47)	
Punjab	1993 & 94	90,585	2,441	274	20,727	338	64 (3)	(NA)	(NA)	(NA)	5,303	99(NA)	5(NA)
			(NA)	(NA)	(870)	(37)		(NA)	(NA)	(NA)	(990)		
Rajasthan	1995	112,897	5,257	997	17,902	943	177 (6)	15,616	604	164	13,137	625(35)	119(5)
			(237)	(31)	(1,643)	(41)		(1,477)	(36)	(5)	(1,050)		
Tripura	1994	5,429	195	70	118	48 (3)	15 (1)	415	26 (2)	7(0)	(NA)	(NA)	(NA)
			(NA)	(NA)	(69)			(163)			(NA)	(NA)	(NA)
West Bengal	1993	51,398	9,515	664	16,966	2,734	184	4,114	676	47	(NA)	(NA)	(NA)
			(NA)	(NA)	(NA)	(NA)	(NA)	(NA)	(NA)	(NA)	(NA)	(NA)	(NA)
Andhra	1995	NA (NA)	14,543	1,093	(NA)	1,660	125 (3)	NA	744	66	(NA)	3,241	245(3)
Pradesh			(1,084)	(20)	(NA).	(129)		(NA)	(59)	(NA)	(NA)	(247)	

Notes: Figures in parenthesis indicate number of Chairpersons. Figures for UP not available (NA) as election process is incomplete.
Source: Ministry of Rural Areas and Employment, 1996.

Table 12.3

Representation of Women Members in the House of People (Lok Sabha)

Lok Sabha	*Total Seats*	*Women Members*	*Per cent of Total*
I	499	22	4.4
II	500	27	5.5
III	503	34	6.7
IV	523	31	5.9
V	521	22	4.2
VI	544	19	3.4
VII	544	28	5.1
VIII	544	44	8.1
IX	529	28	5.3
X	514	39	7.6

Source: Jain, C. K. (1993) Women Parliamentarians in India, Lok Sabha Secretariat.

Table 12.4

Representation of Women Members in Council of States (Rajya Sabha)

Year	*Total Seats*	*Women Members*	*Per cent of Total*
1952	216	15	6.9
1962	236	18	7.6
1972	243	18	7.4
1982	244	24	9.8
1993	233	17	7.3

Source: Jain C. K. (1993) Women Parliamentarians in India, Lok Sabha Secretariat.

Table 12.5

Strength of Women Members in Panchayats, Including Women from Weaker Sections in Some States

	Women Members					
	GP	PS	ZP	GP	PS	ZP
Haryana	17,928 (1,574)	807 (34)	101 (4)	33.0	33.0	33.0
HP	4,066 (8)	288 (1)		28.5	23.5	(N/A)
Karnataka	34,073 (1,877)	1,343 (59)	335 (7)	43.4	40.2	36.4
MP	150,181 (11,953)	3,109 (123)	319 (9)	33.8	34.0	33.7
Punjab	23,990 (158)	326 (47)	89 (5)	26.4	13.3	32.4
Rajasthan	33,566 (3,064)	1,740 (86)	331 (10)	29.7	33.0	33.0
Tripura	1,805 (184)	67 (6)	24 (1)	33.0	34.0	34.0
West Bengal	21,742 (N/A)	3,202 (N/A)	227 (N/A)	35.4	33.6	34.1
AP	N/A (N/A)	5,054 (N/A)	363 (6)	(N/A)	34.5	33.2

Notes: Last three columns of the table represent percentages to total.
Figures in parentheses indicate number of chairpersons; N/A denotes not available.
Source: Government of India, Ministry of Rural Areas and Employment, 1996.

NOTES

1. Teune, H. 1995, *The Annals of American Academy of Political and Social Sciences*, 540 (1 July): 9.
2. Gandhian philosophy inevitably creeps in when the subject is decentralisation. His faith in decentralisation stemmed from his belief that centralisation was inherently violent.
3. Thirty-nine per cent of the rural population is living below the poverty line, earning less than Rs 2,444 per capita per year (National Council of Applied Economic Research [NCAER], 1998, *The India Human Development Report, A Profile of Indian States in the 1990s*. New Delhi: Oxford University Press, 1999.)
4. Dey, S. K. 1961, *Panchayati Raj, A Synthesis*. Bombay: Asia Publishing House, p. 91.

5. Choudhary, Anil K. 1995, 'Panchayati Raj Concerns and Issues', *Vikalp*, 4(2): 4.
6. Dey, S. K. 1986, 'Panchayati Raj in India', in G. Mathew (ed.), *Panchayati Raj in Karnataka Today, Its National Dimensions*. New Delhi: Institute of Social Sciences and Concept Publishing Company.
7. Gandhi, M. K. 1962, *Village Swaraj*. Ahmedabad: Navajivan, p. 12.
8. Unnithan, T. K. N. [n.d.] 'Panchayati Raj and Gandhian Ideal', in M. V. Mathur and I. Narain (eds.), *Panchayati Raj Planning and Democracy*. New York: Asia Publishing House, p. 46.
9. Dr. Ambedkar, one of the founders of the constitution, defended its non-inclusion in the draft constitution on the grounds that the basis of the constitution was the individual and not the village. He was critical of village republics who he regarded as the 'ruination of India'. He condemned the village as a sink of localism, a den of ignorance, narrow-mindedness and communalism. He was glad that 'the constitution has discarded the village and adopted the individual as its unit' (Government of India, 1948, *Constituent Assembly (Legislative) Debates, Official Reports*, Vol. 7, p. 39). The constitution did include a reference to PR but only in the Directive Principles of State Policy (Article 40) which only made it a holy duty of the central and state governments to take steps to organise village panchayats and endow them with the power and authority necessary to enable them to act as units of self-government, since the establishment of PR was not binding on the states, nor justiciable.
10. Government of India, 1957, 'Report of the Team for Study of Community Projects and National Extension Service', Committee on Plan Projects.
11. Tom, R. M. 1994, 'Rural Bureaucracies in Developing Countries', *Prashasanika*, 21(1): 35.
12. Government of India, 1978, 'Report of the Committee on PRI (August)', Ministry of Agriculture and Irrigation, Department of Rural Development.
13. Ibid.
14. Ibid.
15. Adisheshiah, M. S. 1986, 'The Need for Constitutional Safeguards', in M. George (ed.), *Panchayati Raj in Karnataka Today, Its National Dimensions*. New Delhi: Institute of Social Sciences and Concept Publishing Company, p. 25.
16. It is widely believed that the lack of constitutional safeguard was the main impediment to the viability of PR. The G. V. K. Rao Committee reported two recommendations: appropriate improvement in the representative character of panchayats and strengthening their capacity to play an effective role in promoting and managing rural development and local affairs. For this purpose, the Committee recommended that the district should be the basic unit of planning and have its own budget. The Singhvi Committee (1986) recommended constitutional recognition of PR, contending that it should be viewed as a unit of self-government. An additional chapter added to the Constitution would establish the 'identity and integrity of panchayats reasonably and substantially inviolate'. (Singh, S. S. and S. Mishra, 'Legislative Framework of PR in India', *Intellectual* [New Delhi], p. 16.) The primary emphasis was to establish PR as one of the foundation stones of the country's democratic polity; its secondary role was to continue as an administrative agency for promotion and management of rural development. It favoured creation of tribunals for panchayats to

address elections, postponement, dissolution and encroachment on their authority.

The Sarkaria Commission on centre–state relations (1988) addressed the strengthening of local bodies financially and functionally. Regular elections and sessions of these institutions were essential, it advised, and means should be evolved for ensuring this uniformly in all states.

Later, the Thungon Committee also recommended constitutional status for PR. It favoured creation of Nyay (judicial) Panchayats, provision for judicial tribunals, representation of scheduled castes, tribes and women and inclusion of district lists for allocation of financial resources to panchayats. Some expressed the sentiment that it was not lack of constitutional support, but political will that prevented the growth of PR. What further could have prevented ruling parties 'from putting through in the states under their control that which they wanted to provide in the constitution'? (Mukherji, N. 1991, 'Penal Discussion on the 72nd Amendment to the Constitution', Institute of Social Sciences, 25 September.)

17. This Act is not applicable to the states of Nagaland, Mizoram and Meghalaya, where traditional Councils operate.
18. For example, states can adopt a two-tier system to accommodate variations in state population size, and decisions regarding the devolution of power at lower levels and the distribution of responsibilities among the three tiers is left to the states.
19. This article assigns state-level legislative responsibility to design PRI.
20. Exemptions from intermediate-level panchayats are granted to states with a population not exceeding two million.
21. Panchayats may be responsible for implementation of twenty-nine economic development and social justice matters listed in the 11th Schedule.
22. Members of the Commission are to be appointed by the State Governor for five years.
23. TN High Court has ruled that this extent for reservation violates the right to equality under the Indian Constitution.
24. This problem was identified in 1963 by the Santhanam Committee which pointed out that stability and growth of panchayats requires substantial and growing resources that are entirely within their power to exploit and to develop. (Government of India, 1963, *Report of Committee on PR Finance*, p. 4–5.)
25. The Punjab and Uttar Pradesh State Acts are notably opaque in defining tier responsibilities and consequently, the functions of the three tiers tend to overlap. For example, agriculture and agricultural extension is supposed to be administered by all the three tiers. Agriculture is a vast subject and if specific activities are not assigned to a particular tier, then conflicts and inefficiency will result.
26. The listing of functions of three tiers of the PR system in UP, Punjab, and Karnataka is given in Section III.
27. Mukerji, N. 1993, 'Making the Third Stratum Vibrant', *Kurukshetra*, 41(9): 13.
28. Earlier, the objective of the Karnataka PR Act, 1983, was 'decentralisation of powers and functions for promoting development of democratic institutions and securing a greater measure of participation by the people in economic plans, local and governmental affairs'. In this sense, the present Act has taken a step backwards by excluding the spirit of PR.

29. GS, i.e., the entire electorate within a panchayat area, is an important institution of democracy at the village level.
30. Jagannath Mishra, ex-Minister for Rural Areas and Employment. Address to the AIPP 15th Annual National Conference. 8 November 1995, New Delhi.
31. One exception noted is Bihar. In Orissa panchayats were dissolved for political reasons and the Supreme Court ordered elections to be held by December 1996. Panchayati elections in TN were held as late as October 1996, when state political leadership changed.
32. Some villages of UP with larger populations of scheduled castes are categorised as Ambedkar villages and qualify for special treatment in development schemes.
33. Nine-tenths of the cost is borne by funds available under the scheme; the remaining tenth is contributed by the GP itself.
34. The DRDA was created by the Central Government's directive to implement the Integrated Rural Development Programme (IRDP) and other special area development and beneficiary-oriented programmes.
35. This author had the opportunity to interact with these bureaucrats during a workshop on reorientation of bureaucrats at the L. B. S. National Academy of Administration, Mussourie, in August 1996.
36. The formula differs favourably for the hill regions.
37. The Cabinet Minister is chairman and the Chief Development Officer (CDO) is secretary. The Chairman ZP is nominated as vice chairman and MLAs, MPs of the area and the Collector are nominated as its members.
38. The chairman is the DM; the CDO is the member secretary; the District Economic Officer is joint secretary; and the district level officers are its members.
39. As told by the Pradhan.
40. One local source of revenue: the panchayat is entitled dues from the sale of silt. A paltry sum of Rs 200 a year was received by auctioning a pond.
41. Illegal occupation of common lands is also responsible for the loss of revenue of panchayats, since common lands are an important source of income for the panchayats.
42. Further discussion of Punjab in Section III dilates the structure of PRIs in the state.
43. Statistics from the Draft Annual Plan, Government of Punjab, Department of Planning, 1995–96.
44. Randhava, N. S. and G. Kalkat, 1995, 'Multi Level Planning for Successful Implementation of PR and Economic Liberalisation', *Man and Development*, 17(2): 134.
45. Panchayats in border and sub-mountainous areas receive full subsidies.
46. Srinivastava, O. N., J. George and O. Prakash, 1995, 'Panchayati Raj Institutions in Punjab in Panchayati Raj Institutions in India, An Appraisal', National Institute of Rural Development (Hyderabad).
47. Institute of Social Sciences, 1995, *Panchayat Raj Update*, December. New Delhi: Institute of Social Sciences.
48. The Committee recommended, among other things, conferring executive heads designation on the chairpersons of ZP and TP; that state legislators and MPs be debarred from membership of panchayats; that instead of the CE the next higher tier be empowered to suggest dissolution of the lower tier with the

latter having right of appeal. (Government of Karnataka, 'Report of Expert Committee on PR Act, 1993'.)

49. Government of Karnataka, 'Planning, Institutional Finance and Statistics, Science and Technology Department, Draft Annual Plan, Vol. I, 1995–96'.
50. National Institute of Public Finance and Policy (New Delhi), 'Report of the Working Group on Transfers to Local Bodies, October 1995'.
51. For a long time, states have been demanding a 40 per cent share.
52. Rajaraman, I., O. P. Bohra and V. S. Renganathan, 1996, 'Augmentation of Panchayat Resources', *Economic and Political Weekly*, 4 May.
53. Ramanujan, T. C. A. 1996, 'Local Self Governments Powerless and Penniless', *Business Line*, 6 May.
54. Indian Institute of Education, 'Health for All, An Alternative Strategy', Report of the study group set up jointly by Indian Council of Social Science Research and India Council of Medical Research (Pune), 1981.
55. Antia, N. H. 1996, 'Health and Panchayati Raj', Seminar, 438(2): 33–34.
56. Government of India, 1957, *Review of First Five-Year Plan*. New Delhi: Planning Commission, Government of India.
57. Institute of Social Sciences, 1994, *Panchayat Raj Update*, January. New Delhi: Institute of Social Sciences.
58. See note 44.
59. Jain, G. P. 1993, 'Who Trusts A Villager?', *Hindustan Times*, 3 August.
60. Foundation Research in Community Health, 1995, 'Officials Face People's Court', *Panchayati Raj Interactive System* (Bombay), 1(2): 8. One year after this announcement photocopies were still not provided. The crux of agitation was the right to information.
61. In one year of PR operation in Madhya Pradesh, eight sarpanchas were killed due to inter-caste violence. ('MP PR in doldrums', *Hindustan Times*, 4 September 1995.)
62. The world over, women do not enjoy parity with men. The unpaid work that women perform all over the world equals $ 11 trillion, or half the world's income, without the women being recognised or credited for it. (United Nations Development Programme, 1995, *Human Development Report*. Delhi: Oxford University Press.)
63. United Nations Development Programme, 1996, *Human Development Report*. New York: Oxford University Press.
64. The BRMC and the AMC had recommended reservation or cooption of at least two women members in panchayats. The Committee on Status of Women (1976) supported reservation for women in panchayats. The National Perspective Plan for Women 1998–2000 also recommended 35 per cent reservation for women in political bodies. Karnataka PR Act, 1983, for the first time reserved 25 per cent of the seats for women in panchayats.
65. Hindustan Times, 'MP PR in Doldrums', September 9, 1995.
66. Panchayat Sandesh, June–July, 1995, Vol. 3–4, p. 15–16.
67. All-women panchayats number twenty-two today; some were deliberately created, others forced by circumstances, i.e., when most of the men left villages in search of jobs. (Mohanty, B. 1996, 'Women and Political Empowerment', Proceedings of the Women's Political Empowerment Day Celebration, 23–24

April 1995, edited by Bidyut Mohanty. New Delhi: Institute of Social Sciences). Voluntary and non-governmental organisations have extended support to them.

68. Bhandari, C. People's Action, February 1993.
69. The Government of India has instituted several income-generating activities, providing credit facilities and subsidy schemes targeting women. Also, PR Acts, such as those of Rajasthan and Andhra Pradesh, which debar people having more than two children from contesting elections, are radical measures redefining roles of women.

PART V

Reforming the Industrial and Financial Structure

13

Regulation and Reform of the Financial Sector in India: An Analysis of the Underlying Incentives

Pradeep Agrawal

A well-functioning and efficient financial system is important for promoting rapid industrial development in a market economy. By providing relatively liquid assets with reasonable returns on savings, people are encouraged to save and keep their savings in the form of financial assets. Through intermediation of the financial system, these savings are routed to investment firms. The financial system pools savings and distributes risks of investments across a large number of people, thereby making possible large investment projects that may not have been undertaken otherwise. By providing loans to new entrepreneurs, it supports innovation, creativity and a more equitable income distribution, while at the same time creating a larger entrepreneurial base for faster industrial development in the future. By providing loans to buyers, it stimulates demand for industrial goods. Thus, the more efficient the financial system of an economy, the higher the investment rate, and hence the output and employment growth rates of the economy.

The banking sector is the most important part of the financial system in developing countries such as India, and is the focus of study in this chapter. The banking sector in India has remained highly regulated since banks were nationalised in 1969, whether it be in interest rates, loan allocations or the setting up of new banks by private entrepreneurs. The nationalisation of banks helped to provide an initial thrust to the development of banking, especially in rural areas, and increased access to credit for farmers, small firms and weaker sections of the society. Unfortunately, however, it has also stifled competition in the banking sector, leading to inefficient resource use and poor customer service. Similarly, directed lending to 'priority sectors' at concessional rates of interest artificially swelled demand for such loans, some of it from fake borrowers. Ceilings on interest rates have created credit shortages leading to corruption in sanctioning loans.

At the same time, deregulation or reform of the banking sector can unleash its own problems. For example, simultaneous deregulation of interest rates and loan portfolio requirements can create such huge credit demands from the previously credit-starved sectors that interest rates can rise to very high levels for some time. This can lead to the bankruptcy of a large number of firms and can eventually snowball into a major industrial recession, causing a banking crisis due to non-recovery of loans from the bankrupt firms as has happened in a large number of countries in Latin America, Asia and elsewhere.

This chapter examines the consequences of a highly regulated banking environment in India by analysing the incentives and forces it creates for various agents in the economy (Section I). It also describes the banking deregulation and reform that is presently being considered by the Indian government (Section II). It analyses the new incentives that are likely to arise as a result of deregulation and highlights the dangers of rapid banking deregulation by drawing upon the experience of nearly a dozen other countries (Section III). This analysis is used to explain how to deregulate the banking sector in India safely and successfully (Section IV). Finally, the main conclusions of the paper are summarised (Section V).

I REGULATION OF THE BANKING SECTOR IN INDIA: SOME CONSEQUENCES

Since the nationalisation of banks in 1969, the banking sector in India has been heavily regulated. This section explores the incentives created by these regulations and their economic impact. The focus will be on the following regulations: (*a*) entry restrictions on private banks, (*b*) credit allocation requirements, including the priority sector lending requirements and the statutory liquidity requirement (SLR), and (*c*) interest rate controls.

What each of these restrictions stipulated, why they were imposed and what their consequences were will be discussed next.

Entry Restrictions on Private Banks

Since 1969 the entry of private banks to the Indian markets has been restricted. Permission of the Reserve Bank of India is required for starting a new bank or even for opening a new branch of an existing bank. Foreign banks have been allowed to operate only a limited number of branches and foreign equity participation in domestic banks has not been permitted. These restrictions have been eased since reforms were initiated in 1992 in order to stimulate competition.

The entry restrictions on private banks were imposed following the nationalisation in 1969 of the major commercial banks to prevent 'unfair' competition from private banks. The criticism against private banks in 1969 was that they were operating mainly in urban areas and lending mostly to rich individuals and well-established firms. The nationalisation was indeed followed by major expansion of nationalised banks in rural areas, and the government directed lending at subsidised interest rates to weaker sections of the society such as farmers and small-scale industries.

However, an important side effect of the nationalisation has been the virtual elimination of competition among banks. The Reserve Bank began enforcing uniform interest rates, spreads and service charges among nationalised banks on equity grounds. Even when the Reserve Bank directives allowed for some variation in interest rates, the nationalised banks tended to avoid competing with each other, perhaps because bank management gained little from increasing their market share. Further, the private banks were small (the larger ones having been nationalised) and faced the prospect of being nationalised if they grew beyond a certain size. Thus, until 1991, there were limited incentives for existing small banks to try to grow rapidly or for entrepreneurs to start new private banks.

The lack of competition either among the public banks[1] or between the public and private banks, combined with labour policies of the public sector where employees' salaries and promotions were not significantly linked to their job performance, has led to a steady decline in the efficiency and work culture of the banks and an alarming decline in the quality of customer service. Another symptom of this lack of competition was that most banking operations were not computerised until 1991. In the absence of competition, bank managers have had no incentive to improve the efficiency of operations or customer service. Further, fearing job losses, workers have opposed computerisation. Some gradual steps towards computerisation have been initiated recently following the 1992 reforms.

The Credit Allocation Policy

The allocation of bank credit in India is largely determined by the state through the Cash Reserves Requirement (CRR), the Statutory Liquidity Requirement (SLR) and the priority sector lending requirement. For example, in 1991, banks lent to the government 49 per cent of their total deposits at concessional rates through the CRR and SLR. Of the remaining 51 per cent, 40 per cent had to be lent to the priority sectors again at concessional rates. In addition, there were further requirements to lend to the exporters and food procurement programmes at concessional rates. As a result, only about 25 per cent of the bank deposits were left to meet the needs of all the remaining sectors, the allocation of which was determined by market forces (see Table 13.1). Following is a brief description of each of these requirements.

The Cash Reserve and Statutory Liquidity Requirements The Cash Reserve Ratio (CRR) obligates banks to hold a certain fraction of their total deposits as reserves with the Reserve Bank. This requirement has hovered around the statutory maximum of 15 per cent since the late 1980s. The purpose of these reserves is to ensure the liquidity of the banks. However, they also impose a significant cost on the banks since the interest received on the reserves is low (5 per cent per year). While all banking systems require banks to hold some reserves, the magnitude of reserve requirement is relatively high in India. For comparison, the reserve requirement is 8 per cent or less in most East Asian countries (Korea, Singapore, Taiwan, Singapore) and only about 2–3 per cent in most developed countries.

The Statutory Liquidity Requirement (SLR) stipulates that banks must invest a certain fraction of their total deposits in government or government-approved securities which typically carry below-market interest rates. Since the late 1980s, this requirement for Indian banks has been about 38 per cent of their total deposits. While ostensibly this is required to ensure the safety and liquidity of the banks, it is in fact used as a means to divert the bank deposits of households to finance the government budget deficits and other credit needs of the public sector at subsidised interest rates. Table 13.2 shows that the preemption of bank deposits by the government through the CRR and SLR has tended to increase in tandem with the government's fiscal deficit. Table 13.3 shows data on the percentage of domestic credit going to the Central Government in India compared to several East Asian countries. The table shows that this ratio is relatively high for India, pointing to the high SLR on banks in India.

The high CRR and SLR requirements reduce the availability of credit to the private sector. The low interest rates on CRR and SLR implicitly tax the banking sector. The banks, in turn, pass the burden on to their customers in the form of lower interest rates on deposits and/or higher interest rates on loans to the private sector.

Directed Lending After banks have satisfied the CRR and SLR, they are obligated to lend a certain fraction of the remaining funds to the so called 'Priority Sectors', mainly agriculture and small-scale industries, as directed by the Reserve Bank. Since the early 1980s, Indian banks have been required to lend 40 per cent of their total loans (after satisfying the CRR and SLR) to these sectors. In addition, there has been an informal requirement to provide liberal credit to exporters. In 1993 this requirement was formally fixed at 10 per cent of total loans. Foreign banks had a lower directed lending requirement—15 per cent—until 1994. In 1994 this was revised to 32 per cent (inclusive of export credit). Effectively, therefore, even after meeting the CRR and SLR requirements, about one-half of the remaining credit of the domestic banks is directed by the Reserve Bank.

The purpose of the priority sector lending has been to increase the proportion of credit going to the sectors that are important to the national economy with regard to their contribution to growth, employment generation and/or equal income distribution, and that may not receive adequate credit otherwise. These objectives are desirable and have been achieved to some extent. However, by the way the policy has been implemented, many undesirable incentives have been created leading to many problems and costs, as follows:

1. Political control of public sector banks and the consequent lobbying by various pressure groups has resulted in loans, especially those to the priority sectors, being given without adequate safeguards against defaults and with a lax attitude toward enforcing repayment. This, together with widespread mismanagement and corruption in public sector banks, has resulted in large loan arrears. The Ministry of Finance (1993) estimates that 21 per cent of the loans advanced by public sector banks are non-performing.[2] Private estimates are even higher.
2. The priority sector loans have been typically given at concessional interest rates (see Table 13.4). This, together with inadequate safeguards against default, created incentives to borrow under the priority sector loans as much as possible, which sometimes led to cheating in order to qualify. A significant proportion of loans was usurped by those for whom it was not intended. For example, concessional loans and other benefits to small-scale industry has led many larger firms to either subdivide their operations in small fragments or to under-report their capital assets in order to qualify for priority loans for small-scale industry.[3] In some cases, 'ghost firms' have been created for the sole purpose of getting the concessional loans.[4]
3. Loans taken by qualified agents may not always be used for the intended purpose due to the fungibility of funds. For example, a farmer may take a concessional loan for buying a tubewell but use his own funds for buying a television. Assuming that in the absence of concessional loan, he would have bought the tubewell from his funds, the priority sector loan actually finances the purchase of the television.
4. The priority sector lending helps the relatively better-off groups within the priority sector. For example, the wealthiest farmers and largest of the small-scale firms often corner most of the priority sector loans. This happens because the wealthier farmers and larger firms are likely to have better social and political connections, be more creditworthy and involve a smaller transaction cost as a proportion of the amount lent than poor farmers and small firms. The former groups are also more likely to avoid repaying the loans by using their connections to put pressure on banks.
5. The concessional priority sector lending imposes a burden on the rest of the borrowers and the depositors since the banks

pass on the cost of subsidising the priority sector lending to them by offering lower interest rates on deposits and charging higher interest rates on non-priority sector loans. The non-priority sectors are also faced with reduced credit availability.

Thus the social benefits of priority sector lending have proved to be smaller and costs higher than originally expected.

Interest Rate Controls

Since 1969 the interest rates in India have been set by the Reserve Bank. Generally, these interest rates, especially on directed lending to government and priority sectors, have been lower than the market clearing level. This has been justified on the grounds that it will stimulate investment.[5] However, as McKinnon (1973) and Shaw (1973) argue, keeping the interest rates artificially low may result in reduced and less productive investment.[6] Their basic argument against interest rate ceilings is illustrated in Figure 13.1. When the supply of deposits and demand for loans are as depicted in Figure 13.1, the loan market clears at the interest rate r_0 with I_0 amount of funds being loaned out for investments. When an interest rate ceiling of r_C is imposed, interest rates on deposits also go down and many people may save less or divert some of their savings to inflation hedges such as gold or real estate. Thus, the supply of bank deposits goes down to I_C and since less funds are available to be loaned out, the investments must decline from I_0 to I_C.

Furthermore, when the interest rate ceiling r_C prevails on loans, those with investment projects with returns between r_C and r_0 will also seek and receive loans since banks have an incentive to discriminate between borrowers only on the basis of their creditworthiness, not the productivity of their investments. Thus, the average productivity of investments will decline as a result of the interest rate ceiling. This, together with the decline in investments from I_0 to I_C, implies that, *ceteris paribus*, the rate of growth of the GNP will also decline.

For empirical evidence regarding these issues, see, for example, World Bank (1989), Fry (1988), Gelb (1989) and World Bank (1993).[7] The World Bank (1989) shows data based on a sample of eighty developing countries.[8] The countries are subdivided into three groups according to their real (adjusted for inflation) interest rates: positive, moderately negative (0 per cent to – 5 per cent) and strongly negative. The second and third groups are much more likely to have an interest rate ceiling. The table shows that the first group had deeper financial sectors (that is, a higher M2/GDP ratio), moderately higher investment rates and significantly more productive investments (that is, a larger change in GDP/investment) than the other two groups. Fry (1988) and Gelb (1989) run ordinary least squares regression of GDP growth on real interest rates using pooled cross-economy time series data.[9] They find a positive association between GDP growth and real interest rates. However, more recently, World Bank (1993) has provided evidence that a clear positive association between GDP growth and real interest rates exists only for economies with negative real interest rates.[10] This is consistent with the argument advanced in Section III that very high interest rates are harmful to the economy.

Arguments such as those advocated by McKinnon (1973) and Shaw (1973) have led many economists to advocate financial liberalisation, that is, market-determined interest rates and credit allocation, along with privatisation of banks.[11] The financial liberalisation initiated in India since 1992 is discussed next.

II BANKING DEREGULATION IN INDIA SINCE 1992

Financial deregulation has been recommended for India by the government-appointed Narasimham Committee (1991).[12] The Committee recommended the dismantling of barriers to the entry and expansion of private banks, sharp reduction in directed credit and gradual decontrol of interest rates. Following are details of the recommendations and reforms initiated so far.

Dismantling Barriers to Entry and Expansion of Private Banks

In order to increase the efficiency and quality of service of the nationalised banks, the Narasimham Committee recommended that the banking industry be made more competitive by removing restrictions on entry and expansion of private banks, and reducing those on the expansion of foreign banks. The committee also called for an assurance by the government that no new banks would be nationalised. The committee recommended that new private banks should be required to have a minimum initial capital of one billion rupees, and joint ventures between foreign and Indian banks should be permitted, with foreign banks allowed up to 20 per cent equity. The Narasimham Committee also recommended that prudent supervision and regulation of the banks should be undertaken by the Reserve Bank. A new capital adequacy norm of 8 per cent of risky assets has been recommended for banks, to be achieved over the next few years. New accounting norms were also prescribed for banks regarding the classification of non-performing loans.

These recommendations were accepted by the government in April 1992. In a bid to restore health to the bank balance sheets, and eventually sell part of their equity to the public, the government has infused large amounts of capital into the public banks to help write off the non-performing loans. From April 1992 to March 1995, the total capital infusion equalled Rs 110 billion or about 10 per cent of the total bank credit outstanding in 1992 (see Table 13.1). Further, ten new foreign bank branches and ten new domestic private banks had been granted license to operate by early 1995. However, of the ten domestic private banks granted license, only six had actually commenced banking operations. Further, the new domestic banks have only a few branches each, are operating mostly in the major cities and are aiming at the upper segment of the clientele and at the corporate customers. This may indicate that there may still be reservations in the private sector about the viability of private banks, and confidence in the government policy of competition between private and public sector banks may be lacking. Perhaps the minimum initial capital requirement of one billion rupees is also too high.

Deregulating Credit Allocation

The Narasimham Committee also recommended reducing state intervention in credit allocation. Specifically, it recommended that priority sector lending be reduced from 40 per cent to 10 per cent over a three year period. Simultaneously, it called for the institution of preferential refinancing of credit by the Reserve Bank to most of the better-off sectors previously falling under the priority sector. Further, it recommended cutting the SLR requirement from 38.5 per cent to 25 per cent over a three year period and payment of market interest rates on such borrowings.[13]

The government has accepted the recommendation to cut SLR, although it is being phased in at a slower rate than recommended; SLR was reduced to 33.75 per cent in September 1993, and to 31.50 per cent in September 1994 with a marginal rate of 25 per cent for deposits beyond the level reached in September 1994. The interest rates on borrowings under SLR have also been increased to near market rates.

However, the government has not accepted the recommendation to reduce priority sector lending because of strong opposition voiced by the small-scale firms and farmers who are the main beneficiaries of priority sector lending. These groups, including their employees and dependants, account for almost 75 per cent of the population and therefore carry great political clout. However, since 1993 the interest rate subsidy on such loans has been significantly reduced. Eligibility norms for priority sector loans have also been relaxed to make it available to firms with a capital base of up to Rs 7.5 million compared to Rs 3.5 million previously. This makes it easier for banks to meet the priority sector lending requirement.

Decontrolling Interest Rates

The Narasimham Committee recommended a cautious move toward market-determined interest rates as a medium-term objective while correctly warning against allowing interest rates to rise much, as they already were on the high side for the non-priority sectors.[14]

The government accepted these recommendations and began to move gradually towards this goal. Interest rates on deposits were deregulated in 1993, with each bank free to set its own rates on deposits of various maturities, subject to a ceiling, currently set by the Reserve Bank at 11 per cent per year. In October 1994, interest rates on loans for amounts in excess of Rs 200,000 were also deregulated. Interest rates on smaller loans continued at the subsidised rate of 12 per cent for loans smaller than Rs 25,000 and 13.5 per cent for loans in amounts between Rs 25,000 and Rs 200,000. This compares with a prime lending rate of 16 per cent (April 1995) for loans of over Rs 200,000.

Banking deregulation is expected to result in improved efficiency and better service to customers, as well as increased and more productive investments and a higher growth of national income. However, it also needs to be handled very carefully. Following is a discussion of what can go wrong with rapid banking deregulation when the incentives it unleashes are not well understood.

III DANGERS OF RAPID BANKING DEREGULATION

Most of the countries that have attempted financial liberalisation have also experienced a financial crisis—failure of several banking institutions and/or accumulation of a large percentage of non-performing loans by the banking sector, typically exceeding 20 per cent of their loan portfolio.[15] The experience with financial liberalisation has been disastrous in many countries because the incentives unleashed by liberalisation were not well understood.

The financial liberalisation experience of about a dozen countries from Latin America (Argentina, Chile and Uruguay), East Asia (Indonesia, Korea, Malaysia and the Philippines) and elsewhere (Australia, New Zealand, Turkey and the United States) is discussed next. Most of these countries, except Korea, Malaysia and the Philippines, rapidly deregulated the interest rate controls on banks. Usually this was accompanied by a significant and rapid reduction in directed lending and reduction or elimination of credit ceilings on specific sectors or firms. Some of these liberalising countries—namely, Chile, Argentina, Uruguay, the Philippines and Turkey—experienced major crises requiring intervention by the governments to bail out the insolvent banking sectors. In Chile, the central bank holding of bad loans amounted to 19 per cent of GNP in 1988, and in Uruguay, to 7 per cent of GNP in 1983. In Turkey the cost of rescuing the insolvent banks was estimated to exceed 10 per cent of GNP. In the Philippines 30 per cent of bank loans were non-performing in 1987. In most other crises countries also, the non-performing loans were typically in excess of 20 per cent of the total loan portfolio of the banking sector.

Table 13.5 shows that most of the countries experiencing financial crises experienced a sharp increase in the interest rates, often exceeding 8 per cent in real terms. In the Latin American countries and in the Philippines, the real interest rates exceeded 25 per cent in real terms. While some increase in the real interest rates was only to be expected following financial liberalisation, the kind of increases actually experienced were phenomenal, at least in major crisis countries (except Turkey). These real interest rates easily exceeded the real marginal productivity of capital in most countries. For example, the real rates of return on total capital for 1960–80 were estimated to be only 5.18 per cent for the United States.[16] What was the cause of these very high real interest rates? To what extent were they contributing to the financial crisis? These questions can be answered by analysing the incentives unleashed by a sudden liberalisation of the interest rates and credit portfolio restrictions on banks.

Causes of High Real Interest Rates Following Banking Deregulation

The main causes of high real interest rates following banking deregulation are as follows:

1. Pent-up demand for credit from sectors previously denied access to credit can lead to a large upsurge in the demand for credit, and hence the interest rates, for the first few years following liberalisation. Prior to financial liberalisation, in most countries listed in Table 13.5, the banking credit was selectively directed by their governments into preferred sectors such as small-scale industries, exporting firms and public sector firms. At the same time, the credit demands of some of the non-preferred sectors were not fully met. These often included loans for the purchase of equity shares, consumer durables, and in some cases, housing and real estate. In this kind of situation, when government controls on credit allocation and interest rates are suddenly released, the credit-starved sectors try to achieve their desired 'stock' of credit as quickly as possible. In the process, they can create huge 'flows' of demands for credit[17] in the short run, which typically lasts for a few years. During this period, the total demand for credit can

increase very sharply resulting in a sharp increase in the interest rates.

Figure 13.2 shows that the interest rates tend to exhibit an overshooting or 'inverted J' pattern after liberalisation. Starting from an initial credit demand D_o and interest rate ceiling r_c, financial liberalisation leads to the demand for credit shifting to D_1 and the market interest rates rising sharply to r_1. Once the pent-up demand for credit is satisfied and the desired stock of credit is reached, the additional demand for credit from the previously credit-starved sectors will largely decline, and the total credit demand will decline to something like D_2, resulting in the interest rates declining to r_2. Thus, following liberalisation, there will be a tendency for the interest rates to shoot up sharply in the short run and then decline. This pattern was evident in virtually *all* the countries considered as can be seen from Table 13.5 and Figure 13.4.

2. Large credit flows that meet the pent-up demand for credit from share markets, real estate and consumer durables can lead to sharp price increases in these sectors; this further fuels the demand for credit needed to invest in these sectors and puts further upward pressure on the interest rates. For example, if bank credit becomes available for purchase of shares in companies, many individuals who were previously unable to purchase their desired amount of shares due to a liquidity constraint will now be able to do so. As a result, the demand for shares and hence their prices can rise sharply (occasionally this may be delayed until market sentiments turn bullish). When the share prices increase sharply, the real expected return on shares—given by the growth rate of share prices in real terms plus the dividend rate—also increases sharply and may even reach levels above 25 per cent or, in some cases, 50 per cent. For example, after the Chilean banking deregulation in 1975, real[18] share prices nearly quadrupled over the period 1975–80 (see Figure 13.5). These high returns induce many additional individuals to invest in share markets. This leads to additional demand for bank credit even at exorbitant interest rates. This additional demand for credit at high real interest rates can keep the interest rates high for some time. As the pent-up demand for credit from the previously

liquidity-constrained investors is satisfied, the additional demand for shares declines after some time, leading to a decline in the price of shares.

This is illustrated in Figure 13.3: the pre-liberalisation demand for shares is D_0 and the real share price index is at P_0. As credit flow increases after liberalisation, the demand for shares shifts to D_1 and the share prices rise sharply to P_1. When the pent-up credit demand for shares is mostly satisfied, the demand for shares declines to say D_2 and the share prices collapse to P_2. Thus, the share prices, too, will tend to exhibit an overshooting or 'inverted J' effect in countries where interest rates and restrictions on borrowing are liberalised. Figure 13.5 shows the real[19] share price indices for Australia, New Zealand, Chile, Malaysia and Philippines.[20] All of these countries show the 'inverted J' pattern of share prices. A similar pattern is likely to be repeated in the housing and real estate markets.

3. If the inflation rate in the country is high and volatile, real interest rates on loans can become very high simply because of the high risk involved in lending and borrowing in nominal terms. Table 13.6 shows the spread between lending and deposit rates for selected low-inflation (the inflation rate below 5 per cent on the average), high-inflation (the inflation rate between 20 and 100 per cent) and hyperinflation (the inflation rate above 100 per cent on the average) countries. It is seen that while the average spread is only 3 per cent for the low-inflation countries, it increases to 13 per cent for the high-inflation countries and to a whopping 158 per cent for the hyperinflation countries. With spread as high as this, very high real interest rates on loans are not surprising. All of the major crisis countries, Argentina, Chile, Uruguay, the Philippines and Turkey, were either high- or hyperinflation countries.
4. Monetary contraction sometimes accompanies financial liberalisation in an effort to reduce the inflation rate, as was the case in the United States, Turkey and the Philippines. However, a monetary contraction reduces the supply of bank credit at a time when the demand for credit is likely to be increasing due to the liberalisation. This contributes to the phenomenon of high real interest rates following liberalisation.

To summarise, the interest rates can become very high for a few years following financial liberalisation due to pent-up demand from previously credit-starved sectors, due to excessive increases in prices of shares and real estate, for instance, due to high and unstable inflation rates and due to a monetary contraction. These high real interest rates are temporary, except perhaps in countries suffering from high and volatile inflation, and do not represent the true long-run equilibrium interest rates. Their effects on the economy can still be highly debilitating, as will be discussed next.

Consequences of High Real Interest Rates Following Banking Deregulation

A sharp increase in interest rates can lead to a financial crisis, that is, excessive build-up of non-performing loans and bank insolvencies. This can happen through one or more of the following processes:

1. Previously undertaken investments financed by debt can become unviable following sharp and unexpected increases in interest rates. In most developing countries, a large majority of firms depend on bank debt and other corporate debt instruments to finance their investments. When the interest rates suddenly increase, many of these firms, which had based their investment decision on the expectation that the interest rates would stay close to the pre-liberalisation levels, find themselves stuck with investments whose yields are not commensurate with the sharply increased cost of servicing the debt. Thus many of these firms face difficulties and may eventually fail. An industrial recession resulting from the sharp increase in interest rates and/or other factors further exacerbates these difficulties. The firms' inability to service and/or repay their debt leads to a build-up of non-performing loans for the banks.
2. High interest rates can significantly increase the risk involved in lending. This is due to the fact that the relatively safe borrowers with low risk but also lower expected returns may find the interest rates too high for the returns they expect to make and may drop out of the loan market, whereas the relatively

risky borrowers with investment projects that have higher average returns, but also higher risks of failure, remain in the loan market. The risky borrowers remain because if their projects succeed, they keep most of the benefits while the bank simply gets back its loans. If the project fails, the investors walk off leaving the bank to pick up the pieces. Even when the banks have collateral (usually the equipment bought with the loan) they may not be able to fully recover their loans because of the expensive and time-consuming litigation involved in liquidating collateral and the deterioration, lack of proper maintenance or theft of the collateral in the meantime.[21] Also, the banks are likely to be inexperienced in evaluating the risk under the rapidly changing economic scenario that often accompanies financial liberalisation. These factors again contribute to the banks' non-performing loan portfolio.

3. The overshooting effect in share and real estate prices can bankrupt many speculative borrowers. As discussed previously, financial liberalisation often leads to sharply increasing prices of shares and real estate for a few years, inducing many individuals to invest or speculate in these markets with funds borrowed from banks at high real interest rates. When the prices later decline, many of these individuals become insolvent and are unable to repay their loans, leaving the banks with a considerable portfolio of non-performing loans. (The collateral, typically the shares or real estate bought with the loan, may lose so much value that large losses still accrue to banks.)
4. Sudden and unexpected increases in the lending and deposit rates can create severe difficulties for financial intermediaries that do not have a balanced term structure between their deposits and loan portfolios. For example, if a bank has mostly short-term deposits but long-term loans, it will not be able to raise the interest on its pre-committed long-term loans but will be forced to pay higher interest rates on all of its deposits once they mature. In the interim period, the bank can become insolvent. Precisely this process is cited as having contributed to the large-scale bankruptcy of the savings and loan institutions in the United States throughout the 1980s following the sharp increase in interest rates during 1980 to 1982, although in this case, the interest rates rose primarily due to a highly contractionary monetary policy.[22]

Some or all of the effects mentioned above can act simultaneously and add up to bank insolvencies or accumulation of non-performing loans, which leads to the financial crisis. The loan recovery problems are further exacerbated if the economy goes into a recession. This is so because the difficulties faced by enterprises in dealing with sudden increases in interest rates and the risk of failure of an investment project increase significantly if the general economy goes into a recession. Table 13.7 shows that virtually all the countries experiencing financial crisis also experienced a recession for a few years prior to the financial crisis.

A recession can occur due to the sharp increase in interest rates following financial liberalisation and the resulting fall in investment. In addition, financial liberalisation is typically accompanied by other policies such as trade liberalisation, macroeconomic stabilisation and increased international capital mobility. While these policies are desirable in the long run, they can exacerbate the difficulties created by rapid financial liberalisation in the short run if they do lead to a recession or the build-up of excessive foreign debt. Interaction between financial liberalisation, financial crisis and other policies is discussed next.

Financial Crisis: Interaction with Trade Liberalisation, Macroeconomic Stabilisation and International Capital Mobility

Trade liberalisation exposes domestic firms to competition from foreign firms and can lead to a recession as domestic industry adjusts and restructures itself to face the new competition and some of the less efficient domestic firms get weeded out. The process is likely to be more difficult where the levels of protection have been high and the protection is then withdrawn rapidly without giving the firms adequate time to adjust to the increased international competition. This was the case with the Latin American countries and as a result, they went through a severe recession and financial crisis. On the other hand, Korea and Malaysia liberalised their financial markets after the trade liberalisation was over. Thus they experienced relatively minor recessions and financial crises. Even Indonesia, which liberalised its financial markets a few years before it liberalised international trade, experienced a relatively mild recession and financial crisis. Again, this is consistent with the hypothesis that a recession caused by other policy measures acts to exacerbate the severity of the financial crisis.

Macroeconomic stabilisation measures usually take the form of either reduction in government spending in order to reduce the budget deficit or a reduction in the growth of the money supply to reduce inflation. Both of these measures lead to a recession and thus increase the severity of the financial crises. This was the case with the Latin American countries, Turkey, the Philippines and the United States. On the other hand, Australia, Korea and Malaysia did not have to go through a significant macroeconomic stabilisation programme and this contributed to the relatively milder financial crises there.

Relaxation of restrictions on international capital mobility, in countries where they existed, has often accompanied financial liberalisation. When international capital mobility is permitted, the high interest rates following financial liberalisation lead to a large increase in foreign borrowing and thus a faster accumulation of foreign debt. As can be seen from Figure 13.6A and 13.6B, this happened in virtually all the countries except Korea, which had maintained interest rate ceilings during the liberalisation, and the Philippines, which was denied international credit during 1983–85 due to a major political and economic crisis. The debt build-up was particularly strong in Latin America, which allowed domestic banks to accept deposits from foreigners and had very high nominal interest rates along with a controlled exchange rate, providing very high returns to foreign depositors.[23] In the Latin American countries, the large foreign capital inflows not only earned extremely high returns, but also made the domestic currency too strong which hurt the export effort and led to current account deficits. It also created too much liquidity in the economy which led to increased domestic inflation. Even worse, this foreign capital was lent out to domestic private and public firms by the domestic banks whose liabilities were explicitly or implicitly guaranteed by the domestic government. Thus, when the domestic borrowers failed to repay their loans, huge public external debts were built up and repayment has proved to be extremely difficult.

To summarise, the above analysis suggests that interest rate deregulation should be undertaken *after* macroeconomic stabilisation has been achieved. Trade liberalisation should not accompany financial liberalisation;[24] financial liberalisation should follow after the economy has adjusted to trade liberalisation or vice versa. Restrictions on international capital mobility should be removed *after* the interest rate deregulation has been completed and domestic interest rates have settled down to reasonable levels.

IV IMPLICATIONS FOR INDIA: DEREGULATING THE BANKING SECTOR SAFELY

From the above discussion, it is clear that the financial crisis that has followed banking deregulation in most countries is a result of the various economic incentives unleashed by the deregulation process. The proponents of the liberalisation had expected the financial markets to move smoothly towards the long-run equilibrium interest rate and improve the amount and productivity of investment. While their analysis is largely correct in the long run, the short-run turbulence had not been anticipated and has proved too difficult to traverse for most countries, causing many of them to abandon the entire liberalisation attempt.

The analysis developed in Section III suggests ways to minimise the short-run turbulence in the financial markets following deregulation. This can be achieved by liberalising the controls on interest rates and credit allocation gradually over a few years. For example, if ceilings exist on interest rates, it is safer to raise the ceilings to near market rates gradually over a few years before deregulating interest rates completely. Similarly, it is safer to gradually ease credit controls rather than removing them all at once. Further, it is safer to undertake financial liberalisation after macroeconomic stabilisation, especially a moderate inflation rate, has been achieved.

The financial liberalisation initiated in India is moderate and gradual. The credit controls on housing and shares remain unchanged.[25] Interest rates on deposits of different maturities were liberalised in 1993 but a ceiling has been maintained (currently fixed at 11 per cent while the inflation rate is about 10 per cent per year). The interest rates on loans for various maturities and categories were liberalised in late 1994; however the minimum lending rate (currently 16 per cent, except for small loans of under

Rs 200,000) is still prescribed by the Reserve Bank. Thus interest rates have not yet been truly liberalised. Further, control of both the deposit rates and prime lending rate restricts competition among banks and provides them with a spread (between lending and deposit rates) that seems to be too large.

India is well placed to undertake further liberalisation of the financial markets without any undue fear that it may lead to a financial crisis. This is so because India has a moderate inflation rate of around 10 per cent, has no serious macroeconomic stabilisation problems and trade liberalisation has been mostly negotiated. Partial relaxation of controls on some types of foreign capital inflows have led to significant inflows of foreign equity capital which have resulted in a higher than usual expansion of the money supply, and thus, easy credit conditions. Nevertheless, rather than liberalising fully, it would be safer to raise the real deposit rate ceiling while lowering the real lending rate floor gradually, say by 1 per cent per year, until the ceilings are no longer binding. Similarly, the ceilings on loans for personal housing and against shares as collateral can be raised gradually.

A major limitation of the deregulation of banking in India is the heavy dominance of the public sector banks that are used to working in a highly regulated environment. To improve the efficiency of operations and customer service, greater competition from private sector banks is badly needed. Private banks should be set up in larger numbers than has happened so far, indicating the need for more encouragement from the government. Furthermore, the public sector banks should be made more accountable by selling their equity to the public.[26] There is also a need for greater autonomy of public sector banks and greater accountability of bank managers for the performance of their banks.

Priority sector lending has been improved significantly by reducing interest rate subsidies and laying greater emphasis on lending along commercial lines to reduce non-performing loans. This emphasis should be continued by making interest rates on priority sector loans identical to those on non-priority sector loans and taking adequate safeguards against default. Only in cases of small loans to the weakest sections of the society should lending without collateral be considered; in that case other mechanisms for ensuring repayment of the loan need to be created as, for example, in the 'group lending scheme' of the rural banks in Bangladesh. These changes would reduce incentives to cheat in order to qualify for priority sector lending and reduce the misuse and diversion of such loans. Thereby, the availability of credit to the genuine priority sector borrowers would improve. And it is really the availability of credit, rather than its concessional aspect, that is important to the genuine priority sector borrowers. The elimination of concessional interest rates on priority sector loans has been used successfully by several developing countries, for instance, Korea, Singapore and Indonesia. It also reduces the burden of cross-subsidy on the non-priority sectors.

Another refinement in priority sector lending can be to set the loan quota for priority lending, including quotas for its various sub-categories such as agriculture and small-scale industries, for the banking system as a whole rather than for each individual bank. This will not affect the interest of priority sector borrowers but can improve the efficiency of priority sector lending through one of the following mechanisms:

1. Banks can be allowed to trade the priority sector lending liability among themselves. This trading arrangement will encourage cost-reducing specialisation. For example, one bank may specialise in lending to small-scale industry, another to agriculture and a third to exporting industries. It will also allow some banks, such as the foreign banks and the newly emerging private banks, to not be involved in some types of priority sector lending if they so choose. But because such banks will have to 'buy' their lending obligation from other banks at a price, a level playing field will exist among them while reducing their costs.
2. Alternatively, the Reserve Bank can offer preferential treatment of priority loans in the form of a reduced cash reserve requirement or a rediscounting facility. The extent of preference could be varied to attain the desired level of priority lending. It could also be varied across various sub-categories within the priority sector depending upon the relative burden different categories impose; for instance, greater preferential treatment may be given for smaller loans since they involve a greater administrative cost. Such an approach is superior to the present quota approach which encourages loans to the largest enterprises meeting the priority sector requirements

because they involve the least administrative and risk costs for the banks.

While carrying on banking deregulation, the supervision of banks should be increased and banks required to maintain adequate loan–loss provisions and capital-to-loan ratios.[27] The Central Bank should ensure that the riskiness of the banks' loan portfolio is commensurate with its loan–loss provisions. Fortunately, steps in this direction have been initiated in India recently as a result of a major bank scam detected in April 1992.

V CONCLUSION

This chapter analysed the incentives created by the various policies of regulation and deregulation of the banking sector. The main findings are as follows.

Most of the regulations imposed on banks since 1969 have had undesirable effects. For example, restrictions on entry and expansion of private and foreign banks, and lack of competition among public banks (with uniform interest rates, spreads and service charges among nationalised banks being enforced by the Reserve Bank) have led to a steady decline in the efficiency, work culture and the quality of customer service at the banks. An excessively large amount of subsidised borrowing by the government has raised interest costs for other sectors and thus discouraged private investment. Similarly, directed lending to priority sectors at concessional rates of interest artificially swelled demand for such loans, some of it from fake borrowers. Ceilings on interest rates have created credit shortages leading to corruption in the sanctioning of loans.

At the same time, rapid and uncontrolled banking deregulation is not advisable. It has often led to very high real interest rates, and eventually financial crises, in many countries. Financial liberalisation should be undertaken *after* macroeconomic stabilisation has been achieved. Trade liberalisation should not accompany financial liberalisation; financial liberalisation should follow after the economy has adjusted to trade liberalisation or vice versa. Restrictions on international capital mobility should be removed *after* the interest rate deregulation has been completed and domestic interest rates have settled down to reasonable levels. Thus, a controlled and gradual approach to deregulation would be safer and more likely to yield beneficial results. Given that trade liberalisation has been largely negotiated and inflation rate is moderate, India has the right conditions to undertake further gradual liberalisation without much risk of a financial crisis.

Table 13.1
Deposits and Advances of Scheduled Commercial Banks in India 1989–93

	1988–89	*1989–90*	*1990–91*	*1991–92*	*1992–93*
Aggregate Deposits	140150	166959	192541	230758	267147
Net Bank Credit	79234	95132	109298	117443	142149
Credit-Deposit Ratio	.565	.570	.568	.509	.532

Sectoral deployment of Credit (per cent of net Bank Credit)

	1989	*1990*	*1991*	*1992*	*1993*
I.A Priority Sector Credit	43.2	42.4	39.3	38.7	35.0
i. Agriculture	17.6	17.4	15.3	15.5	14.0
ii. Small-scale Industries	16.6	16.30	15.7	15.5	14.0
iii. Other Priority Sector	9.0	8.7	8.3	7.7	7.0
I.B Export Credit	7.8	8.7	8.4	8.8	10.8
I.C Public Food Procurement Credit	0.97	2.11	4.12	3.98	4.74
Total Directed Credit (IA + IB + IC)	52	53.2	51.8	51.5	50.5
II.A Industry (Medium & Large)	40.6	40.2	40.7	40.1	41.2
II.B Wholesale Trade	6.0	5.8	5.4	5.2	4.9

Source: Reserve Bank of India Bulletin, various years.

Table 13.2
Fiscal Deficit and Pre-emption of Resources

Year	*Fiscal Deficit (Central Government)*	*Marginal Pre-emption (as on March 31, in per cent)*		
		CRR	*SLR*	*Total*
1980–81	6.2	6	34@	40
1981–82	5.4	7.75	35@	42.75
1982–83	6.0	7	35@	42
1983–84	6.3	19	35@	54
1984–85	7.5	19*	36	55*
1985–86	8.3	19*	37	56*
1986–87	9.0	19.5*	37	56.5*
1987–88	8.1	20	38	58
1988–89	7.8	21*	38	59*
1989–90	7.8	15	38	53
1990–91	8.4	15	38.5	53.5
1991–92	6.0	25	38.5	63.5

Notes: *In these years, the release of previously impounded balances implies a slightly lower marginal pre-emption than the face value shown here.
@ On gross Demand and Time Liabilities.
Source: Economic Survey, 1992–93 and RBI. Reproduced from Ministry of Finance (1993).

Table 13.3
Selected Interest Rates in India, 1970–1993

Year	*Deposit Rate (3 to 5 years)*	*Lending Rate*				*Inflation Rate**
		General	*Term Lending by Dev. Finance Institutions*	*Small Scale Industry*	*Exporters*	
1970–71	7.0	8.5–12.0	8.5	7.0–8.5		5.24%
1975–76	9.0	15.5	11.0	8.0–11.0	11.5	– 1.09%
1980–81	10.0	19.5	11.9–14	12.5–14.5	11.9–14	17.7%
1985–86	10.0	17.5	14	11.5–16.5	12.0–16.5	4.41%
1990–91	11.0	16.4 (min)	14	11.5–16.5	7.5–15.5	– 9.3%
1991–92	13.0	17–20 (")	18–20	7–15.5	15–24	13.74%
1992–93	12.0	17–19 (")			14–23	7.0%
1993–94	11.0	16.0 (")			11 (min)	

Notes: *Inflation Rate for the following year: Inflation Rate$_t$= $\{[CPL_{t+1} - CPL_t]/CPL_t\} \times 100$.
Source: Basic Statistics Relating to the Indian Economy, August 1993, Centre for Monitoring Indian Economy.

Table 13.4
Credit to Central Government as Percentage of Total Domestic Credit

Year	*India*	*Indonesia*	*Korea*	*Malaysia*	*Thailand*
1980	42.6	–51.1	7.8	2.5	24.7
1981	43.0	–81.5	11.0	9.2	25.9
1982	42.9	–61.6	10.9	12.6	28.5
1983	42.4	–44.6	9.6	9.9	24.2
1984	42.5	–67.0	8.9	9.4	24.0
1985	44.4	–61.4	8.2	3.1	22.5
1986	45.2	–42.0	8.0	4.8	23.3
1987	46.6	–23.9	5.3	8.2	20.1
1988	46.6	–17.6	2.6	6.1	12.7
1989	46.7	–14.8	0.5	6.1	5.7
1990	47.9	–12.5	–0.4	4.3	1.1
1991	49.9	–11.1	1.5	1.7	–4.9
1992	47.3	–12.4	1.7	3.8	–7.1
Average	45.2	–38.6	5.8	6.3	15.4

Source: International Monetary Fund, International Financial Statistics Yearbook 1991 & July 1994.

Table 13.5

Ex-Post Real@ Interest Rates on Short-Term Loans in Countries Experiencing Financial Liberalisation and Crisis

Countries	*1975*	*1976*	*1977*	*1978*	*1979*	*1980*	*1981*	*1982*	*1983*	*1984*	*1985*	*1986*	*1987*	*1988*	*1989*	*1990*	*1991*
Latin American Countries																	
Argentina		– 69.64	*L*74.64	– 11.25	– 11.57	– 3.10	32.58	*C*		25.97	563.16	– 10.18	– 22.53	– 83.33			
Chile	*L*16.0	64.3	87.88	39.56	19.97	22.95	38.26*C*	28.78	19.15*C*	5.84	8.29	8.22	20.57	3.54	7.84	22.23	11.21
Uruguay		*L*2.57	22.93	2.61	2.83	24.28	4.90	6.23*C*	24.68	6.37	10.33	19.03	20.72	11.94	141.88	– 39.82	50.12
East Asian Countries																	
Indonesia			0.69	– 6.13	– 7.64	– 2.89	– 0.45	– 2.48	*L*– 1.39	6.96	5.76	11.30	12.61	14.66	13.27*C*		
Korea	0.16	5.26	1.58	– 1.13	– 7.91	– 2.83	*L*9.63	8.05	7.52	7.36	7.00	6.78	2.63*C*	4.22	2.50		
Malaysia		3.54	2.92	3.71	0.77	– 1.77	*L*2.53	4.90	6.92	10.96	10.72	9.84*C*	6.11	4.31	4.29	2.66	
Philippines	2.59	1.91	4.34	– 4.70	– 3.56	0.82	4.63	7.36	*L*– 20.69	4.13	27.65	13.24	4.21*C*	4.82	5.85	1.74	13.01
Other Countries																	
Australia	– 1.80	– 1.66	2.40	1.22	0.00	0.81	1.60	4.00	*L*9.66	7.25	6.29	10.53	11.71	10.18	13.46	16.51*C*	
New Zealand			– 3.52	– 3.49	– 5.88	– 2.35	– 2.33	5.93	7.26	*L*– 2.55			13.56	10.69	8.10	11.44*C*	
Turkey				– 27.19	– 43.98	*L*– 7.84	3.41	3.54*C*	– 8.68	5.11	14.04*C*	9.92					
USA	2.01	0.33	– 0.76	– 2.00	– 0.73	*L*4.49	11.98	11.27	6.21*C*	8.19	7.92	4.44	4.04	4.29	5.24	13.50	6.65

Notes: @ Ex-Post Real Interest$_t$ = [(1 + Nominal Interest$_t$) (CPI$_{t+1}$ / CPI$_t$) – 1]

L Indicates the year of Liberalisation of interest rates on short-term loans (one year and shorter maturity).

C Indicates the year when major problems of loan default emerged (based primarily on information in World Bank, 1989, Chapter 5, World Bank, 1993, and Cho and Khatkhate, 1989).

Source: International Monetary Fund, International Financial Statistics Yearbook 1992, Washington DC: USA.

Cho and Khatkhate (1989); McKinnon (1988)[28] for Chile 1973–76.

Table 13.6

Inflation Rates and the Spread between Lending and Deposit Interest Rates, 1976–1988

Countries	*Average Inflation rate (Per cent)*	*Average @ Spread*
A. Countries with Hyper Inflation (above 100%)		
1. Argentina	473	248
2. Brazil	256	80
3. Israel*	132	146
Average	287	158
B. Countries with High Inflation (Between 20% and 100%)		
1. Chile	29.1	119.2
2. Uruguay	55.5	22.5
3. Mexico	58.2	6.4
4. Turkey	50.2	4.3
Average	48.2	13.1
C. Countries with Low Inflation (less than 5%)		
1. Japan	3.2	3.4
2. Germany	3.9	4.9
3.Singapore	3.1	2.7
4. Switzerland	3.0	1.1
Average	3.3	3.0

Notes: *For some countries for which data for some years was not available, the average is over a subset of these years.
@ Simple Arithmatic Average of the yearly numbers.
Source: IMF, International Financial Statistics Yearbook, 1991.

Table 13.7

GDP Growth Rates in Countries Experiencing Financial Liberalisation and Crisis

Countries	*1975*	*1976*	*1977*	*1978*	*1979*	*1980*	*1981*	*1982*	*1983*	*1984*	*1985*	*1986*	*1987*	*1988*	*1989*	*1990*	*1991*
Latin American Countries																	
Argentina	−0.7	−0.2	*L*6.2	−3.3	7.3	1.5	−5.7	−3.1C	3.7	1.8	−6.6	7.3	2.6	−1.9	−6.2	0.1	8.9
Chile	*L*−12.9	3.5	9.9	8.2	8.3	7.8	5.5C	−14.1	−0.7C	6.4	2.5	5.6	5.7	7.4	10.0	2.1	6.0
Uruguay	5.9	*L*4.0	1.2	5.3	6.2	6.0	1.9	−9.4	−5.9C	−1.1	1.5	8.9	7.9		1.3	0.9	2.9
East Asian Countries																	
Indonesia	5.0	6.9	8.8	7.8	6.3	9.9	7.9	2.2	*L*4.2	7.0	2.5	5.9	4.9	0.5	13.1C	7.1	6.6
Korea	7.1	12.9	10.1	9.7	7.6	−2.2	*L*6.7	7.3	11.8	9.4	6.9	12.4	12.0C	11.5	6.2	9.2	8.5
Malaysia	0.8	11.6	7.8	6.7	9.3	7.4	*L*6.9	5.9	6.3	7.8	−1.0	1.0C	5.4	8.9	8.7	9.8	
Philippines	6.4	8.0	6.1	5.5	6.3	5.2	3.2	3.6	*L*1.9	−7.6	−7.4	3.4	4.8C	6.3	6.0	2.7	−0.7
Other Countries																	
Australia	2.2	3.3	1.0	3.2	4.8	2.3	3.6	−0.5	*L*1.0	7.4	4.5	1.8	4.6	4.5	4.4	1.2C	−1.1
New Zealand	1.7	0.1	−2.7	−0.3	2.6	1.1	4.9	2.5	4.6	*L*5.2	−1.0	3.3	−0.8	1.2	−1.0	0.2C	−2.0
Turkey	8.0	8.1	3.6	3.0	−0.3	*L*−1.1	4.1	4.6C	3.3	6.0	5.1C	8.1	7.4	3.8	4.9	9.1	
USA	−1.1	5.1	4.6	4.8	2.8	*L*−0.6	1.6	−2.3	3.8C	6.0	2.9	2.8	3.0	4.0	2.4	1.1	−1.2

Notes: L Indicates the year of Liberalisation of interest rate on short term loans.

C Indicates the year when major problems of loan default emerged (See the World Bank, 1989, Chapter 5, World Bank, 1993, and Cho and Khatkhate, 1989).

Sources: International Monetary Fund, International Financial Statistics Yearbook 1992, Washington DC: USA.

Figure 13.1
Pattern of Real Interest Rates

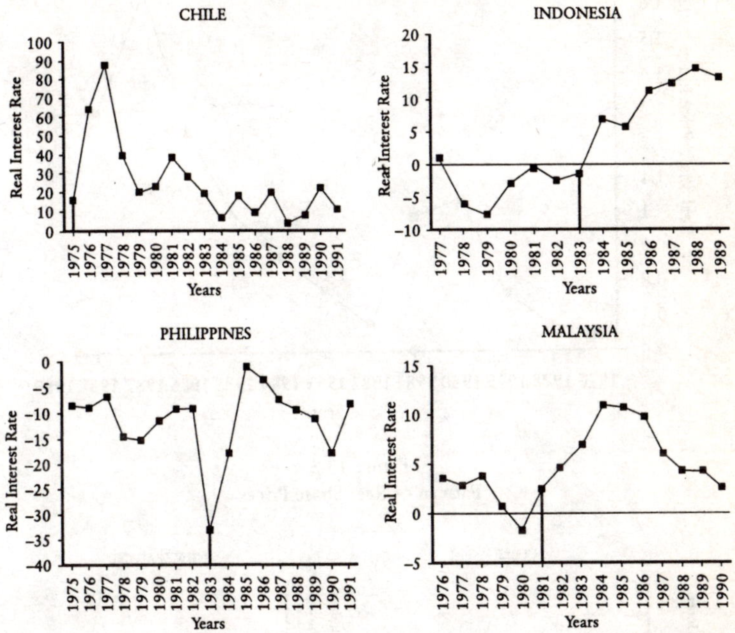

Notes: The vertical line in the graph denotes the year of interest rate deregulation for the concerned country.
Source: Table 1.

Figure 13.2
Australia: Pattern of Real Share Prices

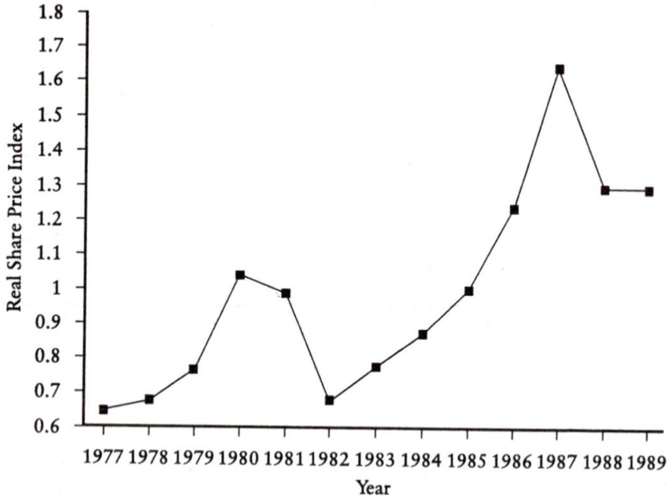

Figure 13.3
Pattern of Real Share Prices

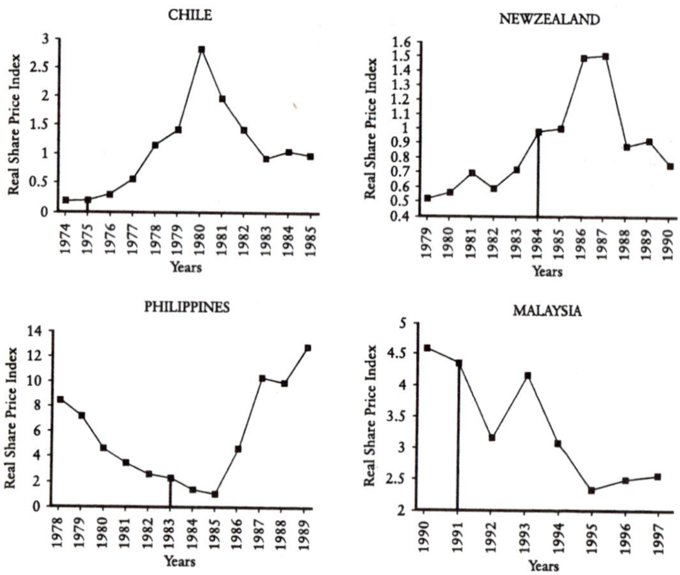

Notes: The vertical line denotes the year of interest rate deregulation for the concerned country.
Source: Based on data from IFC, Emerging Capital Markets Factbook, 1990, 1993.

Figure 13.4
Evolution of Total External Debt in Latin American Countries

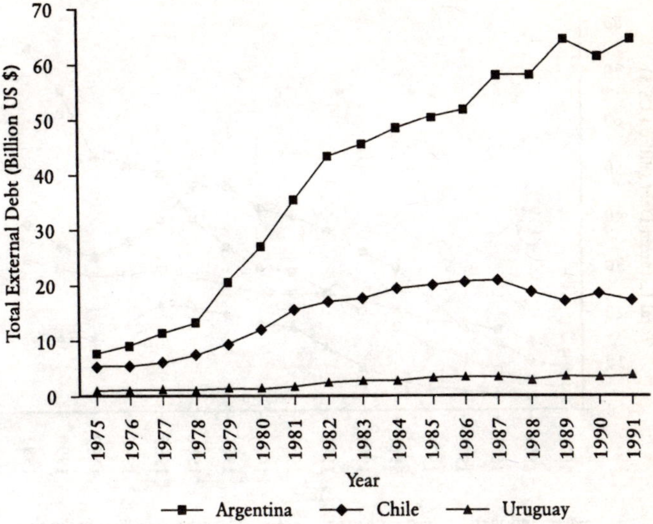

Figure 13.5
Evolution of Total External Debt in East Asian Countries

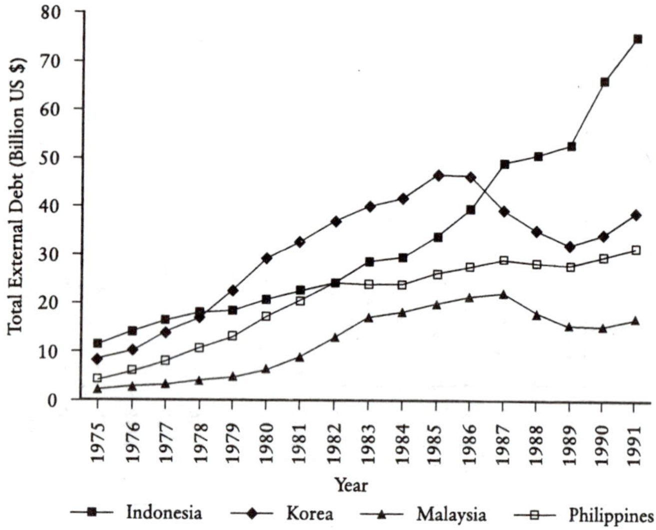

Notes: The vertical line denotes the year of liberalization of the interest rates for the concerned country.
Source: Based on data from the World Bank, World Debt Tables, 1994.

NOTES

1. Public banks refer to the banks nationalised since 1969 plus the State Bank of India group of banks which have always been owned by the government.
2. See, for example, Chapter IV of the Narasimham Committee Report, formally known as 'Report of the Committee on the Financial System', submitted to the Finance Minister of India in November, 1991. See also Ministry of Finance, 1993, 'Public Sector Banks and Financial Sector Reforms: Rebuilding for a Better Future'. Discussion Paper, Government of India, December.
3. Based on private interviews with Mr Kishore Chauker, Industrial Credit and Investment Corporation of India (ICICI) and several managers in the nationalised banks.
4. See, for example, Sandesara, J. C. 1988, 'Small-Scale Industrialisation: The Indian Experience', *Economic and Political Weekly*, 26 March.
5. See, for example, Keynes, J. M. 1936, *The General Theory of Employment Interest and Money*. London: Macmillan.

6. McKinnon, R. I. 1973, *Money and Capital in Economic Development*. Washington, DC: Brookings Institution; Shaw, E. 1973, *Financial Deepening in Economic Development*. New York: Oxford University Press.
7. The World Bank, 1989, *World Development Report*. Washington, DC: The World Bank; Fry, M. 1988, *Money Interest and Banking in Economic Development*. Baltimore: Johns Hopkins University Press; Gelb, A. H. 1989, 'Financial Policies, Growth, and Efficiency'. Working Paper No. WPS 202, Washington, DC: The World Bank. *The East Asian Miracle*. Washington, DC: The World Bank.
8. The World Bank, *World Development Report*, Table 2.3, 31.
9. Fry, *Money Interest*, and Gelb, 'Financial Policies'.
10. The World Bank, *The East Asian Miracle*.
11. See note 6.
12. See note 2.
13. Ibid.
14. Ibid.
15. See The World Bank, *World Development Report*, and Cho, Y. J. and D. Khatkhate, 1989, 'Lessons of Financial Liberalisation in Asia: A Comparative Study'. Discussion Paper No. 50, The World Bank, Washington, DC.
16. See Odagiri, H. and H. Yamawaki, 1990, 'The Persistence of Profits: International Comparison', in D. C. Mueller (ed.), *The Dynamics of Company Profits*. Cambridge: Cambridge University Press.
17. Note that the demand for credit for consumer durables, housing and shares is a demand for a certain 'stock' of credit and it can be very large. For example, if each resident wanted to borrow half a year's income, the total demand for loans would exceed the total amount of loanable funds available with the banks in most developing countries, since they typically have the M2/GDP ratio of less than 0.5.
18. Real share price index equals share price index divided by the consumer price index.
19. See note 18 above.
20. The share price rise in the Philippines seems to have been delayed until 1985 because of the great political uncertainty and turmoil in the last two years (1983–85) of President Marcos' presidency, which would have restrained many investors from investing in the share markets.
21. Also see Stiglitz, J. E. and A. Weiss, 1981, 'Credit Rationing in Markets With Imperfect Information', *American Economic Review*, 71(3): 913–27; and Cho, Y. J. 1986, 'Inefficiencies from Financial Liberalisation in the Absence of Well-Functioning Equity Markets', *Journal of Money Credit and Banking*, 18(2): 191–9.
22. See, for example, Silverberg, S. C. 1990, 'The Savings and Loan Problem in the United States'. Working Paper WPS 351, The World Bank, Washington, DC: and The World Bank, *World Development Report 1989*.
23. Some other forms of foreign capital inflows, such as foreign direct investment and allowing domestic firms to sell bonds and shares in the international capital markets, are not so costly. Countries such as Korea and Malaysia that have used these forms of foreign capital inflows the most have not suffered on this

account. See Agrawal for a detailed discussion of the relative merits of various forms of foreign capital inflows (Agrawal, P. 1994, 'Foreign Capital Inflows: Long Run Desirability and Short Run Management', *Productivity*, July–September).

24. However, it should be possible to gradually raise interest rate ceilings to yield interest rates close to the market levels.
25. Housing loans are allowed only for personal dwellings and are subject to modest ceilings.
26. When selling bank equity to the public, a low ceiling on the voting power of any individual shareholder should be maintained to minimise the take-over of banks by major industrial houses which may be undesirable because it would create excessive concentration of economic power in a few hands and create excessive risk, since such banks may lend mostly to firms belonging to the industrial group. See Agrawal, P. 1992, 'Financial Reforms', in V. Mishra, P. Agrawal, S. Gokarn and B. Saha (eds), *Policy Options for Economic Reform*. Bombay: Indian Merchant's Chamber and Indira Gandhi Institute of Development Research.
27. The Bureau of International Standards (BIS) recommends an 8 per cent capital-to-loan ratio.
28. McKinnon, R. I. 1988, Financial Liberalisation and Economic Development: A Reassessment of the Interest Rate Policies in Asia and Latin America, Occasional Paper No. 6, International Centre for Economic Growth, San Francisco, USA.

14

Labour Markets as Social Institutions in India

Mrinal Datta-Chaudhuri

> Wage rates and jobs are not exactly like other prices and quantities. They are much more deeply involved in the way people see themselves, think about their social status and evaluate whether they are getting a fair share out of the society. . .Social institutions define acceptable and unacceptable modes of behaviour in the weighty context like the labour market.[1]

Robert Solow described the labour market as a social institution. However, as Solow acknowledges, the idea is not new. Alfred Marshall, the great exponent of the principles of demand and supply, spoke of 'fair rates of wages' when he analysed the workings of the labour market in the 1920s.[2] Several other economists and social scientists working in the field of industrial relations have noted the importance of social norms in understanding the workings of the labour market.[3] In fact, empirical studies on industrial organisation clearly reveal widely differing characteristics in the workings of labour markets, even among the mature capitalist economies of Western Europe, North America and East Asia.[4] These differences have much to do with the varied historical experiences and cultural traditions of these societies. They manifest themselves in the workings of what Solow called 'norm-guided behaviour' or the determination of wage rates and labour standards in different economies.[5] Moreover, in many cases non-market institutions have developed that now influence the workings of the labour market directly. The case of the economy-wide apprentice programme, established in Germany, is particularly notable. This programme not only helps in the development of required skills by on-the-job training, it also creates a formal link between job-seeking workers and potential employers.[6]

The purpose of this chapter is to discuss the emergence of institutions—that is, social, political and legal arrangements—that govern labour use in the modern sector of the Indian economy. These institutions have developed in response to the demands of modernisation and industrial development of the economy in the twentieth century, particularly after Indian Independence in 1947. The political process, which gave independent India its constitution as well as the legal and administrative framework for governance, also played a decisive role in the creation of labour market institutions. This process also established new norms of behaviour in the workings of these institutions. However, the manner in which these institutions have evolved has introduced a new set of rigidities that are often inimical to productivity growth, skill formation and learning processes. This is particularly true in the public sector; this sector accounts for a substantial fraction of modern manufacturing industries, financial institutions and facilities in India such as transport, communication and power.

Economists and policymakers understandably attach a great deal of importance to capital formation in the development strategy of a backward economy. However, since the publication of Solow's seminal work,[7] both theorists and empirical researchers working on the processes of economic growth have come to believe that it is not so much the pace of capital accumulation or the expansion in the quantitative base of the factors of production, but the ability of an economic organisation to squeeze more out of given resources that explains much of the performance of a growing economy. Exogenous technical progress alone, however, does not explain all the growth in productivity. The ability of workers and managers to adapt to new and efficient ways of performing their tasks is also important. Contractual arrangements for hiring, firing and wage determination, by creating incentives for workers to perform well, in turn influence this learning process.[8] This is how labour market institutions come to play an important role in influencing the pace of economic development.

The agrarian and the informal sectors of the economy, where most people in India find gainful employment, have by and large remained outside the reach of modern labour laws and labour market institutions. Therefore, the focus of this chapter is on the organised sector of the Indian economy. The organised sector employs only about 8 per cent of the total labour force in India, but consists of all establishments in the public sector and all non-agricultural establishments in the private sector employing ten or more workers. The labour market in the organised sector is governed through legislative, administrative and political measures. The main thrust of economic reforms pursued in India today is directed toward this sector. Therefore, the success of reforms crucially depends on the possibilities of restructuring it, particularly its practices regarding the use of labour and other inputs.

It will be argued here that the institutional framework in which hiring, firing and the working conditions of workers and managers are determined in India has greatly influenced the performance and growth of Indian industries. This framework has discouraged employers from adopting more labour-intensive technology in organised industries, and has reduced the incentives for the workers to improve their productivity. Consequently, the industrial development of India during the last four decades has been accompanied by low rates of growth in total factor productivity. In fact, compared to the fast-growing economies of East Asia, productivity growth in India has been quite dismal.[9] Research work with plant-level data has revealed that the amount of time taken by Indian workers and their managers to master new technology has sometimes been even higher than the economic life of new machines.[10]

After this introduction, the paper proceeds as follows: Section I presents a brief description of the Indian labour markets. Section II outlines the evolution of the legal, administrative and political framework that governs labour use in the organised sector. Section III discusses the Industrial Disputes Act, which is the single most important piece of legislation affecting labour use in organised industries. Section IV discusses the process of wage determination in the organised sector. The chapter concludes with some remarks on the impact of labour market institutions on Indian industries and on the importance of the reform of these institutions in the context of the ongoing economic reforms in India.

I THE INDIAN LABOUR MARKET

Compiling employment statistics for the Indian economy is difficult. This is because about two-thirds of the Indian labour force finds employment in agriculture and rural industries.[11] There is no official machinery for taking a census of the labour force and employment in the rural economy. Moreover, many people are self-employed. In these cases, the duration of work and even the intensity of efforts vary considerably, creating a syndrome of disguised unemployment. In such a situation, there are difficult conceptual problems in identifying the employment status of a person at any point of time. Therefore, estimates of rural employment are dependent on variable concepts and definitions used in compiling employment statistics.[12]

Updated information is available for the organised sector, that is, for all the public sector units, for the non-agricultural private sector units that employ at least ten workers and for the plantations. In the public sector the nature and the duration of employment is easy to measure, because the agencies of the government are required to specify clearly the terms and the conditions of work for their employees. Plantations and the non-agricultural private sector units that employ ten or more workers come in turn under the Factory Act laws governing trade, transport or services. Accordingly, they are required to file annual returns on the various aspects of their activities, including the number of workers of different categories employed by them, to the appropriate regulatory authorities of the government. The Ministry of Labour, Government of India compiles and publishes these data.[13]

For the rest of the economy, there are no censuses to provide complete information. One necessarily needs to rely on sample surveys. The most reliable and comprehensive surveys are those conducted every five years by the National Sample Survey (NSS) of the Government of India. These are two-stage, stratified random samples of households in India. The first stage of the survey picks up a sample of villages or settlements, and the second stage, households within these settlements. Much of India's economic statistics, such as those relating to consumer behaviour, demographic characteristics, employment and earnings, comes from the NSS.

The data presented in Table 14.1 are based on these two sources. The employment statistics relating to the organised sector are based on complete enumeration and compiled by the Ministry of Labour,

Government of India. The data relating to the various unorganised sectors of the economy are estimates based on the sample surveys conducted by the NSS. The totals are the sums of census information and survey estimates.

Table 14.1 indicates that out of the total labour force of 302 million, only about twenty-four million are employed in the organised sector of the economy. This is about 8 per cent of the labour force. Of these twenty-four million employed in the organised sector, nearly seventeen million (or about 70 per cent) are in the public sector. Within the public sector more than half of the people are employed in the service sector, which consists mainly of public administration and defence services. Of the 7.3 million people working in the organised private sector, about 4.4 million (or 60 per cent) are employed in manufacturing. Table 14.1 also reveals that of the various industry groups only mining, quarrying and electricity generation belong predominantly to the organised sector; the rest are predominantly unorganised. Further, over two-thirds of the Indian labour force is engaged in agriculture, which, except for the plantations in the organised sector, consists essentially of peasant farming.

The Indian development strategy since Independence has emphasised the importance of industrialisation and modernisation. This development strategy, spelled out clearly in the successive five-year plans since the early 1950s, has assigned special roles to modern large-scale industries, particularly the industries belonging to the public sector. These industries were supposed to play the role of the 'leading sector' in India's quest for growth and development.[14] The organised sector in Table 14.1 more or less represents this 'leading sector'. It is clear that even four decades after the initiation of this development process, the organised sector has failed to provide gainful employment to even a tenth of India's labour force. An attempt is made in the subsequent sections to show that the labour market institutions in the organised sector have been inimical to the growth of an efficient, labour-intensive industrial economy in India.

II EVOLUTION OF INDIAN LABOUR LAWS

The modalities of labour use in the organised sector in India are dictated primarily by the state, not by the market or by the results of collective bargaining between unionised workers and the management. The state plays a dominant role through labour laws, labour judiciary and administrative officers to 'administer social justice keeping in view the power position and susceptibilities of workers...to eventually lead to a just industrial society'.[15] These arrangements have come to be established during the last fifty years through the workings of India's political process. The evolution of these arrangements is outlined next.

The first legislative actions to control the working conditions in factories and mines were taken by the British administration in colonial India in the last quarter of the nineteenth century. Before that time, the state did not interfere in the working of the factories and mines in India. The British initiated a series of regulatory measures governing child labour, working hours, safety and sanitation beginning with the Factory Act of 1881 and the Mines Act of 1923. The objectives of these acts were to (*a*) specify minimum standards for safety, sanitation and the length of working hours, particularly for women and children, and (*b*) to enable the government to appoint inspectors for factories and mines who could enforce these standards. The major legislative reforms affecting the conditions of work in factories and mines came, however, after 1947, with Indian Independence.

The Factory Act of 1881 came in response to the criticism of the working conditions in Indian factories voiced by the urban intelligentsia in India and their sympathisers in England. There was no organised working class movement in the country to demand such reforms. In fact, there was no legal basis for freedom of association in British India at that time. Nonetheless, the first Indian labour organisation, the Amalgamated Society of Railway Servants, came into existence in 1887. The workers of the Assam-Bengal Railways resorted to strikes for higher wages in 1921–22. This was the first industrial strike in India, which was easily crushed.

However, many of the activists of the Indian independence movement were active among workers in factories and mines. In 1920, they organised the first nation-wide trade union organisation, the All-India Trade Union Congress (AITUC), with affiliated unions all over the country. It is difficult to know the extent of support enjoyed by the AITUC, because union activities were not legal at that time. But it became legal with the passage of the Indian

Trade Unions Act of 1926, which allowed any seven workers to combine in a trade union. By the year 1929, AITUC had fifty-one affiliated unions with a membership of 151,000.

During the colonial period the trade union movement became an important platform for the larger independence movement in India. The entire labour movement remained under the umbrella of the Indian National Congress, a political organisation that led the independence movement. At that time unions were organised as plant-level unions with regional and national affiliation with larger bodies. The leaders of these unions came from urban middle-class intelligentsia associated with the independence movement. For example, Mahatma Gandhi was the organising spirit behind the textile workers' union in Ahmedabad and Jawaharlal Nehru became the President of AITUC in 1929. Consequently, the ideological differences and group rivalries that ran through the body politic determined, to a considerable extent, the organisational characteristics and strategic behaviour of the labour movement in India.

At the time of Independence in 1947, as ideological differences surfaced in the Indian National Congress, the labour movement started to fragment. First, the communists and then the socialists left the Indian National Congress to form separate parties. Various other left-wing groups also splintered away. Since these political groups were important in the labour movement, the labour movement itself experienced successive splits.

Today practically every political party has its trade union wing. Given the flexibility of Indian party structure the number of trade union federations and their respective influence vary considerably over time. In 1989, the Ministry of Labour began an exercise to prepare a register of existing trade union organisations in the country. They listed eight major trade union federations: Indian National Trade Union Congress (INTUC), All-India Trade Union Congress (AITUC), Centre of Indian Trade Unions (CITU), Hind Mazdoor Sabha (HMS), Bharatiya Mazdoor Savha (BMS), Hind Mazdoor Kamgar Party (HMKP), United Trade Union Congress (UTUC), United Trade Union Congress Lenin Sarani (UTUCLS) and National Labour Organisation (NLO), besides a number of small independent unions.[16] Due to the party affiliations, politics at national and regional levels finds its reflection in the trade union activity.

The large number of trade unions has led to inter-union rivalry for members. This rivalry manifests itself in labour militancy. In 1950–75 almost 30 per cent of the industrial disputes in India could be attributed to the problems of union recognition and inter-union rivalry. As Ramaswamy (1984) says: A union has to call an occasional strike to show that it is active in the cause of its members. Without such periodic displays of militant action, it may find it difficult to preserve its following.[17]

Since trade unions are linked to political parties, it is not surprising that narrow partisan considerations, an inevitable feature of politics, has also bedevilled the legal framework regarding the recognition of a union at the plant level. For example, in 1950 the ruling party opposed successfully the introduction of the secret ballot as a method of union recognition on the grounds that it would introduce bribery and poll-rigging. It favoured a system based on the verification of membership through an impartial agency, such as the Labour Department of the Government. The fact that the Congress Party then controlled not only the Central Government, but also the governments at every state capital, was not unrelated to the position it took. As a result, the Labour Department acquired an important position in industrial relations.

Trade unions have been able to steer the evolution of labour legislation in India. The Constitution of the Indian Republic and the various pieces of legislation enacted in the Parliament and the State Assemblies after 1947 tried to uphold the rights of the workers. Since it is difficult to make the laws reach the unorganised sector, the primary beneficiaries from these legislative actions are workers employed in the organised sector.

The behaviour of labour unions and the mechanism of collective bargaining vary considerably even among the developed OECD countries, from decentralised bargaining as in the United States to highly centralised bargaining as in the Nordic countries of Europe. In India, the workers in the organised sector constitute a small fraction of the country's labour force, but the historical association of their unions with the political parties places them in a strategic position. Therefore, the labour movement has found it convenient to operate through the political process with legislative and administrative measures to further their collective goals. How exactly the trade union power shows in the current labour legislation will be discussed next.

III THE INDUSTRIAL DISPUTES ACT (IDA)

The single most important piece of legislation that governs the relationship between the worker and his employer is the Industrial Disputes Act (IDA) of 1947. This act applies to establishments employing fifty or more workers in the organised sector. It confers on the state the power to regulate labour–management relations. In most countries, the state enters the labour–management relationship upon the breakdown of bipartite bargaining. In India, the state assumes the role of the arbiter in lieu of a bargained relationship. According to Ramaswamy (1984), 'the state occupies the centre of the stage. The legal framework of industrial relations is such as to inhibit the growth of voluntary relationship and foster dependence on the state. The state is often forced to play the role, not of a mediator, although it may be so labelled, but of an arbitrator'.[18]

The role of the state as a regulator of labour–management relations has its origin in Section 81A of the Defence of India Rules announced by the British administration in India during the Second World War. These rules armed the government with powers to interfere in labour–management relations. Under their provisions, the government could conciliate in industrial disputes, and if conciliation failed, compel the parties to submit their case to arbitration. The obvious objective of this measure was to maintain industrial peace during the war. When the Defence of India Rules lapsed, these emergency measures of the war years were incorporated into the IDA in 1947. Perhaps, with the various urgent problems faced by the new government at the time of Independence (with partition, religious riots, refugee influx), they found it prudent not to disturb the existing arrangements in too many areas.

The implementation of the provisions of IDA was left to the labour departments of the central and state governments. Once the labour department decides that a particular dispute merits its attention, it sets in motion a process of conciliation. If the process of conciliation fails, the conciliator is required under Section 12(4) of IDA to submit a general report outlining the nature of the dispute, and a confidential report conveying his recommendation regarding adjudication to the government. If the parties fail to agree on voluntary arbitration, then the Ministry of Labour refers the dispute to the labour judiciary for adjudication. Trade unions prefer the adjudication process because the ministries and the labour judiciary, as well as the appellate courts, are expected to be sympathetic to the cause of workers.[19]

In the Statement of Objects and Reasons of Amending IDA in 1982 it was stated: 'a model grievances redressal procedure had been commended for adoption. But this voluntary arrangement has not proved effective. It is therefore proposed to make it obligatory for every industrial establishment employing 100 or more workmen to set up a time-bound grievance redressal procedure'. This procedure has paved the way for what Ramaswamy (1984) calls 'ministerial intervention' or 'political intervention'.[20] In these cases, a minister gets involved in a dispute in the guise of a conciliator interested in settling the case. Since a minister has enormous powers to reward and punish the parties to the dispute, his intervention effectively assumes the character of an imposed solution.

In 1950, the Government of India made an attempt at replacing IDA with two new bills: the Labour Relations Bill and the Trade Unions Bill. The goal of these bills was to encourage labour and management to become self-reliant so that state intervention could be dispensed with. Three of the four trade union federations in existence at that time opposed these bills and successfully lobbied for retaining the existing system. As mentioned earlier, the labour unions felt that with the active involvement of the state and the political process, they would be in a stronger bargaining position vis-à-vis their employers. According to the INTUC, the federation of trade unions affiliated with the ruling Congress Party because, 'only a system of state intervention would ensure the legitimate interests of labor'.[21]

The paramount concern of Indian workers, and thus of their trade unions, relates to the question of job security.[22] Workers and their unions fight for higher wages and bonus payments, but they also fight for job security. Industrial disputes over wages and bonus payments are classified as those due to 'economic causes'. Disputes arising from dismissals, retrenchments or disciplinary actions against individual workers are classified as disputes due to 'non-economic causes'. Between 1951 and 1975, the percentage of disputes arising from non-economic causes varied from 49 to 63.8 per cent. Trade unions fight bitterly even against the imposition of fines and suspensions, because these could go into the building up of a dossier against a worker and eventually be used in a tribunal to get the worker dismissed. According to Ramaswamy, 'Many Union leaders are of the view that there is practically no offence which merits dismissal. A part of the reason for this union condonation of misconduct is humanitarian. A far more important reason is fear of rival union propaganda. A union which accepts punishment to a defaulter is certain to be dubbed a management stooge'.[23]

Due to the pressures from trade unions, IDA itself was amended in 1976 and 1982. According to the 1976 amendment of IDA, if a firm employs 300 or more workers, then the workers cannot be laid off or retrenched without the permission of the government. The 1982 amendment of IDA made this provision applicable to all firms employing 100 or more workers.

Three parts of the amended IDA are of crucial importance to industrial relations. These are Section 9A, and Chapters V-A and V-B. Section 9A stipulates that an employer must give three weeks' notice in writing to the worker of any change in his working conditions. These changes include (*a*) changes in shift work, (*b*) changes in grade classification, (*c*) changes in rules of discipline, (*d*) a technological change that may affect the demand for labour, and (*e*) changes in employment, occupation, process or department. The worker, of course has the right to object to these changes, leading to an industrial dispute with all its implications in terms of time and costs. This provision obviously makes it difficult for an industrial firm to respond quickly to technological changes or changes in its market environment.

Chapter V-A requires an establishment employing fifty or more workers to give a worker (*a*) half pay for forty-five days in case of a layoff (Section 25C), (*b*) thirty days' notice and fifteen days' pay for every year of work in case of retrenchment (Section 25P), and (*c*) in case of a closure for the sale of an establishment the employer must fulfil the same condition as for retrenchment unless his successor takes on these obligations (Sections 25FF and 25FFF). If the employer had the money to pay the workers, even if the firm were loss-making, the question of closure or sale of the firm would not arise. In such a situation the unit is usually declared sick and is allowed to continue functioning on the basis of government subsidies.[24]

The most onerous provision of IDA is Chapter V-B. It states that an establishment employing 100 or more workers must gain a prior permission from the government for layoff, retrenchment or closure. Needless to say, government permission is seldom given. This last provision may sound strange to many outside observers. In fact the only country other than India that has enacted similar laws requiring prior permission of the government before layoffs and retrenchment is Zimbabwe.[25]

It is evident from various High Court and Supreme Court judgements that these laws have acquired over the years a certain measure of moral legitimacy in India. For example, in 1990 a five-judge bench of the Supreme Court denied the management of the Delhi Transport Corporation the discretionary right to retire workers found unsuitable for specific duties.[26] In 1992, a judge on the Calcutta High Court thought that if another private party took over a bankrupt private firm, there would be no guarantee that it would not itself go bankrupt in the future. Therefore, he directed the Government of West Bengal to take over the firm and run it with the existing workers.[27] One cannot fail to notice a similarity between this case and a judgement involving child custody. Paternalistic concern for complete job security of a worker seems to have greater legitimacy than the questions of economic viability of an enterprise.

In an insightful essay, a former Chief Justice of a High Court, Justice Mehta, analysed a large number of important judgements given by the various High Courts and the Supreme Court of India on matters relating to the termination of service by employers. He made the following observations:

> Some judges are overwhelmed by the view that the only object and purpose of the Industrial Disputes Act is to take a view favourable only to labour, ignoring other facts and circumstances as also the necessity of preserving industrial peace. It is sometimes forgotten that the problem confronting industrial adjudication is to promote two fold objectives: (1) security of employment of the workers; and (2) preservation of industrial peace and harmony so that industry can prosper and employment can increase. Any lopsided view, that to favour labour is the only goal of the statute is counterproductive in as such as it ultimately harms the cause of labour itself.[28]

An economist will easily agree with Justice Mehta that excessive concern for job security can be a powerful deterrent to the growth of employment in the economy. It seems, however, that the judicial and the political fraternities in India are prepared to promote job security for few at the cost of job prospects for many.

IV WAGE DETERMINATION IN THE ORGANISED SECTOR

In the organised private sector, salaries and other benefits are determined by the process of collective bargaining between the management and the labour unions. By and large, collective bargaining in India is a decentralised process. In most cases, the management of an enterprise negotiates with the union representing its workers. In some cases, such as the tea plantations of northeast India, or the jute mills around Calcutta, or the coal fields of eastern India before their nationalisation in 1973, there is often industry-wide collective bargaining between the representative associations of the industry and the labour unions. The government, as mentioned earlier, often intervenes in this process either formally or informally, as it has the power under IDA to do so.

In the public sector, the government is both the owner and the regulator. The state-owned enterprises in India do not function as autonomous entities; they are usually run by ministries and departments of the government almost like other administrative departments of the government. In the public sector, wages, salaries, bonus payments and other conditions of work are not determined at the enterprise level. These are determined centrally, keeping in view the parity among government employees in the different sectors.

There is an established procedure for the determination of salaries and other benefits for the employees of the Central Government in public administration, posts and telegraph and the railways. Periodically, the Government of India appoints a Pay Commission.[29] Members of the commission are usually retired judges, members of the Parliament, senior civil servants and academics. The commission holds hearings, solicits opinions and makes recommendations 'having regards among other relevant factors to the prevailing pay structure and retirement benefits, economic conditions in the country, the resources of the Central Government and the demand thereon such as those on account of economic and social development, defence and national security and requirement of some fiscal management'.[30]

The award of the Pay Commission for the Central Government employees becomes the reference point for wage determination in the rest of the public sector, such as the state governments, universities, financial institutions and the industrial and commercial undertakings. For example, the University Grants Commission sets up its own expert committee, which in a similar fashion determines the salary structure of the people employed in Indian universities. A professor or a lecturer is placed on the same scale of salaries irrespective of where he or she is employed.

For the public sector industries the apex body is the Bureau of Public Enterprises (BPE) of the Ministry of Finance, Government of India. BPE sends guidelines for wage settlement to all administrative ministries, setting down norms to be followed in determining basic salaries and the various categories of benefits for different classes of employees. Although individual enterprises technically have the right to offer financial incentives to their employees, BPE strongly discourages such actions. For example, in 1984, BPE sent to all public sector undertakings a circular, which read as follows: 'It has, however, been brought to the notice of the Government that some public sector enterprises have concluded additional or supplementary agreements apart from the main agreements/pay revision in respect of salaries or fringe benefits of the executives. This is not in order. It has to be appreciated that liberalisation of any fringe benefits or revision of the scales pay through separate agreements has serious financial implications and as such requires approval of the Government'.[31]

Mathur analysed the labour standards prevailing in eighteen private and public sector industrial enterprises in India. It is informative to quote him on certain aspects of industrial relations prevailing in one of the best known public sector industrial enterprises in India, Bharat Heavy Electricals Ltd. (BHEL). BHEL is a multiplant conglomerate that produces a wide variety of electrical and electronic goods. Mathur's findings have an important bearing on the nature of the task involved in India's current efforts at economic reform. Mathur (1991: 151–153) observed:

> The centralised bargaining structure for wage negotiations taking all of BHEL units into consideration did not result in any differences in wages between BHEL workers in different units although their financial health varies considerably. Further, the bargain limits are set by the Bureau of Public Enterprises to

ensure parity in wage levels and structures in public enterprises across industries and enterprises.... This has also resulted in the perception that sales are a responsibility of the Government, so are employee costs'.

He goes on to say:

In a recent initiative, the Government has signed Memoranda of Understanding with several public enterprises in 1989 aimed at providing a higher degree of autonomy in decisionmaking. However, this autonomy does not extend to determination of pay and employment levels commensurate with what the consumer is willing to pay in free market conditions. Nor would the enterprise like the freedom from the Government, because so many numbers were employed in the first place due to the Governments' policy of providing employment, one of the stated objectives at the time of establishing public enterprise in the 1960's. In fact, pressure from BHEL executives and officers is in the opposite direction for terms and conditions identical with the Central Government employees.[32]

V ECONOMIC IMPLICATIONS OF THE LABOUR MARKET INSTITUTIONS

What are the economic implications of India's labour laws? It turns out that these labour laws, or more generally the norms of industrial relations in the organised sector of the Indian economy, have created a small privileged class of labour aristocracy, and constrained the growth of employment. In the 1980s the employment in medium-sized and large industries in India remained stagnant even though output and investments of these industries grew at relatively high rates. The Census Sector of the Annual Survey of Industries (ASI) indicates that the value added by these industries grew at the average rate of 7.4 per cent per year between 1980–81 and 1990–91, whereas employment declined at the average rate of (–) 0.6 per cent per year.[33]

This decline in employment during the last decade is partly traceable to the 1976 and 1982 amendments to the Industrial Disputes Act. If an employer is required to obtain the prior permission of the government before laying off a worker, and if he knows that it is impossible to get that permission, he will try to avoid getting into such a rigid and inflexible commitment. He would buy machines instead of hiring a permanent worker, or he would try to perform the job with casual workers or by contracting out work to small enterprises that are not covered by stringent regulations. Goswami shows that employers, like the powerloom industry, have used all these options.[34] According to ASI, the share of the casual workers in the total employment more than doubled from 4.6 per cent in 1980–81 to 10 per cent in 1986–87. Ramaswamy has also found micro level evidence of these phenomena in India.[35] He describes the emerging phenomenon of labour contractors who hire men who do work on the premises of the employer but are not deemed to be his employees. This phenomenon is observed in the capital-intensive fertiliser and chemical industries for packing and storing. Fallon and Lucas report that among the larger Indian plants, the decline in employment is estimated to be largest in industries where the coverage of IDA(V-B) is more extensive, private ownership dominates and there are fewer union members. They did not find any comparable reduction in labour demand in small scale plants uncovered by job security regulations.[36]

IDA introduces economic inefficiencies in two ways: it introduces undesirable automation and thereby reduces employment opportunities; and it increases the resource costs of domestic outputs by sacrificing scale economies. Subcontracting certain operations to small firms sometimes introduces economic inefficiency by sacrificing scale economies. In some cases, as in powerloom industries, inefficient techniques are introduced only in order to evade the rigidities introduced by the labour laws. Moreover, the substitution of permanent workers by casual employees has also the negative dynamic impact on the growth of productivity by discouraging firm-specific learning.

There is some indirect evidence to suggest that the organised private sector has sometimes been able to evade the legal requirements of IDA and restructure its technological and managerial practices.[37] But the cost of overcompensating the affected workers, in the face of opposition from their unions, may have been quite high. Stringent labour laws are proving to be serious barriers to direct foreign investments in the industrial sector.[38] During 1991–94, the flow of foreign investments to India has gone up perceptibly, but the preferred avenue for this investment has been the financial sector rather than manufacturing industries.[39] The fear of not being able to correct mistakes or to alter production plans in response to market signals due to imposed inflexibilities in labour use is a serious deterrent to investments in manufactures.

The reform of labour laws will primarily help the organised private sector. For efficient manpower use in the public sector, more than the reform of the labour laws is necessary. The prevailing practice of letting the Bureau of Public Enterprises (BPE) determine uniform norms of labour use for all enterprises does not allow individual enterprises to seek efficiency in their use of labour and other inputs. These enterprises can operate in a market environment only if their management has greater control over their own commercial activities.

Economic reform programmes everywhere tend to give overwhelming importance to restoring macroeconomic stability and removing barriers to foreign trade. India's current effort towards economic reform also follows this strategy. The basic assumption behind such a strategy is that with price stability and foreign competition, the supply side of the domestic economy will automatically adjust to the norms of efficient industrial progress. The analysis here, however, suggests that without a direct attempt at institutional reforms—particularly of labour laws and of public sector management—current liberalisation efforts may not induce efficient industrial growth in India.

Table 14.1
The Structure of India's Workforce, 1983 (in thousands)

Industry Group	*Total*	*Organised Sector*			*Share of the Organised Sector in Industry (Per cent)*
		Public	*Private*	*Total*	
Agriculture	206,128	498	810	1,308	0.006
Mining & Quarrying	1,829	927	113	1,040	56.86
Manufacturing	32,435	1,717	4,423	6,190	19.08
Electricity	850	732	39	771	90.70
Construction	6,785	1,120	66	1,186	17.47
Trade	19,208	124	276	400	2.08
Transport	7,554	2,864	57	2,921	38.67
Services	26,848	8,895	1,503	10,398	38.73
Total	301,637	16,877	7,287	24,214	7.99

Source: Tendulkar, S. D. and K. Sundaram, 1992, 'Data on the Indian Economy', (mimeo), Delhi School of Economics: Delhi.

NOTES

1. Solow, R. M. 1957, 'Technical Change and the Aggregate Production Function', *Review of Economics and Statistics*, 39 (August): 312–320.
2. Marshall, A. 1925, 'A Fair Rate of Wages', in A. C. Pigou (ed.), *Memorials of Alfred Marshall*. London: Macmillan.
3. For references to studies in various social science disciplines on the importance of social norms in wage determination, see Akerlof, G. A. 1982, 'Labour Contracts as Partial Gift Exchange', *Quarterly Journal of Economics*, 97(4): 543–569; Pigors, P. and C. Myers, 1977, *Personnel Administration*. New York: McGraw-Hill; Goldthorpe, J. H., D. Lockwood, F. Bechhofer and J. Platt, 1968, *The Affluent Worker: Industrial Attitudes and Behaviour* (Cambridge Studies in Sociology 1). Cambridge: Cambridge University Press; Hirschman, A. O. 1970, *Exit, Voice and Loyalty*. Cambridge, Massachusetts: Harvard University Press; Cain, G. G. 1976, 'The Challenge of Segmented Labour Market Theory to the Orthodox Theory', *Journal of Economic Literature*, 14(4): 1215–1257; and Piore, M. J. 1983, 'Labour Market Segmentation: To What Paradigm Does it Belong?', *American Economic Review*, Papers and Proceedings of AEA, 73(2): 249–265.
4. See, for example, Akoki, M., ed. 1984, *The Economic Analysis of the Japanese Firm*. Amsterdam: North-Holland; Akoki, M. 1988, *Information Incentives and Bargaining in the Japanese Economy*, Cambridge: Cambridge University Press; Koike, K. 1990, 'Intellectual Skill and the Role of Employees as Constituent Members of Large Firms in Contemporary Japan', in M. Aoki, B. Gustafsson and O. E. Williamson (eds), *The Firm as a Nexus of Treaties*. London: Sage Publications; Calmfors, L., ed. 1990, *Wage Formation and Macroeconomic Policy in the Nordic Countries*. Oxford: SNS Forlage and Oxford University Press; Gordon, R. J. 1987, 'Why US Wages and Employment Behaviour Differ From That in Britain and Japan', *Economic Journal*, 92(365): 13–44; Yamamura, K. and Y. Yasuba, eds, 1987, *The Political Economy of Japan: Volume One, Domestic Transformation*. Stanford: Stanford University Press; Bain, G., ed. 1983, *Industrial Relations in Britain*. Oxford: Blackwell; Lane, C. 1990, 'Vocational Training, Employment Relations and New Production Concepts in Germany: Some Lessons for Britain', *Industrial Relations Journal*, 21(4): 247; and Williamson, O. E., M. L. Wachter and J. E. Harris, 1975, 'Understanding the Employment Relation: The Analysis of Idiosyncratic Exchange', *Bell Journal of Economics*, 6(1): 250–278.
5. See Solow, R. M. 1990, *The Labour Market as a Social Institution*. Oxford: Blackwell, 71.
6. See Lane, 'Vocational Training'.
7. Since the publication of Solow (see note 1 above), there has been a large volume of empirical research on this all over the world. For an illustration of findings for the OECD countries see Denison, E. F. 1967, *Why Growth Rates Differ: Post-War Experiences in Nine Western Countries*, Washington, DC: Brookings Institution. A similar work for the so-called Asian tigers was done by Chen, E. K. Y. 1977, 'Factor Inputs, Total Factor Productivity and Economic Growth: The Asian Case', *Developing Economies*, 15(2): 121–143. For an example of recent work on India

see Ahluwalia, I. J. 1992, *Productivity and Growth in Indian Manufacturing*. New Delhi: Oxford University Press.

8. Stiglitz, J. E. 1987, 'Learning to Learn, Localised Learning and Technical Progress', in P. Dasgupta and P. Stoneman (eds), *Economic Policy and Technical Performance*. Cambridge: Cambridge University Press.
9. Chen (see note 7) computed Total Factor Productivity (TFP) for the four fast-growing developing economies of East Asia for the period 1960–70. According to his computations, the annual percentage rate of growth of TFP for Hong Kong was 2.03; for Singapore, 3.34; for South Korea, 3.08 and for Taiwan, 3.7. Ahluwalia (see note 7) computed the growth rate of TFP for Indian industries for 1959–79, which was (–) 0.3.
10. Desai, A. 1980, 'The Origin and Direction of Industrial R&D in India', *Research Policy*, 9(1): 74–96; Desai, A. 1984, 'The Slow Rate of Industrialisation: A Second Look', *Economic and Political Weekly*, 1 August.
11. In 1983, about 206 million workers out of an estimated labour force of 302 million were employed in agriculture. If one takes out the organised sector of agriculture, which is mostly plantation, employment in peasant agriculture was about 205 million. See Table 14.1.
12. Sen, A. 1975, *Employment, Technology and Development*. Oxford: Clarendon Press.
13. Different departments of the central and the state governments publish employment statistics for the units under their jurisdiction. Consolidated data for the organised sector of the Indian economy are regularly published in the two journals, *Indian Labour Statistics* (Ministry of Labour, Government of India) and *The Employment Review* (Director-General of Employment and Training, Government of India).
14. For a clear exposition of this strategy, see the first three Five-Year Plans (1951–56, 1956–61, 1961–66), Planning Commission, Government of India.
15. Saini, D. S. 1994, *Labour Judiciary Adjudication and Industrial Response*. New Delhi: Oxford and International Book House Publishing Co, 4.
16. The Labour Ministry of the Government of India also tried to compile statistics relating to the membership of these organisations. Different trade union organisations sent their claims regarding membership, which the officials of the Labour Ministry are trying to verify. Until December 1994, this verification process remained bogged down by objections and disputes. The ministry rejected many of these claims. The rejection rates varied from 25 per cent to 99.3 per cent.
17. Ramaswamy, E. A. 1984, *Power and Justice*. New Delhi: Oxford University Press.
18. Ibid., 14.
19. Mehta, T. U. 1994, 'Contribution of Judiciary to Industrial Equity', in D. S. Saini (ed.), *Labour Judiciary, Adjudication and Industrial Justice*. New Delhi: Oxford and International Book House Publishing Co.
20. See note 17.
21. Ibid.
22. Ramaswamy, *Power and Justice*; Mamoria, C. B. and S. Mamoria, 1991, *Dynamics of Industrial Relations*. Delhi: Himalaya Publishing House.
23. See note 17.

24. By March 1991, there were 1,336 units in the organised private sector that were listed 'sick', with a bad debt of Rs 57.8655 billion. In 1989–90, there were ninety-eight sick enterprises in the public sector incurring a total (annual) loss of Rs 19.59 billion.
25. Fallon, P. R. and R. E. B. Lucas, 1993, 'Job Security Regulations and the Dynamic Demand for Industrial Labour in India and Zimbabwe', *Journal of Development Economics*, 40(2): 241–75.
26. Delhi Transport Corporation vs DTC Mazdoor Congress and others, 1990 (61) FLR 768(SC).
27. Veegal Engine and Engineering Industries Limited (in Liquidation), CP:393 of 1985, Calcutta High Court, Original Jurisdiction.
28. See note 19.
29. Between 1948 and 1994 five Pay Commissions have been appointed by the Government of India: in 1948, 1957, 1970, 1985 and 1995.
30. See The Terms and Conditions of the Fifth Pay Commission, Government of India, April 1994.
31. C. O. No. 2(146)72-BPE(WC) dated June 6, 1984 quoted in Nigam, R. K. 1994, *Policy Referencer For Public Sector Enterprises, Volume Two*. New Delhi: D. C. Publications.
32. Mathur, A. N. 1991, *Industrial Restructuring and Union Power*. Geneva: International Labour Organisation.
33. This sector includes all factories employing fifty or more workers with power and 100 or more workers without power.
34. Goswami, O. 1990, 'Sickness and Growth of India's Textile Industry: Analysis and Policy Options', *Economic and Political Weekly*, 1 August.
35. Ramaswamy, E. A. 1988, *Worker Consciousness and Trade Union Response*. New Delhi: Oxford University Press.
36. Fallon and Lucas (see note 25) estimated a dynamic labour demand function, derived from a CES cost minimisation model for sixty-four manufacturing industries. They attribute 17 per cent of long-term loss in industrial employment to job security regulations.
37. See note 32.
38. Numerous prospective foreign investors have spoken on this. For example, in 1992, the Japanese Ministry of International Trade and Industries (MITI) sent to India a high-powered delegation led by Mr R. Ishikawa, President of the Japanese Chamber of Commerce, to explore investment opportunities in India. Liberalisation of the exit-policy regime figured prominently in the list of 'humble requests' submitted by this delegation to the Government of India. See *The Economic Times* (Bombay and Delhi), 30 January 1992.
39. Less than 20 per cent of the capital flow from abroad during 1992–93 and 1993–94 has been Foreign Direct Investment (FDI).

15

Labour Policies, Employment and Worker Earnings: Indian and International Experiences*

Pradeep Agrawal

Labour is perhaps the most important factor of production considering that all the other factors of production are practically crippled without it. Thus efficient use of a country's labour endowment is crucial to its rapid economic growth. At the same time, labour is a unique factor of production because workers are human beings, not commodities. Therefore labour policies need to have a significant social or welfare dimension to them, which is why opinions remain sharply divided on labour market policies, with one group of economists emphasising the social or welfare aspects of labour policies and the other group laying stress on the efficiency aspects.

Those who have emphasised the welfare or social aspect have often advocated certain labour market interventions to safeguard the interests of workers (who are perceived to be much weaker than the employers on an individual basis) such as the freedom to form unions, minimum wage laws, the provision of some job security, unemployment insurance and subsidised facilities for retraining in case of retrenchment.[1]

On the other hand, those who give greater importance to the efficiency aspect of labour markets have argued that state interventions such as the minimum wage laws and job security provisions may reduce employment, productivity and growth and thus hurt the workers in the long run.[2] They have often advocated policies to:

*This paper was first published in the *Indian Journal of Labour Economics,* vol. 40, no. 4, 1997, pp. 631–653.

(*a*) make labour as productive as possible by providing suitable work incentives for working well through wage, bonus and promotion policies and through appropriate education and training, (*b*) ensure smooth industrial relations by creating proper mechanisms for resolution of conflict between labour and management so that loss of working days due to strikes and other causes can be minimised, (*c*) keep labour use flexible to deal more effectively with various shocks to the economy and with such things as shifts in its sectoral comparative advantage, by allowing easy retrenchment and retraining of workers, and (*d*) minimise distortions and interventions in the labour market.

In reality, both these seemingly contradictory aspects are important and the choice lies not between one and the other, but in striking a proper balance between the two. Thus most countries have followed labour policies that probably fall somewhere in between these extreme positions.

In this chapter, we consider the labour policies and their outcomes in India and several other countries, mostly from East Asia (namely, South Korea, Taiwan, Singapore, Malaysia, Thailand and Indonesia) since the early 1970s. We provide evidence that East Asian countries have achieved a much higher growth of employment and real earnings per employee compared to India despite the latter's having had much stronger unions (Section I). This suggests that the efficiency aspect deserves greater attention, at least in countries like India that have emphasised the welfare aspect to the detriment of efficiency. Thus it is worth analysing the labour policies in East Asia and India to understand the causes of these differing outcomes. With this in mind, we examine the labour laws relating to trade unions, industrial relations and job security in East Asia and India (Section II). We also compare the policies relating to wages, bonus and promotions (Section III), and worker training and productivity enhancement (Section IV) in these countries. We conclude the chapter with suggestions for reforming India's labour laws to make labour more productive and thereby generate more employment and higher earnings per employee (Section V). Labour reforms assume greater importance and urgency in view of the economic reforms undertaken by India over the last five years in order to achieve an economy that is more competitive and globally integrated.

I LABOUR UNIONS, EMPLOYMENT AND WORKERS' EARNINGS

The East Asian countries have achieved their remarkable success in economic growth by using the strategy of export-oriented industrialisation and, often, large inflows of foreign direct investment to augment domestic capital formation. But success in the highly competitive export markets and in attracting foreign capital would not have been achieved if these countries had been unable to provide disciplined, motivated, well-trained and cost-effective labour. Thus it is that East Asian governments have laid much greater emphasis on efficient and flexible use of labour than their counterparts in most other regions of the world.

This emphasis on efficiency at times combined with other socio-political dimensions such as military dictatorships and the excessive fear of communism (for example, South Korea and Taiwan have had highly hostile relations with the communist North Korea and China respectively while the present regime of President Suharto in Indonesia was established by overthrowing the socialist regime of President Sukarno in 1965), led to a certain fear of organised labour, resulting in the unwillingness of many East Asian governments to allow strong and independent labour unions. This was particularly marked in Korea, Taiwan, Indonesia and Thailand. Following democratisation, Korea has moved in the direction of a more balanced industrial relations environment since the late 1980s. Taiwan also seems to be moving in a similar direction following political democratisation in 1987.

Such historic forces were not operating in Singapore and Malaysia, which had inherited liberal labour laws from British colonial rule. However, in Singapore, communist labour unions were purged as part of a major political power struggle in the early 1960s. The government then formed an alliance with the more moderate trade unions under the umbrella of the National Trade Union Congress (NTUC) and the two have cooperated with each other since then (some major labour leaders were even made ministers in the Singapore government) so that while unions were not entirely free, the interests of labour were taken into consideration by the government. New labour laws were passed in 1967–68 (discussed in the following section) that had far-reaching effects on industrial relations in Singapore. Malaysia also tightened its labour laws through its Industrial Relations Act, 1967, following several years of labour strife. Yet, of the six East Asian countries, Malaysia and Singapore probably have the more balanced labour laws and a reasonable judicial system to deal with labour problems.

In sharp contrast to East Asia, India, which also inherited liberal trade union laws from the British era, went the other way and further strengthened protection of labour, including the freedom to form unions, the right to strike and almost complete job security.

A crude measure of the relative strength of the labour unions and their ability to bargain on behalf of workers is provided by the share of workers' earnings in total value added.[3] In addition to the strength of unions, the share of workers earnings in total value added can be expected to depend positively on the human capital endowment of the workforce (since better trained workers can command higher wages) and negatively on the capital intensity of the manufacturing sector (since higher capital per worker also implies a higher share of capital in value added). More developed economies typically have both higher capital intensity and higher human capital endowment of the workforce; these two factors pull the share of workers' earnings in total value added in opposite directions and could counter each other approximately. Hence the share of workers' earnings in value added can be treated as a crude measure of the relative strength of labour unions across economies.

Table 15.1 shows this share for the manufacturing sectors in East Asia and India; for comparison the table also provides the averages for developed countries (the United States, Japan, United Kingdom and France), Latin America (Argentina, Chile, Brazil and Mexico) and South Asia (India, Pakistan and Bangladesh). The table shows that the share has been around 40 per cent in the developed countries, and even higher in India (46 per cent) reflecting the strength of unions in India. Among the East Asian countries, Singapore and Malaysia have the highest share at around 33 per cent and 28 per cent respectively. Korea shows an average share of about 26.5 per cent, which is low for its level of development. It shows some improvement in 1988, following a year of major labour strife and wage increases, but the gain has not been sustained in the 1990s. The share of workers' earnings in total value added appears very low in Indonesia and Thailand at about 22.5 and 16 per cent respectively, suggesting a very poor bargaining position for labour. This evidence is consistent with the discussion of the historical and social factors at the beginning of this section.

Figures 15.1 and 15.2 show indices of employment and real earnings per employee in the manufacturing sector for 1970–93 in East Asia, India and averages for the developed countries, East Asia, South Asia, Latin America and Africa. It is seen that India has achieved very limited success in either increasing employment or real earnings per employee. On the other hand, the East Asian countries have done remarkably well in generating employment for their workers and in improving their real earnings compared to any other group of countries. This is all the more impressive since most of them started from difficult initial economic conditions comparable to those in India, such as large surplus labour and high and growing population density.

Thus, we see that even though India's protective labour laws and strong labour unions have been able to obtain a larger share of the (value-added) pie for their members, it is the East Asian countries, with their emphasis on efficient and flexible use of labour, that have had the better meal in terms of growth of employment and real earnings of workers. While the strong labour unions in India could extract a greater share of the (value-added) pie, the inefficiency induced by the Indian labour (and other) policies have not allowed the pie to grow much. On the other hand, the efficiency-oriented labour (and other) policies of the East Asian economies have led to a rapid growth of the value-added pie in these countries so that workers' earnings have risen rapidly even with a smaller share of the pie going to the workers. This demonstrates that in the long run, one ignores the efficiency aspect at one's own peril. The contrast between India and East Asia is an interesting one and worthy of serious thought by those concerned with the welfare of the working class in India.

A natural question that arises at this point is: To what extent is the higher rate of growth of employment and wages in East Asia a result of labour policies followed in these countries and to what extent is it due to their export orientation and other policies? The question is not easy and entire books have been written on the causes of the East Asian success.[4] However, based on our understanding of the East Asian economies,[5] we offer the following explanation.

The rapid growth of employment in manufacturing sectors in East Asia has been possible due to a rapid expansion of manufacturing sector output. This has been possible due to successfully implemented export-oriented industrialisation policies which emphasised labour intensive manufactures, especially in the early stages of industrialisation *and* the availability of a well-trained, efficient, flexible and productive labour force, which has helped increase exports rapidly due to its price and quality competitiveness in world markets.

These same factors, combined with a peaceful industrial relations climate (see Tables 15.2 and 15.3) and other investment friendly policies, helped attract more capital, both domestic and foreign. This, in turn, increased capital employed per worker (a major determinant of worker productivity). Similarly, improvements in education and worker training, which the East Asian countries have emphasised, help improve the worker productivity. Figures 15.3, 15.4 and 15.5 show the index (1960 = 100) of total physical capital in 1987 constant local prices, logarithm (base 10) of total physical capital in 1987 constant US dollars[6] and the human capital stock (average number of years of formal education for the working population) for East Asia, India and some developed countries. It is seen that virtually all East Asian countries have accumulated physical as well as human capital at much faster rates than India. In fact, India's performance on these vital fronts is dismal and urgent measures to change this state of affairs are called for.

The rapid accumulation of physical and human capital has aided growth of real earnings per employee by increasing worker productivity. The rapid employment growth has improved the bargaining position of the workers by eliminating unemployment, which was reduced to 'natural' levels in most East Asian countries (except Indonesia and Thailand) by the late 1970s—this has also helped raise real earnings per employee.

Thus the rapid growth of employment and real earnings per employee in East Asia is the combined result of labour policies along with a whole range of successfully implemented labour-intensive and export-oriented industrialisation policies that yielded rapid GDP growth. Unless these complementary policies are also successfully implemented, it would be unrealistic to expect such rapid growth in employment and earnings per employee in other countries, such as India, merely through labour policy reforms, as the experience of many countries in Latin America and Africa might suggest. At the same time, success in export-oriented industrialisation itself requires efficient and cost-effective labour, as the East Asian experience testifies. Thus it seems likely that the efficiency-oriented labour policies are likely to be better for workers in developing countries when these are properly implemented in conjunction with other policies (such as the export-oriented industrialisation policies) that lead to rapid GDP growth.

A second question that arises naturally is: Given that the protectionist labour policies in India have been applicable only to the organised sector, what is the relative importance of this sector and how does it compare with the performance of the unorganised sector?

How large is the organised sector relative to the unorganised sector in India? Table 15.4 provides data on the employment, output and output per worker in the two sectors for 1981 and 1991 for India. It is seen that although the organised sector employs only about 10 per cent of the workforce, it contributes about one-third of the Net Domestic Product. Furthermore, the organised sector provides virtually all the infrastructure (railways, ports and airports, electricity and telecommunications) and intermediate products such as steel, iron and aluminium.

In contrast to the organised sector, the unorganised sector workers working in small factories and shops have little protection, partly because some laws are weaker (for instance, the job security laws) or do not even apply to the unorganised sector and partly because of the difficulty of enforcing laws for small establishments. The protective labour laws for the organised sector have created a sharp duality in the labour markets: those with jobs do not work hard due to complete job security and a poor incentive structure for working hard, while the poor productivity of such employees leads to very slow growth of employment in the organised sector, leading to an army of unemployed and underemployed working in the unorganised sector at significantly lower wages and without even minimal protection for the workers.

Consistent with our hypothesis that the overly protective labour laws in the organised sector slow down the growth of employment, the data in Table 15.4 does show that employment has grown more rapidly in the unorganised sector than in the organised sector: the annual growth rates of employment over 1981–91 was 1.58 per cent for the organised sector against 2.73 per cent for the unorganised sector, although the difference is not nearly as dramatic as it was in our comparison of India and East Asia (Figure 15.1). In this regard it should be noted that the organised sector is also the leading sector in the sense that an expansion of the organised sector leads to creation of jobs in the unorganised sector as well since a good part of the latter sector often plays a supporting or ancillary role to the organised sector. Thus if, for example, the organised sector does not grow rapidly because of some capital flight by domestic entrepreneurs and bypassing of India by foreign entrepreneurs owing to poor labour (and other) policies, then the growth of the unorganised sector is likely to be stunted as well. Thus even though the protective labour laws are applicable to the organised sector only, they also affect the growth of the unorganised sector to a significant extent.

Therefore, labour policy reforms that can improve the efficiency of the organised sector can contribute considerably to improving the Indian economy while simultaneously helping the workers as a whole by raising the rate of growth of employment and real wages. Thus it is worth analysing how the East Asian countries have managed to create and sustain an efficient, flexible and well-trained labour force and a peaceful industrial relations climate. We try to understand the economic, social and legal framework behind this in the rest of the chapter. First we examine and compare the labour laws in East Asia and India. This is followed by a discussion of policies relating to wages, bonus and promotions, and then the policies relating to worker training and productivity enhancement.

II COMPARISON OF LABOUR LAWS IN INDIA AND EAST ASIA

In this section, we consider labour laws relating to forming unions, industrial relations (strikes) and job security in India and East Asia. In view of the underdeveloped industrial relations environment in some East Asian countries, a greater emphasis has been placed on the legal framework in Malaysia and Singapore.

Laws Relating to Trade Unions

The usual legal protection for joining labour unions and for undertaking industrial action such as collective bargaining and strikes exists in most East Asian countries. But simultaneously these countries also have provisions to refuse registration of unions considered undesirable by the government, to impose restrictions on causes for which industrial action can be initiated and to specify the procedure to be followed.

To form a union requires the support of at least thirty workers or 20 per cent of the employees in many East Asian countries (Thailand, Malaysia, Singapore). Perhaps due to the Japanese influence (Korea and Taiwan were colonies of Japan prior to the Second World War; other East Asian countries have also had strong economic and cultural ties with Japan), some East Asian countries (South Korea, Taiwan, Indonesia) have in-house unions, that is, only one union per plant or firm representing all employees of that plant or firm. Thus a union must have the support of a majority of workers in the firm. Malaysia and Singapore also allow industry-wide unions, but this is not allowed in the other East Asian countries, at least not for purposes of bargaining or undertaking industrial action. This considerably reduces the power of the unions. At the same time the in-house unions have the advantage that due to continuous contact with management, the two sides have better communication with and understanding of each other. Basically, the concept works well in the case of large firms, now common in Japan and becoming common in Korea. But in Taiwan, where the small firms predominate, application of this concept has led to unions being very weak.

In many East Asian countries, the right to form unions is limited to the private sector; unions are not allowed in the public sector. Even in countries where they are allowed (Malaysia and Singapore), their right to go on strike is quite limited.

In many countries in East Asia (Malaysia, Indonesia, Taiwan), the labour unions are not allowed to have any association with political parties (in practice this has sometimes meant no association with opposition political parties). This has been done to prevent industrial relations from becoming proxy wars for political parties, rather than representing genuine worker concerns.

By contrast, in India, any seven employees could form a union. This provision has led to the mushrooming of a very large number of unions, some of which are floated by employers to counter the more aggressive workers' unions. The workers in the public sector can and often do go on strikes. Further, major trade union confederations are closely associated with political parties. The resulting union rivalries have been an obstacle to the development of a sound industrial relations system in India.

Following the economic reforms beginning in 1991, the Act was revised in 1993 and now requires a minimum membership of 10 per cent of employees in any firm. Although even this revised requirement appears to be too low, it should help reduce to some extent the number of unions and resulting rivalries without compromising workers' interests. The concept of a single enterprise-level union deserves greater encouragement, especially in large enterprises, as such unions are more likely to focus on genuine worker concerns.

Laws Relating to Industrial Relations

In most East Asian countries, trade union laws provide for legal immunity from prosecution for industrial actions such as strikes. However, fairly stringent restrictions have been placed on what constitutes a legal strike. To be legal, strikes usually require approval of the action by a simple majority (two-thirds majority in Malaysia) of voting union members by secret ballot. This has to be followed by a notice to employer and a cooling off and conciliation period (usually fifteen to forty-five days) before the strike can actually be called.

Further, industrial relations laws in most East Asian countries limit the reasons for which legal strikes can be called. For example, in Singapore and Malaysia the following 'fundamental management functions' are the sole right of employers (since 1967–68) and can not be disputed by labour unions: (*a*) recruitment, promotion or internal transfer of an employee, (*b*) assignment or allocation of duties, or specific tasks to an employee, (*c*) retrenchment of an employee due to redundancy or reorganisation, and (*d*) dismissal of an employee for misconduct and his reinstatement. Further, in Malaysia and Singapore, anyone (including union officials) who incites workers to take part in illegal strikes faces prosecution and fines and no worker who refuses to take part in an illegal strike can be expelled from the union or be put to any disadvantage compared to other union members. These changes in the Industrial Relations Acts in 1967–68 had far-reaching effects on the industrial relations climate in Malaysia and Singapore and have drastically reduced the incidence of strikes and lockouts (Table 15.2).

Further, most East Asian countries have developed a system of voluntary and compulsory arbitration of all labour-related disputes by tripartite bodies including representatives of workers, employers and government. Since the government appointees usually end up having the deciding say, a balanced approach on the part of the government is essential for the system to work properly. The system is generally considered to be reasonably fair in Malaysia and Singapore, at least in matters of wage-related disputes, and allows for most disputes to be resolved without having to resort to strikes or lockouts. This explains the very low incidence of strikes or lockouts in Malaysia and Singapore—in fact Singapore has not had a single strike since 1978 (Tables 15.2 and 15.3). However, in some of the other East Asian countries, there have been accusations of governments siding with employers, leading to simmering discontent among workers. This came to a boil in major labour unrest and strikes in Korea in 1987–89 (Table 15.2) following the democratisation of the country in 1987. Taiwan and Indonesia, which have taken a less stringent attitude towards labour unions following pressure of trade sanctions from the United States since 1984, also show an increase in the incidence of strikes since then, implying a somewhat suppressed industrial relations climate in the two countries.

In India, strikes and lockouts are governed by the Industrial Disputes Act (1947). It provides channels (Labour Courts, Industrial Tribunals and National Tribunals) for voluntary arbitration, although the conciliation machinery is generally found inadequate because the role of the conciliation officer was merely to arrange meetings between labour and management representatives. The laws also allow the government discretionary use of even compulsory arbitration if an agreement between employer and employees to mutual satisfaction is not forthcoming. However, compulsory arbitration is not common in practice.

While the Indian legal framework in this respect is not dramatically different from that of East Asian countries, the practice is. For example, although there is a legal requirement of fourteen days advance notice before going on strike, in practice labour unions rarely give an advance notice or go through a cooling off and conciliation procedure before actually going on strike. Indeed, 'flash strikes' are the order of the day due to the tradition of leniency towards the unions even when they break the law. The frequent strikes without warning or conciliation procedures cause employers and the public great inconvenience and create an atmosphere of uncertainty about Indian firms' ability to meet production schedules—a serious problem in these days of global competition that could be costing the Indian economy many export orders and ensuing employment opportunities.

A high level of unionisation in the organised sector and a large number of unions per establishment or industry leads to union rivalries which makes settlement of disputes difficult. A low rate of growth of real earnings per worker (Figure 15.2) has further fuelled worker discontentment. In addition, the employers also tend to resort to lockouts (during which wages do not have to be paid) quite often as ways of disciplining workers or avoiding paying them given the legal difficulty in retrenching them (see the next sub-section). As a result, the industrial relations climate in India is not good and a large number of workdays are lost due to strikes and lockouts, in fact, more than in any other major country (Table 15.3).

However, the industrial relations climate has improved to some extent following the economic reforms initiated since mid-1991, with the number of work days lost per year due to strikes and lockouts declining by nearly 40 per cent since 1991–92 (see Table 15.5). This could be in response to the increasing competition, both domestic and global, faced by Indian firms as well as the increasing willingness of the government to tolerate closure of non-viable firms, making the workers less willing to take disputes beyond a certain point.

While it may not be easy to resolve all the underlying problems of industrial relations in India, one major improvement suggested by the East Asian countries' experience that can considerably reduce the frequency of strikes is to have the requirement that a call for strike must be approved by a majority of union members using secret ballot and to require a cooling-off period of thirty days or so during which strikes can not be called and which is utilised to try to bring about reconciliation between workers and management (with an improved conciliation machinery provided by the government). This will ensure that unnecessary strikes called over matters that can be resolved by negotiations and those called in the heat of the moment or due to ego clashes between union leaders and management representatives are avoided without sacrificing genuine worker interests. The change in law, *and practice*, can be accomplished by educating the workers about the long-run costs to themselves (in terms of reduced growth of employment and wages) of not acting responsibly.

Job Security Laws

In most East Asian countries, it is not difficult for employers to dismiss employees. The grounds on which workers can be dismissed include unjustified absence and misconduct on the job. Retrenchment, through no fault of the employee, can also be undertaken when workers are found redundant owing to technological restructuring of the firm or the need to reduce or cease production.

In most countries, in cases of dismissals, some government-sponsored mechanism for mediation exists. This is probably most developed in Malaysia where roughly 80 per cent of the cases are resolved in this way. If mediation fails, the labour minister can refer the dispute to the industrial court (5 to 10 per cent of the cases) which can order reinstatement or more commonly compensation, if dismissal is found to be unjustified. In the city-state of Singapore, the dismissed employee can appeal, through his union, to the minister of labour, whose decision is final. In Indonesia, government permission is required to retrench workers, although this is not very difficult to get.

In cases of retrenchment, free or highly subsidised retraining facilities are provided in most countries (including Singapore and Malaysia) and efforts are made by the labour ministry to find alternative placement for the retrenched workers. There is no unemployment insurance in most East Asian countries, except some limited benefits in Korea since 1988. However, employers are required to give retrenched workers a written notice of one to three months depending on length of service; this also varies from country to country. Further, retrenchment compensation is also required to be paid (applicable only to employees terminated for redundancy and not to those dismissed for misconduct) to those employees who have completed at least one year (three years in Singapore) of service with the same employer. This is equal to one month's pay for each year worked in Singapore, Taiwan, Malaysia and Indonesia. Malaysia requires 1.25 months' pay per year of service for employees working for over ten years while Indonesia has an upper limit of four months' wages plus one month's service pay for each five years of service. Thailand requires a compensation of one, three and six months' wages for employees employed for four to twelve months, one to three years and over three years, respectively. In Korea severance pay is mandatory at the time of termination and an unemployment insurance scheme is being developed (not available in other East Asian countries).

India once again presents a sharp contrast. Since 1976, large firms in the organised sector, i.e., firms employing over 300 workers (100 since 1982), are not permitted to retrench any worker who has been employed with the firm for at least 240 days, without permission from the government (not applicable to management level employees). If such permission is granted, the firm must give three months' notice to workers, as well as retrenchment compensation of fifteen days wages for each year of service with the employer. However, such permission is in fact almost never granted due to pressure from unions. Thus almost complete job security exists for workers in the organised sector. In the unorganised sector, small-scale firms (employing under 100 workers) may retrench workers but they are required to give one month's notice in writing and a retrenchment compensation equal to fifteen days' pay for each year worked with that employer in the case of employees who have been employed for at least twelve months.

The situation in the organised sector is further compounded by the fact that even the promotions are mostly on the basis of seniority, rather than performance on the job, at least in the public sector, which accounts for about 70 per cent of total employment in the organised sector. This aspect, coupled with the almost complete job security mentioned before, means that there is little incentive for regular employees to work hard or even at all. This leads to serious problems of inefficiency and low productivity from which Indian industry in general and the public sector in particular are suffering.

The almost complete job security for regular employees in the organised sector is unique to India and a handful of other developing countries and leads to many problems. Firms are not able to rationalise their operations and labour force in response to changing market conditions. Even loss-making firms (referred to as 'sick' firms in India) are not allowed to close down but are given subsidised credit through the nationalised banking system and other facilities to continue operation. The subsidies given to loss-making firms sometimes help keep the product prices artificially low which again may cause other firms in the industry to turn 'sick'. This leads to a huge and ever-increasing drain on the resources of the public sector banks (Table 15.6), in addition to the locking up of valuable capital and labour resources in inefficient production.

It is noteworthy that despite their high cost these policies do not increase aggregate employment in the economy and may have actually decreased it by driving away some entrepreneurs, and by making others wary of hiring labour. Furthermore, attempts by firms to avoid the problems caused by an inability to rationalise a regular labour force in response to changing market conditions have led to increasing use of temporary, casual or contract workers who do not have any job security or retrenchment compensation (see Table 15.7). Neither such workers nor their employers have sufficient incentive for proper work training, again leading to inefficient use of resources.

The labour market policies followed in India in the past have led to serious problems due to low labour productivity even in the context of an economy where the firms were shielded from both international competition (by the very high import tariffs) and domestic competition (by the licensing policies). This in turn creates an inefficient and internationally uncompetitive industrial sector which eventually leads to lower wages (Figure 15.2), fewer jobs and higher unemployment (Figure 15.1). These labour policies will be even more difficult to sustain in the new climate of the enhanced level of domestic and international competition under the economic liberalisation policies.

Thus India needs to allow some flexibility in the use of labour while recognising that a reasonable degree of job security is a genuine worker need. However, given our long-entrenched tradition, job security laws may be difficult to change. Thus, small changes in current laws that can significantly improve the productivity of Indian labour are more likely to be feasible and successful. Some such suggestions are:

1. Raise the length of service with one firm required for 'permanent employment' from 240 days to about three years. This allows employers a better opportunity to screen the employees before making a long-term commitment, and longer assignments for short-term employees which would likely raise their prospects for improved training and productivity.

2. Adopt the Japanese-style flexible wage system of giving employees bonuses linked to company profitability (which gives employees a stake in their company's performance) and where promotions are significantly dependent on good job performance. This creates incentives for employees to try to improve their skills and cooperate in improving productivity (see Section III).
3. Allowing non-viable firms to exist on the basis of public subsidies is not sustainable in the long run. Retrenching with a humane face has to be allowed for firms that must reduce or cease production or that need to reorganise technologically to meet competition.
4. Employers have to be given some way out from employees who misbehave or do not work properly at the job. As a counterbalance to prevent misuse of dismissal procedures, employers must be required to prove an employee's misconduct in a court of law and required to pay additional compensation and/or reinstate the worker in case of unjustified dismissals (as in Malaysia).

III POLICIES RELATING TO WAGES, BONUSES AND PROMOTIONS

Minimum wage laws exist in most of the East Asian countries and India mainly for unskilled workers. However, in most cases (including India) the minimum wages so set are close to the market clearing levels and are not enforced seriously except in cities.

Wages for public sector employees are usually set by government-appointed bodies in some countries (for example, India and Singapore) in consultation with representatives of employees.

Wages for private sector employees in East Asia are usually decided by employers or by bilateral agreements between employee unions and employers. When an agreement between the two parties is not forthcoming, there exist mechanisms for government-mediated conciliation proceedings in most countries of East Asia. If these also fail there is provision for voluntary or compulsory arbitration by the labour ministry (Singapore, Indonesia) or by industrial courts (Thailand, Malaysia). Thus in most cases these issues are settled without resorting to strikes.

In Singapore and India, governments have played an active role in the determination of wages even in the private sector. In Singapore since 1972, wages have been mostly decided at the national level by the National Wages Council, a tripartite body with equal representation from labour, management and government, and with a chairman from academia who was without any factional identification. The Council was essentially a negotiating body at the national level with the government serving an integrative third-party role. Although wage guidelines were only advisory, they were generally followed. This had the advantage that wages did not have to be negotiated at each factory or industry level and the resulting friction between labour and management was avoided. However, it also had the drawback that wage increases, being the same across the board, did not reflect the profitability of individual firms or industry. This point hit home when a severe recession struck in 1985 (the first since independence in 1965) after several large wage increases since 1979. The recession resulted in a thorough review of wage (and other) policies. The government accepted the recommendation that Singapore should adopt a Japanese-style flexible wage system with the wage consisting of a fixed component plus a variable component in the form of a bonus of one to three months' wages (subject to a minimum of one month's wages) linked to profitability or worker productivity in individual enterprises. The recommendation was also endorsed by the trade union movement and employers.

In India, the government has appointed over twenty wage boards to determine wages to be paid (to blue-collar workers) in most major industries. The wage boards are typically tripartite, comprising representatives of management, workers and government. The recommendations of the wage boards are not statutorily binding although both labour and management tend to accept them. Some stronger unions can bargain for higher wages than those recommended by wage boards. The settlement of wages through tripartite wage boards has moderated an important source of industrial conflict.

The bargaining power of unions in most countries of East Asia is limited due to factors such as the presence of mostly enterprise-level (rather than industry-level) unions, limited legal scope for strikes and the governments unwillingness to permit strong and independent unions in many of the countries. However, due to the rapid increase in employment opportunities (see Figure 15.1), unemployment levels declined rapidly over the 1970s to close to natural levels of unemployment (except in Indonesia and Thailand) and labour shortages even began to appear in many skilled categories. This has meant that despite the limited bargaining power of unions, wages have grown rapidly in East Asia, especially over the 1980s and early 1990s (Figure 15.2). On the other hand, they have not grown so rapidly in India despite the presence of much stronger unions.

Bonus: The Flexible Wage System

The Japanese-style flexible wage system is becoming increasingly common in East Asia. In this system, applicable to both workers and managers, the wage consists of a fixed component plus a variable component in the form of a bonus. For example, in Singapore the fixed wage component usually includes a basic wage, a small annual increment of about 2 per cent of the basic wage and an Annual Wage Supplement equal to one month's wage. The bonus links wages with performance, that is, performance of the individual, the company and the economy. The bonus can be as much as one to five months' wages in Japan, Korea and Taiwan and one to three months' wages in Singapore. This system helps firms to survive recession by reducing labour costs during recessions. It also helps workers since reduced labour costs also means that the firm can keep more, even all, of the workers employed through the recession. However, the most important benefit of this system may be that by giving the employees a stake in the profitability of the firm, it makes them more cooperative and responsible towards their employers.

In fact, in Singapore and Malaysia the policy of flexible wages has been adopted even for public sector employees with their bonuses linked to the rate of growth of GDP. This has the advantage of reminding the public sector employees that they have a stake in a better performing economy, besides being in tune with government's tax receipts which are roughly proportional to GDP.

Coming back to the private sector, in some countries (Japan and some enterprises in Korea, Taiwan and Singapore), while the total bonus amount is decided by the profitability of the company, the amount given to each individual can vary to reflect his performance on the job. When a good and just performance appraisal system is followed, a strong incentive is created for employees to try to put in their best. Besides monetary gain, recognition as a good employee itself can be a highly motivating force. However, this system of flexible wages can work only when a good and just system is developed to appraise employees and to determine profitability of firms. Otherwise it can lead to disaffection and loss of morale. For example, in 1981, Singapore experimented with performance-related bonuses, but the scheme was abandoned a year later owing to the lack of a satisfactory performance appraisal system in most firms.

In India the Payment of Bonus Act (1965) currently requires the private firms in most industries to pay a bonus to all blue-collar employees. The minimum bonus, which is required to be paid whether or not the firm makes any profits, is 8.33 per cent (4 per cent before 1971) of the annual salary of the worker and the maximum liability is 20 per cent of the annual salary, depending on the profitability of the firm. In practice, a bonus of one month's salary (i.e., 8.33 per cent of the annual salary) is required and more than that is rarely given. Public sector enterprises, though exempt from the act, have also tended to follow the same practice. Thus, essentially, the flexible wage system does not exist in India with the exception of a few large private firms. Furthermore, promotions are mostly on the basis of seniority, at least in the public sector. This leads to a poor incentive for workers to put in hard work resulting in low worker motivation.

We can obtain substantial improvements in the motivation (to improve their skills and work harder) and productivity of employees (both workers and managers) in India by adopting the Japanese-style flexible wage system. Future occasions of wage increases can be used as an opportunity to increase the bonus component for public sector employees, which can gradually be linked to their performance (after an appropriate evaluation system is developed). Alternately, we can follow the example of Singapore and Malaysia and link the bonus of public sector employees to GDP growth.

IV POLICIES TO IMPROVE LABOUR TRAINING AND PRODUCTIVITY

The East Asian countries have made rapid progress in improving the education level of their workforce. This is evident from Figure 15.4 which shows data on the average number of years of formal education for the working population in East Asia and India (the average in developed countries—the United States, Japan, UK and France—is also shown for comparison; data was not available for Taiwan). The performance of Korea and Singapore is seen to be particularly impressive and they are beginning to approach the developed country levels, while the performance of India is the worst.

Most governments in East Asia—for example, Korea, Taiwan and Singapore—have undertaken several programmes to improve training and productivity of workers, especially over the 1970s and 1980s when a restructuring of the economy towards more capital and skill-intensive industries was initiated. Besides doing well in basic and advanced general education, these countries have put much greater emphasis than India has on vocational training, both formal and in-firm. For example, under the Basic Law for Vocational Training, enacted in 1976, Korea required private enterprises with 300 (now 150) or more employees to conduct in-plant training for a stated proportion of their employees or to pay a training levy of 6 per cent (now less) of their wage bill. The levy is used to promote vocational training via government-sponsored vocational training schools.

Similarly Singapore initiated several programmes to improve the skill level of its workers. Some of the main programmes are:

1. Rapid expansion of facilities and enrolment in the universities and polytechnics to provide highly trained manpower.
2. Establishment of the Vocational and Industrial Training Board (VITB) in 1979 for vocational training in commerce and industry.
3. Establishment of the Skills Development Fund (SDF) in 1979, financed initially with a 4 per cent levy on wages (since reduced to 1 per cent) to subsidise efforts to upgrade the skills and expertise of employees or retrain retrenched workers. Between 1981 and 1990, the annual number of worker training places increased by more than twelve times from 32,600 to 405,600. This means that one in three Singapore workers is trained every year.
4. Launching of the Basic Education for Skills Development (BESD) programme to impart to workers basic numeracy and literacy. Similar programmes for higher level attainment were also initiated.

5. Establishment of the National Productivity Board (NPB) in 1972 and the National Productivity Council in 1982 to promote productivity consciousness in Singapore. For example, NPB launched the Productivity 2000 project in 1989 to study key issues relating to productivity. The project's recommendations are being implemented with the tripartite support of employers, government, and the National Trade Union Congress.

Overall, the East Asian countries, especially the more advanced ones such as Korea and Singapore, have made vigorous efforts to create a better educated and well-trained labour force. Besides doing well in general education, these countries have emphasised vocational training (both in-firm and public) for their employed workers as well as free or highly subsidised retraining facilities for retrenched workers. India has lagged behind in both general education and vocational training.

V CONCLUSIONS

In the East Asian countries, labour laws are generally supportive of efficient and flexible use of labour. A peaceful industrial relations climate has been maintained in most countries with the help of laws requiring a cooling-off period (about one month) before a strike can be called and through the use of voluntary and compulsory arbitration. As a result, strikes and work stoppages are uncommon. Further, firms can retrench workers, although they must pay a retrenchment compensation (about one month's wages for each year of employment with the firm). This provides flexibility in the use of labour and also forces a certain discipline on workers. Industrialists therefore want to hire them, leading to a faster growth of employment and wages. The main improvement needed in some of the East Asian countries is greater freedom of operation for the labour unions.

The Japanese-style flexible wage system has also been adopted by Korea, Taiwan, Malaysia and Singapore. Giving the employees a bonus that depends, at least to some extent, on their company's profitability can make employees more cooperative and responsible.

By linking the amount of the bonus (and promotions) each individual employee receives to his work performance, incentives can be created for good performance even in the presence of considerable job security, as is the case in Japan. Finally, East Asian countries have rapidly improved the general education and training of their workers, which has helped make them more productive.

Thus the East Asian countries have generally succeeded in creating a highly disciplined, motivated, flexible and well-trained labour force. For example, the World Economic Forum and IMD (1991) survey rated Singapore's labour as the most motivated among the ten major newly industrialising countries. Korea was rated second, Malaysia third and Thailand fourth. (India came last).

On the other hand, the protective labour laws of India give the organised sector workers in India permanent employment after a brief (typically one year or less) probation period. Employees cannot be fired without government permission, which is rarely given even when the firm becomes non-viable. Public sector employees typically receive fixed annual wage increments unrelated to work performance. There is little incentive to work hard or to strive to improve one's performance. The education and training of workers has improved only slowly (in comparison to East Asia). The result is poor productivity and eventually low wages, fewer jobs and higher unemployment. This is corroborated by the fact that India has high unemployment while most East Asian countries have essentially none, despite wages that are many times that of India's. We need to ponder whether the very high cost of protective labour policies for the small aristocracy of organised sector workers is worth the price. The experience of East Asia and India demonstrates that excessively protective labour policies are not in the long-term interest of the workers and might do them more harm than good.

Thus a proper balance between efficiency and welfare (or protection) aspects has not been maintained in India and the scales have tipped dangerously away from considerations of efficiency. Even if India's different historic and social context may not allow it to go as far as the East Asian countries have gone in the quest for efficiency, it needs to make a reasonable effort to improve the efficiency of labour. For this purpose the following efficiency-enhancing labour policies of East Asia can be adopted in India and should help improve the long-term welfare of Indian workers by improving growth of employment and real earnings of workers:

1. Laws that limit the number of unions, possibly to only one per enterprise. This actually increases the bargaining strength of the workers and at the same time makes it easier to reach agreements by reducing the element of union rivalries. However, such enterprise-level unions should be allowed to have industry-wide federations.
2. The requirement to approve a call for strike by a majority of union members using secret ballot and the cooling-off period of thirty days or so during which strikes cannot be called and which is utilised to try to bring about a reconciliation between workers and management. This ensures that unnecessary strikes called in the heat of the moment or due to ego clashes between a few union leaders and management representatives are avoided without sacrificing genuine worker interests.
3. Some flexibility in the use of labour has to be allowed while recognising that a reasonable degree of job security is a genuine worker need. It is clear that allowing non-viable firms to exist on the basis of public subsidies is not sustainable in the long run. Retrenching with a humane face has to be allowed for firms that must reduce or cease production or that need to reorganise technologically to meet competition. Concurrently, employers have to be given some way out from employees who misbehave or do not work properly at the job. As a counterbalance to prevent misuse of dismissal procedures, employers must be required to prove an employee's misconduct in a court of law and required to pay additional compensation and/or reinstate the worker in case of unjustified dismissals (as in Malaysia). To give blanket job security under all circumstances makes it very difficult to maintain worker discipline and reduces worker motivation and productivity.
4. Raising the length of service after which an employee cannot be easily dismissed from 240 days to about three years and adopting the Japanese-style flexible wage system that gives employees (both workers and managers) a stake in the company's profitability, and where promotions are significantly dependent on good job performance, creates incentives for employees to try to improve their skills and cooperate in improving productivity. This might be a good and politically acceptable way to improve productivity in countries like India with a strong tradition of job security.

5. Greater effort needs to be made towards improving the education and training of the workers to make them more productive. This should include compulsory basic education (eight or more years of schooling) for all children and greater emphasis on vocational training. The former is essential for sustained economic growth over a long period. Similarly, greater effort also needs to be made to increase the availability of physical capital per worker. This includes policies that encourage savings as well as investment, both domestic and foreign.

These features, if incorporated in the labour policy, can considerably enhance India's labour potential. At the same time, it should be noted that the rapid growth of employment and real earnings per employee in East Asia is the combined result of a whole range of labour-intensive and export-oriented industrialisation policies along with the labour policies. Since India has already undertaken most other reforms towards export-oriented industrialisation, it is now well poised to benefit substantially from labour policy reforms in the form of higher growth of employment and real earnings per employee.

Table 15.1
Workers' Earnings as Share of Value Added, Manufacturing Sector, East Asia and india, 1972–92

Year	*India*	*Indonesia*	*Thailand*	*Malaysia*	*Korea*	*Singapore*	*East Asia AVG*[1]	*Developed Country AVG*[1]	*Lat. Amer. AVG*[1]	*South Asia AVG*[1]
1972	54.20	23.50	16.33	29.30	23.50	35.40	25.61	43.80	26.55	36.55
1974	43.60	23.90	16.40	26.90	23.20	30.20	24.12	41.50	22.63	33.94
1976	43.30	21.60	16.33	27.90	24.80	33.10	24.75	42.87	18.90	33.72
1978	48.60	23.80	16.20	26.20	27.10	33.40	25.34	41.77	19.36	33.19
1980	50.70	21.10	15.34	28.00	29.30	29.70	24.69	41.50	20.66	33.83
1982	48.60	25.20	15.54	32.10	27.50	35.10	27.09	41.30	17.70	33.32
1984	50.30	24.00	15.61	28.50	26.30	36.50	26.18	39.33	16.12	32.10
1986	49.40	22.70	15.61	29.10	26.20	31.70	25.06	39.43	15.90	33.23
1988	43.40	22.50		25.90	28.40	28.20	26.25	36.77	15.25	32.43
1990	38.80	19.80		27.00	27.60	31.70	26.53	36.87	16.36	38.13
1992	37.60	19.50		26.90	25.80	33.70	26.48	37.83	8.95	37.60
Average (1972–92)	46.42	22.48	15.89	27.90	26.55	32.83	25.74	40.26	18.06	34.04

Notes: [1]The East Asia average includes South Korea, Taiwan, Singapore, Malaysia, Thailand and Indonesia; the developed country average includes the United States, Japan, United Kingdom and France; the Latin America average includes Argentina, Chile, Brazil and Mexico; the South Asia average includes India, Bangladesh and Pakistan.
Source: World Bank, World Tables, 1995.

Table 15.2

Number of Strikes and Lockouts and Working Days Lost as a Result in East Asia and India, 1958–92

Year	India		Indonesia		Korea		Malaysia		Singapore		Thailand		Taiwan	
	No. of strikes, lockouts	Working days lost (Thousands)	No. of strikes, lockouts	Working days lost (Thousands)	No. of strikes, lockouts	Working days lost (Thousands)	No. of strikes, lockouts	Working days lost (Thousands)	No. of strikes, lockouts	Working days lost (Thousands)	No. of strikes, lockouts	Working days lost (Thousands)	No. of strikes, lockouts	Working days lost (Thousands)
1958	1,524	7,798	55	14	39		69	59	22	78	4	4		
1960	1,583	6,537	64	44	256		37	42	45	152	2	0		
1962	1,491	6,121	34	24			95	459	88	165	3	0	64	
1964	2,151	7,725	21	25	7	2	85	508	39	36	12	1	7	
1966	2,556	13,846	2	0	12	41	60	110	14	45	17	19	3	
1968	2,776	17,244	2	0	16	63	103	280	4	11	14	3	30	
1970	2,889	20,563			4	9	17	2	5	3	22	8	92	
1972	3,243	20,544	1	0			66	33	10	18	34	20	217	
1974	2,938	40,262	6	0	58	17	85	104	10	5	357	508	494	
1976	1,459	12,746	6	1	49	17	70	109	4	3	133	496	371	
1978	3,187	28,340	20	5	102	13	37	35	0	0	21	9	506	
1980	2,856	21,925	198	34	206	61	28	20	0	0	18	5	700	
1982	2,483	74,615	224	73	88	12	26	10	0	0	22	117	1,303	
1984	2,094	56,025	29	2	114	20	19	12	0	0	17	184	1,154	
1986	1,892	32,748	73	109	276	72	27	19	0	0	9	158	1,458	
1988	1,745	33,947	39	109	1,873	5,401	9	6	0	0	7	40		
1990	1,825	24,086	61	317	322	4,487	17	302	0	0	9	72		
1991	1,810	26,428	130	535	234	3,258	23	23	0	0	14	236		
1992	1,388	24,701			235	1,528			0	0	18	155		

Source: For all countries except Taiwan: ILO, Geneva, YEAR BOOK OF LABOUR STATISTICS, 1993, 1985, 1976 and 1966; For Taiwan: Council for Economic Planning and Development, Republic of China, Taiwan Statistical Data Book, 1994.

Table 15.3

Average Number of Work Days Lost per Employee in the Manufacturing Sector in Selected Countries

Country	*1972–81*	*1982–92*
Indonesia	0.004	0.010
Thailand	0.108	0.039
Malaysia		0.004
Korea	0.005	0.216
Singapore	0.010	0.000
Average for East Asia	0.032	0.054
India	4.070	5.736
Pakistan		0.039
Sri Lanka	0.079	1.088
Philippines	0.160	0.646
Japan	0.137	0.009
France	0.333	0.168
UK	1.068	0.240
USA	0.819	0.163
Australia	1.286	0.365

Source: ILO, Geneva, YEAR BOOK OF LABOUR STATISTICS, 1993, 1985, 1976 and 1966 (for all countries except Taiwan); Council for Economic Planning and Development, Republic of China, Taiwan Statistical Data Book, 1994.

Table 15.4
Employment, Output and Output per Worker in the Organised and Unorganised Sectors in India

I Employment (Rs Million)	*1981*	*1991*
a. Total	220.698 (100%)[1]	278.940 (100%)
b. Unorganised	191.890 (86.95%)	252.205 (90.4%)
c. Organised	22.819 (10.34%)	26.735 (9.58%)
c1. Public	15.484 (7.02%)	19.058 (6.83%)
c2. Private	7.395 (3.35%)	7.677 (2.75%)
II Net Domestic Product (Rs Billion at 1980–81 prices)	*1980–81*	*1990–91*
a. Total	1103.40 (100%)	1878.76 (100%)
b. Unorganised	772.67 (70.03%)	1196.56 (63.69%)
c. Organised	330.73 (29.97%)	633.31 (33.7%)
c1. Public	192.76 (17.47%)	402.31 (21.41%)
c2. Private	137.97 (12.5%)	231 (12.29%)
III Output per worker (Rs at 1980–81 prices)	*1980–81*	*1990–91*
a. Total	4999.6	6735.4
b. Unorganised	3905.9	4744.4
c. Organised	14455.6	23688.4
c1. Public	12448.9	211098
c2. Private	18675.2	30089

Notes: [1]Numbers in the parentheses indicate per cent of the total.
Source: Census of India, 1981 and 1991; National Account Statistics, various years. Extracted from Bhattacharya, B. B. and Arup Mitra (1994).

Table 15.5
Man-days Lost (in millions) in India on Account of Strikes and Lockouts since the 1991 Reforms

Quarter	*1991–92*	*1992–93*	*1993–94*	*1994–95**
I	5.11	6.70	4.32	5.97
II	5.56	6.20	6.00	5.15
III	11.00	5.46	5.36	5.10
IV	12.90	4.61	4.76	2.98
Total for year	34.57	22.97	20.44	19.20

Notes: *Provisional.
Source: Labour Bureau, Shimla; Govt. of India, Economic Survey 1995–96.

Table 15.6
Sick Firms In India: Cumulative No. of Units and Outstanding Bank Credit, 1976 to 1990–91

As at end of Dec.	*Units*		*Outstanding Bank Credit (Billion Rs)*		*Total*	
	Large & Medium	*Small*	*Large & Medium*	*Small*	*Number*	*Outstanding Bank Credit (Billion Rs[1])*
1976	241	N.A.	6.09	N.A.	N.A.	N.A.
1978	344	6278	10.61	1.34	6622	11.95
1980	1401	23149	15.02	3.06	24550	18.09
1982	1622	58551	20.17	5.69	60173	25.85
1984	1731	91450	27.59	8.8	93282	36.38
1986	1964	145776	35.68	13.06	147740	48.74
1988	2011	240573	55.64	21.41	242584	77.05
1989–90	2269	218828	69.26	24.27	221097	93.53
1990–91	2337	221472	79.76	29.72	223809	107.68

Source: Centre for Monitoring Indian Economy, 'Basic Statistics Relating to Indian Economy', August 1993.

Table 15.7
Per cent Distribution of all Urban Workers by Employment Status: Usual Status, Adjusted Figures

National Sample Survey Round and Year	*Males*			*Females*		
	Self Emp.	*Regular Wage & Salaried Employees*	*Casual Labour*	*Self Emp.*	*Regular + Salaried*	*Casual Labour*
27th (1972–73)	39.2	50.7	10.1	48.4	27.9	23.7
32nd (1977–78)	40.4	46.4	13.2	49.5	24.9	25.6
38th (1983)	40.9	43.7	15.4	45.8	25.8	28.4
43rd (1987–88)	41.7	43.7	14.6	47.1	27.5	25.4

Source: Sarvekshana, Sept. 1990, Statement 32, p. 92.

Figure 15.1
Index (1970 = 100) of Employment in the Manufacturing Sector, 1970–93

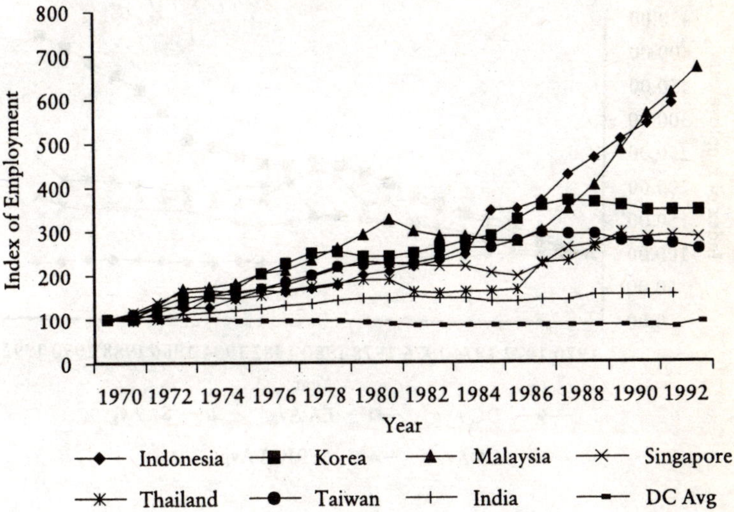

Figure 15.2
Index (1970 = 100) of Employment in the Manufacturing Sector, 1970–93

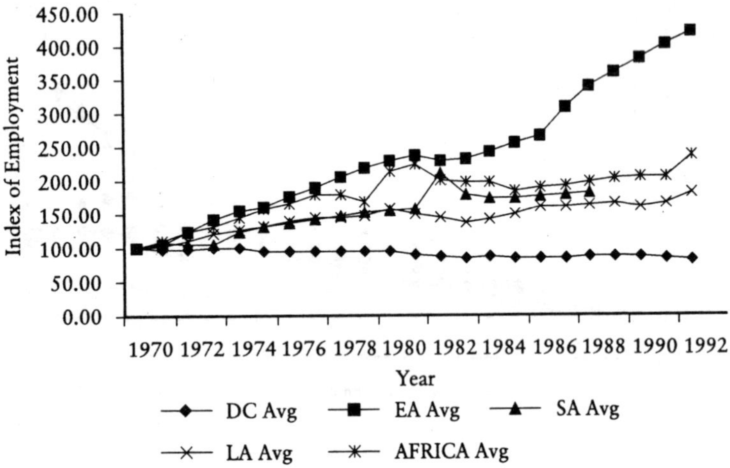

Notes: EA Avg: Average for the Six East Asian Countries
SA Avg: Average for South Asia (India, Bangladesh, Pakistan, Sri lanka)
DC Avg: Average for Developed countries (USA, Japan, UK)
LA Avg: Average for Latin America (Argentina, Chile, Brazil, Venezuela)
AFRICA Avg: Average for African countries (Zimbabwe, Zambia, Kenya, Nigeria).
Source: Based on data from World Bank, World Tables (CD version, 1995).

Figure 15.3
Index of Real Earnings in the Manufacturing Sector, 1970–93

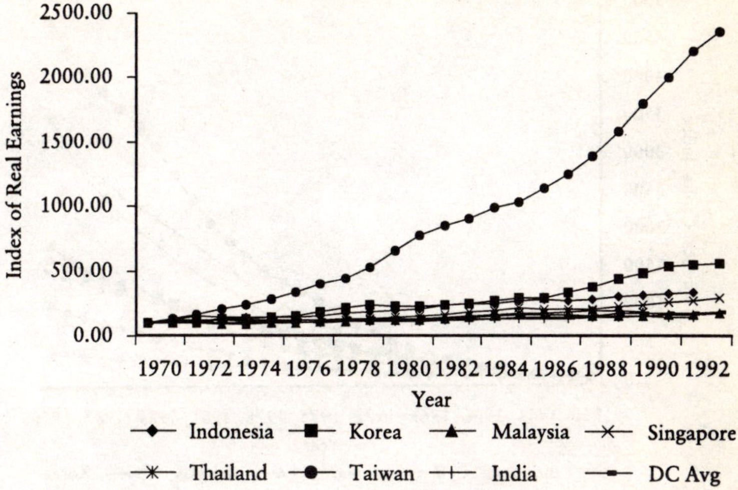

Figure 15.4
Index of Real Earnings in the Manufacturing Sector, 1970–92

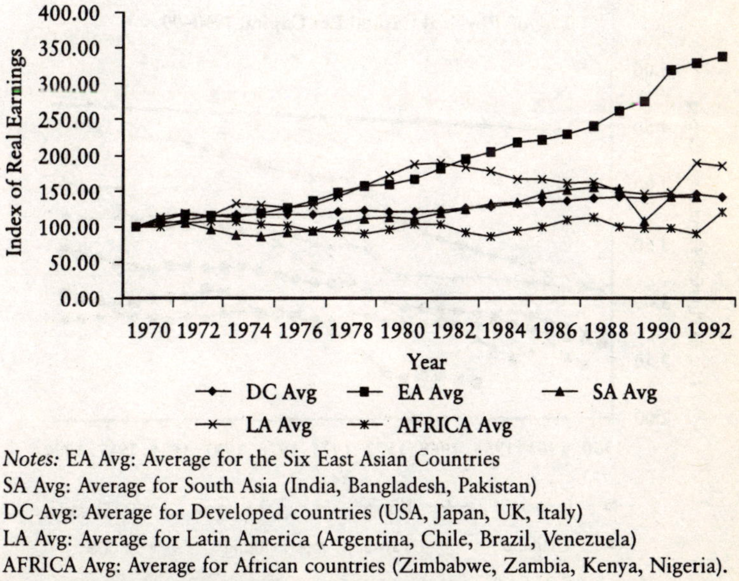

Notes: EA Avg: Average for the Six East Asian Countries
SA Avg: Average for South Asia (India, Bangladesh, Pakistan)
DC Avg: Average for Developed countries (USA, Japan, UK, Italy)
LA Avg: Average for Latin America (Argentina, Chile, Brazil, Venezuela)
AFRICA Avg: Average for African countries (Zimbabwe, Zambia, Kenya, Nigeria).
Source: World Bank, World Tables CD-ROM, 1995.

Figure 15.5

Index (1960 = 100) of Total Physical Capital, 1960–90

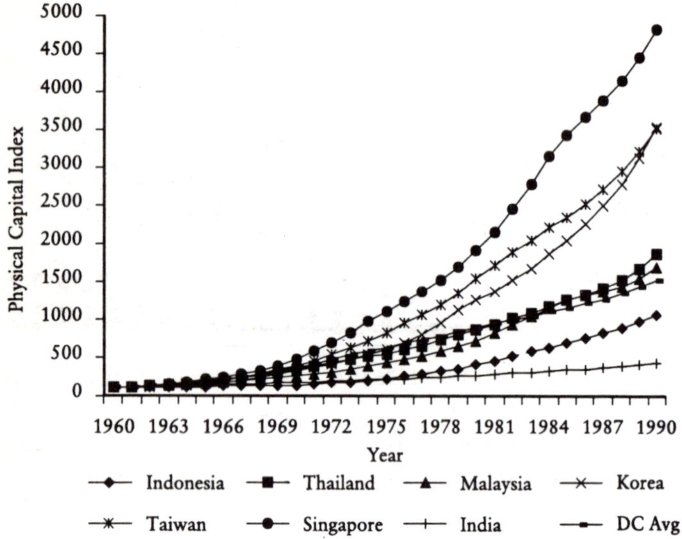

Source: Based on data from World Bank, IEC Capital Stock Data, 1950–90 World Tables (CD version, 1995).

Figure 15.6

Log of Physical Capital Per Capita, 1960–90

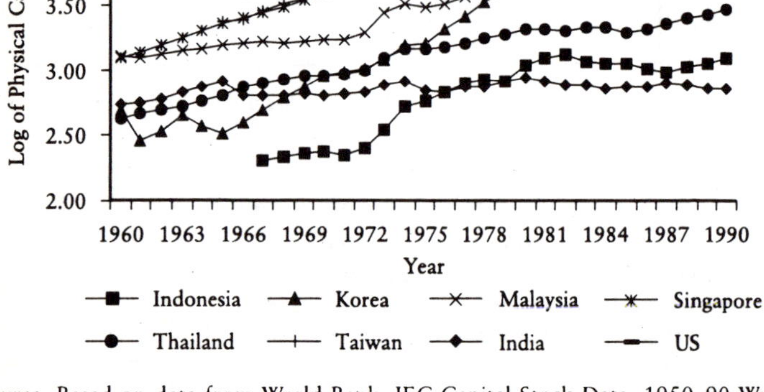

Source: Based on data from World Bank, IEC Capital Stock Data, 1950–90 World Tables (CD version, 1995).

Figure 15.7
Human Capital (Average Years of Education for Working Population), 1960–87

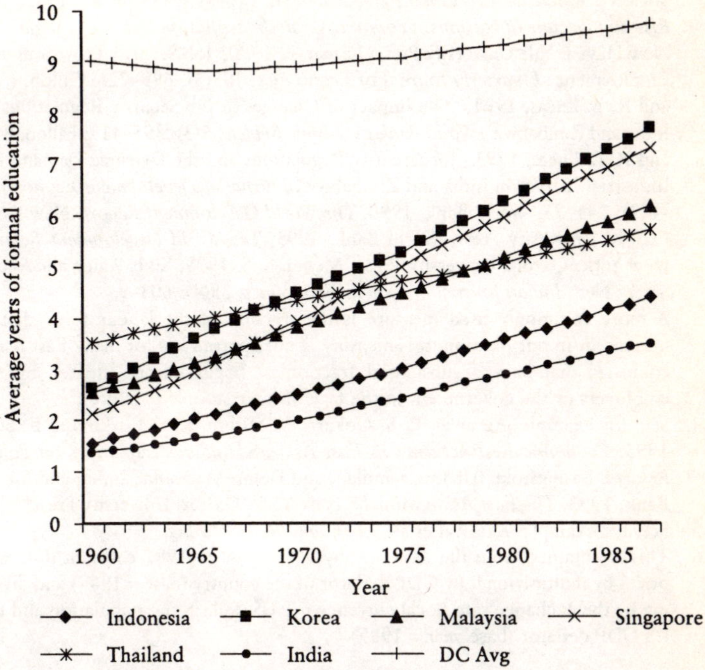

Source: Based on data from Nehru, Swanson and Dubey (1993).

NOTES

An earlier version of this chapter was published in *The Indian Journal of Labour Economics* (1997), 40(4): 631–53, and is reprinted by permission. The author would like to thank Jayatu Sen Chaudhury, Satish Pandey and Brinda Viswanathan for providing valuable research assistance, as well as Joseph S. Lee, Lalit Deshpande, Kirit S. Parikh and Bibhas Saha for helpful comments on an earlier draft.

1. See, for example, Standing, G. and V. Tokman, 1991, *Towards Social Adjustment*. Geneva: International Labour Organisation (ILO); ILO, 1990, 'Wages, Labour Costs and Their Impact on Adjustment, Employment, Growth'. ILO Governing Body Committee on Employment, GB 248/CE/2/1, Geneva;

Bhaduri, A. 1996, 'Employment, Labour Market Flexibility and Economic Liberalisation in India', *Indian Journal of Labour Economics*, 39(1): 13–22.

2. See, for example, Krueger, A. 1974, 'The Political Economy of the Rent-Seeking Society', *American Economic Review*, 64(3): 291–303; Olson, M. 1982, *The Rise and Decline of Nations: Economic Growth Stagflation and Social Rigidities*. New Haven: Yale University Press; Lazear, E. 1990, 'Job Security Provisions and Employment', *Quarterly Journal of Economics*, 105(3): 699–726; Fallon, P. R. and R. E. Lucas, 1991, 'The Impact of Changes in Job Security Regulations in India and Zimbabwe', *World Bank Economic Review*, 5(3): 395–413; Fallon, P. R. and R. E. Lucas, 1993, 'Job Security Regulations and the Dynamic Demand for Industrial Labour in India and Zimbabwe', *Journal of Development Economics*, 40(2): 241–75; World Bank, 1990, *The World Development Report*. New York: Oxford University Press; World Bank, 1995, *The World Development Report*. New York: Oxford University Press; Mehta, S. S. 1995, 'Exit Policy and Social Safety Net', *Indian Journal of Labour Economics*, 38(4): 603–9.
3. A more commonly used measure is the fraction of the labour force that is unionised. In our opinion, this measure is not appropriate for many East Asian countries that have a substantial fraction of bogus unions (floated by the employers or the government in the face of international pressure).
4. See, for example, Agrawal, P., S. Gokarn, V. Mishra, K. S. Parikh and K. Sen, 1995, *Economic Restructuring in East Asia and India: Perspectives on Policy Reform*. Basingstoke (UK): Macmillan, and Delhi: Macmillan India; and World Bank, 1993, *The East Asian Miracle*. New York: Oxford University Press.
5. See, for example, Agrawal et al., *Economic Restructuring*.
6. This is obtained from the data on physical capital in 1987 constant domestic prices by multiplying it by GDP deflator of the country (base = 1987) and dividing by the exchange rate (local currency per US dollar), the population and the US GDP deflator (base year = 1987).

About the Editors and Contributors

Pradeep Agrawal is Associate Professor at the Indira Gandhi Institute of Development Research (IGIDR) Bombay, India. He has published research articles in several journals and co-authored the book *Economic Restructuring in East Asia and India: Perspectives on Economic Reforms.*

Leslie Elliott Armijo is currently a Visiting Scholar at the Mark O. Hatfield School of Government, Portland State University, Oregon. Her publications include *Financial Globalization and Democracy in Emerging Markets* and *Democracy and Inflation*.

Arindam Das-Gupta is a long-term consultant with the Public Economics Group at the World Bank in Washington DC. His research interests focus on tax policy and administration.

Mrinal Datta-Chaudhuri is Professor at the Delhi School of Economics, University of Delhi since 1968. A regular contributor to Indian periodicals and newspapers on economic and political issues, his publications include two books titled *Regional Development: Experience and Prospects in South and South East Asia* and *Development and Change.* He has also been published in several journals and contributed regularly to Indian periodicals and newspapers on economic and political issues.

Anil B. Deolalikar is Professor of Economics at the University of Washington, Seattle. His research interests include human resource modelling, poverty measurement and analysis, health-care reform, and education-sector reform in developing countries. He has done research and policy advising in more than 20 countries in Asia and Africa.

Bhaskar Dutta is a Professor at the Indian Statistical Institute, New Delhi. He has authored numerous publications on subjects such as Game Theory, Political Economy and Social Choice Theory. He is on the editorial board of *Social Choice and Welfare, Mathematical Social Sciences, Review of Economic Design* and *Journal of Quantitative Economics.*

Mukesh Eswaran is a Professor of Economics at the University of British Columbia. His main areas of interest include development economics and industrial organisation. He co-authored a book titled *Why Poverty Persists in India*.

Ashok Gulati is currently a NABARD professor at the Institute of Economic Growth, Delhi. He has written several research papers and books and has recently authored the book, *Indian Agriculture and Trade Liberalisation*.

Chandrika Gulati is a Reader in Political Science at Deshbandhu College, University of Delhi. She has contributed to research papers in national and international journals, and has authored a book titled *Bangladesh-Liberation to Fundamentalism: A Study of Volatile Indo-Bangladesh Relations*.

Anand Gupta is currently working as an Advisor at the FORE School of Management, New Delhi. He has served on several Government of India committees and has also worked as a consultant to many institutions, including the United States–India Business Council and the World Bank. His current consulting and research interests include assessment of India's economic health, design of innovative tariffs for electric power utilities, and management of the privatisation process.

Prem Shankar Jha is a columnist with *The Hindu* and *Business Standard*. He was the editor of the *Hindustan Times* in 1986–87 and information advisor to the prime minister in 1990. He authored the book *Kashmir, 1947: Rival Versions of History*.

Satu Kähkönen is Associate Director of Economic Policy at the Center for Institutional Reform and the Informal Sector (IRIS), University of Maryland, College Park. In addition to conducting research on institutional aspects of economic development, she has undertaken field work in a number of developing and transition economies, and worked as a Consultant to the World Bank. She is the author of *A Not-So-Dismal Science: A Broader View of Economies and Societies*.

Kenneth Kletzer is Professor of Economics at the University of California, Santa Cruz. He has written on subjects such as the economics of development and growth, sovereign debt, public sector solvency, fiscal policy coordination, and European monetary integration.

Anthony Lanyi has been Director of Economic Policy at the Center for Institutional Reform and the Informal Sector (IRIS) of the University of Maryland since 1996. A specialist in macroeconomic and financial policies in developing countries, Dr Lanyi worked for 26 years with the International Monetary Fund, where he was engaged in country operations, research and training. From 1987 to 1996, he was Deputy Director of the IMF Institute, conducting training courses for government officials and seminars for legislators and government leaders. He has also taught at the universities of Princeton and Johns Hopkins.

Dilip Mookherjee has been a Professor of Economics at Boston University since 1995. His current research interests include incentives and institutions in developing countries and theories of organisational design and learning.

M. Govinda Rao is the Director of the Institute for Social and Economic Change (ISEC) in Bangalore, India. He has consulted on several projects for the World Bank, Asian Development Bank, and other UN agencies. He has also been a Fellow at the Australia South Asia Research Center at the Australian National University. He has written seven books and over 40 articles in professional journals and edited volumes.

Pradeep Sharma is a Member of the Indian Economic service and is presently the Director of The Rural Development section of the Planning Commission, Government of India.

Sangeeta Shroff is a Reader in the Gokhale Institute of Politics and Economics, Pune.

Nirvikar Singh is a Professor of Economics at the University of California, Santa Cruz, where he served as Chair of the Department of Economics from 1992 to 1995, and is currently Director of the Business Management Economics Program. He has recently collaborated with Dr Govinda Rao on the book, *The Political Economy of Indian Federalism*.

Prem S. Vashishtha is Director of the Agricultural Economics Research Centre at the University of Delhi, India. He has been a consultant to the ILO and the World Bank. His areas of research interest include agricultural economics, development economics, and human resources.

Index